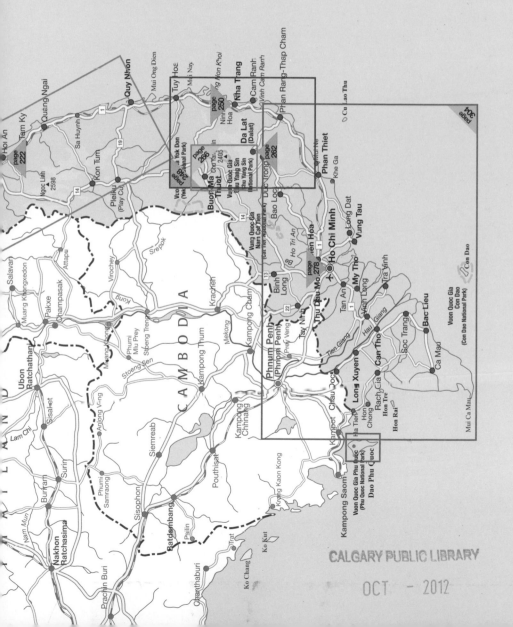

# INSIGHT GUIDES

# VIETNAM

## APA PUBLICATIONS L

Part of the Langenscheidt Publishing Group

## ✻ INSIGHT GUIDE
# VIETNAM

### Editorial
*Project Editor*
**Tom Le Bas**
*Series Manager*
**Rachel Lawrence**
*Designers*
**Richard Cooke, Tom Smyth**
*Map Production*
**Original cartography: Lovell Johns,
updated by Apa Cartography
Department**
*Production*
**Tynan Dean, Linton Donaldson and
Rebeka Ellam**

### Distribution
*UK*
**Dorling Kindersley Ltd**
A Penguin Group company
80 Strand, London, WC2R 0RL
customerservice@dk.com

*United States*
**Ingram Publisher Services**
1 Ingram Boulevard, PO Box 3006,
La Vergne, TN 37086-1986
customer.service@ingrampublisher
services.com

*Australia*
**Universal Publishers**
PO Box 307
St Leonards NSW 1590
sales@universalpublishers.com.au

*New Zealand*
**Brown Knows Publications**
11 Artesia Close, Shamrock Park
Auckland, New Zealand 2016
sales@brownknows.co.nz

*Worldwide*
**Apa Publications GmbH & Co.
Verlag KG (Singapore branch)**
7030 Ang Mo Kio Avenue 5
08-65 Northstar @ AMK
Singapore 569880
apasin@singnet.com.sg

### Printing
**CTPS-China**
© 2012 Apa Publications (UK) Ltd
*All Rights Reserved*
*First Edition 1992*
*Sixth Edition 2012*

# ABOUT THIS BOOK

The first Insight Guide pioneered the use of creative full-colour photography in travel guides in 1970. Since then, we have expanded our range to cater for our readers' needs not only for reliable information but also for a real understanding of a destination, its people and its culture. Today, when the Internet can supply inexhaustible (but not always reliable) facts, our books marry text and pictures to provide those much more elusive qualities: knowledge and discernment. To achieve this, they rely heavily on the authority of locally based writers and photographers.

## How to use this book

*Insight Guide: Vietnam* is structured to convey an understanding of the country and its people as well as to guide readers through its attractions:

◆ The **Features** section, indicated by a pink bar at the top of each page, covers the natural geography and the war-torn history of Vietnam as well as aspects of its culture: its people, religions, performing arts, crafts, cuisine and architecture.

◆ The main **Places** section, indicated by a blue bar, is a complete guide to all the sights and areas worth visiting. Places of special interest are coordinated by number with the maps. A list of recommended restaurants is included at the end of each chapter in this section.

◆ The **Travel Tips** listings section, with a yellow bar, provides all the practical information you'll need, divided into five key sections: transport, accommodation, activities, an A–Z section of essential practical tips, plus a handy section on the Vietnamese language. An

Covering Hanoi, Around Hanoi, Northwest and Northeast Vietnam plus the Tonkin Coast was Canadian freelance journalist **Aviva West**, who lived in Hanoi for almost five years. Currently based in Toronto, Canada, Aviva writes for publications in Asia and North America.

**Adam Bray**, a transplanted American freelance writer, who since 2003 has lived in the laidback beach town of Mui Ne, was responsible for the entire Central Vietnam region. Adam wrote the chapters on Hue, Danang and Hoi An, South to Quy Nhon, Nha Trang and Dalat. In addition, he wrote the Around Ho Chi Minh City chapter (including, of course, his home base, Mui Ne), as well as the information-packed Travel Tips section. He also contributed updates for these chapters in this latest edition.

Making sense of frenetic Ho Chi Minh City and condensing it into a digestible read was English writer **Samantha Coomber**. She has lived in Vietnam for over seven years (first in Hanoi and now in Ho Chi Minh City) and writes for a string of international magazines and travel guides.

**Gemma Price**, another Ho Chi Minh City-based British freelance writer, researched and wrote the chapter on the Mekong Delta.

Bringing Vietnam to life with all its vivid colour and expression was the principal photographer, **Peter Stuckings**. The Australian calls Ho Chi Minh City his home, even though he spends all of his time exploring Vietnam with his trusty camera and motorbike.

The book was copy-edited by **Alyse Dar**, proofread by **Jan McCann** and indexed by **Penny Phenix**.

easy-to-find contents list for the Travel Tips is printed on the back flap, which also serves as a bookmark.

## The contributors

This new edition was supervised and edited by **Tom Le Bas**, a senior editor at Insight's London office, who commissioned local expertise to fully update the guide. Assisting him was a stellar team of Vietnam-based writers who revised and updated the copy.

The entire book has been extensively updated by **Mark Beales**, who has resided in Thailand since 2004. He has written numerous articles for magazines and penned several guidebooks on Southeast Asia.

The bulk of the Places section was compiled by four writers who scoured and researched the length and breadth of Vietnam.

### Map Legend

| | |
|---|---|
| —·— | International boundary |
| ———— | Province boundary |
| —•— | National park / reserve |
| ———— | Ferry route |
| ⊖ | Border crossing |
| ✈ | International airport |
| ✈ | Regional airport |
| ★ | Place of interest |
| ❶ | Tourist information |
| 🚌 | Bus / coach station |
| ⊠ | Main post office |
| ✝ † | Church / ruins |
| ☾ | Mosque |
| ∩ | Cave |
| ▲ | Summit |
| ⚑ | Monument / statue |
| ⚑ | Notable beach |
| ❋ | Viewpoint |

The main places of interest in the Places section are coordinated by number with a full-colour map (eg ❶), and a symbol at the top of every right-hand page tells you where to find the map.

# Contents

**Maps**

## Travel Tips

# THE BEST OF VIETNAM: TOP ATTRACTIONS

From the buzz of Ho Chi Minh City to the languid charm of Hanoi, the eye-popping scenery of Halong Bay and the ethnic diversity of Sa Pa, prioritise with our selection of Vietnam's must-see sights

△ Once home to Vietnam's most notorious prison, the **Con Dao Archipelago** is now the country's finest marine reserve, known for its sea turtle conservation programme and secluded resorts on remote beaches. Page 315.

◁ **Ho Chi Minh City** is Vietnam's economic powerhouse, with all the best that an international city has to offer. Downtown District 1 has trendy bars and cafés, superb restaurants, plus lots of shopping opportunities and historic sites galore. Page 277.

△ Ancient Cham towers, Chinese assembly halls, whale temples and Vietnam's largest reclining Buddha are all located near **Mui Ne**, but it's the sprawling beach and kite-boarding that draw crowds to Vietnam's fastest-growing resort destination. Page 313.

◁ The town of **Sa Pa** is perched amid stunning highland scenery and is home to numerous ethnic minorities with thriving cultures. The Sunday-morning market in Bac Ha hosts merchants from the Nung, Dao, Tay, Thai, Flower Hmong and other hill tribes, in their colourful traditional dress. Page 151.

△ **Nha Trang** has a lively nightlife with a plethora of bars and restaurants around the beach. The main reason to visit, however, is found in the bay, where divers and snorkellers head out to the surrounding islands for a close-up view of the country's finest coral reefs. Page 247.

△ The city of **Hue** sits at the heart of the country, straddling mazes of moats and canals, lotus lakes and the sleepy Perfume River. The Imperial City – a Unesco World Heritage Site – was home to the Nguyen dynasty, whose emperors and empresses now rest in elaborate mausoleums nearby. Page 195.

△ **Hanoi** is both the political and cultural capital of Vietnam. One of its highlights is the Old Quarter, nicknamed "36 Streets" after the 36 merchant guilds located along their respective streets. This and other pockets of nostalgia make for a charming, French-influenced city. Page 109.

△ The Unesco World Heritage Site of **Halong Bay** is a magical landscape of more than 3,000 limestone crags and outcrops riddled with caves and half submerged in the indigo-coloured bay. Spend the night on a sailing junk and visit one of the floating fishing villages. Page 170.

△ Stroll the Unesco World Heritage Site of **Hoi An's Old Town**, along the banks of the Thu Bon River, and experience the old-world ambience of the Japanese Covered Bridge, ancient Chinese assembly halls and old merchant homes built in a fusion of Vietnamese, Chinese, Japanese and French architectural styles. Page 221.

▷ The ancient religious capital of the Indianised Champa kingdom (5th to 15th centuries) is located at **My Son**, central Vietnam, yet another Unesco World Heritage Site. The ruined temples and towers, severely damaged in the war – as well as by the weather – are a concentrated sample of the many Cham towers scattered along the country's long coastline Page 226.

# THE BEST OF VIETNAM: EDITOR'S CHOICE

Brilliant beaches, verdant national parks, ancient ruins and temples, treks to hill-tribe communities, the best museums and world-class hotels... here at a glance are our recommendations on what to see and do

## TOP CULTURAL EXPERIENCES

**Cham Villages: Phan Rang.** Visit villages populated by minority Cham people who live a lifestyle little changed by modernity. See page 256.

**Fish sauce: Phan Thiet and Phu Quoc.** See how fish sauce (nuoc mam) is made and, more importantly, sample the cuisine based around it. See page 312.

**Market shopping.** For an insight into local culture, shop at markets like those in Dalat and Ho Chi Minh City (Benh Thanh). See pages 263, 300.

**Ao Dai.** Women can visit a local tailor and get fitted for a silk ao dai, the national dress of Vietnam. Hanoi, HCMC and Hoi An are the best places for tailored clothes. See page 219.

**Homestays.** Spend a night in a wooden stilt house in a hill-tribe village or Mekong Delta backwater. Book via a tour agency. See page 344.

**Mekong Delta.** Take a boat through the mighty Delta to see how the deep south lives. See page 319.

**LEFT:** traditional dance performance

**ABOVE:** magical, mysterious Halong Bay.

## BEST NATURE EXPERIENCES

**Halong Bay.** Myriad rock formations hide enchanting caves to explore and solitary beaches for swimming. See page 170.

**Bach Ma National Park.** Vietnam's rainiest rain-forest contains countless waterfalls, wild rhododendrons and the rare saola antelope. See page 218.

**Mount Fansipan.** A guide is necessary for the exhilarating climb up Vietnam's highest peak. The hike will take three days. See page 154.

**Tam Coc.** Jagged limestone outcrops sticking out from flooded rice paddies make for some spectacular scenery. See page 181.

**Endangered Primate Rescue Centre: Cuc Phuong National Park.** See some of the rarest primates in the world, including langurs, gibbons and snub-nosed monkeys. See page 185.

**Cat Tien National Park.** Spend the night at Crocodile Lake and catch a glimpse of Siamese crocodiles, and animals like the sambar deer and peafowl. See page 309.

**Con Dao Archipelago.** Go snorkelling to find sea turtles in the reefs, or watch them nesting on shore. See page 315.

## TOP BEACHES

**Jungle Beach.** The Hon Heo Peninsula north of Nha Trang shelters one of Vietnam's finest beaches, backed by rocky mountains and washed by clear, emerald waters. See page 255.

**Mui Ne Beach.** An all-time favourite that is easily accessible from Ho Chi Minh City, with a burgeoning water-sports scene. See page 313.

**Nha Trang.** The hottest nightlife in central Vietnam spills out onto its finely manicured city beach. See page 247.

**China Beach.** One of the longest uninterrupted stretches of sand in Vietnam also has the best surfing. See page 216.

**Cua Dai Beach.** Its easy accessibility from Hoi An makes this the perfect beach to relax by and chill out by day. See page 226.

**Sao Beach.** Located at the southeastern end of Phu Quoc Island, this stretch of paradise is difficult to get to but well worth the effort. See page 334.

**ABOVE:** the wide, sandy expanse of China Beach.

## TOP TEMPLES AND RELIGIOUS SITES

**Temple of Literature: Hanoi.** The city's most important temple is devoted to Confucian teaching. See page 121.

**Cao Dai Great Temple: Tay Ninh.** Part cathedral and part pagoda, the headquarters of this curious indigenous religion attract many visitors. See page 306.

**My Son.** Champa's ancient capital in central Vietnam is a mini, albeit crumbling, counterpart to Cambodia's Angkor Wat. See page 220.

**Perfume Pagoda: near Hanoi.** Built into limestone cliffs, this is one of northern Vietnam's most important religious sites. See page 135.

**Van Thuy Thu Temple: Phan Thiet.** This is the oldest temple devoted to the worship of whales in Vietnam. The whale and dolphin skeletons are a fascinating sight. See page 311.

## BEST OUTDOOR ACTIVITIES

**Kiteboarding and windsurfing: Mui Ne.** Vietnam's premier water-sports and dune-surfing capital. See pages 313, 373.

**Golf: Dalat and Mui Ne.** Play a round at a highland course or a few holes among the ocean dunes. See pages 372, 373.

**Snorkelling and diving: Nha Trang.** Some of Vietnam's best reefs are found in its surrounding waters. See pages 253, 372.

**Kayaking and trekking: Cat Ba Island.** Explore this beautiful location from the water or on dry land.

See pages 173, 371.

**Abseiling: Dalat.** Experience Elephant Falls and other central highland waterfalls up close. See page 372.

**Trekking: Sa Pa.** Hike to the minority villages of the northern highlands. See pages 153, 371.

**Caving:** Experience Phong Nga, the world's largest cave passage, in the seldom-visited Tonkin region. See page 189.

**BELOW:** kiteboarding at gusty Mui Ne Beach.

**ABOVE:** Hanoi's famous Temple of Literature.

## BEST HOTELS AND RESORTS

**The Nam Hai: Cua Dai Beach (near Hoi An).** Combining minimalist chic with tasteful Vietnamese accents, this beachfront luxury hotel is a designer's dream resort. See page 351.
**Park Hyatt Saigon: HCMC.** Built in faux colonial style, this chic luxury hotel is easily the city's most stylish, and atmosphere with modern comforts in Dalat's original, lakefront hotel. See page 354.
**Six Senses Hideaway Ninh Van Bay: Nha Trang.** Accessible only by speedboat, this all-villa hotel is for the seriously rich. See page 353.
**Life Wellness Resort: Quy Nhon.** A stylish beachside spa resort

**BELOW:** pick from three pools at the Nam Hai.

also most expensive, accommodation. See page 355.
**Sofitel Metropole Hotel: Hanoi.** The grande dame of colonial hotels in Vietnam still has heaps of old-world charm despite extensive renovations to its interior. See page 345.
**Caravelle Hotel: HCMC.** Headquarters for journalists and diplomats during the Vietnam War, today it's one of the city's most luxurious hotels. See page 354.
**Dalat Palace.** Enjoy authentic French colonial inspired by ancient Cham architecture. Represents style at a good price. See page 352.
**Ana Mandara Resort: Nha Trang.** An elegant hideaway occupying a stretch of prime beachfront at Nha Trang. See page 352.
**Ana Mandara Villas: Dalat.** Ensconced within snug and refurbished French colonial villas dating from the 1920s and 30s, you will find little reason to venture out to downtown Dalat. See page 354.

## TOP MUSEUMS

**Museum of Vietnamese History: HCMC.** Stroll through halls exhibiting artefacts from all the ancient cultures of Vietnam. See page 291.
**Ho Chi Minh Museum: Hanoi.** The most thorough and definitive showcase of the man behind the Vietnamese communist revolution for independence. See page 123.
**Museum of Cham Sculpture: Danang.** This unmatched collection of artefacts tells the other half of the story found at the ancient Cham sites along coastal Vietnam. See page 213.
**War Remnants Museum: HCMC.** A controversial museum documenting atrocities suffered by the Vietnamese during the war with America. See page 287.

**Lam Dong Museum: Dalat.** Lat gongs, Ma longhouses and Funan relics are interspersed among an outstanding taxidermy collection. See page 265.
**Quang Trung Museum: Quy Nhon.** Dedicated to emperor Quang Trung and the Tay Son brothers, leaders of the infamous rebellion. See page 238.
**Vietnam Museum of Ethnology: Hanoi.** This museum offers a superb introduction to the culture and lifestyles of Vietnam's 54 ethnic minorities. See page 127.
**Hoi An's Old Quarter.** This Unesco World Heritage town is itself a living museum, but several merchant homes have also been turned into remarkable showcases for culture, local folklore and crafts. See page 221.

**BELOW:** Bahnar communal house at the Vietnam Museum of Ethnology.

**ABOVE:** Vietnam's most famous dish – *pho.*

## VIETNAMESE EATS

**Pho.** Served with beef or chicken, *pho* noodle soup is available throughout Vietnam. Diehards swear that Hanoi's version is the best. See page 86.

**Banh Khoai and Banh Beo: Hue.** The best taro-and-rice-batter pancakes and steamed rice-flour dumplings are served at the city's Lac Thien, Lac Thanh and Lac Thuan eateries. See page 209.

**Imperial Banquet: Hue.** Dine like royalty at Phuoc Thanh Restaurant on the elaborate dishes once served exclusively to the Nguyen emperors. See page 209.

**Cao Lau: Hoi An.** This rice noodle dish with pork and sesame crackers is served at all the local eateries in the Old Town. See page 229.

**Goi Cuon:** A southern speciality also known as "summer rolls", with vermicelli, prawns, pork and herbs. See page 89.

**Fresh fruit: Mekong Delta.** Vietnam's fertile southern delta is the best place to sample the country's tropical fruits. See page 320.

**BELOW:** dragonfruit in the Mekong Delta

## VIETNAM FOR FAMILIES

**Water Puppets: Hanoi and Ho Chi Minh City (HCMC).** Enjoy a musical puppet theatre performance with an aquatic twist. See pages 229.

**Vinpearl Land and Underwater World: Hon Tre Island, Nha Trang.** Ride the world's longest ocean-crossing cable car to this island amusement park for exciting rides, games, a water park and an aquarium. See pages 253, 254.

**Oceanographic Institute: Nha Trang.** A splendid aquarium with lots of bizarre sea creatures and live sea turtles. See page 253.

**Hang Nga's Crazy House: Dalat.** Any tree-house-lover will enjoy exploring this whimsical house full of hidden corridors and secret rooms. See page 265.

**Thap Ba Hot Springs: Nha Trang.** Take a therapeutic mineral mud bath and then frolic in the hot-spring pools at this family-friendly site. See page 249.

**BELOW:** water puppetry is a northern Vietnamese art form.

# TRIUMPH OVER ADVERSITY

Having overcome war and deep divisions,
today's Vietnam is now better known for its
breathtaking scenery, beaches and vibrant cities

**M**odern yet traditional, communist yet capitalist, cosmopolitan yet quaint – calling Vietnam diverse doesn't even begin to tell the story. Its associations with war may still be present, but today the tunnels are tourist traps, the tanks are displayed in museums and the divisions are all but healed.

The sheer range of landscapes and attractions makes Vietnam something of a challenge. The long, sandy beaches and the turquoise seas are tempting, but then so are its forested mountains and verdant countryside. Vietnamese cities are dynamic, full of life and colour.

Back in 1975 when the last US troops fled Vietnam, things were not so rosy. The country was reunified but faced a new battle – economic stability. As the government clung firmly to its Marxist–Leninist blueprint, the country floundered. By the mid-1980s, Vietnam was on the brink of bankruptcy; some people were starving, and inflation topped 800 percent. The economic revolution known as *doi moi* began in 1986 and opened up the country to foreign investment – and foreign visitors. From 2000 to 2007 Vietnam was one of the world's fastest-growing economies and the darling of foreign investors.

Today's ruling communist government still keeps a tight reign on cultural and political affairs, and the sheer pace of development means major cities are packed to bursting point. Despite this, there has never been a better time to visit Vietnam as much of the progress is aimed at attracting tourism. The result is that travelling is simpler, the hotels are more luxurious and the restaurants of higher quality than ever before. Vietnam doesn't forget its past – that's why many visitors come, after all – but it is keen to move forward and showcase its natural beauty and its people's friendly nature.

**PRECEDING PAGES:** button-and-sequin portrait of Ho Chi Minh; radish farm, Dalat; ethnic clothing for sale, Bac Ha. **LEFT:** evening market in Hanoi's Old Quarter.
**ABOVE, FROM LEFT:** motorbikes aplenty; bridge over Hoan Kiem Lake.

# GEOGRAPHY AND LANDSCAPE

From the jagged slopes of the northern mountains to the waterways of the Mekong Delta in the deep south, Vietnam is a land endowed with startling physical beauty and a rich biodiversity

Resembling an elongated letter S, Vietnam runs along the length of the Indochinese Peninsula, bordering the Bien Dong (literally Eastern Sea), better known as the South China Sea, to the east. Its 3,730km (2,320-mile) frontier borders China to the north, and Cambodia and Laos to the west. Covering some 327,500 sq km (126,500 sq miles), Vietnam's territory also encompasses a lengthy coastline and thousands of islands reaching from the Gulf of Tonkin to the Gulf of Thailand. These include the disputed Spratly (Truong Sa) and Paracel (Hoang Sa) islands, which China and a number of Southeast Asian nations lay claim to, mostly due to the islands' rich oil and gas deposits.

Vietnam is a long, narrow country. Broadest at its northern and southern ends, it tapers to a mere 50km (30 miles) in the centre. Mountains and forests make up more than three-quarters of the total land area, with roughly 25 percent of the land under cultivation. The 3,000km (1,850-mile) coastline is dotted with beautiful beaches.

## The lie of the land

The northern mountains and steeply carved valleys that separate Vietnam from China and northern Laos include the mighty Hoang Lien Son range, an eastern extension of the Himalayas. This includes Vietnam's highest mountain, Mount Fansipan (3,143 metres/1,030ft), which can be climbed on a three-day trek.

To the south and east of these highlands are the extensive plains of the Song Hong, or Red River, which is home to 90 percent of northern Vietnam's population. The Red River flows from its source in the Yunnan region of China across the north of Vietnam and then southeast via the city of Hanoi to its coastal mouth near Haiphong. The coastline is mostly muddy in the delta area and rocky around Halong Bay, where a stunning archipelago of thousands of limestone outcrops (or karsts) and isles of various sizes and shapes lies scattered in the Gulf of Tonkin.

There are several other areas with karst formations in the far northeast as well as the north-central area of Vietnam, notably in Tam Coc and Hoa Lu, and the area south from Dong Hoi that contains the remarkable Phong Nha Caves. Not yet fully explored, the caves at Phong Nha extend over 35km (20 miles) of underground passages: in 2003, this area became Vietnam's fifth Unesco World Heritage Site.

Central Vietnam, formerly known as Annam, forms a long convex curve within which are narrow plains wedged between the South China Sea and the high plateaux of the Truong Son mountains. This terrain is characterised by coastal dunes and lagoons, and terraces of alluvial deposits towards the mountains.

The narrow coastal strip of central Vietnam is home to much of the region's population, its towns and villages linked by the main north–south railway and Highway 1. The imperial capital of Hue, the large city of Danang and the attractive old town of Hoi An are located here. Further south, the Central Highlands between Danang and Dalat are rich in volcanic basalt soil and contain some of Vietnam's most extensive forests, in addition to vast tea- and coffee-growing plantations. There are various ethnic minority groups in the hills, but many areas are politically sensitive and access is restricted in some areas. The colonial hill station of Dalat is the main tourism hub.

The long stretch of coastline south from Hoi An to Nha Trang has some of the country's most beautiful beaches, largely undeveloped except around Nha Trang, itself Vietnam's leading resort.

The deep south is characterised by extensive lowlands around Ho Chi Minh City (Saigon), one of Vietnam's main rice-growing areas, and more sandy beaches around Mui Ne, Phan Thiet and Vung Tau. To the southwest is the extensive delta of the Mekong River, a maze of waterways and marshes unlike anywhere else in the country. Beyond, in the turquoise waters of the Gulf of Thailand, is the large island of Phu Quoc.

## Flora and fauna

Despite the damage inflicted by American chemical defoliants in the war, and the inevitable decline due to population pressure and logging, Vietnam has retained a significant amount of forest cover and its wildlife has held up relatively well. Yet things are changing rapidly, and the environment is increasingly under threat as habitats continue to vanish and enforcement continues to be slack.

Vietnam's complex climate *(see page 376)* and varied geography provide a wide range of habitats for its remarkable variety of plants and animals – both tropical and temperate species – some of which are unique to the country.

**ABOVE, FROM LEFT:** a traditional Chinese-style junk, Halong Bay; limestone crags amid rice fields at Tam Coc.

## Vietnam's forests

The country's forests are a valuable resource and contain more than 1,200 identified plant species, providing a rich source of oils, resins, timber and medicines. The tropical forests host more than 800 types of wood, including hardwoods such as teak and mahogany.

There are small populations of tigers, leopards and elephants and larger numbers of various primate species, small carnivores such as marbled cats and civets, numerous deer species, wild pigs, pangolins and dozens of rodent species. There are also several reptile species including numerous venomous snakes

as well as crocodiles, and over 800 bird species. The forests occasionally throw up some surprises. In 1989, a Javan rhinoceros thought to be extinct in mainland Asia was rediscovered in Vietnam. Sadly, scientists declared the animal extinct in Vietnam in 2011 following the discovery of a dead individual in Cat Tien National Park, thought to have been killed by poachers.

In the northern mountains, the forests are temperate rather than tropical, and shelter Eurasian species such as black bears, squirrels, civets, otters and foxes. In terms of plant life, the highland areas are home to a wide range of temperate, subtropical and evergreen species, some of which produce timber.

# Conservation Efforts

**The urgent task of protecting rich biodiversity is a major challenge in a rapidly developing nation such as Vietnam**

Vietnam's rapid development has put new pressures on an already fragile environment. A growing population – now estimated to be over 90 million – brings ever greater demands on the land. Much of the country's lowlands are

already intensively farmed, while the forests of the central highlands and the northern mountains continue to be threatened by traditional slash-and-burn farming techniques practised by the hill tribes.

It's a familiar story. The country's forests have, according to some estimates, almost halved in area since 1945, from 45 percent of the land to around 23 percent in 2011 (the use of toxic chemical defoliants during the Vietnam war led to around 5 percent being wiped out): although this figure is still relatively high, it is unlikely to remain so for long. Precious hardwoods are being felled in industrial quantities as timber for export, and minerals are also being extracted. The cost of this destruction could be severe, and not just for the animals whose habitat is being lost. Resulting soil erosion

and flooding are far more likely once the diggers have done their work.

## Reforestation programme

The government has tried to reverse this alarming trend by spearheading a reforestation programme. Yet the 5 million-hectare (12 million-acre) project, started in 1998, involved planting fast-growing cash-crop trees (usually non-native species) that actually masks the ongoing loss of primary and natural forest – and does little to protect wildlife. Therefore, despite more trees being planted than cut in recent years, the fragile ecosystems and biodiversity are finding themselves under even greater stress.

There is now a move to reintroduce native trees to the forests, but these take far longer to mature than cash-crop trees. Logging is illegal, but a black market trade inevitably continues. Logging in the north is a particular problem, and there have been several reports of violence against officials when illegal activity has been unearthed. In 2010, four rangers were killed while trying to stop the loggers.

Several independent groups are working towards improving the situation, including the Vietnam Conservation Fund, an organisation which helps local communities find sustainable and practical ways to earn a living that do not involve damaging the biodiversity of an area.

There are some successes. The Green Corridor project, an international effort, protected 1,340 sq km (500 sq miles) of forest in the central Thua Thien Hue province and led to the discovery of 11 new species of animals and plants. Two hours outside Ho Chi Minh City, the Wildlife Rescue Station has rescued and released 1,000 animals since its launch in 2007.

The government has also set aside large swathes of the country as protected areas, in the form of national parks and nature reserves. But most environmentalists claim these are, in reality, half-hearted measures and not backed up with adequate legislation and enforcement.

**LEFT:** dense tropical rainforest.
**ABOVE:** intensive farming near Dalat

## Endangered marine life

Although the offshore waters contain some 2,000 species of fish, overfishing is a major problem. The government has spoken of creating sustainable breeding programmes for the more economically important species and creating alternative livelihoods for those who depend on the sea to make a living.

Numerous islands are, however, still rich in underwater species and popular with divers, particularly in the south around Nha Trang and the Con Dao archipelago. Species include moray eels, green turtles, various sharks and manta rays.

## The wildlife trade

Fewer than 100 tigers and 100 wild elephants are believed to survive in the wilds of Vietnam, their gene pools already too small to ensure their long-term survival. While the country has been famous over the past two decades for the discovery of new species, it is now on the verge of becoming infamous for the extinction of numerous species.

Exacerbating the problem is the highly lucrative – and illegal – wildlife trade. According to sources, every year nearly 3,300 tonnes of illegal live wildlife and animal products are shipped in and out of Vietnam. Commonly traded creatures include tigers and bears.

Scientists and environmental agencies have voiced concern over Vietnam's lax environmental laws. Anyone can legally keep endangered wildlife species as pets as long as the animals are kept in conditions that meet the government's criteria (which is left up to the village policeman to decide, once he puts down his beer and takes his bribe).

If someone is caught with an endangered species at a private farm, they merely have to pay an administrative fine, which is usually a tiny fraction of the animal's value on the illegal wildlife market, and an undertaking to keep the animal housed in "suitable conditions". What that means, no one really knows, so in reality there is no effective environmental protection at all. The international community is starting to put pressure on the Vietnamese government to be more proactive: in 2010 the Convention on International Trade in Endangered Species of Wild Fauna and Flora (CITES) cited Vietnam as one of the worst offenders.

**RIGHT:** a slow loris at the Primate Rescue Center, Cuc Phuong National Park.

The only way for protection groups to confiscate wildlife is when the animals are caught while in transit. To get around this, smugglers have been to known to create fake permits or use wedding cars or funeral hearses as cover. In one case, a bear was reported to have been smuggled in a hospital ambulance. Fuelling this illicit trade is the Vietnamese affinity for consuming exotic wildlife meat *(see panel)*.

The animal trade is so accepted in Vietnam that traders openly sell animals on city streets. Inspectors do occasionally perform raids, but the traders are adept at packing up and disappearing into the crowds whenever an official is nearby.

### BUSHMEAT

Vietnam's increasing affluence, coupled with an appetite for wildlife meat, is driving some species to extinction. Eating certain animal body parts is often falsely believed to have medicinal or aphrodisiacal effects. Some animals are killed for their skin and teeth, while others are kept in illegal private zoos, but most, over 75 percent, end up in the cooking pot. A 2010 survey of more than 7,000 Ho Chi Minh City residents revealed that about half the respondents admitted using wild animal products, whether it be for food, health or just as ornaments. The most popular dishes were snake, wild boar, deer, porcupine and monitor lizard.

# DECISIVE DATES

**1st millennium BC**
Bronze Age. Dong Son culture flourishes in the Red River basin and Tonkin coast.

**258 BC**
Kingdom of Au Lac.

**208 BC**
Kingdom of Nam Viet.

**AD 39–42**
Trung sisters lead an unsuccessful rebellion against the Chinese. Viet people are placed under Chinese rule.

**542–4**
Ly Bon leads an uprising against China.

**545–938**
Vietnam languishes under periodic Chinese rule.

**939–1009**
A succession of three short dynasties: Ngo, Dinh and Tien Le.

**1010–1225**
Hanoi established as Thang Long by Ly Thai To.

**1225–1400**
Further consolidation under Tran dynasty.

**1400–28**
Ho dynasty.

**1428–1527**
Le dynasty.

**1471**
Le dynasty takes over the southern Champa territory.

**1527–92**
Short-lived Mac dynasty.

**1624**
Jesuit priest Alexandre de Rhodes translates Vietnamese into a Romanised system of writing.

**1672**
The country is divided by rival Trinh and Nguyen lords.

**1771–92**
Tay Son Rebellion.

**1802–1945**
Nguyen dynasty.

**1802**
Capital moved to Hue.

**1861**
French capture Saigon and within six years take over southern Vietnam.

**1883–1907**
Various anti-French movements are crushed.

**1919**
Ho Chi Minh presents an anti-colonial petition at the Versailles Peace Conference.

**1926**
Emperor Bao Dai ascends the throne.

**1930**
Ho Chi Minh rallies communist groups; becomes founder of Indochinese Communist Party.

**1942–3**
Ho Chi Minh imprisoned in China. He is released and recognised as the chief of the Viet Minh.

**1945**
Japan overthrows the French and renders Vietnam "independent" but under Japanese "protection". Japanese later surrender to the Allies, and the Viet Minh takes over the country. Ho Chi Minh declares Vietnam's independence. Emperor Bao Dai abdicates.

**1946**
Hostilities against French begin after the latter try to reclaim Vietnam.

**1951**
Ho Chi Minh consolidates Viet Minh and announces the formation of the Workers' Party

**1954**
The French are defeated at Dien Bien Phu. Geneva Accord divides Vietnam at 17th parallel. Democratic South Vietnam is led by Ngo Dinh Diem; North Vietnam comes under the communist Ho Chi Minh.

**1955**
Escalation of hostilities between North and South Vietnam. Direct US aid to South Vietnam begins.

**1959**
North Vietnam infiltrates South Vietnam via the Ho Chi Minh Trail.

**1960**
North Vietnam forms the National Liberation Front (NLF) in the war against the south.

**1963**
Ngo Dinh Diem is overthrown and assassinated.

**1965**
US bombs military targets in North Vietnam. First American ground combat troops land in

**ABOVE, FROM LEFT:** 13th-century Cham tower at Po Klong Garai; Emperor Bao Dai; Ho Chi Minh; South Vietnamese troops during the Vietnam War.

Vietnam at Danang.

**1968**
The Viet Cong launch the Tet Offensive, the turning point in the Vietnam War. Peace talks begin in Paris.

**1969**
Ho Chi Minh dies, aged 79.

**1973**
Paris Peace Agreement ends hostilities. Last US troops depart.

**1975**
North Vietnamese troops enter Saigon. The South Vietnamese government surrenders. Saigon is renamed Ho Chi Minh City.

**1976**
Vietnam is officially reunified as a communist country.

**1976–85**
A period of severe economic hardship. Millions of refugees, or "boat people", flee from persecution by the new government.

**1977**
Vietnam admitted to the UN.

**1978–9**
Vietnam signs friendship treaty with the Soviet Union.

Hostilities with Cambodia and China.

**1986**
Programme of socio-economic renovation called *doi moi* is launched.

**1994**
US lifts trade embargo.

**1995**
Diplomatic ties are restored with the US. Vietnam is admitted to the Association of Southeast Asian Nations (ASEAN).

**1997**
Asian economic crisis; investors leave Vietnam.

**2000**
Bill Clinton becomes the first US president to visit Vietnam since the war.

**2001**
The US and Vietnam enter a trade agreement. Foreign investment picks up.

**2007**
Vietnam joins the WTO.

**2008**
The economy suffers as food and fuel prices skyrocket.

**2011**
Inflation rises and the currency is devalued.

# EARLY HISTORY

Dynasties quickly rose and fell as Vietnam
fused into a nation. Having initially been
influenced by China in the north, Vietnam later
faced a fresh threat – from French colonialists

Vietnam's ancient history is steeped in the mists of myth, and only by melding Chinese and Vietnamese historical annals with Vietnamese folklore and recent archaeological discoveries have historians managed to piece together the country's origins.

The story of Vietnam begins in the northern Red River Delta, nearly 5,000 years ago, where legend has it that a powerful dragon lord called Lac Long Quan and a mountain fairy named Au Co sired exactly 100 sons. The eldest of these sons was later crowned king of the Lac Viet, naming himself Hung Vuong (Brave King) and his kingdom as Van Lang.

It should be pointed out that the Vietnamese state is generally considered to have started in the north of the country: further south, power lay with the Hindu Cham in the centre and various Khmer kingdoms in and around the

> Extending from northern Vietnam into Cambodia, Laos and even Indonesia, the Dong Son culture, named after a small village in northern Vietnam, produced exquisite bronze works as early as 300 BC.

Mekong Delta, and these areas were only assimilated into the Vietnamese state much later in its history.

French colonialists later dismissed the story of Van Lang, claiming they were mere myths. But we now know this kingdom was well organised and powerful, encompassing most of present-day

northern and central Vietnam. It is said to have prospered under the rule of 18 successive Hung kings during the 1st millennium BC until Thuc Phan, king of neighbouring Au Viet, defeated the Lac Viet in 258 BC. He then renamed himself An Duong Vuong (Peaceful Sun King) and established the new kingdom called Au Lac, establishing his capital at Phuc An. The remains of his citadel are located in the present-day village of Co Loa, to the north of Hanoi.

A matriarchal society, which is sometimes referred to as the Dong Son culture, is thought to have prevailed at this time. At its peak around 500–200 BC, Dong Son is best known for its ornately carved wooden drums and fine bronze ornaments.

**LEFT:** red-brick Cham tower at My Son, near Hoi An.
**RIGHT:** Dong Son bronze drum, 500-100BC

## China's influence

Around 200 BC, the Au Lac kingdom fell to the northern hordes led by an ambitious general called Trieu Da from the south of China. He founded the independent kingdom of Nam Viet, which included much of present-day southern China, and established the Trieu dynasty in 208 BC. His capital was located near present-day Guangzhou (Canton).

Nam Viet gradually came under the Chinese sphere of influence as the Han dynasty unified China. By 111 BC, the plains of northern Vietnam had become a colonial province of China called Giao Chi (Jiaozhi). Administrators from China were appointed as governors to rule the country, but their efforts to impose Chinese culture on the Viet people were met with fierce resistance.

Frustrated by decades of Chinese influence and culture, the Vietnamese not only guarded their national identity but fought fiercely to preserve it. One dauntless woman called Trung Trach, a member of an indigenous elite class, sparked the leap from protest to revolt. In AD 39, together with her sister Trung Nhi, she led a swift rebellion that forced the Chinese authorities to flee. Trung Trach was made queen but her reign was short-lived. Three years later, the

## THE RISE AND FALL OF THE CHAM CIVILISATION

The earliest records of the Cham civilisation date back to the end of the 2nd century AD. The Cham grew in strength on the basis of maritime trade and became more Indianised through commercial relations with India and Southeast Asia. By the 4th century, Hinduism had been adopted and Sanskrit was the language of communication. At the height of its power, Champa controlled the entire central coast from the Hoanh Son Pass in the north to the area around Vung Tau in the south.

The Cham civilisation is best known for its brick temples and towers, remnants of which are scattered along the south-central coast where the Cham kingdom once dominated. While the Cham ruins cannot compare with the similarly Indian-influenced Angkor in Cambodia or Pagan in Burma, their masterful masonry and exquisite sculpting are still apparent in the ruins of Po Nagar at Nha Trang and My Son near Hoi An.

The territorial ambitions of later Viet kings would eventually reduce Champa to a sliver of territory near Nha Trang by the end of the 15th century. In 1720, the last Cham king and his subjects fled to neighbouring Cambodia. Today, only about 100,000 Cham people are left in southern Vietnam. Most converted to Islam centuries ago, but there are still small communities of Hindu and Buddhist Cham people. For more on the Cham, *see page* 240.

better-equipped Chinese army brought the country again under their control. The two sisters, known to Vietnamese as Hai Ba Trung (Two Trung Ladies), committed suicide. Today, they are honoured as national heroes.

## Khmer and Cham kingdoms

Direct Chinese control did not extend into present-day central and southern Vietnam, which were heavily influenced by maritime trade with India and Southeast Asia. The far south was part of the Khmer Funan kingdom, and later the Chen La kingdom which led on to the foundation of Angkor. From the second century AD, much of the centre was ruled by the powerful Cham kings (*see page* 28).

## Rebels with a cause

After the Trung sisters' rebellion was crushed, Nam Viet was administered as a Chinese province known as Giao Chau (Jiaozhou) until the 6th century, when a scholar named Ly Bon led an armed revolt and succeeded in routing the Chinese. Ly Bon was declared emperor and he renamed the empire Van Xuan (Eternal Spring), changing his own name to Ly Nam De (the Southern Emperor) in AD 544. His kingdom was short-lived, however; the Chinese quickly regained supremacy in the area in 545. Ly Nam De fled to Laos where he died in exile. His successor, Triet Viet Vuong, an accomplished general, managed to drive the Chinese out of Van Xuan in 550, but eventually the Chinese returned and resumed occupation in 603.

The Chinese, now under the prosperous Tang dynasty, again made concerted efforts to impose their culture and civilisation on Nam Viet, which they renamed An Nam. Nonetheless, armed revolts by the Vietnamese remained a thorn in their side. Rebel leaders such as Mai Hac De in 722 and Phung Hung in 791 successfully rallied locals and managed to overthrow the Chinese rulers. Their brief reigns ended when China inevitably sent reinforcements. However, with each revolt a new folk hero was born, inspiring more shrines and more legends, which only served to fuel the desire to remove the Chinese.

**Above, from Left:** the big cat (China) receives tribute from servile mice (Vietnam); Temple of Literature, Hanoi.

## The early dynasties

Disorder accompanied the decline of the Tang dynasty in China, giving the Vietnamese the chance to stake their claim for independence. In a protracted war a general called Ngo Quyen defeated the Chinese reinforcements and founded the first Vietnamese dynasty in 939. He renamed the country Dai Viet and moved the capital back to Co Loa. After his death in 967, the kingdom fell into chaos and remained fragmented for more than 20 years, while the threat from China's Song dynasty loomed large to the north.

The most powerful of the feudal lords, Dinh

Bo Linh, eventually reunified the fragmented country under the name of Dai Co Viet and took the imperial title of Dinh Tien Hoang De (The First August Emperor Dinh). He wisely negotiated a non-aggression treaty in exchange for tributes payable to the Chinese every three years.

Dinh Tien Hoang established his royal court in the new capital of Hoa Lu in Ninh Binh province, 100km (62 miles) south of Hanoi. He instated a rigorous justice system and introduced the death penalty to anyone who threatened his rule. Security and order were progressively re-established, inaugurating a new era of peace. However, the emperor was assassinated in 979 by a palace guard. The heir to the throne was only six years old, so the court's commander, Le Hoan, seized power and pro-claimed himself Emperor Le Dai Hanh. He succeeded in warding off the Chinese but also continued paying them tribute.

With relative peace assured on the northern border, Le Dai Hanh sought to pacify the south. In 982, a military expedition was launched against the Champa kingdom, which would gradually be absorbed over the following centuries. The emperor also sought to consolidate the Viet nation. He developed a road network in order to administer the country better. However, a succession of local revolts assured 24 years of difficult rule until Le Dai Hanh died.

dynasty. In 1070, the Temple of Literature dedicated to Confucius was constructed in Thang Long.

The Ly dynasty consolidated the monarchy along Confucianist principles. It established a centralised government, a tax system, a judiciary and a professional army. Important public works, including the building of dykes and canals in the Red River Delta region, were undertaken to develop agriculture.

## Tran and Ho dynasties

An ambitious commoner, Tran Canh, married into the Ly dynasty royalty and shrewdly

## Ly dynasty

The Ly dynasty (1009–1225), which reigned over the country for more than two centuries, was the first of the more enduring national dynasties. Ly Cong Uan was a disciple of a monk, Van Hanh, who helped him rise to power. After assuming the name Ly Thai To, the new sovereign moved the capital to present-day Hanoi, naming it Thang Long (Ascending Dragon) after seeing the apparition of an ascending dragon on the proposed site.

During the Ly dynasty, Buddhism flourished as the national religion. Buddhist masters assisted the Ly kings as advisers. Several Ly kings also led Buddhist sects. Confucian studies were also encouraged under the Ly

manoeuvred his way to power to found the Tran dynasty (1225–1400). During this period the Viet armies repelled three invasions – in 1257, 1284 and 1288 – by the Mongols under Kublai Khan, who had occupied China and founded the Yuan dynasty. The mastermind behind the latter two victories was Tran Quoc Toan (better known as Tran Hung Dao), one of Vietnam's greatest military heroes. The key to his success was to avoid the Mongols' strength in open field battles and city sieges (the Tran court abandoned the capital and the cities), then counter them at their weak points in swampy areas and on rivers. The Mongols retreated only to be routed at the Bach Dang River in 1288.

In the 16th century, Ho Chi Minh City was a Khmervillage called Prei Kor. When the Viet settled this area in later years, ethnic Khmers were resettled in the Mekong Delta, where today they are a minority race.

The country's territorial ambitions to the south also continued. The king's sister married the king of Champa in 1307, thus extending the territory southwards with the peaceful annexation of the Hue region through a diplomatic marriage.

Towards the end of the 14th century, the Tran dynasty went into swift decline. A political opportunist called Le Quy Ly shrewdly manoeuvred his way to power and founded a dynasty under his ancestral name of Ho. While successful for initiating many economic, financial and educational reforms, his reign prompted another attack from China. Aware that the new king had usurped the throne, the Chinese Ming dynasty emperor sent 5,000 soldiers under the pretext of helping the faithful followers of the deposed Tran dynasty. The Ming intervention led to the fall of the Ho dynasty in 1407. During the short period of Chinese occupation that followed, the Vietnamese suffered inhumane exploitation. The Chinese strove to destroy the Vietnamese national identity – Vietnamese literature, artistic and historical works were burnt or taken to China, and in schools, books were replaced with Chinese classics. The Chinese style of dress and hair was imposed on Vietnamese women, local religious rites and festivals were replaced or banished by the Chinese and private fortunes were confiscated.

## Le dynasty

It took a man called Le Loi, renowned for his courage and generosity, to organise a resistance movement from his village and wage a guerrilla war against the Chinese. Through surprise attacks, Le Loi weakened the enemy and at the same time avoided combat with the superior Chinese forces. His strict military discipline ensured that no pillaging was carried out by his troops in the regions under his control, making him a popular military hero.

**ABOVE, FROM LEFT:** old print of traditional village in the Hue area; Vietnamese court official

Le Loi founded the Le dynasty in 1428 and became king under the name of Le Thai To. He renamed the country Dai Viet and immediately began the task of its reconstruction after the devastation caused by the war. He reduced his army from 250,000 to 10,000 men and adopted a rotation system that enabled soldiers to return to the countryside to work and help boost food production. The legal system was reorganised and the penal system revised. A new college was founded to educate future administrators, with admission based entirely on merit and not on social or family status.

Le Thai To died in 1443, leaving the throne to

his son, Le Thai Tong, whose sudden death not long after was followed by a decade of confusion and plots within the royal court. This troubled period ceased when Le Thanh Tong began his 36-year reign in 1460 and the country prospered as never before. He revised the fiscal system, encouraged agriculture and placed great emphasis on customs and moral principles. He penned the first volume of Vietnamese history.

Le Thanh Tong's reorganised army also won an easy victory over the southern Champa army in 1471. His farmer-soldiers excelled not only on the battlefields but also in the fields where they set up militarised agricultural communities wherever they went. In this way the national territory gradually expanded southwards, until finally the Champa kingdom was completely absorbed and assimilated.

## Secession wars

The increasing decadence of the Le dynasty in the late 16th century and the corrupt and idle kings who succeeded Le Thanh Tong led to the country's division into two rival principalities. Mac Dang Dung, a shrewd and scheming adviser at the court, seized control of the north (including Hanoi) and founded the short-lived Mac dynasty in 1527. Meanwhile, descendants of the Le dynasty rallied around Nguyen Kim, a former official in the Le court, and his

son-in-law Trinh Kiem founded the southern court near Thanh Hoa, 120km (75 miles) south of Hanoi, in 1543. A protracted civil war continued indecisively until the death of the Mac dynasty's last king, Mac Mau Hop, in 1592.

In an effort to restore law and order to the territory controlled by the Mac dynasty, Trinh Kiem left the southern court under the temporary control of Nguyen Kim's nephew, Nguyen Hoang, and set out for the north. After pacifying the region, Trinh Kiem returned to find Nguyen Hoang well entrenched in the southern court as lord and master of all.

This led to a drawn-out standoff. Between 1627 and 1672, the Trinh Lords of the north and the Nguyen Lords of the south battled indecisively for over 40 years. Eventually, the Trinh Lords consented to the partition of the country just north of Phu Xuan (Hue).

Relative peace between both sides lasted for a century, during which time the Nguyen Lords made further inroads into the Mekong Delta. In 1771 revolution broke out in Quy Nhon province, south of Phu Xuan. Provoked by corruption within the imperial court and the north–south feud, a man named Nguyen Hue (no relation to the Nguyen Lords), along with his two brothers, led a peasant uprising known as the Tay Son Rebellion, which overthrew the Nguyen Lords. The Tay Son brothers took control of the south of Vietnam before defeating the Trinh Lords in the north and, most audaciously, the Chinese forces occupying Thanh Long. A peasant uprising had, incredibly, unified Vietnam.

## Nguyen dynasty

Nguyen Hue pronounced himself Emperor Quang Trung in 1788 and devoted his energies to rebuilding the country. Sadly, his promising reign was cut short by his premature death in 1792.

In the meantime, one of the surviving Nguyen Lords, Nguyen Anh, had not given up hope of securing power for himself. He befriended a French Catholic, Pigneau de Behaine, the Bishop of Adran. De Behaine saw an opportunity to expand the Catholic Church's influence and negotiate a promise of military aid for Nguyen Anh from the French government in exchange for territorial and commercial rights in Vietnam. However, the French were busy with other internal disputes and the promised aid never materialised. Undaunted, the bishop

**From Nam Viet to Vietnam**

In the early 19th century, the Nguyen Emperor Gia Long sent his ambassador to China to seek approval for the reunification of the old land of An Nam and the new land of Viet Thuong, and to change the country's name to Nam Viet. But the Chinese emperor was advised that the name Nam Viet would bring to mind the ancient kingdom of Nam Viet Dong, which had included two Chinese provinces, and might also conceal territorial ambitions on the part of Gia Long. Therefore, the two words Viet (people) and Nam (south) were simply reversed.

organised funds and recruited troops himself. Training in Western military techniques proved invaluable to Nguyen Anh and his army, and it facilitated victory in 1801 when he defeated the last of the Tay Sons. In 1802, he proclaimed himself Emperor Gia Long, the founder of the Nguyen dynasty.

Nguyen Anh may have owed his accession to the French, but he was suspicious of France's designs. Therefore, he relied more on the assistance of Confucian mandarins than the Catholic missionaries in the consolidation of his empire. The reunified and renamed Viet Nam *(see panel)* extended from the Chinese frontier to the Ca Mau Peninsula at the country's southernmost tip. Serious efforts were made to codify the law and develop the national administration along Confucian principles. Hue became the country's new administrative capital, and elaborate palaces, mausoleums, temples and pagodas were built.

The Nguyen kings extended Vietnam's border into Laos and Cambodia, incorporating parts of these two kingdoms as vassal states. They closed the country off to Western penetration from the seas, fearing that the expansion of trade links would undermine the inherent structure of the Nguyen monarchy.

## The French connection

Prince Canh, Nguyen Anh's eldest son, accompanied de Behaine to France during his negotiations with the French government. The prince was later educated at a missionary school in Malacca and converted to Catholicism. This made Canh the first Viet prince to be given a Western education. Military leaders within Nguyen Anh's army realised the superiority of modern Western military technology and so wanted to utilise Prince Canh's knowledge to rebuild the country after the war. Canh was seen as the one who could modernise Vietnam.

But after Gia Long died in 1820, court ministers from the Chinese faction supported Canh's younger brother, Mien Tong, to take the throne. Prince Canh, supported by the French faction, reportedly died of measles at the age of 21, though missionaries close to the court claimed

**ABOVE, FROM LEFT:** the young Prince Canh received a Western education; depiction of French troops entering Hung Hoa in 1884.

*Alexandre de Rhodes, a French Jesuit priest, arrived in Vietnam in 1619 and began work on the first Portuguese-Latin-Vietnamese dictionary. This was later used to develop the Romanised Vietnamese alphabet called quoc ngu.*

he had been poisoned. Once Mien Tong was crowned as Emperor Minh Mang, the French-Chinese divide officially ended. Most of Canh's followers were demoted or executed.

In the meantime, Catholic missions began to accelerate their proselytising efforts, provoking

Emperor Minh Mang into taking a vigorous anti-Catholic stance, "lest they spread darkness in the kingdom".

This gave the French the perfect excuse to intervene in Vietnam. The old cycle of invasion and occupation began anew, but this time from afar. The landing of a French party in Danang in 1858 heralded the beginning of colonial occupation that would last almost a century. The French government wanted a strategic and religious sphere of influence in Indochina (present-day Vietnam, Laos and Cambodia), but their demands for a French consulate and commercial attaché in Danang were rejected by the Vietnamese imperial court in Hue. The French responded to the affront by seizing Danang.

# THE ROAD TO WAR

A century of French colonialism culminated in a
bloody war of independence, swiftly followed by
the catastrophic Vietnam War. The country
emerged from these conflicts battered but unified

In 1861 the French took Saigon and within six years the entire southern part of the country had been annexed as a French colony and rechristened Cochinchina. In the 1880s, central and northern Vietnam became French protectorates under the nominal rule of the Nguyen dynasty. Central Vietnam was renamed Annam, while the north became Tonkin.

The Vietnamese were no happier under French domination than they had been under the Chinese. Resistance movements took shape in occupied areas, some led by former court officers, others by peasants. Even the teenage Nguyen emperor Ham Nghi started an anti-French movement, only to be captured and exiled to Algeria.

One influential resistance movement, composed mainly of aristocrats, intellectuals and young people, was led by the radical Confucian scholars Phan Boi Chau and Phan Chau Trinh, who embraced the idea of democracy. This movement had been inspired by the Japanese victory over Russia in 1904, which convinced them that Western powers were not invincible.

Phan Boi Chau established the Eastward Movement (Dong Du) in 1907 and secretly sent students to learn from the Japanese. The French authorities discovered the scheme and negotiated with Japan to extradite the Vietnamese students. However, Japanese officials helped some escape to China, where they witnessed the 1911 revolution led by Sun Yat-sen. This convinced them that Vietnam was ready for a similar kind of coup.

But the revolutionaries were not united. A rift widened between the Westernised reformer

Phan Chu Trinh and the nationalist Phan Boi Chau. The latter created the Vietnam Quang Phu Hoi Party and planned armed resistance against the French, while Phan Chu Trinh maintained that Vietnam could regain independence through the democratic process. In 1915, he went to Paris to rally Vietnamese exiles and radical French politicians into supporting the struggle against colonial rule.

## A young leader in the making

The Russian Revolution of 1917 had a tremendous impact on shaping Vietnamese history, primarily because of its influence on a young revolutionary called Nguyen Tat Thanh, later known as Ho Chi Minh.

**LEFT:** the Ho Chi Minh Mausoleum in Hanoi.
**RIGHT:** the legendary Ho Chi Minh in the 1950s.

# Vietnam's Last Emperor

**A pawn in the power struggle between the French and Ho Chi Minh, Bao Dai was an enigmatic figure who lived most of his life in exile**

The last ruling monarch of Vietnam, Prince Nguyen Vinh Thuy, was born in 1913 and spent his youth in France where he was edu-

cated according to Western principles. On becoming emperor in 1926, when he took the name Bao Dai, he was just 12 years old. Too young to take up his royal duties, the young monarch returned to France to continue his studies. A council of regency, made up of French loyalists, ruled Vietnam in his absence.

When Bao Dai returned home to the imperial city of Hue in 1932, he tried to reform the judicial and educational systems, but soon became better known as the "Playboy Emperor" thanks to his lavish lifestyle. He is said to have devoted weeks at a time to hunting tigers in the Vietnamese rainforests. But when faced with political peril he was less brave. After the Japanese swept across Southeast Asia and occupied Vietnam during World War II, he was allowed to retain his throne,

as the Japanese hoped his presence would demonstrate some continuity. After the Japanese departed in 1945, the Viet Minh quickly "persuaded" Bao Dai to abdicate.

Despite his face-saving offer to be Ho Chi Minh's supreme adviser, the communists had no intention of sharing power with the former emperor. With war on the horizon, Bao Dai left for Hong Kong and China, but in 1949 he was coaxed back to Vietnam by the French, who needed a recognised figurehead as head of state. As before, Bao Dai left the major decisions to his French-backed advisers, preferring to spend time with his mistress at his hunting lodge in the central highlands.

When the 1954 peace accord between the French and the communists resulted in the division of Vietnam into North and South, Bao Dai and his advisers tried to assume true power in South Vietnam. In response, the American-backed premier, Ngo Dinh Diem, organised a referendum on the issue of monarchy versus republicanism. The corrupt Ngo won 98.2 percent of the votes in a remarkable election which saw 605,000 votes cast in the Saigon-Cholon area, where only 450,000 voters were registered.

Even though the fraudulent election was discredited and Ngo was later assassinated, the monarch returned to France where he remained until his death. In a rare public statement, made in 1972, he appealed to the Vietnamese people for national reconciliation. That same year, his mother, who remained in Vietnam, reportedly sold the family porcelain to help her only son survive in exile. He spent the final years of his life in a modest Paris apartment before his death in 1997.

**LEFT:** Emperor Bao Dai. **ABOVE:** Bao Dai Palace, Dalat

Under the alias Nguyen Ai Quoc, Ho submitted an anti-colonial petition at the Versailles Conference in 1919. He became involved with French intellectuals who formed the French Communist Party in 1920, and then went to Moscow to be trained as an agent of Communist International.

In 1924, Ho was sent to China where he contacted young Vietnamese revolutionaries and founded the Association of Vietnamese Youth. Emperor Khai Dinh died in 1925, and his son Bao Dai ascended the throne in 1926, aged just 12. Bao Dai *(see page 36)* was sent to France for his education and would not return to Vietnam until 1932.

## Communism consolidates

For Vietnam, the onset of World War II in 1939 was a landmark event as significant as the French occupation of Danang in 1858. The pro-Nazi Vichy government of France accepted the Japanese occupation of Indochina, but on condition that it could continue administering Vietnam. Earlier, the Central Committee of the Indochinese Communist Party had met in China and announced the formation of the Revolutionary League for the Independence of Vietnam, later known as the Viet Minh.

At the end of World War II in 1945, Vietnam faced a political void as Japan overthrew the

The Vietnamese waited to see if the French would adopt more liberal politics, but it soon became clear they would make no real concessions. In 1930, Ho rallied several communist groups and founded the Indochinese Communist Party. In the same year, under the leadership of the revolutionary Nguyen Thai Hoc, the Quoc Dan Dang (Vietnam Nationalist Party) launched a military revolt while communist groups staged several peasant uprisings. The French took severe measures against the fledgling movements, but the apparent calm that reigned after the reprisals was shattered with the first battles of World War II.

**ABOVE:** Hang Bo Street, Hanoi, in the late 1930s.

French, imprisoned their civil servants and rendered Vietnam "independent" under Japanese "protection", with Bao Dai as head of state. By the middle of August, following the Japanese defeat, chaos and uncertainty reigned. Using the clandestine Indochinese Communist Party and the Viet Minh as intermediaries, Ho tried to become the dominant political force by occupying as much territory as possible.

## The August Revolution

On 16 August 1945, the Viet Minh announced the formation of a National Committee of Liberation for Vietnam. Three days later, Ho's guerrilla forces took Hanoi. Hue's turn came four days later when Bao Dai's government was besieged and "asked" to hand over the royal seal. After Bao Dai's abdication, Ho announced the formation of a provisional government in Hanoi, and proclaimed himself president of the new Democratic Republic of Vietnam.

However, the situation was precarious. The British arrived in Saigon looking to disarm the Japanese and restore order, while the French tried to reclaim their former colony. From the north, the Chinese entered Vietnam looking to disarm the Japanese.

In the general elections, organised in early 1946, the Viet Minh won a majority in the first National Assembly. The country's first national constitution was approved, and the French were allowed to stay for five years in return for recognising the Democratic Republic of Vietnam as a free state within the French Union. However, relations between the French and the Viet Minh deteriorated. Hostilities reached a peak with the French bombing of Haiphong port, east of Hanoi. In December 1946, Ho ordered an offensive against the French in Hanoi and at the French garrisons in northern and central Vietnam. A war for independence had begun that would rage for 30 years.

## THE BATTLE OF DIEN BIEN PHU

The battle of Dien Bien Phu in 1954, masterminded by General Vo Nguyen Giap, marked a turning point in Vietnamese history. The French strategy was to force the Viet Minh into a large-scale battle which France would, presumably, win. In December 1953, a defensive complex was built at Dien Bien Phu, which would block the route of the Viet Minh forces trying to return to camps in neighbouring Laos.

General Vo's first task was to dig a trench that encircled the French fortification. From the outer trench, more tunnels were dug inwards towards the centre. In this way the Viet Minh could close in on the French troops while escaping fire. Meanwhile, reinforcements arrived.

Soon General Vo had 70,000 soldiers surrounding Dien Bien Phu, five times the number of French troops. Employing recently obtained anti-aircraft guns and howitzers from China, he severely restricted the ability of the French to supply their forces in Dien Bien Phu.

On 13 March 1954, General Vo launched his offensive and for 56 days the Viet Minh pushed the French forces back until they only occupied a small area of Dien Bien Phu. The French surrendered on 7 May, after 13,000 of their men and another 25,000 of the Viet Minh had died. Shortly after, the war ended with the 1954 Geneva Accord, under which France agreed to withdraw from its former Indochinese colonies in Asia.

## War of resistance

Thousands of Vietnamese took up arms against the French, yet few knew the identity and allegiance of their new leader and his party. On Ho's orders, his principal collaborator, General Vo Nguyen Giap, launched a general offensive against the colonial forces, but in the face of superior firepower the Vietnamese troops retreated to the countryside. They adopted Mao Zedong's guerrilla strategy of a "people's war and people's army" by attacking and sabotaging isolated French units, rather than becoming embroiled in large-scale battles, a tactic reminiscent of that used by Le Loi against the Chinese in the 15th century.

Party that had officially disbanded but in reality was still active. The nationalists and non-communists were forced to choose between the new regime and the French colonialists.

## The Geneva Agreement

In May 1954, the French base at Dien Bien Phu suffered a humiliating and historic defeat after a heavy artillery attack from General Vo Nguyen Giap's forces, which famously used bicycles to carry supplies. The French forces in northern Vietnam evacuated to below the 16th parallel at Danang. The war officially ended on 20 July, after long negotiations in Geneva.

After Ho's guerrillas had wiped out several French posts on the Chinese border, China and Vietnam established direct contact for the first time. China, the old aggressor, was now an ally, supplying the young republic with military equipment and substantial provisions.

On his side, Ho attempted to shore up the nationalist support. In 1951, he merged the Viet Minh with the Lien Viet, or Patriotic Front, into the National Union of Vietnam. He also announced the formation of the Workers' Party (Lao Dong), a disguise for the Communist

**ABOVE, FROM LEFT:** General Vo Nguyen Giap on the 40th anniversary of the French defeat; battle of Dien Bien Phu.

In finally gaining national independence, however, Vietnam lost its unity. The Geneva Agreement signed in August divided the country at the 17th parallel, pending general elections scheduled for 1956. The north of the country became the Democratic Republic of Vietnam – communist North Vietnam – under the leadership of Ho Chi Minh; and the south became the Republic of South Vietnam.

By this time, the last French troops had left Vietnam and Indochina. Bao Dai, who had been persuaded to return from exile by the French after his abdication, appealed on behalf of the royalists and asked Ngo Dinh Diem, a former minister at Bao Dai's court, to become prime minister of what would become South

By the time the dust settled on the Vietnam War, some 2 million civilian Vietnamese, along with 1 million soldiers from North Vietnam, 250,000 soldiers from South Vietnam and 57,605 Americans had perished.

Vietnam. Ngo was a curious choice, a Catholic in a predominantly Buddhist country who had been away from Vietnam for two decades. In a subsequent fraudulent referendum, Bao Dai was deposed by Ngo Dinh Diem, marking the beginning of the Republic of South Vietnam.

## THE MY LAI MASSACRE

The My Lai massacre of 16 March 1968 was a turning point in the public perception of the Vietnam War. In just three hours more than 500 Vietnamese civilians were killed in cold blood by US troops. The soldiers had been on a "search and destroy" mission to root out communist fighters in what was fertile Viet Cong territory. However, there had been no firefight with the enemy. In fact not a single shot was fired at the American soldiers. When the story of My Lai was exposed, it tarnished the name of the US army, as well as adding momentum to the anti-war movement that was spreading across the US at the time.

But rather than creating stability, it set the stage for Vietnam's next, and bloodiest, conflict.

## The North–South divide

The elections stipulated by the Geneva Agreement to take place in 1956 never occurred. From 1954 to 1974, the two Vietnams had no diplomatic, cultural or commercial relations with each other. Immediately after the Geneva Agreement, a virtual state of war existed between the two divided parts of the country. North Vietnam's intensified armed and revolutionary activities made the prospect of reunification increasingly unlikely.

Meanwhile, the US saw the conflict in Vietnam as part of a larger global fight against communism. It reinforced Ngo's troops, in effect turning South Vietnam into an American military protectorate. In December 1960, North Vietnam formed the National Liberation Front (NLF), which began revolutionary activities against Ngo's increasingly repressive and unstable regime. Its communist ally in South Vietnam, dubbed the Viet Cong, which fought against Ngo's government and the US, grew stronger in the early 1960s. To bolster the Viet Cong, North Vietnam sent additional reinforcements in the form of North Vietnamese Army (NVA) troops.

Facing mounting pressures from his own people, Ngo ordered oppressive measures against the Buddhist establishment, provoking a wave of suicides by Buddhist monks, who set fire to themselves. In June 1963, Thich Quang Duc, a 66-year-old monk, immolated himself on a street corner in Saigon.

This signalled the end for Ngo's regime. He and his brother, Ngo Dinh Nhu, head of the security forces, were murdered five months later by Ngo's own officers following a US-backed coup.

## American involvement

The beginning of 1965 marked the escalation of direct American involvement in Vietnam, when US President Lyndon Johnson sent in large

political and social legitimacy as the American public got wind of atrocities like the My Lai massacre *(see panel)*. Eventually, Johnson announced he would not run for re election. His successor, Richard Nixon, had promised a secret plan to end the war during the election campaign, but this turned out to be nothing more than turning the bulk of fighting over to the South Vietnamese.

In 1969, Ho Chi Minh died without seeing his work completed, and peace negotiations dragged on in Paris between 1968 and 1973. Eventually Americans troops left in 1973, as part of the Paris Peace Agreement, although

numbers of troops. By the end of 1967, there were more than 500,000 American and 100,000 Allied troops (mostly from Korea, Australia and New Zealand) in Vietnam.

What many consider the war's turning point came in 1968, when the Viet Cong launched surprise attacks on Saigon and other cities throughout the south during the Lunar New Year, or Tet. The "Tet Offensive" included a raid on the American embassy in Saigon that stunned and embarrassed the US. Domestic opposition in the US increasingly took on

**ABOVE, FROM LEFT:** a Viet Cong base camp being burnt by the Marines; the Son My Memorial; troops enter Saigon, 1975.

the US continued funding the Southern Vietnamese military efforts. In 1975, when the communist forces from North Vietnam steadily moved south and the Saigon regime finally crumbled, the US Congress refused to offer additional military aid, in effect ending South Vietnam's ability to continue the war.

The north launched its final offensive, and on 30 April 1975 the Northern Vietnamese Army (NVA) entered Saigon as the very last American troops and diplomats fled by helicopter from the American embassy. The Communist Party's long struggle for power had finally ended in victory. Vietnam was now independent of foreign troops and control, and it could set its sights on unification.

# MODERN HISTORY

Vietnam's journey towards unity and development has been long, and often painful, but since the 1990s the nation has made rapid economic progress. Freedom of speech may take a little longer

Following the unification of Vietnam in 1975, it looked as though years of oppression and suffering were at an end. Yet the dreams for national rehabilitation never fully materialised. Several strategic errors, later admitted by Hanoi's communist leaders, destroyed any hopes that this may have been the dawning of a progressive new era.

In July 1976, Vietnam was officially reunified into one country, and a radical programme of socialist construction was put forward by the Communist Party government. It called for the rapid socialisation of the southern economy, with the forced collectivisation of agriculture, small industry and commerce. The South's intellectual and government leaders were also sent to so-called "re-education camps". This policy quickly resulted in an unprecedented economic disaster, prompting more than a million refugees (or "boat people"), many of whom were southerners facing political persecution by the new government, to flee the country *(see panel)*.

## THE BOAT PEOPLE

In 1979 alone, more than 270,000 refugees left Vietnam, the vast majority taking to the seas as other routes were impractical. The exodus became a global issue as images of crowded fishing boats packed with Vietnamese became commonplace. Thousands died at sea and countless others were robbed by pirates, while those that did find refuge were often poorly treated. Camps were set up in Hong Kong, Malaysia, the Philippines, Indonesia and Thailand. When ethnic Chinese started to be persecuted in Vietnam in 1979, Hong Kong gave them refuge. The US, meanwhile, accepted more than 800,000 Vietnamese and set up a resettlement programme, while the Catholic Church, with its long-standing connections to Vietnam, also played a major role. Others were granted asylum in Great Britain and elsewhere in Europe. Hong Kong later began to view some Vietnamese as economic migrants and, controversially, started forcible repatriation. The final camp closed in June 2000 and its residents were offered residency in Hong Kong.

By the late 1980s there were fewer and fewer refugees, while financial rewards to return to Vietnam and a growing economy through the 1990s meant many people did come back. In 2008 a final group of 200 refugees who had been living in the Philippines were accepted into the US, Norway and Canada, bringing to an end the Boat People's long journey.

## War with Cambodia and China

Just a few years after reunification, Vietnam found itself fighting again – this time with neighbouring Cambodia's Khmer Rouge and its leader Pol Pot. This led to a clash with China in the north in 1979 in a brief but bloody battle (to this day, both sides of the conflict claim victory). The invasion of Cambodia (then known as Kampuchea) and the subsequent entanglement with China absorbed most of Vietnam's post-war energies and delayed its long-overdue recovery.

For the next decade, the presence of Vietnamese troops in Cambodia remained a central issue in the international arena. China, the US and the members of ASEAN (Association of Southeast Asian Nations) managed to garner international support to isolate Vietnam, which in turn had lost most of its hard-earned international sympathy. At the Fifth Party Congress in 1982, the old guard, under the guidance of party secretary-general Le Duan, stubbornly maintained Vietnam's course, hoping that, against all odds, it could consolidate its political and military edge in Cambodia, and at the same time stabilise Vietnam's own economic and social situation. It was a policy that would drive the country to the brink of disaster.

## Economic shifts and doi moi

The 1980s are remembered bitterly by most Vietnamese as a time of wretched poverty. People were starving, there wasn't enough rice to go around and meat was rationed. People had to stand in line for monthly and weekly allotments of food. It was only in 1986, following the Soviet example of *glasnost* and *perestroika*, that the party decided to reinvent the country with an ambitious programme of socio-economic renovation called *doi moi*.

Under the new leadership of Nguyen Van Linh, the motto of the party was "to change or to die". A new contract system was implemented in 1988 to encourage Vietnamese farmers to cultivate their land, and, as a result, rice production witnessed an immediate upsurge in 1989. Progress was also recorded in the sector of manufactured goods and commodities exports.

---

**ABOVE, FROM LEFT:** fleeing the communist takeover in 1975; sign of the times in Hanoi: propaganda posters for sale as souvenirs.

Until the end of 1988, socialist Vietnam followed the path of Soviet *perestroika*, but the Vietnamese leaders were soon aghast to see the direction of Mikhail Gorbachev's "new thinking" and its social and political consequences. Hastily, while reaffirming the Communist Party's commitment to reform, Nguyen Van Linh repeatedly rejected any idea of political pluralism in Vietnam.

Vietnamese forces withdrew from Cambodia in 1989. With the fall of the Soviet Union in 1991, a valued ally, Vietnam changed tack and adopted a new course in foreign affairs: it started to court China. By the early 1990s,

European and Asian companies started flooding into Vietnam seeking investment opportunities in what many saw as the last economic frontier. Hanoi and Ho Chi Minh City were soon buzzing with developments. Hotels were renovated and new ones built, international airline services increased, and telecoms and other infrastructures upgraded. In 1993, the American administration led by Bill Clinton allowed the release of International Monetary Fund loans to Hanoi. Foreign investment in Vietnam leapt. In early 1994, the US lifted its trade embargo, and in the following year Clinton restored diplomatic ties between Vietnam and the US, and an embassy opened in Hanoi. In 1995, Vietnam became a full member of ASEAN, ending an era of costly international ostracism.

## A growing economy

The Asian financial crisis in the late 1990s slowed the pace of economic growth that marked the earlier part of the decade. However, from 2000 onwards, the economy picked up, primarily as the result of ongoing economic and trade liberalisation. In 2001, a bilateral trade pact was signed with the US, and investors returned in large numbers.

The subsequent period of rapid economic growth transformed the country from an economic backwater into one of the world's hottest economies. US president George W. Bush arrived in 2006 to strengthen economic ties at an Asia-Pacific summit hosted in Hanoi. In 2007, the country joined the World Trade Organization, further cementing its position as a dynamic player in the global economy. Vietnam had become a "poster child" of the benefits of market-oriented reforms. In Ho Chi Minh City and Hanoi, where real-estate prices are among the highest in Asia, a frenzy of construction has brought a rash of luxury apartments, shopping malls and five-star hotels.

## ISLAND DISPUTE

Long-standing tension between China and Vietnam has been heating up in recent years over a disputed group of islands. The Paracel and Spratly island chains, rich in oil and natural gas, are claimed by several countries: China claims that the islands have been under its sovereignty for 2,000 years, Vietnam says it has ruled them for 400 years, while the Philippines feels it has a legitimate claim because the islands lie closer to its territory than any other country's. Taiwan, Indonesia, Malaysia and Brunei have also staked claims.

Violent clashes flare up from time to time, with China allegedly scuppering a Vietnamese expedition, while Vietnam has angered Beijing with live-firing exercises. Following alleged damage to a Vietnamese vessel's cables by the Chinese, hundreds of residents in Hanoi and Ho Chi Minh City held peaceful street protests in June 2011.

The islands are minuscule: if grouped together, Spratly's 750 reefs and seamounts would comprise a mere 5 sq km (2 sq miles), but they are spread out over 425,000 sq km (160,000 sq miles). France held the islands until World War II, when Japan used them as a submarine base. Today most of the countries that stake a claim have soldiers or some form of base on several of the islets.

## Recent developments

In 2008, against the backdrop of an impending global recession, Vietnam's economy started to lose its fizz. Compounded by a looming trade deficit, a widening urban–rural income gap and a major rise in food and oil prices that caused inflation levels to hit 25 percent, workers at many of Vietnam's factories went on strike, demanding higher salaries in order to survive. This led to panic in the local stock market and rumours of a currency depreciation. In 2009 exports plunged by 10 percent, prompting the government to respond with lending schemes and stimulus spending. Help came in part from foreign donors who promised US$8 billion in investments. The result was that growth turned the corner in 2010 and returned to healthy levels.

However inflation rates began creeping up in 2011, the country's credit rating was downgraded and state-run companies began to face difficulties. In its five-year plan, ending in 2015, the government predicts gross domestic product to grow annually by around 7 percent, but sceptics say serious reforms are again needed if such targets are to be met.

## Challenges for the future

Accompanying the doubts about the economy's staying power, an array of other issues hinders Vietnam's progress. Corruption has always been rampant in business – foreigners and Vietnamese alike complain that they are nickel-and-dimed to death, with bureaucrats at all levels demanding "tokens" in order to get paperwork completed, licences approved and offices opened. Following a number of high-profile trials, there are signs that the government is trying to confront this issue. But anecdotal evidence will tell you that corruption is still entrenched in Vietnamese society.

Almost as bad as the corruption is the glacial speed of legislative and bureaucratic processes; proposed laws have to be shoved through all sorts of hoops before taking effect. Efforts are under way by the government to trim the fat from the bloated bureaucracy and streamline wieldy official procedures.

Although the press enjoys much more freedom of speech these days, and the internet provides the public with access to the world

**ABOVE, FROM LEFT:** soldiers at Hanoi's Museum of Vietnamese Revolution; economic boom in HCMC.

*When a local paper, Tuoi Tre (Youth), conducted a survey asking young people to name their idols, Microsoft's Bill Gates nearly outpolled Ho Chi Minh, much to older generations' dismay.*

at large, domestic coverage of the government and its leaders is strictly censored. "Dissident voices" are swiftly silenced, while overseas anti-government websites are firewalled. All this is proof that despite a liberal attitude towards the economy, the government remains nervous at

the thought of losing its firm grip on society.

Despite the impressive economic turnaround of the past 20 years, Vietnam remains a predominantly agricultural country, with over 70 percent of its people still engaged in this sector. Income levels nationwide are relatively low – the average per capita income in 2010 was just US$1,168 a year – and large swathes of rural areas are mired in poverty. Unemployment during non-harvest periods routinely hits 25 to 35 percent. The presence of a new urban class of unskilled workers who have left the countryside for work in the cities but still struggle to make ends meet, and the increasing visibility of Vietnam's nouveaux riches, is already causing some social friction.

# PEOPLE

Vietnam is trying to balance rapid economic and population growth rates with a fiercely traditional culture – all the while under the watchful eye of a communist government

round 5,000 years ago in the foothills and valleys of the Red River Delta, a distinctive culture emerged that can be traced to the people who now call themselves Vietnamese. This is where the kingdom of Van Lang came into being, considered the cradle of Vietnamese culture. Its line of kings, known as the Hung, were the forefathers of the Vietnamese people.

Studies on the origins of the Vietnamese show that the people who settled in the Indochinese Peninsula and its bordering regions most likely came from southern and eastern China, the high plateaux of Central Asia, islands in the South Pacific and also other parts of the world. Vietnam can thus be considered the proverbial melting pot into which the major Asiatic and Oceanic migrations converged.

## The main racial groups

Almost 87 percent of Vietnam's 90 million-strong population lists its ethnicity as Kinh (or Viet) – the commonly accepted term for its main indigenous race – but in reality, most Vietnamese have evolved from a mixture of races and ethnicities over thousands of years. That mixture is the result of repeated invasions from outside Vietnam, particularly from China, along with continual migrations within the country, most commonly from north to south. As a result, you will find in Vietnam today the predominant Kinh as well as distinct ethnic minority groups, like the hill tribes (see page 58) of the northern and central

highlands, and small pockets of Cham and Khmer people in the south, whose kingdoms were vanquished by Vietnamese armies from the north.

The Cham people mainly inhabit the Phan Rang and Phan Thiet regions in southern Vietnam. Today they number about 100,000 – but the Chàmpa kingdom was once home to a distinctive culture that lasted for several centuries. Ethnic Khmers, part of the same ethnic stock as Cambodians, number around 900,000 and are concentrated in the Mekong Delta area.

Minority groups have been among the last to reap the rewards of Vietnam's new-found prosperity – with one exception. Ethnic Chinese, who as recently as the late 1970s were ostracised

**PRECEDING PAGES:** Vietnamese men enjoying a mineral mud bath at Nha Trang. **LEFT:** Dalat vendor. **RIGHT:** Flower Hmong ethnic minority in Sapa.

– if not run out of the country – because of tensions arising from the northern border clash with China, have not only benefited from Vietnam's economic progress but, in many ways, fuelled the country's economic growth. This is particularly pronounced in Ho Chi Minh City, the country's main economic hub.

Most of Vietnam's 1.7 million Chinese, known as Hoa, have adopted Vietnamese citizenship. Most are shopkeepers and business-people who settled in Ho Chi Minh City's Cholon district, which has long flourished as the Chinese community's primary commercial centre in southern Vietnam.

## Village and family bonds

Much of Vietnamese culture has been heavily influenced by the Chinese, who colonised Vietnam over 2,000 years ago. Among their number were the usual tyrants and exploiters, but also administrators and teachers who brought with them religions, philosophies, organisational skills, and a written language, the *chu han*.

In Vietnam, the family is considered to be a small world unto itself. Deeply influenced by Confucian principles, children are taught the importance of *hieu* (filial piety) – respecting one's elders, in fact, was once enshrined by the law. The family in turn is duty-bound to pay

## VIETNAMESE NAMES

All Vietnamese names follow a simple structure: family name, middle name and given name. When a Vietnamese hands you a business card you should address the person with the name on the far right. A man named Nguyen Manh Hung, for example, should be addressed as Hung.

There are roughly 140 Vietnamese family names in use today. The most common is Nguyen, which was also the name of the last royal dynasty. Other royal surnames still in use today include Tran, Trinh and Le. The name was probably acquired to show loyalty to the monarch in power, or taken on as a mark of respect when a new dynasty rose to power.

Only around 30 of the 140 or so family names used in Vietnam are actually of Vietnamese origin. For the most part, family names are of Chinese (Khong, Luu, Truong, Lu, Lam), Cambodian (Thach, Kim, Danh, Son), or ethnic minority origins (Linh, Giap, Ma, Deo).

The most common middle names are Van for men and Thi for women. The middle name is traditionally used to indicate a person's generation, or the separate branches of a big family, or a person's position within the family – for instance, Ba is for the first son of the first wife, Manh for the first son of the second wife, and Trong for a second son.

homage to its ancestors. A traditional family home would typically have as many as three generations under the one roof: grandparents, parents, married sons with wives and children, and unmarried children. In the event that one member needed money for an investment or for university studies, the entire family would chip in to help. Family connections are strong and the family tree can have dozens of branches.

Traditionally, having a boy in the family was a "must" as the eldest son would assume the duties of his father as head of the family when the latter died. Women were generally brought up for domestic duties, and were less educated than men. Despite growing affluence and gender equality today, especially in urban areas, there is a still a clear preference for boys, as witnessed by the number of sex-selective abortions in the country. Vietnamese law states that families may only have two children.

Greater prosperity, as well as the inevitable rise in materialism brought by television and the internet, has spurred a desire for personal independence and individualism among younger Vietnamese. Increasingly, young married couples are buying apartments and moving out of the family home. While the older generation, especially in the north, may cling to Ho Chi Minh's ideals, Vietnam's younger generation is far more interested in their iPods than ideology. This shift has caused annoyance among some of Vietnam's elderly population, who can remember the bombs and destruction. As younger people start to outnumber the old and more and more look for careers in the cities, this divide becomes ever greater. Young Vietnamese now are more confident and embrace fashion, won't be told whom to date and are more outgoing than their predecessors.

Overall, though, this is still a conservative and traditional country where the new-found wealth has created a gulf between rich and poor. Changing demographics mean that it is Vietnam's youthful population – 72 percent of its citizens are under 35 years of age – which dominates society, despite the collective influence of the state and that of older generations raised on Confucianist principles during less privileged times.

**ABOVE, FROM LEFT:** the modern faces of Vietnam; Vietnamese children now pick up English from an early age.

Many of those who emigrated during the war have now returned. Known as Viet Kieu, they were once seen as privileged and the elite, but today they are generally accepted.

## Vietnamese society

Although the country is now technically united, there are plenty of divisions that are clear to see. North and south view each other with some cynicism. Northerners tend to see Ho Chi Minh City dwellers as business-orientated and keen on displaying their new wealth; southerners claim northerners are tough and lack any sense of fun. Maybe that shouldn't be a surprise, given that

each region took entirely separate paths for so long, yet it would be too simplistic to say the north hangs on to its communist roots while the south retains capitalist dreams. Vietnam may still officially be communist, but the hammer and sickle have been all but forgotten and replaced by the dollar and dong.

Along with an increasing desire for Western ideals of wealth has come a desire to speak English. Older generations may speak French, Russian or even German, but today's young people are far more likely to want to learn English; it is the language of business, after all.

Children in urban areas learn English at school and at private language schools. Their confidence with the language and easy

*While Vietnam doesn't have a reputation for sex tourism like Thailand or Cambodia, prostitution is more widespread than it appears. Often, karaoke bars and massage parlours serve as fronts for illicit activities.*

interaction with foreigners are noticeable. Teenagers will commonly listen to English songs and watch Hollywood movies on DVD, while everyday speech and online chats are liberally sprinkled with English words and slang. Students are quite likely to approach tourists

in major cities for the opportunity to practise their English skills.

But whatever language they use, almost no subject is taboo (the major exception is political reform in Vietnam). So at your very first encounter with a Vietnamese, you are likely to be asked where you're from, whether you are married, how much you earn, what car you drive, and so on, in whatever fractured English the speaker can muster. This curiosity should not be misinterpreted as nosiness. There is a genuine fascination with foreigners, especially in the less visited areas of Vietnam.

The Vietnamese are proud of what their country has achieved. When it comes to China, there is a guarded welcome to improved relations.

Trade links are strong and there is talk of economic corridors and economic zones. But old habits die hard, and old wounds still fester, with the disputed Spratly islands (*see panel page 44*) a particularly emotive issue.

## Sex and marriage

Marriages were once seen as a form of business transaction between two families. Spouses were screened and selected by parents and other senior family members rather than by the prospective partners. These days, it is more common for couples to court each other before the wedding, though family approval is still a symbolic part of the process. Wedding rituals include the bride and her family bringing an odd number of gifts to the groom's family. Given the tight family structure, a wedding is a huge event in any community. In order to demonstrate this, families often spend far more than they can afford to ensure everyone sees just how lavish their family's wedding is.

Even today the wife is expected to move to the husband's house upon marriage. This is a stressful and daunting prospect for any young bride as she is expected to please the whole family and follow the rules of the house.

Vietnam is still a very traditional country, though not necessarily a prudish one. Pre-marital sex is taboo for the older, more conservative generations, but attitudes are changing rapidly. Internet chat rooms, websites, blogs and columns in the state-run media have become forums for young people to discuss subjects like love, sex and sexual orientation. In the past few years there has been an upsurge in short stories or novels written by female writers on female sexuality.

## Socialising

Vietnamese people of all ages love to *di choi* (go out to play). This means going out to have fun, hanging out with friends at a bar or café, singing karaoke, etc. When Vietnamese *di choi*, it's often a case of the more the merrier. Whether it's celebrating a birthday or a job promotion, they will invite all their friends and partners/spouses out for a meal. Vietnamese typically drink with a meal, so local restaurants are often filled with boisterous drinkers shouting "*Tram phan tram*" (literally 100 percent) before downing a glass of beer or shot of *ruou* (rice liquor).

It's customary for the person who extended the invitation to pick up the tab. In fact,

Vietnamese rarely split the bill, even if it isn't a special occasion. Friends are forever trying to grab the bill in cafés and restaurants or surreptitiously bribing the waiter in an attempt to be presented with the bill first.

## Street life

Living in cramped houses filled with extended three-generation families means that life often spills onto the streets. Itinerant vendors on bicycles and on foot, streetside barbers, shoeshine boys, not to mention the constant and chaotic flow of traffic, will assail your senses. Even in quieter residential areas, families often gather

*Vietnamese can come across as quite blunt; being called beo (fat) can be a well-intentioned remark that someone's just looking well and happy rather than overweight.*

## Customs and etiquette

Face, and not losing it, is an important part of nearly every Asian culture. In Vietnam it is particularly crucial. People will go to all sorts of lengths to avoid causing embarrassment to others, and visitors should be particularly mindful of this. Direct criticism and raised voices

in the lanes to gossip with neighbours or buy fruit from passing vendors.

With a lot more cars, motorbikes and people than ever before, Vietnam's major cities suffer from chronic congestion, leading the government to impose restrictions on street activity. Street vendors, shopkeepers and food stalls are perpetually playing hide and seek with local police and district authorities who will confiscate goods – plastic stools, baskets, whatever – if these items are deemed to be blocking traffic or pushing pedestrians onto the road.

**ABOVE, FROM LEFT:** modern wedding ceremony; trendy shops along Hanoi's Nha Tho (Church) Street.

### KEEP SMILING

Vietnamese often smile when embarrassed, confused or when they're being scolded by an older person or their boss, or when they don't understand what a foreigner is asking – which can be rather disconcerting. If you lose your temper and this happens, it doesn't mean they are not taking the situation seriously, but rather that he or she is embarrassed for you. Likewise, when a traffic accident is averted, Vietnamese often crack into a wide smile, especially if you're a foreigner. It means, "I'm sorry!" or "Aren't we lucky nothing serious happened!"

are ideal ways to lose any argument. When things do go wrong, they can go wrong in spectacular fashion as the Vietnamese have a fiery temperament and public arguments occur far more frequently than in other Southeast Asian countries.

As tourist numbers increase, some values are changing. Vietnamese sometimes have no qualms about overcharging visitors, and no amount of complaining will stop this. If visitors do feel they have been ripped off, polite but firm discussions are the best way to proceed. In some areas, a particularly resolute approach is required. The northwestern town of Sa Pa is

one such place, as here the Hmong people will follow tourists relentlessly around town in a bid to sell them souvenirs, and polite refusals often fall on deaf ears.

Other customs include never touching somebody on the head, not pointing, passing items with both hands and not touching members of the opposite sex. When eating, be sure not to leave chopsticks poking up in a rice bowl as this resembles incense sticks at a funeral, an extremely offensive sign. If you are invited to a person's home, it is customary to bring a small gift, such as a basket of fruit – but never wrap it in black or white paper. When eating with Vietnamese, wait until the oldest member of the party begins to eat before starting to feast. If people do constantly ask your age, they aren't being rude – they are simply trying to ascertain how to address you, as hierarchy is an important part of Vietnamese culture.

## Education

Children begin primary education aged around six and remain there for five years. After this time, students will sit a test, which determines the kind of secondary school they will attend.

At the end of grade 12, students take one more test, which they need to pass to gain their high-school diploma. Getting into university is an important first step towards almost any successful career. Most universities are state-run, though the number of private and foreign-run establishments is increasing.

Vietnam has a literacy rate of more than 90 percent, but the quality of teaching is questionable. Rote-learning and teacher-centred

### THE VIETNAMESE LANGUAGE

The country shares one common tongue, a blend of several languages – ancient and modern – that has evolved from a mixture of the Austro-Asiatic, Austronesian and Sino-Tibetan sources. Yet there are distinct

Despite D dialects across the country, and northerners and southerners often find it impossible to understand each other. Some letters of the alphabet are pronounced differently, and the vocabularies of northerners and southerners contain distinct words. Even the syntax is different. In addition to Vietnamese, the country's many ethnic minorities speak their own distinct languages and dialects. In the Mekong Delta,

for example, a large number of people speak the Khmer language of Cambodia.

Thousands of words in contemporary Vietnamese – as much as 70 percent – are derived from Chinese. There is a touch of French too, with words that entered the lexicon during the colonial period. Several food items are recognisably French – ca phe (café), pho mat (fromage), ga to (gâteau) and bia (bière).

Learning to speak Vietnamese is challenging. Despite the Romanised alphabet, the use of tones alters the sounds of words. The city of Hue, for example, is pronounced "whey", not "Hugh", and the popular beef noodle soup pho bo is pronounced "fuh baw", not "foe bow".

classrooms are the norm. In order to pass classes, many students study after school and so it is not uncommon to be walking home at night and hear a chorus of English coming from a crowded room-full of students.

## Competitive spirit

Once the working day is done, Vietnamese tend to pull on their tracksuits and head outside. Many towns and cities have open areas where locals play badminton, practise t'ai chi or join in mass aerobics.

Tennis and golf are now the sports of choice for the well-heeled, but football is by the far the

> With 72 percent of its people under the age of 35, Vietnam has one of the youngest populations in the world, a powerful engine for driving the country's growth.

preferential treatment from people in positions of authority. Even teachers frequently receive "gifts" from parents in the hope their child might receive extra attention at school. When accidents occur, traffic policemen will skip the paperwork and issue a verbal warning in return for an outright bribe.

most popular working-class sport. Vietnamese men play (and watch) the game with great enthusiasm. In the height of summer, matches are played early in the morning as it would be too hot by the afternoon. It is not uncommon for Vietnamese men to stay up all night to watch European football matches – and then go to work the next day bleary-eyed.

## Under the table

Corruption is an entrenched part of Vietnamese society. Palms are greased to skip bureaucratic hurdles, win contracts and invite

**ABOVE, FROM LEFT:** smiling boy, Can Tho; palying football in front of St Joseph's Cathedral, Hanoi

There are occasional reports of protests and even riots from disgruntled locals, but little changes. The pro-democracy movement Bloc 8406 (so called as it was formed on 8 April 2006) has had some impact, but authorities continue to crack down hard on those who speak out of line. Catholic priest Nguyen Van Ly was jailed for eight years in 2007 for supporting the group.

The government is reportedly trying to root out corruption, but it's an uphill task given the fact that it is so deeply ingrained. In the past, Vietnamese would have blamed the war for the country's poverty; these days, corruption is often cited as the main reason for any perceived ills.

# The Legacy of War

**The war may be over, but its aftermath is omnipresent. From rusty bullets for sale on street corners to the politics of international relations, the war's impact can still be felt**

In the years following the war with the US, Vietnam survived largely in isolation from the West. From 1975 until 1994 it was illegal for US firms to trade

with Vietnam, with the only form of help coming from Soviet quarters (until the late 1980s). But by the early 1990s relations with America were thawing and in 1995 formal diplomatic relations were restored by the then US president Bill Clinton. In 2000 Clinton became the first US head of state to visit the country since the war, which played a large part in normalising relations. A raft of trade deals has since been signed that has catapulted Vietnam's economy forwards, and by the end of 2011 the Vietnam Trade Commission predicted that bilateral trade would reach US$20 billion, a 10 percent rise on 2010's figures.

In addition to economics, it is in the USA's strategic interests to have Vietnam close, even if only to help keep rivals China in check. In turn, Vietnam

values its relationship with the US for financial reasons, but it walks a fine line as it must be careful not to allow its growing US links to damage its ties with China. Vietnam therefore views links with the US as a useful buffer against any Chinese aggression while paradoxically looking to repair relations with China. This delicate balancing act, amid US calls for improved human rights, has placed limits on how far the relationship with the USA can progress.

## Interest in the war

Nonetheless, despite the healthy trade relations and Vietnam's welcoming attitude to tourists – be they American, British or French – it would be a mistake to think that all is forgotten and forgiven. The war is still within living memory of many Vietnamese and Americans and there are scars on both sides that will take generations to heal. Still, most Vietnamese have few qualms about discussing the war and tourists should not consider it a taboo subject. Indeed, it would be virtually impossible to visit Vietnam and not have a conversation about the country's recent history.

The war has an influence on nearly everyone. Its effects on the physical landscape are clear, from the devastating impact of Agent Orange on the country's fields to the still-visible bomb craters and, more significantly, the thousands of landmines that still lie undiscovered. For some, the war remnants offer an entrepreneurial edge as they sell allegedly genuine war medals and memorabilia to tourists – and some war sites (notably the Cu Chi Tunnels near Ho Chi Minh City) are full-scale tourist attractions.

Interest in the war is inevitable and Vietnam does its best to oblige, even toning down some of the jingoistic propaganda. A case in point is the museum in Ho Chi Minh City originally known as "The House for Displaying War Crimes of American

**ABOVE:** the site of a crashed US B52 bomber in a lake in Hanoi, downed by a rocket in 1972.
**LEFT:** Tourist on the firing range at Cu Chi Tunnels.

Imperialism and the Puppet Government". This was later changed to the slightly less inflammatory "Museum of American War Crimes" and today it's known far more euphemistically as the War Remnants Museum.

Another factor is the inevitable change as the country develops and new generations grow up. Younger citizens seem happy to embrace Western ideals. Many are now pushing traditional boundaries in terms of lifestyle choices, while the number of English-language schools is proof of how important the tourist industry is now. Maybe the biggest post-war change has come in terms of attitudes to the West. Ask Vietnamese teenagers whom they

details the hundreds of notes that Herr, a former journalist, amassed after front-line reporting in Vietnam. The result is a part-fictitious, part-factual narrative that brilliantly captures the swirling, horrific mess of war. Robert Timburg's *The Nightingale's Song* (Simon & Schuster, 1995) looks at the experiences of several notable veterans, including author Oliver Stone and US politician John McCain, while *Born on the Fourth of July* (2005, Akashic) details the memoirs of Ron Kovic, who was paralysed by a bullet. The book was later made into a movie of the same name. *Victnam: Rising Dragon* by Bill Hayton (Yale University Press, 2010) gives a comprehensive overview of

most admire today and they are more likely to name an English Premier League footballer than Uncle Ho (Chi Minh).

## The war in literature and film

Among the numerous books on the war, several stand out. *A Bright Shining Lie* by Neil Sheehan (Pimlico, 1998) tells of this journalist's conversations with Lt Col John Paul Vann, who was so appalled by the incompetence of the South Vietnamese and US generals that he started briefing reporters on what was really happening. *Dispatches* by Michael Herr (Picador, 1991)

**ABOVE:** My Lai Massacre exhibit at the War Remnants Museum in Ho Chi Minh City.

contemporary Vietnamese history. See also Further Reading on page 385.

Perhaps the ultimate Vietnam war movie is actually based on a book about Africa. *Apocalypse Now* is Francis Ford Coppola's seminal film, and is heavily influenced by Joseph Conrad's Heart of Darkness. Marlon Brando plays Kurtz, a colonel who has lost his mind due to the horrors of war. *Full Metal Jacket*, director Stanley Kubrick's tale of a teenage recruit who ends up in Hue during the 1968 Tet Offensive, is a gripping, no-holds-barred vision of war, while *Platoon* is a violent, gripping tale that tells things from a soldier's perspective, as does the powerful and brutally blunt *Full Metal Jacket*. *Hamburger Hill* is based on the 101st Airborne Division's battle for survival in the heart of Vietnam's dense jungle.

# HILL TRIBES

Living in remote mountainous regions with little fertile ground for agriculture, Vietnam's hill tribes inhabit a world far removed from the bustle of the country's urban centres

There are 54 ethnic minority groups in Vietnam, the bulk of which comprise those hill tribes that inhabit the mountainous areas that extend through much of the length of the country. Each has its own language, lifestyle and heritage. Collectively referred to as the Montagnards (or mountain people) by the French, the hill tribes live in the most remote and inaccessible parts of Vietnam. Although the government has tried to reduce poverty and provide access to education and other facilities, the hill tribes have been left behind in Vietnam's race towards modernisation.

Fully aware of the lucrative potential of tourism, the government has encouraged the hill tribes to preserve their traditional identity and heritage. Northern hill tribes such as the Hmong, Dao and Tai in particular have successfully tapped into Vietnam's growing tourism industry, offering homestay accommodation and producing handicrafts for sale. The hill tribes living in the central highlands, however, do not feature on many tourist itineraries. Much of this region is sensitive, and there have been uprisings over land disputes and accusations by international human rights groups of religious oppression.

The following text identifies the major groups.

## NORTHERN HIGHLANDS

### Dao

The Dao (pronounced "Zao") first arrived from China in the 18th century. Part of the Hmong-Dao language group, they number about 630,000 and are found all across Vietnam's northern provinces, living in large villages

or small isolated hamlets and cultivating rice using the slash-and-burn method. The Dao can also be broken up into subgroups based on customs and the women's clothing. These include the Dao Quan Trang (White Trousers Dao), Dao Ao Dai (Long Tunic Dao), Dao Dau Troc (Shaven-Headed Dao) and Dao Do (Red Dao). The Red Dao wear a striking scarlet turban decorated with tassels or bells.

The Dao are expert artisans and highly skilled at making their own paper. For centuries they have used Chinese characters to record their genealogies, popular songs and rhymes, as well as folk tales and fables. The women plant cotton, which they weave and then dye with indigo. Dao embroidery is worked directly onto the cloth from memory, the traditional designs fixed in the weavers' minds.

## Hmong

The Hmong, or Meo, who number about 800,000, are found in villages known as *giao* throughout the highlands of northern Vietnam. Unrest and warfare encouraged the Hmong to migrate to Vietnam from the southern Chinese kingdom of Bach Viet at the beginning of the 19th century.

The Hmong minority group has been sub-divided into branches classified by women's costume, dialect and customs. For example,

> Since the mid-1990s the former French hill station of Sa Pa has become one of the main tourist attractions in the country, and villagers have benefited from selling various handicrafts to tourists.

cloth, paper, silver jewellery, leather goods, baskets and embroidery. The Hmong have no written language. Their legends, songs, folklore and proverbs have been passed down from one generation to the next through the spoken word.

the Hmong of Sa Pa are called Black Hmong because of their predominantly black clothing. The most colourful sub-group are the Flower Hmong, found in large numbers around Bac Ha in Lao Cai province, who wear bright-coloured clothes with embroidery.

Corn is the main staple of Hmong people, but rice is often grown on terraces watered with the aid of irrigation. Hemp is grown to be woven into textiles, and cotton is also cultivated in some villages. As skilled artisans, the Hmong produce a variety of items, including handwoven indigo-dyed

**ABOVE, FROM LEFT:** Red Dao woman from a village near Sa Pa; a Flower Hmong trader at Bac Ha market.

## Muong

Numbering around 1.2 million, the Muong people inhabit the mountainous parts of Hoa Binh and Thanh Hoa provinces. They are most closely related to the Kinh majority. Ethnologists believe that the Muong remained in the mountains and developed independently, while the majority Kinh moved to the lowlands and became influenced by Chinese culture after the 11 BC invasion led by the Han emperor Wu Ti.

## Nung

The Nung share the same language, culture and customs as the Tay *(see below)*. Numbering about 875,000, they live in Cao Bang and Lang

Son provinces in the northeast bordering China. They are known for their rich folk-art traditions, including music and poetry, as well as a variety of handicrafts.

### San Chi

There are more than 150,000 San Chi living in villages mainly in Ha Giang, Tuyen Quang and Bac Tai provinces, but they are also found in certain regions of Lao Cai, Yen Bai, Vinh Phu, Ha Bac and Quang Ninh provinces. They are of the Tay-Tai language group and arrived from China at the beginning of the 19th century. San Chi ritual dances are elaborate: boys and young

Kinh culture is evident in their customs and traditions, the Tay prefer to speak in their own indigenous language.

### Tai

There are more than 1.3 million Tai living along the Song Hong (Red River), in the north-west of Vietnam, often together with other ethnic minorities. Their bamboo or wooden stilt houses are constructed in two distinct styles. The Black Tai build homes shaped like tortoise shells, while the White Tai construct rectangular dwellings. The women wear long, black sarongs and short tops with silver buttons.

girls perform traditional love songs in festivities that can last all night.

### Tay

The highlands of northern Vietnam are home to the 1.5 million-strong Tay, Vietnam's largest minority group. Tay villages are found in the provinces of Cao Bang, Lang Son, Bac Tai, Quang Ninh, Ha Giang and Tuyen Quang, and also in the Dien Bien Phu region. Their villages, or *ban*, are located in valleys near flowing water, where they build their houses, usually on stilts. A patriarchal society, the Tays cultivate a variety of crops, including rice, tobacco, spices and a variety of fruit on the steep mountainsides. Although the influence of Vietnam's dominant

They are skilled weavers and produce beautiful embroidery using motifs of flowers, birds, animals and dragons.

### SOUTHERN AND CENTRAL HIGHLANDS

### Bahnar

The Bahnar (also spelt Ba Na), one of Vietnam's poorest ethnic groups, live primarily in the central highland provinces of Gia Lai and Kon Tum as well as the coastal provinces of Binh Dinh and Phu Yen. There are around 180,000 Bahnar people, for whom life revolves around a traditional calendar, in which 10 months are set aside for cultivation and the remaining two months for social and personal duties such as marriage, weaving, ceremonies and festivals. One of their unique traditions is the ear-piercing ceremony. When babies turn a month old, their ear lobes are pierced, signifying the official acceptance of the child as a member of the village. Those who die without ear piercings are believed to be banished to a land of monkeys headed by a black-eared goddess called Duydai.

## Jarai (Gia Rai)

The Jarai, or Gia Rai, numbering around 320,000, live in the central highland provinces of Gia Lai, Kon Tum and Dak Lak. They belong to the Malay-Polynesian language group and arrived in the Tay Nguyen highlands around 2,000 years ago. They live a sedentary lifestyle in villages known as *ploi*, or sometimes *bon*. Jarai villages, with at least 50 homes, are built around a central *nha rong*, a communal house. The community has small matriarchal families.

Young Jarai girls take the first step in choosing a marriage partner, making their approach through an intermediary. The promise of marriage is sealed with the exchange of bronze bracelets, with the ceremony proceeding in three steps. First, the bracelet-exchanging rite is performed in front of the two families and the intermediary. Then the young couple's dreams are interpreted, a ritual that predicts their future prospects. Finally, the wedding ceremony is held at the home of the groom's parents.

## Rhade (Ede)

The Rhade, or Ede, found mainly in Dak Lak province in the central highlands, number more than 270,000. Like the Jarai, they belong to the Malay-Polynesian language group. They live in wooden longhouses built on stilts in villages known as *buon*. Each longhouse shelters a large matriarchal family under the authority of a *koa sang*, the most senior and respected woman. She directs community affairs, settles internal conflicts, and is also responsible for the safekeeping of all the communal heirlooms, especially the bronze gongs and ancient jars used for preparing rice beer for important festivals. The village's autonomous organisation is run by the *po pin ea*,

*Vietnamese hill tribes often serve sweet rice liquor called ruou can in a communal jar with a bunch of bamboo shoots for straws.*

the chief who is elected to take care of its communal affairs.

The Rhade employ slash-and-burn techniques to clear the land for agriculture. Rice, the main crop, is cultivated along with sugar cane, melons, cotton and tobacco. Nearly every village has its own forge to produce and repair metal farming implements. Basketry, pottery and indigo cloth are produced by the Rhade for their own use.

**ABOVE, FROM LEFT:** drinking ruou can, sweet rice liquor, in Mai Chau; rice terraces surrounding Sa Pa.

# RELIGION

Nearly every religion can be found in Vietnam, including Buddhism, Confucianism, Taoism, animism, Christianity, Islam, and the unique fusion of the Cao Dai faith

When the government started relaxing its grip on organised religion in 1986 as part of the country's *doi moi* (economic renovation) policy, it sparked a religious revival. Across the country, thousands of pagodas were resurrected as centres of spiritual life. Temples which had been closed or turned into schools or granaries returned to their original use. Rituals and festivals were revived, and congregations at Roman Catholic and Protestant masses were suddenly spilling out onto the streets. Suppressed for decades, religion was back in vogue.

Organised religion in Vietnam has long been a thorn in the side of the Communist Party. Although the government's decision to permit religion has filled a spiritual and ideological void, religious practice is still closely monitored.

> Astrological charts are often consulted to select an auspicious date for ceremonies, such as weddings, and other important events.

## Religious fusion

Vietnam is often regarded as a Buddhist country. The reality is rather more complex. Although up to 85 percent of the population regularly visits Buddhist pagodas, only 16 percent would be considered strictly Buddhist if you go by the book.

**LEFT:** Buddhist statuette, Long Khanh Pagoda, Qui Nhon. **RIGHT:** Catholic worshippers at Phat Diem Cathedral.

Over the centuries, Taoism, Buddhism and Confucianism have become simplified, intertwined and Vietnamised to constitute – along with other indigenous animistic beliefs – a core religion that is shared to some extent by all Vietnamese. This religion is sometimes referred to as *tam giao* (triple religion). There is no sense of contradiction for a Vietnamese person to make offerings to Buddha at a pagoda, a national saint at a temple and a deceased grandparent at the family altar. Even some church-going Christians practise ancestor worship at home, while Vietnamese who regard themselves as non-religious routinely visit temples on festival days. The everyday behaviour

> *The small mirrored octagonal disc with the Yin Yang symbol fixed above the front door of houses and shops throughout the country is believed to bar wandering spirits and ghosts from entering.*

and attitude of the typical Vietnamese is shaped by a complex synthesis of Asian religious traditions.

To complicate matters, Vietnam also has its own indigenous spirituality. Together, the gods of the earth, water and mountains

define and transform the geomantic structures and rules that determine – in the same way that the Chinese use *feng shui* – the orientation of houses, businesses, cities, graves and temples, and configure the good and bad luck of families, communities and nations. Between heaven and earth, but never separate from them, are humans, both male and female, the dead and the living, the ancestors and the descendants.

Each of the realms – heaven, earth and human – has its own rules, regulations, elements of good, bad, ugly and beautiful, and, above all, its own deities. These deities are found everywhere – in stones, trees, lakes and animals – and they are praised, fed, housed and revered with ritual offerings and prescribed modes of behaviour.

## Chinese influence

When the Chinese imposed their rule on Vietnam, they brought along their agricultural know-how and their books on religion, philosophy and other ideas, written in one of the most complicated scripts ever devised. While a new Vietnamese written language replaced Chinese script in the 13th century, the Vietnamese are still attached to the old Chinese characters, which visually and stylistically represented the meaning and feeling attached to each word.

Although the Vietnamese fought against Chinese cultural hegemony, they selectively screened and assimilated what they considered the best aspects. Chinese teachers, some of whom were administrators, were usually

## THE CAO DAI CULT

In 1921 a former civil servant of the French colonial administration called Ngo Minh Chieu received a message from a "superior spirit" called Cao Dai, meaning High Spirit or Supreme Being. Disillusioned by existing religions, Ngo was urged to create a new religion that meshed the world's main creeds together.

Today, the Cao Dai religion has an estimated 3 million followers in Vietnam. Cao Dai incorporates the teachings and philosophies of Buddhism, Taoism and Confucianism. Before God existed, there was the Tao, that nameless, formless, unchanging and eternal source referenced in the Tao Te Ching. Then a Big Bang occurred, out of

which God was born. The universe could not yet be formed and to do so, God created yin and yang. He took control of yang and shed a part of himself, creating the Goddess to preside over yin as Mother Buddha.

The religion's three original prophets were a disparate bunch of people: French novelist Victor Hugo, Chinese Nationalist Party leader Sun Yat-sen and Vietnamese poet Trang Trinh, while the extensive list of Cao Dai saints includes William Shakespeare, Joan of Arc, Julius Caesar, René Descartes and Thomas Jefferson. British author Graham Greene described the Cao Dai faith as "a game that had gone on too long".

accompanied by Confucian scholars, Buddhist masters and Taoist diviners. The Vietnamese absorbed much of what they had to offer, and these religious influences persist in Vietnam today, as do the religions introduced later – Hinduism and Islam brought from India, and Christianity from Europe and America.

## Confucianism

Confucianism is based on the teachings of Confucius, who was born in northern China around 550 BC and lived at a time of great political turmoil. As a teacher and unsolicited adviser to kings, he compiled rules and ideas

the Vietnamese imperial dynasties adopted Confucianism because of its ability to sustain a system of social order without much repression, and for its code of social mobility based on merit. It became the official doctrine of the imperial government examinations, the first of which was held in 1706. The Vietnamese monarchy recruited its high officials according to the results of these competitive examinations, which were in theory open to all men, except (for some reason) actors.

Those who earned their degrees received a hat and tunic from the emperor and were welcomed home as wise scholars by the entire

to define the relationships between ruler and subject, parents and children, husband and wife, student and teacher. Confucius was more of a moral and ethical guide than a spiritual leader. He refused to discuss life after death, as well as the unseen or the mystical, and he was primarily interested in a social order based upon compassion, etiquette, loyalty, knowledge and trust.

Confucianism reached Vietnam over 2,000 years ago and it has remained a pillar of the Vietnamese moral and spiritual establishment ever since. Officially, and pragmatically,

population. Those who failed the examinations would most likely have returned home and made a living as teachers. In this way, whole villages were indirectly introduced to the teachings of Confucianism.

## Buddhism

Vietnamese Buddhism is a fascinating blend of several branches of Buddhism. Introduced across the sea from India and overland from China, Buddhism extended the question of knowledge from the social order and rules of Confucianism to the general human condition.

From the 2nd to the 10th century, two popular Buddhist sects – the A-Ham (Agama) and the Thien (Dhyana in Sanskrit and Zen in

**ABOVE, FROM LEFT:** devotees at Dien Huu Pagoda in Hanoi; Temple of Literature in Hanoi.

Japanese) – competed peacefully for followers and believers in Vietnam. Eventually Thien prevailed, despite its exacting practice that requires continual training in self-discipline and in mastering the techniques of breathing, meditation and concentration.

Thien is one of the many sects of Mahayana Buddhism widely observed in China, Japan, Korea and Vietnam. Less dogmatic than others, it is more receptive to the diverse cultural and social conditions of different countries. The other branch of Buddhism, the Hinayana or Theravada (found in Sri Lanka, Burma, Thailand, Laos, Cambodia and parts of south-

## Hoa Hao

Hoa Hao is a religious tradition based on Buddhism founded in 1939 by Huynh Phu So. Adherents consider Huynh to be a prophet and Hoa Hao a continuation of a 19th-century Buddhist ministry known as Buu Son Ky Huong (Strange Perfume from Precious Mountains, referring to the That Son range on the Vietnamese–Cambodian border).

The religion claims approximately 2 million followers in Vietnam; in some provinces near its Mekong Delta birthplace, as many as 90 percent of the population practises this tradition. An important characteristic

ern Vietnam), is more orthodox yet co-exists with Mahayana. The main doctrinal division between the two schools is that the Mahayana sect maintains that lay people can attain nirvana, whereas the Theravada school believes that only ordained monks and nuns can do so.

Few Vietnamese outside the clergy, however, are acquainted with Buddhism's elaborate cosmology. What appealed to them at the time it was introduced was the ritual and imagery of Mahayana Buddhism. Mahayana ceremony easily conformed to indigenous Vietnamese beliefs, which combined folklore with Confucian and Taoist teachings, and Mahayana saints were often venerated alongside various animist spirits.

of Hoa Hao is its emphasis on the practice of Buddhism by laypeople in the home, rather than at the temple. Aid to the poor is favoured over pagoda-building or expensive rituals. Religious ceremonies are simple and modest, and do not include food offerings or divination services.

## Taoism

The *tao* is the highest and most active level of an otherwise static consciousness, the general law of the motion of the universe and of all things. It is both energy and matter, and the moment when the contradictory forces of yin and yang fuse in temporary harmony. In Chinese writing, it is represented by a character meaning "way" or "path".

In Vietnamese villages where Buddhism, Confucianism, animism and other forms of worship co-existed, Taoist priests were also welcomed. Introduced to Vietnam about the same time as Confucianism, Vietnamese Taoism does not have the hierarchy of schools and systems typical of China.

## Ancestor worship

A French Jesuit priest, Léopold Cadière, who spent decades in Vietnam studying religion, wrote in 1944 that Europeans were deluded about the importance of Buddhism in Vietnam. He believed that if there was one uniform religion, it was "the cult of spirits". Ancestor veneration is one of the most unifying aspects of Vietnamese culture, as practically all Vietnamese, regardless of religious affinity, usually have an altar dedicated to ancestors in their home or business place. This concept of filial piety has roots in the teachings of Confucianism. Failing to worship one's ancestors is considered sinful, and condemns the ancestors to a life of hellish wandering.

Vietnamese believe that burning votive objects will help their loved ones settle into a comfortable afterlife. On the anniversary of the person's death, the extended family will gather together to feast and pay their respects by burning incense and votive offerings at the tomb or shrine of the ancestor. In the past, typical offerings were paper replicas of household goods, clothes and fake money. Nowadays, the offerings can be more ostentatious – real houses, cars, iPods and credit cards

## Whale worship

If there is one place where whales can swim safely, it is off the coasts of Vietnam. That is because of a religious practice that worships these giants of the sea. Ngu Ong is a whale god that is feared and revered by followers, while living whales are given special respect. In 2010 a dead 15-tonne individual was found in Bac Lieu province and was buried in a giant glass tomb. In Danang province an annual festival is held in the third lunar month of the year where boats are brightly coloured and special thanks are

**ABOVE, FROM LEFT:** gilded Buddha statue at Tay Phuong Pagoda; prayerful Catholic nuns.

*While travelling in Vietnam, you will hear locals exclaim, either in excitement or exasperation, "Oi Gioi oi"! (pronounced "oi zoi oi"), which means, "Oh my God"!*

given to the whales for protecting the community's fishermen.

## Christianity

The first Western missionaries set foot in Tonkin, in northern Vietnam, in 1533, and more arrived in central Vietnam in 1596. But

their stay was brief. It was not until 1615 that the first permanent Christian missions were founded – in Hoi An, Danang and Hanoi – by the Portuguese Jesuits. The introduction of this organised and culturally alien religion generated, unavoidably, misunderstanding and conflict.

Many Vietnamese from all classes of society converted to Catholicism. This development worried the mandarins and ruling classes, who saw the new religion as a threat to the traditional order of society and its rites, particularly the belief in *nam giao* and ancestor worship. Between 1712 and 1720, a decree forbidding Christianity was enforced in the north. In the south, foreign missionaries were sent packing in 1750 when Christianity became forbidden.

Levels of tolerance towards Christianity varied among leaders. Under Emperor Minh Mang, who viewed Christianity as "the perverse religion of Europeans" that "corrupts the heart of men", a decree was enforced forbidding the entry of Christian missionaries to Vietnam. Thieu Tri was more tolerant, but his successor, Tu Duc, reinforced the prohibition of Christianity. This period of persecution lasted until the mid-1860s, when a treaty ceded territory and commercial rights to the French and granted freedom for Christians to practise their

While there is significantly more freedom of religion for the Catholic Church, the government remains cautious of Protestant hill tribes in the central highlands and followers of Hoa Hao Buddhism. Protestantism is the country's fastest-growing religion. Thanks to a six-fold increase in the past decade, there are now nearly 1 million followers practising in over 400 churches in Vietnam. Local authorities keep an eye on proceedings. The Saigon Protestant Church in Ho Chi Minh City, for instance, one of the biggest in the country, has to submit a list of its event schedules, financial records and appointments of

faith. Between 1882 and 1884, another wave of persecution hit the Catholic Church, and many followers paid with their lives. The persecution ended in 1885 with the French conquest of the entire country.

After the signing of the Geneva Agreement in 1954 and the division of the country, over half a million Catholics fled North Vietnam for the tolerance of the former South Vietnam. Since the reunification of Vietnam in 1975, the Catholic Church has operated under the written law of the Socialist Republic of Vietnam, which guarantees the freedom of religion or non-religion under an official Marxist-Leninist ideology. All Catholic schools in the country have been nationalised.

Church leaders to government officials for their prior approval.

## Islam

Vietnam's small Muslim community consists mainly of ethnic Chams and South Asians. A 10th-century stela inscribed in Arabic, found near the central coastal town of Phan Rang, provides the earliest record of Islam's presence in Vietnam. Although they consider themselves as Muslim, their religious practices are not fully orthodox. They don't make the pilgrimage to Mecca, and although they avoid eating pork, Vietnamese Muslims drink alcohol and observe Ramadan for only three days instead of a full month. Their rituals also co-exist with other animistic and Hindu-based worship.

# Tet: The Lunar New Year

**Similar to its Chinese counterpart, Vietnam's colourful New Year festival is a time of parades, fireworks and family gatherings**

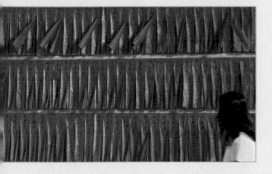

Tet Nguyen Dan (Festival of the First Morning of the Year), often called simply Tet, is Vietnam's most important festival and marks the beginning of the lunar year. It is celebrated in either January or February, depending on the lunar calendar.

Tet rites begin a week before Mung Mot (the first day of the Lunar New Year). This is when the Kitchen God (Ong Tao) returns to the Kingdom of Heaven and presents his annual report on the state of earthly matters to the Jade Emperor before returning to earth on New Year's Eve. During his week-long journey to heaven, the Vietnamese guard themselves against bad spirits. In the countryside, you will often find a *cay neu* (signal tree), a bamboo pole with a clay tablet and a piece of yellow cloth attached, in front of the home. Another indispensable feature in the north is a branch of peach blossom, or *cay dao*. In southern and central Vietnam, *cay mai*, a branch of yellow apricot blossom, is more common. The kumquat tree is another popular decorative feature in the north. This tree is carefully selected to ensure it has both golden-orange ripe fruit and unripe green fruit, representing prosperity now (ripe fruit) and prosperity to come (green fruit).

During the holiday the family table will be laden with food. There will be plenty of *banh chung*, glutinous rice cakes stuffed with pork beans and onion,

**ABOVE, FROM LEFT:** St Joseph's Cathedral in Hanoi; New Year wishes at a temple; dancing dragons.

*xoi* (sticky rice) with pork and pickled onions as well as a variety of *mut*, or candied sweets.

The Vietnamese traditionally lit firecrackers to scare off bad spirits. However, firecrackers had turned the cities and countryside into a battle zone, and in 1995 they were outlawed. Today, extravagant fireworks displays are organised in every major city to celebrate the start of the New Year.

The first day of Tet is for the worship of ancestors, who are ceremoniously welcomed back from heaven on New Year's Eve during the Giao Thua, the transition as one year passes to the next. Elaborately prepared food offerings, together with burning incense, await the ancestors at the altar. All events – whether favourable or unfavourable – that take place on the first day of Tet are believed to affect the course of one's life for the year ahead. Homeowners will also consider carefully who should be the first

person to walk through their door after the New Year begins, a custom known as *xong nha*. It must be a person who has had a prosperous year or a person with a reputation for bringing good luck.

The rest of the week will be spent visiting relatives, family friends, temples and pagodas. Children will receive *mung tuoi* (or *li xi*), meaning lucky money, in slim red envelopes from elders. Employees will often visit their boss, sometimes bearing lavish gifts to curry favour for the working year ahead.

Traditionally, people would have stopped working for at least a week. Now in most cities many businesses only close for three days, forcing reluctant staff back to work prematurely. Still, during Tet, tourists should anticipate services to be running more sluggishly than usual, if at all.

# VIETNAMESE TEMPLES AND PAGODAS

**Pagodas and temples reflect the cultural diversity of religious practice in Vietnam and are a focus of social, political and religious life**

Most Vietnamese villages have their own complex of temple buildings, including the *dinh* (communal house), where the village founder is venerated and the village council, an assembly of male leaders, traditionally meets to debate local affairs and conduct important meetings. The *chua* (pagoda) is regarded as an important social centre for women and is generally devoted to the worship of the Buddha. The *den* (temple) and *mieu* are shrines to the ancestors of individual families. Temples often have Taoist and Confucian elements, dedicated to other gods, national heroes or guardian spirits.

Vietnamese religious practice is eclectic, and this is reflected in the layout of the temple buildings. Large temple complexes may include a *phuong dinh* (front hall), a *ngoai cung* (central hall), a *noi cung* or main altar hall, and a *cay tien huong*, which acts as a gate to the main temple complex. The choice of temple gods also varies from one village to the next. In some temples, statues of Confucius sit alongside Taoist or Buddhist images. In the north, it is common to find Vietnam war heroes joining the statue line up. Many offer the chance to burn joss sticks before a life-size statue of the national hero Ho Chi Minh.

After 1945, religious activity was discouraged, but since the 1980s there has been a revival and many Vietnamese have donated money towards temple renovations in their villages.

**BELOW:** first built in wood in 1049, Hanoi's Chua Mot Cot (One Pillar Pagoda) was destroyed in 1954 and has since been reconstructed in sturdy concrete.

**RIGHT:** Hanoi's Tran Quoc Pagoda, near West Lake, is one of Vietnam's oldest.

## The Importance of Incense

Worship in pagodas is informal, as people come and go, chat with the monks, drink tea and present offerings. But nobody visits a pagoda without burning incense. On festival days, packets of joss sticks can be bought outside the pagoda building. One may burn the whole packet or a small number of sticks, depending on the occasion. But the total burnt must add up to an odd number – it is taboo to burn an even number of sticks.

After lighting the incense, worshippers stand in contemplation before the altar for a few moments. They then make respectful bowing movements before placing the burning sticks in a small urn filled with ash.

The rising smoke from the joss sticks symbolises communication with the other world. It allows people to maintain contact with ancestors, ask for wishes to be granted, or act as a thanksgiving to one of the many gods in the Vietnamese religious pantheon.

**Above:** every temple gate has its quan bao ve, or guardian soldiers, one malevolent and one benevolent, as pictured here at the Co Tien Temple near Sam Son Beach in north Vietnam.

**Below:** incense offerings are made in the form of joss sticks. They are an essential part of all worship, both in the home and, as here, in temples and pagodas.

**Above:** Chinese influence on Vietnam's culture is reflected in temple architecture, and Chinese characters are common features of religious buildings. Pictured here is the Fujian Assembly Hall in Hoi An, central Vietnam.

# PERFORMING ARTS

## After decades of neglect, Vietnam's traditional performing arts must now compete with more modern forms of entertainment to survive

The ancient Dong Son bronze drums, which depict dancers performing to the accompaniment of musical instruments, testify to the long-standing importance of musical and dance traditions in Vietnam. For a long time, however, music played an integral part in religious ceremonies and not as a means of public entertainment. It wasn't until much later that music became part of the cultural landscape in a broader sense.

## A MUSICAL TRADITION

The majority Kinh or Viet population, and many of Vietnam's 54 ethnic minorities, have a rich musical heritage. Generally Vietnamese music falls into two groups: *dieu bac*, literally northern mode, which exhibits more of a Chinese influence, and *dieu nam*, southern mode, which features the slower tempo and sentimentality of ancient Cham culture.

Folk music takes the form of tunes sung by villagers illustrating their life in the countryside. There are several categories: lullabies, known as *hat ru* in the north, *ru em* in the centre and *au o* in the south; work songs or *ho*; and mushy love songs, known as *ly*.

Perhaps the most important catalyst in the development of contemporary Vietnamese folk entertainment was the appearance of the call-and-response dialogue song, a genre found widely throughout Southeast Asia. Most ethnic minorities have a version of a flirtatious male–female courting game in which boys and girls sing poetic dialogue that tests each other's skills.

## Quan ho

Among the Kinh majority, the call-and-response dialogue song developed into various forms, including the unique Red River Delta art form known as *quan ho*, a complex and technically demanding style of romantic folk singing. *Quan ho* has close links to the custom of *ket cha* (establishing friendship between villages) in which male and female singers, accompanied by a small traditional music ensemble and sometimes by a small chorus, perform songs interspersed with improvised repartee.

*Quan ho* is sung a cappella and is characterised by a special vibrato technique called *nay hat*. More than 180 different *quan ho* songs are

---

**LEFT:** a folk music and dance performance in Hoi An's old town. **RIGHT:** Hoi An is a leading centre for the Vietnamese cultural arts.

*While traditional performing arts have struggled to survive, there is no shortage of willing participants for talent shows, cabaret nights and beauty pageants, all extremely popular with modern audiences.*

still performed in around 40 villages in Bac Ninh and Bac Giang provinces. Various *quan ho* festivals are held throughout the region after the Tet festival, the largest and most important being the Hoi Lim Quan Ho festival in Bac Ninh province.

## THE RISE AND FALL OF THE CIRCUS

Travelling acrobatic troupes were once a prominent feature of village entertainment in Vietnam. During the French colonial period, professional circus companies from Europe inspired the establishment of local circus troupes, and in the post-war period in the 1950s a number of prestigious Vietnamese groups were established with Soviet aid. In recent years, many provincial troupes have been disbanded and the remaining companies have struggled due to a lack of funds. In areas with strong Chinese connections acrobatic groups still exist, while lion and dragon dances continue to draw crowds, especially during festivals as they are seen as harbingers of good fortune.

## Court music

Despite the establishment of an independent Viet kingdom in the 10th century, successive Vietnamese rulers continued to mimic the courtly traditions of their powerful Chinese neighbour. In subsequent centuries, Confucian music and dance traditions were increasingly appropriated from the Chinese imperial court. Court music was also influenced by the music of the old Hindu kingdom of Champa, in the southern part of present-day Vietnam.

During the Le dynasty (1428–1527), a system of court music was established. A number of musical categories was invented for different religious and social occasions, although the majority of royal dances functioned as a means to wish the sovereign and his family happiness, prosperity and longevity.

From the turn of the 20th century onwards, the royal court at Hue became increasingly Westernised and, during the reign of French-educated Bao Dai (1926–45), the last of the Nguyen kings, traditional royal music and dances were rarely performed. Since the late 1980s, court music has been revived in the old imperial capital by the Thua Thien Hue Provincial Traditional Arts Company and the Hue Royal Palace Arts Troupe.

## Ca tru

One traditional Vietnamese folk art enjoying a revival is *ca tru*, which scholars trace back to a form of music widely performed as an expression of worship during the Ly dynasty (1010–1225). *Ca tru* is often described as sung poetry, but the accompanying music is an integral part of the performance.

A group usually consists of three performers. The singer, always a woman, plays the *phach*, an instrument made of wood or bamboo beaten with two wooden sticks. A musician called *kep* accompanies the singer on the *dan day*, a long-necked lute with three silk strings and 10 frets. There is also a drummer, *trong chau*, who moves with the rhythm of the singer or the songs.

Traditionally, before enjoying the music at a communal house, private home or inn, guests would purchase a stack of bamboo cards. These cards were given to the singers in appreciation of the performance, each singer receiving payment in proportion to the number of cards received. This explains how the name *ca tru* was born. Literally, *tru* means card in Chinese, *ca* means song in Vietnamese, hence the name *ca tru*, or card songs.

Although *ca tru* flourished during the French colonial period, it had shady implications as a geisha-style form of entertainment. Attractive young singers known as *co dau* were assigned to help rich male listeners relax while plying them with drinks and opium.

Because of this sleazy reputation, *ca tru* was suppressed after the August Revolution in 1945. In recent years, *ca tru* has been rediscovered and performed at a number of clubs, foremost among which is the Hanoi Ca Tru Club. Besides hosting regular performances, the club organises an annual *ca tru* festival to help promote this traditional art form.

## THEATRE

Vietnam's oldest recorded theatrical performance is *tro he*, a farce created during the Tien Le dynasty (980–1009). During the Tran period (1225–1400), two new types of theatre emerged: *hat giau mat*, masked performances, and *hat coi tran*, coat-less performances. These archaic forms of theatre no longer exist today. Today's varieties – *cheo*, *hat tuong* and *cai luong* – are a blend of court theatre and folk performances with some foreign influences.

### Cheo

*Cheo* is as old as the Vietnamese nation itself and has been depicted on the engravings of Bronze Age drums and urns. The word "*cheo*" is a distortion of *tieu*, the Chinese word for laughter. Although it hails from and is performed almost exclusively in the north of the country, *cheo* is promoted as a national art form. Generally presented in accordance with conventions laid down in 1501 by a theorist called Luong The Vinh, *cheo* dramas provide a framework within which the players improvise; the troupe is judged according to its ability to vary and reinvent a familiar theme.

Musicians sit to the right of the stage area with drums, gongs, rattles, stringed instruments and a flute. To start the play, someone from the audience beats a large drum. When a performer sings well, this drum will be beaten by a member of the audience to register

approval; when the performance is poor, the drum's wooden barrel is struck instead.

Costumes and make-up are simple, in marked contrast to that of *hat tuong* (*see below*). Characterisation (of stock character types such as the drunk old man, the Confucian scholar, the coquette and the clown) has much in common with that of Italian commedia dell'arte, with interaction between the performers and the audience always an important feature of the action.

In addition to restoring and performing ancient *cheo* classics, the Cheo Theatre in Hanoi also sponsors the writing of new works aimed at rural audiences, many of which relate to con-

temporary issues such as drug abuse and Aids. Unfortunately, as with their counterparts from other branches of Vietnamese traditional theatre, *cheo* artists have seen their audiences decline significantly in recent years. Many of the country's professional *cheo* companies have been obliged to diversify their activities into more commercial forms of entertainment to survive.

### Hat tuong

Unlike *cheo*, which is uniquely Vietnamese, *hat tuong* arrived from China in the 13th century during the Tran dynasty. An individual named Ly Nguyen Cat – a prisoner of war captured after the defeat of the Mongols – was a master of Chinese theatre who later became a

**ABOVE, FROM LEFT:** musicians at the Royal Theatre in Hue; xylophone at the Temple of Literature, Hanoi.

Vietnamese citizen and taught Chinese drama to the Vietnamese court. From China also came make-up, ceremonial costumes, masks, stylised gestures, percussion and wind-instrument music, and the emphasis on heroic and noble themes.

Hat tuong originated as a theatre for the elite. It begins with a song introducing the drama's story-line. Each player describes his character and role. The stage is nearly empty save for symbolic props: a branch represents a forest, a painted wheel stands for a cart. The dramatic action is guided by Confucian moral virtues and concepts – for example,

loyalty to kings or devotion to parents. The orchestra sits on the stage's side, accompanying not only the singing but also details of the activity and movement on stage. Hat tuong was adapted to the Vietnamese character, with women replacing men in the female roles, and the orchestra was enlarged, incorporating Indian influences from the Cham culture.

Today, the hat tuong orchestra includes cymbals, gongs, drums, tambourines, flutes and an arsenal of stringed instruments, including the dan nhi, a violin with a high register played by drawing two strings tight over a drum skin, and the dan bau, whose single string, stretched over a long lacquered sound box, is both bowed and plucked to produce vibrato effects and long resonances of great subtlety.

## Cai luong

Cai luong made its first appearance in southern Vietnam in 1920. It interprets classical Chinese stories in a more accessible style. Influenced by the European stage, cai luong has evolved into its present spoken-drama form, abandoning the cumbersome epic style in favour of shorter acts, emotional and psychological themes, and free dialogue.

Whilst audiences for other traditional Vietnamese theatre genres have declined over the years, cai luong has to a certain extent retained its appeal by continually appropriating elements from contemporary culture, including popular characters, plot scenarios and hit songs.

Today, cai luong continues to develop in tandem with Vietnamese spoken drama; indeed many of its leading practitioners are active in both fields. Nowadays the musical accompaniment to cai luong takes the form of a mixed ensemble of Vietnamese and Western instruments. There are currently around 30 professional cai luong troupes nationwide.

## Ballroom dancing

One of the few Western art forms to take off in Vietnam is ballroom dancing. Major towns, especially Hanoi, have halls dedicated to couples who want to waltz or tango their way through the night. Waiters sometimes double as dance partners, as there tend to be more women present than men.

### FUNERAL MUSIC

Some genres of Vietnamese music originally evolved as a means of celebrating social events such as marriage, birth and death. Of these, only funeral music is still commonly heard – and it came close to dying itself when the government clamped down on religious and superstitious beliefs in the 1960s. Now revived as an art form, musicians and singers are hired by grieving families to perform laments. This service is known as khoc thue, which literally means "rented tears". Only men are allowed to perform.

**ABOVE, FROM LEFT:** preparation for a cai luong performance.

# Puppetry in Motion

**A visit to one of Vietnam's unique water puppet shows is an entertaining way to get closer to the country's culture and heritage**

**D**uring the 11th-century Ly dynasty, before a series of dykes was built, the Red River would swell each year, bursting its banks and flooding much of the region. This annual flooding of the lowlands inspired a form of entertainment that is found only in Vietnam, namely water puppetry (mua roi nuoc).

The flooded paddies were the perfect platform to conceal both the puppeteer and the long bamboo poles used to control the puppet. Gradually, these theatrical events transferred to the small ponds and lakes beside the communal houses (dinh) found in a typical 11th-century Vietnamese village.

Today, the puppeteers still perform in a chest-deep pool of water but behind a curtain on stage. The water is kept deliberately murky so as to obscure the poles and mechanics used to control the puppets, which are protected from the elements by a layer of lacquer. The puppets usually range from 30 to 100cm (12 to 39ins) in height and weigh from 1 to 5kg (2 to 11lbs). Larger puppets can weigh up to 20kg (44lbs) and need four people to manipulate them.

As its origins and themes hark back to farming communities in feudal times, water puppetry is not merely enjoyable theatre, but also portrays part of Vietnamese culture. A performance will consist of 12 to 18 acts, each telling a mythological story about Vietnam and its history, while a

**ABOVE AND RIGHT:** water puppet performance.

small ensemble of traditional musicians and cheo singers provides background music. One story, for example, tells of how a tortoise living in Hanoi's Hoan Kiem Lake supposedly emerged from the depths to provide King Ly Thai To with the sword he needed to fight off Chinese invaders.

Characters can be heroic, legendary or mythical, but most are ordinary peasants with plot lines that tend to be action-oriented as the puppets are unable to convey emotional conflicts. The water's surface also reflects what is taking place: calm and serene when fairies sing and dance, but a heaving tempest when a battle breaks out with fire-spitting dragons.

In an attempt to win over modern-day audiences, some scriptwriters have adjusted traditional plots.

The Hong Phong puppet troupe from Hai Duong province, for example, has adapted a story called The Frog Sues Heaven, in which a thief sneaks into a Buddhist pagoda under the cover of a dark and stormy night and steals antique statues, aiming to sell them to overseas buyers. The thief is caught, and after a quick trial under Article 272 of the Criminal Code he is dispatched to jail for three years.

Water puppetry dropped off the radar during the Vietnam War but was revived in the 1980s. While it took time to redevelop the art form due to a lack of numbers and poor facilities, thanks to Vietnam's booming tourism industry, water puppetry has found its way back onto the stage.

# ART, CRAFTS AND LITERATURE

The Vietnamese are among the world's most literate and poetic people, and their contemporary crafts and art are popular with collectors around the world

A fter decades of obscurity and isolation, Vietnamese artists have started to make inroads into the international arena. Sold in galleries and exhibited in museums worldwide, Vietnamese paintings are routinely featured in auctions of Southeast Asian art at Christie's and Sotheby's.

Much of the work making waves in the international art scene shares a gentle, lyrical quality – rarely is any self-indulgent anger expressed – with styles ranging from figurative to abstract and surrealist, at other times expressionist or realist. The abundance of this impressionist and figurative art is testament to the tenacious influence of Western culture within Vietnam.

## Painting traditions

While China, Japan and Korea share long painting histories, Vietnam's artistic tradition emerged during 19th-century French colonial rule. Prior to this time, local artistic achievements had been restricted to decorative arts for religious and communal purposes, with only a limited output of paintings, coloured embossments and silk portraits.

In spite of the largely destructive arrival of the French, new opportunities for creative achievement arose during the colonial period, with painting becoming the most developed artistic expression. Through this Western influx, a unique French–Vietnamese amalgamation of cultures emerged. In 1925, under the initiative of the French painter Victor Tardieu, the École des Beaux-Arts de l'Indochine (EBAI) was founded in Hanoi. Scores of painters and

**LEFT:** Green Harmony: Two Sisters, c.1938, by Le Pho.
**RIGHT:** modern Vietnamese art.

sculptors were schooled in the European tradition during its 20-year existence. The establishment was responsible for creating the "first generation" of Vietnamese masters, most notable of whom were Nguyen Gia Tri, Nguyen Phan Chanh, To Ngoc Van, Bui Xuan Phai, Nguyen Sang and Nguyen Tu Nghiem.

While the influence of these first graduates was felt in the 1930s, the artistic importance of the last group of notable graduates – Bui Xuan Phai, Nguyen Sang and Nguyen Tu Nghiem – was not apparent until the 1960s and 1970s. While not all of these artists shared the same vision or even style, each shared a desire to champion European modernism while remaining true to their Vietnamese spirit and heritage.

*The works of Vietnam's artists are becoming less homogeneous and more complex and experimental, ensuring their future in Asia's vibrant art scene.*

Through their innovative use of traditional materials and their depiction of domestic themes in warm colours, all these artists can be accredited with freeing Vietnamese painting from its colonial academism.

These philosophies were then passed on to their students at the Hanoi College of Fine Arts – the EBAI's successor – and the College of Applied

### GUARDED AESTHETICS

With Vietnamese art now in the international art market, authorities are ever careful to oversee foreigners' perceptions of the country, and paintings with political overtones and opinions opposing the government's ideals are potential firecrackers. Truong Tan is a controversial artist who blatantly depicts his own individual sexuality by confronting traditional family values and hierarchy, and some of his work has been confiscated by the government. After rejecting the conservative art scene of the 1990s, he moved to Paris and is now one of Vietnam's most established artists. He works in France and Hanoi.

Arts in Hanoi. The result is that most Vietnamese painters have their roots, in some way, in the traditional European school of painting.

## A new beginning

After decades of war, isolation and censorship, however, the artistic community was torn apart. Nearly everything, from nudes to abstraction, even impressionism, was banned. It was not until the late 1980s, with increasing openness in economic and cultural intercourse and the overall freeing up of Vietnamese society as a whole, that artistic enterprise began to flourish once again.

Nowhere was this rebirth better captured than in the 1991 exhibition Uncorked Soul, organised by Plum Blossoms Gallery in Hong Kong, the first full-scale post-war show of Vietnamese contemporary art outside of Vietnam. Since then, the art scene has not looked back.

Today, a new generation of artists is emerging, who enjoy more freedom and international recognition than ever before. Artists are also working in more diversified media. You can find experimental performance art, video and installations as well as neo-traditionalists who paint nudes, calligraphy and Chinese-style scrolls.

## Galleries

Both Hanoi and Ho Chi Minh City are awash with highly commercialised art. With fine Vietnamese art selling for six-figure sums or more in international art circles compared to the paltry US$200 or so it used to fetch two decades ago, it's not surprising that a rash of mediocre Vietnamese artists is trying to cash in on its popularity. The sheer number of art shops can be overwhelming for first-time visitors.

In Hanoi, a number of galleries, such as Art Vietnam, L'Espace and Mai Gallery, regularly showcase the country's finest talents while nurturing some of the most promising emerging artists (check www.hanoigrapevine.com for a list of exhibitions). The art scene in Ho Chi Minh City, traditionally less dynamic than in Hanoi, is now improving, with galleries such as Apricot Gallery, Galerie Quynh and Thanh Mai Gallery leading the charge (*see Shopping, page 360*).

## Craft villages

In the past, entire Vietnamese villages would have specialised in making certain crafts, such as lacquerware, pottery, parasols, conical hats or fishing nets.

In time, the village would become associated with the handicraft it produced. Today, certain villages near Hanoi are synonymous with specific products, for instance Van Phuc for silk, Bat Trang for pottery and Dong Ky for furniture (see page 131).

Vietnamese folk art and crafts declined with the onset of French colonisation at the end of the 19th century. By the end of the 20th century, however, village handicrafts were thriving once again. Today, the government recognises 1,500 genuine handicraft villages scattered all over Vietnam. This has helped preserve the villages' cultural heritage and also helped alleviate poverty in rural areas.

combine informality with great technical skill, lies somewhere between these two.

The most famous and longest-standing pottery village in Vietnam is Bat Trang, which is found just outside Hanoi. Nguyen Trai, a great politician, strategist, diplomat and poet, recorded in the 15th century that Bat Trang had provided 70 sets of bowls and plates as tribute paid to China, proof of the villagers' sophisticated craftwork.

## Woodcut

The best examples of woodcuts are known as Dong Ho paintings, an art form which

## Pottery

One expert summed up the freedom and individualism of the Vietnamese ceramic tradition when he said: "Chinese pottery is good for the eye; Vietnamese pottery is good for the heart." The combination of skilled potting, fine finishing and glazing, as well as free and calligraphic embellishing, are all features typical of the Vietnamese ceramic tradition. While the Chinese potter aims for perfect technique and the Japanese tradition strives for accidentally achieved beauty, the aesthetic appeal of Vietnamese ceramics, which

**ABOVE, FROM LEFT:** Apricot Gallery, Hanoi; woodcarver in the Old Quarter, Hanoi; drying silk at Van Phuc village.

existed as early as the 11th century during the Ly dynasty. At first the prints were limited to black and white, but after the 15th century colour was introduced. The village craftsmen make their own paper and natural colours, and prepare the blocks in variations of classic motifs depicting good luck, historical figures and battles, spirits, as well as popular allegories and social commentary.

Good fortune is symbolised by a corpulent pig decorated with garlands, often accompanied by a litter of suckling piglets. A hen surrounded by chicks symbolises prosperity. The cockerel, herald of the dawn, is the symbol of peace and courage. Social criticism is expressed by caricatures of mandarins, represented by croaking frogs and rats marching with drums and trumpets.

## Lacquerware

Lacquered wood objects have been found in tombs dating from the 3rd century AD. Today, lacquerware *(son mai)* – including paintings, screens, boxes, vases and trays – has become a relatively lucrative export item. Its quality is a result of the meticulous attention given to the preparation of the lacquer and to the designs of a 1,000-year-old tradition. However, most of the lacquerware sold in the tourist centres is mass-produced and not very durable.

Lacquer is prepared from the resin of the *cay son*, or lacquer tree, which is collected in the same way as latex (from the rubber tree). The resin is then diluted with water and the dark-brown surface layer known as *oil lac* is skimmed off. Two types of lacquer are used. Varnish lacquer is obtained by mixing lacquer resin with *mu* oil, while pumice lacquer, a higher-quality and more durable form, is produced by mixing lacquer resin with pine resin. Unlike varnish lacquer, it is rubbed and smoothed in water after painting to bring out a high gloss finish. With the addition of various ingredients and dyes, including mother of pearl, bone and egg-

shell fragments, this is used for the upper layer of lacquer paintings.

## Home accessories

A community of Vietnamese and locally based foreign designers has created a vibrant scene in this area. Homeowners will be spoilt for choice with the range of home accessories that combine Asian accents and local materials like wood, silk, lacquer and bamboo with modern design.

Boutique stores in Ho Chi Minh City, Hanoi and Hoi An sell contemporary products – luxurious cushion covers, silk lamps, vases, candle stands and the like – that mesh seemingly disparate colours, materials and styles (*see* Shopping, page 368).

# The Literary Scene

From the *Tale of Kieu* – practically Vietnam's national text – to more recent and controversial works, Vietnamese literature has a rich tradition

Classical Vietnamese literature has been fed by the country's seemingly endless wealth of oral storytelling traditions – comprising myths, songs, legends, folk and fairy tales. These stories, passed from one generation to the other, are imaginative and captivating, funny and sometimes tragic, and have remained popular and culturally significant for Vietnamese for thousands of years.

Nearly every Vietnamese reads and remembers the *Tale of Kieu*, a 3,254-verse story published over 200 years ago. During the 19th century it would have been circulated orally in the villages. Today, pupils begin studying it in the sixth grade. *Kieu* was written by one of Vietnam's most respected writers, Nguyen Du (1765–1820), and is considered to be the cultural window to the soul of the Vietnamese people. What makes the book as relevant today as it was two centuries ago is Nguyen Du's ability to lay bare the whole spectrum of society. Vices and virtues, ugliness and beauty, nobility and trickery – all are entangled in a seemingly hopeless tragic comedy reflecting the face of Vietnam.

By the time *Tale of Kieu* had become entrenched in the psyche of the Vietnamese people, the French had already colonised their country. During the early half of the 20th century, the Romanised Vietnamese script called *quoc ngu* grew popular. As the literary traditions of France and the rest of Europe became more accessible, Vietnamese literature was enriched with new ideas of Western thought and culture.

One of the finest Vietnamese novels of this era is *Dumb Luck*, a sharp satire on modernisation in Vietnam during the late colonial era. Written by Vu Trong Phung and first published in 1936, it follows the absurd and unexpected rise within colonial society of a street-smart vagabond named Red-Haired Xuan. The novel still has relevance in Vietnam as the country succumbs to another wave of modernisation.

During the Vietnam War, writers mostly restricted themselves to penning stories that were meant to unify and inspire people. After the war ended in 1975,

**ABOVE, FROM LEFT:** lacquer trays make interesting souvenirs for the home; Vietnamese author Duong Thu Huong.

Communist Party cadres controlled publishing; even today, government censors must approve writings before publication. In the 1980s authors and poets often used analogy and parody to evade censorship and publish stories that would send ripples of amusement and scandal through the reading public.

Some authors did not skirt around the issue. Duong Thu Huong's anti-establishment novels have been banned in Vietnam and she was even placed under house arrest. Nguyen Huy Thiep's 1987 short story, *The General Retires*, about the emptiness of Vietnamese society, generated much criticism, with some heatedly

denouncing its author on moral grounds. In the early 1990s, *The Sorrow of War*, written by a Vietnamese War veteran under the pseudonym of Bao Ninh, was the first war novel to confront the gruesome realities of armed conflict and the psychological effects upon soldiers.

Despite interest in Vietnamese literature, the lack of English-language translations limits readership. Wayne Karlin, a Vietnam veteran and author, has translated numerous modern works. Together with Ho Anh Thai, one of the country's most acclaimed authors, he edited the short-story anthology *Love after War*, which features the work of several leading contemporary writers. Their stories reveal the relationships and concerns of everyday life, and the erosion of life in modern Vietnam.

# VIETNAMESE CUISINE

Piquant rather than fiery, uncommonly healthy
Vietnamese food practically dances on your
palate with its distinctive mix of sweet and
sour, zesty and herbal accents

Vietnam's cuisine reflects not only its geographical position but also the country's contacts with other cultures over the centuries. From China in the north came the use of chopsticks, the art of stir-frying in a hot wok and the widespread consumption of noodles. From the streets of Paris came freshly baked baguettes *(banh mi)* and pâté as well as the art of sautéing and the use of meats such as beef.

Despite these influences, Vietnamese cuisine has retained its distinctive character. Thanks to an abundance of fresh local ingredients, it has formed its own flavours and nuances with wonderfully contrasting textures and colours. The national dish may be *pho* noodles, but the seafood found along the coastline is just as tempting and the coconut-influenced dishes of the south have a distinctive edge.

## Culinary divides

The Mekong Delta and Red River Delta have been described by Vietnamese as the great rice baskets on either end of a bamboo pole. The Red River Delta provides rice and vegetables for north Vietnam, while the fertile Mekong Delta produces rice and an amazing variety of fruits and vegetables for the southern and central regions.

To add flavour to the abundance of fresh food available, Vietnamese cooks use a riot of fresh herbs such as lemongrass, basil, coriander, mint and parsley – as well as garlic, lime, star anise and ginger. In general, as Vietnamese chefs use spices sparingly, its food is milder than that of Thailand and Cambodia.

**LEFT:** Hue "royal" cuisine. **RIGHT:** fried spring rolls, cha gio, are popular appetisers.

Vietnamese cuisine varies greatly from one region to the other. Northern food tends to be blander, and uses fewer spices and herbs. In central Vietnam, the food can be a bit spicier. Southern cooking, familiar to Westerners who have eaten in Vietnamese restaurants overseas, tends to be more flavourful and robust.

Many northerners complain they cannot eat southern food, claiming that southern cooks dump sugar into everything. This is not entirely true: sugar is used in southern cooking, in dishes such as *pho (see below)*, but not in great amounts, and coconut milk is often used to round out the flavours.

Equally, southerners will moan about northern food. The south has one essential advantage:

> *There is a local expression that goes "Eating alone hurts". Meal times are very much a communal affair in Vietnam.*

better access to fresh fruit and vegetables. There is a wider variety of food grown in the south and the growing seasons are longer.

## Signature dishes

Northerners and southerners can also argue endlessly over who has the best *pho*, Vietnam's signature noodle dish. A Hanoian will complain that the *pho* of Ho Chi Minh City is

too sweet, while someone from Saigon will complain that Hanoi's broth is too bland. Nonetheless, with a large Vietnamese diaspora scattered throughout Asia, Europe, Australia and the USA, the clear but subtle flavours of this simple and intoxicatingly delicious dish are known throughout the world.

Pronounced *fuh*, this noodle soup can be eaten for breakfast or as a late-night snack. Steaming hot broth is poured over a bowl of rice noodles topped with chicken or beef, fresh herbs and onion. Sometimes, a raw egg yolk is added, and Vietnamese might also add lime juice, hot peppers, chilli sauce or vinegar to liven up the dish. It is usually served with *quay* – a deep-fried piece of flour dough and a side dish of *rau thom (see page 89)*.

Based on literary accounts, *pho* surfaced sometime after the French occupation of Hanoi in the mid-1880s. While its roots remain the subject of debate, there is compelling evidence that it sprang from an unlikely marriage of Chinese and French culinary influences. It is said the French popularised the use of bones and lesser cuts of beef to make the broth, which forms the base of the soup. Some say that *pho* was devised by Vietnamese who learned to make *pot-au-feu* for their French employers. The theory goes that the name actually comes from the French *feu*.

The other great Vietnamese staple is *nuoc mam* (fish sauce), which is used as an ingredient as well as a dipping sauce for dishes such as spring rolls or *banh xeo* pancakes. *Nuoc mam* has a pungent aroma and biting saltiness that is an acquired taste, but it's the perfect complement

---

### VIETNAMESE RESTAURANTS

There's a wide choice of places to eat in Vietnamese cities. Whether you opt for budget meals or high-class dining, the quality will generally be high. Starting with the simplest variety, you can join locals as they pull up a plastic stall at roadside stalls that offer quintessential pho (noodle soup). Each of the small tables will have a mix of chillies, bean sprouts, mint and basil that diners add according to their own tastes.

Food markets are ideal places to find cheap and tasty snacks. Each usually has a collection of small restaurants selling everything from freshly baked baguettes to pickled vegetables. As well as roadside stalls, there are hundreds of basic restaurants with bare floors and grey concrete walls that specialise in noodles, and more sophisticated restaurants that focus on local cuisine and cater for wealthy locals and tourists. Street food can be bought from 7am to 10pm in most towns, while restaurants tend to open from 7am to 9pm. See page 90 for more on street food.

More upmarket restaurants in the main cities offer ambient settings and a mix of styles, from local to Indian, Thai and French. Service in such places is often far friendlier than in the cheaper, roadside spots. Most restaurants will not have English menus but many have photos of the food, and fellow diners are usually happy to recommend a dish to visitors.

to the subtle flavours of the food. Produced in coastal cities such as Phan Thiet and Phu Quoc, fish sauce is made by fermenting anchovies and salt in large wooden barrels for about six months. *For more, see page 312.*

## Seafood galore

Vietnam's 3,000km (1,800-mile) coastline and numerous rivers and waterways provide an ample supply of fresh fish and seafood all year round. Crabs, prawns, lobsters and squid are often simply boiled or steamed and served with a dip of salt, lemon and chilli. Fresh- and saltwater fish are usually steamed in a hotpot or

*Drinking alcohol is a still a predominantly male pursuit in Vietnam. Boisterous locals raise a toast by saying "Tram phan tram" (100 percent), which means "Drink it in one!"*

to declare "*toi an chay*" (I'm a vegetarian) when ordering.

## Family affair

Rice, or *com*, is the mainstay of a Vietnamese meal. A typical lunch or dinner for a Vietnamese family will almost always feature steaming

boiled in a broth in which the flavours mingle with the vegetables and herbs. One of the most popular dishes is *ca kho to* – catfish fillet with slices of coconut served in a clay pot and glazed with a rich, caramelised sauce.

Restaurant menus tend to be dominated by meat, fish and seafood. However, there are plenty of delicious options for vegetarians, too, such as stir-fried spinach with garlic, crunchy green (unripe) papaya salad, or tofu served in a variety of styles. Fried rice may be cooked with pork or squid, so it's best for non-meat-eaters

**ABOVE, FROM LEFT:** banh xeo, a savoury pancake made from rice flour, corn flour and egg; seafood platter.

### DOG MEAT

Dog, snake and turtle occasionally end up on Vietnamese menus, but as these places are often situated on the outskirts of town or in the countryside, tourists hardly notice them. None of these meats is everyday fare and, typically, friends will choose to eat at such an establishment to celebrate a special occasion.

Dog-meat (thit cho) consumption is generally more widespread during wintertime in the north, but you can find it throughout Vietnam. It is believed to aid sexual potency: older men eat dog meat in the belief that it will boost virility while young men like to gather at a dog-meat restaurant before a night on the town.

> *If you are invited to a wedding, funeral or festival, there will usually be two main courses, one salty and the other sweet. A typical feast will include meatballs, local sausages, chicken stew and a salad.*

bowls of rice accompanied by a few side dishes. It is so much part of the cuisine that people refer to both lunch and dinner simply as *com*.

Wherever you are in Vietnam, a standard meal will consist of rice plus a meat or fish dish, stir-fried vegetables and a bowl of soup *(canh)*. The soup, usually a light, sour broth with vegetables and sometimes seafood, is used to wash down the rice. Also on the table will be various dipping sauces, including soy sauce, salt moistened with lime juice and the ubiquitous fish sauce. Each dish will have its own particular dipping sauce. For example, duck will be dipped in soy sauce, chicken in salt with lime, and pork in fish sauce.

While you can find Vietnamese desserts such as *che*, a sweet bean dessert served in cafés and restaurants, there is no real post-dinner dessert culture in Vietnam. It is most likely your meal will finish off with a platter of fresh fruit, such as watermelon or dragon fruit.

A great way to enjoy a shared dining experi-

## CHANGING TIMES

With so many fresh vegetables, a wealth of fresh herbs, minimal use of oil, and the use of meat as a condiment rather than a main course, Vietnamese food is healthy. Inevitably, as elsewhere in the world, the younger generation has a taste for mass-produced Western hamburgers and pizzas. Fast-food chains are everywhere in Hanoi and Ho Chi Minh City. Offering free Wi-Fi and air conditioning, they are seen by young Vietnamese as hip places to hang out. A taste for burgers is also seen as an urbane trait in a country where older generations are notoriously reluctant to try foreign food.

ence is a hotpot *(lau)* or steamboat meal. This DIY feast includes plates of assorted meats or seafood, and fresh vegetables and noodles, which are added to a communal pot of boiling broth at the diner's discretion. Vietnamese can sit over a hotpot for hours, adding more stock and ingredients, while chatting and clinking glasses throughout the evening.

## Must-eat dishes

Apart from pho and other staples mentioned earlier in the chapter, here are some Vietnamese specialities visitors are likely to encounter.

*Banh cuon:* rice-flour crêpes stuffed with pork, mushrooms, onion and coriander, and topped with fried onions, alongside fresh herbs and fish sauce.

**Banh flan:** A delicious dessert with a strong French influence, it is sometimes known as banh caramel. It strongly resembles crème caramel, though the Vietnamese version occasionally substitutes the caramel with black coffee.

**Banh khoai:** a rice- and corn-flour and egg pancake filled with pork or shrimp, onions, bean sprouts and mushrooms. A Hue speciality.

**Banh mi thit/pate/trung:** baguette served with either *thit* (meat), pâté or eggs, along with sliced carrots, coriander and other fresh herbs.

**Banh xeo:** a rice-flour pancake studded with shrimp and crunchy bean sprouts.

**Bit tet:** Vietnamese beefsteak served in thick is rolled in a lettuce leaf with fresh herbs and dipped in *nuoc cham*.

**Che:** A popular dessert, made with sticky rice and beans. Often sold in plastic containers, it comes in several varieties, depending on the type of bean that is used.

**Ga** or **muc xao sa ot:** sautéed chicken or squid with lemongrass, fish sauce, garlic, onion and chillies.

**Goi cuon:** a cold spring roll of vermicelli, prawns, pork and herbs wrapped in rice paper. It sometimes appears on English menus as "summer rolls".

**Mi Quang:** A complex noodle dish that features strong, opposing flavours mixed with vegetables, rice and herbs.

gravy with a fresh baguette, French fries and salad.

**Bo luc lac:** stir-fried beef cubes and onions served over greens and tomatoes. Usually eaten with rice.

**Bun bo:** a Hue speciality of fried beef, served over noodles with coriander, onion, garlic, cucumber, chillies and tomato paste.

**Bun cha:** charcoal-grilled minced pork patties or strips of lean pork, served in a bowl of *nuoc cham* with cold rice noodles. While ubiquitous in the north, *bun cha* is rarely found in the south.

**Cha gio** (often called *nem Saigon* in the north): small rolls of minced pork, prawn, crab meat, mushrooms and vegetables wrapped in thin rice paper and deep-fried until crisp. *Cha gio*

**ABOVE, FROM LEFT:** preparing banh cuon; pho noodles.

### HERBS AND VEGETABLES

Vietnam is blessed with a bounty of fresh veg and herbs that are often served with pho noodles, spring rolls and other dishes. Collectively referred to as rau thom ("leafy fragrant"), mint, marjoram, bean sprouts, coriander, purple perilla, sawtooth herb and dill are likely to be found, as well as good old-fashioned lettuce and other temperate vegetables grown in the cooler highlands. Tourists are understandably nervous about eating raw greens in Vietnam, so pick a restaurant that looks clean and is well patronised. Rau thom adds an explosion of flavours when mixed into your food.

# STREET FOOD

**To experience satisfying Vietnamese cuisine as the locals do, head to an inexpensive street market**

Hanoi and Ho Chi Minh City have numerous upmarket restaurants with flickering candles and soft music, but the tastiest food is often found outside at the street stalls. It may look basic, with little more than plastic stools and knee-high tables, but Vietnamese street food nearly always delivers. Vendors normally operate from early morning to late evening.

Roadside shacks are found in almost every town and offer quick and simple dishes – a bowl of steaming noodles or a beef stew filled with vegetables. Also ubiquitous are sliced and diced pineapples, mangos and guavas. For those who just want a drink, Vietnam's café culture extends to the street: pull up a stool and wait for the thick, rich coffee to come. For those who want something more filling, the list of options is immense.

Most vendors have the names of their wares printed on their carts. Among the most popular options are bite-size snacks that are deep-fried or grilled. The nation's favourite noodles, *pho*, or snacks such as *ca vien* (fish balls on a stick) are packed with flavour.

Each region has its own culinary quirk. In the north, dishes such as *bun cha*, sliced pork with vermicelli, are famous. In the central provinces, the best-known snack is *banh bao*, a soft, dumpling-like creation. Down south, the use of coconut milk and lime juice is more in evidence. Hu tieu mi, a mass of noodles and vegetables, is a classic southern dish, as is *banh bot chien* (nothing to do with dogs!), a fried rice-flour cake.

Street food is generally safe to eat, but the normal rules apply: go for ice cubes, not the crushed variety, and remember that peeled fruits have been less exposed to germs than those that have been laid out in the open for hours.

**ABOVE:** street food seller in Hanoi.

**BELOW:** *Banh Mi, Xuo Xich,* warmed baguette stuffed with sausage, sliced cucumber and covered in fish sauce.

**LEFT:** a Hmong boy at Tam Duong market near Sa Pa.

**ABOVE:** crowded roadside tables in the Old City, Hanoi.

## TABLE MANNERS

Chopsticks are commonly used throughout Vietnam. Correct eating etiquette involves holding the bottom of the bowl with your left hand so it is near your face, then using the chopsticks in the right hand to shovel in the noodles or rice. Any other method may result in bemused stares from locals. Other dishes require a fork and spoon, with the spoon held in the right hand.

As with most Asian cultures, avoid sticking your chopsticks upright into a bowl of rice as this is thought to resemble incense sticks at a funeral and so has connotations of death. If you are a guest, be sure to leave some food on your plate. And lastly, you don't need a litre of water at the ready when eating Vietnamese food, as it is far less spicy than other Asian cuisines.

**BELOW:** *Ca Vien*, prawn balls and assorted street food including barbecued meatballs with shredded pork, cucumber, beansprouts, herbs, roasted peanuts and rice vermicelli.

**ABOVE:** *Banh Cuon Nhan Thit*, soft spring rolls filled with pork with a sweet chilli sauce.
**BELOW:** *Pho*, the classic Vietnamese noodle dish.

# ARCHITECTURE

Vietnamese urban architecture is a wonderful blend of Chinese, colonial and socialist influences. There are also Buddhist pagodas and Khmer temples plus vestiges of the fallen Cham civilisation

**A**ccording to the architect William S. Logan, Vietnamese cultural and national survival came about through "bending with the wind". Throughout its history Vietnam has assimilated the cultures of invading countries while preserving its own traditions. As a result, architecture in Vietnam is "characteristically multi-layered" – each layer is an example of the external powers' cultural and political influence.

The Chinese, the ancient Chams and Khmers, the French and the Russians have all made an indelible impression on Vietnam with their distinctive architectural styles. Today, Western architecture makes its presence felt in the urban centres of Hanoi and Ho Chi Minh City, where luxury high-rise offices and apartments are sprouting.

## The Chinese stamp

There is no escaping the Chinese influence on Vietnamese architecture: the string of Vietnamese dynasties that ruled from the 10th to the 19th centuries all incorporated Chinese influences into their buildings. Some of the best examples of Chinese architecture are found in Hanoi, founded in 1010 by King Ly Thai To, who constructed a new citadel according to Chinese principles. In 2003, the foundations of several royal palace buildings, a drainage system, wells and thousands of artefacts were discovered when construction work on a new government building began.

Perhaps the most significant Chinese-style building of this period is the Temple of Literature (Van Mieu), established in Hanoi in 1070 in honour of Confucius. The original structure was demolished in the 19th century to make way for a royal temple, which in turn was razed in 1946 during fighting with the French, and rebuilt later in the 20th century according to the original specifications.

The old imperial capital of Hue is another treasure trove of Chinese architecture. When Nguyen Anh took the throne as Emperor Gia Long in 1802 he transferred the royal seat of government to Hue. In 1805 he set about constructing the new royal citadel on the north bank of the Huong (Perfume) River. Stylistically, the Imperial City is a reasonably faithful copy of Beijing's Forbidden City. By 1975 only 20 of the original 148 palaces and buildings were left standing. What remained was still sufficiently magnificent for the Imperial City to be recognised as a Unesco World Heritage Site in 1993.

Since 1996, significant progress has been made in restoring the surviving monuments.

Another repository of Chinese architecture is found at Hoi An, another Unesco World Heritage Site in central Vietnam. Settled by a Chinese community in the 15th century, the historic town was a thriving port that was regularly visited by ships from all over Europe and Asia. The town features Chinese temples, assembly halls and traditional houses. Japanese traders also constructed wooden temples and homes in the town. While most of these have now disappeared, a Japanese-style bridge acts as a reminder of Hoi An's past. A handful of the

form of brick temples and towers scattered over the coastal lowlands and some inland areas. There are several outstanding Cham sites, but the most famous is My Son in Quang Nam province. My Son, which served as the spiritual and intellectual capital of the Champa kingdom, is considered to be the Cham equivalent to the grand cities of Southeast Asia's other Indian-influenced civilisations, like Angkor in Cambodia, Pagan in Myanmar and Ayuthaya in Thailand.

At one time, the mighty Khmer empire stretched across modern Cambodia, Thailand, Laos and Vietnam. Ancient Khmer architecture

merchant houses display an interesting blend of Chinese, Japanese and Vietnamese styles, and many of the town's pagodas also have similar influences.

## Cham ruins and Khmer pagodas

The Champa kingdom was established in central Vietnam in the 2nd century, and for about 1,000 years, from the 5th to the 15th centuries, Cham rulers presided over an extraordinary renaissance of Hindu art and architecture. What is left of the Champa kingdom is mainly in the

**LEFT:** Nine Dynastic Urns at the restored Pavilion of Splendour at the Imperial City in Hue. **ABOVE:** the red-brick towers of Po Nagar at Nha Trang.

### A SENSE OF BALANCE

When it comes to architecture, Vietnamese people strongly believe in the principles of feng shui, or phong thuy as it's known in Vietnamese. New construction must commence on an auspicious date on the lunar calendar that is decided after consultation with a feng shui master. Entire villages have been developed according to these principles.

Another Chinese-style belief relates to numbers: modern Vietnamese office or apartment blocks frequently omit the number four when naming floors as tu (four) sounds like the Sino-Vietnamese word for death.

has survived unscathed in parts of southern Vietnam, and the sparkling golden roofs of elaborate Khmer pagodas can be found across the Mekong Delta, especially in the former Khmer stronghold of Soc Trang province. Its 18th-century Kh'leng Pagoda is especially striking.

## French urban planning

The origins of Vietnam's contemporary architecture can be traced to the arrival of the French colonialists. Before the 19th century, the main building material used in Vietnamese architecture was wood. The French brought modern materials and technology as well as ambitious plans for

Dame Cathedral in Ho Chi Minh City, built between 1877 and 1883, is a superb example of classical French colonial architecture. Remarkably, every single stone used in its creation was shipped from France. Many of these places of worship are pink in colour, including the distinctive Danang Cathedral, or Con Ga, and Tan Dinh Church in Ho Chi Minh City, known locally as the Pink Church.

## East meets west

Auguste-Henri Vildieu, the official French architect for Vietnam at the start of the 20th century, imposed traditional oriental architectural features

urban redevelopment in Saigon and Hanoi as part of its *mission civilisatrice* (civilising mission).

Towards the end of 19th century, the French began developing both cities' commerce and infrastructure by reclaiming land and constructing roads and waterways. This transplanted European urban model came with the attendant neoclassical public buildings, a grand opera house, tree-lined boulevards, parks and generous squares. Today, a stroll down Trang Tien Street in Hanoi or Dong Khoi Street in Ho Chi Minh City will give you a sense of the French architectural vision.

Another legacy from the French was the numerous churches and cathedrals that were built to spread the Catholic faith. The Notre

on Western structures. He adapted European design to the climatic conditions of Hanoi, incorporating long lobbies, thick walls, roof canopies, verandas, patios and ventilation holes, helping to keep the essentially Western-style buildings warm in winter, cool in summer, and to provide protection from the heavy rainfalls and tropical sunshine, while allowing sufficient air circulation.

Vildieu built the Presidential Palace of Vietnam, located beside the Ho Chi Minh Mausoleum, between 1900 and 1906 to house the French governor-general of Indochina. From the outside, the palace is pointedly European; the only visual cues that you are still in Vietnam are the mango trees growing on the grounds. When Vietnam achieved independence in

1954, Ho Chi Minh refused to live in this grand structure. Instead, a traditional Vietnamese stilt house overlooking a carp pond was built on the grounds to accommodate the president.

Ernest Hébrard, who was appointed head of the Indochina Architecture and Town Planning Service in 1923, later continued developing this "Indochinese" style of architecture. By the 1940s, this style would be apparent in the designs of residential housing.

Another striking edifice fusing cross-cultural design is the late 19th-century Phat Diem Cathedral in Ninh Binh province near Hanoi. This is an extraordinary example of an eclectic architectural style. Designed by a Vietnamese priest, Father Sau, who rallied the local population to build the cathedral, the roof is in the style of a pagoda while the walls are those of a Western church. The interior walls are filled with Catholic iconography but also, curiously enough, Eastern religious symbols such as dragons, unicorns, tortoises and phoenixes.

In Vietnam's larger cities, shopfronts often alternative between old Chinese-style wooden shutters and smart, modern, glass-fronted units that are further proof of how varied Vietnamese architecture has become. On the downside, modern Vietnamese architects seem to favour bland blocks of concrete.

## Soviet influences

One of the most important pre-Reunification architectural projects in Hanoi was the Ho Chi Minh Mausoleum, designed by Nguyen Ngoc Chan. Constructed between 1969 and 1975, it successfully combines Soviet-style realism with the simplicity of ethnic minority architecture.

In the wake of Reunification, all efforts were focused on the need to re-establish the national infrastructure. Many new public buildings were constructed in monumental Soviet style during the 1970s and 1980s, their design intended to reflect the power of the state and its ideology. The Ho Chi Minh Museum in Hanoi and the Hoa Binh Theatre in Ho Chi Minh City are among the most significant buildings dating from this period.

## Modern times

Since the turn of the 21st century, the Vietnamese economy has by and large been buoyant. In major urban centres like Hanoi, Ho Chi Minh City, Danang and Haiphong, a rash of high-end shopping malls, office and apartment complexes has been built to accommodate Vietnam's business community and the newly minted rich. Modern villas built to house Vietnam's growing middle class have mushroomed, sometimes resulting in a garish clash of Vietnamese and Western architectural styles. To meet the demand for premium office and retail space, several large building projects are under way. High taxes on the frontages of townhouses have had an unexpected side-effect – the creation of unusual, long,

thin properties that became known as "tube houses". Examples of these are particularly common in Hanoi and Hoi An. Their French-style balconies would look rather appealing, were it not for the giant iron security gates that tend to be attached to such homes to prevent break-ins.

Real-estate prices in Vietnam's urban centres reached ridiculous levels by 2007, with some commercial areas in Ho Chi Minh City costing around US$180,000 per square metre – more than their equivalent in Hollywood. Since then, spiralling inflation and high interest rates have brought prices back down to more realistic levels and resulted in a rather flat market.

**ABOVE, FROM LEFT:** a curious amalgam of styles at the Phat Diem Cathedral; Ho Chi Minh Mausoleum.

# PLACES

A detailed guide to the entire country, with
principal sites cross-referenced by number to
the accompanying maps

**G**iven the decades of war and destruction, you may
be forgiven for imagining that Vietnam's infrastructure is not going to be set up for travellers. However,
although the delays and red tape can be tiring, the rewards
are immense.

In today's Vietnam the remnants of war have become
tourist attractions rather than eyesores. The scars and memorials are a now
a part of the country's tourism pull, whether you're burrowing into the
depths of the Cu Chi tunnels near Ho Chi Minh City (formerly Saigon) or
viewing the rusting heaps of wartime hardware at Hanoi's Military History
Museum. The vestiges of a more remote past, from Champa ruins and
Hue's imperial city to the elegant colonial streets of Hanoi, are a
major lure, as are the glorious natural attractions – from a coastline of powder-soft beaches to the impressive forested mountains.

Northern Vietnam's signature city is Hanoi, an appealing place
full of the old villas and facades of the French colonial era which
give it a unique ambience. Farther on, the pancake-flat Red River
Delta is bordered on the east by the Gulf of Tonkin, where the
fabled limestone islands of Halong Bay sit. Beyond the delta's
plains, cooler mountain regions, populated by hill tribes, ascend
towards the west and Laos and northwards towards China.

Heading south, the country narrows through a chain of
increasingly tropical provinces washed by the warm waters of the South
China Sea. In the old Imperial City of Hue, a sense of the past pervades,
carried over into the nearby town of Hoi An. In the lands of the ancient
Champa kingdom further south are decaying temples that testify to the
conquest by the Viet people from the north. And all along the serpentine
coast are stretches of largely undeveloped white-sand beaches lapped by
aquamarine waters.

Beyond the resort of Dalat in the picturesque southern highlands is
Ho Chi Minh City, Vietnam's vibrant commercial centre. The far south is
dominated by the Mekong Delta, an extensive area of farms and orchards
and numerous waterways best explored by boat. Offshore are the newly
touristed islands of Phu Quoc and, further east, the Con Dao archipelago.

---

**PRECEDING PAGES:** spectacular Halong Bay; Ban Gioc Waterfall spans the Vietnam-
China border; picturesque Hue and the Perfume River. **LEFT:** Phu Quoc Island.
**TOP:** Cu Chi tunnels. **ABOVE RIGHT:** Tam Coc.

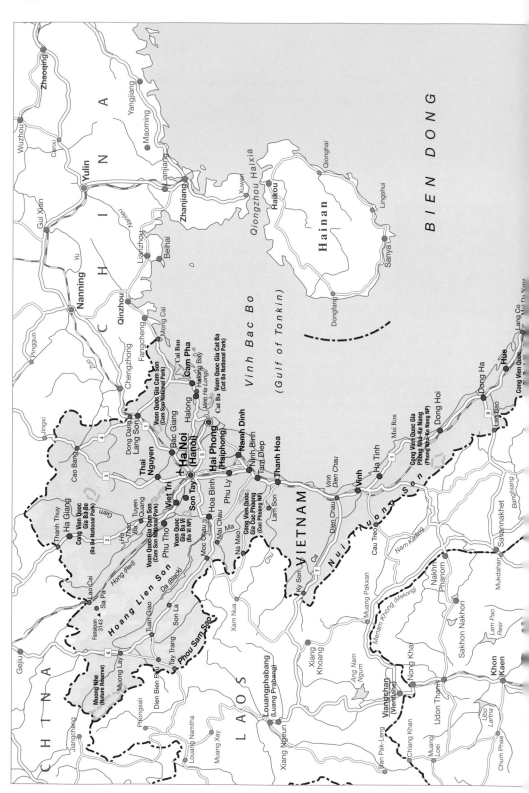

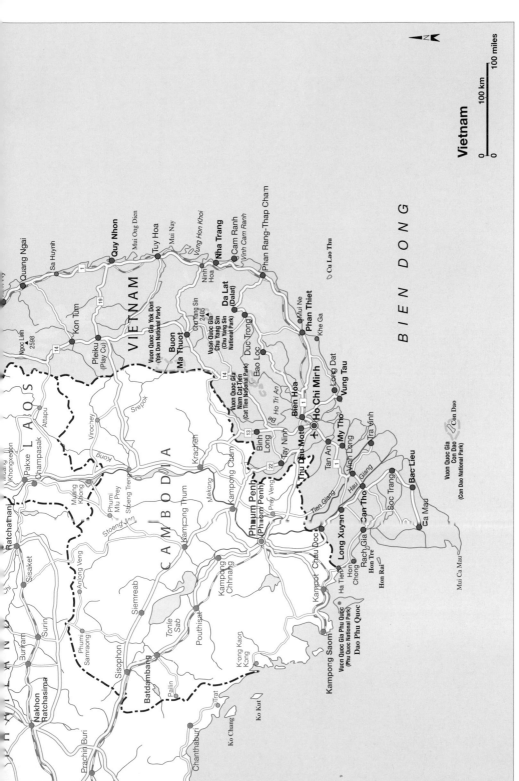

**Vietnam**

0   100 km
0   100 miles

# NORTHERN VIETNAM

Home to many of Vietnam's foremost attractions, the north offers jagged mountain ranges and a picturesque coast, as well as the historic capital city of Hanoi

For those hankering to experience dramatic scenery and colourful ethnic groups, northern Vietnam ticks all the boxes. While parts of the region rush headlong towards modernisation, with many communities becoming increasingly aware of tourist lucre, the north remains a traditionalist stronghold.

Encapsulating the bewildering blend of modernity and traditionalism, Hanoi – the country's political and administrative centre – is the ideal place to start any journey. Always evolving, the 1,000-year-old city's fortunes are reflected in the architecture of its many temples and pagodas, in the lingering presence of a French colonial past, and in the whir of construction as luxury high-rise buildings emerge in old neighbourhoods.

Beyond Hanoi lie timelessly sedate and picturesque provincial regions, where the waters of the Red River (Song Hong) feed brilliant-green rice paddies and fruit orchards. In small, far-flung villages, groves of trees and bamboo enclose modest communities where life revolves around the local communal house and pagoda, and where traditions continue as they have for centuries. In other areas, factories and large-scale assembly plants have sprouted

like weeds, providing livelihoods for workers but polluting the local environment and appropriating farmlands.

On the eastern coast, in the Gulf of Tonkin, is the busy port of Haiphong, gateway to the breathtaking scenery of Halong Bay. The city is recognised as a Unesco World Heritage Site and is famous for its dramatic, mist-shrouded seascape of limestone cliffs and caves. Farther east is the Tonkin Coast, which is speckled with national parks, ancient sites and more beaches.

The highlands of the northern interior are home to several ethnic minority peoples, many of whom live high in the mountains and farm on stunning terraced fields. In Lao Cai province, the picturesque hill retreat of Sa Pa has become famous as a high-altitude getaway with treks into minority villages and homestays in stilt houses, though here more than anywhere the presence of tourists is starting to influence traditional ways of life.

---

**LEFT:** lanterns of all colours. **TOP:** ceremonial headgear of the Dao minority.
**ABOVE RIGHT:** Mai Chau farm.

# HANOI

Brimming with a complex history yet full of
modern energy and potential, Hanoi is an
attractive and enjoyable city, and a great place
to get the measure of 21st-century Vietnam

For decades the bastion of Vietnamese ideology and conservatism, Hanoi is fast becoming a modern, thriving city: luxury shopping malls and apartments now sit alongside 200-year-old temples, while trendy coffee shops line busy streets.

Despite the changes, Hanoians are passionate about protecting their age-old traditions and culture, and a number of preservation works have been announced to preserve important historic sites. The French-influenced architecture and an abundance of trees and lakes give Hanoi a romantic air. Hanoi may be the Vietnamese capital, but it is far smaller than its southern counterpart Ho Chi Minh City, and thus far easier to navigate. From the charismatic French Quarter to the various parks and open spaces, Hanoi's appeal is instant.

Its long history also means that several major historical attractions are based here, including the Ho Chi Minh Mausoleum and several war museums.

Hanoi is a relatively small capital, with an urban population of 3.2 million. However, in August 2008, the government announced that the city boundaries had been expanded to swallow up the entire province of Ha Tay and Me Linh District in Vinh Phuc province, as well as four communes within Hoa Binh province's Luong

Son District. In one fell swoop, a whopping 3,300 sq km (1,274 sq miles) have been added, now encompassing a population of around 6.2 million.

At the heart of the city is Hoan Kiem District, which comprises the Old Quarter just north of Hoan Kiem Lake and the French Quarter, just east and south of the lake. Most of the action takes place in the Old Quarter, also known as the 36 Streets. In the early 13th century, a collection of small-scale artisan villages evolved into craft

**Main attractions**

OLD QUARTER
THANG LONG WATER PUPPET
  THEATRE
SOFITEL LEGEND METROPOLE HOTEL
OPERA HOUSE
NATIONAL MUSEUM OF VIETNAMESE
  HISTORY
ST JOSEPH'S CATHEDRAL
VIETNAM FINE ARTS MUSEUM
TEMPLE OF LITERATURE
HO CHI MINH MAUSOLEUM
WEST LAKE
VIETNAM MUSEUM OF ETHNOLOGY

**LEFT:** Opera House. **RIGHT:** West Lake at sunset.

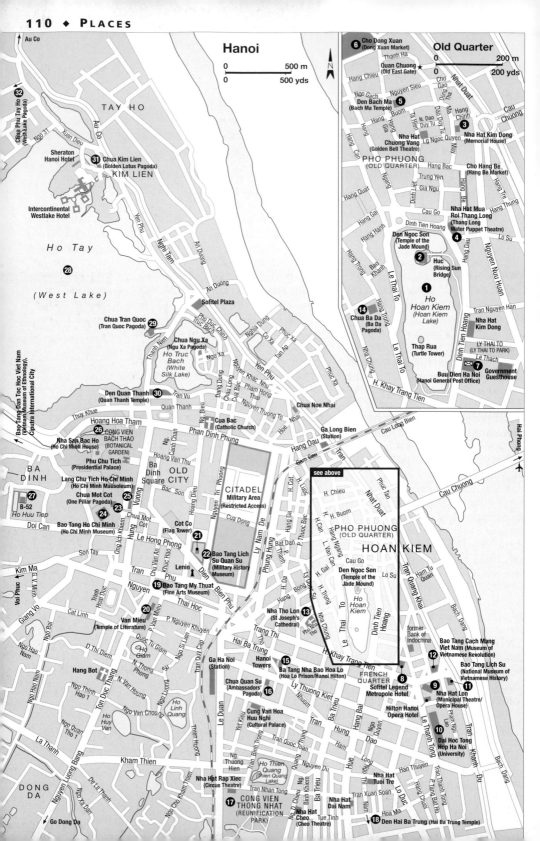

**Hanoi**

0 ____ 500 m
0 ____ 500 yds

**Old Quarter**

0 ____ 200 m
0 ____ 200 yds

Au Co

**TAY HO**

32 Chua Phu Tay Ho
(WestLake Pagoda)

Sheraton
Hanoi Hotel

31 Chua Kim Lien
(Golden Lotus Pagoda)

**KIM LIEN**

Intercontinental
Westlake Hotel

*Ho Tay*
*(West Lake)*

28

Sofitel Plaza

Chua Tran Quoc 29
(Tran Quoc Pagoda)

Chua Ngu Xa
(Ngu Xa Pagoda)

*Ho Truc Bach*
*(White Silk Lake)*

Bao Tang Dan Toc Hoc Viet Nam
(Vietnam Museum of Ethnology),
Ciputra International City

Den Quan Thanh 30
(Quan Thanh Temple)

Chua Noe Nhai

Nha San Bac Ho 26
(Ho Chi Minh House)

CONG VIEN
BACH THAO
(BOTANICAL
GARDEN)

Cua Bac
(Catholic Church)

Ga Long Bien
(Station)

Phu Chu Tich
(Presidential Palace)

**BA
DINH**

Lang Chu Tich Ho Chi Minh
(Ho Chi Minh Mausoleum)

**Ba
Dinh
Square**

**OLD
CITY**

**CITADEL
Military Area
(Restricted Access)**

27 B-52
Ho Huu Tiep

Chua Mot Cot 25
(One Pillar Pagoda)

Bao Tang Ho Chi Minh 24
(Ho Chi Minh Museum)

23

Cot Co
(Flag Tower) 21

22 Bao Tang Lich
Su Quan Su
(Military History
Museum)

Lenin

19 Bao Tang My Thuat
(Fine Arts Museum)

20

Van Mieu
(Temple of Literature)

Hang Bot

Ga Ha Noi
(Station)

Hanoi
Towers

Nha Tho Lon 13
(St Joseph's
Cathedral)

15 Ba Tang Nha Bao Hoa Lo
(Hoa Lo Prison/Hanoi Hilton)

Chua Quan Su
(Ambassadors'
Pagoda) 16

**FRENCH
QUARTER**

Sofitel Legend
Metropole Hotel 8

Hilton Hanoi
Opera Hotel

Bao Tang Cach Mang
Viet Nam (Museum of
Vietnamese Revolution)

Bao Tang Lich Su
(National Museum of
Vietnamese History)

12

9 Nha Hat Lon
(Municipal Theatre/
Opera House)

11

*Ho
Linh
Quang*

Cung Van Hoa
Huu Nghi
(Cultural Palace)

Dai Hoc Tong
Hop Ha Noi
(University) 10

**DONG
DA**

Go Dong Da

Nha Hat Rap Xiec
(Circus Theatre)

*Ho Thien
Quang
Thien Quang
Lake*

17 CONG VIEN
THONG NHAT
(REUNIFICATION
PARK)

Nha Hat
Cheo
(Cheo Theatre)

Nha Hat
Dai Nam

Nha Hat
Tuoi Tre

18 Den Hai Ba Trung (Hai Ba Trung Temple)

---

**Old Quarter detail:**

6 Cho Dong Xuan
(Dong Xuan Market)

Quan Chuong
(Old East Gate)

Thanh Ha

Den Bach Ma 5
(Bach Ma Temple)

3 Nha Hat Kim Dong
(Memorial House)

Nha Hat
Chuong Vang
(Golden Bell Theatre)

**PHO PHUONG
(OLD QUARTER)**

Cho Hang Be
(Hang Be Market)

Nha Hat Mua
Roi Thang Long
(Thang Long
Water Puppet Theatre) 4

Den Ngoc Son
(Temple of the
Jade Mound) 2

Huc
(Rising Sun
Bridge)

1

*Ho
Hoan Kiem
(Hoan Kiem
Lake)*

Nha Hat
Kim Dong

14 Chua Ba Da
(Ba Da
Pagoda)

Thap Rua
(Turtle Tower)

7 Buu Dien Ha Noi
(Hanoi General Post Office)

Government
Guesthouse

LY THAI TO
(LY THAI TO PARK)
Le Thach

---

see above

**PHO PHUONG
(OLD QUARTER)**

**HOAN KIEM**

Den Ngoc Son
(Temple of the
Jade Mound)

*Ho
Hoan
Kiem*

former
Bank of
Indochina

guilds, and the streets were named after the products they made, the service they rendered or their location. Today, some road names still reflect the trade that takes place there, but they now share space with backpacker hotels, cafés, shops and restaurants.

Ba Dinh District, to the west of the Old Quarter, is the political and administrative heart of Hanoi, and hosts several sites of historic interest, including the mausoleum of Ho Chi Minh.

North of Ba Dinh and Hoan Kiem districts is West Lake District (Tay Ho District). In this burgeoning area are huge five-star hotels, expensive shops and restaurants, and the extravagant villas of Hanoi's newly minted rich.

Visitors tend to stick to the main urban areas of Hoan Kiem, Ba Dinh and Tay Ho.

In Vietnamese, Hanoi is written as two words: Ha meaning river, in reference to the Red River, or Song Hong, and noi, meaning inside. The city's rich and complex history dates back to the Neolithic era, when the ancient Viet people settled in Bach Hac and Viet Tri regions (present-day Vinh Phuc province), at the confluence of the Red and Lo rivers.

## The origins of Hanoi

Northern Vietnam once formed the Van Lang and Au Lac kingdoms of antiquity (see page 27). From around the 3rd century BC, the influence of China grew, and by the first century BC much of the region (Nam Viet) had been absorbed into a Han Chinese colony named Giao Chi (Jiaozhi).

After a long period of Chinese domination and periodic local struggles for independence, the Chinese were expelled in the 10th century.

Ly Thai To, founder of the Ly dynasty, is thought to have arrived in Dai La – an ancient city along the Red River – in the early 11th century. Legend says he saw an enormous golden dragon emerge from a lake and soar into the sky above the site. Based on this omen, he moved the capital from Hoa Lu to Dai La, which he renamed Thang Long (Ascending Dragon), present-day Hanoi.

*Legend has it that in a dream King Ly Thai To saw the goddess Quan Am seated on a lotus leaf offering him a male child in her outstretched arms. Shortly after his dream, the king married a young peasant girl who bore him the male heir of whom he had dreamt. As a sign of his gratitude, he is said to have built Hanoi's One Pillar Pagoda (see page 123).*

**BELOW:** early morning activity at Reunification Park.

*Local women gather by Hoan Kiem Lake for a daily dose of exercise.*

The area between West Lake and the citadel became the administrative city (Kinh Thanh) and at the heart of this was the Royal City (Hoang Thanh). In 1010, the Royal City contained eight palaces and three pavilions, with eight more palaces built during the 11th century. The Temple of Literature, the One Pillar Pagoda and the Tran Quoc Pagoda were all built during this time.

Following the fall of the Tran dynasty (which had succeeded the Ly in 1225), the capital was moved to Thanh Hoa in 1400. Seven years later the armies of the Chinese Ming dynasty invaded, maintaining control of the region until Le Loi defeated the Chinese and moved the capital back to Thang Long (Hanoi) in 1428, renaming it as Dong Kinh (later corrupted by the French as Tonkin). Le Loi took on the name Le Thai To and founded the Le dynasty.

### European influences

Dutch, Portuguese and French traders arrived during the 17th century, quickly followed by Christian missionaries. With the rise of the Nguyen dynasty in 1802, the centre of power shifted to Hue in central Vietnam and Dong Kinh was renamed Ha Noi. When Hanoi fell into the hands of France in 1883, the city underwent a dramatic transformation.

Hanoi and the north finally defeated the French in 1954, but followed this with a new conflict, as it tried to impose communist rule on southern Vietnam. During the Vietnam War, nearly a quarter of Hanoi was bombed flat by American warplanes. After North and South Vietnam were reunified in 1976, Hanoi was declared capital of the new Socialist Republic but social and economic problems hampered reconstruction efforts.

Today, Hanoi is a rapidly developing city with striking European embellishments. For a city full of fiercely independent people, it's somewhat ironic that it possesses a decidedly European air. Hanoians may brag about their beautiful city while eating baguette sandwiches and sipping café au lait, but few like to concede that much of this is down to the French.

## HOAN KIEM DISTRICT

### Hoan Kiem Lake

Picturesque **Hoan Kiem Lake ❶** (Ho Hoan Kiem) is hugely popular with locals as a recreational site. Set in the heart of the Old Quarter, the lake – known to Hanoians as Ho Guom (Green Lake) – comes alive at dawn as t'ai chi, badminton and jogging take place around its shore.

Every evening the lake has a convivial vibe as traders sell all manner of food and toys, the air is filled with music and locals sip coffee or enjoy ice cream in one of several lakeside cafés.

Known as the Lake of the Restored Sword, it is also the stuff of legend. Folklore says that King Le Thai To of the 15th-century Le dynasty received a magical sword from an ancient tortoise. He used the weapon during his 10-year resistance against the Chinese in the early 1400s. After liberating the

country, the king took a boat to the centre of the lake to return the sword to the divine tortoise. The tortoise is said to have snatched the sword from his hand and disappeared into the lake. In 2011 a clean-up operation was launched to improve the polluted lake and succeeded in saving a giant freshwater turtle that had been spotted there.

## Ngoc Son Temple

Look towards the middle of the lake to see a small 18th-century structure called the **Tortoise Tower** (Thap Rua). Perched on a tiny islet at the north end of the lake is **Ngoc Son Temple**, also known as the **Temple of the Jade Mound ❷** (Den Ngoc Son; daily 8am–5pm; charge). The temple is reached from the shore via an arched bridge, painted bright red and known as The Huc, or the **Rising Sun Bridge**. On the small hillock at the end of the bridge stands a stone column in the form of a brush next to an ink well. Inscribed on the column are three Chinese characters: *ta tien qing*, or "written on the blue sky". Ngoc Son

Temple is dedicated to, among others, the famous General Tran Hung Dao *(see page 30)* and La To, the patron saint of doctors. Inside is a huge 250kg (550lb) stuffed tortoise caught in Hoan Kiem Lake in the 1960s.

## THE OLD QUARTER

### The "36 Streets"

North of Hoan Kiem Lake is an area known as the **36 Streets**, or the **Old Quarter** (Pho Phuong), one of the oldest parts of Hanoi. Formerly a centre for resistance against the French, this part of town evolved in the 13th century when artisan guilds were concentrated along each of the original 36 lanes. The guilds developed independently, separated from each other by walls and gates that were locked each night. Tinsmiths were found on Hang Thiec (Tin Street), bamboo basket makers on Hang Bo (Bamboo Basket Street), and so on. The present-day commercial frenzy that the Old Quarter has become (along with its intense motorbike and bicycle traffic) is all the more amazing considering

*The 18th-century Tortoise Tower on Hoan Kiem Lake.*

**BELOW:** Rising Sun Bridge (The Huc), leading to Ngoc Son Temple.

*The much-delayed, much-maligned Hanoi Metro rail project is on track for an opening in 2016. When it finally does begin running, it should consist of eight lines. The city's first metro will go a long way to alleviating traffic congestion.*

that, with few exceptions, the communists prohibited private trade until as recently as 1986.

The new tradespeople still cluster along each street by speciality, but the trade doesn't necessarily match the street name any longer. Silver jewellery, as well as gravestones, can still be found on **Hang Bac** (Silver Street), but also here now are travel agencies and tourist cafés. The street called **Hang Gai** (Hemp) specialises in silk, clothing and embroidered articles, while **Hang Dau** (Cooking Oil) is full of shoe shops. However, **Hang Chieu** (Mats) is still the place to find mats, **Hang Ma** (Paper Votive Objects) has mainly stationery shops, and Thuoc Bac does a steady trade in herbal medicines.

Each of the 36 craft guilds once had its own *dinh* (communal house). However, like most of the quarter's pagodas and temples, they were shut down during the communist takeover and transformed into schools or public housing. Similarly, the narrow storefronts, some less than 3 metres (10ft) wide, once contained

single-family dwellings. These *nha ong*, or tube houses, extend far to the back and are punctuated by tiny courtyards. Today, in most cases, they have been re-apportioned among several families. You can take a look inside a typical Chinese merchant's well-preserved *nha ong* at the **Memorial House** ❸ (Nha Hat Kim Dong; 87 Ma May Street; daily 9–11.30am and 2–5pm; charge). If you look along Tran Quang Khai you can see the dikes that once kept floodwaters at bay. Also note the narrow fronts to many houses – this was done to avoid taxes, which were once based on a property's width. The best way to experience this area is simply to wander and browse among the endless range of artwork, silk and traditional clothing.

Sweet-toothed tourists head to Hang Buom Street for its astonishing selection of sweets. The street's name means "shop of sails" and derives from the Chinese vessels that used to drop off goods here. They have long gone and today this lively part of the Old Quarter gets particularly busy when there is a forthcoming festival.

## Water Puppet Theatre

Vietnam's most famous show is a fascinating display of traditional water puppetry. Dating back at least 1,000 years, the performance is a collection of short scenes that depict everything from everyday life through to mythical stories. You can book tickets in advance at the **Thang Long Water Puppet Theatre** ❹ (Nha Hat Mua Roi Thang Long; tel: 04-3824 9494; www.thanglongwaterpuppet.org; shows Mon–Sat 3.30pm, 5pm, 6.30pm, 8pm and 9.15pm, Sun 9.30am; charge). The theatre is on the northeast corner of Hoan Kiem Lake along Dinh Tien Hoang Street. An integral part of the nightly performances is the live music, all played with traditional instruments *(see page 77)*.

## Bach Ma Temple

From Hang Buom Street, you should be able to hear the chanting or smell

the incense coming from **Bach Ma Temple 5** (Den Bach Ma; daily 8am–5pm; charge), at 78 Hang Buom Street (Sail Street). This is the Old Quarter's most revered temple and honours the white horse that appeared to King Ly Thai To in a dream and led him to build the walls of the old city. A statue of the giant wooden horse is inside, along with a lacquered palanquin adorned with carvings of phoenixes, cranes and tortoises. Originally built in the 9th century, the temple was reconstructed in the 18th and 19th centuries. In regular use, it remains in a good state of repair.

## Dong Xuan Market

The area around **Dong Xuan Market 6** (Cho Dong Xuan; daily 8am–5pm) in the northern part of the Old Quarter rewards exploration. The original colonial-era market was rebuilt following a huge fire in 1994 and resembles its original state. This site is the wholesale source for many dry goods and is the largest undercover market in Hanoi. The counterfeit D&G bags and other low-quality apparel seem intended for Vietnamese customers, but it's a good place to shop for home wares or cheap souvenirs. In the surrounding streets, farmers squat on the pavement selling their produce, while florists add a welcome splash of colour with their fragrant blooms. Look out for performances of Ca Tru, a traditional music form sung by women. On **Lang Ong Street**, traditional medicine shops sell all manner of exotic cures, including snake wine and lizards preserved in alcohol.

Nearby, at the end of Hang Chieu and close to Tran Nhat Duat Street, is the crumbling brick gate of **Quan Chuong**, the last remnant of the wall that once encircled the Old Quarter.

## SOUTHEAST OF HOAN KIEM LAKE

On the southeast side of the lake at 75 Dinh Tien Hoang Street is the city's **General Post Office 7** (Buu Dien), designed by French architects in 1942. One block north is a small patch of greenery known as **Ly Thai To Park** (formerly Indira Gandhi Park). The park is a good place to watch local life go by, from skateboarding youngsters

*Gravestone carving is one of the many trades found in the Old Quarter.*

**BELOW:** fabrics galore at Dong Xuan Market.

and budding footballers, to friends and couples out for a stroll. A large statue of King Ly Thai To, the founder of the Ly dynasty, dominates the park.

To the east of the park on Ly Thai To Street is the striking Art Deco-style **former Bank of Indochina**. Across from the park's southeastern corner is the arresting **Government Guesthouse** (no entry) at 12 Ngo Quyen Street. Yellow with green trim and protected by a wrought-iron fence, the building was inaugurated in 1918 as the palace of the French governor of Tonkin.

## Sofitel Legend Metropole

Southwards, straddling Ly Thai To and Ngo Quyen streets, is the stunning **Sofitel Legend Metropole Hotel ❽**. This gem of a hotel was the only international-standard hotel – called the Grand Hotel Metropole Palace then – in French colonial days and was the epicentre for colonial society people.

Former guests include writers Noël Coward and Somerset Maugham and actors such as Charlie Chaplin (who spent his honeymoon here after his secret wedding to Paulette Goddard) and anti-Vietnam War activist Jane Fonda (who famously took cover at the hotel during American air raids). Writer Graham Greene wrote a few chapters of his visionary novel *The Quiet American at the hotel* in the 1950s. During the Vietnam War years, the hotel was used as a base by diplomats and journalists. In the 1980s its condition had severely deteriorated, but a French management team restored the hotel to its former glories and relaunched it in 1992. Its historical value, elegance and high-quality French restaurants make it more than just a hotel.

## Opera House

From here it's only a short walk south on Ly Thai To Street to the grand columned **Municipal Theatre**, often referred to as the **Opera House ❾** (Nha Hat Lon). This performing arts centre was built at the turn of the 20th century to keep the French entertained. After years of renovation, this renewed beauty reopened in 1997 and hosts regular performances. Its basement boasts a gourmet restaurant called **Nineteen11** *(see page 128)*.

Days after the Japanese surrender in World War II cadres rushed in to Hanoi, and on 19 August 1945 they declared the establishment of an independent democratic republic – from the theatre's balcony. Tens of thousands of peasants armed with machetes and bamboo spears were joined by equal numbers of city residents. Only a few days before, few of the latter had ever heard of the Viet Minh, but they were soon caught up in patriotic euphoria and obeyed orders to seize important buildings from the Japanese and their Vietnamese collaborators.

The Opera House is stunning, its interior embellished with a sweeping marble staircase, crystal chandelier, and red and gold-leaf decor. To be able to see around you will need

**BELOW:** facade of the old-world Sofitel Metropole Hotel.

to buy a ticket for a show (www.ticketvn.com), as there are no guided tours). Adjacent is the luxury **Hilton Hanoi Opera**, with a facade that replicates the style of the Opera House; the interior, however, is contemporary in style. Interestingly, the more obvious title of The Hanoi Hilton was not considered, as this was the ironic name given to a prison used to torture US troops during the Vietnam War. Today, performances include everything from Flamenco and Tchaikovsky to more traditional Vietnamese music.

## Trang Tien Street

Heading back west and skirting the southern tip of the lake, **Trang Tien Street**, which ends in front of the **Opera House**, was once the main shopping street of the French Quarter. When the communists closed private enterprises, Trang Tien Street was one of the few areas that retained any commerce; today it houses upmarket art galleries, bookshops, and – in the once drab old government department store – the **Hanoi Securities Trading Centre**. While the street is predominantly known for its range of books, it is also popular as a place to try local ice cream – one delicious option comes with sticky rice. Look out for the blocks to the south and west, on sedate tree-lined streets, as this is where the colonialists' elegant former villas now house embassies, diplomatic residences and the headquarters of non-governmental organisations.

## Vietnam National University

The road southeast of the Opera House, Le Thanh Tong Street, runs by **Vietnam National University ⑩** (Dai Hoc Tong Hop Ha Noi) and its Frenchera buildings. Walk into the main courtyard, to view the fusion of colonial and Vietnamese architecture. Founded in 1906 as the University of Indochina, schools of law, medicine, science and arts were added in the 1930s. The Indochinese students who studied here, including the future General Vo Nguyen Giap, were part of Vietnam's intellectual (and probably financial) elite. The French

*Hanoi's General Post Office (Buu Dien Ha Noi) sits by the calm Hoan Kiem Lake.*

**BELOW:** the Hanoi Opera House is a visual treat.

*A bronze figurine by the facade of St Joseph's Cathedral.*

**BELOW:** a life-size statue of Ho Chi Minh at the Museum of Vietnamese Revolution.

commitment to education and literacy was somewhat half-baked: in 1937, the student body here numbered only 631.

## National Museum of Vietnamese History

Behind the Opera House, with a cupola resembling a pagoda, is the **National Museum of Vietnamese History** ⓫ (Bao Tang Lich Su Viet Nam; tel: 04-3824 1384; www.nmvnh.com.vn; Tue–Sun 8–11.30am and 1.30–4.30pm; charge). The museum occupies the old archaeological research institution of the French School of the Far East, which opened in 1910 and was substantially renovated in the 1920s. High on content and low on propaganda, this may be the best museum in town. The excellent archaeological collection includes relics from the Hung era and Neolithic graves, Bronze Age implements, axe heads, Cham relics, and an eerie sculpture of the Goddess of Mercy, Quan Am, with 1,000 eyes and arms. An ornate throne, clothing and artefacts belonging to the 13

Nguyen-dynasty emperors are also on display. The museum is worth visiting for its stunning architecture alone as it blends French and Chinese features to great effect.

## Museum of Vietnamese Revolution

Nearby, the **Museum of Vietnamese Revolution** ⓬ (Bao Tang Cach Mang; tel: 04-3825 4151; Tue–Sun 8–11.45am and 1.30–4.15pm; charge), at 216 Tran Quang Khai Street, offers a carefully scripted version of the struggles of the Vietnamese people from ancient times up to 1975. Among the thousands of items on display are the long wooden stakes that crippled the Mongol fleet in Halong Bay during one of three invasion attempts in the 13th century, and a bronze drum from 2400 BC.

## WEST OF HOAN KIEM LAKE

### St Joseph's Cathedral

Resembling a miniature version of Paris's Notre-Dame, **St Joseph's Cathedral** ⓭ (Nha Tho Lon; the Vietnamese simply call it the "big church") sits just west of Hoan Kiem Lake, where Pho Nha Chung joins Ly Quoc Su Street. Gothic in style, with distinctive square towers, the cathedral was consecrated on Christmas night in 1886. St Joseph's was built on the site of the Bao Thien Pagoda, which was razed by the French to build the cathedral. Celebration of Mass resumed here only in 1990 after more than 30 years of repression. On Sundays, the Masses are packed. Inside are beautiful stained-glass windows and an ornate altar decorated with gold leaf.

For a completely different environment, simply walk across the road to **Pho Nha Tho Street** (Church Street), as this and adjoining thoroughfares form a trendy shopping area that specialises in high-end tailors, handicrafts and home decor shops, local designer boutiques and jewellers. There are also

lots of restaurants and charming cafés where you can take a breather.

## Ba Da Pagoda

A narrow passageway on 5 Pho Nha Tho Street leads to **Ba Da Pagoda** ⑭ (Chua Ba Da; daily 8am–5pm; free), tucked between St Joseph's Cathedral and Hoan Kiem Lake. This lovely pagoda was built in the 15th century – though the site itself dates back to the 11th century – after the discovery of a stone statue of a woman (hence its name, Stone Lady Pagoda) during the construction of the Thang Long citadel to the west. The statue, which was thought to have magical powers, disappeared and has since been replaced by a replica. The pagoda's modest exterior belies its exquisite interior. An impressive line-up of gilt Buddha statues forms the central altar. A sizeable number of resident monks and nuns live on site. This was once one of three pagodas in the area, but one was knocked down by the French to make way for St Joseph's Cathedral. The other, Ly Quoc Su, still exists.

## Hoa Lo Prison

Better known by its more ironic name, The Hanoi Hilton, this prison site is about three blocks south of Hoan Kiem Lake. **Hoa Lo Prison Museum** ⑮ (tel: 04-3824 6358; Tue–Sun 8–11.30am and 1–4.30pm; charge) once held the likes of US Republican senator and failed presidential candidate John McCain and the US ambassador to Vietnam in the late 1990s, Pete Peterson. The prison is of significance to Vietnamese, too, as the French imprisoned, tortured and guillotined countless revolutionaries within the walled compound, which until recently occupied an entire block.

In 1994, the prison was almost entirely demolished to make way for an enormous foreign-financed steel and glass office and shopping complex called **Hanoi Towers**. The small section that remained was turned into the Hoa Lo Prison Museum. Topped with barbed and electric wire, Hoa Lo's yellow concrete main gate (which reads "Maison Centrale") and a few cells have been preserved along with exhibits of instruments of torture and

*Elements of torture and abuse are depicted at the Hoa Lo Prison Museum.*

**BELOW LEFT:** the entrance to Hoa Lo Prison.
**BELOW RIGHT:** worshippers at St Joseph's Cathedral

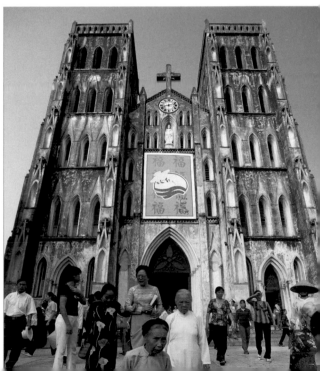

*The Vietnam Fine Arts Museum is a veritable treasure trove of Vietnamese art history.*

a guillotine. The images of American and Vietnamese who were kept here are particularly poignant.

## Ambassadors' Pagoda

One block southwest, the **Ambassadors' Pagoda** ⓰ (Chua Quan Su; daily 8am–5pm; free), located at 73 Pho Quan Su Street, is perhaps the busiest pagoda in town. On the first and 15th days of each lunar month, crowds gather to make offerings of incense, foodstuffs and paper goods. In the 17th century, the site was a guesthouse for envoys from other Buddhist countries, hence its name. The long, low buildings surrounding the temples are schoolrooms for novice monks and contain a small library of parchment and texts in Vietnamese and Chinese. A handful of monks and nuns still live here.

## HAI BA TRUNG DISTRICT

## Reunification Park

About 500 metres/yds south of the Ambassadors' Pagoda is the small but lovely **Thien Quang Lake** (Ho Thien Quang), where visitors can rent paddle boats. To the south, just across the street, is an entrance to **Reunification Park** ⓱ (Cong Vien Thong Nhat; daily daylight hours; charge). This pleasant and shady area, still known locally by its old name of Lenin Park, is said to have been built by volunteer workers on marshy land once used as a dumping ground. The park is designed around the large **Bay Mau Lake** (Ho Bay Mau) and operates a number of children's rides at the weekend. At other times locals come out to jog or couples head out for a stroll in the scenic grounds.

## Hai Ba Trung Temple

Southeast of Reunification Park is the **Hai Ba Trung Temple** ⓲ (Den Hai Ba Trung), also known as the Dong Nhan Temple after the village that surrounded the site back when it was built in 1142. The temple is dedicated to two famous Trung sisters who organised an uprising against the Chinese Han invaders in AD 39 and who later committed suicide together by jumping into the river. Two unusually formed stone statues recovered from the Red River, said to represent the two sisters, are kept in a small room inside the temple. Each February the statues are brought out for a grand procession, where they are dressed in new clothes and displayed in reverence.

## BA DINH DISTRICT AND WESTERN HANOI

## Vietnam Fine Arts Museum

To the far west of Ho Hoan Kiem Lake is the excellent **Vietnam Fine Arts Museum** ⓳ (Bao Tang My Thuat; tel: 04-3846 5081; Tue–Sun 8.30am–5pm; charge) at 66 Nguyen Thai Hoc Street. Built in the 1930s as a boarding school for children of Indochinese officials, today the exhibits include displays on minority folk art and history, Dong Son bronze drums, Dong Noi stone carvings, Cham statues

and carvings, ceramics, 16th-century communal house decorations and 18th-century wooden Buddha statues in some surprisingly undignified poses. Particularly impressive are the displays tracing the development of Vietnamese paintings from the 20th century to the present. Note the rare examples of lacquer painting on paper. Guided tours in English are available.

## Temple of Literature

One of Hanoi's must-see attractions is the **Temple of Literature** ㉚ (Van Mieu; tel: 04-3845 2917; Tue–Sun 8.30–11.30am and 1.30–4.30pm; charge). This historically rich museum is south of the Fine Arts Museum at Pho Quoc Tu Giam Street. Built in 1070 under the reign of King Ly Thanh Tong, the temple is dedicated to Confucius. When it was first built, the Quoc Tu Giam, or School of the Elite of the Nation – Vietnam's first university – adjoined the temple's grounds. Under the Tran dynasty, the school was renamed the Quoc Hoc Vien, or the National College, in 1235.

After passing exams at the local levels, scholars aspiring to become senior mandarins came here to study for rigorous examinations. Subjects included literature, philosophy and Vietnamese history. Van Mieu became known as the Temple of Literature when the capital was transferred to Hue at the beginning of the 19th century. Above the main gate is an inscription requesting that visitors dismount from horses before entering.

Each of the five walled courtyards inside the temple hosts its own unique story. After passing through the main **Van Mieu Gate** (Van Mieu Mon) and the first two courtyards past this gate, one arrives at the **Pleiade Constellation Pavilion** (Gac Khue Van), where the men of letters recited their poems. Through the **Great Wall Gate** (Dai Thanh Mon), an open courtyard surrounds a large, central pool known as the **Well of Heavenly Clarity** (Thien Quang Tinh). Now regrouped and sheltered under a roof, the **82 stone stelae**, survivors of an original 117, rest on the backs of stone tortoises. Students come to

**TIP**

Most Hanoi businesses and shops close every day for an hour or two over lunch. In the summertime, Hanoians tend to start their day around 5am, and retreat indoors once the heat of the day sets in. Government offices close at 4.30pm and are shut on Sunday.

**BELOW:** classical Chinese architecture at the Temple of Literature.

*It is hard to miss the Cot Co Flag Tower, sole surviving remnant of the old citadel and 33 metres (108ft) tall.*

**BELOW:** reliving the days of war at the Military History Museum.

rub the heads of the tortoises as it is believed this will bring them good fortune – and good grades. Before they were restored a few years ago, the stone stelae under the trees on either side of the courtyard were exposed to the elements. The stelae are inscribed with the names, works and academic records of some 1,306 scholars who succeeded in the 82 examinations held between 1442 and 1779 (as well as some less academic modern-day graffiti. The French halted examinations here in 1915 (and in Hue in 1918). By then, the importation of Chinese-language materials had been prohibited for seven years.

Facing the temple is the **House of Ceremonies** (Bai Duong), where sacrifices were offered in honour of Confucius. Today, musicians perform traditional music and charge a fee to those who care to sit and listen. Nearby are the Eastern Gate and the Great Success Sanctuary.

In the final courtyard was once the National Academy, destroyed by French aerial bombing in 1947. These were the academy buildings where the final examinations were held. A two-storey building contains a small museum and shrines to great scholars.

## Cot Co Flag Tower and Military History Museum

Virtually all that remains of the former Hanoi citadel can be found several blocks north on Dien Bien Phu Street. **Cot Co Flag Tower ㉑ was built** in 1812 by the Nguyen dynasty as part of the citadel. The main structure was ravaged by fire at the end of the 19th century and now this hexagonal, 33-metre (108ft) -high tower is all that remains. A branch of the upscale domestic café chain **Highlands Coffee** has an outdoor outlet at the base of the tower.

Next door is the **Military History Museum ㉒** (Bao Tang Lich Su Quan Su; tel: 04-3733 4682; www.btlsqsvn. org.vn; Tue–Thur, Sat and Sun, 8–11.30am and 1–4.30pm; charge), which details Vietnam's battles for independence and unification against the French and American patrons of South Vietnam. The uniforms of captured US pilots and images of Vietnam's war heroes are interesting,

but the real draw here is the wreckage of a decrepit B-52 bomber that sits in the outside courtyard.

## One Pillar Pagoda

Continuing northwest up Dien Bien Phu Street, a small road called Chua Mot Cot leads to the **One Pillar Pagoda ㉓** (Chua Mot Cot) and the Ho Chi Minh complex. Originally built in 1049 by King Ly Thai Thong, this unique wooden pagoda rests on a single concrete pillar rising out of a murky green pool – it is supposed to symbolise the sacred lotus sprouting from the waters of suffering. It is said the king saw a goddess who, while seated on a lotus flower, handed him a male heir. The king later married a peasant girl who gave him a son, and the pagoda was built in gratitude for the premonition. The pillar is a late 1950s replacement after French soldiers cynically blew up the original structure in 1954. Prime Minister Nehru of India planted the banyan tree behind the pagoda in 1958 during an official visit to the then fledgling Vietnamese republic.

## Ho Chi Minh Museum

Behind the park with the pagoda is the eclectic **Ho Chi Minh Museum ㉔** (Bao Tang Ho Chi Minh; tel: 04-3846 3752; Tue–Thur and Sat–Sun 8–11.30am and 2–4.30pm; charge). The museum, arranged into chronological sections and opened on 19 May 1990 (the 100th anniversary of Ho's birth), chronicles the great man's revolutionary life and the pivotal role he played in Vietnam's history and international development. Part of the museum focuses on the past, with a collection of photos, documents and personal effects, such as the actual disguise he used to flee to Hong Kong. The modern section is far more obscure and symbolic, from the gigantic lopsided table scene to the car that seems to be crashing through a wall. Jingoistic explanations accompany most displays, though the meaning of the battered mortars that lie in front of ornate plates seems to have eluded even the caption writers.

*The One Pillar Pagoda is a familiar Hanoi city landmark.*

**BELOW:** the body of the revered Uncle Ho lies within the Ho Chi Minh Mausoleum.

*Escape the bustle of Hanoi at the serene Botanical Gardens.*

## Ho Chi Minh Mausoleum

Immediately north looms the imposing marble-and-granite-clad **Ho Chi Minh Mausoleum** ㉕ (Lang Chu Tich Ho Chi Minh; Tue–Thur, Sat–Sun 8–11am; charge), built on the spot in **Ba Dinh Square** where Ho Chi Minh delivered Vietnam's declaration of independence in 1945. The embalmed corpse of Uncle Ho lies in a glass casket within this monumental tomb, despite his wish to be cremated and have his ashes scattered in the north, centre and south of the country. In late autumn/early winter it is advisable to check beforehand whether his body is in residence. Rumour has it he is packed off to Russia for embalming three months out of every year. Dressed in his trademark khaki suit, the heavily guarded body lies displayed on an elevated platform in a dark and chilly room.

Upon entering the mausoleum, visitors are ushered quickly past either side of the body. No cameras or handbags may be taken inside so these have to be checked in at the entrance. The white-uniformed guards who control

**BELOW:** Ho Chi Minh's humble abode.

the flow of traffic will not hesitate to eject anyone not displaying the proper decorum – so talking or laughing is out, and hats are off. Part of the fascination is watching the Vietnamese reverence for Ho, which is unfailing. The changing of the guards outside is worth waiting around for as it is a rather grand event. Ho Chi Minh died in 1969, on the same date as his declaration of independence.

## Ho Chi Minh House

The wooded grounds of the Presidential Palace are right by the mausoleum, and although it is closed to the public there are two buildings within the grounds that are worth exploring. Built in 1906, the palace was formerly the residence of the French governor-general. Today, it has been turned into a government guesthouse for foreign dignitaries. Ho led a simple life, and it's not surprising that he preferred not to stay in the palace, using it only for government council meetings and receiving guests.

Instead, Ho lived in two unassuming houses on the same grounds: the first (said to be the electrician's house) was his home from 1954 to 1958, before he moved to a specially constructed but still austere house built on stilts. The **Ho Chi Minh House** (Nha San Bac Ho; Tue–Thur, Sat–Sun 7.30–11.30am; charge), with its immaculately varnished wooden exterior, overlooks a carp pond in a quiet and leafy section of the park. The modest living quarters consist of two small rooms with an open-air meeting room below. Ho lived here from May 1958 to August 1969. Vietnam is clearly intent on preserving not just Ho's body, but also his personal items, as everything from his furniture to his pens is here. There is even a garage housing his Peugeot 404.

## Botanical Gardens

Behind the Presidential Palace, but best reached from Hoang Hoa Tham Street, are the **Botanical Gardens** ㉖

(Cong Vien Bach Thao; daily daylight hours; charge after 7am), with rolling hills, peaceful lakes and numerous trees for shade. The park was designed by French landscape engineers in 1890 on the site of a former zoo; a few monkeys and peacocks are still kept here today. A handful of sculptures add character to this park, which is a fantastic spot for a picnic. This is one of the few genuinely quiet places in Hanoi, and so it makes for an ideal picnic lunch location.

## B-52 Lake

Wander a kilometre from the Ho Chi Minh Mausoleum on Hoang Hoa Tham Street and duck down a winding alley and you'll be greeted by a **B-52 ②** sticking out of a small, brackish pond. This is the remains of the *Rose 1*, an American B-52 bomber that was shot down on 19 December 1972. Of its crew of six, four survived the attack and were taken prisoner and two were killed. Sadly, the "lake" is often used as a garbage dump by local residents.

# WEST LAKE (HO TAY) DISTRICT

## West Lake and surroundings

North of the main city centre lies the vast **West Lake ㉘** (Ho Tay), formerly known as the Lake of Mists, an area popular with wealthy expats. This lake, the largest in Hanoi, lies on an ancient bed of the Red River (Song Hong). The palaces of emperors and generals once graced its banks, all of which have been destroyed in feudal battles. One legend says the lake was formed when a golden buffalo calf mistook the sound of a giant bell for that of its mother's call, and trampled the land, thus creating the lake. Another myth says a dragon king formed the lake after slaying a nine-tailed fox. Since the 1990s, the area surrounding the lake has seen considerable building activity – particularly along its northeast bank.

## Tran Quoc Pagoda

During an uprising against the occupying Chinese in 545, national hero

*The area around West Lake has seen recent development, mainly in the form of expensive housing.*

**LEFT:** Ho Chi Minh in 1954.

# Uncle Ho

**H**o Chi Minh, or Uncle Ho as he is known locally, was a Marxist revolutionary who helped secure Vietnam's independence. Today much of his ideology has been forgotten, but his image remains as cherished as ever: his face is on every banknote, the nation's capital is named after him and nearly every town has a statue of him. Unravelling the man behind the myth is difficult: Ho Chi Minh was only one of several pseudonyms he used and he rarely gave interviews; even his birthday is disputed.

Ho Chi Minh lived in the USA and the UK before heading to France, where he studied communism and began calling for the French to leave his homeland. After studying further in the Soviet Union and China, he returned to Vietnam in 1941 to fight the French. As president of North Vietnam, he inspired the fight against the US-backed administration in the south.

He did not live to see the North's victory. News of his death, on 2 September 1969, was carefully managed – an announcement was made 48 hours afterwards to prevent it from coinciding with the anniversary of the founding of the Democratic Republic of Vietnam. Today, his legacy and image are fiercely guarded by the government, which regularly censors anything that does not match with the official version of Ho's life.

*The Quan Thanh Temple is steeped in rich history.*

**BELOW:** the area around White Silk Lake is a wining and dining hotspot.

Ly Bon built the National Foundation Pagoda (Chua Khai Quoc) beside the Red River. In the 17th century, the pagoda was transferred to its present site on a tiny peninsula off West Lake and renamed the **Tran Quoc Pagoda** ㉙, or the National Defence Pagoda (Chua Tran Quoc; daily 8am–5pm; free). Tran Quoc is perhaps Vietnam's oldest pagoda; the stela, dating from the year 1639, recounts its long history.

## White Silk Lake and Quan Thanh Temple

Separated from the lake by Thanh Nien Road is **White Silk Lake** (Ho Truc Bach). This was the ancient site of Lord Trinh's summer palace, which later became a harem where he detained his wayward concubines. The lake derives its name from the beautiful white silk these concubines were forced to weave for the princesses.

Nearby, the ornate **Quan Thanh Temple** ㉚ (Den Quan Thanh; daily 8am–5pm; free) beside the lake was originally built during the Ly dynasty (1010–1225). This temple has a huge bronze bell and a 4-tonne bronze

statue of Tran Vu, guardian deity of the north, to whom the temple is dedicated. The street that runs along the perimeter of White Silk Lake is famous for its street stalls that serve *pho cuon*, tender slices of beef wrapped in rice noodles with herbs, and is a popular nightspot among Vietnamese teenagers.

## Kim Lien Pagoda and Flower Village

Further up the northern bank of West Lake, tucked away in a small neighbourhood beside the plush Intercontinental Hotel, are **Kim Lien Pagoda** ㉛, also known as Golden Lotus Pagoda (Chua Kim Lien; daily 8am–5pm; free), and the **Kim Lien Flower Village**. In the three small lanes that wind their way towards the lake from the pagoda, courtyards spill over with tropical flowers of unimaginable variety, in particular many exotic varieties of orchid. The Kim Lien Pagoda, built in its present form in 1711 and recently renovated, is dedicated to the Buddha and to Princess Tu Hoa, the daughter of King Ly Than

Tong who is said to have taught local villagers how to cultivate mulberries, raise silkworms and weave silk.

## West Lake Pagoda

Even further north, at the tip of a small peninsula at the end of Dang Thai Mai Street, is **West Lake Pagoda** ❷ (Chua Phu Tay Ho; daily 8am– 5pm; free), a popular destination for pilgrims and unmarried Vietnamese, particularly on the 15th day of each lunar month. The lane just before the pagoda is lined with lakeside restaurants specialising in *banh tom* (shrimp cakes). Inside the pagoda, the hall to the right is especially garish, its altars crammed with statuettes of strange beasts, grottoes and miniature sailing ships. Worshippers bring heaps of fruit and packets of biscuits, among other things, and pile them in front of the altars as offerings to the deities.

From West Lake Pagoda, visitors can take a pleasant walk north, passing large villas on the right and serene lotus ponds on the left. Restaurants near here are renowned for their *bun oc*, or snail soup.

## NORTHERN HANOI

### Vietnam Museum of Ethnology

The **Vietnam Museum of Ethnology** (Bao Tang Dan Toc Hoc Viet Nam; tel: 04-3756 2193; www.vme.org.vn; Tue– Sun 8.30am–5.30pm; charge) on Nguyen Van Huyen Street is Hanoi's most modern museum. Located about 20 minutes by taxi from the city centre, the museum brilliantly details the lives and history of the country's 54 ethnic minorities. Many special events – like artisan demonstrations, traditional games, films and lectures – are held here, especially at weekends and during the holidays.

The open-plan two-storey museum was designed by a member of the Tay ethnic group in the form of an ancient Dong Son drum. There are displays of handicrafts, garments, weapons, musical instruments and various artefacts as well as audio and video recordings and full-scale models of village communal houses. The displays are labelled in English and French and, for a small extra fee, a guide is available. The museum is also wheelchair-friendly.

*The Vietnam Museum of Ethnology gives an insight into the culture and lifestyles of Vietnam's 54 ethnic groups.*

**BELOW LEFT AND RIGHT:** displays at the Vietnam Museum of Ethnology.

# RESTAURANTS AND CAFÉS

Years ago, eating in Hanoi involved munching on simple rice or slurping down a bowl of noodles while balanced on a plastic chair by a dusty sidewalk. While that option still exists, there are now dozens of excellent restaurants, serving a variety of cuisines, including a fusion of French and Vietnamese dishes. Hanoi's culinary scene is as cosmopolitan as it gets. Unlike in Ho Chi Minh City, the capital's best eateries are well spaced out; the largest concentration is in the central Hoan Kiem District.

## Hoan Kiem District

### Vietnamese

**69 Bar Restaurant**
69 Ma May St, Hoan Kiem District. Open: daily B, L & D. **$$$**
Set in a wonderfully atmospheric wooden property, the 69 Bar has a good range of food that is tourist-friendly, although it also has a few traditional local dishes if you ask.

**Blue Butterfly**
61 Hang Buom St, Hoan Kiem District. Open: daily L & D. **$**
As well as offering its own cookery school, the Blue Butterfly does a reasonable line in Vietnamese cuisine with a Western influence.

**Bun Cha**
20 Ta Hien St, Hoan Kiem District. Open: daily L & D. **$$**
*Bun cha*, seasoned and grilled pork pieces served with fresh rice noodles and drenched with a piquant sweet and sour sauce, is a lunch-time favourite for most Hanoians. This small streetside restaurant in the Old Quarter serves some of the best *bun cha* in town. Be prepared to share a table.

**Cha Ca La Vong**
14 Cha Ca St, Hoan Kiem District. Tel: 04-3825 3929. Open: daily L & D. **$$$**
One of the oldest restaurants in Vietnam. Since 1871, generations of this family have been serving *cha ca*: tender fried fish fillets served with dill and rice noodles, all cooked at your table on a charcoal-fired brazier. Prices have gone up, but the quality is still high. Worth it for the experience alone, but ask your waitress to go easy on the oil if greasy food bothers you.

**Chim Sao**
65 Ngo Hue St, Hoan Kiem District. Tel: 04-3976 0633. Open: daily L & D. **$**
www.chimsao.com
This Vietnamese boho-chic restaurant is a top favourite among both expats in the know and locals. Great local food at reasonable prices (try the ethnic minority sausages) set in comfortable but low-key surroundings. Its art gallery always has an interesting exhibition going on.

**Club De L'Oriental**
22 Ton Dan St, Hoan Kiem District. Tel: 04-3826 8801. Open: daily L & D. **$$$$**
This is the new incarnation of the Emperor, a former fine-dining landmark which closed in 2007. It features four separate dining rooms, each with its own distinct design. Service and food are excellent, and in dining room number 2 you can watch your dinner being prepared by the chefs.

**Quan An Ngon**
18 Phan Boi Chau St, Hoan Kiem District. Tel: 04-3942 8162. Open: daily B, L & D. **$$$**
This always packed outdoor eatery serves the best of Vietnamese cuisine at reasonable prices. With a large menu and solidly good food, be sure to arrive early before the best dishes are het roi (finished). A sister restaurant, **Quan Hai San Ngon** (199A Nghi Tam, West Lake District), specialises in seafood and is also worth a visit.

### Indian

**Tandoor**
24 Hang Be St, Hoan Kiem District. Tel: 04-3824 2252. Open: daily L & D. **$$$**
www.tandoorvietnam.com
Hanoi's premier North Indian curry house is situated in the heart of the Old Quarter. Extensive menu and reasonable prices, as well as some of the best naan breads in town. Upstairs is a nice balcony overlooking busy Hang Be Street.

### International

**Al Fresco's**
23L Hai Ba Trung St, Hoan Kiem District. Tel: 04-3826 7782. Open: daily B, L & D. **$$$**
www.alfrescosgroup.com
The place to go in Hanoi if you're looking for steak, pizza, pasta or other standard Western dishes. Large, good value, wellprepared meals. Get an upstairs table to enjoy the lakefront view. There are other branches around town, too.

**Hanoi Press Club**
59 A Ly Thai To St. Tel: 04-3934 0888. Open: daily L & D. **$$$$**
This six-storey restaurant exudes style with its subtle decor and top-notch service. Dishes range from steak to more experimental options; the orange pumpkin soup is recommended. At the top level is a club with Latino DJs and some of Hanoi's best-dressed crowd.

**La Badiane**
10 Nam Ngu, Hoan Kiem District. Tel: 04-3942 4509. Open: Mon-Sat L & D. **$$$$.**
Stylish and contemporary, La Badiane provides exceptional French and international cuisine with first-class table service. Dishes are nothing short of spectacular and it lives up to its claim of being one of the city's, if not the country's, finest restaurants.

**La Salsa**
25 Nha Tho St, Hoan Kiem District. Tel: 04-3828 9052. Open: daily B, L & D. **$$$**
A popular hangout among the city's French expats, this is the place to go for tapas and paella. If things get a little wild at the bar, escape upstairs to the balcony overlooking St Joseph's Cathedral.

**La Verticale**
19 Ngo Van So St, Hoan Kiem District. Tel: 04-3944 6317. Open: daily L & D. **$$$$**
www.verticale-hanoi.com
Outstanding Franco-Vietnamese fusion dishes in a classy restaurant set in a 1930s French villa. The first floor is a gourmet spice shop. Elegant and refined dining at its best. Set lunches and dinners are real value for money.

**Le Beaulieu**
Sofitel Legend Metropole, 15 Ngo Quyen St, Hoan Kiem District. Tel: 04-3826 6919. Open: daily B, L & D. **$$$**
When it comes to classic French food in Hanoi, Le Beaulieu sets the bar with its superlative dishes and excellent wine list. The lavish Sunday brunch is an institution among Hanoi's moneyed class.

**Nineteen11**
1 Trang Tien St, Hoan Kiem District (basement of the Opera House). Tel: 04-3933 4801. Open: daily L & D. **$$$$**
www.nineteen11.com.vn
Named after the year the Hanoi Opera House was completed, this smart restaurant features a walk-in wine cellar and serves gourmet Continental dishes (along with some refined Vietnamese ones) in a

modern, multi-tiered dining room. Both the service and the food are exquisite.

## Vegetarian

### Com Chay Nang Tam
79A Tran Hung Dao St, Hoan Kiem District. Tel: 04-3942 4140. Open: daily L & D. $ Popular vegetarian restaurant tucked down an alley, serving delicious Vietnamese dishes using meat substitutes. It's usually packed on even-numbered days of the lunar calendar, when Vietnam's Buddhists eat vegetarian meals. Don't miss the quirkily named Snowball potatoes.

### Tamarind Café
80 Ma May St, Hoan Kiem District. Tel: 04-3926 0580. Open: daily B, L & D. $ Features imaginative and contemporary vegetarian dishes with an Asian twist. All-day breakfasts, spring rolls and quesadillas are recommended. Even non-vegetarians will love this delightful eatery in the Old Quarter. Excellent juice bar.

## Ba Dinh District

## Vietnamese

### Brother's Café
26 Nguyen Thai Hoc St, Ba Dinh District. Tel: 04-3733 3866. Open: daily L & D. $$$$ A Vietnamese restaurant set in a former shrine that caters almost exclusively to tour groups. Most dishes are – nonetheless – of

above-average quality and served buffet-style, with both indoor and outdoor seating available. Service can sometimes be a bit erratic, but it's a good introduction to Vietnamese cuisine.

### Highway 4
54 Mai Hac De St, Ba Dinh District. Tel: 04-3976 2647. Open: daily B, L & D; $$$ Specialises in flavoured rice wines and traditional northern Vietnamese cuisine. Great atmosphere. Make sure you don't miss the fried catfish spring rolls with hot wasabi. There are other branches in Ba Dinh and Hoan Kiem districts.

### Seasons of Hanoi
95B Quan Thanh St, Ba Dinh District. Tel: 04-3843 5444. Open: daily L & D. $$$ Artfully prepared northern Vietnamese cuisine in a beautiful French-style villa. Almost everything on the menu is good, but don't miss the seafood spring rolls and deep-fried fish with five spices. Book ahead.

## Italian

### Luna d'Autunno
11B Dien Bien Phu St, Ba Dinh District. Tel: 04-3823 7338. Open: daily L & D. $$$ Some of the best Italian food in Hanoi is found at this long-standing restaurant. Great pasta, pizza and friendly if unhurried staff. Particular highlights are the

Scampagnata and Quattro Formaggi pizzas.

## Japanese

### Kamon
104 Van Phuc St, Ba Dinh District. Tel: 04-3762 4428. Open: daily L & D. $$$ A small, well-put-together Japanese restaurant specialising in the pizza-like okonomiyaki (Japanese pancakes). There's no sashimi or sushi on the menu, but it's still worth a visit.

## West Lake District

## International

### Kitchen
9 Xuan Dieu St, West Lake District. Tel: 04-3719 2679. Open: daily B, L & D. $$$ www.so-9.com An ingenious little diner/café tucked away in the driveway entrance to the Sheraton West Lake Hotel. Features great sandwiches and salads all day long, and Mexican dishes for dinner only. The weekend breakfast specials are delicious.

### Restaurant Bobby Chinn
77 Xuan Dieu St, West Lake District. Tel: 04-3934 8577. Open: daily L & D. $$$$ Run by the eponymous celebrity chef, Bobby Chinn's eaterie is justly regarded as one of the finest places to dine in Hanoi. Cleverly designed dining rooms set in silk-draped dining rooms. Always busy.

### Vine Wine Boutique Bar and Café
1A Xuan Dieu St, West Lake District. Tel: 04-3719 8000. Open: daily B, L & D. $$$$ www.vine-group.com A delightful restaurant and bar near West Lake. A varied selection of world-class wines complements an eclectic menu that includes Thai-inspired spaghetti and gourmet pizzas. Its Sunday brunch is a good deal.

## Other areas

## Vietnamese

### KOTO (Know One, Teach One)
59 Van Mieu St, Dong Da District. Tel: 04-3747 0337. Open: daily B, L & D. $$ www.koto.com.au/ A restaurant and training school that offers disadvantaged kids a chance at a productive life. Its mixed menu of foreigner-friendly Vietnamese dishes as well as salads, sandwiches and fruit juices are popular citywide. Try to get a table upstairs in the "temple" room.

## Chinese

### Tao Li Restaurant
Nikko Hotel, 84 Tran Nhan Tong St, Hai Ba Trung District. Tel: 04-3822 3535. Open: daily B, L & D. $$$ Hanoi's premier Chinese eatery serves excellent Cantonese fare, including dim sum for lunch.

# CAFÉS

Coffee shops are an integral part of life in Hanoi. Simply cradling a latte isn't enough for Hanoi's trendy residents, though; more and more offbeat, arty and chic cafés are catering for the discerning customer. The coffee itself remains cheap and high quality, which isn't surprising as Vietnam is one of the world's largest producers of coffee.

### Ailu Café
Xuong Phim 4, Thuy Khue, Tay Ho District. Open: daily B, L & D. $

Cats, not coffee, take centre stage in what may be Hanoi's quirkiest café. More than a dozen cats are in permanent residency here and are more than happy to be stroked or fussed over by customers. Food options are limited but there is an interesting range of coffee, fruit teas and smoothies.

### Dice Café
111 Trieu Viet Vuong, Hai Ba Trung District. Tel: 09-0429 5955. Open: daily B, L & D. $ So much more than just a

coffee shop, the Dice Café also provides customers with all manner of games to play while sipping their filtered coffee. Everything from Jenga to card games is available for VND9,000 per hour. And if that isn't cool enough – they have squeaky cushions.

### Duy Tri
43A Yen Phu St, Tay Ho District. Tel: 04-3829 1386. Open: daily B, L & D. $ Serious coffee-lovers get their caffeine fix here, in this tiny but charming café. Head

for the upstairs balcony and order a fabulous coffee with frozen yoghurt; it really does taste a lot better than it sounds.

### Kinh Do Café
252 Hang Bong, Hoan Kiem District. Tel: 04-3825 0216. Open: daily B, L & D. $ A cosy little spot with a range of fantastic pastries and drinks, Kinh Do Café's main claim to fame is that actress Catherine Deneuve used to stop by for refreshments while making a movie in Hanoi.

# AROUND HANOI

The urban and rural areas that surround Hanoi are rich in history and natural beauty. Many of the sacred pagodas, ancient citadels, traditional craft villages and national parks can easily be visited on a day trip from the capital

Excursions to the scattering of pagodas, parks and villages around **Hanoi** ➊ are worth the effort. Most day trips can be booked with tour agencies in the city, while others may require the use of slow and uncomfortable local buses or hired cars (the more adventurous can jump on a motorbike or even bicycle). The land surrounding the capital is agriculturally rich, nurtured by the Red River (Song Hong) which spreads its alluvial deposits over much of northern Vietnam. Beyond the rice paddies and occasional rocky outcrops, several ancient pagodas are just a few hours' drive away, as are a number of highland escapes. Boat trips pass by limestone cliffs bedecked with spectacular pagodas, the national parks are full of wildlife and treks through thick tropical forests end up at tumbling waterfalls. Closer to Hanoi are traditional craft villages which produce fine silks, pottery and woodcarvings. Several old French hill stations give a glimpse of how life used to be.

## SOUTH OF HANOI

### Bat Trang village

Some 10km (6 miles) southeast of Hanoi, potters carry on a 500-year-old tradition in the village of **Bat Trang** ➋. Rather incongruously, large showrooms with wide glass windows dominate the main street, while the oldest part of town, near the river, is threaded with walled alleyways. What appear to be cowpats stuck on the brick walls are really blobs of coal drying out for use as fuel. A ceramics market has been built for tour groups, but the most interesting areas are hidden in the alleys behind the modern shop fronts. Inside these tiny workspaces are brick kilns and great vats of white liquid clay fed by a network of troughs. Bat Trang artisans used to make bricks,

**Main attractions**

BAT TRANG
DAU PAGODA
VAN PHUC
PERFUME PAGODA
THAY PAGODA
TAY PHUONG PAGODA
BA VI NATIONAL PARK
HUNG KINGS' TEMPLES
TAM DAO

**LEFT:** steps leading up to Tay Phuong Pagoda. **RIGHT:** ceramic urns at Bat Trang.

*Thrill-seekers can witness a deadly cobra being slaughtered before having it for dinner at Le Mat snake village.*

but now they concentrate solely on glazed ceramics, which include teapots, dinnerware and 3-metre (12ft)-tall blue-and-white urns destined for temples and pagodas.

Along the riverside is the village **communal house**, dedicated to Bach Ma (White Horse), King Le Thanh Tong's guardian spirit, as well as five village heroes, including Hua Chi Cao, who introduced ceramics to the area. A wall plaque, villagers say, was a gift from Emperor Gia Long and honours Bat Trang for making the bricks used to construct the imperial city of Hue in the early 19th century.

## Le Mat snake village

The return from Bat Trang to Hanoi can include a snake dinner at **Le Mat**, only 7km (4 miles) outside the city. Le Mat locals are experts in hunting snakes, raising snakes, serving snake cuisine and creating snake-based medicinal tonics. Restaurants in the touristy village offer cobra and buffalo snake in soups, entrées and appetisers. Traditionally the domain of men, these days women are also welcome to

partake of snake meat. Guests are welcome to watch the snake being seized from its cage, gutted, and then to witness its blood squeezed into a glass of rice alcohol. Bottles of this snake "elixir" with a small cobra suspended inside are sold everywhere, and are said to act as a natural form of Viagra. Be sure to check prices before ordering, as certain snakes are far more expensive than others. On the 23rd day of the 3rd lunar month a special festival is held, featuring ritualistic performances that celebrate the slaying of a giant mythical snake.

## EAST OF HANOI

### Dong Ky village

The once infamous craft village of **Dong Ky**, about 15km (9 miles) northeast of Hanoi, was the country's firecracker factory until 1995, when firecrackers were banned throughout Vietnam. At one time the highlight of the year was the January firecracker festival, when competitors armed with pillar-sized creations vied to produce the loudest bang. The festival probably

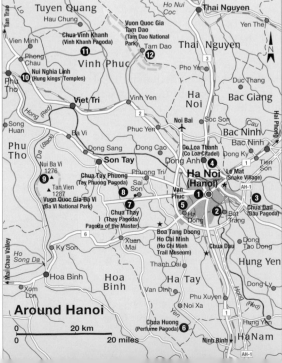

Around Hanoi

evolved from ancient religious rites that invoked thunder, lightning and rain. With the demise of their explosives business, Dong Ky villagers have taken on a more serene occupation – the crafting of intricately carved hardwood furniture, sold locally and in numerous shops in Hanoi.

## Dau Pagoda

**Dau Pagoda** ❸ (Chua Dau; daily 8am–5pm; free), 30km (20 miles) east of Hanoi in Bac Ninh province, dates from the 13th century. The pagoda is off the beaten track, but the trip is rewarding as the route passes through picturesque countryside and gives glimpses of traditional village life.

Officially called Thanh Dao Tu or Phap Vu Tu, the pagoda is dedicated to the Buddha as well as the Goddess of Rain. Its most interesting attributes are the two lacquered statues that contain the **mummified remains** of two monks – Vu Khac Minh and Vu Khach Truong – who lived here centuries ago. The story goes that when Vu Khac Minh was approaching death in 1639, he and his nephew

locked themselves in the pagoda and asked their disciples to leave them alone for 100 days so they could meditate in peace. When the disciples eventually entered the building, they found the monks motionless but perfectly preserved. The disciples concluded that the monks had attained nirvana and decided to preserve their bodies by covering them in lacquer. In 2007, the two statues were removed from the pagoda and restored; they are now back in place. The detailed architecture around the pagoda is noteworthy as it reflects all kinds of folklore.

## NORTH OF HANOI

### Co Loa citadel

North of Hanoi, 16km (10 miles) away in Dong Anh District, is Vietnam's first fortified citadel, **Co Loa** ❹ (Co Loa Thanh; daily 8am–5pm; charge), built in the third century BC by King An Duong. The citadel briefly contained the national capital (AD 939–44), and was constructed within walls in three concentric circles that formed

*Buddha figurines in a temple at the Co Loa Citadel.*

**BELOW:** entrance to the temple dedicated to King An Duong at Co Loa.

## TIP

Day trips to the Perfume Pagoda booked in Hanoi should include transport, entrance fees, boat fees and lunch. With just about every tour agent offering the trip, prices can vary anywhere from US$20–60 per person, with the cheaper trips likely to involve large groups. Be prepared for persistent souvenir peddlers. (See Travel Tips, page 370, for a list of reputable travel agents in Hanoi.)

an 8km (5-mile) battlement, parts of which still survive today.

Inside the ramparts is a temple dedicated to King An Duong (257–208 BC) and his daughter Princess My Chau, which has been rebuilt in the last 50 years. According to legend, King An Duong was given a magic crossbow by a golden tortoise that made him invincible in battle. His daughter, married to the son of a Chinese general, showed her husband the crossbow and he in turn stole it and gave it to his father. As a result, the Chinese were able to invade and defeat King An Duong and claim large tracts of his land. Realising he was doomed, the king killed the princess and then himself. A pond also houses a statue of King An Duong shooting the legendary crossbow.

One of the pagodas is dedicated to the princess My Chau, while another, **Am Mi Chau**, contains an array of archaeological finds that are of limited interest. Government attempts to upgrade the site have not wholly succeeded and the extant ramparts of the citadel are now rather hidden.

A festival held at the start of the first lunar month remembers the unfortunate king and his crossbow.

## WEST OF HANOI: HA TAY PROVINCE

The area west of Hanoi and the provinces to the southeast and southwest are the most interesting and diverse destinations within touching distance of the capital. Technically, Ha Tay is still a part of the capital, as Hanoi extended its administrative boundaries in 2008 to include all of this province.

Leave Hanoi by the southwest on Highway 6. It can take up to an hour to negotiate the sprawl of vehicles and construction around the city, but the traffic will eventually thin out, and the two-lane road is flat and in good condition. The first point of interest is **Van Phuc** ❺. This is a traditional silk-weaving village within the town of **Ha Dong**, which is sometimes a stop on day tours to the Perfume Pagoda *(see below)*.

Families in Van Phuc have been producing silk for centuries, but it was only during the late 1990s that the numerous

**BELOW:** The annual festival at Co Loa.

## Co Loa Festival

The annual Co Loa festival held in the first lunar month honours King An Duong Vuong. It takes place over several days and is a great way to see numerous traditional celebrations and activities. A procession of a dozen sedan chairs arrives at the village gate, followed by an incense-offering ceremony, with village elders resplendent in their ceremonial silk gowns. On the main day, the sixth of the first lunar month, another procession takes place featuring a small statue of the king and another, headless, statue of his daughter. The decapitated figure symbolises her punishment for revealing a magic crossbow to her Chinese husband. Festivities involve ear-splittingly loud firecrackers, traditional games, cock fighting, archery, human chess, wrestling and dance.

retail shops lining the main street sprang up. Many of the shop owners here also own silk shops along Hanoi's Hang Gai Street, but prices are, not surprisingly, lower here. As well as purchasing silk fabrics by the metre and ordering made-to-measure clothes, you can also see old-fashioned electric looms introduced by the French still being used in the workshops.

A short distance further on, the **Ho Chi Minh Trail Museum** (Bao Tang Duong Ho Chi Minh; Tue–Sun 8–11.30am and 1.30–4pm; charge) lies 13km (8 miles) southwest of Hanoi. Heavy on propaganda, the three floors of exhibits focus on the efforts of the thousands of people who struggled to create and maintain the vital arms supply route through Vietnam, Laos and Cambodia. War buffs will appreciate the incredible displays of weaponry.

## Perfume Pagoda

When it comes to visiting the **Perfume Pagoda** ❻ (Chua Huong; daily 7.30am–6pm), the journey is just as important as the destination. Around 60km (38 miles) southwest of Hanoi, this sacred pilgrimage site is best approached by rowing boat on the dramatic and swiftly flowing Yen River (Song Yen). Looming over the quiet countryside are the jagged karsts of the Hoang Son mountains.

The dreamy landscape has been compared to Guilin in China. An oarswoman, rowing in a particularly strenuous fashion, will propel the flat-bottomed boat that will take you to the Perfume Pagoda. If a Vietnamese interpreter accompanies you on the ride, the oarswoman can point out peaks with such quaint names as the Crouching Elephant, Nun and Rice Tray – otherwise you will just have to make out the shapes for yourself.

After a winding 4km (2.5-mile) river journey that takes about 90 minutes, the boat will pull up to a cluster of pavilions and market stalls. A short walk up the bottom slopes of

**Huong Tich Mountain** (Mountain of the Fragrant Traces) **leads** visitors to a path that ascends 4km (2.5 miles) to the pagoda complex. The hike is arduous and slippery and can take 1–1½ hours. To improve access, a **chairlift** (daily 7am–6pm; charge) takes pilgrims up and down in a few minutes – the views are stunning.

The collection of pagodas and Buddhist shrines at the top of the mountain is built into the limestone cliffs and caves. Among the sites are **Pagoda to Heaven** (Chua Thien Chu), **Pagoda of Purgatory** (Giai Oan Chu) and the main attraction itself, the **Pagoda of the Perfumed-Vestige** (Huong Tich Chu). The latter is located inside the **Huong Tich Grotto**, which lies just below the summit of the mountain. Some 120 stone steps bedecked with Buddhist flags lead down to the "dragon's mouth" entrance, where worshippers jostle to rub banknotes on a large, wet

*A shrine at the Pagoda of the Perfumed Vestige (Huong Tich Chu).*

**BELOW:** visitors arrive by rowing boat at the Perfume Pagoda, set amid beautiful limestone hills.

*The statues of Buddhist saints at the Tay Phuong Pagoda are carved from jackfruit wood.*

**BELOW:** ornate dragon motifs on the roofs of the Tay Phuong Pagoda.

stalactite said to bestow wealth. In the darkness of the 50-metre (160ft) -high cave, surrounded by stalactites and stalagmites, are numerous gilded Buddhist statues with altar offerings of fruit and incense. Centre stage is an image of Quan Am – Goddess of Mercy and the female personification of Buddha.

Visiting during the pagoda's annual seven-week festival, from March to April, is not advised, as the grounds are thronged with thousands of worshippers and it can be a struggle to get around. At any time of year overly aggressive vendors can be a problem.

## Thay Pagoda

One of Vietnam's oldest pagodas, **Thay Pagoda** ❼ (Chua Thay; daily 8am–5pm; free), also known as the Pagoda of the Master, is nestled against the hillside in **Sai Son Village**, about 37km (23 miles) west of Hanoi. It shares its compound with the smaller **Ca Pagoda** (Chua Ca).

Founded in 1132 by King Ly Thai To, Thay Pagoda has been renovated a number of times. It is dedicated to three individuals: Ly Than Tong, king of the Ly dynasty from 1127 to 1138; Sakyamuni, the historical Buddha and his 18 *arhat*, or disciples; and the venerable monk Dao Hanh. All are represented by elaborate lacquer statues, some dating back to the 12th and 13th centuries. The pagoda complex itself is divided into three sections: the outer section is for ceremonies, the middle section is a Buddhist shrine, while the inner temple is dedicated to Dao Hanh. Known as The Master, Dao Hanh was a great herbalist who is said to have created the water puppet theatre. Dao Hanh is commemorated by a large sandalwood statue within the main pagoda.

On the fifth, sixth and seventh days of the third lunar month, the district's premier puppet troupes stage elaborate shows on the pond in front of the pagoda. Folk plays, chess games, a recital of Dao Hanh's feats and a procession of tablets also take place. The two arched, covered bridges – **Moon Bridge** and **Sun Bridge** – date from 1602.

A climb up the hillside leads to two more small shrines and a superb view of the pagoda complex and surrounding countryside. Several limestone grottoes in the vicinity are worth exploring, notably **Hang Cac Co**. As the pagoda grounds are vast, it is worthwhile hiring a local guide.

## Tay Phuong Pagoda

About 6km (4 miles) from the Thay Pagoda complex – and usually visited in conjunction with day trips from Hanoi – is **Tay Phuong Pagoda** ❽ or the Pagoda of the West (Chua Tay Phuong; daily 8am–5pm; free), in the picturesque village of **Thac Xa**. It is perched atop the 50-metre (164ft) Tay Phuong hill, which is said to resemble a buffalo. The pagoda dates from the 8th century, though the present structure was rebuilt in 1794. It is famous

for its 74 statues of *arhats* (Buddhist saints) carved from jackfruit wood, which illustrate stories from the Buddhist scriptures and all aspects of the human condition.

The pagoda is reached by climbing 238 laterite steps, closely pursued by incense and souvenir vendors. Built of ironwood with bare brick walls, the pagoda comprises the **Prostration Hall** (Bai Duong), the **Central Hall** (Chinh Dien) and the **Back Hall** (Hau Cung). The overlapping roofing of the halls is decorated with ornate carvings and lacquer figures of dragons and animals. Day tours to the Thay and Tay Phuong pagodas sometimes stop at nearby **So village**, which specialises in the age-old trade of making noodles from the flour of yams and manioc.

## Ba Vi National Park

Some 48km (30 miles) west of Hanoi and still within Ha Tay province is the scenic **Ba Vi Mountain** (Nui Ba Vi) and **Ba Vi National Park ❾** (Vuon Quoc Gia Ba Vi; daily daylight hours; charge). The park's protected forest boasts a number of rare and endangered plants and animals, including several varieties of flying squirrel, though tourist activity in the area means your chances of seeing them are limited. Regardless, the park's large orchid garden and many hiking paths make it a favourite destination for many city-weary Hanoians looking to commune with nature.

At the summit of the 1,276-metre (4,861ft) Ba Vi Mountain is a temple dedicated to Ho Chi Minh. The walk is gruelling but rewards from the summit are astounding views of the surrounding countryside and even Hanoi on clear days. At the base of the mountain is Vietnam's oldest golf course, the public **Kings' Island Golf Club** (tel: 04-3368 6555; www.kingsislandgolf.com).

## PHU THO PROVINCE

To the northwest of Hanoi is the province of Phu Tho, which is considered to be the cradle of the pre-Vietnamese

Hung Lac people and the ancestral home of the Viet, who settled in the area before moving into the Red River Delta. Ancient bronze relics up to 4,000 years old have been discovered in the region, including the famous Dong Son drums, and the area still bears the marks of its early settlers, evidenced by the remains of the Hung kings' temples.

## Hung kings' temples

The original Hung temples date back to the 3rd century BC, when a line of 18 Hung kings graced the throne of Vang Lang, as the kingdom was then known. In the third month of the lunar calendar, a major festival is held at **Thuong Temple** (Den Thuong; daily 8am–5pm; free) in Phu Tho province to celebrate the lives of the Hung kings. The event is a major event and draws thousands of devotees from Hanoi.

Altogether there are three **Hung kings' temples ❿** (open daily; free) on the slopes of **Nghia Linh Mountain** (Nui Nghia Linh), some 90km (56 miles) northwest of Hanoi. The **Lowest Temple** (Den Ha) is reached by climbing up 225 steps and is dedicated to Au Co,

**TIP**

In some areas surrounding Hanoi it's not uncommon to find all manner of wildlife on restaurant menus. Despite legislation, leopards, bears, gibbons, macaques, pangolins, lizards, turtles, cobras, pythons and tigers are illegally hunted for food and medicine. Visitors should avoid buying these wildlife products.

**BELOW:** Ba Vi National Park is a green getaway for city-dwellers.

*Image of a
3rd-century BC
guardian warrior,
protector of the Hung
kings.*

the legendary mother of the Viet people. At the back of this temple is an incredible statue of a Buddha with 1,000 arms and eyes. Below the temple, at the foot of the hill, is an arched portal flanked by two huge stone columns engraved with two parallel sentences glorifying the origins of the Vietnamese people.

A further 168 steps lead up to the **Middle Temple** (Den Hung), where the seventh Hung king was crowned and where the rulers would gather to discuss state affairs. Only another 102 steps remain to reach the **Superior Temple** (Den Thuong). This temple is dedicated to the deities of heaven, earth and rice, as well as to Than Giong, the infant hero who in the 3rd century BC is said to have chased out the Chinese Han invaders, assisted by a genie that took the form of an iron horse. The temple, rebuilt in the 15th century, is adorned with dragon and guardian warriors. The well at the foot of the mountain is said to be where the 18th Hung king's daughter brushed her hair and watched her reflection in its clear water.

**BELOW:** Tam Dao.

## VINH PHUC PROVINCE

### Binh Son Tower and Vinh Son Snake Farm

Northeast of Phu To province is Vinh Phuc province, where **Binh Son Tower**, part of the **Vinh Khanh Pagoda** ⓫ (Chua Vinh Khanh; daily 8am–5pm; free), rises some 16 metres (52ft) into the sky in Lap Thach District. Built in the 13th century during the Tran dynasty, the impressive 11-tiered baked-clay tower of the pagoda is adorned with many intricate carvings.

Nearby, in Vinh Lac District, is the **Vinh Son Snake Farm** (daily 8am–5pm; free). Established in the 1990s, the farm breeds indigenous snakes and produces snake wine and an ointment containing snake venom that is used by Vietnamese to relieve muscle and joint inflammation.

### Tam Dao

**Tam Dao** ⓬ is a popular place to escape the capital's summer heat and humidity. Established as a hill station by the French in the early 1900s, Tam Dao sits at an altitude of 880 metres (2,886ft) on a large plateau some 70km (43 miles) north of Hanoi in the Tam Dao mountain range.

These mountains stretch 80km (50 miles) from northwest to southeast, separating Vinh Phuc province from Thai Nguyen province in the north.

Tam Dao means "three islands", the name deriving from three mountains – **Thien Thi**, **Thach Ban** and **Phu Nghia** – which rise to about 1,400 metres (4,592ft) and dominate the landscape. From a distance they resemble three islands jutting above a sea of clouds.

Tam Dao hill station is part of the **Tam Dao National Park** (Vuon Quoc Gia Tam Dao; daily daylight hours; charge). Rare trees and plants cover the mountain slopes, while the forests teem with more than 200 bird species and dozens of kinds of mammal, but you will need a local guide to see anything other than the butterflies and birds. It can be chilly and damp throughout the year, but it's a refreshing escape from Hanoi during the enervating summer heat. Facilities and accommodation are rather run-down. The town's restaurants and shops sadly do booming

business in illegal game meat and animal parts. During the high season from May to August, bus loads of Vietnamese arrive to dine at the game meat restaurants, then drink and sing at karaoke bars. As far as hiking options go, a 20-minute walk from Tam Dao leads to the popular 45-metre (148ft) -high **Silver Waterfall** (Thac Ba). To reach the more remote forested areas is a full day's walk.

For the Vietnamese, Tam Dao also has melancholy revolutionary significance. After the disastrous Thai Nguyen mutiny and uprising in August 1917, nearly 100 survivors fled here to make a doomed three-month last stand against the French army. Close to the end, one legendary leader, Sgt Trinh Van Can, committed suicide. The French made every effort to track down and kill every last rebel soldier and political prisoner who escaped; in the end, the French claimed that only five eluded them. The Tam Dao Golf Course (www.tamdaogolf.com) opened in 2007 and is a notable addition to the area's facilities.

*Take a trek to forest waterfalls at the Tam Dao National Park – a cool respite during the summer.*

## RESTAURANTS

### Le Mat

**Quoc Trieu Snake Restaurant**
Le Mat Snake Village, Long Bien. Tel (mobile): 091-322 7045. Open: daily B, L & D. **$$$**
Diners are treated to a seven- to eight-course esoteric meal that includes snake meat, snake bones, snake heart and, of course, a shot of snake blood mixed in rice wine. Definitely not for the faint of heart.

**Son Que Restaurant**
742 Quang Trung, Ba La, Ha Dong District, Ha Tay province. Open: daily L & D. **$$$**
This large but simply designed restaurant provides a good range of Vietnamese dishes, from

simmered frog with banana and soya curd to the slightly safer-sounding roasted crab. A bottle of the locally produced wine is worth sampling.

**Tan Da Restaurant**
Tan Da Spa Resort, Tan Linh Mountain, Ba Vi District, Ha Tay province. Tel: 034-388 1047. Open: daily B, L & D. **$$$**
This resort in Ba Vi National Park features two restaurants – an outdoor buffet with traditional northern dishes and an indoor dining room serving a variety of adequate Western and Asian standards. You can also ask for a table in the adjoining traditional Muong stilt house.

### Tam Dao

**Bamboo Restaurant**
Mela Hotel, Thi Tran, Tam Dao Town, Van Phuc province. Tel: 021-182 4321. Open: daily B, L & D. **$$$**
A good spot to find relatively decent Western meals while in Tam Dao. Also serves a selection of Vietnamese dishes, which perhaps come closer to hitting the mark.

### Phu Tho province

**The Riverside Fish Restaurant**
Song Thao Street, Tien Cat Ward, Viet Tri City, Phu Tho province. Tel: 021-084 6013, mobile tel: 091-257 7816. Open: daily L & D. **$$**
Despite its name, this

restaurant is not on the water. Instead it serves the rare *anh vu* fish caught in the Thao River, which costs upwards of US$45/kilo and was once reserved only for royalty. The other dishes are more reasonably priced; many recommend the *lang* fish hotpot with an assortment of pineapple, tomato, fennel, taro, cabbage and rice noodles.

Prices for a three-course dinner per person:
**$** = under US$5
**$$** = US$5–10
**$$$** = US$10–20
**$$$$** = over US$20

C H I N A

Yizu Zizhixian

Ta Fou San

A Pa Chai

Ban Pa Thang

Giang Mung Pho

Muong Nhe (Nature Reserve)

Muong Nhe

Sop Pong

Muang Hat Hin

Muang Va

Phongsali
Boun Nua

Sen Soi

Bo Kong

Sop Nhom

Ban Khana

Ban Naluang

Pak Ban

Pak Pe

Muang Khoua

Muang Mai

Sop Kai

Taxoum

Sam Phou

Sao Phai

Muang Ngoy

P h o u   D e n   D i n

L a i   C h a u

Muong Te

Muong Boum

Muong Nhe

Ban Cheng Nuo

Ban Po Bai

Nam Cum

Ma Li Chai

Ngu dai son 3120

Jinping

Phong Tho

Lai Chau

Ban Nam Che

Sinh Ho

Ban Nam Muong

Xiaohekou

Phan Si Pan (Fansipan) 3143

Ban Ko La

Nam Bon

Pac Tha

Nam Bai

Hekou

Lao Cai

Tram Ton

Thac Bac (Silver Falls)

Sa Pa

Day Hoang Lien (Hoang Lien Nature Reserve)

Kunming

Lahadi

Pingbian

Dulong

Kunming

Ha Giang

Nam Ric

Ban Thuy

Lang Cay

Yen Binh Xa

Vinh Tuy

Bac Ba

Ham Y

Tchoung Sao

Bac Ha

Nam Khap

Ban Tang

Pho Lu

Bao Ha

Pho Rang

H o a n g   L i e n   S o n

Van Ban

Lang Na

Lang Than

Tu Le

Poun Loung

Phu Luong 2985

Lao Phou Vao

Ban Na Tong

Yen Bai

Nghia Lo

Van An

Ba Khe

Bac Yen

Phu Yen

Xom Tang

P h u

Muong Lay

Muong Tong

Ban Na Pheo

Luan Chau

Tuan Giao

Ban Nam Nen

Quynh Nhai

Ban Pa Hoang

Pha Din

Ban Veng

Ban Vay

Son La

D i e n   B i e n

Dien Bien Phu

Ban Cong Deng

Tay Trang

M a

S o n   L a

D a   (B l a c k)

Co Noi

1235

Yen Chau

Chieng Pan

Moc Chau

Ho Jong Da

Song Ma

Ban Beng

Muong Leo

Muang Peu

Muong Het

Ban Loup

Sop Long

Muang Hom

Thac Dai Yem

Thao Nguyen

Pa Luong 1880

Ban Tat Loi

Xam Nua

Xiangmen

Muang Ven

Ban Phung

Muong Lat 1418

T h a n h   H o a

Na Meo

Ban Na Mang

Ban Na Chang

Ban Houay Tieng

Muang Nai

Poungthak 2452

Muang Hin

Ban Chieng

Muang Lam

Nam Can

Ky Son

N g h e  A

Tuong Duong

Canh Trap

Ca Khe Bo

Phu Xai Lai Leng 2711

Ban Ko Oi

Ban Muangngat

Con Cuong

Muang Mok

Na Mang

Ban Thamnou

Nui   Tuong   Son

P h o u   S i a m   S a o

L A O S

L A O S

⑤
⑥
⑦
⑧
⑨
⑩
④
③

INSET MAP:

Nghe An

Tap Phuc

Nghi Loc

Hon Mat

Luong Khe

Bich Thi

Vinh

Cua Lo

Ho Thong

Hoang Tru / Kim Lien

Nui Ba Mu 1357

Linh Cam

Kim Cuong

Can Loc

Cua Sot

Dien Xa

Truc Lam

Ha Tinh

Cua Nhuong

Cau Thuong

Ha Tinh

Cam Xuyen

Ky Anh

Cua Khau

Hon Son Duong

Xuan Lung

Tuan Thuong

Ban Vangchang

Bau Mon

Thanh Lang Xa

Tuyen Hoa

Ngang Pass

Mui Doc

Vinh Son

Ron

Yen Lac

Cha Noi

Quang Trach

Don Bai Dinh

Phong Nga

Quang Binh

Ly Nhon Bac

Dong Hoi

Cong Vien Quoc Gia Phong Nha-Ke Nang (Phong Nha-Ke Nang NP)

Chap Le

Quang Tri

DMZ

Donh Ha

Vinh Bac Bo (Gulf of Tonkin)

N u i   T u o n g   S o n

㉕
㉖
㉗

0   10 km
0   10 miles

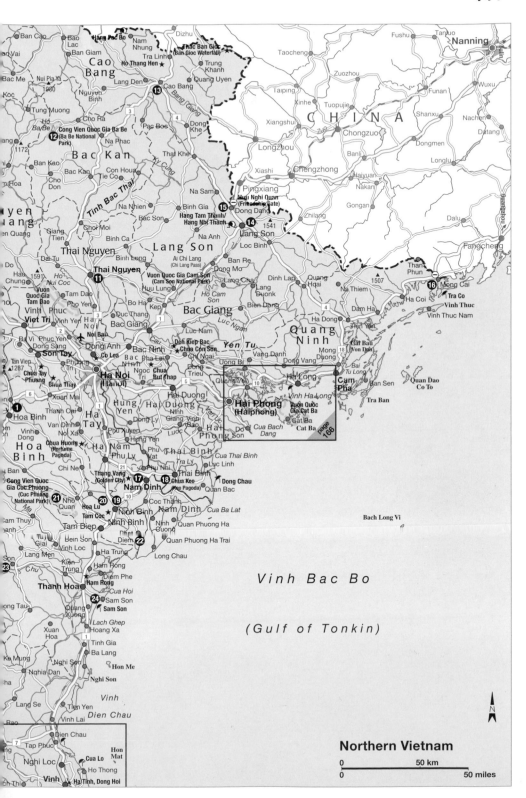

Ban Cao
Bao Lac
Ban Giam
Cao Bang
Hang Pac Bo
Nam Nhung
Tra Linh
Ho Thang Hen ★
Dizhu
Thac Ban Gioc (Ban Gioc Waterfall) ★
Trung Khanh
Fushu
Tanuo
**Nanning**

Nui Vai
Bac Me
Nui Pia Ya 1980
Lang Den
Nguyen Binh
Quang Uyen
Taocheng
Taiping
Xinhe
Zuozhou
Tuopujie
Wuxu

Koc
Tung Muong
Ho Ba/Be)
**13**
Cao Bang
Xiangshui
C H I N A
Funan
Nachen
Datang

1172
Cong Vien Quoc Gia Ba Be (Ba Be National Park)
**12**
Pac Bos
Dong Khe
Longzhou
Chongzuo
Dongmen
Longlu

Ban Kao
Bac Kan
Con Houa
Tie Co
**B a c  K a n**
That Khe
Xiashi
Chengzhong
Banli
Haiyuan
Nakan
Dalu

Cho Don
Na Phac
Ky Cung
Na Sam
Pingxiang
Zhilang
Gongan
Fangcheng

Hoa
Tinh Bac Thai
Na Nhien
Binh Gia
Huu Nghi Quan (Friendship Gate)
Dong Dang
Thanh Phun
1507

yen quang
Giang Tien
Choi Moi
Bac Son
**15**
Hang Tam Thanh/ Hang Nhi Thanh
**14**
1541
Mong Cai
**16**
Tra Co

en Quang
Binh Ca
Na Anh
**L a n g  S o n**
Loc Binh
Ha Coi
Vinh Thuc
Vinh Thuc Nam

Do
Hau Chung 1591
Dai Tu
Binh Long
**Thai Nguyen**
Ai Chi Lang (Chi Lang Pass)
Ban Re
Dong Mo
Dinh Lap
Quang Hqai
Na Thiem
Dam Ha

Chung
Ho Nui Coc
Tam Dao
Vuon Quoc Gia Cam Son (Cam Son National Park)
Lang Chai
Lang Buonk
**11**
Pho Yen
Bo Ha
Kep
Bien Dong
Ha Dong
Ban Sen

Vuon Quoc Gia Tam Dao
Duc Thang
H, Noi Ban
**B a c  G i a n g**
Luc Ngan
Ha Dong
Mong Duong
**18**
Cat Bau (Von Dinh)

Vinh Phuc
**Viet Tri**
Vinh Yen
Bac Giang
Luc Nam
**Q u a n g  N i n h**
Bai Tu Long
Quan Dao Co To

Ba Vi
Phuc Yen
Dong Anh
Bac Ninh
Den Kiep Bac
Chua Con Son
Yen Tu
Vang Danh
Dong Vang
**Cam Pha**
Tra Ban

Son Tay
Phuong
Cu Loa
Bac Pha Lai
Chi Ngai
Uong Bi
**Ha Long**
Bai Tu Long

Tan Vien 1287
Chua Tay Phuong
Ngoc Chua But Thap
Dong Trieu
**Vinh Ha Long**

Xuan Mai
**Ha Noi (Hanoi)**
**Hai Duong**
Vuon Quoc Gia Cat Ba

**1**
**Hoa Binh**
Thanh Oai
**Hung Yen**
**Hai Duong**
Ninh
Giang Vinh
Cat Ba

Vinh Dong
Van Dinh
Noi Xa
Dong Ly
Phu Xuyen
**Hai Phong**
Cua Bach Dang
page 166

**Hoa Binh**
Chua Huong (Perfume Pagoda)
**Ha Nam**
Phu Ly
Phu Vat
**Thai Binh**
Cua Thai Binh

Ban
Chi Ne
21
Tra Ly
Phu Nhi
Luc Linh

Cong Vien Quoc Gia Cuc Phuong (Cuc Phuong National Park)
Thang Vang (Golden City) ★
**17**
**18**
Chua Keo (Keo Pagoda) ★
Dong Chau

**21**
Nho Quan
**20** **19**
Hoa Lu
**Nam Dinh**
Coc Thanh
Quan Bac
Quan Phuong Ha

Cam Thuy
Tam Coc
**Ninh Binh**
**Nam Dinh**
Cua Ba Lat

anh
Tam Diep
Hein Son
Diem
Ninh Cuong
Quan Phuong Ha Trai

Giai
Vinh Loc
**22**
Quan Phuong Ha
Bach Long Vi

**23**
Lang Men
Kien Trung
Ha Trung
Long Chau

Son
Chu
Ham Rong
Diem Phe

**Thanh Hoa**
Ham Rong
Cua Hoi
*V i n h  B a c  B o*

ong Tau
**24**
Sam Son
*(G u l f  o f  T o n k i n)*

Xuan Hoa
Quang Xuong
Lach Ghep
Hoang Xa

Ke Mung
Tinh Gia
Ba Lang

Nghi Son
Hon Me

Nghia Dan
Nghi Son

ha
*Vinh*
Lang Se
Tien Yen
Vinh Lai
*Dien Chau*

Bao
**7**
Tap Phuc
Dien Chau
Hon Mat

Nghi Loc
Cua Lo
Ho Thong

Thi
**Vinh**
Ha Tinh, Dong Hoi

N

**Northern Vietnam**

0                    50 km
0                    50 miles

# NORTHWEST VIETNAM

The far northwest is a wild, untamed land that demands exploration. Those who dare to brave the perilous roads and rough terrain are treated to magnificent scenery and remote minority villages

To the west and northwest of Hanoi, the flat-as-a-pancake, rice-growing delta of the Red River (Song Hong) soon gives way to deep green valleys and craggy mountain ranges inhabited by a number of ethnic minority groups. These days, the people farm in the shadow of modern hydroelectric dams supplying power to much of the rest of the country. Bounded on the north by lengthy borders with Laos and China, this is a stunningly wild and picturesque region, but those who venture this far on the "northwest loop" can expect poor roads, treacherous passes and few modern tourist amenities. Travellers who do make the journey are rewarded for their efforts with serene valleys and some of the most spectacular mountain vistas anywhere in Southeast Asia. These include the Son La and Moc Chau highlands and the enormous Hoang Lien Son mountain range in the extreme northwest.

Heading southwest from Hanoi, Hoa Binh province's scenic Mai Chau Valley offers a chance to explore the lush landscape and stay overnight in an authentic White Tai minority village. Further northwest, French colonial rule met its end in a mountainous valley known as Dien Bien Phu. From here, a trip north takes visitors to the hill retreat of Sa Pa, the most popular destination in the northwest. Sa Pa is a lively mountain town filled with colourful ethnic minority markets, serious trekking opportunities and access to the highest peak in Vietnam: Fansipan Mountain. Development has been rapid, with hotels and more souvenir sellers, while ethnic groups, notably the Hmong, have embraced the town's new-found fame and many work as guides. Reaching the northwest is easy as trains connect Hanoi to Lao Cai, near Sa Pa, followed by a short minibus ride. Getting around

**Main attractions**
DIEN BIEN PHU CITY
SA PA
MOUNT FANSIPAN
MAI CHAU VALLEY
BAC HA

**LEFT:** terraced farms near Sa Pa.
**RIGHT:** Flower Hmong ethnic minority girls.

the region can be more time-consuming, though here it really is as much about the journey through the mountains as it is the final destination.

## HOA BINH PROVINCE

### Hoa Binh City

Those who arrive in **Hoa Binh City** ❶ may wonder what its appeal is. While it may appear rather industrial and plain, the city is a great base from which to visit ethnic groups and natural sites. Among those who make their home near here are Muong, Hmong, Tai, Tay and Dao (pronounced "Zao") ethnic groups.

**Hoa Binh**, about 75km (47 miles) west of Hanoi, was the site of much bloodshed during the early 1950s when the French and Viet Minh forces battled for control of the area. Some of the bloodiest battles were waged on the Black River (Song Da) around the so-called Notre Dame Rock. In the end, the French forces retreated, but for the Viet Minh, Hoa Binh was a dress rehearsal for a later, decisive showdown at Dien Bien Phu (*see page 147*).

Today, **Hoa Binh City**, the provincial capital, is a sprawling industrial area. Just outside of the urban area is the **Hoa Binh Dam** and hydroelectric power station, which supplies energy to towns as far away as the Mekong Delta. Built in 1979 with technical assistance and money from the former Soviet Union, construction of the dam took 15 years and displaced approximately 50,000 people from the Black River Valley, which is now submerged. Vietnam is so dependent on the energy generated at Hoa Binh that when water levels drop during the dry season, large sections of the country suffer extended blackouts.

While few ethnic minority people wear their traditional clothing, it is possible to visit more rural areas and stay overnight in nearby villages where their presence and culture are obvious. Hoa Binh's markets and shops are good sources of tribal souvenirs, in particular brocade garments and weaving. Local dishes include rice cooked in bamboo. On the whole, though, foreign tourists generally give Hoa Binh a miss, stopping only briefly before heading for the pleasantly rural ambience of nearby Mai Chau Valley, a picturesque Thai ethnic minority area.

### Mai Chau

Located 135km (84 miles), or 3.5 hours' driving time, from Hanoi on Highway 6 is the serene **Mai Chau Valley** ❷. If you've stopped at Hoa Binh City, Mai Chau is only 60km (40 miles) further along the road. The valley makes for an excellent weekend outing and is an ideal base for treks to nearby highland villages, with none of the hassling hawkers that plague other areas. Famous for its *ruou can* (a rice wine drunk through long bamboo straws), Mai Chau is a collection of small villages, farms and individual stilt houses spread out over a vast, verdant valley. Peaceful and charming, it is also the closest place from Hanoi where countryside trekking can be

**BELOW:** the Hoa Binh Dam is an important source of energy for the country.

done, along with overnight stays in an authentic ethnic minority village.

While most tour agencies drop off guests at **Lac Village** (Ban Lac), a commercial White Tai village popular with Vietnamese tourist groups, it's better not to linger here. Stop for a meal after the drive from Hanoi and then set off with a guide to one of the farther-flung and more authentic White Tai villages deeper in the valley.

White Tai women are renowned master weavers. Beneath their stilt houses is usually a loom or two where they create their fine textiles. At the village centre are shops with displays of beautiful shawls and scarves. White Tai womenfolk wear tight blouses held together in front by a row of silver clasps. Their sarong-style skirts are usually dark-coloured with thin plain or warp *ikat* horizontal stripes and embroidered hems. The Sunday market is the highlight of the week for most, and sees women from nearby ethnic groups come to sell fruit. Traditional dances are also an integral part of the market.

## SON LA PROVINCE

Continuing northwest, **Moc Chau** in neighbouring Son La province is a stunningly beautiful highland valley surrounded by low mountains. Sprinkled with prosperous villages of Muong and White Tai and Black Tai people, it is laced with a vast irrigation network that feeds the fields of wet rice as well as the stilt-house villages. Traditionally fishermen, each Tai household has its own fish pond and prominently displayed nets.

### Moc Chau

Moc Chau owes much of its current fame to the Dutch. Cows from the Netherlands were imported to the area, and a dairy industry was born: you'll know when you are approaching Moc Chau when you see the black-and-white dairy cows wandering across the road. Much of the area is devoted to dairy farming (many farmers relocated here following the building of the new Son La hydropower plant), so be sure to try out some of the famously rich yoghurt, ice cream or Moc Chau-branded chocolate bars.

*Farmland amid rolling hills and expansive valleys at Mai Chau.*

**BELOW:** ethnic music and dance performance at Mai Chau.

*Vendor selling barbecued corn at a Son La Market.*

**BELOW:** former prison cell at the restored Son La Provincial Museum.

Visitors can even get closer to nature by milking the cows themselves. During the coldest months, January and February, the temperature can fall to –3°C (27°F). With central heating nearly impossible to find, visitors need to pack appropriate clothing.

Highway 6 from Moc Chau climbs west past hills cultivated with tea, coffee, cotton, and fruit trees, including mulberry, whose leaves feed silkworms. The road winds through the mountainous landscapes of Son La province close to the border with Laos. The region is home to many ethnic minorities, including Hmong, Mnong, Muong, Mun, Kho Mu, Dao, Tay, White Tai and Black Tai, Xinh Mun and Hoa peoples.

Further northwest along Highway 6, the road passes through idyllic Muong and Black Tai villages with their long, precarious suspension bridges and miniature hydroelectric generators. While the forest edging the road here seems thick, locals have long plundered it for firewood and house-building materials. From here on, one will often see Black Tai and Muong people walking along the roadside. Black Tai women can be identified by the elaborately embroidered folded cloths that they balance precariously on their heads. Muong women usually wear white rectangular scarves, long skirts and short vests open at the front. Their skirts are usually adorned with a large silk belt embroidered with all kinds of fantastic creatures.

Dai Yem Fall is about 4km (2.5 miles) from Moc Chau. Two streams join together here and fall from a height of 100 metres (330ft) into a clear lake, surrounded by scenic forest.

## Son La City

The capital of Son La province, **Son La City ❸** is 100km (60 miles) northwest from Moc Chau. The minuscule "city" runs for just over a kilometre on the southwestern bank of the **Nam La River** (Song Nam La). Despite increased development and a scattering of shiny new government buildings, it is still the familiar, faceless Vietnamese provincial town of dusty roads and tall, narrow houses. In the early mornings, many traditionally dressed Hmong, Muong, Xinh Mun, and Black and White Tai minority people gather to trade in the market.

The city's main **To Hieu Street** is named after a political prisoner jailed for sedition in the 1940s. He died in prison from malaria, and is best known for planting the prison compound's single, symbolic peach tree. A number of local landmarks bear his name.

Above To Hieu Street, on a wooded promontory, the brick ruins of the former French prison have been converted into the **Son La Provincial Museum** (Bao Tang Tinh Son La; tel: 02-285 2022; daily 7.30–11am and 1.30–5.30pm; charge). Originally built in 1908, the prison was once the residence of thousands of political prisoners. Visitors can view the prison's original cells, complete with their food slots and leg shackles. Partially rebuilt for tourists, most of the compound was blasted away during the war with

the French. The site also sustained heavy damage when it was used as a dumping ground for unused ammunition by US bombers returning from missions to Hanoi and Haiphong. As well as being a historically important site, it also has an interesting display of objects belonging to the dozen ethnic groups that live in the area.

## Around Son La

After the drabness of the city, Son La's environs are refreshingly verdant and lush, offering rice fields, fruit orchards and attractive ethnic minority villages. **Ban Mong**, a Black Tai village outside of Son La, about 6km (4 miles) south of the prison, has some scummy-looking public hot springs that are best avoided. The **Tham Coong Cave**, northwest of town, isn't worth the admission price, but there are nice walks in the countryside. Ask at your hotel for directions. Tham Tet Tong is a series of caves just over 1km (½ mile) from Son La and is worth checking out.

The Vietnamese government has big plans in store for Son La as it is expected to become part of a planned trade corridor that extends into northern Lao. However, this development comes at the expense of the 170km (106-mile) stretch of Highway 6 between Son La and Dien Bien Phu, which will be torn up, re-cut and re-laid in the future.

## DIEN BIEN PROVINCE

Continuing west from Son La for about 90km (56 miles) brings you to the small town of **Tuan Giao**. The intersecting road to the west is Highway 279, the route to **Dien Bien Phu ❹**, which is a further 80km (50 miles) and at least 3.5 hours' driving time away.

### Dien Bien Phu City

**Famed for being the site of a battle that signalled the end of French colonialism in Asia, Dien Bien Phu City**, the capital of Dien Bien province, lies on the east bank of the **Nam Rom River** (Song Nam Rom) at the northern end of the Muong Thanh valley. Named Muong Thanh by its Tai rice farmers, the heart-shaped, pancake-flat valley extends 20km (12

*The significance of Dien Bien Phu's past is easily lost on the younger generation. Pictured here is A1 Hill, which was the scene of much bloodshed.*

**BELOW:** a strong military presence remains in Dien Bien Phu City.

## The End of French Rule

French colonial forces tried, and ultimately failed, to tame the wild northwest for 40 years. In 1953, as part of Vietnamese efforts to eject the French, General Vo Nguyen Giap and his Viet Minh soldiers launched excursions into northern Laos, reaching the outskirts of the royal city of Luang Prabang. The French, believing Dien Bien Phu was key to preventing a communist takeover of Laos – a French protectorate – easily recaptured it in late 1953. At that time, Dien Bien Phu was an old and ramshackle trading village at the intersection of three major drug routes.

General Vo and his Viet Minh forces launched decisive attacks starting on 13 March 1954, and 56 days later the Viet Minh had managed to rout the French troops, led by General Christian de Castries, and planted their flag on the main command bunker. The Battle of Dien Bien Phu is hugely significant as it finally booted the French out of Vietnam and its other colonies in Indochina. But the victory was bittersweet: the Geneva Agreement, signed months after the war in August 1954, resulted in Vietnam being divided at the 17th parallel – a communist north and a capitalist south, with tragic consequences in the following years.

*Figurines of soldiers in the tunnel at A1 Hill.*

**BELOW:** Artefacts from the battle of Dien Bien Phu – such as the charred remains of military jeeps – are on display at the Museum of the Dien Bien Phu Victory.

miles) from north to south and 6km (4 miles) east to west. This valley was the site of a 57-day siege – the famous Battle of Dien Pien Phu – which spelt the ignominious end to French colonialism in Asia. It is encircled by steep, green hills from which tens of thousands of Viet Minh troops launched their assault on the French garrisons in 1954. The road leads on from Dien Bien Phu to the border with Laos, just 35km (22 miles) away, but is not generally open to tourists.

Dien Bien Phu was just another grey, concrete town until 2003, when it was bestowed city status in preparation for its new role as provincial capital. In 2004, the celebration of the 50th anniversary of the French defeat brought about a mini tourism surge and building boom, soon to be followed by an increase in the number of flights from Hanoi. Despite such efforts, however, tourists are something of a rarity and facilities are limited, with only basic accommodation available. For the hardier traveller, the route from Sa Pa has gorgeous views.

## Battleground sights

Tourists can visit a reconstruction of **General de Castries's main command bunker** (daily 7.30–11am, 1.30–4.30pm; a guided tour is included in the price of admission to the Museum of the Dien Bien Phu Victory; see below), set amid a litter of rusty tanks and artillery. Not far away, **A1 Hill**, known as "Eliane 2" to the French, was the scene of fierce fighting and is now a war memorial dedicated to the Viet Minh who died here. There's also a bunker and entrance to a tunnel dug by coal miners. The miners stuffed the tunnel with 1,000kg (2,205lbs) of explosives and detonated it on 6 May to signal the final assault on the French bases.

On the edge of downtown, the site of the **Museum of the Dien Bien Phu Victory** (Nha Trung Bay Thang Lich Su Dien Bien Phu; daily 7–11am and 1.30–4pm; charge) has black-and-white battle photos, an illuminated electronic model of the valley and battle positions, and a selection of Chinese, American and French weapons. A guide here is useful to explain exactly what is displayed, as there are few signs in English. Across the street is a **Viet Minh Cemetery** where some of the Viet Minh soldiers are buried.

Towering over town from its vantage position at D1 Hill is the Dien Bien Phu Victory Monument, a huge bronze statue measuring 12.6 metres (41ft) and weighing 220 tonnes. It depicts three soldiers standing atop the French garrison, one holding a flag, another holding a gun, and the third carrying a child with flowers. On the flag is written *"Quyet chien, quyet thang"* (determined to fight, determined to win).

## LAI CHAU PROVINCE

Wedged in between China to the north and Laos to the west, Lai Chau province is covered in thick forests. It was once known for its wildlife, including tigers, bears, bison and pheasants, but sadly this is now

hugely diminished due to rampant deforestation, slash-and-burn farming and increased trade in illegal animal products.

## Muong Lay

Running due north of Dien Bien Phu, Highway 12 connects with the historic Thai town formerly known as Lai Chau, some 104km (65 miles) away. Today known as **Muong Lay** ❺, this small town is a good place to stop for lunch or an overnight stay on the way to Sa Pa. Here, the surroundings are striking in their contrast: jagged, unforgiving peaks are set against dense tiers of thick forest. The road into town is in good condition but during the rainy season between May and August, landslides can cause serious delays.

## Black River dam

There is much discussion about the damming and inundation of the **Black River** (Song Da) into the Muong Lay Valley for the construction of the **Son La hydroelectric power plant**, which is the biggest in Southeast Asia. The first turbines were connected to the national grid in 2010 and the project is expected to be completed by 2015. While most of the present downtown will be sacrificed to the new reservoir, Muong Lay will continue to exist. It is estimated that 100,000 people, mainly from ethnic groups, will have to relocate. The US$2 billion project has a capacity of 2,400 megawatts. Earlier plans for an even grander dam were scaled down owing to environmental and safety concerns.

## Lai Chau town

The new capital of Lai Chau province was moved 150km (93 miles) northeast to the (new) **Lai Chau** ❻ town, which was formerly known as **Tam Duong**. New shops and hotels are a sign of how bustling this town has become. Much of the appeal comes from the White Hmong and Flower Hmong, White Tai and Black Tai, Dao Khau and Giay hill tribes. Visits to ethnic minority villages are popular, but most are only accessible by motorbike. The immediate surroundings here are dirty and dusty, as the nearby hills

**BELOW:** always ask permission before photographing local people.

## Hill-tribe Etiquette

While it is essential to be patient when photographing ethnic minority people, it is even more important to be respectful. It is tempting for the beautiful surroundings, striking beauty of the people and their costumes to make photographers forget basic etiquette. Taking a picture without the subject's permission may be interpreted as offensive. Once permission is given, children and adults alike will clamber over travellers to get a glimpse of themselves on the camera's screen. In Sa Pa, industrious Hmong have become used to being photographed (though they often insist that you buy something from them in return). Other ethnic minority groups, including some Red Dao, believe that having their picture taken is bad for their health. Always ask first.

# Opium in the Northwest

**Despite government efforts, the lucrative rewards for growing opium are hard to resist for the poor farmers of northwest Vietnam**

Lan, a 27-year-old Black Hmong woman from Lai Chau province, toils at her family's small patch of rice paddy at least eight hours a day. Each morning well before dawn, she and her husband trek for 9km (6 miles) down a hillside to a piece of land given to them by the government. Lan and her husband Mo were given the land because both their parents are opium addicts, as are a number of their neighbours. Under a programme to provide arable land to ethnic minorities in the rugged northwestern highlands, the government hopes to curb the region's propensity for cultivating – and using – opium.

Though pleased to have a good plot of land, Lan says the government doesn't do enough to lift Hmong like her out of poverty, leaving many to feel they have no choice but to grow and trade the illicit drug. Struggling with poverty and a lack of alternatives, Lai Chau and other provinces in northwestern Vietnam – in common with other countries in the so-called Golden Triangle, such as Laos and Burma – have a long history of opium cultivation and use. A valuable cash crop, ethnic minorities have used opium not only medicinally but also as a means of alleviating hunger.

## Government programmes

After Vietnam achieved independence from the French, the central government tried hard to eradicate opium cultivation, but demand for heroin – processed from the opium poppy – became so great in the 1960s as a result of the US military presence in the south that its production in places like Lai Chau boomed. After the US Army departed in 1975, demand for opium dropped back down to pre-1945 levels.

Since then, the government has done much to destroy poppy fields, though little to provide economic alternatives. According to estimates, poppy cultivation in Lai Chau fell from 12,200 hectares (30,144 acres) in 1992 to just 32 hectares (80 acres) in June 2004, the last time the Vietnamese government released official figures. However, the scale of the problem remains vast: in 2009 heroin users consumed 15 tonnes of pure heroin in Indonesia, Malaysia and Vietnam, yet only 600kg (1,200lbs) were seized.

The region's proximity to Laos and China and its porous borders have long made northwest Vietnam a major transit point. Also driving production is the fact that drug abuse has surged sharply in Vietnam's big cities in the past decade.

Today, those selected for the government-run crop diversification programme from Lan's village grow rice, cotton, fruit, tea and spices at the bottom of a remote valley. But due to the long, backbreaking work that brings in less than half the worth of a season's poppy crop, Lan is tempted to return to the old ways.

The consequences of buying, possessing or using opium, heroin or any other drugs are extremely harsh in Vietnam. Traffickers are subject to the death penalty, and charges of simple possession can land a foreigner up to five years in jail. Purchasing opium from ethnic minority people reinforces an unhealthy practice, and some sellers are known to work for the police.

**LEFT:** harvesting the opium poppy for heroin is lucrative but illegal.

have been dug out to create more flat land for construction.

## LAO CAI PROVINCE

### Towards Sa Pa

The 90km (56-mile) stretch of road from **Lai Chau** to the hill-town retreat of **Sa Pa** – Highway 4D – runs southeast along the dramatic Hoang Lien mountain range. Here, the mountains become higher and craggier and are more thickly forested. The road winds through **Tram Ton Pass**, the highest mountain pass in the country. The sealed road carved into the steep mountainsides was once unstable and subject to landslides because the dirt, laterite and gravel road was repaired by manual labour. Nowadays, this work is performed by heavy machinery and the road is in good condition. During the winter, thick fog and mists can make for a terrifying but eerily beautiful ride.

### Sa Pa town

The picturesque town of **Sa Pa** ❼ is rightly renowned as the jewel in the northwest's crown. At around 1,600 metres (5,500ft) above sea level, its cool climate and rich mix of ethnic groups makes it an unmissable part of any northwest itinerary. It is a relatively small town though, and its sudden rise in popularity has also resulted in an increasingly determined group of locals keen to exploit Sa Pa's new-found fame.

Travellers will know they are approaching once they reach the village of **Binh Lu**. The ethnic minority people who live around here are neither shy nor indifferent to tourists or their cameras. On the contrary, they often take off their metal jewellery and headpieces and proffer them for sale. Primarily villages of Dao people, the women traditionally have close-cropped hair, usually hidden under a black turban, which holds the headpiece, a kind of metal cap with a small box-like crown.

Originally a Black Hmong settlement, Sa Pa was used by the French as a hill-station retreat during the summer months. The temperate climate at an elevation of 1,650 metres (5,413ft) was a welcome respite from the stifling humidity at the lower levels, and reminded the French of home. While the French made it a favourite spot in the 1940s, Sa Pa's current incarnation as a bustling tourist town only took place in the mid-1990s, with the arrival of large numbers of backpackers.

Dramatically perched on the edge of a high plateau, it is surrounded on all sides by theatrical dark-blue peaks enveloped by shifting mist and cloud. All along the lower hillsides of the valleys are terraced rice fields interspersed with minority hill-tribe villages. It is all unbelievably scenic, and best of all, it doesn't take more than 10 minutes to stroll beyond this small frontier town to the breathtaking countryside.

### When to visit

Sa Pa can be uncomfortably cold in the winter, especially in January and

*Silver bracelets traditionally worn by the ethnic minority women can be purchased in Sa Pa.*

**BELOW:** Black Hmong people in the hills outside Sa Pa – although increasingly touristy these days, Sa Pa still retains its idyllic feel.

February when temperatures frequently drop below freezing. It's at times like these that the French open fires are particularly welcome. The busiest tourist season is summer, when the Vietnamese arrive to escape the heat – although this period also coincides with the rainy season. The optimum times for a visit are September to November and March to May, when the skies are bright and the weather is nippy at night.

Any time of year, Sa Pa experiences a tourist surge from Fridays to Sundays. Just about every travel agency in Hanoi offers a weekend getaway to the hill retreat, with many hyping the so-called weekend "love market". No doubt local ethnic minority youth do come to town in the hope of meeting the opposite sex from other villages, but they are wise enough to avoid the gawking tourists and their cameras. What foreigners will see is the weekly rendezvous when villagers come to town to buy, sell and socialise at the bustling marketplace.

## Ethnic minorities

With one of the largest populations of ethnic groups in Vietnam, Sa Pa is the ideal place to interact and learn about the hill tribes. Ethnic Vietnamese make up 15 percent of Sa Pa's population of 36,000, with more than half belonging to the Hmong group. Both Black Hmong men and women in this area wear dark-blue, almost black, clothing. It's been dyed with indigo, and there are always indigo fields near Hmong villages. The women and girls wear indigo turbans, skirts, vests and leggings, accessorised with big silver hoop earrings. Their hands are often stained a mixture of blue and green from working with the dye. Men wear baggy shirts and trousers and a long vest, as well as silver and bronze necklaces. Although their embroidered decorations are minimal, the motifs are very similar to those used by the Hmong in Thailand and Laos. Hmong babies here also wear colourful little tasselled caps.

The clothing of the Red Dao people, like their culture and architecture, varies considerably throughout

**BELOW LEFT:** Red Dao woman doing embroidery work.
**BELOW RIGHT:** Black Hmong farmhands.

Vietnam. In Sa Pa, the Dao men's attire is similar to the Hmong, but the little patches of embroidered decoration instantly identify them. Like that of their counterparts in Laos and Thailand, Dao embroidery is incredibly dense and colourful and often incorporates dozens of coins and silver beads. Dao women wear loose trousers that stop below the knee. However, Dao women here wear a jacket with a very long back panel, and a cushion-like red turban.

## Sa Pa Market

All manner of hill-tribe clothing, jewellery and handicrafts, some quite old, are sold – after fierce bargaining – in the main **Sa Pa Market**. The ethnic minority attire on sale has been adroitly altered for foreign body shapes. Vendors gather at the market every day, but the best time to visit is early on Saturday and Sunday mornings. Throughout the week, Black Hmong and Red Dao women wander about town aggressively touting their clothing and jewellery. Long accustomed to dealing with foreign tourists, these women – some barely in their teens – can usually string together a few words in a number of languages, and English and French quite well. They can be decidedly tenacious, so don't even glance at their goods unless you're really interested in buying something. While this market is notoriously geared towards tourists these days, markets outside of town are far better places to see how locals live and trade.

## Sa Pa Church

Replaced in the last decade with all manner of mini-hotels and karaoke bars, only a few original buildings – with balconies and cupolas – linger from Sa Pa's days as a French hill station. One of the most noteworthy is **Sa Pa Catholic Church**. Built in 1930, it was shelled in 1952 by the French and again in 1979 by the Chinese. Repaired in 1994, a priest

comes in from Lao Cai twice a week to preach to a packed congregation able to recite mass from memory. In the courtyard is the tomb of Father Trinh, a priest who was brutally decapitated on the church grounds in 1952 after confronting a young monk who was having a romantic affair with a village girl.

## Sa Pa Treks

Trekking is one of the main activities in Sa Pa and the town has several companies that can arrange trips. Most treks follow a similar pattern, heading out from the town for a few hours' trekking, then sleeping over in a remote village – where facilities are understandably basic – before awaking for another morning along makeshift paths. Such tours usually ensure trekkers get to visit the villages of various ethnic groups so a variety of cultures can be seen. Physically, some of the trekking is tough, so those taking part need to be in good physical health, although softer trekking options head for outlying villages like Ta Van, Sin Chai and Ta Phin.

*Red Dao women at the Sa Pa Market.*

**BELOW:** Sa Pa Catholic Church.

**TIP**

To enhance the experience of trekking around Sa Pa's surrounding villages, hire a guide from a local hotel. Most of the hotels in town (see page 347) will have a stable of energetic English-speaking guides, usually young Hmong women, who are experienced in leading groups of foreigners through the picturesque valleys. Non-English-speakers can request French-, German- or Chinese-speaking guides.

**BELOW:** view of Mount Fansipan, Vietnam's highest peak.

One of the most popular destinations is just 3km (2 miles) outside of Sa Pa: the well-trodden Black Hmong village of **Cat Cat**. The Black Hmong children here squat bare-bottomed in the dirt and pose for tourists' cameras (naturally, in return for money). Dozens of visitors tramp through this small stilt-house village daily on their way to the nearby **Silver Falls** (Thac Bac), about 12km (7 miles) out of town. Also near the falls is a long, wooden suspension bridge called **Cloud Bridge** (Cau May). Another place of interest is **Can Cau**, up near the border with China. Its Saturday market draws ethnic groups from all around, including some from across the border. Several outlying villages like Ta Vin, Sin Chai and Ta Phin make for pleasant and relatively easy treks.

Hotels and travel agencies in Sa Pa will have more details on all trekking options. Another ideal way to see Sa Pa is by bicycle. Companies around the town have similar packages on offer: most involve overnight stays in a village and some challenging routes through the countryside. Cycling around Sa Pa is increasingly popular and allows

visitors to see several different villages within a relatively short space of time.

## Mount Fansipan

For the truly adventurous (or fool-hardy), there is **Mount Fansipan ⑧** (Nui Phan Si Pan) to conquer. At 3,143 metres (10,310ft) and directly west of Sa Pa, this is Vietnam's highest peak. A guide is mandatory, although there is a trail blazed by previous trekkers. Most visitors book a tour with a travel agency, such as All Sapa Tours (www. allsapatours.com). Located in **Hoang Lien Nature Reserve**, the scenery is magnificent, notable for its rhodo-dendron-rich forests and exceptional birdlife. Don't count on seeing any animals though – most of them have either been poached or are extinct.

While there is some rather thread-bare camping equipment available for rent in Sa Pa, most climbers choose to outfit themselves for the trek in Hanoi, where it's easy to find good fleece jackets and sturdy shoes. While not technically demanding, the excursion to Mount Fansipan takes at least three days, often longer in rain or misty conditions. Closer to the top, the ascent involves negotiating a number of steep, rocky patches and can be treacherous if the ground is wet. March is perhaps the best time to visit as this is the peak of the dry season. If you decide to make the trip, be sure to book with an experienced local operator.

## Lao Cai Town

There's little reason to linger in the town of **Lao Cai ⑨** on the Chinese border. The 40km (25-mile) descent from Sa Pa, however, has spectacular views and the road is in excellent condition. Most travellers who skip the northwest loop and travel directly from Hanoi to Sa Pa take the overnight train for the 320km (199-mile) journey to Lao Cai's terminus first, from where they get off and transfer by bus or car for the road trip to Sa Pa.

In the French days, the colonial elite were carried up and down this route on sedan chairs. Unless tensions crank up

again between China and Vietnam, it's perfectly legal to enter and exit China by walking across the **Lao Cai international border** gate bridge during daylight hours. Beyond is the Chinese town of Hekou, where you can take the train to Kunming. Travellers must have a Chinese visa in hand, issued in either Hanoi or Beijing, if they wish to go across the border.

Lao Cai is an ugly, sterile town, partly because it was flattened when China invaded in 1979. It was not the first time it had been occupied by the Chinese. Ironically, the Vietnamese rebuilt it to resemble just another communist Chinese city, with lots of grim cement boxes, wide streets and very little greenery. But the Chinese aren't solely to blame. In early 1951, while testing out his new heavy artillery and the ins and outs of offensive warfare, General Giap set his sights on Lao Cai. With Viet Minh troops outnumbering French five to one, he took the town within a few days. Now there is little here except a casino that plays host to bus loads of Chinese tourists and a bustling market filled with crates of cheap electronics and other goods destined for Hanoi or Beijing.

## Bac Ha Market

About 63km (39 miles) northeast of Lao Cai, little **Bac Ha** ⑩ is best known for its colourful and lively **Sunday market**. The town itself is smaller, usually warmer, and has more of a frontier feel than Sa Pa. The market's appeal stems from the sheer variety of hill-tribe minorities represented. Most people in this area belong to one of the Hmong groups, including the colourfully dressed Flower Hmong people, but there are also Dao, Giay, Laichi, Lolo, Nhang, Nung, Phulao, Tai, Thulao and Hoa as well as Vietnamese. Each Sunday, the women gather to socialise and trade, while their husbands drink themselves under the table on rice wine.

Some 2km (1.2 miles) from Bac Ha, through cornfields, is a Flower Hmong village called **Ban Pho**, famous for its maize alcohol. Further afield, the **Can Cau Market**, in a village 18km (11 miles) north of Bac Ha, runs on Saturday and was originally a livestock market.

*Flower Hmong women at Bac Ha sell their ebulliently coloured ethnic clothing to tourists to make a living.*

## RESTAURANTS

Prices for a three-course dinner per person with a half-bottle of house wine:
**$** = under $20
**$$** = $20–45
**$$$** = $45–60
**$$$$** = over $60

In the northwest, travellers eat where they can, and food is merely a fuel to push onwards into the mountains. At pit stops along the way, restaurants mainly serve ethnic minority delicacies heavy with grilled pork, beef and vegetables. Not to be missed is the region's famous rice wine *(ruou)*, served warm and flavoured with sour apples.

### Dien Bien Phu

**Lien Tuoi Restaurant**
64 Muong Thanh St, Dien Bien Phu. Tel: 023-382 4919. Open: daily B, L & D. **$$**
Popular for its quality Vietnamese and Chinese dishes. The translated English and French menu often produces a few smiles.

### Sa Pa

**Auberge**
7 Muong Hoa St, Sa Pa. Tel: 020-387 1243. Open: daily B, L & D. **$$$**
This guesthouse has a restaurant on a terrace overlooking the owner's delightful garden. Delicious snacks and mains (both Vietnamese and Western), with a nice selection of vegetarian options.

**Baguette & Chocolat**
Thac Bac St, Sa Pa. Tel: 020-387 1766. Open: daily B, L & D. **$$$**
The ground floor of this guesthouse is a quaint restaurant and café, with a bakery attached. They can do a packed picnic lunch if you're heading out on a trek.

**Camellia**
22 Tue Tinh, Sa Pa. Tel: 020-387 1455. Open: daily B, L & D. **$$$**
A warm, friendly eatery with delicious and reasonably priced Vietnamese comfort food. The spring rolls and salads are fantastic, as is the warm and toasty mountain-apple rice wine.

**Delta Restaurant**
33 Cau May St, Sa Pa. Tel: 020-387 1799. Open: daily B, L & D. **$$$**
This Italian restaurant features the best pizzas, pastas, soups and steaks that you're going to find in these parts. Warm and cosy, upstairs is a romantic wine bar with private booths. Great for those who need to take on some carbs before heading out on a trek. Credit cards accepted.

**Red Dao Restaurant**
4B Thac Bac St, Sa Pa. Tel: 020-387 2927. Open daily B, L & D. **$$$**
With staff dressed in the attire of the Red Dao people, this charming restaurant serves quality local food. The set menus are a good bet.

### Mai Chau

**Mai Chau Lodge**
Mai Chau Town. Tel: 218-386 8959. Open: daily B, L & D. **$$$$**
This upscale resort has a lovely open-air restaurant overlooking the valley. There is a good variety of quality Western and Vietnamese dishes, but they are on the pricey side for this neck of the woods.

# ETHNIC MINORITY CULTURE AND CLOTHING

**Vietnam's ethnic minorities live mostly in isolated highland areas, but their traditional culture is under threat from an influx of curious tourists**

The ethnic minorities of Vietnam can be divided into the northern group and the south/central group. Each has its own distinct origins, cultural practices and reactions to change.

In the northern highlands, populations of Tai, Dao, Hmong, Tay and Nung people have migrated from southern China over the past 500 years. They live in stilt houses, wear homespun costumes and sustain some of the best-preserved traditional highland cultures in Southeast Asia.

The central highlands are inhabited by the indigenous Bahnar, Ra De (Ede), Jarai and Sedang people. The rolling hills are suitable for coffee cultivation, and have recently been settled by large numbers of Vietnamese.

The ever-growing number of visitors to Vietnam has given the country's ethnic groups a dilemma: how can they generate an income from tourism but not destroy their culture in the process. In some towns, the push for tourist dollars means certain groups are in danger of becoming caricatures of themselves as their true heritage fades away.

Many minorities have adapted to modern life, building houses on the ground and abandoning their loincloth for clothes. In some areas, notably around Sa Pa, the tourist trade provides a good living. Others, wishing to maintain their traditional lifestyle, move deep into the remaining forest to live in isolation and sustain themselves through slash-and-burn agriculture. They can be seen in urban centres on market days trading their produce.

**ABOVE:** Tai women in the northwest still wear the *khan pieu*, or headscarf. Men traditionally give young women a khan pieu in declaration of their love.

**LEFT:** Hmong girl in traditional indigo-coloured clothing.

**BELOW:** Flower Hmong women in their trademark colourful garb. They gather at Bac Ha Market near Sa Pa every Sunday to sell handicrafts and silver jewellery.

## HILL-TRIBE TEXTILES

All the hill tribes of the northern highlands have retained their own textile industries, and these are currently enjoying a revival as the number of overseas tourists and Vietnamese visitors increases.

White Tai people in Mai Chau Valley use hand looms to weave long cotton scarves, which are then dyed in brightly coloured stripes using traditional vegetable dyes and tied at the ends into elaborate tassels. In the Sa Pa region, Hmong women carry their embroidery with them to the terraced rice fields and work on their bags and hats during rest periods.

Large numbers of imitation embroidered items are now sold at the market. Visitors are urged to make their purchases with caution if they want the genuine article.

Intricate silver jewellery figures prominently in the cultures of the hill-tribe minorities. Pictured above are examples of elaborate silver jewellery used by Red Dao women on festival days.

**RIGHT:** this Ede woman's clothes look traditional, but are in fact a modern

**ABOVE:** embroidery is a thriving trade as hill-tribe minorities find a ready market among visitors in the northern and central highlands.

# NORTHEAST VIETNAM

The northeast is characterised by dramatic karst scenery and the beautiful coastline around Halong Bay. Bordering China, the region has been a frequent battleground over the centuries

**B**etween the Red River Delta and the sea, northeast Vietnam is an area rich in agriculture and history, as well as a regional engine of growth for industry and tourism. Scenic Halong Bay and Cat Ba Island draw crowds who sail peacefully through a dreamy seascape of rocky limestone outcrops, while the bustle of Haiphong makes it clear that this area is a vital artery in the country's industry and trade.

Few visitors venture much beyond Halong Bay, but farther north the landscape is filled with dramatic mountain passes, towering waterfalls, lush national parks and ancient royal citadels. Ethnic hill-tribe minority villages, tucked away at the foot of mountains, offer trekking opportunities, while lakeside retreats are an escape from the stifling summer heat. Cao Bang province has some of the country's most beautiful scenery, with sweeping verdant hills and waterfalls. At Mong Cai, the easternmost border gate with China, goods (and people) pass in and out between the two countries, and beach resorts and colourful markets abound. China invaded, occupied and generally interfered with Vietnam for centuries, with the northeast being their principal gateway. Chinese forces last invaded in 1979 as

retaliation for the Vietnamese occupation of Cambodia, and the resulting war devastated parts of the region. These days, border trade is buoyant in some parts of the northeast, but the Vietnamese remain guarded about how much China and its now vast economic power may influence life here.

## THAI NGUYEN PROVINCE
### Museum of the Cultures of Vietnam's Ethnic Groups

Some 80km (50 miles) north from Hanoi on Highway 3, **Thai Nguyen** ⓫

**Main attractions**
MUSEUM OF THE CULTURES OF VIETNAM'S ETHNIC GROUPS
BA BE NATIONAL PARK
BAN GIOC WATERFALL
HAIPHONG CITY
HALONG BAY
CAT BA ISLAND

**LEFT:** Chinese-style junk on Halong Bay.
**RIGHT:** display at the Museum of the Cultures of Vietnam's Ethnic Groups.

*Life-size figurines of ethnic warriors at the Museum of the Cultures of Vietnam's Ethnic Groups.*

**BELOW:** tranquil Ba Be Lake.

is a grimy industrial city and home of Southeast Asia's first steel mill, built with Chinese aid in the 1950s. The sole reason to stop here is to visit the city's excellent **Museum of the Cultures of Vietnam's Ethnic Groups** (Bao Tang Van Hoa Cac Don Thoc Viet Nam; Tue–Sun 8–11am and 2–4.30pm; charge). The museum has a number of displays featuring the culture and artefacts of the country's 54 ethnic groups. Of particular interest are the clothes used by some ethnic groups that are said to be able to identify magical sounds, along with hunting tools and examples of handicraft. Although they can't be recognised by their everyday attire, many of the city's factory workers come from the Muong, Nung, Tay and Tai minority communities.

A Communist Party stronghold, Thai Nguyen claims a landmark in revolutionary history. In 1917, Luong Ngoc Quyen, a nationalist student, was imprisoned and tortured by the French authorities here. This spurred the local garrison to mutiny and to seize the town. Peasants and miners, under the banner of the League for the Restoration of Vietnam, supported the soldiers. French troops from Hanoi suppressed the rebellion within a few days and Luong was killed. Surviving members of the group who fled westwards were ultimately slaughtered in Tam Dao in 1918. During the First Indochina War, Thai Nguyen had considerable strategic importance as a key Viet Minh base for supplies from China in the fight against the French.

## BAC KAN PROVINCE

### Ba Be National Park

North of Thai Nguyen is Bac Kan province, where the top attraction is **Ba Be National Park** ⑫ (Cong Vien Quoc Gia Ba Be; daily daylight hours; charge). The national park covers more than 7,000 hectares (17,300 acres) and is home to high mountains and deep valleys, as well as waterfalls, lakes and caves. More than 300 animal species live here, including bears, macaques, pheasants and, supposedly, tigers. A few small colonies of the indigenous Tonkin snub-nosed monkey, recently thought to be extinct, have also been found here. One reason for the park's fabulous flora is a government initiative that pays villagers not to lop down trees. Such schemes are often little more than an uneasy truce between villagers and nature though, so visit Ba Be while it's still looking good.

### Ba Be Lake

In the southwest of the national park, **Ba Be Lake** (Ho Ba Be), or Three Seas Lake, is the largest natural body of water in the country. Comprising three linked lakes stretching 9km (6 miles) long and over 1km (0.6 miles) in width, it reaches a depth of over 30 metres (98ft) and is surrounded by limestone cliffs and lush forests. The lake's major attractions are boat trips to nearby caves, waterfalls and minority villages where visitors can stay overnight. In July and August, the height of the tourist season for Vietnamese, the normally peaceful lake is crowded with tour boats for hire.

Highlights in the area include **Dau Dang Waterfall** (Thac Dau Dang), which can only be reached by boat, and **Puong Cave** (Hang Puong), which runs completely through a mountain and is traversed by a river, meaning it can be explored by boat. Regular trips go into the cave and guides are available.

For visitors wishing to spend the night, there are two options. The Tay minority who live in the park and surrounding areas have cottages and rooms for rent inside the park boundaries. Outside the park, slightly more expensive lodgings in the form of guesthouses and air-conditioned villas are available.

## CAO BANG PROVINCE

### National Highway 4

Wildly beautiful Cao Bang province to the northeast has only opened its borders to foreigners in the past 15 years. **National Highway 4** runs down to the coast through ravines and mountain passes parallel to the Chinese border. This highway was the site of numerous clashes in the late 1940s between French colonial troops and the Viet Minh guerrillas. Protected by a thin string of French forts that were constantly under attack, French-speaking soldiers dubbed the then-Highway 4 "the Street without Joy".

### Cao Bang City

The provincial capital is also called **Cao Bang ⑬**. Shelled by the Chinese in 1979, the town itself has limited tourist appeal, but it does serve as a launching pad for visits to the nearby mountains and the Chinese border. In the past few years, the town has undergone significant development, with new government buildings, hotels and shops popping up all over. Its market is said to be the biggest in the country, selling all manner of fruit and vegetables and some household items. When it comes to eating, try breakfast favourite *bahn mi*, a satisfying baguette that

is toasted and filled with meat, salads and a spicy sauce. To walk off your food, climb the hill that leads to a war memorial and enjoy the spectacular views at the summit. Cao Bang's relatively high altitude gives it a pleasant climate.

Throngs of hill tribes, including Tay, Hmong, Nung, Dao and Lolo, gather at the morning markets in the surrounding villages. Enquire at your hotel about these markets, and be prepared to make an early start.

## Around Cao Bang

Cao Bang province shares a long border with China. Forests make up the majority of the province and the climate is quite cool, with chilly winters. The culturally diverse province has a population of about 800,000 people, and it covers an area of 8,450 sq km (5,400 sq miles) of high, rocky terrain. Due to the lack of available farmland, Cao Bang's economic value lies in its rivers, which have been harnessed by hydroelectric stations to generate power, as well as its recently

*According to scientists, Ba Be Lake, one of the world's largest freshwater lakes, is at risk of running dry within the next 100 years due to the build-up of alluvium deposited by rivers that empty into it. Based on data collected between 1975 and 2002, experts say that some 700,000 tonnes of alluvium fill the lake each year.*

**BELOW:** lakeside lodge at Ba Be Lake.

*The Nung tribe originated in Thailand.*

**BELOW:** Pac Bo Cave.

upgraded roads that link Vietnam's inland provinces with China.

## Pac Bo Cave

A two-hour drive north of Cao Bang City, along potholed roads, is **Pac Bo Cave** (Hang Pac Bo), yet another stop on the Ho Chi Minh pilgrimage trail. As well as being a fantastically scenic spot, just a kilometre (0.6 miles) from the Chinese border, it also has great historical importance. Here, in 1941, a man then known as Nguyen Ai Quoc crossed into his homeland for the first time in almost 30 years. Later, after taking the name Ho Chi Minh, he lived in the cave near the Nung village of Pac Bo – the proximity of the Chinese border providing a quick escape route if French soldiers discovered his hiding spot. Ho returned to China in 1942 for two years, spending some of that time in prison before heading back south.

In Pac Bo there is a small **museum** (daily 7.30–11.30am and 1.30–4.30pm; charge) with information on the surrounding area as well as artefacts that belong to Ho, his jungle hut, a replica of his simple bed and, of course, tourist trinkets. In true communist style, Ho named the stream flowing in front of the cave as **Lenin Creek** and christened a nearby mountain **Karl Marx Peak**.

## Ban Gioc Waterfall

Vietnam's largest waterfall is Ban Gioc, sometimes known as Ban Doc. Close to the Chinese border and about 80km (50 miles) northeast from Cao Bang, the falls are hugely popular with Vietnamese and Chinese tourists. The 300-metre (984ft) width of the falls stretches from Vietnam and across the border into China and is at its most spectacular during the rainy season from May to September. Ask your hotel to arrange a visit, as the land around Ban Gioc is a military area and access can be restricted. Boat trips can be arranged to within fairly close range of the falls.

## Nguom Ngao Cave and Thang Hen Lake

Some 2km (1.2 miles) away from the waterfall is **Nguom Ngao Cave** (daily daylight hours; charge). The

### Nung Hill Tribes

Along with Lang Son and Bac Kan provinces, Cao Bang province is home to almost all of Vietnam's 900,000-strong Nung community. They farm at both valley floors and high altitudes like the 1,000-metre (3,300ft) -high Dong May Plateau. The Nung are excellent weavers and makers of bamboo furniture and baskets, and are known for their musical traditions. The women wear long indigo dresses and headscarves. Linguistically and culturally, the Nung share much with their neighbours, the Tay, who number over 1.5 million. Their shared language is clearly Thai, but because both the Nung and Tay have lived in Vietnam for over 2,000 years and have been isolated from most other Thai, their cultural practices are closer to the Vietnamese and Chinese. Their practice of ancestral worship, for instance, includes Confucian and Buddhist elements.

3km (2-mile) -long cave network is so extensive that you will need a guide. There are two sections to the cave; the smaller cave is beautifully lit, therefore simple to navigate, but to explore the second, larger cave you need a torch and a guide. The latter cave apparently has a secret entrance near Ban Gioc Waterfall. In the low season, visitors are scarce so tourists that do visit often have the caves to themselves.

Limestone mountains and lush forests surround another of the province's beauty spots, **Thang Hen Lake**. This is one of seven scenic lakes in the area, but access to it can be difficult and tourism infrastructure is scant. Wild orchids grow in profusion throughout the region. It is best visited during the rainy season, when rafts can be taken out onto the lake.

## LANG SON PROVINCE

South of Cao Bang is Lang Son province, which shares a border with China's Guangxi province. High mountains and thick forests cover around 75 percent of the land area and shelter wildlife including leopards, pangolins and monitor lizards as well as a variety of primates and various species of deer.

Tay, Nung, Hmong, Dao, Nghia and Hoa are among the ethnic minorities living in this part of Vietnam. The **Ky Cung River** that flows through the province is unique in that it flows northwards to China – the other rivers in the region all flow south.

### Chi Lang Pass

The narrow gorge at **Chi Lang**, a series of passes connected by tortuous tracks forged between high mountains south of the Chinese-Vietnamese border, is a battleground where the Vietnamese have fought many major battles against Chinese invaders throughout history. In 1076, the Vietnamese defeated 300,000 Chinese Song-dynasty troops here, and in 1427 nearly 100,000 Ming-dynasty troops received the same treatment. The gorge's northern entrance is known as the **Barbarian Invaders Gate** (Quy Quan Mon) and the southern exit is called the **Swearing Path** (Ngo The).

## Lang Son City

National Highway 1A, which originates here and travels the length of the country, intersects with Highway 4 in the provincial capital of **Lang Son ⓮**, 150km (94 miles) northeast of Hanoi. Today, unsightly bombed-out buildings are being replaced by equally unsightly new ones. When 85,000 Chinese troops invaded Vietnam in February 1979, Lang Son was a prime target. Sixteen days later, 80 percent of the buildings were rubble, with both sides counting the costs. After the Chinese troops withdrew, the town was rebuilt and entrepreneurs on both sides of the border re-established trade. Today all manner of commerce – both legal and illegal – flourishes here.

The city is situated on the banks of the Ky Sung River, which is also home to the Ky Lua market. While walking across the bridge to the market, look for a mountain summit that resembles

*Numerous fierce battles have been fought through the ages at Chi Lang Pass between the Vietnamese and Chinese.*

**BELOW LEFT:** Nguom Ngao Cave.

a mother holding a child. Known as Vong Phu Mountain (Waiting for Her Husband), folklore says a woman waited at the spot so long for her husband to return from war that she and her child were turned to stone.

### Tam Thanh/Nhi Thanh caves

Several kilometres west of the city is an area riddled with numerous caves and grottoes, many of which are used for the worship of spirits. The two main examples, **Tam Thanh Cave** and **Nhi Thanh Cave** (both daily daylight hours; charge), are illuminated and contain Buddhist altars. Tam Thanh is 2.5km (1.5 miles) from Lang Son, and Nhi Thanh is about 500 metres/yds beyond Tam Thanh. A short walk from Tam Thanh Cave, up a flight of stone stairs, are the ruins of an ancient city wall that belonged to the 16th-century **Mac Dynasty Citadel**. Within the winding passages is a mass of graffiti and carvings left behind by some of the cave's erstwhile visitors. Some of these scribes were poets who came here to write their works. The grotto at Nhi Thanh has more than a dozen carvings, which provide valuable insights into the history of the area. Inside is an engraved statue of Ngo Thi Si, the leader who found the caves, probably in the 1770s.

### Bac Son Valley

In the mountains just west of Lang Son is a highland valley called **Bac Son** and a market town inhabited by Tay (Tho) and Nung people. Briefly allied with the newly arrived Japanese, in 1940 Tay guerrilla bands attacked isolated French military posts. While the Japanese soon reconciled with the French, the guerrilla insurgency had significant momentum, and in 1940 it staged a general uprising in Bac Son and eight southern provinces – collectively known as the **Bac Son Uprisings**. The French stamped out the rebellion and executed 100 cadres. The repercussions were especially devastating for the Communist Party in the south. However, it meant that Bac Son and the far north became the base from which the communists would rebuild from virtually nothing.

**BELOW:** Buddhist altar, Tam Thanh Cave.

## Museum of Bac Son

An unmarked white building perched on stilts, the **Museum of Bac Son** (Bao Tang Bac Son; tel: 02-581 2631, mobile tel: 091-337 6661; open on request; donation) contains a small collection of artefacts from the Bac Son period (5000–3000 BC), as well as exhibits and displays related to the Bac Son Uprising of 1940, including documents penned by Ho Chi Minh. Unfortunately, no English translation is available.

## Dong Dang

In 1979 **Dong Dang** ⓯ was flattened during a Chinese invasion. Today the town, about 18km (11 miles) northwest of Lang Son City, has made a comeback thanks to cross-border trade. The crossing here is known as the **Friendship Gate** (Huu Nghi Quan), a somewhat ironic moniker given the sporadic exchanges of gunfire between Vietnam and China that happened until as recently as 1992.

For foreigners, this is probably the most popular exit to China from Vietnam, and it is possible to board a train here for the 45-hour (direct) journey to Beijing. Visas, however, must be issued either in Hanoi or Beijing. Once called Porte de Chine, it was through here that Japanese troops entered Vietnam in 1940 before attacking Lang Son.

## QUANG NINH PROVINCE

### Mong Cai

About 180km (112 miles) southeast from Lang Son is **Mong Cai** ⓰, a bustling coastal city on the border with China. The town was destroyed by retreating Chinese troops in 1979 and reconstruction began only when the border was reopened in 1991. This is one of three land-border gates to China open to foreigners, though visas must be issued in either Hanoi or Beijing. Business here is brisk as Vietnamese come here to buy cheap Chinese goods; Chinese flock here to gamble in its two casinos. Despite its dreary appearance, this is one of the wealthiest places in Vietnam, with a significant proportion of households enjoying incomes of up to US$20,000 per year.

## Tra Co Beach

Tra Co is a relatively undeveloped beach resort in the far northeast which hosts a growing number of Chinese and Vietnamese tourists. Located at the starting point of Vietnam's famous "S" shape, the beach stretches for 17km (11 miles). The sand is coarse and uninviting and there is litter but that doesn't deter the thousands of visitors who flock here. Unless you don't mind large crowds, avoid visiting the area from May to August, as this is when both Chinese and Vietnamese tourists arrive in droves. The resort's seafood restaurants serve up seriously fresh food at reasonable prices. A few kilometres offshore is the Con Mang sandbank, the perfect place to see the sunset. About 1km (0.6 miles) north of the beach is the large and impressive **Tra Co**

*Border trade – illicit or otherwise – spells big bucks in Vietnam. In 2007, it was estimated that trade between Vietnam and China across the Mong Cai border hit a whopping US$2.4 billion.*

**BELOW:** ancient ruins, Mac-dynasty Citadel.

**Church**, built in 1880 and restored by the French in 1914.

At the southern end of the beach, **Mui Ngoc** is where you can catch a hydrofoil to **Van Don Island** (Dao Cai Bauwq), which is part of Halong Bay. From here, it is 240km (150 miles) southwest to Haiphong.

## HAIPHONG

Further along the coast, northern Vietnam's most important port, Haiphong, gladly yields to what lies beyond: Halong Bay (Vinh Ha Long), a wondrous cove that was created when an ancient dragon swished its immense tail – or so the story goes.

### Getting to Haiphong City

From Dan Tien Port in Mong Cai, it is possible to take a Russian-made hydrofoil for the 4.5 -hour ride – departing daily at 12.30pm – southwest along the coast to **Haiphong City Ⓐ**. A hydrofoil also travels twice daily from Dan Tien Port direct to Halong Bay's Bai Chay area at 9am and 2pm. Just show up

at the port ahead of time and tell the person in charge where you want to go.

From Hanoi, the two-hour drive on the upgraded 100km (62-mile) road to Haiphong heads deep into the densely populated Red River Valley. In the late 1940s and early 1950s at the height of the guerrilla campaign against the French, this road, **Highway 5**, was lined with garrisons, watchtowers and massive forts surrounded by barbed-wire fences, trenches, bunkers and minefields. Vehicles ventured along this road only in convoys and during daylight hours. At night, the road was officially closed – though not to elusive Viet Minh guerrillas.

Today, trucks, cars, bicycles and motorbikes on their way to and from Haiphong's busy port constantly trammel the well-maintained road. Many of Haiphong's outer industrial areas sprang up after the French left; approaching the city you will see numerous large, ugly industrial plants and factories.

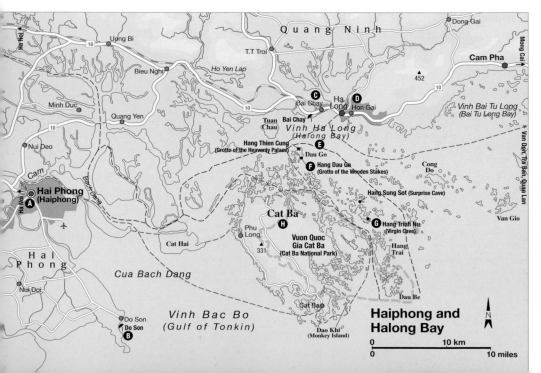

**Haiphong and Halong Bay**

## Haiphong's history

Haiphong, Vietnam's third most populous city and the north's most important port, is located in the northeast of the **Bac Bo Delta**. A small port town at the time of the French conquest in 1873, it quickly grew as the Europeans set about draining swamps and constructing monumental buildings. As 16 rivers cross the city, setting the foundations in the soggy ground was no simple task.

The most famous of Haiphong's waterways is the **Bach Dang River**. The first of the French warships arrived in Haiphong in 1872 seeking access, via the Red River, to China's Yunnan region. Coincidentally, the last of the French expeditionary forces exited the same way in 1955.

More was to come: during the war with the US, Haiphong was sporadically bombed from air and sea between 1965 and 1972. In 1972, US president Richard Nixon ordered the mining of the harbour to stem the influx of Soviet military supplies. However, less than a year later, the US led efforts to remove the mines under the terms of the Paris ceasefire agreement.

Haiphong's troubles didn't end after the Americans left in 1975. For more than a decade, the harbour was the most popular departure point for the "boat people" fleeing economic and political hardship. Persecuted during the 1979 war with China, most members of the city's large ethnic Chinese community joined the exodus, if they hadn't already fled by then.

*During the 1970s and '80s, Haiphong was a significant port of departure for many Vietnamese refugees.*

## Downtown Haiphong

Haiphong doesn't attract many tourists, which means those that do arrive can enjoy its laid-back feel without being hassled by touts. Inside the boundaries of the Old City, wide shady streets, well-tended spots of greenery and a surprising number of colonial-era buildings are still in excellent condition.

The city centre curves around the **Tam Bac River** (Song Tam Bac). In this area are several impressive hotels, administrative buildings and the raspberry-coloured **Haiphong Museum** (Bao Tang Haiphong; Tuc and Thur

**BELOW:** a busy street in Haiphong City.

*Do Son Resort Hotel in Haiphong is Vietnam's first casino and gets very mixed reports. It is aimed primarily at the Chinese crowd, not Westerners, while most Vietnamese aren't allowed through the front door.*

8am–10.30pm, Wed and Sun 7.30am–9.30pm; charge).

At 56 Dinh Tien Hoang is a square overlooked by the yellow, neocolonial **Grand Theatre**, which dates back to 1912. During the first days of the 1946 French attack, actors with antique muskets held off French troops here. In 2003, the government spent US$6.3 million to renovate the interior.

Another sight worth seeing is the **Haiphong Cathedral** (daily 8am–5pm; free), on Hoang Van Thu Street. Built in the late 1800s, the church has an unusual statue of the Virgin Mary.

Haiphong has far more of a café culture than a pumping nightlife, but after dark there are some interesting places to hang out, the best of which is Maxim's Bar, with live music nightly (see page 175).

## Temples and pagodas

The **Du Hang Pagoda** (Chua Du Hang; daily 8am–5pm; charge) in the south of the city was built in 1672 by a wealthy mandarin-turned-monk.

Since then it has been restored many times. It is dedicated to Le Chan, a female warrior who aided the Trung sisters in the uprising against the Chinese in AD 39. The long, low wooden building with its magnificent carvings and swooping roof is reached by passing through a triple-tiered bell tower and an open courtyard. Behind the carved offering table is a baby Buddha protected by nine dragons.

It is easy to confuse – as do many locals and even some *xe om* drivers – Du Hang Pagoda with the nearby **Hang Kenh Communal House** (Dinh Hang Kenh; daily 8am–5pm; charge). The communal house, built in 1856, is just off Nguyen Cong Tru Street and is fronted by a lotus pond. Beyond the spacious courtyard is a similar wooden building to that of the Du Hang structure, with a curling, tiled roof. Within the dim interior, 32 ironwood pillars support the roof, and there is an enormous palanquin decorated with carvings of dragons. The beams of the ceiling are adorned with 308 carved dragons.

**BELOW:** Haiphong's neocolonial Grand Theatre.

## Do Son Beach

About 20km (12.5 miles) southeast of Haiphong, at the tip of a peninsula, is **Do Son Beach** ❸, home of one of a few legal casinos and an area famous for gory buffalo fights. These take place on the ninth day of the eighth lunar month and are very popular with Vietnamese tourists. Aside from this, there is little worth seeing. The hotels and guesthouses are shabby and the beach disappears completely during high tide. While the sand here is better than in Tra Co, the sea has an unappealing rust colour, a result of silt deposited by the Red River.

## HALONG CITY

### Bai Chay

Formally established in 1994, **Halong City** – about 165km (102 miles) from Hanoi and about 3.5 hours by car – comprises two smaller towns, **Bai Chay** and **Hon Gai**, as well as their surrounding districts.

Most hotels, tour agencies and restaurants can be found in **Bai Chay** ❸. Shops specialise in kitschy souvenirs fashioned from pearl, coral and limestone rock. There are dozens of expensive hotels and even more tacky mini-hotels with karaoke bars. On summer weekends, the latter are filled with Vietnamese tourists and their overseas relatives. During the winter months, Bai Chay is nearly deserted.

Bai Chay's saving grace is its fresh and well-prepared seafood. Most popular are the open-air restaurants lining the main avenue, which runs along the waterfront. A short walk along this avenue reveals two swimming beaches that are packed in the summer. Hundreds of tonnes of clean white sand have been dumped on the original muddy beach to make it more picturesque, and, although crowded and noisy, the view over the bay at sunset is spectacular.

### Hon Gai

Across the bay, **Hon Gai** ❹ has a much more bustling feel. The ferry from Bai Chay to Hon Gai only takes a few minutes, but it is also possible to take the 903-metre (2,691ft) **Bai Chay Bridge** which connects both points. Hon Gai, which means "coal mine" in Vietnamese, is known for its open-pit mining in the surrounding hills,

*A gilded statue of Buddha at the Du Hang Pagoda.*

**BELOW:** Bai Chay's beachfront hotels.

**BELOW:** sunset at
Halong Bay.

as well as its coal warehouses. When the French launched their final successful campaign in the north, they seized Hon Gai in 1883 to safeguard the coal mines. Despite its association with the coal industry, Hong Gai has turned into a busy spot with new shops, hotels and houses.

Near the Hon Gai ferry dock is the 106-metre (348ft) -high **Poem Mountain** (Nui Bao Tho), named after King Le Thanh Tong who etched a poem about its beauty into the rock in 1486. At the foot of the mountain, the gaudy **Long Tien Pagoda** (Chua Long Tien; daily 8am–5pm; free), guarded by statues of fierce armoured soldiers, was built in 1941 and is dedicated to the popular General Tran Hung Dao of the Tran dynasty. A bomb-damaged colonial church is just north of Hon Gai and has some of the best views of the area.

## HALONG BAY

Halong Bay's exquisite limestone islands and numerous outcrops are amongst the most outstanding sights in Southeast Asia. Any trip to

northern Vietnam must include a visit to **Halong Bay** (Vinh Ha Long).

The bay's tranquil beauty encompasses some 1,500 sq km (579 sq miles) of indigo sea and is dotted with more than 3,000 limestone islands and rocky outcrops, or karsts, most of them uninhabited. Weirdly shaped rock sculptures jut dramatically from the sea, and numerous grottoes create an enchanted, timeless and almost mystical world. The soaring sails of Chinese-style junk boats and sampans gliding on the bay add to the beauty of the scene. Not surprisingly, the bay has been declared a Unesco World Heritage Site – twice, in fact: in 1994 for its natural scenic beauty, and then again in 2000 for its biological diversity. Between March and April, visibility can be poor.

## Legend of the dragon

Halong means "dragon descending", and its name is steeped in local legend. The story goes that a heavenly celestial dragon and her offspring were ordered by the Jade Emperor to halt an invasion from the sea. To combat this, the dragons spewed out bits of jade and jewels that turned into wondrous islands and karst formations on contact with the water, thereby scuppering enemy ships.

Other versions of the legend claim the bay was created when the dragon flung herself into the water. In the process, her swishing tail gorged deep valleys and crevices in the mainland, which were subsequently filled by the sea. The dragon was so pleased with her creations that she settled among them and is said to now live under the bay. Some people claim to have seen this Vietnamese equivalent of the Loch Ness Monster, a black creature resembling a snake about 30 metres (98ft) in length. Called a *Tarasque* by former French residents of the area, enterprising boat owners have made a career out of taking tourists in search of the beast.

The more practical explanation for the karst outcrops says that they were formed by a giant limestone sea bed that eroded over the centuries until only their pinnacles were left behind. Many of these limestone piles have strange and otherworldly shapes, some of which are known to local fishermen by fanciful nicknames such as the Dog, Turtle and Toad, derived from the rocks' uncanny resemblance to the shape of certain animals. Over time, rain and the elements created caves within some of these limestone rocks, several of which can be visited.

## Exploring the bay

A rushed one-day tour from Hanoi is a far from ideal way to experience this wonderful place; by the time you get to Halong Bay and board your boat, almost half the day is gone. Those with time and specific sites in mind could spend a few days cruising around the bay. Tickets for the many tour boats are available at the pier in Bai Chay, though a better option is to book a package from a Hanoi-based tour operator *(see panel, opposite, and also page* 370). As some of the caves are wet (and dark), a sturdy pair of shoes and a flashlight are handy items to have.

Another alternative is to use Cat Ba Island, the bay's largest island and a national park, as a base from which to explore. Not only is it cleaner and less crowded than some other parts of the bay, it is also closer to many of the most dramatic grottoes.

*Explore Halong's caves, created by the gradual erosion of limestone formations.*

**BELOW:** touring Halong Bay.

## Halong's caves

*A new cave discovered at Halong Bay is being touted as one of the best in the area. Named Golden Fruit Cave and in Cat Hai district, it is 30 metres (98ft) wide and 100 metres (328ft) deep and is divided into two parts, both filled with stalactites and stalagmites.*

The most spectacular cave at Halong Bay is on the island closest to Bai Chay, the vast **Grotto of the Wooden Stakes** **⑤** (Hang Dau Go). There are three chambers filled with an assortment of stalactites and stalagmites that resemble beasts, birds and human forms. It was here that General Tran Hung Dao stored hundreds of wooden stakes that were used to destroy the ships of Kublai Khan's invading Mongol hordes in 1288. It was christened the Grotte des Merveilles (Cave of Wonders) by the first French tourists to visit in the late 19th century. Unfortunately, modern-day tourists have left their mark in the form of graffiti and piles of litter.

Also worth seeing on the same island is the **Grotto of the Heavenly Palace** (Hang Thien Cung), which is adorned with stalagmites, stalactites and limestone growths that look like cauliflower heads.

On another nearby island, folklore claims that the **Virgin Cave** **⑥** (Hang Trinh Nu) was named after a young girl whose parents were poor and could not afford a boat. They had to rent one from a rich man, but when they could

not pay what they owed him, the rich man demanded their beautiful daughter in lieu of the debt, and so forced her to marry him. The poor girl refused all his advances. He had her beaten but she still refused to submit to him. He finally exiled her to a grotto, where she starved to death and was subsequently immortalised in stone by a rock that resembled her figure, which magically emerged from her burial site.

**Tunnel Cave** (Hang Hanh) extends underground for 2km (1.2 miles) and features some amazing stalactites. Getting there is tricky, however, as you need to arrive at half tide. **Surprise Cave** (Hang Sung Sot) is also very popular, with three large chambers filled with strange rock formations, including one that resembles a giant phallus.

Several other caves are open to the public. Boats usually visit a number of caves en route, admission to which is covered by the flat entrance fee included in the price of your boat tour. The caves that boats visit depend on the weather, tide levels and the number of other vessels out on the water on that day.

**BELOW:** Surprise Cave.

Some boats stop off at **Tuan Chau Island** (Dau Tuan Chau), 5km (3 miles) west of Bai Chay. The island once served as an exclusive retreat for the colonials. Today, its decaying villas have been replaced with resorts catering to wealthy Vietnamese. Ho Chi Minh used to spend his summers here and his house, of course, has been preserved as a memorial.

## Cat Ba Island

The **Cat Ba Archipelago** consists of 366 islets and islands that cover 200 sq km (77 sq miles) of sea and are peppered with beautiful beaches and grottoes. Just 20km (12 miles) from Haiphong, with the Gulf of Tonkin to the west and Halong Bay to the east, the main **Cat Ba Island** ❶ covers about 354 sq km (137 sq miles), with a stunning landscape of lush forested hills, coastal mangroves and freshwater swamps, as well as lakes, waterfalls and reefs.

These days the island's permanent population is just over 20,000, less than half the number some 20 years ago. With its remote harbours, Cat Ba's fishing fleet was ideally situated to serve the needs of fleeing "boat people"

in the late 1970s. When Vietnam began persecuting its Chinese minority shortly before its war with China in 1979, Cat Ba islanders, most of whom were ethnic Chinese, joined the exodus to safer lands. As a consequence, many of those left behind today have relatives in the US, Canada and Australia.

Gifts and loans from overseas relatives helped to build the narrow mini-hotels, shops and restaurants in the clunky cement village of **Cat Ba**. Overlooking the Gulf of Tonkin, it is the island's main settlement and port. Scattered along the coast are a number of floating fishing villages, though these are best visited by boat. Each one tends to have a small number of families who increasingly are starting to welcome tourists to help boost their meagre income.

## Cat Ba National Park

Half of the island and 52 sq km (20 sq miles) of the surrounding inland waters are part of the **Cat Ba National Park** (Vuon Quoc Gia Cat Ba; tel: 031-368 8686; park office daily 7–11.30am and noon–5.30pm; charge). The thickly forested island has a rich diversity of

**BELOW LEFT:** Cruise in style on scenic Halong Bay from the comfort of a Chinese-style junk.

## Halong Bay Sailing Options

Almost all Hanoi tour operators arrange boat trips to Halong Bay lasting one to four days. These include transportation, meals and accommodation. Valiant efforts have been made by the Halong authorities to regulate the local boats and the haphazard ticketing system, but it's still best to book with a well-known, reputable agent. For those with limited time, one-day tours from Hanoi are available, but these are usually rushed affairs; Halong should be savoured at a more languid pace. Trips that last several days allow travellers to explore the lagoons, virgin beaches and caves dotted around this spectacular area in greater detail. Hopping in a kayak to paddle out to some spots is the preferred form of transport here.

Most tour operators use standard engine-powered wooden boats with dormitory-style cabins. Luxury junks, with top-notch dining, large sundecks and en-suite cabins, are also available. **Handspan** (tel: 04-3926 2828; www.handspan.com) operates the most economical trips aboard its 18-cabin *Aloha Junk*. **Buffalo Tours** (tel: 04-3828 0702; www.buffalotours.com) operates the mid-priced *Jewel of the Bay* luxury junk with five cabins, and a three-day trip to Bai Tu Long Bay on one-, two- or four-cabin junks. **Emeraude Classic Cruises** (tel:04-3935 1888; www.emeraude-cruises.com) runs the most expensive cruises on its 36-cabin luxury replica paddle steamer.

*A vista of Halong Bay from a cave on Cat Ba Island.*

**BELOW:** kayaking at Cat Ba Island.

flora and fauna, including 69 species of bird – including the hornbill – numerous reptiles and 32 species of mammals, such as wild cats, boar, porcupines, various monkeys and deer. However, you are unlikely to see anything other than birds and insects – and possibly primates – whilst hiking the park's many paths. Poaching is still a problem on Cat Ba, despite educational programmes, increased surveillance by park rangers and greater affluence brought about by tourism. The golden-headed langur, for example, is unique to Cat Ba Island and is in danger of extinction as there are only around 65 left. Human remains and stone tools from the Neolithic era have been discovered in some of the island's caves.

Despite its considerable size, the park boasts only a handful of good beaches, and all of these are within easy access of Cat Ba village; they are inventively named Cat Co 1, 2 and 3. Rocky cliffs line most of the island, with a few sandy beaches tucked in between the coves. Cat Ba can be easily explored by motorbike along its limited network of roads. There are

several trails that lead deep into the forest; the easiest hike extends just 2.5km (1.5 miles). As long as it's not rainy (and muddy) the walk isn't difficult, but it's a good idea to buy a trail map from the park office. The forest path is clearly marked with numbered signs, and these correspond to the informative descriptions on the map. Alternatively, hire a local guide at the park office who will be more adept at spotting forest life. Trekking trips can also be arranged with Cat Ba's hotels. Camping is allowed in the park (check with the park office), but you'll need to bring or rent your own gear. Rock climbing is perhaps the ultimate activity here, given the views from their peaks. Several companies, such as Slo Pony (www.slopony.com), offer day trips that include a range of routes up, offering various degrees of difficulty. Top-rope systems are generally used to make things as safe as possible.

Improved infrastructure, including a bridge, due for completion in 2012, could mean that things will get a lot busier here.

## Bai Tu Long

While nearly all visitors to this area stick to Halong Bay, Bai Tu Long is every bit as jaw-droppingly gorgeous. To some, this national park may hold even more appeal as it has all the beauty but far fewer visitors than Halong Bay; the downside of this is that are fewer tourist facilities. Bai Tu Long, which sits northeast of Halong Bay, was created when a limestone plateau sank, revealing its numerous islands. Van Don island, the largest and busiest of these, has the greatest number of amenities, which isn't saying much. A bridge connects the island to the mainland. Boats leave from Van Don for another substantial isle, Tra Ban, which has dense jungle and incredible views. Or there is Quan Lan, an island with a small community, a handful of guesthouses and plenty of unexplored land. To reach Bai Tu Long it's possible to take a five-hour boat ride from Halong Bay or hop on a hydrofoil, which makes the same trip in an hour. Another option is to go by land to Cai Rong and catch a boat from there.

# RESTAURANTS

Prices for a three-course
dinner per person:
**$** = under US$5
**$$** = US$5–10
**$$$** = US$10–20
**$$$$** = over US$20

It's not surprising that
northeast Vietnam offers up
great seafood, given its
proximity to the South
China Sea. What's amazing
is just how good it is. In
Haiphong and Halong City,
check out the street stalls
and crack open some
freshly caught crabs and
prawns. Deeper in the interior, wild mushrooms, roots
and pungent spices aug-
ment the local Vietnamese
and Chinese dishes. In
these areas, however, don't
expect anything more than
basic (but decent)
restaurants.

Thai Nguyen

**Mot Thoang Huong Tram
Restaurant**
19 Hoang Van Thu St, Thai
Nguyen City, Thai Nguyen
province. Open: daily B, L & D. **$**
Located directly across from
the Thang Long Hotel, this
small café specialises in
local (and strong)
Vietnamese coffee. It also
serves a reasonable variety
of Western and Vietnamese
dishes, with surprisingly
good fish and chips for this
neck of the woods.

**Cao Bang**

**Huong Sen Restaurant**
On the banks of the Bang Giang
River near the market, Cao Bang
City, Cao Bang province. Open:
daily B, L & D. **$$**
This small restaurant
does decent rice and
noodle dishes, and a
few of the servers speak
a word or two of English
– enough to understand
what you want to eat.
Try the roasted duck if
they have it that day.

**Lang Son**

**Cua Hang An Uong**
Corner of Le Loi St and the
market, Lang Son City, Lang Son
province. Open: daily L & D. **$**
Try the cheap but delicious
*lau* (hot po meal) and revel
in the English clubhouse
decor.

**Mong Cai**

**Hoai Len Restaurant**
14 Van Don St, Mong Cai City,
Quang Ninh province. Open:
daily L & D. **$**
In the evening the streets
near the market transform
into open-air restaurants,
and this is the best of them.
Ask for help and the genial
owner will usher you down
the alley to help choose your
ingredients.

**Haiphong**

*Thai*
**BKK**
22 Minh Khai St, Haiphong. Tel:
031-382 1018. Open: daily L &
D. **$$–$$$**
Set in a beautifully restored
building in the heart of
Haiphong, BKK serves up
excellent, authentic Thai
dishes. Great service, with
English spoken. Highly
recommended.

*Vegetarian*
**Au Lac Vegetarian
Restaurant**
276 Cat Dai St, Haiphong. Tel:
031-383 3781. Open: daily B, L
& D. **$**
Open year-round, this res-
taurant is most popular on
the first and fifteenth days
of the lunar month when
tradition dictates that
Buddhists eat vegetarian
meals.

*Vietnamese & Western*
**Maxim's Restaurant and
Bar**
51B Dien Bien Phu St, Haiphong.
Tel: 031-383 3781. Open: daily
B, L & D. **$$$**
A pleasant coffee shop-type

restaurant that serves passable Western standards
along with cheaper
Vietnamese dishes. The
breakfast set meals are particularly good.

**Halong Bay**

*Vietnamese*
**Bien Mo Floating
Restaurant**
35 Ben Tau St, Bay Chay, Halong
City. Tel: 03-382 8951. Open:
daily L & D. **$$$**
Climb aboard this floating
restaurant and dig into
some of Halong Bay's best
seafood dishes.
Specialities here include
succulent oysters, crabs,
lobster and prawns – all
cooked local-style.
Extremely popular, it can be
crowded and noisy during
dinner hours.

**Co Ngu**
Halong Rd, Bai Chay, Halong
City. Tel: 03-351 1363. Open:
daily L & D. **$$**
The sea views to the front
and great mountain views to
the rear are almost enough
of a selling point; the fact
that the seafood is fresh
and fabulous is a great
bonus.

*International*
**Asia Restaurant**
24 Vuon Dao, Bay Chay, Halong
City. Tel: 03-384 6927. Open:
daily B, L & D. **$$**
A reliable place for
Vietnamese standards plus a
few Western dishes.

*Western*
**Emeraude Café**
Royal Park Resort, Bay Chay,
Halong City. Tel: 03-384 9266.
Open: daily B, L & D. **$$$**
Part of the reception
office of Emeraude
Cruises, the café here
mainly caters to guests
embarking on its luxury
cruisers, but it's open to
other guests as well.
There is a good range of

tasty Western standards,
as well as a reasonable
wine list.

**Cat Ba Island**

*Vietnamese*
**Bamboo Forest (Truc Lam)
Restaurant**
Group 19, Zone 4, Cat Ba Town,
Cat Ba Island. Open: daily B, L &
D. **$$**
Bamboo Forest serves a
good variety of the area's
justifiably famous seafood,
as well as many vegetarian
options. The owner, Mr Dau,
is very friendly and has a
wealth of information on the
area.

**Duc Tuan**
1/4 St, Group 17, 4th, Zone, Cat
Ba Town, Cat Ba Island. Tel:
09-8897 1685. Open: daily L &
D. **$$$**
Part of a large, slightly dated
hotel, this restaurant has an
interesting menu consisting
of local food with a few
twists. The spring rolls and
fish dishes are particularly
good.

**Hoang Y**
D1-4, Cat Ba Town, Cat Ba
Island. Tel: 09-0403 7902. Open:
daily L & D. **$$$**
A big menu and equally big
portions ensure this place is
nearly always busy. There
are plenty of options for
every preference, but it's the
seafood that steals the
show.

*International*
**Green Mango**
Group 19, Block 4, 1-4 St, Cat
Ba Town, Cat Ba Island. Tel:
03-188 7151. Open: daily B, L &
D. **$$$**
A hip restaurant and bar
overlooking Cat Ba
Harbour. Serves an eclec-
tic mix of Vietnamese,
Asian and Western cui-
sines, along with some
creative fusion dishes.
Relax in comfortable yet
classy surroundings and
chill.

# THE TONKIN COAST

One of the poorest parts of Vietnam's north central region, the Tonkin Coast has several priceless natural wonders and some good beaches

**H**eading south out of Hanoi, **National Highway 1A** passes through varied landscapes as it enters an area known to the French as the Tonkin Coast. Comprising several provinces that contain just about every terrain imaginable, the vistas include mountains, limestone hills, low-lying plains, inland waterways, rice paddies and long stretches of sand. Rich in culture and revolutionary history, the area is home to ancient citadels and temples and was the birthplace of Ho Chi Minh himself. One of the poorest parts of the country, the people here are among the friendliest anywhere in Vietnam. The Tonkin Coast's Sam Son Beach, popular among Vietnamese tourists, is rarely visited by foreigners.

National Highway 1A stretches for 2,300km (1,430 miles) along the length of the entire country, from the Huu Nghi Quan border gate to China in Lang Son province all the way to Nam Cam township in southern Ca Mau province. Recent development projects have drastically improved the condition of the roads – previously in poor repair – and the **Ho Chi Minh Highway** (Duong Ho Chi Min) has helped take the pressure off the coastal road.

On the arterial roads, however, traffic still moves at snail's pace as buffalo and bicycles vie for space. It doesn't

help that farm produce is often placed to dry on the dusty edges of the road – everything from straw, rice and corn to chilli peppers, peanuts and tea.

## NAM DINH PROVINCE

### Nam Dinh City

The city of **Nam Dinh** ⑰, on Highway 21 about 90km (56 miles) south of Hanoi, is the capital of Nam Dinh province. Nam Dinh City and the surrounding areas are a Catholic stronghold, although many former residents

**Main attractions**
GOLDEN CITY RUINS
KEO PAGODA
HOA LU
TAM COC
CUC PHUONG NATIONAL PARK
PHAT DIEM CATHEDRAL

**LEFT AND RIGHT:** flooded rice fields framed against limestone hills in Ninh Binh province.

*Rural scene in Thai Binh province*

**BELOW:** a trader sells her wares on a rowing boat in Thai Binh.

were among the 500,000 Vietnamese who fled south after the communist takeover in 1954. Portuguese, Spanish and French missionaries converted their ancestors to Catholicism in the 16th and 17th centuries, long before the French colonial conquest.

Nam Dinh is a large industrial city that lies on the bank of the **Nam Dinh River** (Song Nam Dinh) and is famous for its textiles. In 1899, the French built the **Nam Dinh Textile Mill**, which still operates today. In the early 19th century, a large citadel surrounded Nam Dinh. The French dismantled it after occupying the area in 1882, but a single lookout tower survives. Head to the old riverside, where artisans and merchants still congregate in an area similar to Hanoi's Old Quarter.

### Tran-dynasty ruins

Just 3km (2 miles) north of Nam Dinh is the village of **Tuc Mac** and the ancient Tran-dynasty ruins of the **Golden City** (Thang Vang). These ruins are all that remain of the palaces built by the Tran kings who defeated the Mongol Yuan-dynasty invaders

from China three times in the 13th century. Among the ruins are the **Thien Truong Temple** (Den Thien Truong; daily 8am–5pm; free), built in 1238 and dedicated to the 14 Tran kings, and the beautiful **Pho Minh Pagoda** (Chua Pho Minh; daily 8am–5pm; free), built in 1305. The pagoda contains an impressive 13-storey tower and an amazing statue of King Tran Nhan Tong lying on his side, about to enter nirvana.

### THAI BINH PROVINCE

To the east of Nam Dinh, the tiny Thai Binh province has one of the highest population densities in the country, with approximately 1,200 people per square kilometre. Salt flats cover extensive areas on the coastal shores. Under the French, all salt had to be produced under the aegis of the government's salt monopoly. With a monopoly also on opium sales, the government reaped great revenues, but at tremendous cost to peasants and fishermen who were crippled (and sometimes inspired to revolt) by prices that continued to rise regardless of demand.

### Sons of Thai Binh

Thai Binh province, known best for its salt flats and tropical storms, is also the birthplace of several influential people, including the first Vietnamese man to travel into space (in 1980), Pham Tuan. Also from Thai Binh was Ta Quoc Luat, the soldier who captured French commander Christian de Castries and who planted the victory flag in the battle of Dien Bien Phu. Some Thai Binh natives are among the richest in Vietnam, including Vu Quang Hoi, owner of the Bitexco Financial Tower in Ho Chi Minh City, and Vu Van Tien, founder of AB Bank. Quach Tuan Ngoc, as a professor of computer science at the Hanoi University of Technology, authored the first successfully commercial domestic software for processing and translating Vietnamese text, the *Bach Khoa Editor*.

Private production of salt during this time was severely punished.

## Keo Pagoda

East of Nam Dinh on the road to Haiphong is the site of 11th-century **Keo Pagoda** ⑱ (Chua Keo; daily 8am–5pm; free). Destroyed by a flood in 1611, the pagoda has undergone significant reconstruction but still retains the spirit of the original design. Considered one of the finer examples of traditional Vietnamese architecture, it is dedicated to the Buddha, his disciples, and an 11th-century monk named Minh Khong who is said to have cured King Ly Thanh Ton of leprosy. Look out for the many traditional rituals and diverse forms of entertainment that are performed at the pagoda – some of them centuries old – particularly during the Tet holidays.

## NINH BINH PROVINCE

## Ninh Binh City

At the intersection of National Highway 1A and Highway 10, about 30km (20 miles) from Nam Dinh and 91km (57 miles) south of Hanoi, the dusty city of **Ninh Binh** ⑲ in the eponymous province has few redeeming features. However, as it's only two hours from Hanoi, the city is a good base for explorations of the far more interesting ancient capital of **Hoa Lu**, the scenic beauty of **Tam Coc** and several other interesting sights.

Ninh Binh City is dusty mainly because of a nearby rock quarry. Most of the city's inhabitants are employed by the quarry, either carting around large rocks and transporting them by truck or working in the tourism industry. With an increasing number of people visiting the city on their way to nearby tourist sites, new mini-hotels and restaurant stalls are appearing all over town.

Across the river rises a large, bare crag. In the French colonial days, a fort was perched on top. In 1951 the Viet Minh temporarily overran the French positions in and around Ninh Binh. Eighty French soldiers holed up in the local Catholic Church, of whom only 19 survived. In the eastern part of town, in front of the train

*No nails were used in the 11th-century construction of Keo Pagoda.*

**BELOW:** Buddha statue at Keo Pagoda.

station, stands the Catholic Ninh Binh Cathedral with its decidedly Asian spire; the eave and window treatments echo the curved lines of a temple.

## Hoa Lu

Only 13km (8 miles) northwest of Ninh Binh is **Hoa Lu ⑳**, site of the 10th-century capital of the Vietnamese kingdom known as Dai Co Viet, or Great Viet Land. This was a rather small feudal kingdom, covering an area of 300 hectares (741 acres), and was ruled by the Dinh and then the Le dynasty from AD 968–1010. A citadel that bordered the Hoang Long River (Song Hoan Long) and stretched along the Yen Ngua limestone hills originally enclosed the kingdom. The enemy at the time were the Chinese, who had been expelled in 939.

Though much of the capital has long since been destroyed, there remain vestiges of the earthen citadels, palaces, shrines and temples, albeit in a state only archaeologists could appreciate. What has survived are two 17th-century temples modelled on 11th-century originals, which were built after the capital was transferred from Hoa Lu to Thang Long (now Hanoi) in 1010.

## Dinh Tien Hoang Temple

The **Dinh Tien Hoang Temple** (Den Dinh Tien Hoang; daily 8am–5pm; free) was originally built in the 11th century and was reconstructed in 1696. Dedicated to the founder of the Dinh dynasty, Dinh Tien Hoang, who reigned in the late 10th century, the temple now faces east, although the original faced north. It is entered by passing through two brick arches, the so-called **Outer Triumphant Arch** and the **Inner Triumphant Arch**. The 17th-century **Dragon Bed**, in an area once used for sacrifices, lies in the centre of the courtyard in front of the main building. It was carved out of a single rock. Lightly carved on the surface is a strange-looking dragon floating in a mass of clouds: it has a long beard, the head and ears of a buffalo, paws resembling human hands, and fish-like scaly skin. Surrounding it are carvings of a carp, shrimp and mice. Gifts and food

**BELOW:** picturesque mountain ranges and valleys frame Dinh Tien Hoang Temple in Ho Loa.

offerings are placed on the slab during festivals.

Crude statues of mythical animals – part-dog, part-lion – guard the doorway of the small temple. A huge drum in the forecourt was used by peasants to get the attention of mandarins. Inside the temple, King Dinh Tien Hoang, also known as Dinh Bo Linh, is worshipped at a central altar. On one of the temple pillars is written "Dai Co Viet", the name Dinh Tien Hoang gave Vietnam. Behind the altar, past some heavy carved beams, is a windowless back room with a 19th-century wooden statue of a paunchy Dinh Tien Hoang, framed by statues of his three sons. While Dinh Quoc Lien was the eldest, he was not chosen as heir apparent, and as a result, he masterminded the assassination of the anointed heir, his infant brother Dinh Hang Lan, in 979. The next year, a palace official assassinated both the king and Dinh Quoc Lien. The six-year-old youngest son (whose statue does not appear childlike at all), Dinh Toan, became king but only ruled for six months. Le Hoan, seizing the opportunity, eliminated him and founded the 29-year-long Le, or "Earlier Le", dynasty and went on to repel invasions by the Chinese.

## Le Hoan Temple

The second temple, called **Le Hoan** (Den Le Hoan; daily 8am–5pm; free), is a miniature of the Dinh Tien Hoang temple and is dedicated to Le Hoan (who later assumed the title King Le Dai Hanh). In addition to fending off the Chinese, Le Hoan is known for launching a military expedition against the Champa kingdom in 982, sacking the citadel in present-day Quang Nam province. The 17th-century carvings around the entrance door and on the roof beams portray dragons holding a pearl in their mouths, surrounded by clouds. The temple has a series of three chambers: the **Hall of Worship**, **Hall of Heavenly Fragrance** and **Inner Shrine**. In this last, dimly lit

back room are statues of Le Hoan, his queen Duong Van Nga (supposedly the widow of Dinh Tien Hoang) and his two sons.

## Nhat Tru Pagoda

Not far from Dinh Tien Hoang Temple is **Nhat Tru Pagoda** (Chua Nhat Tru; daily 8am–5pm; free), a lively and active place of worship. In front of the entrance stands a stone column engraved with Buddhist sutras dating from 988.

Adjacent to Dinh Tien Hoang Temple is the steep **Ma Yen Hill** (Nui Ma Yen). Those who are willing to climb the 260-plus stone steps (and ignore aggressive hawkers flogging souvenirs) will be rewarded with a panoramic view of the ancient kingdom as well as the site of **Dinh Tien Hoang's tomb**.

## Tam Coc

The enchanting scenery of **Tam Coc** (Three Caves) is known as "Halong Bay on Rice Paddies" owing to the jagged limestone outcrops that jut out dramatically from the flooded

*Devotees burn joss sticks and present offerings in remembrance of Dinh Tien Hoang atop Ma Yen Hill.*

**BELOW:** Dinh Tien Hoang Temple.

**TIP**

Use plenty of sunscreen and wear a hat on the boat trip up the scenic Ngo Dong River in Tam Coc. The open boats offer no protection from the fierce sun.

rice paddies. Usually combined with a visit to Hoa Lu on day trips from Hanoi, Tam Coc can also be accessed from the Van Lam Wharf, 9km (6 miles) southwest of Ninh Binh City. If not travelling with a tour group, this is where travellers can hire a small, flat-bottomed boat manned by two people (a rower and poler, both usually women) for the stunning journey – which was immortalised in the 1992 film *Indochine* – along the atmospheric **Ngo Dong River** (Song Ngo Dong).

In the initial segment of the two- to three-hour journey, the narrow and lazy river blends into the adjacent flooded rice fields. In the dry season, the river meanders alongside the rice fields, but during the height of the rainy season the river can sometimes merge with the adjacent paddy fields. Soon, the waterway meanders through three large tunnel caves (*tam coc*) that have bored through the limestone hills over the centuries. The last cave is so low passengers need to duck down. The largest cave has stalactites and stalagmites. In between are shallow, glass-smooth lagoons encircled by verdant

limestone cliffs. Birdwatchers might catch sight of herons and kingfishers. Note how the oarsmen and women row the boat with their feet.

After numerous complaints of aggressive vendors and pushy boat operators, the tourist police have issued strict rules that have minimised such hassle. The vendors will still push you to buy embroidery, drinks and snacks, but at least they wait until the boat has turned around and is on the way back to the wharf.

Past the wharf and the stalls of T-shirt sellers is **Van Lam**, a village where shirts and table linen are embroidered. This is where most of the similar items sold in Hanoi's Old Quarter originate. At least one member of every family is engaged in the art of embroidery, and tourists are welcome to browse. Prices here are cheaper than in Hanoi.

## Bich Dong Pagoda

About 2km (1.2 miles) southwest of the boat wharf is the Jade Grotto, better known as **Bich Dong Pagoda** (Chua Bich Dong; daily 8am–5pm;

**BELOW:** picturesque boat ride along the Ngo Dong River, Tam Coc.

charge). At the pagoda entrance, stone steps hewn into a limestone rock dotted with shrines lead up to a cave entrance where three Buddhas sit atop lotus thrones. Walk through here and climb up the steps cut into the cliff face, where there are more Buddhist shrines and a terrace with stunning valley views. The complex dates back to the early 15th century, when King Le Thai To was in power.

## Trang An Grotto Complex

The **Trang An Grotto Eco-Tourism Complex** (tel: 03-062 0334; daily 8am–6pm; charge) comprises a series of caves with lyrical names such as Three Drops (Ba Giot), Holy Land (Dia Linh) and Cloud (May), beautiful limestone mountains and a vast network of underground rivers. There is also the 200-metre (650ft) **Bai Dinh Pagoda Mountain**, which is being developed as a pilgrimage site to rival the Perfume Pagoda near Hanoi.

Trang An is located 4km (2.5 miles) southwest of Hoa Lu. Locals here boast that the area is 10 times more beautiful than Tam Coc and will no doubt be the biggest attraction when it opens. However, considering that the government is spending almost US$60 million developing the site, don't come expecting a quiet, back-to-nature type of environment.

## Kenh Ga fishing village

Just 21km (13 miles) northwest from Ninh Binh, **Kenh Ga** was once a charming little fishing village, with most of its residents living on houseboats and earning a living from fishing. In the past five years, however, many of the wealthier villagers have built concrete homes on the land, and only the poorest remain on the water. Kenh Ga, or Chicken Canal, supposedly got its name from the wild chickens that used to live in the area, and can be reached by boat and motorbike.

Kenh Ga residents' pride and joy is their rustic **Catholic Church**, with its ancient wooden shutters on the outside, and heavy wooden beams and pillars with interesting carvings within.

A 15-minute boat ride from the Dong Chua Port in Kenh Ga are the **Kenh Ga Hot Springs** (tel: 03-083

*Kenh Ga is a sleepy backwater village.*

**BELOW:** the Bich Dong Pagoda is set in limestone caves.

*The critically endangered grey-shanked Douc langur species can only be found at Cuc Phuong's Endangered Primate Rescue Center.*

**BELOW:** educational tour at Cuc Phong's Endangered Primate Rescue Center.

1006; daily 8am–6pm; charge), a large tourist development geared towards wealthy Vietnamese. Chaotic and noisy, the mammoth complex includes a 20-room hotel, a stilt house, a 150-seater restaurant and a series of hot spring and whirlpool tubs.

## Cuc Phuong National Park

Continuing west 24km (15 miles) along on the same road that runs by the Kenh Ga pier, you will arrive at the entrance to the 25,000-hectare (61,000-acre) **Cuc Phuong National Park** ㉑ (Cong Vien Quoc Gia Cuc Phuong; tel: 03-084 8006; www.cucphuong-tourism.com; daily daylight hours; charge). If visitors can only visit one national park in northern Vietnam, this should be the one.

Declared open by Ho Chi Minh himself in 1962, the biodiversity here is compelling. The park was established to shelter 250 bird and 64 mammal species, including tigers, leopards, bats, boars, civet cats and flying squirrels, as well as the endangered Delacour langur. However, given the propensity for poaching and Vietnam's lax

environment protection laws, there is little likelihood of most visitors coming across any animal (and least of all a dangerous one). Unlike staff at other parks in Vietnam, however, the park wardens at Cuc Phuong seem to have a genuine interest in wildlife and environmental protection.

Even without glimpsing the larger wildlife, visitors can get a sense of the great diversity of insects and flora within the park. Some of the trees (*Parashorea stellata* and *Terminalia myriocarpa*) reach over 50 metres (165ft) in height, and are estimated to be over 1,000 years old, and close to 500 medicinal plants and herbs, of both native and foreign origin, have been discovered in the park. Some of Cuc Phuong's many caves and grottoes are also easily accessible within two mountain ranges that enclose a valley with a microclimate quite different from that of the surrounding region. Three tombs, excavated in one of the grottoes in 1966, contained shells, animal teeth, rudimentary stone tools and prehistoric human remains.

As Cuc Phuong is only 45km (30 miles) from Ninh Binh (and 140km/87 miles from Hanoi), it can be easily visited on a day trip. It will be a rushed day trip, however, and visitors will not have time to explore the various hiking trails, including the popular 7km (4-mile) trail that starts at the park centre. Visitors can go on longer hikes in the national reserve but guides are mandatory. You can stay either at the bungalows run by the park authorities or at one of the Muong villages within the park.

## Endangered Primate Rescue Center

A highlight of any visit to Cuc Phuong is the **Endangered Primate Rescue Center** (tel: 03-084 8002; www.primatecenter.org; daily 9–11.30am and 1.30–4pm; charge), located 500 metres/yds in front of the park reception office. Run by a team of German and Vietnamese biologists, the goal of the centre is to protect, study and breed the park's rare primates.

Founded in 1993, the centre is home to more than 140 primates, including six langur species found nowhere else in the world – the endangered grey-shanked Douc langur, the Delacour langur, the Cat Ba langur, the Hatinh langur, the black langur and the Laos langur. The work of the centre is funded primarily by donors, so visitors can help out by buying postcards and souvenirs, or by participating in their "Adopt-a-Monkey" programme.

## Phat Diem Cathedral

The towering stone edifice called **Phat Diem Cathedral** (Mass held Mon–Sat 5am and 5pm, Sun 5am, 9.30am and 5pm) is an architectural wonder that is little known outside of Vietnam. It is located in the town of **Phat Diem** ㉒ (also known as **Kim Son**), about 25km (16 miles) southeast of Ninh Binh. While the road is a bit bumpy, traffic is thin, making it well suited for motorbikes or bicycles. It is best to visit the church during Mass times as the main buildings are locked for most of the day – although if this is the case, ask the staff at the tour kiosk just outside the main entrance to open up the buildings for you; Phat Diem is a popular tourist site for Vietnamese and the staff will usually oblige.

Built in 1891, the Sino-Vietnamese-style cathedral with elements of European Gothic has sturdy stone walls and is fringed with boxy cupolas with upturned tiled roofs. It was designed by a Vietnamese priest, Father Tran Luc (more popularly known as Father Six), who insisted that the stone used to construct the church be towed from hundreds of kilometres away. Father Six's tomb is in the square in front of the cathedral. Not counting the bishop's quarters behind a rear wall, there are half a dozen other structures in the complex, including a tomb-like stone chapel and a magnificent bell tower.

The **main cathedral** has a nave that extends for 74 metres (240ft) and is supported by 52 iron-wood pillars, 16 of which are 11 metres (36ft) high. The front sanctuary area above the single-slab altar is decorated with orthodox-style lacquered

*Container for holy water at the Phat Diem Cathedral.*

**BELOW:** Sunday-morning Mass at Phat Diem Cathedral.

*The Ham Rong Bridge was a formidable target that proved tough to destroy during the Vietnam War.*

**BELOW:** the wooden Phat Diem Bridge over the Day River.

and gilded carved woodwork. Note the angels with Vietnamese faces near the vaulted ceiling.

The two-tonne bronze bell in the **bell tower** was hauled up there on a ramp of earth. Climb to the top for sweeping views of the town.

Phat Diem and its surroundings are Catholic country (about 6 million of Vietnam's 86 million-strong population are staunchly Roman Catholic). There are also at least 10 well-maintained churches in the vicinity.

On the road back to Ninh Binh, look out for the quaint 19th-century covered **Phat Diem Bridge**, made of wood and arching across the **Day River** (Song Day).

## THANH HOA PROVINCE

Leaving behind Ninh Binh province, one enters Annam, the traditional central region of Vietnam, and the beautiful but impoverished Thanh Hoa province. This is the first of a succession of seven coastal provinces hemmed between the South China Sea – known to the Vietnamese as the "East Sea" – and the Truong Son mountain range.

From Thanh Hoa down to the former Demilitarised Zone (DMZ) – that is, through Thanh Hoa, Nghe An, Ha Tinh and Quanh Binh provinces – National Highway 1A is crowded with trucks, cars, motorbikes, bicycles, buffalo carts and pedestrians. Given the sporadic road construction along the way, the train is an attractive option. Provincial governments are charged with road maintenance, so the state of the road reflects a province's poverty, and Thanh Hoa is among the poorest in the country. The sandy soil has never made for good harvests and is only able to grow one rice crop a year, with peasant families scraping by on manioc and peanuts. However, since the 1980s, with seed money from Britain, many farmers in Thanh Hoa have become successful apiarists and honey producers.

### Ham Rong Bridge

There is little to see in the provincial capital, **Thanh Hoa City**, although just 3km (2 miles) to the northeast of the city limits, the historic 160-metre (525ft) -long **Ham Rong Bridge** (Cau Han Rong) crosses the Ma River (Song Ma) to link the central and northern sections of Vietnam. A crucial transport link for the Vietcong during the Vietnam War, the bridge was continuously targeted by the US Air Force from 1965. It was only in 1972, however, that the Americans finally managed to destroy the bridge with laser-guided bombs, but the enterprising Vietnamese quickly built a replacement pontoon. All in all, the US is said to have lost 70 planes in missions to destroy Ham Rong, more than against any other wartime target.

## Dong Son culture

Thanh Hoa is well known as the cradle of **Dong Son culture**. The province harbours a number of ancient historical sites and is also an important settlement area for the Muong minority. At the beginning of the 20th century, archaeologists discovered many relics of the Dong Son civilisation (which lasted for approximately the entire millennium from 1000 bc) dispersed along the length of the **Ma River** (Song Ma) **Valley**: bronze drums, musical instruments, statues, jewellery, various tools and domestic objects. Some of these are now displayed at the Fine Arts Museum in Hanoi. The Muong still adhere to their ancient language, similar to Vietnamese, and use the bronze drums in their unique culture and festivals. Although there has been much intermarriage and cultural melding over the centuries, the Muong probably predated the Viets in Vietnam.

## Lam Son village

Thanh Hoa's highlands are relatively untouched and support an array of wildlife and various hill tribes. The Muong village of **Lam Son** ㉓, in the Thanh Hoa highlands, about 50km (30 miles) west of Thanh Hoa City, was the birthplace of Vietnam's national hero, Le Loi, who became King Le Thai To. It was from here that Le Loi launched a decade-long uprising against the Chinese Ming-dynasty occupiers of Vietnam in the 15th century. The struggle, waged from 1418 to 1428 in this mountainous region, finally ended in victory for Le Loi and his troops.

In the village is the **Le Loi Temple** (Den Le Loi; daily 8am–5pm; free), dedicated to Le Loi. It contains a bronze bust of his likeness cast in 1532. Nguyen Trai, Le Loi's adviser, penned the epitaph on the large stone stela, dedicated to the life and works of Le Loi.

## Sam Son Beach

Some 16km (10 miles) southeast from the city of Thanh Hoa, the white sands of **Sam Son Beach** ㉔ stretch for 3km (2 miles) along the coast of the South China Sea. There are actually two beaches here, separated by rocks. Both are busy, but more businesses are located on the northern beach. Superb scenery surrounds Sam Son, named after the coastal mountains. A popular spot for domestic tourists, rapid development has unfortunately left the area buzzing with seedy karaoke bars, sex workers and aggressive beachside vendors. Accommodation is of the mini-hotel variety, though prices will spike during the summer. The resort is packed in the summer months but mostly deserted the rest of the year.

## NGHE AN PROVINCE

South of Thanh Hoa is Nghe An province. With a long history of peasant uprisings, this is the birthplace of several revolutionaries, including Phan Boi Chau and Nguyen Ai Quoc (more famously known as Ho Chi Minh). It was also the birthplace of national poet Nguyen Du (1765–1820), author of the *Tale of Kieu*, Vietnam's famous poetic epic *(see*

*Vendors at Sam Son Beach inflate prices during the summer months, when the beach is often crowded.*

**BELOW:** fishing boats along Sam Son Beach.

page 83). The city of **Vinh** is the capital of Nghe An province but it isn't very exciting. A modern industrial base, it was bombed by the US Air Force and then completely rebuilt in a drab, grey Soviet style. Most travellers use Vinh as a rest stop, or use the city as a transit point en route to the Lao border.

In Nghe An province and its neighbour to the south, Ha Tinh, the mountains give way to wide plains along a 230km (143-mile) coastline, and forests cover more than half of the land. The climate is harsh – the area is frequently hit with severe typhoons and flooding. There are more than 100 rivers and streams, the longest of which is the **Lam Dong River** (Song Lam Dong) that feeds the two provinces.

## Hoang Tru and Kim Lien villages

In 1959, the inhabitants of **Hoang Tru village** ㉕, 14km (7 miles) northwest of the nondescript provincial capital, **Vinh**, re-created the humble three-room house, with

bamboo walls and a palm-leaf roof, where Ho Chi Minh was born as Nguyen Sinh Cung in 1890. Ho's family moved from here to Hue when he was five.

Ho's father, a mandarin and minor official in the Hue court, became disillusioned with the French rulers and was eventually dismissed. He returned to this area in 1901 and settled close to Hoang Tru, in nearby **Kim Lien village**, where he and Ho Chi Minh's grandfather taught. Young Ho Chi Minh spent a few years here before he and his father returned to Hue.

Kim Lien villagers constructed a replica of the second house, also in 1959, and turned it into yet another Ho Chi Minh shrine. It is very similar to the one in Hoang Tru. Nearby is a dusty three-room museum displaying memorabilia, old photographs, Ho's poems and some actual shirts he wore. All the sites can be visited daily from 7.30–11.30am and 1.30–5pm, and depending on who is working, visitors may be asked to pay a small

**BELOW:** the house in Kim Lien village, where Ho Chi Minh once lived.

fee, or alternatively to buy flowers to leave at the shrines.

It's easy to confuse these two Ho Chi Minh houses since there is little English-language information at either. It is not obvious that these are replicas of the original homes or that Ho spent little of his life in either place. During his 30-year odyssey, Ho rarely contacted his family, and he returned to his childhood homes just once in his life, in 1961.

## Cua Lo Beach

About 20km (12 miles) north of Vinh is **Cua Lo Beach**, which, like Sam Son Beach, attracts mostly local Vietnamese. The waters are clean and the stretch of sand is inviting, but the karaoke bars, massage parlours and general tackiness may deter many.

## QUANG BINH PROVINCE

Quang Binh province was one of the earliest battlegrounds between the Viets and the Champa, in their struggle to control Vietnam. Although now a quiet backwater, it was the home of several well-known historical figures in Vietnam,

including the poet Han Mac Tu, former president Ngo Dnh Diem, and one of the most respected Communist war veterans in the country, Vo Nguyen Giap.

The Unesco World Heritage Site **Phong Nha-Ke Bang National Park** ㉖ was created to protect some of the world's most extensive karst landscapes. The park is best known for its caves, including **Phong Nga**, which is home to the world's longest underground river, and the world's largest cave passage, Son Doong, discovered by British explorers in 2009. It is possible to explore both the huge cave and river with guided tours. A boat tour of the cave is the highlight of any visit to this region.

## Dong Hoi

About 55km (34 miles) from Phong Nga, quaint **Dong Hoi** ㉗ makes a good base for day trips to the caves and exploring the DMZ. There was once an ancient citadel here but little remains other than moats and vestiges. The local beach, Nha Le, is a lovely and very quiet place to get away – there's little there in the way of service and accommodation, apart from Sun Spa Resort.

*A re-created house in Kim Lien village bears a shrine bestowing reverence on Ho Chi Minh.*

# RESTAURANTS

Prices for a three-course dinner per person:
**$** = under US$5
**$$** = US$5–10
**$$$** = US$10–20
**$$$$** = over US$20

Many restaurants cater to domestic tourists heading to or from the beach. Some of the least desirable places here serve wild game meat, and some of the best offer Vietnamese standards with a unique Tonkin Coast twist that includes twice the normal amount of chillies. Seafood restaurants dominate along the coast itself.

## Ninh Binh

**Anh Dzung**
Bich Dong St, Ninh Binh City.
Tel: 030-618 020. Open: daily B, L & D. **$$**

Set in a pleasant two-storey wooden building and with great service, this is one of the best places in town. Simple and cheap set menus.
**Lounge Bar & Lighthouse Café**
Thuy Anh Hotel, 55A Truong Han Sieu St, Ninh Binh City, Ninh Binh province. Tel: 030-387 1602. Open: daily B, L & D. **$$$**
Head to the rooftop terrace to choose from simple but well-prepared local dishes and some Western standards in the Lighthouse Café.

## Hoa Lu

**Van Xuan Hotel & Restaurant**
Thien Ton St, Hoa Lu, Ninh Binh province. Open: daily L & D. **$**
A good lunch-time stop when travelling to or from the Hoa Lu complex. Has a selection

of Vietnamese and Western dishes.

## Cuc Phuong N.P.

**Cuc Phuong National Park Restaurant**
Park entrance (second branch located 1km inside park), Ninh Binh province. Tel: 030-384 8006. Open: daily B, L & D. **$**
Two simple but efficient restaurants serving local fare are found at the entrance just inside the Cuc Phuong National Park.

## Thanh Hoa

**Hoa Hong Hotel & Restaurant**
102 Trieu Quoc Dat St, Thanh Hoa City, Thanh Hoa province. Tel: 037-385 5195. Open: daily B, L & D. **$$**
This nondescript hotel restaurant offers generously sized

meals. Mostly Vietnamese standards, with a few pasta dishes thrown in.

## Sam Son Beach

**Vanchai Resort**
Quang Cu, Sam Son Beach, Thanh Hoa province. Tel: 037-379 3333. Open: daily B, L & D. **$$$**
Tucked away on the edge of a private beach, a great place to lunch on fresh crabs or steamed grouper. Set dinners are good value.

## Vinh

**Saigon Kimlien**
25 Quang Trung St, Vinh City, Nghe An province. Tel: 04-716 4132. Open: daily B, L & D. **$$**
One of the best restaurants in the city, staff are friendly and the food, a mix of local and international dishes, is reliably good.

# CENTRAL VIETNAM

**The central stretch of Vietnam offers some of the country's most alluring attractions, including a trio of Unesco World Heritage sites – Hue, Hoi An and My Son**

The central region of Vietnam is a showpiece of the country's rich history, from the ancient Sa Huynh culture centred in Quang Ngai province to the devastation of war in the former DMZ, or Demilitarized Zone. At the heart of Vietnam is Hue, the imperial capital of the Nguyen kings. A few hours south, the charming old town of Hoi An makes for an exquisitely relaxing break.

The Nguyen dynasty ruled from Hue for 143 years, leaving behind a substantial imperial city as well as a revered collection of tombs which dot the countryside along the fabled Perfume River. In contrast to the brief reign of the Nguyens, the Champa kingdom ruled most of central Vietnam from the 7th to 15th centuries. Its most celebrated ancient red-brick temple-towers are found at My Son, but there are several other Champa sites scattered across the entire central coast. These ancient structures stand as silent testimony to the kingdom that flourished here before its absorption by the Vietnamese descending from the north.

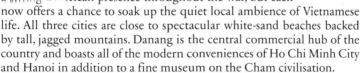

Outside Hue, the narrow, central coastal provinces of Quang Tri and Dong Ha, positioned directly south of the DMZ, suffered immeasurably during the Vietnam War. The cities of Danang, Quang Ngai and Qui Nhon all had a strong American presence throughout the war, but each now offers a chance to soak up the quiet local ambience of Vietnamese life. All three cities are close to spectacular white-sand beaches backed by tall, jagged mountains. Danang is the central commercial hub of the country and boasts all of the modern conveniences of Ho Chi Minh City and Hanoi in addition to a fine museum on the Cham civilisation.

The 15th-century town of Hoi An was once the biggest seaport and most important centre of trade in the country, when it was known to Europeans as Faifo. Its beautifully preserved assembly halls, merchant shops and family homes reflect the influence of the Chinese, Japanese and Westerners who settled in the region. Today, numerous tailor shops, cafés and restaurants jostle for space with an assortment of older buildings.

---

**PRECEDING PAGES:** bucolic setting at Thanh Toan Bridge, near Hue. **LEFT:** Buddha image among the Cham ruins at My Son. **TOP:** fishermen at Lang Co, near Danang. **ABOVE RIGHT:** To Mieu Temple, Hue.

# HUE

The former imperial capital is a sleepy, romantic city, badly damaged during the Vietnam War. Nearby, along the Perfume River, are the ancient tombs of the Nguyen emperors

**A**n imperial citadel still stands proudly in Hue, despite violent bombardment during the Vietnam War (1954–75) by the Viet Cong and the Americans. Ask Vietnamese about Hue and they'll often remark that it's a sad and sleepy city. This may have something to do with the old architecture and crumbling ruins (many of Hue's residents have built a livelihood based around the city's past). Hue is also prone to exceptionally rainy weather compared to the rest of Vietnam, particularly in the second half of the year.

Once the capital of Vietnam and the seat of the Nguyen dynasty (1802–1945), **Hue ❶** is located 12km (7.5 miles) from the coast on a narrow stretch of land in Thua Thien-Hue province, which borders Laos in the west. It is roughly midway between Hanoi to the north and Ho Chi Minh City to the south. Today, the city is one of Vietnam's more noteworthy attractions, thanks to its eventful history as well as its cultural and intellectual connections, made all the more inviting by its scenic location along the banks of **Song Huong** – the Vietnamese name for the Perfume River.

Hue is a pretty city, crisscrossed by dozens of bridges, lakes, moats and canals. On the river's north bank is the ancient imperial citadel and residential areas, while the new commercial area, the old French quarter and the hotel district are all on the south bank. Further south are several tombs that belong to the emperors of the Nguyen dynasty.

## HUE'S HISTORY

Hue's modern history goes back to 1601, when Nguyen Hoang, of the powerful Nguyen Lords faction (see page 32), arrived. The Nguyen Lords administered the whole region with

Main attractions

IMPERIAL CITY
ROYAL ANTIQUITIES MUSEUM
THIEN MU PAGODA
TU DUC'S TOMB
MINH MANG'S TOMB
KHAI DINH'S TOMB
THE DMZ

**LEFT:** the extravagant tomb of Khai Dinh.
**RIGHT:** a pavilion within the Imperial City grounds.

Central Vietnam

0    25 km

0    25 miles

the agreement of the – often rival – Trinh lords. This arrangement operated smoothly at first, but hostilities soon flared as the territory extended southwards. Bloody battles broke out between the two warring families, but eventually the Nguyen Lords gained the upper hand. The Nguyens also managed to crush the remnant of Champa in the south along the way, gradually dissolving their autonomy. Nguyen feudal lords ruled over the area until 1802. That year, after quelling the Tay Son uprising, the 10th Nguyen Lord proclaimed himself Emperor Gia Long and founded the Nguyen dynasty, which would last for 143 years, until 1945.

Just 33 years into the dynasty's reign, the French invaded Hue. They retained the Nguyen as something of a puppet regime, with nominal governance over central Vietnam (Annam) and northern Vietnam (Tonkin). Thanks to French manipulation, a quick succession of emperors occupied the throne. The anti-French demonstrations and strikes of the colonial era were followed by the Japanese occupation in World War II and the abdication of Bao Dai, the last of the Nguyen emperors, at the end of the war.

The relative peace that reigned after 1954, when Hue became part of South Vietnam following the country's division into two by the UN, was short-lived. During the Tet Offensive of 1968, Hue's imperial city suffered extensive damage when the Viet Cong held out in the fortified ancient citadel against American attack for nearly two months. Many priceless historical monuments and relics were destroyed in the battle. In the ensuing years, typhoons and flooding caused further damage, and what remained was generally neglected until Hue began to develop as a tourist destination in the 1990s.

## THE IMPERIAL CITY

On the northern side of the Perfume River, Hue's **Citadel** (Kinh Thanh) covers some 520 hectares (1,285 acres) and is enclosed by a wall made of stone, brick and earth and measuring 8 metres (26ft) high and 20 metres (65ft) thick. The wall – all 10km (6 miles) of it – is punctuated by 10 large fortified gates, each topped with watchtowers, and surrounded by a moat. On the southern side of the wall, facing the river, is the large Flag Tower (Cot Co), visible from all over the city.

A second, 6-metre (20ft) -high defensive wall within the Citadel guards a far smaller area, the **Imperial Enclosure** (Hoang Thanh; daily 7am–5.30pm; charge), with its palaces, temples and flower gardens. Most of what visitors come to see today is found within this inner zone, which was fashioned after Beijing's Imperial City and built during the reign of Emperor Gia Long. Four richly decorated gates provided access: Hoa Binh (northern gate), Hien Nhon (eastern gate), Chuong Duc (western gate) and the **Ngo Mon Gate Ⓐ** (southern gate, or noon gate), first built of granite in 1834 during the reign of Emperor Minh Mang. The main entrance point into the Imperial Enclosure, this gate is topped by the **Five Phoenix Watchtower** (Lau Ngu Phung), with its roofs brightly tiled in yellow over the middle section and green on either side. From here, the emperor used to preside over formal ceremonies and rites. It is perhaps the most recognisable structure in the entire city.

Outside of the gate – between it and the outer wall (and the Flag Tower) – are the **Nine Deities' Cannons Ⓑ** (Sung Than Cong). The five cannons on the western side represent the five elements – metal, water, wood, fire and earth – while the four to the east represent the four seasons. Each cannon weighs about 10 tonnes.

## Thai Hoa Palace

Pass through Ngo Mon Gate and walk across the **Golden Water Bridge** (Trung Dao), which at one time was reserved for the emperor. It leads to **Thai Hoa Palace Ⓒ** (Dien Thai Hoa), or Palace of Supreme Harmony, the most important administrative structure in the Imperial City. Here the emperor would hold bimonthly

**TIP**

You may exit the Imperial Enclosure and re-enter later in the day to attend a performance at the royal theatre. Just check with the ticket booth at the front gate when you exit.

**BELOW:** the Ngo Mon Gate, entrance to the Imperial Enclosure.

*Sights within the grounds of the Forbidden Purple City include the Hall of Mandarins*

audiences with the court, including male members of the royal family; civil mandarins on the left, and military mandarins on the right.

## Forbidden Purple City

Beyond Thai Hoa lies the third and final enclosure, the **Forbidden Purple City** (Tu Cam Thanh). This city within a city was reserved solely for the emperor and the royal family, who resided here behind a brick wall. The Forbidden Purple City was almost completely destroyed during the Tet Offensive of 1968 when the Viet Cong used it as a bunker. Today, the structures within are undergoing reconstruction work.

To the left and right are the **Halls of the Mandarins**, which are annexes to the demolished Can Chanh Palace. In the **Left Hall** (Ta Vu), visitors can be photographed in period costumes, while the **Right Hall** (Huu Vu) houses an extension of the **Royal Antiquities Museum**, with small but representative exhibits of silver, bronze and wood belonging to the Nguyen royalty.

The **Royal Theatre ❶** (Duyet Thi Duong) behind and to the right (east), stages 30-minute shows (daily 9.30am, 10.30am, 2.30pm and 3.30pm) that feature dancers in elaborate costumes backed by a traditional orchestra.

The emperor's **Reading Pavilion** (Thai Binh Lau) sits behind the theatre, ornately decorated with ceramic tiles. This is one of the few structures to have survived the Tet Offensive, although it is in a poor state of repair and looks like it could collapse at any time.

Beyond, a number of **covered walking corridors** (*truong lan*) are still under construction, imitating the Nguyen-dynasty style. In the empty expanse behind to the left and right

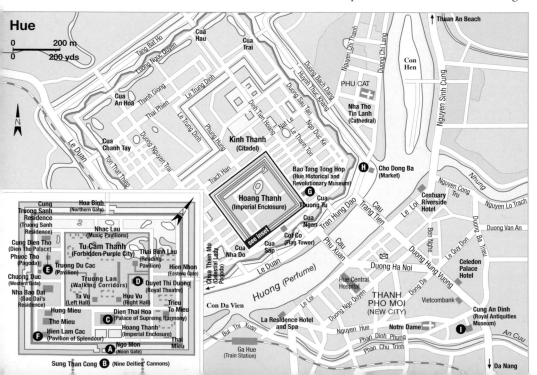

is a pair of octagonal **Music Pavilions** (Nhac Lau).

## Dien Tho Palace

To the west, between the walls of the Forbidden City and the Imperial Enclosure, is **Dien Tho Palace ⊜**, the traditional residence of the various queen mothers. There are some 20 structures at this site, most notably the **Phuoc Tho Pagoda**, the **residence of Emperor Bao Dai** and the lovely **Truong Du Pavilion**, which is nestled over a small lotus pond. The beauty of this complex rivals that of Thai Hoa Palace.

Just behind Dien Tho Palace is **Truong Sanh Residence**, which served as a sort of social area for the queen mothers. Constructed during the time of Emperor Minh Manh, the building is in a severe state of disrepair and not easily accessible.

## The temples

The temples within the Imperial Enclosure are dedicated to various lords and royal family members: in the southeast corner, the temple of **Trieu To Mieu** (now used as a plant

nursery) was built to honour Nguyen Kim, while the adjacent **Thai Mieu** was dedicated to Nguyen Hoang and his successors.

The **To Mieu** complex in the southwest corner houses numerous shrines of significance as well. The **Hung Mieu** is devoted to Nguyen Phuc Luan, Gia Long's father. To its left is the well-preserved **The Mieu**, dedicated to the sovereigns of the Nguyen dynasty.

In front of The Mieu temple and completely restored is the magnificent **Pavilion of Splendour ⊜** (Hien Lam Cac), with the **Nine Dynastic**

*The impressive Pavilion of Splendour and the Nine Dynastic Urns.*

**BELOW:** aspects of Dien Tho Palace.

Trang Tien Bridge and Phu Xuan Bridge. Trang Tien Bridge is the most recognisable modern structure in the city and is lit up every evening in a multicoloured light show. The hotel, shopping and restaurant district is concentrated within a triangle formed by Ben Nghe and Ha Noi streets; the main nightlife hub is in the northeast corner of that triangle, between Le Loi and Tran Cao Van streets.

There are attractive parks on both sides of the river, abuzz with stalls and cafés in the evening.

*The resplendent Trang Tien Bridge across the Perfume River.*

Urns (Cuu Dinh) lined up before it. The urns are decorated with motifs of the sun, moon, clouds, birds, animals, dragons, mountains, rivers, historic events and scenes from everyday life. Each urn represents an emperor of the Nguyen dynasty and weighs up to 2,500kg (5,600lbs).

## BEYOND THE IMPERIAL CITY

**BELOW:** cyclos passing in front of the Ngo Mon Gate.

Another world lies beyond the walls of the Imperial City, which is flanked to the south and east by Hue's commercial centre. The modern downtown area is south of the river between

## Hue Historical and Revolutionary Museum

Near the east gate of the Imperial City, the **Hue Historical and Revolutionary Museum** ◗ (Bao Tang Tong Hop; Tue–Sun 7.30–11am, 1.30–5pm; free) is easily recognised by the tanks and artillery sitting out front. The central building, built in the style of a traditional *dinh* (communal house), contains a humble collection of archaeological discoveries (mainly pottery and Cham relics) from the area. To the left, in a separate pavilion,

is an uninspiring presentation of the First Indochina War (against the French) with plenty of photos but few artefacts. The pavilion on the right is dedicated to the Second Indochina War (against the Americans) in similar fashion.

## Phu Cat

Northeast of the museum is the neighbourhood of **Phu Cat** – home of the Hoa people (Vietnamese-Chinese), who arrived as "boat people" from China in the early 1800s. The lively **Cho Dong Ba** 🚩 is the city's main market and offers a great variety of local products and food delights. Buy one of the famous "poem hats" which, when held up to a light source, reveals the shadow of a scene or a poem.

## Thuan An Beach

Thuan An Beach is located about 30km (19 miles) east from Hue. Ancient Cham relics and ruins found scattered in the nearby coastal dunes long pre-date the nearby imperial city. Seldom visited by tourists, Thuan An is undeveloped and lined with seafood shacks and drink stands. Reclining chairs occupied by Vietnamese families sit under tattered umbrellas. The beach itself isn't as nice as the stretch from Danang to Hoi An, but it is a pleasant escape from town for visitors with ample free time. The Ana Mandara is arguably the best resort on the beach (see page 350).

## Royal Antiquities Museum

Southeast of Trang Tien Bridge is the **Royal Antiquities Museum** ❶ (Cunh An Dinh; daily 7am–5pm; charge) at 150 Nguyen Hue Street, which occupies the former private residence of Emperor Khai Dinh and his adopted son, Bao Dai. Although not usually acknowledged in Vietnam, letters and communications within the royal court and royal family indicate that Khai Dinh was gay, suggesting that this residence was in part his attempt to live his lifestyle freely, away from the watchful eye of the royal court. The elaborately ornamented facade of the house (facing the river),

**TIP**

The Imperial City, and most Nguyen tombs, have entrance fees of VND55,000 each. Add another VND5,000 for parking if you take your own motorbike. English-speaking guides are also available for hire at the Ngo Mon Gate.

**BELOW:** the octagonal Phuoc Duyen tower at Thien Mu Pagoda.

*Longtail boats are a leisurely way to travel along the Perfume River.*

gazebo and the murals and gaudy finishes reflect Khai Dinh's flamboyant personality. The less inspiring rear of the house (which faces the entrance to the grounds) would have had an equally ornate facade, but the decorative aspects were removed when a third floor and theatre were added (but since demolished). Khai Dinh was obsessed with French fashion and lifestyle. Visitors will note that the residence (much like his tomb) departs from typical Nguyen style and is more French than Vietnamese in character.

The exhibits in the museum are scant, and include a few pieces of porcelain, silver objects and items from the royal wardrobe. Some items were given as gifts to the Nguyen emperors by dignitaries, while others represent the high level of craftsmanship during the Nguyen dynasty (1802–1945).

**BELOW:** the evocatively named Perfume River.

## Thien Mu Pagoda

Some 3km (2 miles) to the west of the Imperial City, situated on a hill overlooking the Perfume River, is **Thien Mu Pagoda ❶** (Celestial Lady Pagoda; daily 8am–5pm; free). Built by Nguyen Hoang in 1601, the seven tiers of the temple's octagonal tower – **Phuoc Duyen** – each represent a different reincarnation of the Buddha. Six images of deities guard the pagoda, which contains a gilt statue of the laughing Buddha and three other glass-enclosed statues. Many generations have heard the tolling of the pagoda's enormous 2,000kg (4,410lb), 2-metre (6ft) bell since it was cast in 1701. It makes such a resounding racket that it can be heard up to 16km (10 miles) away.

In 1963, Thich Quang Duc, a monk from this temple, travelled to Saigon and burnt himself to death in protest at President Ngo Dinh Diem's repressive regime in South Vietnam. The Austin car which he drove to Saigon, as well as the famous photo of the monk alight in flames that captured headlines

all over the world, are on display behind the pagoda.

## THE NGUYEN TOMBS

The Nguyen imperial tombs lie scattered on the hillsides on either side of the Perfume River, to the west and south of Hue. Although the dynasty had 13 sovereigns, only seven of them reigned until their deaths, and only these are laid to rest in this valley: Gia Long, Minh Mang, Thieu Tri, Tu Duc, Kien Phuc, Dong Khanh and Kai Dinh. Three generations of emperors forcibly removed from power are buried at Duc Duc's Tomb: Duc Duc himself (and his wife), their son Thanh Thai and their grandson Duy Tan.

The tombs of the Nguyen emperors are well spread out and could easily take up two full days if you visited all of them. However, many people choose to skip the tombs of Gia Long and Kien Phuc because they are further afield.

The poor state of the roads leading to the tombs is surprising given that this is one of Vietnam's most important cultural sites. The road from Khai Dinh's tomb to the Perfume River, for instance, is little more than a pavement. It's also very easy to get lost as there are many turn-offs (beware of locals sending you along forest trails that lead nowhere). Roads are poorly and infrequently signposted, and often in Vietnamese only.

There is no one efficient way of touring the tombs, so if you choose to see the majority, it may require some backtracking.

## General tomb layouts

Each tomb has a large brick-paved courtyard, called *bia dinh*, that contains several stone figures of elephants, saddled horses, soldiers, and civil and military mandarins. In front of this stands the stelae pavilion, containing the tall marble or stone stela engraved with the biography of the deceased king, usually written by his successor. Beyond this is the temple, or *tam dien*, where the deceased king and queen are worshipped by their families and their royal belongings are displayed. The king's widows would keep incense and aloe wood perpetually

**BELOW:** Emperor Tu Duc's tomb.

**BELOW:** the understated beauty of Minh Mang's tomb.

burning before the altar until their own deaths. Behind and on either side of the temple are the houses built for the king's concubines, servants and the soldiers who guarded the royal tomb. The emperor's body would be laid in a concealed place, or *bao thanh*, enclosed by high walls behind well-locked metal doors.

## Nam Giao Dan

To reach the tombs from Hue, head south on Dien Bien Phu Street, first passing **Nam Giao Dan** ⓚ (Terrace of Heavenly Sacrifice; daily 8am–5pm; free) on your left, an esplanade surrounded by a park of pine trees around 2km (1.2 miles) from Hue's commercial centre. Built by Gia Long in 1802, in its day it was considered a most sacred and solemn place. Composed of three terraces – two square and one circular, the esplanade represents the sky and the earth. There is little actually to see here and nothing is marked, although new gates and walkways are under construction and an old temple complex sits in the distance.

During the Nguyen dynasty, the Nam Giao (Festival of Sacrifice) took place at the centre of the circular esplanade once every three years. Here, the emperor would have a buffalo sacrificed to the Vietnamese God of the Sky, who is believed to govern the destiny of the entire world.

## Tu Duc's tomb

The **tomb of Tu Duc** ⓛ (daily 8am–5pm; charge) is less than 3km (2 miles) west of Nam Giao Dan via Xuan Thuong 4 Street, and is surrounded by a clutch of incense and souvenir shops. The mausoleum construction began in 1864 and took three years to complete. The result resembles a royal palace in miniature and harmonises beautifully with the natural surroundings. It is perhaps the loveliest of all the Nguyen tombs and certainly the most visited. Live traditional music is periodically performed within the tomb grounds.

Tu Duc, the son of Thieu Tri and the Nguyen dynasty's fourth king, reigned for 36 years, the longest reign of any of

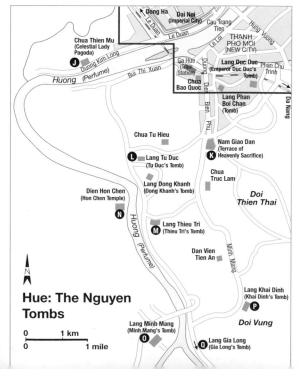

**Hue: The Nguyen Tombs**

the Nguyen kings. He spent his leisure hours in the two pavilions beside the lake, Luu Khiem. The more popular of the two lakeside pagodas is **Xung Khiem Pavilion**. A staircase leads to the Luong Khiem mausoleum, which contains a collection of furniture, vases and jewellery boxes. Further on is the terrace leading to the tomb, with its stone elephants, horses and mandarins. The actual crypt, which is inaccessible, is covered by dense pine forest. The tombs of Tu Duc's adopted son, Kien Phu, and Queen Le Thien An, lie beside the lake.

The **tomb of Dong Khanh**, the nephew and adopted son of Tu Duc who ruled for just four years from 1885, lies just outside the complex. The smallest of the Nguyen tombs is currently closed for restoration work.

## Thieu Tri's tomb

The **tomb of Thieu Tri**  (daily 8am–5pm; charge) is located a few kilometres to the south. Thieu Tri, Minh Mang's son, was the third Nguyen emperor and reigned from 1841 to 1847. His tomb was built in the same elegant architectural style as his father's but on a much smaller scale. Now crumbling, the mausoleum sprawls across several lakes and is largely open, and, unlike most other tombs, is not enclosed by walls.

## Hon Chen Temple

On the western bank of the Perfume River is **Hon Chen Temple** ❶, where the goddess Po Nagar, protector of the Champa kingdom, is worshipped. Po Nagar, greatly venerated by the Cham people, is also to a lesser extent worshipped today by some local Vietnamese as Tien Y Ana. A festival takes place here on the 15th day of the seventh lunar month every year, when worshippers march in a long procession accompanied by ceremonial music and a heavy cloud of incense.

## Minh Mang's tomb

The **tomb of Minh Mang** ❶ (daily 8am–5pm; charge) is located about

*In Vietnamese folklore, the dragon represents the emperor, prosperity and power.*

**BELOW:** Khai Dinh's tomb.

*Several weather-beaten stone statues line the courtyard of Khai Dinh's tomb.*

**BELOW:** Dan Vien Tien An, which houses a cathedral and monastery, combines Catholic and Buddhist elements.

5km (3 miles) south, where the Ta Trach and Huu Trach tributaries of the Perfume River meet. Minh Mang was Gia Long's fourth son and the Nguyen dynasty's second king. He was responsible for the building of the Imperial City and was highly respected for his Confucian outlook and opposition to the French presence in Vietnam. The construction of the tomb was begun a year before his death, in 1840, and was finished by his successor Thieu Tri in 1843. The setting blends the beauty of nature with majestic architecture and superb stone sculpture.

## Khai Dinh's tomb

About 4km (2.5 miles) south of Nam Giao Dan, on Minh Mang Street, the tomb of **Khai Dinh** ⓟ (daily 8am–5pm; charge) somewhat resembles a European castle, its architecture a blend of the oriental and the occidental. Made of reinforced concrete, it took 11 years to complete and was only finished in 1931. Khai Dinh, Bao Dai's adopted father, ruled for nine years during the colonial era. A grandiose dragon staircase leads up to the first courtyard, from where further stairs lead to a courtyard lined with stone statues of elephants, horses, and civil and military mandarins. In the centre of the courtyard stands the stela inscribed with Chinese characters composed by Bao Dai in memory of his father.

Once inside, however, the contrast is striking and more identifiable with the ostentatious character of the emperor. Coloured tiles pave the floor, and a huge "dragon in the clouds" mural, painted by artists using their feet, adorns the ceiling of the middle chamber. Jade-green antechambers

lead off to the left and right. Bright frescoes composed of many thousands of inlaid ceramic and glass fragments depict various themes. Animals, trees and flowers provide a visual feast after the morbid, blackened exterior of the mausoleum. The back room contains a small museum of the emperor's possessions, including photos, clothing, ceramics, crystal, furniture and a clock. A life-size bronze statue of Khai Dinh, made in France in 1922, rests on a dais on top of the tomb.

## Gia Long's tomb

The rarely visited tomb of **Gia Long** ⊙ (daily 8am–5pm; charge), located 16km (10 miles) south from Hue and on a hillside, is somewhat inaccessible by road; a more pleasant way to reach it is by boat on the river. The tomb, begun in 1814, was completed a year after Gia Long's death in 1820. Gia Long was the founder of the Nguyen dynasty, and his tomb perhaps served as a model for the later tombs. Unfortunately, the site was located right in the middle of a particularly active battleground during the Vietnam War and bombs damaged the tombs. The tomb has become rather neglected, but the wild beauty of the site itself, with its mountainous backdrop, makes the effort to get there worthwhile.

## The DMZ

The **Demilitarized Zone**, or DMZ, is where some of the bloodiest fighting of the Vietnam War took place. The DMZ stretched for 8km (5 miles) on either side of the **Ben Hai River**, 100km (60 miles) north of Hue. It was the line of demarcation between North Vietnam and South Vietnam, established at the Geneva Conference in 1954 after the end of the war against the French. Following the 17th parallel, the border was supposed to be temporary, until elections could be held in 1956. The elections never took place and Vietnam remained divided along this line until the two countries were officially reunified in 1976, following the collapse of South Vietnam.

Today, there are still desolate stretches of scorched earth. Just south of the Ben Hai, Highway 9 passes

**TIP**

A tour of the DMZ will often take all day, but this is mainly due to the long driving distances. Many agencies in Hue conduct tours of the DMZ. Note: remnant mines and other unexploded ordnance are another problem, so even if you get off the bus, be sure to stay on the paths.

**BELOW:** cannon and reconstructed bunkers at Khe Sanh base.

*The pronunciation of "Hue" is somewhere between "hey" and "h-way". The vowel combination forms an odd sound to English-speakers due to the "high rising" tone on the final "e".*

sites of famous Vietnam War battles and old US military bases like **Con Thien** and **Khe Sanh**. It is believed that 10,000 North Vietnamese, around 500 US soldiers and countless civilians were killed at the 1968 battle of **Khe Sanh ②** (daily 7am–5pm; charge). After being nearly obliterated by more than 100,000 tonnes of bombs and assorted chemical weapons, vegetation has only recently begun to regrow here.

North of the DMZ, in **Vinh Moc ③** (daily 7am–5pm; charge), a series of tunnels that are similar but more developed than those of Cu Chi *(see page 303)* is located where an entire village camped out for several years to escape the constant bombings. Most of the people evacuated to other parts of the country after the bombings began, but some stayed put. For five years, from 1966 to 1971, some 300 people lived in the 2,000-metre (6,500ft) long network of tunnels. Seventeen babies were said to have been born in this subterranean home. Unlike Cu Chi to the south, the tunnels here are easy to walk through, and so tend to be popular with visitors.

Another important DMZ site is the **Truong Son National Cemetery ④**. Located 17km (11 miles) off Highway 1A and 13km (8 miles) north of Dong Ha, this large memorial is dedicated to the North Vietnamese soldiers who died along the Ho Chi Minh Trail in the Truong Son Mountains during the war. It is a sobering testament to the cost of war, with more than 10,000 tombstones dotting the hillsides. Each bears the Vietnamese words *Liet Si*, which means "martyr". It should be noted that there are no memorials, here or anywhere else in the country, for soldiers who fought for the South and were killed during the war.

Most visitors see sights in the DMZ as part of a shared all-day bus or shuttle tour with a large group. While this may be an easier and cheaper route, it means spending many boring hours in transit and waiting for the group. For a more enjoyable time, rent a motorbike and explore independently, or a private car and guide.

**BELOW:** Preserving the national heritage.

## Rush to Preserve

For a country with a long and rich history, Vietnam boasts relatively few ancient architectural landmarks. Those that have managed to survive the centuries of war, typhoons and the effects of the tropical climate have subsequently suffered from neglect. In the last decade, however, Vietnam has shown an active interest in saving its historical sites. In part, this movement to preserve is part of the government's emphasis on nationalism. Restoring architectural ruins is one way to develop national pride. But more significantly, it is now perceived as commercially viable. All government officials needed to do was notice tourists flocking to Cambodia's Angkor Wat to figure out that there is money in a pile of old ruins. If the ruins are well maintained and easily accessed, that is.

# RESTAURANTS

Prices for a three-course dinner per person:

**$** = under US$5
**$$** = US$5–10
**$$$** = US$10–20
**$$$$** = over US$20

Hue's famous cuisine is regarded as the food of the emperors – so you know it must be good. A meal in Hue is not complete if you haven't sampled some of its famous delicacies. *Banh khoai* is a rice-flour, egg and taro-based pancake, pan-fried with a filling of bean sprouts, pork and shrimp, then topped with *nuoc leo* (a local peanut sauce). *Banh beo* are tiny dishes of steamed rice flour, topped with spices and pork rinds, and then dipped in *nuoc mam* (fish sauce). *Bun* are noodle dishes that come with a variety of meats: *Bun Bo Hue* (Hue-style rice noodle soup with beef) and *Bun Bo Nuong* (rice noodles with grilled beef, mint and lettuce, topped with peanut sauce) are the most common.

The main area for eating out is centered on the streets off Le Loi, close to the river north of Duong Hung Vuong in Thanh Pho Moi (the new city).

## Hue

### *Vietnamese*
**Club Garden**
8 Vo Thi Sau St.
Tel: 054-382 6327. Open: daily B, L & D. **$$**
This eatery specialises in traditional Hue cuisine, with both à la carte and set menus. Tables are set in a lovely garden or in air-conditioned dining rooms.
**Lac Thien, Lac Thanh and Lac Thuan**
06 Dinh Tien Hoang St.
Tel: 054-352 7348. Open: daily B, L & D. **$**
Opened in 1965 and

perhaps the most famous restaurants in Hue, largely because they have been featured in all the major guidebooks and the *Globe Trekker* TV series. The three eateries, which stand back to back, are owned by deaf siblings who are known for giving customers their trademark wooden bottle openers as souvenirs. The traditional Hue cuisine served is excellent and still dirt-cheap despite the restaurants' popularity.
**Ngo Co Nhan**
47D Nguyen Bieu St.
Tel: 054-351 3399. Open: daily B, L & D. **$$**
Located inside the citadel walls, Ngo Co Nhan is a good place to sit beside locals and enjoy a wide spread of local dishes. Be aware that the restaurant has two menus – a cheaper menu for Vietnamese-speaking customers, and an expensive one with a few extra Western dishes. Ask for the Vietnamese menu.
**Nina's Café**
16/34 Nguyen Tri Phuong St.
Tel: 054-383 8636. Open: daily B, L & D. **$**
Nina's is a popular restaurant for its good food, wide range of dishes, cheap prices and friendly service. Nina takes her culinary and service reputation seriously: if something isn't right, let her know and she'll fix it! A range of good vegetarian options.
**Phuoc Thanh Restaurant**
30 Pham Ngu Lao St.
Tel: 054-383 0989. Open: daily B, L & D. **$$$**
Another eatery specialising in royal Hue cuisine. The set menus with seven to eight courses are very popular, and the place is often packed to the rafters. The ornate traditional design of the restaurant gives way to a surprisingly minimalist interior.

**Phuong Nam Café**
38 Tran Cao Van St.
Tel: 054-384 9317.
Open: daily B, L & D. **$**
Despite attracting plenty of foreign customers, prices have remained reasonably low. Mainly Vietnamese menu, except for the pancakes. Service is slow but friendly. Try the *bun thit nuong* (grilled meat and noodles) or any of the Hue specialities.
**Tropical Garden**
27 Chu Van An St.
Tel: 054-384 7143. Open: daily B, L & D. **$$**
Traditional Hue cuisine is served here to the accompaniment of a four-piece traditional orchestra (7–9pm every night). Try any of the good-value set menus or just come for ice cream and the music.
**Y Thao Garden**
3D Thac Han St. Tel: 054 352 3018. Open: daily B, L & D. **$$$**
Situated in a lovely garden with fairy lights outside an old home located within the citadel walls. Y Thao Garden offers a set menu or royal cuisine served by a friendly family.

### *French*
**La Boulangerie Française**
46 Nguyen Tri Phuong St. Tel: 054-383 7437. Open: daily B, L & D. **$**
One of the finest French bakeries in Vietnam. We can't sing their praises enough here. Not only do the pasties, tarts, cakes and crusty breads look scrumptious, they taste even better. The place is run by a charity that does excellent work in training disadvantaged street kids to become bakers and pastry chefs.

### *Indian*
**Omar Khayyam's**
22 Pham Ngu Lao.
Tel: 054-381 0310. Open: daily L & D. **$$$**

Omar's is a lively location with flashy décor and great food. The Tandoori and curry is consistently excellent. Their pot of chai is a great bargain too. There are two branches – the original venue is at 34 Nguyen Tri Phuong.

### *International*
**Hung Vuong Vinh**
20 Hung Vuong.
Open: daily B, L & D. **$$**
Popular with backpackers, this is a friendly place with excellent baguettes and pastries.
**La Carambole**
19 Pham Ngu Lao St.
Tel: 054-381 0491. Open: daily B, L & D. **$$**
A festive atmosphere with a packed house in the evenings. The menu includes English, French and Vietnamese favourites. The quiche and the homemade lemon sorbet are recommended. English is spoken by the waiting staff, and the service is fast.
**Minh and Coco**
1 Hung Vuong St. Open: daily B, L & D. **$**
Bargain basement prices for a bite to eat, this is also a good place for a beer in the evening.

### *Japanese*
**JASS Japanese Restaurant**
12 Chu Van An St.
Tel: 054-382 8177. Open: daily D only. **$$$**
The menu is small but the dishes are near perfect, with flavours that are clean and delicate. The Japanese Associate of Supporting Streetchildren (JASS), founded by Michio Koyama, runs an excellent programme to house, educate and train disadvantaged youth. JASS has changed the lives of hundreds of young people, and the restaurant is part of a new initiative.

# DANANG AND HOI AN

Anchoring the centre of the country is busy Danang, one of Vietnam's largest cities. Nearby – but worlds apart – is Hoi An, a delightful old port town. All along the coast are sandy beaches interspersed with ancient Cham sites

**D**anang, the business and commercial centre of central Vietnam, is an overlooked treasure trove of natural beauty and local culture. Fronted by the renowned "China Beach", the broad stretch of pristine sandy coastline changes name several times on its way past the Marble Mountains. These limestone outcrops were once host to ancient Cham temple sites, burrowed in their damp caves.

Nearby is the once-important port of Hoi An, preserved today as a Unesco World Heritage Site. It still retains its lovely old-town atmosphere and architecture, but also has the dubious honour of being central Vietnam's top shopping destination – there are more bespoke tailors per square metre here than anywhere else in the country. Hoi An was once the commercial hub for an extensive trade route spanning much of central Vietnam and far into the mountains. Cham, and then later the Chinese, Portuguese, French, Japanese and Vietnamese came here to trade cinnamon, ceramics, textiles and other goods, most of which went to China. Hidden away in the green folds of nearby foothills, the ancient temple city of My Son was the holy land of the Champa kingdom, and is today another Unesco World Heritage Site.

**LEFT:** Linh Ung Pagoda, Marble Mountains.
**RIGHT:** fishermen, Lang Co Beach.

## HAI VAN PASS TO DANANG

The 110km (68-mile) route from Hue to **Danang** via the 1,200-metre (4,000ft) **Hai Van Pass** is one of the most dramatic in Vietnam. The 3.5-hour drive over Highway 1A follows a vertiginous route up, down and around mountains that hug the coast.

Along the way is the peninsula of **Lang Co** ❺, which rates as one of the most superb beaches in the country. To one side lies a stunning blue-green lagoon, and, on the other, kilometres

### Main attractions
LANG CO
MUSEUM OF CHAM SCULPTURE
CHINA BEACH
MARBLE MOUNTAINS
BACH MA NATIONAL PARK
HOI AN OLD TOWN
CUA DAI BEACH
CU LAO CHAM MARINE PARK
MY SON

*A ceremony at Danang's Cao Dai Temple. It is estimated that there are 6 million Cao Dai followers in Vietnam.*

of white sandy beach. Lang Co was once the resort playground of the Nguyen Kings; the ruins of their villas are still visible. Lang Co Beach Resort is the primary accommodation at the beach. Nearby excursions include visits to nearby streams, waterfalls, lagoons, villages and activities like snorkelling, fishing and camping. Despite the beach's fame, most tour buses today speed past without stopping. The climate becomes noticeably warmer and more humid after you pass the summit of Hai Van Pass and descend into the scenic coastal region. Taking the 6km (4-mile) -long **Hai Van Tunnel** shaves 30 minutes off the ride from Hue to Danang (Lang Co is itself 30 minutes from Danang) but you do miss out on some nice scenery. If you wish to take the Hai Van Pass route you'll need your own transport, as buses take the tunnel.

**Danang** ❻ lies at the midpoint of the country, about 800km (500 miles) from both Hanoi and Ho Chi Minh City. It broke away from Quang Nam province in 1996 to become an independent municipality, and is now Vietnam's fourth-largest city. Danang straddles the east and west bank of the Han River, between Nam O Beach to the north and China Beach to the south. While it's not as hectic as Hanoi or Ho Chi Minh City, this is central Vietnam's main economic centre and host to the country's third-busiest port. With its international airport, Danang is also a jump-off point for tourists, and resorts and numerous golf course developments are sprouting up all along the nearby coast.

Danang is as good a place as any to gauge the flavour of modern Vietnam, and has prospered in the economic boom of recent years. There are glitzy new shopping centres and high-rise buildings, and all the conveniences and entertainment of Ho Chi Minh City, generally without the attendant traffic and crowds.

## History

Known as Tourane to the French, Danang is perhaps best remembered for the role it played at the beginning and end of the Vietnam War. Because

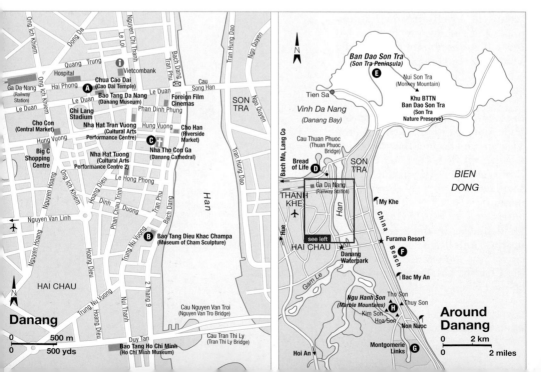

of its location in the centre of the country, it found itself a city divided during the war. Many people in the area supported the South Vietnamese government, while others quietly worked for the Viet Cong.

It was at Danang that the first 3,500 US Marines came ashore on Vietnamese soil in 1965. Ten years later, communist troops rolled into town, facing little resistance as South Vietnamese soldiers shed their uniforms along the side of the road and fled. Two American 727 jets evacuated refugees, most of them soldiers, in a scene of panic broadcast around the world. So many people tried to climb onto the planes that, as one of them took off, people clinging to the wheels fell into the sea.

Other foreigners came to this part of Vietnam long before the Americans, however. In the 17th and 18th centuries, the first Spanish and French landings were made here. In the course of the 19th century, Danang superseded Faifo (present-day Hoi An) as the most important port and commercial centre in the central region.

## Cao Dai Temple

Danang's **Cao Dai Temple** Ⓐ (63 Haiphong Street) dates back to 1956, and locals claim it is the second-largest temple for the religion outside its base in Tay Ninh *(see page 306)*. In reality, the fact is overstated as Cao Dai temples of approximate size can be found in numerous cities throughout Vietnam. An archbishop and 15 priests serve Danang's congregation of about 20,000 people. Like other Cao Dai temples, daily services are held every six hours: 6am, noon, 6pm and midnight. Visitors are not allowed into the temple, but are welcome to observe from the periphery.

## Museum of Cham Sculpture

For an insight into Vietnam's ancient Cham civilisation, visit the **Museum of Cham Sculpture** Ⓑ (Bao Tang Dieu Khac Champa; daily 8am–5pm; charge) at the corner of Trung Nu Vuong and Bach Dang streets in the southern part of the town. Danang's most noteworthy attraction was established in 1915 by the Ecole Française

*Regional products include cinnamon from Tra, pepper from Tien Phuoc, tobacco from Cam Le, silk from Hoa Vang, saffron from Tam Ky, carvings in rosewood, ironwood and ebony, and sea swallow nests from the Cham Islands.*

**BELOW LEFT:** Danang Cathedral.
**BELOW RIGHT:** Museum of Cham Sculpture.

*Danang was the first landing point for Christian missionaries in Vietnam, and has retained a thriving Protestant population. Altogether there are a total of nine authorised churches, as well as an international church for foreigners only. There are also several Catholic churches dotted around the city.*

**BELOW:** Cham figurines on display at Danang's Museum of Cham Sculpture.

d'Extrême-Orient as an open-plan colonial structure embellished with Cham-inspired motifs. The museum contains the largest display of Cham artefacts in the world, with each room dedicated to a different Cham era and city of origin: My Son, Tra Kieu, Dong Duong and Thap Mam. In total, the rooms cover over 1,000 years of Cham history.

Finely crafted figures from the pantheon of Hindu deities, notably Vishnu, Shiva, Uma, Ganesh and Nandi, are a recurrent theme, as indeed is the female breast, an important icon of Cham religious art. Perhaps the most famous of all the carvings is the exquisite dancing *apsara* of Tra Kieu (late 10th century) on display in the northwest corner of Gallery Three. The top floor has displays of traditional instruments and costumes.

Guides are available at the museum for a small fee. You can also buy a copy of the booklet called *Museum of Cham Culture: Danang*, written by the museum curator, Tran Ky Phuong, on sale at the entrance (US$10). Don't expect a guide to the museum collection, however; the book covers

the general art history of the Cham civilisation.

## Danang Cathedral

Pastel-pink **Danang Cathedral** ⓒ, at 156 Tran Phu Street (English Mass Sun 10am), was built in 1923 and is one of the most recognisable landmarks in the city. Locals refer to the church as Nha Tho Con Ga (Rooster Church) because of the weathercock above the steeple.

The church runs the **Thanh Tam School** at 47 Yen Bay Street (tel: 0511-381 8402) for deaf and disabled children. Visitors are welcomed, so be sure to stop by their gift shop, internet café and fruit-shake stand outside the gate on Yen Bay Street (directly behind the cathedral). Deaf students not only make all the crafts but also run all three shops.

## Bread of Life

**Bread of Life** ⓓ (tel: 0511-356 5185; www.partnersincompassion.org; Mon–Sat 7am–9.30pm), at the riverside roundabout on the intersection of Bach Dang and Dong Da streets, is more than an outstanding bakery,

Wi-fi café and restaurant which happens to be run by deaf staff. It is an organisation that has brought heart and hope to the deaf community of Danang and Quang Nam province and beyond. The deaf in Vietnam are generally viewed as a burden, incapable of learning basic life skills. Most have never been taught to read or write, nor do they know anything about sign language. Bread of Life teaches young people a Vietnamese version of sign language as well as training them in vocational skills so that young deaf people can build a future for themselves. Committed foreign volunteers are welcomed.

## AROUND DANANG

Danang's countryside is more famous for its natural beauty than for any historical landmarks. Surrounded by three nature reserves, jagged mountains and many kilometres of wide sandy beaches, this area invites leisurely exploration.

### Son Tra Peninsula

The **Son Tra Peninsula** ❺, also known as Monkey Mountain to US

servicemen during the Vietnam War, is a beautiful nature reserve just northwest of Danang. The mountain is best explored by motorbike or bicycle, taking the new road winding around steep cliffs and dense rainforest. Macaques and civet cats are among the wildlife sometimes spotted. There is a lighthouse at the far eastern end of the peninsula, but unfortunately, visitors are not welcome. Likewise, a number of beautiful beaches line the coves below, but most of them have been taken over by new resort hotels.

A military base previously occupied the mountain, but now you can wander freely to the abandoned observatory or the highest pinnacle for views (weather permitting) of the coast, city and surrounding mountains.

### China Beach

Several bridges connect Danang over the Han River with the beach, but the most striking is **Song Han Bridge**. The swing suspension bridge is lit up at night and has become one of the city's modern symbols. Two smaller bridges lead to the beach further

*Painted deities sit on altars in caves at the Marble Mountains.*

**BELOW:** fine sand and clear waters at China Beach.

*The French villas at the 1920s Ba Na Hill Station were recently given a new lease of life.*

**BELOW:** the Marble Mountains near Danang.

south. To the north, at the river's mouth, is the huge **Thuan Phuoc Bridge**, currently under construction.

**China Beach** ❻ is the name given by American servicemen during the Vietnam War to the 30km (19-mile) stretch of white-sand beach extending from Son Tra Peninsula past Danang all the way east to Cua Dai Beach near Hoi An. The Vietnamese refer to specific stretches of China Beach by different names, like **My Khe**, **Bac My An**, **Non Nuoc** (just adjacent to the Marble Mountains), **An Bang** and finally **Cua Dai** *(see page 226)* just east of Hoi An.

The section of China Beach closest to Danang, called My Khe, was the R&R hangout of American soldiers seeking reprieve from the rigours of the Vietnam War. For nearly three decades following the war, much of the beach remained deserted. But not any more. Investors who've realised the tourism potential of this famous stretch of sand have bought up tracts of prime beachfront. Several upmarket hotels, such as the Furama Resort,

are already up and running, and more are on the way.

Danang has a burgeoning golf scene. Both the **Montgomerie Links** ❼ (www.montgomerielinks.com), designed by Scottish golfer Colin Montgomerie, and the Danang Golf Club (www.dananggolfclub.com), designed by Australian Greg Norman, are 18-hole courses located across from China Beach.

## Marble Mountains

About 11km (7 miles) south of Danang, not far from Non Nuoc Beach, stand five large hills known as the **Marble Mountains** ❽ (Ngu Hanh Son). Each hill is named after one of the five Taoist elements: **Kim Son** (metal), **Thuy Son** (water), **Moc Son** (wood), **Hoa Son** (fire) and **Tho Son** (earth). These mountains were once a group of five offshore islets, but due to silting over the years they eventually became part of the mainland. The caves within were once used by Cham people and now shelter altars dedicated to the Buddha, and various *bodhisattvas* and

local deities worshipped by the area's inhabitants.

The most famous peak, which is riddled with caves, temples and paths, is **Thuy Son** (daily 7am–5pm; charge). Nearly all tour buses stop at the large cave at the base. The paths weaving through the mountain are well marked and easy to navigate. The highest cave, **Huyen Khong**, has a small tunnel that leads to the very top of the hill, where there is a lookout with views of the sea and the countryside. During the Vietnam War, the Marble Mountains became a hideout for the Viet Cong because of the view over the surrounding area.

The mountains were once a valuable source of red, white and blue-green marble. At the foot of Thuy Son and the other mountains, skilful marble carvers chisel out a great variety of objects, ranging from small souvenirs to giant statuary. Some will proudly tell you that they worked on the construction of Ho Chi Minh's mausoleum, but most will pester you incessantly until you visit their shop.

## Ba Na Hill Station/Suoi Mo

Just west of Danang, at an elevation of 1,136 metres (3,727ft), is the **Ba Na Hill Station** ❼ (daily daylight hours; charge), built by the French on **Chua Mountain** (Pagoda Mountain) in the 1920s to escape the summer heat. The hill station, where temperatures are typically around 10°C (18°F) lower than at the coast, was later abandoned and reclaimed by the jungle and the ravages of war. In recent years the government and private enterprise have sought to revive the old villas by turning the hill station into an ecotourism destination. In Vietnamese fashion, however, some of this has translated into loud karaoke, monkeys in small cages and restaurants serving exotic animal meat. Still, a great variety of flora and fauna can be seen along walking trails at **Ba Na-Nui Chua Nature Reserve**, including lively monkeys and birdlife, colourful butterflies, bizarre insects and delicate orchids – many of which cannot be found in the valleys below.

Construction of the new Ba Na Hills Resort has been completed, and

**TIP**

As you approach the Marble Mountains you'll be swarmed by drivers offering to guide you there, just to be friendly. Most seem to be shop owners who will first direct you to their place of business. Beware, however, of more serious scams.

**BELOW:** Ba Na Hill Station.

*A trip to Danang is incomplete without a visit to the picture-perfect beach of Lang Co.*

**BELOW:** insect life at Bach Ma National Park.

the mega-tourism complex dominates the top of the mountain. **Linh Ung Pagoda** sits nearby on a cliff, where a giant 24-metre (79ft) high-seated Buddha gazes over the valleys below. Near the pagoda is a **gondola** service (charge), which is one of the highlights of a visit to the hill station, and now runs regularly.

Some, however, may find that **Suoi Mo** (Dream Spring; daily daylight hours; charge) is actually more enjoyable than Ba Na, even though it's only a side-trip on the way. Just 2km (1.2 miles) from the Ba Na turn-off, this pristine mountain river offers swimming and several waterfalls. The water

is so clear that the bottom can be seen at virtually any depth. Bring a picnic lunch and watch the swarms of butterflies and the colourful birdlife.

## Bach Ma National Park

Towering 1,450 metres (4,757ft) northwest of Danang is **Bach Ma Mountain**, which, like Ba Na, served as a hill-station resort for the French in the 1930s. Even before the French discovered it, the area had caught the attention of conservationists seeking to protect the resident population of rare Edward's pheasants. In the 1940s, the species was thought to be extinct, but more than 50 years later it was rediscovered at Bach Ma. The hill station was abandoned when the French left Vietnam, and over the course of time, the 139 villas that once hosted the French were reduced to rubble.

Today, **Bach Ma National Park** ❽ (tel: 054-387 1258; www.bachma.vnn. vn; daily daylight hours; charge) is a 22,031-hectare (8,916-acre) treasure trove of flora and fauna, with numerous species unique to Vietnam. At the last count some 2,147 plant species,

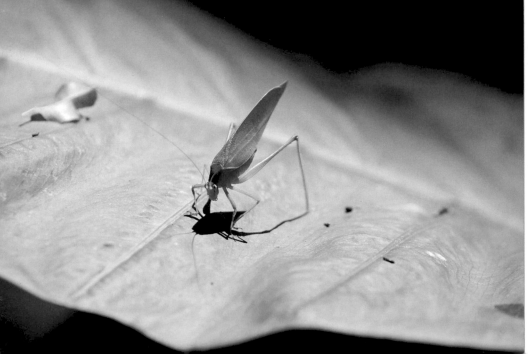

132 mammals, 358 birds, more than 50 reptiles and amphibians, 57 fish and 894 species of insects (identified thus far) have been documented. Nine species of primate have been recorded in Bach Ma, including various macaques, langurs, loris and gibbons. The rare saola (*Pseudoryx nghetinhensis*), a type of antelope, was discovered in Vietnam only in 1992 and is also present in the park. Tigers and leopards may still lurk in remote areas.

Bach Ma has a unique climate thanks to its high altitude. It is considered the wettest place in Vietnam, with approximately 8 metres/yds of rainfall each year, much of which falls in a series of deluges between September and December. The summit of Bach Ma Mountain is several degrees cooler than the surrounding lowlands as well. Warm clothing and rain gear are necessary during the rainy and winter seasons.

Several drinking fountains have been built along the summit road at the head of each trail, allowing hikers to fill their water bottles while exploring the park's numerous trails.

The **Rhododendron Trail** descends 689 steps to a cliffside waterfall that plunges 300 metres (990ft) and eventually feeds the Perfume River in Hue. The park is famous for the red rhododendrons, which bloom from February to March. The **Five Lakes Cascade Trail** follows a series of waterfalls and pristine swimming areas. Several waterfalls can also be visited near the **Visitor Centre**, including **Thuy Dien** and **Da Dung**. The **Summit Trail** is one of Vietnam's most spectacular spots for watching the sunrise and sunset. Some 5km (3 miles) from the park gate, the **Pheasant Trail** leads you through rainforest to a waterfall and swimming hole of the same name. As the name suggests, several species of pheasant can be spotted along the trail.

Bach Ma is located 60km (37 miles) northwest of Danang. Just after the Hai Van Pass and past Lang Co Beach (*see page* 211), drive another 15km (9 miles) to the turn-off for **Suoi Voi** (Elephant Springs; daily daylight hours; charge), a mountain stream with numerous crystal-clear swimming holes. Continuing west on

*Tourists flock to Hoi An to have suits and dresses tailor-made.*

**BELOW:** Traditional *ao dai* dresses.

## Allure of the Ao Dai

The national dress of Vietnamese women is the *ao dai*, alluring, beautiful, and provocative yet discreet. In 1744, the Nguyen dynasty, ruling central and southern Vietnam, dictated a change in dress towards the lines of the Chinese style. Buttoned coats and trousers replaced skirts and split coats tied in front. Emperor Minh Mang imposed the wearing of trousers for all women. In the 1930s, an artist from a liberal reform group attempted to modernise the Vietnamese woman's dress through diversity in colour and design. His new creation of a longer coat used different materials and could even be bare-shouldered. His innovations evolved to become today's *ao dai*.

WHERE

To get to Ba Na from Danang, head west on Hung Vuong Street. Turn left on Road No. 601 and pass the commercial zone outside Danang. The turn-off for Ba Na to the left and Suoi Mo to the right is about 28km (17 miles) from town. Stop at the reception desk at the foot of the mountain to pay the admission charge. As it's a steep uphill climb from here, you have to take the shuttle bus for the final 20km (12 miles) to the

**BELOW:** fresh produce at Hoi An's Central Market.

Highway 1A, the entrance to Bach Ma is 3km (2 miles) from the turn-off at the town of Cau Hai. Visitors are required to park at the entrance and take a shuttle bus to the top.

## HOI AN

Located some 25km (15 miles) southeast of Danang is the ancient town of **Hoi An ⑨**. One of the key attractions of central Vietnam, it occupies a scenic location along the banks of the **Thu Bon River**, just a few kilometres inland from the coast and the charms of lovely Cua Dai Beach *(see page 226)*.

### Background and history

Hoi An traces its roots back to the ancient Champa kingdom, when it was a seaport known as Dai Chien. In the 13th and 14th centuries, it developed under the control of the Tran dynasty (1225–1400). At the beginning of the 16th century, the first Portuguese arrived to explore the coastline of central Vietnam, to be followed by expeditions led by the Chinese, Japanese, Dutch, British and French. The Europeans brought the

first Catholic missionaries (and later the Protestants), making Hoi An one of the earliest places to be exposed to Christianity. Among them was the Jesuit priest Alexandre de Rhodes, who devised the Romanised form of the Vietnamese language.

Hoi An appeared in Western travelogues in the 17th and 18th centuries as Faifo or Hai Po. For several centuries, it was one of the most important trading ports in all of Southeast Asia and an important centre of cultural exchange between Europe and the Orient. By the beginning of the 19th century, however, its fortunes were in free fall. The conflict between the Trinh and Nguyen Lords and the Tay Son faction caused considerable damage, while the mouth of the Thu Bon River silted up and prevented the flow of sea traffic. Another port was built at the mouth of the Song Han River, and Danang replaced Hoi An as the centre of trade.

In the early 1980s, Unesco took the initiative and funded a restoration programme to safeguard Hoi An's Old Quarter and historic monuments,

leading to its achieving the status of World Heritage Site in 1999. Unfortunately many of Hoi An's monuments are threatened by annual floods (mainly between October and November) when the water spills over the river banks and submerges streets in up to 3 metres (10ft) of water, causing serious damage.

These days, Hoi An is a relaxed town of about 120,000 people, 10 percent of whom live in the Old Quarter, which has been turned into a historical showpiece for tourists. Many of the older homes, with their wooden beams, carved doors and airy, open rooms, have been turned into souvenir shops masquerading as museums. While it's certainly the old architecture that draws the tourist buses, there's no denying that shopping is the new heart and soul of Hoi An. Bespoke tailor shops are found everywhere, and its not uncommon to see tourists lugging entire suitcases filled with newly tailored suits and dresses. In fact, some worry that the very thing that makes Hoi An attractive – its quiet charm and peaceful atmosphere – is being ruined. Nearly all the buildings in the Old Town have been turned into shops or restaurants, and about 80 percent of the residents now derive their income directly from tourism.

An admission ticket (sold by various tourist offices around the perimeter of the Old Town) gains you entry to one each of four museums, four old houses, three assembly halls, the Handicraft Workshop (with traditional music performance) and either the Japanese Bridge or the Quan Cong Temple. The complicated system is designed so that you need to purchase a total of four tickets to see everything – something that people rarely do. Most sites are open daily from 7am to 6pm, unless otherwise stated.

## Old Town Walking Tour: West Side and Japanese Quarter

The oldest part of town is in the southern section bordering the Thu Bon River. Running perpendicular to the river, Le Loi was the first street to be built in the middle of the 16th century.

**TIP**

Don't wait for the tour buses at Ba Na Hill Station to show you around the mountain – their job is to direct you to the restaurants. Agree on the time you'll finally leave and hike the rest on your own.

**BELOW:** restaurants by Hoi An's Thu Bon River.

## Hoi An Architecture

Hoi An is an amalgamation of Chinese, Japanese, French and Vietnamese architectural styles. Pristine examples of each culture can be seen in the Japanese Covered Bridge, the colonial villas of the French quarter and the many Chinese assembly halls. Most buildings combine features from the four cultures however, such as the Chinese tile roofs, French balconies and window shutters, Japanese support joists, and Vietnamese tube-house configurations with multiple courtyards. While examples of Chinese temples, French villas and Japanese bridges can actually be found in other parts of the country, such a large collection of architectural styles in a small area, as well as the blending of these traditions, is unique to Hoi An.

*A fusion of Japanese and Chinese cultures at the Phung Hung House.*

**BELOW:** tailor shop assistant.

The Japanese quarter, with its covered bridge and Japanese-style shops and houses, followed half a century later on the west side of town. Next came the Cantonese quarter 50 years later.

Hoi An's past is superbly preserved in its architecture. The Old Quarter is a fascinating blend of temples, pagodas, community houses, shrines, clan houses, shophouses and homes. Twenty clan houses stand in the centre of the Old Town. Most of these were built by the Chinese migrant community between 1845 and 1885. It is the dense concentration of heritage structures in such a small area that gives Hoi An its unique ambience.

Le Loi Street is centrally located and a good place to start your exploration. Heading south towards the river, buy your ticket at the **ticket office** on your right as you enter the Old Quarter. Turn right on Tran Phu Street and head to the **Cantonese Assembly Hall ❹** at No. 176, founded in 1786. It's a pleasant spot with a fountain in the middle of the courtyard, with statues of a twisted dragon trying to devour a carp, and a turtle spying from

behind. Large red coils of incense hang from the ceilings, hung by worshippers as offerings.

Just opposite, the **Museum of Sa Huynh Culture ❸** (daily 8am–5pm) at 149 Tran Phu Street has a collection of pottery and jewellery from excavations of the Sa Huynh cultural site (see page 235). The upstairs houses a fairly typical communist **Museum of the Revolution**.

Continue down Tran Phu Street to one of the most remarkable architectural highlights in town, the **Japanese Covered Bridge ❻**. Built by the Japanese community in the late 16th century and renovated several times since, it links the Chinese and Japanese quarters, and Tran Phu Street with Nguyen Thi Minh Khai Street. The bridge's curved shape and undulating green-and-yellow tiled roof give the impression of moving water. According to legend, a monster with his head in India, his tail in Japan and his heart in Hoi An was causing mayhem by causing earthquakes and disasters to occur. The bridge was subsequently erected in Hoi An (the

heart) to kill this monster. Apparently, work on the bridge was started in the year of the monkey and finished in the year of the dog. Thus, a pair of stone replicas of each animal now stands at either end of the bridge as guardians. In the middle of the bridge is a shrine, **Chua Cau**, dedicated to Tran Vo Bac De, Emperor of the North. There is nothing really to see at the shrine other than a modest altar with a small idol and a pair of phoenixes.

Further up on the right at 4R Nguyen Thi Minh Khai Street is **Phung Hung House ⓓ** (daily 8am–5pm; free), which has both Japanese and Chinese architectural influences and is still family-owned after nearly 230 years. The family conducts guided tours and operates an embroidery shop in the back and a gift shop upstairs.

From here, turn back to the Japanese Bridge and make your way to the right on Nguyen Thai Hoc Street, continuing until you reach **Tan Ky House ⓔ** at No. 10 (daily 8am–noon and 2–4.30pm). This elongated house extends all the way to Bach Dang Street behind, which faces the river.

Typical of the old houses in Hoi An, it is built of wood in a very refined, two-storey style. An inner courtyard is open to the sky with a veranda linking several living quarters. Although many of the old Hoi An homes have been restored over the years, they retain their original wooden framework, distinctive crab-shell ceilings, carved doors and windows, and decorative stuccos. Many of the houses also contain rare antiques from China, Japan and France, as well as Vietnam.

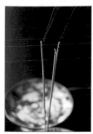

*Burning joss sticks at a Hoi An temple.*

## Old Town Walking Tour: East Side and French Quarter

Continue down Nguyen Thai Hoc Street, passing **Hoi An's Department of Swallow Nests ⓕ** at No. 53. Since the nests are only gathered from Cham Island *(see page 226)* twice each year, there is only a remote chance of seeing any activity here. The swallows' nests, more precisely the dried saliva the birds produce to bind their nests, are a prized delicacy among the Chinese, forming the main ingredient for bird's nest soup and prized for

**BELOW:** Tan Ky House.

*Wells in Hoi An were dug by the ancient Cham more than 1,000 years ago. The waters, once considered sacred by the Cham, are required to make "authentic" Hoi An noodle dishes.*

their reputed energy-enhancing and healing properties.

Further down the same street at No. 33 is the **Museum of Folklore in Hoi An G** (daily 8am–5pm; free), which occupies a large old house with a craft shop on the ground floor, and an excellent museum upstairs with exhibits of artisan tools, ancient crafts and local folklore.

The **Hoi An Artcraft Manufacturing Workshop H** is located in a 200-year-old Chinese merchant shop at 9 Nguyen Thai Hoc Street. Lanterns and other souvenir crafts are made and sold in the back of the shop. While there is a large selection, there's nothing here you won't find in most shops in Hoi An. The main draw is the traditional music and dance show at 10.15am and 3.15pm each day.

Continue east and make your way through the **Central Market** (Cho Hoi An), which is a great place to pick up snacks, fresh fruit and better bargains than at most streetside shops.

Take a left on Hoang Dieu Street, then a right on Nguyen Duy Hieu

**BELOW:** Quan Cong Temple entrance.

Street, heading northeast to No. 157, **Chaozhou Chinese Assembly Hall ●** (daily 8am–5pm), also known as the Trieu Chau Assembly Hall. Dating back to 1776, its altars are considered to be among the finest examples of woodcarvings in Hoi An. The roofs of the structure are decorated with elaborate miniature figures of soldiers, deities, dragons and mythical beasts – all made from colourful ceramic tiles.

Continue along Nguyen Duy Hieu Street, which after the junction becomes Tran Phu Street. The **Hainan Chinese Assembly Hall ●** (daily 8am–5pm; free) on the right at No. 10, built in 1851, is a memorial to the 107 Chinese merchants who were murdered by a rogue commanding officer in Emperor Tu Duc's navy. Ton That Thieu looted the ships and massacred those on board, claiming that they were pirates. The crimes were later discovered and the officer and his men were executed.

Further along at 24 Tran Phu Street, across from the market, is **Quan Cong Temple ●**, also known as Chua Ong. Built in 1653, the temple

is dedicated to Quan Cong, a general from the Three Kingdoms period (AD 221–65) who is deified for his loyalty and sincerity. Inside the temple is a large papier-mâché statue of Quan Cong, flanked by his general Chau Xuong and the mandarin Quan Binh. The temple is really more interesting outside than inside. Behind it, at 7 Nguyen Hue Street, is the **Hoi An Museum of History and Culture** **L** (daily 8am–5pm). It houses a single, underwhelming exhibition room filled with a few artefacts tracing the history of Hoi An.

Continue on Tran Phu Street to the **Fujian Chinese Assembly Hall M**. The largest and most elaborate of Hoi An's assembly halls, it dates to 1792 (the triple-arched gateway at the entrance, however, was built in 1975). Inside is a temple dedicated to Thien Hau (Tin Hau) and other minor Chinese deities. Worshippers believe Thien Hau, who sits in the back chamber, rescues sailors from sinking ships. Her assistants, Thuan Phong Nhi (red skinned) and Thien Ly

Nhan (green-skinned), stand in glass cases on either side of the room. They are said to inform her whenever the calls of sailors in peril are heard.

Pass the **All-Chinese Assembly Hall** at 64 Tran Phu Street on your right. It is unmarked and empty other than a small shrine in the back. Next up is the **Museum of Trading Ceramics** at No. 80, which is set in a lovely old wooden house and contains a modest display of broken ceramics. You would expect to find a ceramics souvenir shop in the back, but oddly enough the shop sells

*Quan Thang House at 77 Tran Phu Street is a typical Chinese-style house.*

**BELOW:** entrance to the Fujian Chinese Assembly Hall..

*Cua Dai is a great beach to repair to after you've seen the sights at Hoi An.*

handbags. On the opposite side at No. 77 is **Quan Thang House** , which is more than 300 years old and has been in the current family for more than six generations. It is sparsely decorated with two family altars and a small courtyard. The highlights are the beautiful and well-preserved carvings on the inner walls.

## AROUND HOI AN

### Cua Dai Beach

Just 5km (3 miles) from Hoi An is the broad, silvery expanse of **Cua Dai Beach**. This stretch of sand is lined with several good beachside hotels, including one of Vietnam's most expensive resorts, the fabulously indulgent **Nam Hai** *(see page 351)*. The sprawling low-rise resort sits on 25 hectares (62 acres) of prime beachfront land and many of its elegant villas have their own private pools.

Palm-fringed Cua Dai beach is perfect for those looking to combine the pleasures of sun and surf with the sightseeing and dining options of Hoi An town.

**BELOW:** idyllic Cua Dai Beach.

## Cu Lao Cham Marine Park

Some 20km (12 miles) or 25 minutes by speedboat from Hoi An and Cua Dai Beach is **Cu Lao Cham Marine Park** ⑩, which comprises eight islands that make up the **Cham Islands** archipelago. The marine park is one of the finest diving spots in central Vietnam and harbours a large variety of fish and coral. Diving trips – the best months are from June to September – can be organised with Rainbow Divers (tel: 0510-392 7678). The main **Cham Island** is known for its rich bounty of swallows' nests (the species in question is, in fact, German's swiftlet), a prized delicacy all over Asia. Numerous boats take visitors to swim along the reefs each day, but few tourists venture onto the island.

## My Son

The ancient kingdom of Champa, which dates back to the 2nd century AD and flourished from the 5th to 15th centuries, once occupied the central Vietnamese coast all the way to Nha Trang in the south. The Chams soon became Hinduised through

commercial contacts with India, and their kingdom functioned as a loose confederation of five states named after regions of India – Indrapura (Quang Tri), Amaravati (Quang Nam), Vijaya (Binh Dinh), Kauthara (Nha Trang) and Panduranga (Phan Rang).

At the beginning of the 10th century, Champa came under severe pressure from the successive Viet rulers, who were beginning their long push to the south. In 1069 Indrapura was lost, and by 1306 Champa's northern frontier had been pushed back as far as the Hai Van Pass with the subsequent loss of Amaravati. The process of Vietnamese expansion proved inexorable, with Vijaya falling in 1471 and Champa – now reduced to the rump kingdoms of Kauthara and Panduranga – effectively a broken power. The final absorption by Vietnam was delayed until the reign of Minh Mang in 1832, by which time the Vietnamese were already engaged in the occupation of the lower Cambodian regions of Prey Nokor (later renamed Saigon) and the Mekong Delta.

Thus Champa disappeared – but not the Cham people. As their kingdom was swallowed piecemeal by the invading Viet, increasing numbers of Cham fled to neighbouring Cambodia, though others chose to remain under Viet tutelage in their former homelands. Today, there are approximately 100,000 Cham people left in southern Vietnam.

**My Son** ❶ (daily 7am–4.30pm; charge), nestled under the green slopes of Cat's Tooth Mountain (Nui Rang Meo) some 50km (31 miles) from Hoi An, is the site of Vietnam's most important Cham monuments and was declared a Unesco World Heritage Site in 1999. It is one of the most atmospheric locations anywhere in the country, with the crumbling ruins set in a verdant jungle. Chosen as a religious sanctuary by King Bhadravarman I in the 4th century, many temples and towers (kalan) were built in this area. Most were dedicated to kings and Brahman divinities, especially the god Shiva, who was

**TIP**

Stay on marked paths at My Son as there may be unexploded ordnances beyond the tombs and temples. The walk is long but easy. Bring sunscreen and water. There are no shops inside the complex.

**BELOW:** My Son's Group B cluster of temples.

*My Son's Cham ruins have often been compared to Cambodia's more famous Angkor Wat complex.*

**BELOW:** remains at My Son.

There are 11 designated temple groups in My Son, and there are likely to be other groups of ruins that are either unpublicised or undiscovered. Of the listed groups, H, G and L are off-limits. The first cluster of temples at B, C and D are the most intact. Two *mandapa* (meditation halls) in D have been turned into small galleries with modest sculpture displays, although the best pieces have been carted off to other museums. Stone symbols abound throughout the temples, in the form of the male phallic *linga* and female spout-like *yoni*. As you walk among these ancient structures, imagine them humming with monks' incantations. At the height of the Champa kingdom, only a handful of attendants would have resided here, leaving the area a place of quiet mysticism for the gods to live in.

considered the creator and defender of the ancient Champa kingdom.

According to legend, the Cham towers were ingeniously constructed from raw bricks and fired in a giant "bonfire". Recent research has shown that the bricks were actually bonded using a vegetable resin *(dau rai)*, allowing them to withstand the onslaught of time and the elements, but not, however, the Vietnam War. In 1969, American B-52s bombed the temples, where the Viet Cong had established a base and mined the valley. Many of the ancient buildings were badly damaged or completely destroyed.

Note: the route to My Son is not clearly signposted, so it's better to book a tour in Hoi An or Danang. Seeing all the temples requires a significant amount of walking, so be sure to wear comfortable shoes and a hat.

# RESTAURANTS

Prices for a three-course
dinner per person:
**$** = under US$5
**$$** = US$5–10
**$$$** = US$10–20
**$$$$** = over US$20

## Danang

Danang is street food
heaven. For grilled meats
try Chen at 29 Pham Hong
Thai Street. Ba Thoi has
cheap grilled seafood
served from 11pm until
past midnight at 100 Le
Dinh Duong Street. *Mi
quang*, the local noodle
soup speciality, is available
at 1A Hai Phong Street. Tu
Tai offers *com ga* (chicken
rice) for lunch and dinner
on 62 Hai Phong St. Eat the
best *bun thit nuong*
(grilled meat with rice noodles) at Kim Anh on 239
Phan Chu Trinh Street.
Finally, Danang-style *ban
xeo* (seafood pancakes) is
best at K280/21 Hoang
Dieu Street.

### Vietnamese
**Apsara Restaurant**
222 Tran Phu St. Tel: 0511-356
1409. Open: daily L & D. **$$$**
This upscale restaurant –
the priciest in town – near
the Cham Museum serves
fresh seafood and local deli-
cacies with Cham influences.
A re-created Cham tower in
miniature (although it still
looms high above) sets the
mood. Nightly traditional
Cham music and dance
shows.
**Com Nieu**
25 Yen Bai St. Tel: 0511-384
9969. Open: daily B, L & D. **$$**
www.truclamvien.com.vn
The interior decor of this
establishment is not as eye-
catching as the outside, but
the food is good, the service
is friendly, and it's all reasonably priced. Try the spicy
beef salad and stir-fried
pork and aubergine
(eggplant).

**Garden View Café**
37 Le Dinh Duong St. Tel: 0511-
358 2482. Open: daily B, L, D.
**$$**
www.truclamvien.com.vn
The owners of the popular
"Pho 24" and "Com Nieu"
chains throughout Vietnam
own this truly unique café,
set in four ancient wooden
houses. There is a central
garden with waterfalls and
goldfish ponds. Prices are
higher than a typical Da
Nang café but the food is
exceptional. Breakfast is the
main draw.

### Japanese
**Kita Guni**
24 Le Hong Phong St. Tel: 0511-
356 2435. Open: daily L & D.
**$$**
Japanese-owned and pri-
marily catering to Japanese
businessmen, this eatery
serves delicious traditional
cuisine plus a few surprises.
Try the 'Japanese pancake'
and quail eggs wrapped in
bacon.

### Western
**Bread of Life**
Bach Dang St roundabout at
Dong Da St. Tel: 0511-356 5185.
Open: daily B, L & D. **$$**
www.breadoflifedanang.com
This bakery, café and restau-
rant, serving American com-
fort food, is staffed almost
entirely by the hearing-
impaired. The menu includes
pizza, pasta, burgers, sand-
wiches and baked macaroni.
Free Wi-fi.

## Hoi An

There is very little street food
in the Old Town, so your best
bet is to order traditional
favourites like *cao lau*
(shredded pork on top of
thick rice noodles with gar-
nishes of rice, sesame
crackers and herbs), "white
rose" (dumplings with
minced shrimp filling) and
*hoanh thanh* (Chinese
wonton noodles) at any one

of Hoi An's superlative res-
taurants. There are plenty of
choices in tourist-friendly
Hoi An.

### Vietnamese
**Cao Lau 296 Cua Dai**
296 Cua Dai St. Open: daily B
only. **$**
This is a morning sidewalk
stand located down an alley.
It serves *cao lau* (delicious
rice noodle speciality which
is exclusive to Hoi An), *bun
cary* (Vietnamese sweet
curry on rice noodles with a
baguette; a national dish)
and *mi quang* (rather dry and
bland rice noodle speciality
of Danang).
**Mango Rooms**
111 Nguyen Thai Hoc St. Tel:
0510-391 0839. Open: daily B, L
& D. **$$$** www.mangorooms.
com
A bright and breezy place
that serves an inventive
Vietnamese menu. The
Vietnamese chef grew up in
the USA and gives a decidedly Californian spin to the
dishes. Very popular with
tourists, so be sure to book
ahead.
**Morning Glory**
106 Nguyen Thai Hoc St. Tel:
0510-2241 555. Open: daily B, L
& D. **$**
www.hoianhospitality.com
A cosy restaurant serving
the best of Vietnamese
street food, all conceived
by its owner, Ms Vy.
Housed in an elegant old
French colonial villa in the
middle of the historic quarter. There is also a good
cookery school in the
premises, with lessons
taught by Ms Vy.

### Vietnamese & Western
**Cargo Club Restaurant and
Patisserie**
107–109 Nguyen Thai Hoc St.
Tel: 0510-391 0839. Open: daily
B, L & D. **$$**
www.hoianhospitality.com
Charming and popular eatery
with a menu of international

and Vietnamese dishes,
French pastries, cakes,
home-made ice cream and a
well-stocked wine bar.
**Jenny's Café and Bamboo
Restaurant**
15 Tran Huong Dao St. Open:
daily B, L & D. **$$**
This popular eatery special-
ises in local Hoi An dishes,
plus other Vietnamese and
backpacker favourites like
pizzas, pastas and sand-
wiches. Its fried wontons
topped with sweet and sour
shrimp are potentially
addictive.
**Moon Restaurant &
Lounge**
321 Nguyen Duy Hieu St. Tel:
0510-324 1396. Open: daily B,
L, D; **$$**
www.hoianmoonrestaurant.com
Service is very friendly in
this "classical Vietnamese
restaurant with a modern
twist". Set in an old French
colonial building with
wooden interior and
furniture and decorated with
a gallery of paintings. It has
a cosy atmosphere and a
nice bar.

### Indian
**Ganesh Indian Restaurant**
24 Tran Hung Dao St. Tel: 0510-
386 4538. Open: daily D, L & D.
**$$$**
www.ganeshindianrestaurant.
com
Set just outside the Old
Town, so you can walk or
drive there. Lots of curry, tandoori and vegetarian
options.

### Italian
**Good Morning Vietnam**
102 Nguyen Thai Hoc St. Tel:
0510-391 0227. Open: daily L &
D. **$$**
Despite having no serious
Italian competition in Hoi An,
Good Morning Vietnam
offers consistently good ser-
vice and quality pastas, pizza
and other traditional fare,
making it a perennial
favourite.

# SOUTH TO QUY NHON

Lofty mountains, empty beaches and isolated vestiges of the Cham civilisation mark the stretch of coast south to Quy Nhon. In stark contrast is the poignant and chilling My Lai memorial

The road south from Hoi An to Quy Nhon is one of the least touristy stretches of coastline in Vietnam, following scores of pristine, uncrowded beaches, hot springs, waterfalls and rocky mountains spanning the provinces of Quang Nam, Quang Ngai and Binh Dinh. The natural beauty is matched only by the rich cultural history surrounding the region, from the Long Wall of Quang Ngai – a Nguyen Dynasty barrier between the Vietnamese and indigenous people – to the ancient Champa capital at Quy Nhon. This is also the site of the My Lai massacre, one of the worst atrocities of the Vietnam War. The scenic stretch remains relatively unexplored by tourists, thanks in part to authorities that have only recently warmed up to the idea of tourism.

## AROUND TAM KY

About 50km (31 miles) south of Hoi An, Highway 1A passes through **Tam Ky**, the provincial capital of Quang Nam province. Some 5km (3 miles) before Tam Ky, three Cham towers dating from the 11th century rise from a walled enclosure at **Thap Chien Dang** ⓬ (daily 8–11.30am and 1–5pm; charge). A small museum here has fine sculptures of creatures from Hindu mythology as well as more everyday images of dancers, musicians and elephants.

---

**LEFT:**: Cham towers. **RIGHT:** Cham sculpture.

A short distance south of Tam Ky is **Thap Khuong My** ⓭ (daily 8am–5pm; free), another important Cham site. The temple complex here dates from the 10th century and is renowned for the richness of its decorated pillars, pilasters and arches. Both sites provide a sneak preview of Cham monuments yet to come further south in Binh Dinh province.

## QUANG NGAI PROVINCE

Quang Ngai is a name shared by both the Quang Ngai province and its

### Main attractions

THAP CHIEN DANG
THAP KHUONG MY
QUANG NGAI PROVINCIAL MUSEUM
THIEN AN PAGODA
SON MY MEMORIAL MUSEUM
QUY NHON
QUANG TRUNG MUSEUM
THAP BANH IT

*A replica of a hill-tribe bamboo longhouse at the Quang Ngai Provincial Museum.*

**BELOW:** Quang Ngai Water Tower.

capital. **Quang Ngai City**  is located on the southern bank of the **Tra Khuc River**, about 15km (9 miles) from the coast. Locals gather along the riverfront at sunset, when the area is transformed nightly into a long succession of stalls offering fruit shakes and fresh seafood.

Few tourists venture to these parts, other than to visit the memorial museum at neighbouring **My Lai**. Visitors who choose to stay, however, will be rewarded with cultural treasures and scenic vistas of rainforest-clad mountains, pristine lakes, rivers, beaches, ancient relics of the Sa Huynh civilisation, and also ethnic minority villages of the Koor, H're and C'dong peoples. At least 35 ruins of Cham origin, dating to as early as the 8th century, are scattered throughout the province, although most are undocumented and difficult to reach.

Quang Ngai is not as progressive as its neighbouring provinces. The Communist Party fervour of the local provincial government is evident in the many red banners, slogans and party symbols that are hung up all over town. Indeed, there

are a number of infamous hamlets in the province, including Ba To and Van Tuong, which have been highly honoured in the past for their unflagging support of the Viet Cong during the Vietnam War. Numerous *nghia trang liet si* ("martyrs' cemeteries") for Viet Cong who fought against the Americans dot the hillside, clustered around large communist monuments. Big Brother keeps himself busy here – everything requires a few more papers signed and questions answered.

Still, the fact that Quang Ngai is not a major stop on the tourist track has many advantages. Prices are much cheaper – there is often little need to haggle in the markets – and people are friendlier and more hospitable than in other areas of Vietnam. Scenic areas are much less developed and pollution is minimal. In many ways Quang Ngai is the Vietnam of the early 1990s.

Change is on the horizon, however, with construction of the **Dung Quat Deep Sea Port and Oil Refinery**. Quang Ngai is poised to become an industrial powerhouse over the next decade. New hospitals, schools, housing complexes and high-rise hotels have already been constructed to support the anticipated growth.

There are few notable landmarks within the city. The **Quang Ngai Water Tower**, built in the 1930s to collect and store water, is the city's most recognisable piece of architecture, with little "horns" decorating the rim of its roof. The tower, which is found at the edge of the city square, is no longer in use today.

## Quang Ngai Museum

The **Quang Ngai Provincial Museum** (daily 7.30–11am and 1.30–4pm; free), at 99 Le Trung Dinh/Hung Vuong streets, is definitely worth a visit. The ground floor has an impressive exhibit of ancient Sa Huynh artefacts, including pottery, jewellery, weapons, burial displays and a giant bronze kettle. An adjoining section has displays of ancient Champa relics. Most of the floor, however, is devoted to cultural displays and artefacts from the Koor, Hre and C'dong minority hill tribes, as well as 16th-century antique clothing displays from the dominant Kinh people.

The upper floor is a typical museum tracing the communist revolution. Outside the museum, amid cannons, artillery and broken Cham statues, is a replica of a hill-tribe bamboo communal longhouse.

## Thach Nham Lake

Road 626, heading west out of Quang Ngai City, passes by the old **Quang Phu Airstrip**, which was used by the Americans during the war. It is still in remarkably good condition and actually forms part of the road. The road continues for some 25km (16 miles) through rice paddies and minority villages before climbing into the mountains to meet the Tra Khuc River once again, at **Thach Nham Lake and Dam**. This is a superb place to swim or have a picnic, surrounded by lush green mountain slopes.

## Thien An Pagoda

Sitting on the northeastern banks of the Tra Khuc River, **Thien An Mountain** offers fabulous views of Quang Ngai and the surrounding valleys. Built in 1627, **Thien An Pagoda** (daily 8am–5pm; free) is perched on the highest point. The temple was founded by a Chinese monk who is buried underneath an enormous nine-tiered tower. A bronze bell, more than 350 years old, sits inside the temple, while a much newer replica hangs out front. Don't be confused by the Disney-style cement animals outside the entrance. This is the oldest and most famous pagoda in the province, with an active monastery.

To reach Thien An Mountain, first head north out of Quang Ngai City on the Tra Khuc Bridge. Turn right on the other side of the river in Son Tinh village, heading towards My Khe Beach. A large sign of the pagoda hangs at the base of the mountain, on the left, just outside Son Tinh.

*Quang Ngai is famous for cinnamon and sugar cane. Cinnamon is grown by the Koor minority in the mountainous district of Tra Bong, and shipped worldwide. Heavenly smells waft from the Quang Ngai Sugar Factory, the source of unique local candies.*

**BELOW:** tableau, Son My Memorial Museum.

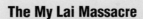

## The My Lai Massacre

US intelligence had suggested that Son My (My Lai) was a Viet Cong stronghold, yet not a single shot was fired against the American soldiers during the massacre. It is believed that the killings were motivated by revenge after heavy US casualties were inflicted by the 48th Local Forces Battalion of the North Vietnamese Army (NVA), who led the Tet Offensive against Quang Ngai in the previous month. In the course of a few hours, not only were the residents murdered, but all of the homes were burnt, the livestock killed, wells poisoned, and several women and children were raped.

Of the 25 men sentenced, only Lieutenant William Calley was convicted, but even then, his punishment was a travesty: Calley served only three days of his life sentence of hard labour before it was commuted to house arrest by President Nixon. He was paroled three years later. In 1998, three US veterans were awarded medals by the US government, including Warrant Officer Hugh Thompson, Jr, for protecting some of the villagers during the carnage.

*Four Hours in My Lai,* by Michael Bilton and Kevin Sim, is perhaps the most exhaustive account of the events of the My Lai massacre and its aftermath.

### Son My (My Lai)

On 16 March 1968, Lieutenant William Calley led Charlie Company from the First Battalion of the American forces in the most infamous atrocity of the entire Vietnam War. Shortly after 7am the soldiers attacked the My Lai and My Khe hamlets of **Son My** ⓯, killing perhaps 500 of its residents (the actual number is still in question today), half of whom were children, the elderly and pregnant women. Although the American military tried to cover up the massacre, the truth was eventually uncovered by journalist Seymore Hersh, working for *Newsweek* magazine, with the assistance of former GI Ronald Ridenhour and photographer Ron Haeberle.

The **Son My Memorial Museum** (tel: 055-384 3222; daily 7am–5pm; charge), 12km (8 miles) east after crossing the Tra Khuc Bridge, is a stark reminder of the horrors that took place here. The grounds contain a re-creation of the village in cement, as it would have been just after the massacre, with a few mass graves off to the side. Inside, the museum retells the gruesome story through photographs, dioramas, mannequins and mementoes of the victims.

Just a few minutes further down the road from the Son My Memorial is a pleasant stretch of white sand – a good spot for a rest after the museum but not particularly remarkable. There isn't much development along the shore, accommodation is scant, but a few cafés offer parking, beach chairs and drinks.

### Binh Hai Beach

About 30km (19 miles) northeast of Quang Ngai via the turn-off for Dung Quat Bay is **Binh Hai Beach**, nestled against high coastal bluffs on the Batangan Peninsula. The beach is a long crescent of powdery white sand, and encroaching upon it is an ancient fossilised reef that extends from the shore to the sea like a flat concrete pavement. Formed by shell deposits over millions of years, it forms a living reef that attracts schools of vividly coloured tropical fish. With the Dung Quat Oil Refinery project looming over the horizon, however, the future of this natural phenomenon is uncertain.

### The Long Wall of Quang Ngai

In 2005 Dr Andrew Hardy, head of the Hanoi branch of École française d'Extrême-Orient (EFEO; the same organisation that founded the Museum of Cham Sculpture in Danang and which is responsible for cataloguing and preserving many of the ancient monuments in Vietnam), discovered a Nguyen-dynasty document referring to a previously undocumented "Long Wall of Quang Ngai" (Truong luy Quang Ngai). After years of research and exploration, he and a team of archaeologists announced the discovery in late 2010.

The wall, which spans 127.4km (79.2 miles) from northern Quang Ngai to the province of Binh Dinh, was built in 1819 as a protective barrier

**BELOW:** Binh Hai Beach with seaweed piled on its shores.

separating the ethnic Vietnamese from the Hre people. The Hre – once part of the Champa Kingdom – did not always get along well with their new neighbours, who vanquished Champa in 1471. Besides security, the wall also helped to regulate commerce along an adjacent, much older trade route connecting Hoi An, Quang Ngai, Binh Dinh and the Central Highlands. While still largely undeveloped for tourism, the wall – along with the associated 50 or more military forts, surrounding minority villages, hot springs, rugged mountains and beautiful countryside dotted with waterfalls – presents a fascinating opportunity for exploration. A few sites are signposted but exploring with a guide is recommended.

## SA HUYNH

Highway 1A continues south towards **Sa Huynh** ⑯, where the coastal estuaries have been turned into shrimp farms and salt-evaporation ponds. The pungent aroma of the Sa Huynh Fish Sauce Factory on the edge of town wafts across the highway. Sa Huynh,

which means "golden sands", is a small town 60km (37 miles) south of Quang Ngai with nearby pristine, yellow-sand beaches interspersed by boulder-strewn capes.

The town is most famous for its archaeological discoveries of the Sa Huynh culture, beginning in 1909. A contemporary of the Dong Son culture in the north and Oc Eo of the Funan empire in the south, the Sa Huynh (1000 BC–AD 200) are believed to be the predecessors of the Champa people. The Sa Huynh cremated their dead and buried them in large clay jars, some of which are on display at museums in Quang Ngai City and Hoi An. The Sa Huynh women wore ear ornaments that featured two-headed animals, usually made of jade or glass. Virtually all of these artefacts were removed from the excavation sites in the area, and locals were apparently never educated about the important discoveries made here. A sundial and a few unmarked excavation sites remain scattered in the surrounding hills.

*A jade-green Buddha statue stands atop a lotus throne at the Long Khanh Pagoda, Quy Nhon City.*

**BELOW:** bustling fish market along the coast of Quy Nhon.

*The Thap Doi Chan Towers stand as a reminder of Quy Nhon's ancient Cham past.*

**BELOW:** blue-green waters off Quy Hoa Beach.

## QUY NHON

Situated at the southern coastal tip of Binh Dinh province, 115km (72 miles) south of Sa Huynh, the capital city of **Quy Nhon** ⑰ (also spelt Qui Nhon) has held a prominent place in Vietnam's political and cultural history for nearly 1,000 years. After Emperor Le Hoan of the Ly dynasty in northern Vietnam sacked the Cham capital of Indrapura in AD 982, the Cham people were forced to move their capital to Cha Ban, just west of Quy Nhon. The new kingdom, which was firmly established by the early 10th century, was named Vijaya (Victory). Despite its name, however, the kingdom suffered frequent wars and conquest by the Dai Viet (the northern Vietnamese empire) and the Khmers to the west. Weakened by constant conflict, the empire suffered a gradual decline until the capital city was captured and destroyed in 1471 by the Dai Viet emperor Le Thanh Ton. As many as 60,000 Cham people were killed in the process, and another 30,000 carried off as slaves.

Nearby Tay Son village was the birthplace of the infamous Tay Son Rebellion, which began in 1771. The area encompassing Quy Nhon was used as a launching point for the armies of Nguyen Hue and his two brothers, who eventually conquered the entire country by overthrowing the Le-dynasty emperor and the two rival feudal houses of Trinh in the north and Nguyen in the south. Nguyen Hue changed his name to Quang Trung and crowned himself emperor of a united Vietnam in 1778.

More recently, during the war with America, Quy Nhon was a strategic military port. Viet Cong, South Vietnamese and American soldiers were all active here during the war. Its Thi Nai Port is still an active commercial port today.

A team of New Zealand surgeons was stationed in Quy Nhon during the war. After the country opened up to foreigners in the 1990s, medical missions from New Zealand returned to assist the community and a small group of Kiwis still live here.

It is amazing that with so much natural beauty and a rich history, Quy Nhon has never figured very much on the popular tourist trail. Perhaps this adds to its charm. Despite its relatively large size, this inexpensive, sleepy beach town is a great place to escape the crowds of Nha Trang to the south and soak up the ambience of a Vietnamese culture as yet untainted by mass tourism.

## Phuong Mai Peninsula

**Thi Nai Bridge**, built in 2006 and the longest sea bridge in Vietnam, crosses the Thi Nai Lagoon and connects Quy Nhon with the **Phuong Mai Peninsula**. The crossing is actually a series of connected bridges (the final one stretching 2,500 metres/yds), passing over mangrove forests and shrimp farms. At the far end of the peninsula, above Phuong Hai fishing village (reachable only by boat), stands the **Tran Hung Dao Statue**, pointing north. The legendary general thwarted two Mongol invasions led by Kublai Khan during the 13th century.

## Thap Doi Cham towers

Located right in the middle of a busy neighbourhood in Quy Nhon city are the pair of Cham towers called **Thap Doi** (886 Tran Hung Dao; daily 8am–5pm; free). Built in the late 12th century, both towers have pyramidal peaks rather than the characteristic terracing found on most Cham towers. Although the peaks are original, some of the decorative carvings you see on the towers are a recent addition by overzealous restoration workers who have taken creative liberties. A garden surrounding the towers and a small visitor centre were constructed in 2008.

## Binh Dinh Museum

The only museum in Quy Nhon is the **Binh Dinh Museum** (daily 8am–5pm; free) at 30 Nguyen Hue Street. It has four wings containing Champa statuary as well as ceramics of Cham and other foreign origin, but most of the exhibits recount Vietnam's more recent war history. In the central atrium is an elaborate wooden loom, typical of the ones used by local minority hill-tribe communities.

## Quy Nhon's beaches

The city's main **Central Beach** sprawls before Xuan Dieu Street and is one of the most popular night-time hangouts in town. Hundreds of homes were torn down in 2008 to make way for a large boulevard and parks along the beachfront. Locals don't usually swim here as the beach fronts an active fishing harbour and the water is not very clean.

At the far southern end of An Duong Vuong Street, **Queen's Beach** (Bai Tam Hoang Hau) is not actually a beach but a scenic coastal drive. Said to have been a favourite holiday spot of Queen Nam Phuong (wife of Emperor Bao Dai), the road climbs Ghenh Rang Mountain, providing scenic views of the bay, the offshore islands and the Quy Nhon cityscape. The grave of the popular romantic poet Han Mac Tu (1912–40) is signposted.

*Religious architecture in Quy Nhon includes the eerie orange Phong Trien Lam Pagoda on 141 Tran Cao Van Street, the giant Buddha at Long Kanh Pagoda near 143D Tran Cao Van Street, and the pastel Quy Nhon Cathedral on Tran Hung Dao Street.*

**BELOW:** statue of Emperor Quang Trung at the Quang Trung Museum.

*The Quang Trung Museum celebrates the three Nguyen brothers who instigated the Tay Son Rebellion.*

The road then descends to a quiet cove near the **Quy Hoa Leper Hospital**, which is right in front of **Quy Hoa Beach**, easily Quy Nhon's finest. It is clean and the water is a transparent emerald green. A drink shop, souvenir stand and beach shacks are scattered under a grove of palm and pine trees. A small village sits at the southern end of the beach.

All of the tiny beaches and coves for the next couple of kilometres have been taken over by small local-style resorts and snack and drink shacks.

A few kilometres past **Bai Xep village** – a picturesque little fishing settlement facing three small islands offshore – is **Bai Bau Beach** (Pregnant Beach). The enormous theme-park-style billboard at the entrance greatly exaggerates Bai Bau's modest facilities. It's a lovely spot for a picnic and a swim, though, if you ignore the monkeys (in dirty cages).

## AROUND QUY NHON

The following sites can be visited on a single day trip by motorbike or car using Qhy Nhon as a base.

**BELOW:** swimming spot at Ham Ho.

## Quang Trung Museum

Binh Dinh province's **Quang Trung Museum** ❶❽ (daily 8am–5pm; charge), also known as Tay Son Palace, is located in the town of Phu Phong, 50km (31 miles) west of Quy Nhon via Highway 19. The museum exhibits highlight the military campaigns of Emperor Quang Trung (Nguyen Hue) and the Tay Son dynasty (1778–1802) that followed after. Other exhibits include clothing, jewellery and weapons used by the local Banar and Ede ethnic minorities; two brass pagoda bells dating from the 18th and 19th centuries; and coins and ceramics from local excavations. The museum is well kept and air-conditioned, a rare luxury in this part of central Vietnam.

To the right of the museum is the **Temple of Tay Son**, which is dedicated to the worship of the generals involved in the Tay Son Rebellion. Built in 1978, the temple represents a common religious practice in Vietnam that is condoned by the communist government: the formal worship of historical military leaders.

A **performance pavilion** on the far left of the museum grounds is reserved for daily performances of Tay Son martial arts, and cultural shows with Ede and Banar performers, although there is no strict performance schedule. In front of the pavilion is the most striking structure at the museum – an enormous **Banar thatched longhouse**. The interior is creatively decorated with weapons, deer antlers, jars, drums, gongs and other traditional instruments.

## Ham Ho

The mountain river of **Ham Ho** (daily 8am–5pm; charge) is a beautiful swimming spot about 5km (3 miles) from the Quang Trung Museum. The water here is a little dark-coloured, not caused by pollution but by the natural tannins that seep from the lush jungles that cling to the mountains on either side. A restaurant is located at the first swimming hole, and there are beaches and other choice swimming spots among the giant boulders.

# Quy Nhon's Cham towers

Several Cham towers are scattered in the vicinity of Quy Nhon. The ancient Cham people could not have picked a lovelier spot for the cluster of four towers called **Thap Banh It** ⑲ (daily 8am–5pm; free). It is located some 20km (12 miles) north of Quy Nhon on a hill overlooking a river valley inhabited by a quaint village and surrounded by lush green mountains. One tower sits apart from the others, claimed by a Buddhist temple seeking to benefit from the spiritual energy of the site. A gate and ticket office stands at the entrance, but no fee is collected.

Another 30km (19 miles) north is another important Cham site, **Thap Duong Long** (daily 8am–5pm; free). The three enormous towers here are under renovation. Although shrouded in scaffolding, there isn't much definition or ornamentation to see underneath anyway as the towers have been ravaged by time and weather over the years.

Other lesser-known Cham towers are difficult to find, largely because they are not part of the usual tourist circuit. About 40km (25 miles) northwest of Quy Nhon on Highway 1A, **Thap Canh Tien** (daily 8am–5pm; free), the "Fairy Wing Tower", rises above the trees like a giant candelabra behind an expanse of rice paddies. The tower and outer wall foundations are all that remain of the citadel of **Cha Ban**, the former capital of the Champa kingdom of Vijaya.

On the other side of Highway 1A, on a hill above the river, stands the solitary **Thap Phu Loc** (Golden Tower). **Thap Thu Thien** is located just off Highway 19, halfway between Thap Banh It and the Quang Trung Museum. Once a treasure trove of ancient relics, the 11th-century tower has been greatly damaged by pillaging over the years.

**Thap Binh Lam**, the most difficult Cham tower to reach, is located about 20km (12 miles) north of Quy Nhon near the far end of Thi Nai estuary. It is believed that this tower marks an ancient port and the transitional capital city for the Champa kingdom of Vijaya, before Cha Ban was constructed.

*The rustic beauty of the red-brick Thap Banh is often understated.*

# RESTAURANTS

Prices for a three-course dinner per person:
**$** = under US$5
**$$** = US$5–10
**$$$** = US$10–20
**$$$$** = over US$20

Quang Ngai

Quang Ngai bursts with great street food. Quan 468 on the corner of Quang Trung and Nguyen Nhiem streets is one of the most popular noodle spots in town. *Banh xeo* and another local speciality, *ram bap* (tiny corn spring rolls),are sold at 124 Phan Dinh Phuong Street.
**Cung Dinh Restaurant**
LO 127 Truong Dinh St. Tel: 055-381 8555. Open: daily B, L & D. **$$**.

Dine on delicious Vietnamese cuisine and local specialities. Service is fast and friendly, and English is spoken by many of the staff. Popular local specialities include the little stewed Tra River mudskipper fish and grilled sugar cane birds.
**Com Nieu Hoa Sua**
28 Nguyen Khuyen St. Tel: 055-381 7799. Open: daily B, L & D. **$$**
A rustic, family and group-dining setting, Com Nieu has some of the best food in the province, served at reasonable prices. Try the caramelised pork in a clay pot, fried morning glory or the many seafood items.

Quy Nhon

Quy Nhon is one of the cheapest cities on the coast for dining. Head to the beachside and around the parks in the evening for cheap and tasty seafood at roadside stands. Such seafood venues are always preferable to restaurants in terms of price and quality.
**Bun Thit Nuong**
168 Phan Boi Chau St. Tel (mobile): 094-351 5444. Open: daily B, L & D. **$**
Located in the centre of town, this humble eatery serves a single eponymous dish. Bun thiet nuong is grilled pork or other meats served on rice noodles with fresh herbs, tangy, shredded green papaya or mango and a rich sweet-and-sour sauce.

**Vietnamese Bay Quan**
120A Tran Phu St. Open; daily B, L & D.
**$**
This popular corner diner serves rice meals, beefsteak and a few noodle dishes. The service is fast, the menu and prices are posted on the wall, and the food is delicious.

*Western*
**Barbara's "The Kiwi Connection"**
19 Xuan Dieu St. Tel: 056-389 2921. Open: daily B, L & D.
**$$**
Barbara offers a light menu of family recipes and Western favourites. She is also a traveller's best friend. Her extensive knowledge of the area and personalised tours are unmatched.

# CHAM ART, ARCHITECTURE AND SCULPTURE

**The remains of its magnificent temples all over central and southern Vietnam serve as a reminder of the once-powerful Champa kingdom**

The Cham people have always had a thriving artistic culture, of which their ancient temples are most lauded. **My Son**, inland from Hoi An, has the highest concentrations of known temples. Other well-preserved temples worth visiting include **Po Shanu** in Mui Ne, **Po Rome** and **Po Klong Garai** in Phan Rang, and **Po Nagar** in Nha Trang.

Temple buildings contain a single inner chamber with cathedral ceilings, no windows, and only one eastward-facing door. Cham temple complexes usually consist of three or more buildings, all made of red-baked bricks. In the centre of the main building sits a *linga* (male phallus) and/or *yoni* (female counterpart).

The best examples of Cham statuary can be found at the **Museum of Cham Sculpture** in Danang. Common subjects include Hindu gods, particularly Shiva, as well as Vishnu, Brahma, Ganesh, Nandin the bull, Garuda (a bird-like deity), historical kings and uniquely Cham deities such as the goddess Po Nagar.

The Cham have always been known for their brightly coloured and very beautiful textiles, which are still woven on looms in homes. Cham holy men wear bright white robes with orange or red sashes and satchel, and a white turban with red tassels. The village of **My Nghiep** near Phan Rang is most famous for its textile weaving.

**ABOVE:** Cham dancers perform in traditional style at the Po Nagar Cham Towers, Nha Trang.

**LEFT:** Sandstone carving of the Goddess Uma at the Museum of Cham Sculpture, Danang.

**BELOW:** Intricate carving at Chien Dan Cham Tower, near Quang Ngai.

**LEFT:** A carved phallic symbol – known as a *lingam* stone – at the My Son temple ruins.

## PRESERVING CHAM CULTURE

Frenchman M.C. Paris rediscovered the holy city of My Son in 1898. A year later, members of the scholarly society, École française d'Extrême Orient (EFEO), began to study the inscriptions, architecture and art of My Son. In 1900, Frenchman Henri Parmentier began his work rediscovering and cataloguing most known Cham temple sites across the country. EFEO set up the Museum of Cham Sculpture in Danang to protect much of the best artwork retrieved from temples and archaeological sites around Vietnam. EFEO has continued to spearhead preservation work and study at My Son, but many of Champa's other monuments have been left largely unprotected and continue to be destroyed both by local residents and the government, hoping to exploit the resources where the temples are located. A few have indeed been imaginatively "restored" by local workers or foreign organisations using unproven techniques. However, the original technology used by the Cham to create the temples so far cannot be duplicated. Restorations tend to erode within a few years and cause the original structure – often more than 1,000 years old – to disintegrate along with it.

**ABOVE:** The Po Klong Garai Cham Towers date back to the 14th Century rule of King Jaya Simharvarman III.

**RIGHT:** Restoration work at the Duong Long Cham Towers near Qui Nhon.

# NHA TRANG AND DALAT

These two popular holiday spots could not be more different. Nha Trang is all sea, sand and sun, while Dalat is an elegant old hill station

The cities of Nha Trang and Dalat are a dynamic contrast. Both are popular vacation spots for locals, but while Nha Trang offers modern tourism infrastructure and sunny beaches, Dalat has a pleasantly cool climate and the rustic elegance of an old-world French colonial mountain retreat. Nha Trang is a transition zone of climate and culture between southern and central Vietnam, while Dalat is the gateway to the central highlands and the minorities that inhabit them. Both cities, but particularly Dalat, have much to explore outside their metro area. Many visitors spend a few days with a motorbike guide driving through the central highlands, north of Dalat.

Nha Trang is larger and livelier than Mui Ne to the south, but has far fewer resorts. The emphasis here is on the beach and the urban nightlife – the latter rivalled only by Ho Chi Minh City and Hanoi. Dozens of bars and restaurants ribbon the beach, including well-known haunts like the Sailing Club and Louisiane. Additionally, the islands off Nha Trang shelter some of the most popular scuba-diving spots in Vietnam. Visitors can earn diving certifications while they explore the beautiful reefs during their stay.

Dalat is all about ambience. Old colonial villas and historic hotels perch around lakes, gardens and a golf course. Mist rolls through the pine-forested hillsides each morning and down to the beds of roses, strawberries and bountiful produce grown nowhere else in the country. On the hillsides, the K'ho minority grow coffee and tea amid spectacular waterfalls and forested mountain peaks. K'ho women produce some of Vietnam's most beautiful handwoven silk fabrics, embossed with traditional tribal patterns.

Vietnam's most beloved Frenchman, the extraordinary Dr Alexandre Yersin, made his home in Nha Trang and was the first European to explore the central highlands. As a result of his time in the hills, he encouraged the French to build a hill station in Dalat. Yersin is most famous for discovering the cause of the bubonic plague, and for opening a branch of the Pasteur Institute in Nha Trang (another was built later in Dalat, too) to develop the serum and cure the disease.

---

**PRECEDING PAGES:** Whale Island Resort, off Nha Trang. **LEFT:** a gondola connects Nha Trang to Hon Tre Island. **TOP:** strawberry farm, Dalat. **ABOVE RIGHT:** Ana Mandara Resort, Dalat.

# NHA TRANG AND SURROUNDINGS

When travel in Vietnam gets too wearying, consider an escape to Nha Trang with its fine beaches, tourist facilities and nightlife. Nearby are the crumbling ruins of the old Champa empire

**B**eaches. Nightlife. Diving. These three words encapsulate the experience of **Nha Trang ❶** for most travellers. Vietnam's favourite party town has many hidden charms, however, for those who delve deeper and explore its museums, aquariums and rich ethnic culture. Within striking distance in the hinterland are several important sites where the ancient Cham culture has left its mark. What is more, Nha Trang is serviced by daily flights from Hanoi, Danang and Ho Chi Minh City, making an idyllic beach holiday within easy reach when these big cities start to grate on your nerves.

Nha Trang is the ideal place to break a journey, relax and soak up the sun. With its population of about 400,000, it is the fifth largest city in Vietnam, and the capital of Khanh Hoa province. The province is relatively unexplored in regard to tourism. The countryside is inhabited by Raglai, Churu and other hill tribes whose villages sit along small mountain and river roads.

## NHA TRANG

Nha Trang has a stunning location, bordered by mountains one side and a beautiful stretch of **beach** on the other. There are always visitors basting away in the warm sun, and a cool breeze blowing at popular beach spots fronted by bars and restaurants such as the **Sailing Club** and **Louisiane Brewhouse**. Upmarket resorts like the plush **Ana Mandara** shield their patrons from the persistent hawkers selling fruit, barbecued seafood and sunglasses.

As a tourism showpiece, Nha Trang's golden sandy beach is kept pretty clean, but the water quality can vary during the year from clear and sparkling blue to murky and speckled with bits of garbage from the Cai

**Main attractions**

PO NAGAR CHAM TOWERS
THAP BA HOT SPRINGS
HON CHONG PROMONTORY
DAM MARKET
ALEXANDRE YERSIN MUSEUM
OCEANOGRAPHIC INSTITUTE
HON TRE
HON HEO PENINSULA
PO KLONG GARAI

**LEFT:** scuba-diver takes the plunge in Nha Trang. **RIGHT:** fishing boats at Nha Trang

**TIP**

The best diving in Nha Trang is during the dry season from June to September. The optimum time to take advantage of these conditions is during late August and September when the crowds tend to be at their thinnest.

**BELOW:** rinsing off the mud at Thap Ba Hot Springs.

River; the latter usually happens after heavy rain causes the river to run off into the bay.

Activities abound on the beach: there is an amusement park, jet-ski rentals, sailing, windsurfing and parasailing. There are no designated areas for most of these activities, so water-sports enthusiasts constantly launch and land among groups of swimmers – not an ideal situation.

The main tourist area lies mostly on the north-south parallel streets of Tran Phu, Hung Vuong and Nguyen Thien Thuat, in the four blocks between Nguyen Thi Minh Khai and Tran Quang Khai streets. This is where the largest concentration of hotels, bars and restaurants is found. A seedy element has grown in tandem with the tourist industry – prostitutes, pickpockets, and even elements of the Vietnamese mafia, mingle among the tourists at night – so keep an eye on your belongings and be careful about flaunting expensive camera equipment or jewellery.

## Po Nagar Cham towers

On a hill above the **Cai River**, at the city's northern entrance, stand the majestic towers of the famous Cham sanctuary and temple **Po Nagar** Ⓐ (tel: 058-383 1569; daily 8am–6pm; charge). The 25-metre (82ft) main tower is dedicated to the Cham goddess Po Yan Inu Nagar (worshipped by local Buddhists as the goddess Thien Y Ana), the "Holy Mother" of the Champa kingdom, and considered to be Shiva's female form. Her statue resides in the main temple, but it was decapitated during French rule; the original head now resides in the Guimet Museum in Paris. Only four of the sanctuary's original eight temples, all of which face east, remain standing. These were apparently constructed over an extended period of time between the 7th and 12th centuries. The 22 pillars and steep steps leading up to the main tower hint at the grandeur of the original temple. In the late 1990s the towers were carefully restored, and today they are swamped by tourists – both Vietnamese and foreign – throughout the day.

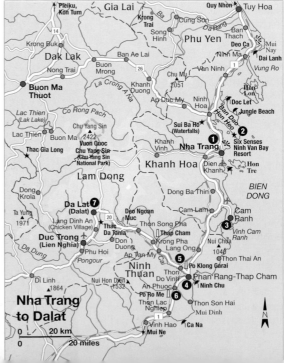

Personal religious expression is highly restricted by the local government in this part of Vietnam. Signs around the temple forbid the burning of incense or what are deemed to be superstitious behaviours. Cham people who try to worship here and place offerings of flowers and incense in front of the phallic *linga* at the main tower are sometimes forcibly removed by the police.

Ethnic Cham performers from Phan Rang present live traditional music and dances daily from 7.30 to 11am and 2.30 to 4.30pm. Shops behind the temples sell a variety of Cham crafts. Some of the textiles sold here are woven using traditional looms on site.

## Xom Bom village

Opposite the Po Nagar Cham towers, across Xom Bong Bridge at the mouth of the Cai River, is a picturesque fishing village called **Xom Bom**. Although the settlement is being chipped away by new resorts moving in, it occupies a remarkable natural harbour punctuated by small islets and boulders. From either **Xom Bong Bridge** or **Tran Phu Bridge**, you can watch the blue and red fishing boats returning with their fresh catches; early mornings are best.

## Thap Ba Hot Springs

Following the Cai River west of Po Nagar are the **Thap Ba Hot Springs** **B** (15 Ngoc Son St; tel: 058-383 5335; www.thapbahotspring.com.vn; daily 7am–7.30pm; charge), famous for their mineral mud baths, although there are also a number of thermal pools with the water simmering at a toasty 40°C (104°F), and a swimming pool with a man-made waterfall. The natural spring water here does not bubble to the surface. It is pumped via a well from a short depth. Apparently much of the mud is also brought from another location, and it's not entirely clear how sanitation is ensured.

This is one of the rare tourist attractions that appeals equally to both local and foreign tourists. If the thought of sharing a bath with strangers does not appeal, book a special "VIP Spa" with private soaking pools, steam bath and massage. A number of good restaurants are located at the park, making Thap Ba a convenient place for families to spend the afternoon. Do avoid the souvenir shops if they are found selling lacquered sea turtles, however.

Little known to visitors (or, for that matter, most Vietnamese), hot springs are a fairly common phenomenon throughout Vietnam. Many other coastal provinces also have them, though not all have been developed for tourists. Unfortunately, their popularity in some places has spawned a few fake "mineral hot springs" and "mineral mud baths" in tourist areas around the country. When visiting water parks, be sure to ask where the hot water and mineral mud actually come from.

## Hon Chong promontory

Just northeast of Xom Bom, the promontory of **Hon Chong** **C** juts out into the aquamarine waters of the

*The sheltered bay at Hon Chong is perfect for swimming.*

**BELOW:** the Po Nagar Cham towers are among the most famous Cham monuments in Vietnam.

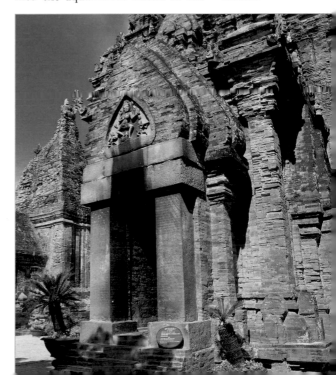

**Nha Trang**

0       500 m
0       500 yds

South China Sea. The spot is a perfect place for swimming as it's a bit more sheltered than the main beach at Nha Trang. The beach here is usually crowded with children at the weekend. An on-duty policeman keeps things in order.

North, across the bay, is **Co Tien Mountain** (Nui Co Tien), or Fairy Mountain. Its three summits are thought to resemble a fairy lying on her back; the first peak on the right resembles her face, the middle one her breasts and the third (and highest) her crossed legs.

## Dam Market

Some of Nha Trang's most interesting French colonial architecture and crumbling 19th-century Chinese houses can be seen around **Dam Market** Ⓓ (Cho Dam), near the Cai River. This former Chinese quarter is truly the most underrated part of town. The busy market sees surprisingly few foreign tourists, and is a welcome contrast to the rest of the modernised city – and a great place to snack on local foods. While souvenirs abound, please refrain from purchasing dried sea products, including sharks' fins, sea horses, puffer fish and other reef animals. Buying these goods only encourages further destruction of Nha Trang's already frail coral reefs.

## Nha Trang Cathedral

Just east of the Nha Trang railway station stands the large **Nha Trang Cathedral** Ⓔ (Nha Tho Nui Nha Trang; tel: 058-382 3335; Mass Mon–Sat 5am and 4.30pm, Sun 5am, 7am and 4.30pm) at 31 Thai Nguyen Street. Built in a Gothic style between 1928 and 1934, this Catholic cathedral is one of the city's defining landmarks. Its beautiful stained-glass windows depicting Jesus, Mary and a variety of saints reflect the coloured neon lights that encircle the statues inside.

## Long Son Pagoda

On the top of Trai Thuy Hill and to the west of the city centre a white, 19-metre (62ft) statue of the Sakyamuni Buddha overlooks the city from behind **Long Son Pagoda** ❺ (daily 8am–5pm; free). The original pagoda was built here in 1886 and has been renovated several times since.

The Buddha statue at Long Son Pagoda, which is seated on a lotus blossom throne, was erected in 1963 to commemorate the Buddhist struggle against the repressive South Vietnamese regime of Ngo Dinh Diem, which was overthrown that same year. Images of the Buddhist nuns and monks who killed themselves as a final protest are displayed at the base of the statue. The most famous of them, Thich Quang Duc, made headlines when he immolated himself in the centre of Saigon in 1963.

## Nha Trang Evangelical Church

The large, cathedral-style **Nha Trang Evangelical Church** ❻ (Sun service 8am) at 29 Le Thanh Phuong Street is the administrative centre for the large Protestant population of Khanh Hoa province. Several of the pastors here have spent years in and out of prison for openly expressing their faith under the communist system. The Sunday service is always packed to the rafters.

## Alexandre Yersin Museum

The **Pasteur Institute** ❼, on Nha Trang's seafront at 10D Tran Phu Street, was founded in 1895 by Dr Alexandre Yersin (1863–1943), a French microbiologist, military doctor, explorer and overall Renaissance man who had worked at the Pasteur Institute in Paris, where he helped Emile Roux discover the diphtheria bacterium. He arrived in Vietnam (via Nha Trang) in 1891 and was one of the first Europeans to explore extensively the Mekong Delta area and the central highlands.

Yersin was instrumental in the development of the hill station at Dalat and was also responsible for introducing Brazilian rubber trees and establishing *quinquina* plantations – quinine-producing trees – in the Suoi Dau region southwest of Nha Trang. He is buried here among his rubber trees, with a pagoda built nearby to honour him.

In 1894, Yersin was sent to Hong Kong by the French government and the Pasteur Institute to investigate an outbreak of the bubonic plague. He soon discovered the link between rats, fleas and eventually the bacteria that cause it (later renamed *Yersinia pestis* in his honour). Returning to Nha Trang in 1895, he built a laboratory to manufacture the serum for the disease. Ten years later, in 1905, the lab became an official branch of the Pasteur Institute. Today, Nha Trang's Pasteur Institute still produces vaccines and carries out research, despite being constrained by a very tight budget.

The small **Alexandre Yersin Museum** (tel: 058-382 2355; Mon–Fri 7.30–11am and 2–4.30pm;

*The statue of Buddha at Long Son Pagoda overlooks Nha Trang from the top of Trai Thuy Hill.*

**BELOW:** Alexandre Yersin and his telescope.

charge) attached to the institute displays many of the great man's personal effects, furniture, documents and antique laboratory equipment (including an enormous telescope). Many of his old books are still kept in the library.

## Khanh Hoa Provincial Museum

A few doors down from the Pasteur Institute is the small **Khanh Hoa Museum** ❶ (tel: 058-382 2277; Tue–Fri 8–11am and 2–5pm; free) at 16D Tran Phu Street. The museum's left wing contains relics from the Xom Con (about 3,000 years old), the Dong Son (c.2000 BC–AD 200) and Cham (which peaked between the 7th and 12th centuries) cultures. The most unusual item is the ancient stone lithograph (a musical instrument similar to a marimba) estimated to be 3,000 years old. The museum's right wing contains photos of modern Khanh Hoa province and a random mix of old ceramics. Notably absent are exhibits on Vietnam's wartime history or about Ho Chi Minh.

## Bao Dai's Villas

At the southern end of Nha Trang, near the Cau Da Port, are **Bao Dai Villas** ❶ (Vinh Nguyen; tel: 058-359 0147; www.vngold.com/nt/baodai). The five ageing villas are set on three hills amongst well-manicured trees and shrubs, and date back to the 1920s when they were built for Bao Dai (the last emperor of Vietnam's Nguyen dynasty) and his family. From the mid-1950s until 1975, high-ranking officials of the South Vietnamese government used the villa as a holiday home. After 1975, communist leaders from Hanoi supplanted them. Today, the buildings have been restored and the provincial tourism authorities run the complex as a hotel. The grounds, restaurants and a somewhat scruffy little beach facing the port are all open to the public. The rates are slightly overpriced, but it's a nice spot to take some photos and have a picnic. You can sneak into the tower of the main house for a better view of the bay.

**BELOW:** water sports at Nha Trang.

## Oceanographic Institute

Sandwiched between the Bao Dai Villas and Cau Da Port is the **Oceanographic Institute** Ⓚ (tel: 058-539 8188; daily 6am–6pm; charge), founded in 1923 and housed in a large French-colonial complex. The institute has about a dozen large, open tanks – most notable are the prowling sharks, inquisitive rays and the seemingly oblivious sea turtles. Smaller tanks are filled with bizarre reef fish and sea horses. The main building houses a large collection of preserved specimens. Impressive are the giant humpback whale and dugong skeletons, as well as an entire pickled dugong (which might turn a few stomachs).

## NHA TRANG'S ISLANDS

### Hon Tre (Bamboo Island)

From Nha Trang Beach, the outline of large **Hon Tre** Ⓛ (Bamboo Island) in the distance is clearly visible. The island is rather dominated these days by the **Vinpearl**

**Land Amusement Park** (tel: 058-395 8188; wwwvinpearlland.com; daily 8am–10pm; charge) and **Vinpearl Resort**. The blinding-white, Hollywood-style lettering on the mountain proudly announces who is responsible for the environmental degradation. Thankfully the park looks much better on the inside. A **gondola** (charge) – which incidentally holds the Guinness World Record for the longest ocean-crossing cable car at 3,320 metres (10,892ft) – departs from **Phu Quy Port** and delivers visitors to the centre of the amusement park. If you find the idea of a 10-minute cable-car ride daunting, take the

*Hon Tre's Vinpearl Resort operates an impressive Underwater World, an ideal excursion for families with young children.*

**BELOW LEFT:** preserved specimens at the Oceanographic Institute.

## Underwater Nha Trang

**O**ne of the star attractions of Nha Trang is its beautiful coral reefs – largely encompassed by the Hon Mun Marine Protected Area, which includes nine offshore islands. During marine surveys in the 1990s, some 190 species of coral and 176 species of marine life were documented in its waters.

Sadly, and predictably, Nha Trang's reefs are rapidly deteriorating due to pollution, overfishing and mismanagement by the government. Visibility, which was once 30 metres (98ft), is typically restricted to 10 metres (33ft). Of the 19 original dive sites, only five are still around. Boats supplied to the government by NGOs to monitor the reefs now sit idly by while fishermen in full view drop nets and, even worse, dynamite and cyanide, on marked dive spots.

Visitors should support eco-friendly companies that help conserve the reefs. Safety is also paramount, as some companies have had their licences revoked for abandoning divers at sea. See the Activities section (*page 372*) for recommendations of safe and responsible dive centres.

In 2010, *National Geographic Traveller* ranked Nha Trang, together with Mui Ne, among the world's worst beaches, largely on environmental grounds. The sensational listing got the attention of the provincial government. Whether they take positive steps to improve the situation is yet to be seen.

*Many islands, such as Hon Yen (Bird's Nest Island), are home to German's swiftlets, whose famous nests – gathered in vast quantities – are a source of nutrition and income.*

**BELOW:** idyllic Whale Island Resort.

ferry instead (20 minutes) from Phu Quy Port. The park contains a number of rides and a roller-coaster, a games area, water park, a shopping centre and several restaurants. The large amphitheatre was the centre of attraction when it hosted the 2008 Miss Universe swimsuit competition.

The crowning feature of the park is the modern **Underwater World**, with more than 20 fresh- and seawater tanks of varying sizes, including an impressive walk-through wrap-around tank featuring sharks, rays, morays and a large variety of reef animals. The aquarium is controversial within Nha Trang's diving community, however; some have accused it of pillaging the local reefs for the marine specimens, including a well-known moray that divers used to seek out.

The park is a fun way to spend a day with children, but the near US$20 basic entry fee for the park and aquarium will keep out most local Vietnamese and budget travellers. Visitors can choose to stay on the island's five-star Vinpearl Resort, an over-the-top beach-front resort with 400 rooms, Vietnam's largest swimming pool and myriad facilities.

## Other Islands

From Phu Quy Port, visitors can take a 20-minute boat ride to **Hon Mieu**, where the large **Tri Nguyen Aquarium** (tel: 058-359 9689; daily 8am–5pm; charge), designed to look like a tall ship that has been sunken and fossilised, is located. The facility also serves as a fish and crustacean hatchery.

Several other islands are located in the vicinity of Nha Trang, including **Hon Mot** (no popular English translation), **Hon Mun** (Ebony Island), **Hon Yen** (Bird's Nest Island), **Hon Ong** (Whale Island) and **Hon Lao** (Monkey Island). Most of these islands, as well as beaches on Hon Mieu and Hon Tre, are easily visited on a boat tour (which can be booked at any tour office or guesthouse in Nha Trang). Tours include snorkelling at various reef spots. Most require additional marine park fees, not included in the tour price.

A word of caution: **Hon Lao**, though tempting to visit, is best avoided. The large population of macaques running free there is highly aggressive and some of them are bred for scientific research. Due to the genetic experiments and the conditions they live in, it's not only possible but also likely that the monkeys carry dangerous diseases communicable to humans. Many would also consider the circus-style animal shows held here to be inhumane.

**Hon Ong** is occupied by the French-run **Whale Island Resort** (tel: 058-384 0501; www.whaleislandresort.com) and is a permanent diving station for **Rainbow Divers** (*see page 372*). The island's future and its pristine coral reefs, however, are hanging in the balance as the government has proposed dredging the channel and building a steel mill on the island in the near future.

# NORTH OF NHA TRANG

## Ba Ho Waterfalls

About 25km (16 miles) north of Nha Trang, near the village of Phu Huu, are the **Ba Ho Waterfalls** (Sui Ba Ho; daily 7.30am–5pm; charge). Here, amid lush green forests, are three pools in ascending height, formed by water cascading over large boulders. Enterprising youngsters will follow you the entire 2km (1.2-mile) -long trek, offering helping hands (and selling drinks), all of which become much appreciated as the climb grows increasingly steep and slippery.

## Doc Let Beach

Further north on its own peninsula is the lovely and secluded **Doc Let Beach**, which looks out over the South China Sea. This palm-tree-fringed expanse of gently sloping sand has relatively calm waters and is very popular with Vietnamese tourists at weekends. Several small and low-key resorts here offer budget accommodation. Some rubbish from the nearby fishing village tends to mar the beach at times, but thankfully most resorts keep their own respective beaches quite clean.

In the west, **Me Con Mountain** (Nui Me Con) reaches a height of about 2,000 metres (6,600ft). From a distance, its silhouette resembles that of a woman carrying a child, hence its name, Mother and Child Mountain.

## Hon Heo Peninsula

North of Nha Trang is the **Hon Heo Peninsula ❷**, an idyllic world of secluded beaches and tall boulder-strewn mountains, inhabited by large populations of one of Indochina's rarest primates – the black-shanked Douc langur (*Pygathix nemaeus nigripes*). The two beaches on the peninsula have become legendary destinations themselves. The first, **Jungle Beach**, is on the northern side, some 40km (25 miles) from Nha Trang, about an hour's drive away. The beach here is pristine and the water sparkling and clear year-round, with permanent populations of bioluminescent algae that magically light up when swimmers stir the water at night. The rustic **Jungle Beach Resort** (*see page 353*) occupies the prime position here. On the southern side of the peninsula, reachable only by boat, is an exclusive getaway for people with money to burn. The **Six Senses Ninh Van Bay** (*see page 353*) offers luxury private villas, each with its own personal butler, swimming pool and private terrace and deck which has a ladder descending into the clear waters below.

# SOUTH OF NHA TRANG

Heading 35km (22 miles) south of Nha Trang, the coastal road passes Cam Ranh Airport and then arrives at **Cam Ranh Bay ❸** (Vinh Cam Ranh), the deep-water bay used as a naval base, first by the Americans, later by the Soviets, and finally by the Vietnamese. The bay has been opened to tourists, but tourism infrastructure has yet to be developed. While the water itself is clear and inviting, the beaches are often littered with rubbish. South of Cam Ranh, the road enters Ninh Thuan province. The coastal road passes through a rather monotonous, sand-covered landscape.

*The sand from Cam Ranh Bay is of a quality much sought-after for manufacturing lenses and high-quality crystal. Before the war, enormous quantities of sand were exported to Japan, Europe and America.*

**BELOW:** the exclusive Six Senses Hideaway resort.

*Carving at Po Ro Me tower, named after the last king to rule the Champa kingdom in the 17th century.*

## Phan Rang and Thap Cham

The town of **Phan Rang** ❹ and its sister city of **Thap Cham**, 7km (4 miles) to the west, are co-capitals of Ninh Thuan province, and the modern cultural centre of the Cham people, who are now settled along the **Cai River**. Local residents often walk about town in traditional dress, the men in white gowns and turbans with red sashes, and women with heads covered in Muslim fashion. The towns are located in an extremely arid landscape dotted with menacinglooking cacti and poinciana trees. This is one of Vietnam's poorest areas, due to the lack of agricultural resources and discriminatory policies of the communist government. Grape-growing has recently taken root, however, and more and more vineyards can be seen in the countryside.

## Po Klong Garai

Four 13th-century Cham towers known as **Po Klong Garai** ❺ (daily 8am–6pm; charge) stand on an arid hill about 7km (4 miles) west of Phan Rang, toward Dalat on Highway 20. These brick towers were built under the reign of the

**BELOW:** Po Klong Garai.

Cham king Jaya Simhavarman III to worship King Po Klong Garai, who had constructed a much-needed local irrigation system. The entrance to the largest tower is graced with a dancing, six-armed Shiva, and inside a statue of the bull Nandi, recipient of offerings brought by farmers to ensure a good harvest. A *linga* (stone phallus) painted with a human face sits below the main tower.

## Po Ro Me

About 15km (10 miles) south of Phan Rang is the tower of **Po Ro Me** ❻ (daily 8am–6pm; free), named after the last king of Champa, who ruled from 1629 to 1651 and died a captive of the Vietnamese. Po Ro Me, which dates back to the early 16th century, is one of the last towers built by the Champa kingdom. An image of King Po Ro Me is found at the top of the tower, flanked by reliefs of the bull, Nandi.

Like Po Klong Garai, the tower is a focal point of the annual Kate Festival (Cham New Year), but receives fewer holiday revellers. To reach the tower, head south from Phan Rang on Highway 1A for about 9km (6 miles), and then head west at Hau Sanh for the remaining 6km (4 miles).

# RESTAURANTS

Nha Trang's main dining district – around Biet Thu and Tran Quang Khai streets, around 1km (0.6 mile) south of the Cathedral and close to the beach – is home to a variety of restaurants serving fare, from Indian to Italian as well as seafood. If you want something cheap and local, try the stand serving *bun thit nuong* (grilled pork with rice noodles), and the signature here – a boiled quail egg and spring roll on top – in the evenings at **20 Tran Quang Khai Street**, for under US$1. Also recomended is the *pho bo* (beef and rice noodle soup) at **Pho Huong Bac** on 109 Nguyen Thien Thuat Street.

## *Vietnamese*
### Lac Canh Restaurant
44 Nguyen Binh Khiem Street. Tel: 012-382 1391. Open: daily L & D.**$**
Always crowded with locals, the Lac Canh is one of the best places for seafood in Nha Trang. Décor is basic, and it's possible to grill prawns, fish etc to your own taste on the tabletop barbecues. An authentic Vietnamese experience.

### Lanterns
72 Nguyen Thien Thuat St. Tel: 058-247 1674. Open: daily L & D. **$$**
www.lanternsvietnam.com
Lanterns is a long-time favourite serving delicious local dishes like hotpot, seafood and braised pork in a clay pot, in a tasteful setting surrounded by ubiquitous hanging lanterns. Lanterns also runs a popular cooking class.

### Nha Hang Yen's Restaurant
3/3 Tran Quang Khai St. Tel: 012 1955 6861. Open: daily B, L & D. **$**
www.in2vietnam.com
This popular restaurant is a recent addition to the backpacker neighbourhood, not far from the beach. Dishes include street-food favourites like *banh xeo* (seafood crepes) and *bun bo hue* (beef noodle soup). The owner, Yen, is friendly and takes service seriously.

### Truc Linh
11 Biet Thu St. Tel: 058-352 6742. Open: daily B, L & D. **$$**
www.truclinhrest.vn
Popular seafood restaurant, with the catch of the day displayed in enormous tanks outside along the street. A few doors down on 21 Biet Thu St is sister restaurant **Truc Linh 2**, which also serves Thai dishes, in addition to the regular Vietnamese menu.

## *French*
### Le Petit Bistro
26D Tran Quang Khai Street. Tel: 012-352 7201. Open: daily B, L & D. **$$$**
Quality French dining, a good wine list and an attractive, intimate space make this a popular choice. Note that you'll pay extra for sauces. If the air-con is too fierce, there's also a minuscule courtyard.

## *International*
### Booze Cruise Bar & Grill
110 Nguyen Thien Thuat St. Tel: 012-6750 7551. Open: daily L & D. **$$**
A popular nightspot, particularly with the older gentlemen and younger lady crowd, and famous for its burgers and pizza. Booze Cruise is well grounded as a sports bar, showing most of the North American sports games and any other games to be had on its big flat screen.

### The Grill House
1/18 Tran Quang Khai St. Tel: 058-352 8087. Open: daily B, L & D. **$$$**
The Grill House serves tasty Australian steaks, burgers and seafood, all cooked on a charcoal grill. The atmosphere is pleasant and staff generally outgoing. Be sure to try the tiramisu, made by their Italian chef.

### Louisiane Brewhouse
Lot 29, Tran Phu St. Tel: 058-352 1948. Open: daily B, L & D. **$$$**
www.louisianebrewhouse.com.vn
One of the most expensive spots, but definitely the best atmosphere in town. The beachside restaurant with swimming pool offers mostly Vietnamese seafood, with some steaks, burgers, pizza and sushi thrown in for variety. The home-made brews are excellent – try its signature ginger ale with lemongrass.

### Rainbow Divers
90A Hung Vuong St. Tel: 058-352 4351. Open: daily B, L & D. **$$**
www.divevietnam.com
The head office of Vietnam's top dive shop has an excellent bar and restaurant. The easy all-wood interior feels like the cabin of a ship. Menu includes steak sandwiches, burgers, pizza, pasta, meat pies and steaks, fish and chips, and imported ice cream.

### The Sailing Club
72–74 Tran Phu St. Tel: 058-382 6528. Open: daily B, L & D. **$$$**
www.sailingclubvietnam.com
One of the most famous expat haunts in Vietnam, with a sister resort in Mui Ne. This is one of the more expensive venues in town, but you get the quality you pay for. Menu includes an eclectic mix of wraps, salads, plus Indian, Vietnamese and Italian dishes.

### Texas BarBQ & Steaks
26 Tran Quang Khai St. Tel: 058-352 5084. Open: daily L & D. **$$$**
www.texasbbqvietnam.com
This authentic American-style restaurant serves US imported beef, ribs, burgers, fish, chicken and seafood. Prices are high but the food is outstanding. Be sure to try the apple pie and ice cream for dessert, if you still have room.

## *Italian*
### Da Fernando
96 Nguyen Thien Thuat St. Tel: 058-352 8034. Open: daily L & D. **$$$**
Fernando formerly helmed the *Good Morning Vietnam* eatery in Mui Ne, but has come into his own in Nha Trang. The menu includes the usual Italian favourites – pizzas, pastas, gnocchi and risotto, but moves beyond the basics with a few delightful surprises. Easily the best Italian eatery in Nha Trang.

### La Taverna
115 Nguyen Thien Thuat St. Tel: 058-352 2259. Open: daily L & D. **$$$**
www.latavernavietnam.com
Swiss-Italian owner Atheo was the original manager of *Good Morning Vietnam* in Nha Trang and has moved on to this fine restaurant serving all the popular Italian basics (pizzas, pastas, lasagne, gnocchi and ravioli) as well as a few good Swiss dishes.

## *Spanish*
### La Mancha
78 Nguyen Thien Thuat St Tel (mobile): 091-456 9782. Open: daily B, L & D. **$$**
This excellent tapas restaurant has a great atmosphere, lively Spanish music and a fountain at the centre. Complimentary fresh bread is served throughout the meal. Try the stewed Spanish sausages.

# VIETNAMESE FESTIVALS

**Festivals in Vietnam are a time of fun. The main festival of Tet is especially vibrant as the whole country joins together in celebration**

Vietnam is a great place for festival-lovers. Colourful festivities, most with a strong Chinese cultural influence, take place throughout the year, although the most interesting ones occur in spring and autumn. Nearly all coincide with the lunar calendar. For a complete list of festivals (including many region-specific events) and precise dates, check www. vietnamtourism.com. Here are a few nationwide highlights.

**Jan/Feb, Tet**: The first seven days of the Lunar New Year mark the most important holiday in Vietnam (Tet Nguyen Dan), although only the first four days are a national holiday (see page 69 for more details).

**Mar/Apr, Thanh Minh**: Many people visit the graves of their ancestors to make offerings.

**May/June, Buddha's Birthday**: Better known as Vesak, this is a big day at temples, with religious processions and ceremonies.

**May/June, Tiet Doan Ngo**: Summer Solstice Day is observed by making offerings to spirits to ward off summer epidemics. It is often celebrated with dragon-boat races.

**Aug, Trang Nguyen**: Wandering Souls Day is the second-largest celebration after Tet.

**Sept/Oct, Trung Thu**: The Mid-Autumn Festival is a time for eating "moon cakes" filled with nuts, seeds and egg yolks. Children are given lanterns in the shape of dragons, carps and stars to play with.

**ABOVE:** ancestor worship is widely practised in Vietnam, co-existing with Buddhist, Confucian and Taoist beliefs. The ancestor cult is a homely affair but it is also celebrated publicly with effigies placed on pagoda altars.

**BELOW:** on the eve of Tet, and during Wandering Souls Day, families burn paper offerings to their ancestors. They often do so right on the pavement outside their house, so watch your feet!

**LEFT:** Buddhist monks and nuns, dressed in simple brown tunics, welcome visiting worshippers. Most are are happy to sit over a cup of green tea, explaining in detail the history and the imagery of their pagoda or temple. Vesak is the main Buddhist festival.

**Above:** beautifully crafted candlelit lanterns are carried by children during the atmospheric Mid-Autumn Festival in either September or October. This is also the time when "moon cakes" are eaten.

## VILLAGE FESTIVALS

The best time to observe village festivals is just after Tet, a word which itself means "festival". During the first two lunar months (February and March), most villages organise a fête of some sort. Families will visit the village pagoda and light incense to local deities and their ancestors. Youngsters play games, swinging on giant bamboo swings or playing "human chess" with people or metre-high models moving between squares marked on a courtyard.

Villages near the Red River (Song Hong) in northern Vietnam send boats to collect ceremonial water to offer to the water god, Ha Ba. The most spectacular of these traditions is when young men put on the elaborate costumes of the dancing lion and dance energetically among the revellers to the sound of beating drums. One of the most popular of these occasions is the quan ho festival at Lim village, near Hanoi. Here, young couples sing love songs to each other in a fertility rite to welcome the spring, a time-honoured tradition that goes back to ancient times.

**Above:** Liberation Day is celebrated on 30 April. This nationwide holiday marks the surrender of South Vietnam to the North Vietnamese Army in 1975. A year later Vietnam was officially united under the Communist Party. Other national holidays include the Founding of the Vietnamese Communist Party (3 February), and National Day (2 September).

**Left:** the colourful *rong mua lan*, or dancing lion, is a centrepiece of Tet festivals and other major festivals in villages throughout the country. The dance is said to scare away evil spirits and usher in good luck.

# DALAT AND SURROUNDINGS

A cool and tranquil retreat from the crowded lowland cities, Dalat is situated among pine-covered mountains and misty forests. A bounty of fresh produce and flowers flourishes here

**Main attractions**
DALAT PALACE HOTEL
CENTRAL MARKET
HANG NGA'S CRAZY HOUSE
BAO DAI'S SUMMER PALACE
LAM DONG MUSEUM
TIGER FALLS
LANG DINH AN VILLAGE
ELEPHANT FALLS
XQ HISTORICAL VILLAGE

The bracing cool mountain climate that **Dalat** ❼ enjoys at an altitude of 1,500 metres (4,920ft), its large open spaces, picturesque waterfalls, colonial architecture and incredibly fresh produce provide respite for those wishing to escape the heat and humidity of Ho Chi Minh City and the lowlands of southern Vietnam. It is easy to see why the French were so enamoured of Dalat during the colonial days and why it was the favourite getaway for Vietnam's last emperor, Bao Dai. For those seeking culture and exotic adventures, Dalat is also the gateway to the central highands area where hill-tribe villages abound.

In 1893 Dr Alexandre Yersin (see page 251) was the first European to survey the area, under the authority of Paul Doumer, the French governor-general of Indochina at the time. He suggested that a hill station and sanatorium be built here to take advantage of the mild climate and beautiful scenery. The area surrounding the Cam Ly River was eventually developed from a small fort in 1899 into a thriving resort town over the next few decades.

Annual temperatures range between a comfortable 16°C (61°F) and 24°C (75°F), making Dalat one of Vietnam's most popular retreats and its top honeymoon destination. The dry-weather months run from December to April, while the wet season is from May to November. These latter months are not so good for a visit. Nights can be quite chilly.

Dalat is a well-connected holiday hub, with major highways leading conveniently to Ho Chi Minh City (320km/200 miles; 6-7 hours' drive), Mui Ne (247km/153 miles; 5–6 hours), Phan Rang (108km/67 miles; 4–5 hours) and Nha Trang (205km/127 miles; 5–6 hours).

**LEFT:** Dalat Cathedral. **RIGHT:** radish farm in the lush highland countryside.

*Lat ethnic minority girl dressed in traditional costume.*

## Tourism in Dalat

The town receives plenty of domestic tourists. Some of its attractions, therefore, are geared towards Vietnamese tastes, and often seem rather kitsch to international visitors. At some of its parks and lakes, men in American cowboy costumes lead tourists on pony rides, while actors in monkey suits twirl spears for photo opportunities. Scores of souvenir sellers jostle for space with giant, brightly painted concrete statues of animals, mushrooms and Disney characters. You may want to avoid the notably kitsch **Valley of Love** (Thung Lung Tinh Yeu), 6km (4 miles) north of town, and the **Lake of Sighs** (Ho Than Tho), 5km (3 miles) northeast.

This does not have to be your Dalat experience, however. The city has been spared the ravages of war suffered by the rest of the country. During the Vietnam war, representatives from both sides came here for rest and recuperation (and probably for a bit of spying on each other). As a result, the beautiful colonial architecture has been preserved like nowhere else in Vietnam.

Most of the old villas and government buildings can be found in the French Quarter along the south side of Xuan Huong Lake and Cam Ly River.

Dalat is a wonderful place for walking with its many gardens and lakes, but it is difficult to navigate without a map in hand, as the narrow streets wrap themselves haphazardly around the hills. Elephant rides and horse carriages, once common, have fallen out of favour due to the harsh treatment of the animals. A paddle boat, available for rent at several lakes in and around Dalat, is a pleasant way to spend an afternoon.

## Two historic hotels

The hill resort was originally built around the grand Langbian Palace Hotel in the early years of the 20th century, a historic hotel that was renovated and reopened as the **Sofitel Dalat Palace** in 1995. Construction of the original Langbian Palace began in 1902 and laboured on for 20 years (at the time, travel from the coast took more than a week, making any new construction a slow and difficult task). The

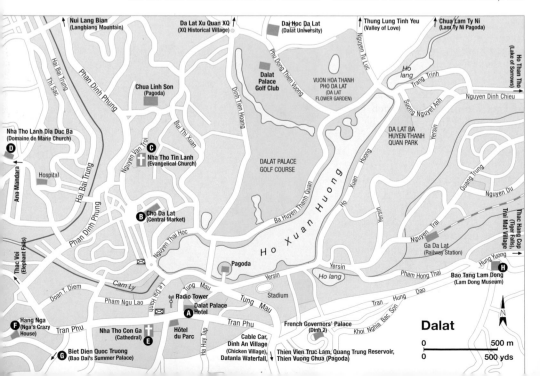

Hôtel du Parc, just diagonally opposite, followed in 1932. It has regained its old name after a series of recent re-brandings. The Sofitel, likewise, is now simply the **Dalat Palace** Ⓐ. Both retain much of their original architectural charm and the Dalat Palace still maintains over 4 hectares (10 acres) of grassy lawn, a rarity in Vietnam.

Just north of the Palace, **Xuan Huong Lake** (Ho Xuan Huong), formerly part of the town's colonial-era golf course before it was flooded, extends through the heart of the town. The surrounding hills, French-style villas and pine forests provide a lovely backdrop, although the water itself is muddy with red clay after the rains.

On the northern banks of the lake, a golf course originally built for the last emperor, Bao Dai, has been supplanted and expanded into the **Dalat Palace Golf Club** (tel: 063-382 1201). The 18-hole championship course is a sister club to the Ocean Dunes Golf Club in Phan Thiet.

## Central Market

Dalat's **Central Market** Ⓑ (Cho Da Lat; daily 6am–10pm) is one of the largest in the country, and one of the city's principal attractions. Set in a deep hollow of a hillside and surrounded by rows of cafés and shops selling wine and candied fruit, the current market was built in the 1960s. The original market, sitting on the hill above, was built in the 1920s and later converted into a cinema. The series of three central buildings can be confusing to navigate, and it may take several sweeps to find all the floors.

The food is the highlight here. The second floor of the middle building is devoted entirely to food stalls – mostly rice served with local specialities, and bowls of *che*, a dessert made with sweetened beans and candied fruit.

The ground floor of the market offers a peek into the great diversity of produce grown in the region: strawberries, tomatoes, avocados, asparagus and just about any fruit, flower and vegetable found in countries with temperate climates.

On Saturdays and Sundays from 7–10pm, the streets surrounding the market are closed to vehicles and a carnival-like atmosphere ensues with an influx of pedestrians, souvenir and clothing pedlars, and more food vendors.

## Churches and pagodas

North of the Central Market is the yellow **Dalat Evangelical Church** Ⓒ (Nha Tho Tin Lanh; Sun services with interpreter at 8am) at 72 Nguyen Van Troi Street. Built in 1940, most of the congregation is composed of impoverished hill-tribe minorities. Since 1975, local Protestants have suffered persecution as the communist government associates Protestants with the former American military presence. Even today the government restricts the activities of this church.

To the west, perched on the hilltop at Ngo Quyen Street, is **Domaine de Marie Convent Church** Ⓓ (daily 8am–noon and 2–5pm; free). Constructed in 1942, this French

**TIP**

Avoid buying the tiger and bear claws in the market shops (sold with the full knowledge of the police), as it encourages poaching of endangered wildlife around Langbiang Mountain. The animal teeth in the shops tend to be plastic fakes, but the claws are generally the real thing.

**BELOW:** fresh produce and dried goods at the Central Market.

*Dalat is famous for growing many things – especially the flowers that fill the market. Roses and tulips are shipped internationally, and Dalat's flowers supply most of the night markets in southern and central Vietnam.*

convent used to have almost 350 nuns in residence. Today, only 25 or so remain, running an orphanage and selling unique handmade crafts, embroidery, knitted sweaters and ginger candy to raise funds for local orphans, the homeless and the disabled.

In the southern part of town is the large, pink-coloured **Dalat Cathedral** Ⓔ (Nha Tho Con Ga; Mon–Sat Mass at 5.15am and 5.15pm, Sun Mass 5.15am, 7am, 8.30am, 4pm and 6pm). Located at the intersection of Tran Phu and Le Dai Hanh streets, the church is more popularly known as the Rooster Church on account of the rooster weathervane on top of the steeple. The cathedral was built in 1942, with stained-glass windows made by Louis Balmet, in Grenoble, France. Sunday Masses see large and enthusiastic crowds turning up. Across from the cathedral, taking the form of a mini Eiffel Tower, is Dalat's telecommunications tower.

Dalat's Buddhist temples were all built in the last century, but most are atmospheric and provide important places of worship for Chinese and ethnic Vietnamese immigrants. Thien Vuong Pagoda (also known as the Chinese Pagoda) is located 3km (2 miles) southeast of town on Khe Sanh Street. The temple, built in 1958, is fairly unremarkable but for the three giant sandalwood Buddha images that it houses.

The highlight of a visit to Lam Ty Ni Pagoda (2 Thien My Street) is not the architecture or the idols, but rather the solitary monk, Mar Thuc, who lives there. Made famous by an episode of the TV series *Globetrekker*, the "Crazy Monk" draws poems and writes poetry, which he sells to visitors.

Linh Son Pagoda sits on top of a hill at 120 Nguyen Van Troi Street, in the centre of town. The building has an attractive entrance and beautiful carved wooden doors, which lead behind to one of the largest monasteries in the central highlands.

### Hang Nga's Crazy House

For anyone travelling with children, or those who have played in tree houses themselves as children, **Hang Nga's**

**BELOW:** Dalat Palace Golf Club.

**Crazy House ⒻF** (tel: 063-382 2070; daily 7am–6pm; charge) at 3 Huynh Thuc Khang Street will surely appeal. This is a whimsical and inspiring piece of architecture that is guaranteed to delight. The never-completed house is continuously being added to, with tunnels, stairways and halls meandering into secret rooms and towers, and reading nooks occupied by statues of giant kangaroos, giraffes, eagles and bears.

The master architect, Dr Dang Viet Nga, daughter of the deceased General Secretary of the Communist Party in Vietnam, began construction of the fantasy house in 1990. Gift shops occupy a couple of rooms, selling unique handmade crafts. The other rooms may be rented as accommodation, but guests may find the constant stream of visitors rather intrusive.

## Bao Dai's Summer Palace

Tucked away under pine trees on a hill about 1km (0.6 miles) from Nga's Crazy House at Trieu Viet Vuong Street is the **Summer Palace of Bao Dai ⒼG** (Biet Dien Quoc Truong; tel: 063-382 6858; daily 7.30–11am and 1.30–4pm; charge). This Art Deco-influenced abode of Vietnam's last emperor was built between 1933 and 1938. Also referred to as Dinh III, this is actually one of three palaces (the others being Dinh I and Dinh II, neither of which is currently open to the public) belonging to Bao Dai in Dalat. It's said that all three are connected by tunnels so that the emperor could secretly visit his mistresses in each one. Although guides will say that the furnishings and artefacts in the house were used by Bao Dai, it is a well-known fact that many of his belongings were carted away in the early years. Outside the mansion, a carnival-like atmosphere prevails, with souvenir vendors, pony rides and Disney characters. To appreciate the villa better, visit it right after it opens in the morning, or just before lunch.

## Lam Dong Museum

On Hung Vuong Street in the eastern part of town is the **Lam Dong Museum ⒽH** (Bao Tang Lam Dong; tel: 063-382 2339; daily 7.30–11.30am and 1.30–4.30pm; charge), recognised by the United Nations for its extensive collections of musical gongs used by the local K'ho, Ma and Churu minorities. Other exhibits at this former colonial villa include an impressive taxidermy collection of local wildlife; relics from the Champa or Funan empire (this is debatable) excavated at Cat Tien National Park; artefacts found in recent excavations from still unidentified cultures; and full-sized Ma and K'ho tribal longhouses, decorated with musical instruments, weapons and common household items

**Dalat University** in the north of the city is one of the top schools in the country, and its many students live in tiny boarding houses that line most of the surrounding alleys. The city owes its abundance of cheap, delicious street food to the presence of so many students.

*A peek into the Summer Palace of Emperor Bao Dai reveals his Western tastes.*

**BELOW LEFT:** the unconventional Crazy House.

*The Lam Dong Museum has a wide array of exhibits and makes for an interesting afternoon.*

**BELOW:** Dalat railway station.

## EAST OF DALAT

Outside of the main town centre are several sights in the surroundings of Dalat that can be easily visited on half- or full-day trips. It is best to hire a car, taxi or motorbike to get to these places.

### Dalat Train Station and Trai Mat Village

The picturesque colonial-style **Dalat Train Station** (Ga Dalat) at Quang Trung Street opened in 1932, and was once the terminus of a train service that ran all the way to Phan Rang, just east of Nha Trang on the coast. The track, however, was damaged during the Vietnam War and never repaired. The only line that exists today is a short 7km (4-mile) stretch that carries a small diesel-run train transporting tourists to **Trai Mat village** east of the city. There are five daily departures, at 8am, 9.30am, 11am, 2pm and 3.30pm; a minimum of six passengers is required. The ride takes 30 minutes and passes through some lovely countryside.

There isn't much to see in Trai Mat for the moment, save for the grandiose

**Linh Phuoc Pagoda** (Chua Ling Phuoc; daily 8am–5pm; free). Built in 1952, the imposing seven-tiered pagoda is just a few hundred metres from the train station, on the other side of the street.

### Tiger Falls

**Tiger Falls** (Thac Hang Cop; daily daylight hours; charge) is the grandest waterfall in Dalat's environs, and thankfully the least visited or developed, largely because of the long drive down a poor road and a further walk down a very steep hill. The falls are an ideal outing for nature-lovers who wish to do a bit of adventure trekking, following the stream as it crashes among the boulders in the rainforest canyon below. Tiger Falls is 14km (9 miles) east of Dalat, past Trai Mat village, where there is a signposted turning on the left.

## SOUTH OF DALAT

### Dalat Cable Car

The **Dalat Cable Car** (Cap Treo Dalat; Tue–Fri 7.30–11.30am and 1.30–5pm,

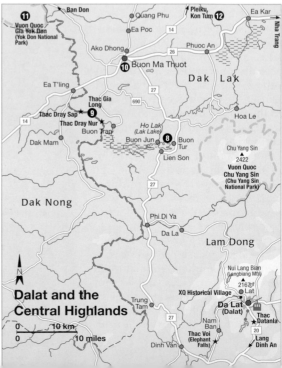

**Dalat and the Central Highlands**

0    10 km
0         10 miles

Mon 7.30–11.30am only; charge) is located about 3km (1.8 miles) south of town. The cable-car ride stretches over 2km (1.2 miles) and offers lovely panoramas of villages and mountain forests, all the way to the **Bamboo Forest Meditation Centre** (Thien Vien Truc Lam).

This Zen-style Buddhist monastery was built in 1993 and has about 100 monks and 80 nuns in residence. The temple is famous because of its perfect *feng shui* placement, with **Pin Haat Mountain** (Nui Pin Haat) behind and **Quang Trung Reservoir** (Ho Tuyen Lam) below. Below the monastery is a picnic area with tables and chairs that overlooks the tranquil reservoir. The artificial lake is now a recreational area with rowing boats and canoes for rent.

## Datanla Waterfall

The turn-off for **Datanla Waterfall** (Thac Da Tanla; daily daylight hours; charge) is about 5km (3 miles) south of Dalat, or just a few hundred metres past the turn-off for the Bamboo Forest Meditation Centre. There is a 10-minute walk through rainforest, down to the falls below (allow 20 minutes for the return walk). The waterfall makes for great photos, if you can overlook the kitschy pony rides, girls in fake minority costumes and men in bear suits. The mechanised toboggan run (extra charge) down to the falls and back is the most enjoyable aspect of the commercialism that has taken root here.

## Lang Dinh An village

Once a favourite stop for tourists wishing to see the K'ho ethnic minority, **Lang Dinh An village** (more popularly known as Chicken Village), 17km (11 miles) south from highway 20, today resembles most other villages in Dalat's environs, with one exception. Its unique focal point is a giant concrete chicken, which isn't at all as tacky as it sounds. It's actually a rather striking sculpture with an interesting story behind it.

The K'ho were once a nomadic tribe, subsisting on slash-and-burn agriculture. After 1975, the communist government tried to get them to move out of the hills and to one of the villages closer to Dalat, where they could assimilate with the Kinh colonists, and thus be under the watchful eye of the government. The local K'ho chief, however, said that the tribe would only agree if the government built a giant chicken statue, with nine claws, to adorn the centre of the new village.

According to an ancient K'ho legend, a girl had approached the mother of her lover, asking permission to marry her son (as is the custom in the matriarchal K'ho culture). The mother, who disapproved of the pairing, told the girl that she would only consent if she could bring her a chicken with nine claws (knowing this to be impossible). The girl thus began an epic search for the unlikely chicken, but eventually died in her quest.

This rooster statue that the chief requested stands as a symbolic offering to the legendary maiden, putting her finally at peace. The irony, which

*Dalat's surrounding forests, as lovely as they may be, are not entirely natural. In an effort to make their surroundings more familiar, the French burnt much of the grasslands and reseeded the hills with pine, which spread rapidly in the rich soils and mild climate.*

**BELOW:** the Dalat Cable Car connects to a few attractions worth visiting.

*The resourceful K'ho and Ma women are excellent weavers and still dye their cloth using natural bark extracts. The impoverished minority women also sell street food in the Dalat Central Market.*

many have missed altogether, is that much like the mother who sent the maiden on a fool's errand, the chief probably never expected the government to accede to his strange request. As a result of the agreement, however, many K'ho families were forced to move out of the hills, much against their wishes, to this new village.

Shops around the chicken statue sell lovely handwoven blankets, handbags, tablecloths and other items with brightly coloured tribal patterns that prominently feature horses and elephants.

## WEST OF DALAT

**Elephant Falls** (Thac Voi), 30km (19 miles) southwest of Dalat, is a favourite stop on tours of Dalat's countryside led by local guides. The dramatic rock formations are just as arresting as the falls themselves, which look like a movie set from Peter Jackson's *King Kong*. It's a bit of a climb down to the bottom of the falls for the best views, but steps have been skilfully carved into the rocks to make the trek easier. A shop above the falls sells beautiful

**BELOW:** the mighty Elephant Falls.

handwoven K'ho blankets and crafts, all made on-site.

## NORTH OF DALAT

### Langbiang Mountain

The 12km (7-mile) drive from Dalat to **Langbiang Mountain** (Nui Lang Bian) passes through quaint **Lat Village**, inhabited by K'ho, Lat and Ma minorities. The villagers make a meagre living from the squash, tobacco, coffee, tea and cotton that they grow on the hillsides.

Visitors can explore Langbian Mountain's hiking trails on their own, but hiring a guide offers more options. The mountain is a favourite trekking location of adventure tour companies such as Groovy Gecko and Phat Tire (*see page* 372). There are breathtaking vistas of the countryside, and the surrounding pine forests are said to harbour a surviving few bears, deer, leopards and boar.

### XQ Historical Village

About 6km (4 miles) north of town and across the street from the Valley

of Love is the **XQ Historical Village** (tel: 063-383 1343; www.xqhandembroidery.com; open daily 8am–8pm; free). Although run as a commercial enterprise and not really a village, this attraction offers an entertaining and informative experience, engaging all the senses in a way that few other tourist attractions in Dalat can. XQ is Vietnam's top brand of embroidered paintings – its works are a favourite gift from the government to visiting dignitaries and celebrities.

XQ's high-quality embroidery is one of Vietnam's success stories. The company has a presence in every major city in Vietnam – but it goes far beyond mere shops. Most include live music shows, serve inexpensive but delicious local cuisine at in-house restaurants, and have extensive art galleries of embroidery works which are not for sale. Its outlet in Dalat includes all of this plus a fine museum on the culture of embroidery as well as local minority handicrafts. A cluster of gift shops and a café (in addition to the restaurant) await customers at the end of the village tour. XQ has two much

smaller store outlets in Dalat, one on the top floor of the Central Market, and another across the street.

## CENTRAL HIGHLANDS

Far north of Dalat, the area known as the central highlands is a tempting lure for the adventurous traveller. The cities of the north do not feature significantly in most travellers' itineraries, however. This is mainly because police do not allow tourists to travel very far from the cities and into the surrounding countryside.

The largely Protestant (and impoverished) hill-tribe communities in these provinces, also known as Montagnards, supported the Americans during the war, and have been a source of grief for the communist government ever since. Needless to say, the government's attempts to encourage the Kinh majority from other parts of Vietnam to settle down in the central highlands have not been received favourably by the Montagnards. As such, this is an area of periodic unrest, and the government requires that all foreigners

*Many of the K'ho people still live in their traditional houses.*

**BELOW LEFT:** Langbiang Mountain.

### Dalat's Easy Riders

The best way to explore the central highlands is to book a tour with an adventure guide company like Groovy Gecko or Dalat's Easy Riders, rather than go it alone. The Easy Riders is a loose association of motorbike guides, and they are a popular option. Just stand on the street above Dalat's Central Market and one will surely find you. Usually no particular preparations are needed when you travel with a guide. They tend to take care of all your needs.

Tours of varying lengths including stays in hill-tribe villages can be arranged to end in either Nha Trang, Quy Nhon or Hoi An. It is possible to drive yourself but not advised. Driving can be dangerous in Vietnam, more so because of the other people sharing the road, rather than the actual road conditions. Also, while police don't normally enforce the law in the highlands, technically foreign drivers are required to have a Vietnamese licence (Vietnam does not honour its commitment to accept the International Driving Permit) and this is not easy to get. That being said, due to the climate, scenery and absence of traffic, the central highlands are the best place in Vietnam to drive or ride a motorbike. See the Dalat activities section *(page 372)* for more details.

*Silk embroidery craftswoman, XQ Historical Village.*

**BELOW:** Dray Sap Waterfall in Buon Ma Thuot.

obtain permits (virtually impossible to do without a government recommendation and professional credentials) to travel off the main highways, unless travelling to the three provincial capitals, Yuk Don National Park, and a few of the main lakes and waterfalls.

About a day's drive north of Dalat, the shores of **Lak Lake** ❽ (Ho Lak) are inhabited by displaced members of the M'nong tribe. A number of villages can be visited by boat.

Originating from Cu Yang Sin Mountain, the three waterfalls of Dray Sap, Dray Nur and **Gia Long** ❾ (daily 7am–5pm; charge) form a 100m/yds-wide cascade.

Two hours east of the falls, and 200km (124 miles) north of Dalat, is **Buon Ma Thuot** ❿, the capital of Dak Lak province, as well as the capital of Vietnam's coffee production. Just south of the city centre, on the corner of Le Duan and Y Nong streets, the Museum of Ethnology (Tue–Sun 7.30–11am, 2–5pm; charge) has one of the finest collections of central highlands hill-tribe crafts and relics.

Drive another hour west and spend the evening inside **Yok Don National Park** ⓫ (Vuon Quoc Gia Yok Don, Buon Don District; yokdonecotourism@vnn.vn; daily during daylight hours; charge). This 115,545-hectare wildlife reserve contains at least 63 species of mammals and 250 species of birds. There are known to be around 50 Asian elephants, 10 tigers, golden jackal, leopard and green peafowl living in the park.

Foreigners are not allowed to venture outside the capital **Pleiku** (200km/124 miles north of Buon Ma Thuot) or off Highway 14 without signing up for a government bus tour. Just north of town on the east side of the highway is Sea Lake (Ho Bien), a volcanic crater that forms a lake.

**Kon Tum** ⓬ is the provincial capital of the province by the same name, and the last city of the central highlands. The city is situated 47km (29 miles) north of Pleiku. Communal stilt homes (known as rong) of ethnic Banhar and S'tieng fill the suburbs of Kon Tum, their thatched roofs towering above the villages. There are several points of interest in the city, besides the obvious cultural richness, including the beautiful wooden cathedral, French seminary, and provincial museum.

# RESTAURANTS

Prices for a three-course dinner per person:

**$** = under US$5
**$$** = US$5–10
**$$$** = US$10–20
**$$$$** = over US$20

With a tiny expat community and more domestic than foreign tourists, Dalat has fewer outstanding restaurants catering to foreigners than other tourist destinations in Vietnam. Some of the best food can be bought in the evenings from street vendors on the ramps and stairs leading into the **Central Market**, as well as the second floor of the middle building, at any time of the day.

## Vietnamese

**Da Quy**
49D Truong Cong Dinh St. Tel: 063-351 0883. Open: daily B, L & D. **$**
Da Quy is a popular restaurant specialising in local Vietnamese dishes. Service is friendly and attentive, but prices are cheap (in the range of street food). Try the clay pot dishes, BBQ meats and Vietnamese desserts. The setting is a little more romantic than most, with candles on the tables.

**Hoa Sen**
62 Phan Dinh Phung St. Tel: 063-356 7999. Open: daily B, L & D. **$**
While the street-side, open-air atmosphere isn't anything to get excited about, the vegetarian menu is more diverse – and much tastier – than most of the places in town that actually serve meat. From hotpot, to stir-fry, clay pot dishes and spring rolls, Hoa Sen is popular even with non-vegetarians.

**Phu Dong**
1A/1B Quang Trung St. Tel: 063-354 2222. Open: daily B, L & D. **$$**
www.nhahangphudong.com.vn
Ambience is the main draw here in this French-style castle. The

beautiful stonework, mosaic floors and fountains offer a romantic departure from typical run-of-the-mill Vietnamese restaurants. Classical music serenades you as you dine on traditional Vietnamese cuisine as well as local specialities.

**XQ Historical Village**
258 Mai Anh Dao St. Tel: 063-383 1343. Open: daily B, L & D. **$**
www.xqhandembroidery.com
Enjoy an exquisite three-course meal for less than US$2. The menu of traditional Hue and Dalat dishes is priced cheaply in order to lure customers into buying the pricey (but excellent) embroidery the craft village is known for. A separate café in the complex serves pastries and desserts.

## International

**Dalat Palace Golf Club**
Phu Dong Thien Vuong St. Tel: 063-382 1201. Open: daily B, L & D. **$$$**
www.vietnamgolfresorts.com
Set in the original colonial clubhouse, the restaurant serves an eclectic mix of Tex-Mex, Korean, Japanese, Thai and Vietnamese specialities. The home-made chips and salsa, buffalo wings and chicken fingers are all top-notch. Outdoor seating offers a lovely view of the greens and the lake.

**Café de la Poste**
Tran Phu St. Tel: 063-382 5444. Open: daily B, L & D. **$$$**
Set between the Hôtel du Parc and Dalat Palace hotels, and in partnership with both, this charming French-style diner serves a select menu of sandwiches, pasta, Asian and French entrées. Service is friendly, and meals are prepared with great care. Even the grilled ham and cheese is a memorable gourmet treat. Its excellent breakfast buffets are a real treat.

**Tu An's Peace Café**
57 Truong Cong Dinh St. Tel: 063-351 1524. Open: daily B, L & D. **$$**
With her outgoing and

flamboyant personality, Tu An is a bit of a local celebrity herself. She insists hers is the original Peace Café, as she is surrounded by several venues by the same name. Both the Vietnamese and foreign food is great. Try the goulash, pasta or simply ask for whatever you want and she can usually make it.

## Cafés

**Art Café**
74 Truong Cong Dinh St. Tel: 063-351 0089. Open: daily L & D. **$**
Beside the *Peace Hotel* (and the other *Peace Café*), this small but cosy nook serves good coffee and standard Vietnamese fare at reasonable prices. This strip is very popular with backpackers and Dalat Easy Rider guides.

**Café Nam Huy**
26 Phan Dinh Phung St. Tel: 063-352 0205. Open: daily B, L & D. **$**
Walking distance from the backpacker district but also

frequented by locals looking for bargains, this cosy café has lots of comfortable nooks to lounge in. Serves great street dishes like pho and beef curry, most of which is priced under US$1.

**Whynot Café**
24 Nguyen Chi Thanh St. Tel: 063-383 2540. Open: daily B, L & D. **$**
One of the nicest Vietnamese cafés in town, it sits above the Central Market and has a menu that includes Western favourites like burgers, pasta and pizza. A flat-screen TV shows mainly Hollywood films. Free Wi-fi on site.

**100 Rooms Café**
57 Phan Boi Chau St. Tel: 063-383 7518. Open: daily B, L & D. **$**
This creative wonderland is designed to look like a jungle. *100 Rooms* is constructed in a similar vein as the "Crazy House" with the addition of serving good coffee and inexpensive meals. Especially popular for kids.

**RIGHT:** harvesting strawberries in Dalat.

# SOUTHERN VIETNAM

Defined by the vibrant capital city, the lush
Mekong Delta and some superb beaches,
Vietnam's deep south is one of the most
appealing parts of the country

That southern Vietnam has a character quite different from the north should come as no surprise given their separate histories: rather than a millennium of Chinese rule, the south evolved from centuries of Indian and Khmer civilisations. Where the north is traditionally perceived as authoritarian and disciplined, the south is considered more entrepreneurial.

The southern character is epitomised in Ho Chi Minh City, the nation's largest city and its commercial and industrial hub. Cosmopolitan, urbane and frenetic, the erstwhile Saigon is all about consumerism. In turn, Ho Chi Minh's neighbours prosper; the Mekong Delta is Vietnam's most productive agricultural area. The Southern Economic Zone (Ho Chi Minh and surrounding provinces) is Vietnam's new industrial powerhouse, its investment in various industries accounting for nearly half of the nation's GDP. The south is helped by plenty of natural resources and an inherent southern entrepreneurial spirit, driven mostly by the Overseas Vietnamese (Viet Kieu), many of whom were the original boat people who fled in the 1970s and 1980s.

Blessed with a beautiful landscape, from sand dunes to scenic beaches and lush rainforests, as well as an array of cultural attractions and the best windsurfing in Southeast Asia, this region has plenty to offer. Ho Chi Minh City makes an ideal base from which to explore the wetlands of the Mekong Delta or Cat Tien National Park, one of the country's largest areas of lowland tropical rainforest. There is also an abundance of beautiful beaches, islands and coastline at Vung Tau and Mui Ne. Off the coast are Phu Quoc and the Con Dao archipelago, with gorgeous white-sand beaches, jungle-clad mountains and rich marine life.

---

**PRECEDING PAGES:** People's Committee Building, HCMC. **LEFT:** drying shrimps, Phu Quoc. **TOP:** fisherman, Mui Ne. **ABOVE RIGHT:** Ben Thanh Market.

# HO CHI MINH CITY

Big and bold, Vietnam's capital is its most vibrant and exciting city. Filled with historic attractions and, increasingly, world-class tourism facilities, it still retains plenty of old Saigonese charm

Compared to other cities in Vietnam, **Ho Chi Minh City** (HCMC; Thanh Pho Ho Chi Minh) is relatively young, celebrating its 300th anniversary only in 1998. Yet this chaotic and mesmerising city has always been the backdrop to momentous history. Although the pace of development is furious, reminders of the past are inescapable in HCMC. History makes up its very essence, and evokes memories of French, Vietnamese, Chinese, Soviet and US influence.

## Background and history

Situated 40km (25 miles) inland from the South China Sea, northeast of the Mekong Delta and alongside the Saigon River (Song Sai Gon), Ho Chi Minh City sits on top of what was once a Khmer settlement – the name "Sai Gon" comes from the Khmer word "Prei Kor", meaning "Kapok Tree Forest".

Until the 17th century, this was a thinly populated area of forest and swamps. The southern outpost of Saigon was established in 1698 as a territory and governmental base of Gia Dinh Prefecture. Due to its strategic riverside location, it became an important trading centre for foreign merchants. Towards the late 18th century, ethnic Chinese (Hoa) from the southeastern seaboard of China settled in present-day Cholon (*see page* 293), establishing a thriving trading area.

Advancing south, French forces captured Saigon in 1861, which emerged as capital of the French Protectorate of Cochinchina (South Vietnam). In 1887, it became part of the French Union of Indochina and was transformed into a major port city. As in Hanoi, the colonials modelled the city after their own image and it soon acquired the air of a French provincial town, albeit with an oriental edge (*see page* 284).

### Main attractions

REUNIFICATION PALACE
NOTRE DAME CATHEDRAL
DONG KHOI STREET AREA
MUNICIPAL THEATRE
PEOPLE'S COMMITTEE BLDG
REX HOTEL
WAR REMNANTS MUSEUM
BEN THANH MARKET
MUSEUM OF VIETNAMESE HISTORY
JADE EMPEROR PAGODA
CHOLON AREA

**LEFT:** Ho Chi Minh statue (People's Committee Bldg). **RIGHT:** food vendor.

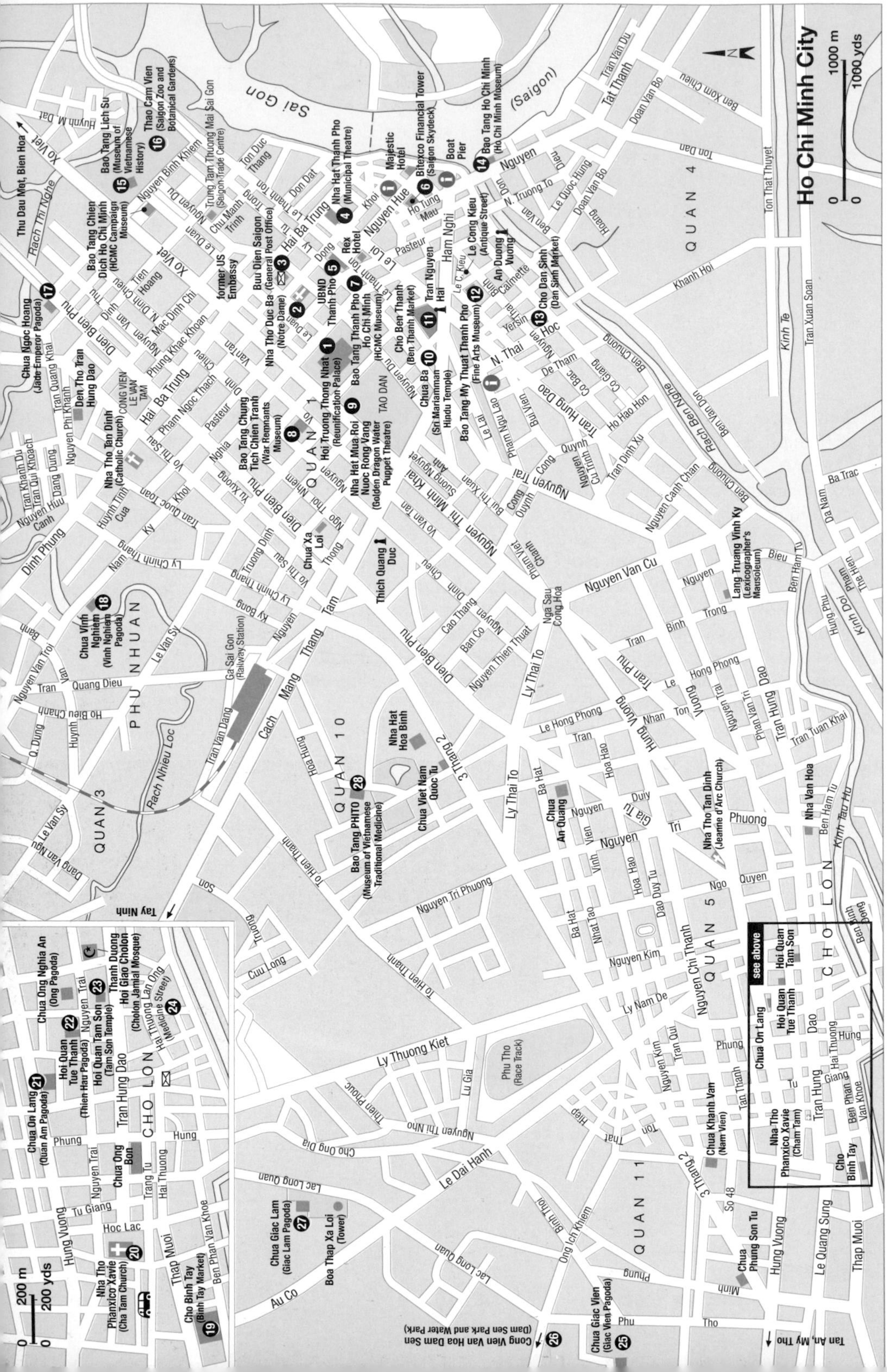

# Ho Chi Minh City

N

0          1000 m
0          1000 yds

QUAN 1
QUAN 3
QUAN 4
QUAN 5
QUAN 10
QUAN 11
PHU NHUAN
CHO LON

Sai Gon (Saigon)

**1** Nha Hat Thanh Pho (Municipal Theatre)
**2** Bhexco Financial Tower (Saigon Skydeck)
**3** Buu Dien Saigon (General Post Office)
**4** Nha Hat Thanh Pho (Municipal Theatre)
**5** Rex Hotel
**6** Majestic Hotel
**7** Bao Tang Thanh Pho Ho Chi Minh (HCMC Museum)
**8** Bao Tang Chung Tich Chien Tranh (War Remnants Museum)
**9** Hoi Truong Thong Nhat (Reunification Palace)
**10** Bao Tang My Thuat Thanh Pho (Fine Arts Museum)
**11** Cho Ben Thanh (Ben Thanh Market)
**12** Cho Dan Sinh (Dan Sinh Market)
**13** An Duong Vuong (Antique Street)
**14** Bao Tang Ho Chi Minh (Ho Chi Minh Museum)
**15** Bao Tang Lich Su (Museum of Vietnamese History)
**16** Thao Cam Vien (Saigon Zoo and Botanical Gardens)
**17** Chua Ngoc Hoang (Jade Emperor Pagoda)
**18** Chua Vinh Nghiem (Vinh Nghiem Pagoda)
**19** Cho Binh Tay (Binh Tay Market)
**20** Nha Tho Phanxico Xavie (Cha Tam Church)
**21** Chua On Lang (Quan Am Pagoda)
**22** Chua Ong Nghia An (Ong Pagoda)
**23** Hoi Quan Tue Thanh (Thien Hau Pagoda)
**24** Thanh Duong Hoi Giao Cholon (Cholon Jamial Mosque)
**25** Chua Giac Vien (Giac Vien Pagoda)
**26** Cong Vien Van Hoa Dam Sen (Dam Sen Park and Water Park)
**27** Chua Giac Lam (Giac Lam Pagoda)
**28** Bao Tang PHITO (Museum of Vietnamese Traditional Medicine)

Den Tho Tran Hung Dao
Nha Tho Duc Ba (Notre Dame)
Cho Ba (Sri Mariamman Hindu Temple)
Nha Hat Mua Roi Nuoc Rong Vang (Golden Dragon Water Puppet Theatre)
Thich Quang Duc
Nha Hat Hoa Binh
Chua Viet Nam Quoc Tu
Nha Tho Tan Dinh (Jeanne d'Arc Church)
Lang Truong Vinh Ky (Lexicographer's Mausoleum)
Chua An Quang
Nha Van Hoa
Chua Khanh Van (Nam Vien)
Nha Tho Phanxico Xavie (Cham Tam)
Cho Binh Tay
Chua Phung Son Tu
Boa Thap Xa Loi (Tower)
Ga Sai Gon (Railway Station)
Former US Embassy
Hoi Quan Tam Son
Chua On Tam Lang
Chua On Lang (Quan An Pagoda)
Hoi Quan Tue Thanh
Hoi Quan Tam Son

see above

0     200 m
0     200 yds

Tan An, My Tho
Tay Ninh

After being defeated in 1954, the French withdrew and the Geneva Convention divided Vietnam into two independent states: communists in North Vietnam and non-communists in the Republic of South Vietnam.

Saigon subsequently suffered from poor leadership, corruption, demonstrations and coups – in addition to communist attacks from the north. The US supported South Vietnam's regime, and during the Vietnam War Saigon became the nerve centre of US military operations. On 30 April 1975 the North Vietnam Army arrived in Saigon and, on 30 April 1975, overthrew the government, leading to reunification of the North and South. Saigon was renamed Thanh Pho Ho Chi Minh in 1976, after the founder of the modern Vietnamese state.

Shutting its doors to the outside world, southern Vietnam was economically restructured in line with the North and large-scale political repression followed. It took until the 1980s and the *doi moi* ("economic renovation") for the city's fortunes to improve. Northerners moved south to grab official posts and residences. Widespread turmoil, inflation and poverty ensued. Fearing communist reprisals, re-education camps, conscription and abject poverty, many thousands of Saigonese fled the country.

In 1997 the Asian economic crash left many buildings and projects half-built or abandoned for years and prompted disgruntled foreign businesses to pull out, slowing down but not completely derailing progress.

## Changing economy

Dynamic and increasingly cosmopolitan, HCMC has wasted no time catapulting itself into the 21st century and is now Vietnam's main commercial and economic hub. Always noted for its savvy business acumen, the city now enjoys feverish commercial enterprise and development, and exudes a tangible air of confidence. With massive multi-national investments and business pouring in, the only "exploding booms" nowadays come from the omnipresent

**BELOW:** cityscape at dusk.

**TIP**

Ho Chi Minh City has two distinct seasons: the dry season, running from November/December to April/May, and the rainy season through the remainder of the year. During the latter, there are frequent heavy downpours (usually in the afternoon), so it's worth carrying a raincoat or umbrella at all times. Highest temperatures occur in April at the end of the dry season.

**BELOW:**
Reunification
Palace facade.

construction work. The skyline over the last decade has dramatically changed from a low-rise cityscape to a downtown dotted with glitzy high-rises of international five-star hotels, corporate offices and luxury apartments. As a result, some real-estate prices are now higher than in Tokyo's notoriously expensive Ginza district. The emerging *nouveaux riches* and middle classes with their high incomes are all too evident, seen in the flashy cars, flashy restaurants, buzzing nightspots, chic boutiques and shopping malls selling all manner of international designer goods.

HCMC hasn't succumbed to full-scale globalisation quite yet and in some ways lags behind other more sophisticated regional hotspots. Most development is concentrated in the centre, contrasting with other parts of the city where general day-to-day living hasn't changed much. Although a legacy of its strife-torn past, the city still clings to its impressive colonial architecture and romantic Gallic-oriental charm, as well as its unique Saigonese identity.

## Orientation

Sprawling across 2,090 sq km (807 sq miles), with a population approaching 8 million, HCMC is Vietnam's largest city, and one of the densest urban areas on earth. The city is divided into 19 urban districts plus five outer districts, although the main points of interest are mostly found in Districts 1, 3 and 5.

**District 1** is the city centre, where most of the main shops, upmarket hotels, restaurants, bars and tourist attractions are located. It contains the original French Quarter, dissected by the city's main tourist magnet, Dong Khoi Street. The magnificent buildings constructed by the French house some of the city's major attractions. Fortunately, most tourist sites and entertainment venues are concentrated in a compact area and are eminently walkable. Also in District 1 are the backpacker haunts along Pham Ngu Lao Street. With more tourists than Vietnamese, the area can be hectic and noisy, but it does have more foreign restaurants and travel agents than anywhere else, too. The main nightlife area for visitors is also here.

North and west of District 1, the more sedate **District 3** also offers colonial architecture, parks and wide, tree-lined boulevards interspersed with a few dining and shopping diversions.

To the southwest of the centre is sprawling **District 5** (which overlaps into Districts 6, 10 and 11), incorporating bustling **Chinatown** (Cholon) with its vibrant markets, pagodas and temples, and restaurants.

Except for a few other attractions scattered further afield in Districts 10 and 11, visitors don't usually travel beyond these areas. **District 7** and, across the river, **District 2** have developed as expatriate and middle-class suburbs.

## CENTRAL DISTRICT 1

### Reunification Palace

Prominently located in the centre of District 1 at 135 Nam Ky Khoi Nghia Street is the former Presidential Palace of South Vietnam, now known as **Reunification Palace ❶** (Hoi Truong Thong Nhat; tel: 08-3822 3652/3808 5038; www.dinhdoclap.gov.vn; daily

7.30–11am and 1–4pm; charge includes guide). To the communists, this piece of ostentation – sometimes referred to as the **Independence Palace** – will forever symbolise the decadence of the Saigon regime.

Surrounded by extensive gardens, this monolith of a concrete building stands on the site of the Governor-General of Indochina Residence, or Norodom Palace, which dates back to 1871. After the French left in 1954, the new president of the Republic of South Vietnam, Ngo Dinh Diem, installed himself here. In 1962, the left wing was bombed and damaged beyond repair during an air raid; Ngo ordered the palace to be demolished, and a new edifice was constructed on top, although he never lived to see its completion as he was assassinated in 1963.

The new Presidential Palace was the headquarters of South Vietnam's President Nguyen Van Thieu from October 1967 to 21 April 1975. In one of the most enduring images of the Vietnam War, communist tanks stormed the city on 30 April 1975 and crashed through the palace's front

*Little has changed inside the Reunification Palace, which used to house the president of South Vietnam. It survives as a museum and "historical relic".*

**BELOW LEFT:** Saigon street food vendor.

## What's in a Name?

When the newly formed Socialist Republic of Vietnam compelled Saigon to take the name of Ho Chi Minh City in 1976, it was like rubbing salt into the wounds of its inhabitants. Today, most locals still defiantly refer to their city as Saigon as a matter of principle (they also prefer to call themselves Saigonese). At the very least, people use the name Saigon for downtown District 1, one of the first sectors of the city to be built and the original French Quarter. One reason might be that 'Saigon' is just so much easier to say than 'Thanh Pho Ho Chi Minh', the full Vietnamese name for the metropolis.

Although great measures have been taken – even to this day – to extinguish the Saigon name in most official capacities (some publications, for example, are not allowed to use the Saigon title), it is still, confusingly, allowed to be used in some forms: notably, the river winding its way around the city remains Saigon River, the main city newspaper is the *Saigon Times* and the city's state-owned tour company is Saigontourism. Place names like Saigon Zoo, Port of Saigon and Saigon Railway Station are still in use, and the three-letter ticket code for the city's Tan Son Nhat International Airport is SGN. No wonder visitors get confused.

**TIP**

The Vietnamese consider lunch to be the most important meal of the day – the nation literally "downs tools" from around 11.30am to 1.30pm (often with a brief siesta thrown in afterwards). Most state-run banks, offices and businesses close for lunch, but even some museums, pagodas, temples and churches are not immune. Your day should be planned with this midday interruption in mind

**BELOW LEFT:**
Diamond Plaza.
**BELOW RIGHT:** Notre Dame Cathedral.

gates (these tanks are now displayed on the front lawns). This was *the* defining moment of the fall of Saigon, resulting in reunification and the subsequent creation of the Socialist Republic of Vietnam.

The former palace's multiple floors and nearly 100 rooms resemble a time capsule with everything left largely unchanged. The first floor houses the cabinet meeting room, used for military briefings (the 35 chairs equalling the number of the Saigon cabinet members). The president's reception rooms and private residential quarters, complete with Catholic chapel and bedrooms, are on the second floor, while the third floor features a private cinema and gambling room, plus a helipad. This and the top floor offer excellent views over **Le Duan Boulevard** (Dai Lo Le Duan).

The fascinating bomb-proof basement yields an eerie warren of tunnels and rooms, including a war command room with original war maps, a communications room and the president's combat duty bedroom. The ground floor features a photo gallery with frequent screenings of a documentary film. Directly in front, a small park offers a shaded oasis, edged by several cafés.

## Notre Dame Cathedral

Heading northeast and walking across the park, you'll come to Cong Truong Cong Xa Paris (Paris Commune Square) and one of Ho Chi Minh's most iconic landmarks, **Notre Dame** ❷ or Cathedral of Our Lady (Nha Tho Duc Ba; 8–11am and 3–4pm; Mass at 5.30am and 5pm Mon–Sat, seven Masses on Sun; free).

The French colonial architect Pavrard designed the neo-Romanesque structure to represent the glory of the French empire and mirror the original Notre-Dame de Paris. Inaugurated in 1880, making it the oldest church in Vietnam, this was one of France's most ambitious projects in Indochina at the time; bricks used in the construction were shipped from Marseilles in France.

The Catholic cathedral has two main central bays and an interior that features stained-glass windows, Stations of the Cross in marble relief and Gothic

vaults. A small square at the far end of the church is anchored by a white marble statue of the Virgin Mary.

## General Post Office

Adjacent to the cathedral, at 2 Cong Truong Cong Xa Paris, is the **General Post Office ❸** (Buu Dien Saigon; tel: 08-3824 4244; daily 7am–10pm), an impressive salmon-hued colonial-era building. Also known as Saigon Central Post Office, the city's main post office is also a tourist attraction in its own right, and certainly the loveliest place in HCMC to post a letter or postcard.

This classic colonial building, based on the design of the French architect Auguste-Henri Vildieu, appears little changed since its completion in 1891, with green wrought-iron work, handsome arched ceilings – even old-fashioned pots of glue for stamps. The cavernous main hall, complete with over 30 service counters and old-style phone booths, is dominated by a huge portrait of Ho Chi Minh, plus two original map-murals dated 1892 and 1936. Full postal and telephone services are available here. The post office

and cathedral are hugely popular for fashion photo shoots and weddings, as both buildings provide perfect backdrops.

## Dong Khoi Street

Running about a kilometre from Le Duan Street to the Saigon River through the heart of District 1 and original French Quarter, **Dong Khoi Street** (Duong Dong Khoi) is the city's main commercial drag. This wide, tree-lined boulevard is home to shops, galleries, trendy cafés and luxury hotels. During French colonial times, this was known as the elegant Rue Catinat, the epicentre of colonial life and where the French built some of their most important buildings.

With France's departure in 1954, Catinat became Tu Do Street (Freedom Street), later notorious for its sleazy bars, clubs and massage parlours catering to American GIs seeking R&R. North Vietnamese communist tanks rolled down this street during the fall of Saigon. Following the south's "liberation" in 1975, it was renamed Dong Khoi (Popular Uprising) Street and for

*The economic boom in Ho Chi Minh City has brought an influx of Vietnamese from all over the country, making it one of the most densely populated cities in the world.*

**BELOW:** the General Post Office.

# The French Factor

The French may have gone from Ho Chi Minh City but they left behind some elegant colonial architecture and a café culture that encapsulates its spirit

Among the fascinating melange of architectural influences, it's the mark of the French that is most evident – the legacy of nearly a century of colonial rule in Indochina. Many parts of HCMC, especially central District 1, still bear the French architectural stamp.

## Architecture

When Saigon was declared the capital of French Cochinchina in the 1860s, the French filled in the ancient canals, drained the marshlands and reclaimed land. They then created leafy parks, built wide, tree-lined boulevards and introduced steam-powered trams. Impressive new edifices were constructed to serve the city's administrative role and to accommodate its burgeoning expatriates. Grandiose public buildings included hotels like The Majestic (one of Southeast Asia's classic colonial hotels), the GPO, the Cochinchina Governor's Palace (now HCMC

Museum), Hôtel de Ville (People's Committee Building) and Ben Thanh Market (known then as Les Halles Centrales), among others. Norodom Boulevard (now Le Duan) developed as – and still is – a diplomatic and residential enclave with rows of pastel-hued villas. This French-designed quarter evolved as the playground of the French during Indochina: cafés and bars, boutiques, the Opera House and Botanical Gardens were established to keep the French amused. Cultivated by them into a mini-French metropolis, Saigon was christened the "Paris of the Orient".

## Cafés and cuisine

Other French influences go deeper than bricks and mortar. French missionaries were responsible for the spread of Catholicism in the country, and a number of Catholic churches, including Saigon's own Notre Dame, were built in Saigon. Although only some 6 million of Vietnam's 86 million population are Catholics today, the country has the largest Catholic population in Southeast Asia after the Philippines.

The Westernised idea of drinking coffee and socialising in sidewalk cafés was introduced by the French – and embraced wholeheartedly by locals. Cafés are found all over town, fuelled by the Vietnamese love of coffee (ca phe) and tête-à-tête.

Naturellement, the French also left their hallmark on local cuisine: baguettes, pâtés, pastries, jambon (ham) and yoghurt are now part of daily life. The national dish pho (rice noodle soup with slices of beef) allegedly originated from the Gallic dish pot-au-feu. The French also successfully introduced European produce like cauliflowers, artichokes, berries and roses, in the cool-climate highland region of Dalat – itself founded by a Frenchman, Alexandre Yersin.

Other notable contributions include the Pasteur Institute, a foundation dedicated to the research of viruses, vaccination and bacteria. Inaugurated in 1891 and named after its founder, Saigon hosted the first foreign Pasteur Institute, initiating an international network. The Fine Arts University (formerly L'Ecole de Dessin) was established in 1913 by two Frenchmen and continues today in the same role.

**ABOVE:** alfresco café. **LEFT:** colonial buildings bear witness to French influence on the city.

a time went to seed. Today, Dong Khoi and its offshoots reflect the city's accelerating economic boom, increasingly dominated by international designer boutiques and upmarket shopping malls. Yet despite its prominence, Dong Khoi Street still yields a surprisingly languid, amiable air and is eminently walkable.

## Municipal Theatre

At the junction of Le Loi and Dong Khoi streets at **Lam Son Square** (Cong Truong Lam Son) stands the **Municipal Theatre** ❹ (Nha Hat Thanh Pho; 08-3829 9976). Also called the **Opera House**, it was designed by French architect Ferret Eugène, and features a grandiose, neoclassical pink facade, white classical statues and a domed entrance. It was opened in 1899 to keep the colonial French entertained. Post-1954, this became the Republic of South Vietnam's National Assembly headquarters for the next two decades. Following reunification, the authorities returned it to its municipal theatre function. Restored to its former glory to celebrate the city's 300th anniversary in 1998, it received a complete face-lift, modern lighting and sound systems, a rotating stage and an 800-seater hall. Today, the Municipal Theatre presents occasional classical music and dance performances.

## Old-world hotels

Lam Son Square is sandwiched between two historic hotels. The first is the **Hôtel Continental**, built in 1880. In the early 20th century, this was where the cream of French high society gathered. The hotel was also a meeting point for a motley assortment of diplomats and spies, high-society people and journalists. During World War II, the Continental was dubbed "Radio Catinat", as many American press corps had their bureaus operating here. In the 1950s, British novelist Graham Greene resided in Room 214, where he wrote much of *The Quiet American*, the hotel and its surrounds finding their way onto the pages of Greene's acclaimed book.

On the opposite side is the glitzy five-star **Caravelle Hotel**. The hotel's

**BELOW:** classical and modern styles: the Municipal Theatre, with the Caravelle Hotel on the right.

**TIP**

Crossing the road in HCMC is not for the faint-hearted. The sheer amount of traffic, particularly the 4 million motorbikes, can be daunting, but if you wait for traffic to stop, you could be kerb-side all day. The trick is to take a deep breath, walk out slowly, constantly looking left and right, and continue walking across (don't suddenly freeze), and the traffic will generally flow around you. Take care on the pavements – motorbikes sometimes ride up here too.

older 10-storey wing was home to the offices of the Associated Press, NBC, CBS, the *New York Times* and the *Washington Post* during the Vietnam War. The rooftop bar (now the Saigon Saigon Bar) was a favourite watering hole for many war correspondents, some recording the action without ever vacating their bar stools.

Further south down Dong Khoi Street, at the junction of the water-front Ton Duc Thang Street, stands the aptly named **Majestic Hotel**. Built in 1925 by the French, the Majestic is one of Southeast Asia's classic colonial hotels. Despite several extensive reno-vations and now state-run, the elegant building still radiates an old-world colonial charm, with its Art Deco stained-glass windows, a grand, mar-bled lobby with crystal chandeliers, and its helpful dapper bellboys. The rooftop bars afford wonderful views of the Saigon River.

## People's Committee Building

If the Reunification Palace sym-bolises the former South Vietnam

regime, then the **People's Committee Building ❺** (UBND Thanh Pho), at the northern end of Nguyen Hue Street, is one of the strongest symbols of colonial rule. The Hôtel de Ville was completed in 1908, after 16 years of ferment over its structure and style. Its Baroque yellow-and-white facade encloses an equally ornate interior of crystal chandeliers and wall-sized murals. Now the headquarters of the HCMC People's Committee, visitors are not permitted inside. One of the city's loveliest landmarks, the building is beautifully illuminated at night.

## Rex Hotel

Situated on Nguyen Hue Street and overlooking both plazas, the legend-ary **Rex Hotel** (Khach San Rex) is part of Saigon history. Originally a French garage and American Cultural Centre, it became headquarters for the US Information Service and home to billeted US servicemen dur-ing the Vietnam War. The US mili-tary also hosted daily press briefings here, which came to be known as the "Five o'Clock Follies". The building only opened as a hotel in 1976, after reunification.

## Bitexco Financial Tower (Saigon Skydeck)

HCMC's loftiest building is a stun-ning, 68-storey creation, designed to resemble a lotus bud. The **Saigon Skydeck ❻** (36 Ho Tung Mau, Ben Nghe Ward; 08-3915 6156; daily Sun–Thur 9.30am–9.30pm, Fri–Sat 9.30am–10pm; charge), Vietnam's second-tallest structure after Hanoi's Landmark Tower, gives panoramic views and features a touch-screen monitor that allows visitors to call up information on major landmarks. The helicopter pad that juts out 22 metres/yds on the 52nd floor includes a bar and restaurant. A lift whisks visitors up at a rate of 7 metres (23ft) per sec-ond. A small exhibition explains how the tower was constructed, using 6,000 individually cut glass panels.

**BELOW:** the historic Rex Hotel.

## Ho Chi Minh City Museum

One block west of the People's Committee Building, at 65 Ly Tu Trong Street, is the **Ho Chi Minh City Museum** ❼ (Bao Tang Thanh Pho Ho Chi Minh; tel: 08-3829 9741; www.HCMC-museum.edu.vn; daily 8am–4pm; charge). The neoclassical exterior is impressive, completed in 1890 and cleverly blending Western and oriental styles. Its faded interiors feature high ceilings, a sweeping staircase and chandeliers.

Spread over two floors, the displays are slightly less appealing but include handicrafts and an exhibition of southern beliefs and wedding rituals. The collection of war items upstairs with exhibits such as an old Vespa scooter and an accordion and banjo used to play propaganda songs, is more interesting. Underneath is a network of reinforced bunkers, built by Ngo in 1962, though they are not open to the public. The underground shelter comprises six rooms with 1-metre (3ft) -thick walls, including a living room and communications centre. Ngo and his brother hid down here during a coup in November 1963, before fleeing to Cholon. At the rear of the museum is a collection of classic cars.

To the northwest of the museum, the mustard-yellow building on Nam Ky Khoi Nghia Street is the **City People's Court** (Toa An Nhan Dan Thanh Pho), another impressive remnant of colonial-style architecture.

## WEST OF DISTRICT 1

### War Remnants Museum

Two blocks north of the Reunification Palace at 28 Vo Van Tan Street is the **War Remnants Museum** ❽ (Bao Tang Chung Tich Chien Tranh; tel: 08-3930 2112; daily 7.30am–noon and 1.30–5pm; charge). A visit here is a sobering reminder of the heavy toll of war. Occupying the former US Information Agency, this was hurriedly opened as the Museum of American War Crimes after reunification in 1975. Its controversial name was changed in 1997 as part of conditions dictated by the US government over trade pacts.

*Exhibit in the Ho Chi Minh City Museum.*

**BELOW:** military hardware at the War Remnants Museum.

*Hindu religious image at the Sri Mariamman Temple. The temple caters to the city's small Tamil population, but is also used by local Vietnamese.*

**BELOW:** seeking blessings at Sri Mariamman Hindu Temple.

A series of numbered exhibition halls displays the horrors of the French and American wars; these include graphic photographs, bell jars of deformed foetuses showing the effects of US-sprayed chemical defoliants, plus a guillotine used by the French and mock-up of the notorious "tiger cages". The poignant Requiem Hall features a large collection of photos taken by 134 photojournalists from 11 nations, themselves killed during both conflicts, and shows a rare, non-North Vietnamese war perspective. Although the exhibits are distressing to see, this is one of the city's biggest tourist attractions.

## Golden Dragon Water Puppet Theatre

Moving south, one block west of the Reunification Palace at 55B Nguyen Thi Minh Khai Street is the **Golden Dragon Water Puppet Theatre ❾** (Nha Hat Mua Roi Nuoc Rong Vang; tel: 08-3930 2196; daily performance 5pm and 6.30pm; charge). Water puppetry *(Mua Roi Nuoc)* is unique to northern Vietnam's Red River Delta – where

rice farmers for centuries practised this recreational art form in flooded rice paddies. Wooden puppets manipulated by bamboo sticks hidden beneath the water play out original stories based on folk tales and daily events, accompanied by traditional Vietnamese music.

## Sri Mariamman Hindu Temple

Several blocks southwest from the museum is the **Sri Mariamman Hindu Temple ❿** (daily 7am–7pm; free) at 45 Truong Dinh Street. The temple caters to the city's small population of Hindu Tamils and has a stunning multi-tiered *gopuram* (ornate tower) over the main entrance. Built in the late 19th century, the ground-floor open complex has statues of the Hindu gods Mariamman, Maduraiveeran and Pechiamman in the sanctuaries. The Hindu temple is also frequented by a number of ethnic Vietnamese – the influence of local customs and practices apparent in the use of incense sticks placed in Chinese-style bronze urns.

## Ben Thanh Market

A few blocks southeast, at the intersection of Ham Nghi, Le Loi, Le Lai and Tran Hung Dao streets, is **Ben Thanh Market** ⑪ (Cho Ben Thanh; daily 6.30am–6.30pm). Opened in 1914 by the French and covering 11,000 sq metres (118,400 sq ft), its distinctive pill-box-style clock over the main entrance tower on Le Loi Street has iconic status. Under one roof is practically every conceivable product sold at countless stalls, located along alleys leading off a main central aisle. The market is busy but not so crowded that it's uncomfortable.

Predominantly still a market for locals, selling basic necessities like household wares, fabrics and food-stuffs, Ben Thanh is increasingly geared towards the lucrative tourist market, with some specialist goods on sale. Situated at the rear are food and drink stalls, plus an open-air fresh produce market.

Once the main market shuts, the **Ben Thanh Night Market** springs into action, operating until late at night along the streets immediately surrounding the building. The main attraction is the open-air makeshift food stalls *(see page 300)* serving authentic – and cheap – Vietnamese fare.

## Ho Chi Minh City Fine Arts Museum

On the other side of the intersection, at 97A Pho Duc Chinh Street, is the **Ho Chi Minh City Fine Arts Museum** ⑫ (Bao Tang My Thuat Thanh Pho Ho Chi Minh; tel: 08-3821 6331; Tue–Sun 9am–5pm; charge). Although the museum has displays of some interesting Vietnamese art, this is somewhat of a disappointment and a poor cousin to the infinitely superior Fine Arts Museum in Hanoi. Housed in a vast space, the actual collection is quite small and poorly displayed.

More riveting is the building that houses the museum. A fine example of colonial architecture, the building was constructed in the early 20th century as the residence of a Chinese businessman. It bears typical

*The clock tower is a well-known feature of the bustling Ben Thanh Market.*

**BELOW:** Ben Thanh Market at night.

*Dan Sinh Market is well worth a visit even if you are not intending to buy anything.*

Asian-European characteristics of the era, and the original Art Deco stained-glass windows and antique elevator are still in place.

## Le Cong Kieu Street

Across from the HCMC Fine Arts Museum, narrow **Le Cong Kieu Street** (Duong Le Cong Kieu) has long been known as "Antique Street". One of the city's most atmospheric quarters, the row of narrow, open-fronted dwellings along this small stretch is devoted to selling a chaotic jumble of Asian and colonial-era bric-a-brac, furniture and home decor.

Formerly Rue Reims, this quiet residential street was home to Saigon's small Arab community, most of whom fled when the communists invaded in 1975. Today, the houses have been turned into shops that sell oriental mother-of-pearl mahogany chests, Art Deco bronze lamps, old *piastre* coins and black-and-white photographs. It used to be antique-hunting grounds, but not any more: most goods today are massproduced reproductions.

## Dan Sinh Market

A few blocks southwest, on the corner of Yersin and Nguyen Cong Tru streets is **Dan Sinh Market** ⓭ (Cho Dan Sinh; daily 7am–7pm), also known as the "War Surplus Market" for obvious reasons. The back of this run-down building houses several stalls selling a vast jumble of armed forces clothing and goods, as well as wartime memorabilia. This includes army, navy, air force and police stock from Vietnam (including pre-1975), Korea, the Soviet Union and the USA. While some stock is genuine vintage, most is new surplus or mass-produced stuff. You will find everything from Vietnamese berets to US Army hard helmets and flak jackets, gas masks, fake GI dog tags and Zippo lighters – even medical bags and stretcher beds.

## Ho Chi Minh Museum

The striking **Ho Chi Minh Museum** ⓮ (Bao Tang Ho Chi Minh; tel: 08-3825 5740; Tue–Sun 7.30–11.30am and 1.30–5pm; charge) is easily visible just across the bridge in **District**

**4**, where Ben Nghe Canal (Rach Ben Nghe) enters the Saigon River. Oriental dragons slithering across the rooftop explain its alternative name, **Dragon House** (Nha Rong). One of the first buildings constructed by the French in Cochinchina in 1863, this was originally the head office of a French shipping company. It was from this wharf that Ho Chi Minh, using his real name, Nguyen Tat Thanh, left Vietnam in 1911 on a French merchant ship for 30 years of self-imposed exile. There are over two floors of photographs, documents, artefacts and Ho's personal items. You can even buy a Ho Chi Minh bust at the museum shop. The large, airy building, set in pleasant riverside gardens, offers wonderful river views and cooling breezes.

## NORTHEAST OF DISTRICT 1

### Former US Embassy

Head eastwards from Notre Dame Cathedral to 4 Le Duan Boulevard, the site of the **US Consulate**, which was built over the **former US Embassy**, a highly symbolic building of the US involvement in Vietnam. During the 1968 Tet Offensive, in an event marking a turning point in the war, Viet Cong guerrillas broke into the embassy grounds where a running battle ensued for several hours. The building had another starring role seven years later: on 30 April 1975, as North Vietnamese communist troops advanced on Saigon, the US ambassador and remaining troops were airlifted from the rooftop by helicopter. In 1999, the embassy was pulled down to make way for the new US Consulate – viewed as another step in eradicating the physical evidence of more turbulent times.

### Museum of Vietnamese History

At the end of Le Duan Street, along Nguyen Binh Khiem Street, is the **Museum of Vietnamese History ⓰** (Bao Tang Lich Su, tel. 08-3829 8146; www.baotanglichsuvn.com; Tue–Sun 8–11am and 1.30–4.30pm; charge), housed in another stunning example of French-Chinese hybrid architecture,

*The Ho Chi Minh Museum is a must-see for those wanting to find out more about the extraordinary life of Vietnam's famous founding father.*

**BELOW:** Ho Chi Minh Museum.

with a distinctive pagoda-style roof. Formerly the Musée Blanchard de la Brosse under French rule, the museum today gives an excellent introduction to Vietnamese history and culture from prehistory to the founding of the Democratic Republic in 1945.

Exhibits are displayed in a series of numbered rooms in historical sequence starting on the ground floor and covering relics, artefacts, dioramas, photographs and artworks. Highlights include outdoor displays of 18th- and 19th-century cannons, a 2,500-year-old bronze drum, ancient sandstone sculptures from the Champa and Cambodian civilisations and the preserved mummy of a woman who is thought to have died in 1860.

## Saigon Zoo and Botanical Gardens

Adjoining the museum are the expansive grounds of **Saigon Zoo and Botanical Gardens**  (Thao Cam Vien; tel: 08-3829 1425; daily 7am–6pm; charge). Established in 1864 by two Frenchmen for the benefit of the colonials, the shady landscaped gardens are vast. The Zoo and Botanical Gardens house some 800 specimens from 120 species (many endangered), as well as 2,000 trees, and various cactus, orchid and bonsai plants. Among the celebrity animals on show are tigers, Asian elephants, giraffes and leopards, though animal-lovers may feel their enclosures are rather small and basic. Try to visit during animal feeding times (usually 3–5pm) and special events, like weekend elephant shows. A children's zoo features goats, sheep and hippos.

## Military Museum

Close by the Botanical Gardens is the rather bare **Military Museum** (Bao Tang Quan Doi; 2 L St; daily 7.30–11am and 1.30–4.30pm). However, it is worth dropping by to see the collection of war-related items in its front yard. These include anti-aircraft guns, armoured vehicles and the mangled remains of US military hardware.

## Jade Emperor Pagoda

One of the city's most colourful and captivating places of worship is the **Jade Emperor Pagoda** (Chua Ngoc Hoang; daily 8am–5pm; free), located on Mai Thi Luu Street, on the northern fringes of District 1. Built in 1909 by Cantonese Buddhists who settled in Saigon, its unique interior architectural style is heavily influenced by southern Chinese elements. A dense fog of smoke from spiral incense coils suspended from the rafters envelops a fascinating array of weird and wonderful elaborate statues – some Buddhist, others Taoist-inspired. The ornately robed Jade Emperor surveys the main sanctuary from his central altar, while to his right, the triple-headed, 18-armed statue of Phat Mau Chau De, mother of the Buddhas of the Middle, North, East, West and South, looks out in three directions from her encasement. Left of the Jade Emperor's chamber, the Hall of Ten Hells features

*A bust of Ho Chi Minh on display at the Museum of Vietnamese History.*

**BELOW:** Vinh Nghiem Pagoda.

intricately carved wood reliefs portraying the fate awaiting those sentenced to the diverse tortures found in the 10 levels of hell.

## WEST TO DISTRICT 3

### Vinh Nghiem Pagoda

Heading west to **District 3**, the **Vinh Nghiem Pagoda** ⓲ (Chua Vinh Nghiem; daily 8am–5pm; free) on Nam Ky Khoi Nghia Street opened in 1971, and is one of the city's newest pagodas – and also the largest. Built with aid from the JapanVietnam Friendship Association, this striking Buddhist pagoda bears distinct Japanese and Zen elements. The large main hall is dominated by a huge golden Buddha perched on a lotus and flanked by disciples. Behind are altars consecrated to the dead, where funerary tablets and their corresponding photographs are placed for the first 100 days after their deaths.

An elevated terrace runs from the hall to a seven-storey tower containing Quan Am statues on each level. The large bell opposite was presented as a gift from Japanese Buddhists during the Vietnam War, as the embodiment of prayers for an early end to the conflict. The three-storey repository tower behind the main temple houses neatly stacked ceramic burial urns containing the ashes of deceased souls. The busy pagoda is home to numerous monks as well as a Buddhist college for nuns.

## CHINATOWN (CHOLON)

About 5km (3 miles) west of downtown, HCMC's sprawling Chinatown, or Cholon, is a bustling place packed with Chinese shops and French architecture. "Cho Lon" translates as "big market", and aptly describes this endlessly buzzing maze of streets and alleyways. Ethnic Chinese (Hoa) originating from southwest China first settled here in the late 18th century. Once Cholon became entrenched as a successful trading area, Chinese immigrants arrived in droves, reaching a peak during the early 20th century. Today there are half a million Hoa here, making it the largest Chinese community in Vietnam.

**EAT**

Cholon (District 5) offers excellent authentic Chinese food, but restaurants are not generally geared to tourists. Hardly any English is spoken by staff, and menus are often written in Chinese. That said, they are well worth exploring – best if you can take a guide with you. Chinese food outlets are everywhere in Cholon, but reliable introductions are food stalls in covered markets like Binh Tay (see page 294), plus restaurants in large shopping centres.

**BELOW LEFT:** the Golden Dragon Water Puppet Theatre.

## Activities for Children

H o Chi Minh City is particularly good for those travelling with children. The range of activities here will keep even the fussiest youngster entertained. In the heart of the city, **Saigon Skydeck** (see page 286) gives incredible views from the 49th floor of the new Bitexco building, and has interactive features to occupy young fingers. The **Golden Dragon Water Puppet Theatre** (see page 288) is a great 50-minute spectacle near the Reunification Palace, while **Saigon Zoo and Botanical Gardens**, with giraffe-feeding and a children's zoo among the highlights, is a good way to spend an afternoon. Also in town is **Diamond Superbowl** (34 Le Duan Street; Mon–Sat 10am–1am, Sun 9am–1am),,,, on the fourth floor of the excellent Diamond Plaza shopping centre. It is a modern place, with computerised scoring and some fluorescent lanes. Outside of the city, **Dam Sen Park** (see page 298) has a host of rides and activities, including a roller-coaster, monorail and dinosaur park, while **Dam Sen Water Park** has more than a dozen rides designed to soak and amuse. About an hour outside HCMC is **Suoi Tien** (www.suoitien.com), a US$150 million theme park. Among the 50-plus attractions on this 105-hectare (250-acre) site are a roller-coaster, cinemas, crocodile kingdom, bumper cars, the Space Drop Tower and an array of mythical statues.

*Shophouses in Cholon have a unique blend of French and Chinese Baroque architecture.*

Evolving as a separate municipality, Cholon was officially established as a Chinese community in 1879 by the French governor of Cochinchina. Despite thousands of Chinese fleeing Vietnam after 1975, exacerbated by the country's increased tensions with China, over half a million Hoa still reside here – the largest Chinese community in Vietnam. With the city's boundaries being constantly expanded, Cholon now spills over into Districts 6, 10 and 11.

Cholon, which is largely contained within District 5, is a great place simply to wander around, taking in the sights and smells, particularly along Trieu Quang Phuc Street, where all manner of herbs are sold. As with all of HCMC, though, development is coming. Some of the historical Chinese shophouses and colonial edifices are being demolished or have fallen into disrepair. The once atmospheric canal where trading and cargo boats sailed in is being widened, and characterless modern buildings are appearing. Despite such development, Cholon is still a fascinating and authentic working and living area, offering the visitor bustling markets and commerce, excellent Chinese food and richly decorated Chinese temples and pagodas (the latter are noticeably different from their Vietnamese counterparts). Listen out for the blaring Mandarin pop coming from shops and look out for the stores selling all manner of colourful ritualistic items. There are a handful of three-star hotels but most choose to make it a half-day trip from District 1.

Eating options include a handful of bakeries, offering everything from dim sum to custard tarts. Trung Nguyen Café (347 Tran Hung Dao) is the perfect place to sip their fantastic iced coffees and people-watch. The main points of interest in Cholon are found principally in the southwest.

## Binh Tay Market

**Binh Tay Market ⓳** (Cho Binh Tay; tel: 08-3857 1512; www.chobinhtay. gov.vn; daily 6am–7pm) at Thap Muoi Street is Cholon's biggest market and epitomises its vibrant commercialism.

**BELOW:** Binh Tay Market in Cholon.

Built in 1928, its exterior is a fine example of early 20th-century Chinese-influenced French architecture: oriental-style multi-tiered roofs stalked by serpentine dragons blend with distinctive French mustard-yellow walls and a clock tower with four faces.

Although predominantly a wholesale market, Binh Tay is far less commercialised than Ben Thanh Market and thus offers a more authentic cultural experience. Spread over a vast 17,000 sq metres (183,000 sq ft) on two levels, the market is divided into organised sections, with more than 2,300 stalls. Not surprisingly, its goods have a more Chinese leaning than other city markets, with stalls crammed with joss sticks, herbs and dried goods used for traditional Chinese medicine and an array of Chinese food stalls. In the middle of the ground floor is a statue of the market's founder, Quach Dam.

## Cha Tam Church

Several blocks northeast of the market, at 25 Hoc Lac Street, is the Catholic **Cha Tam Church** ⑳ (Nha Tho

Phanxico Xavie; daily 8am–6pm; free). A brilliant example of architectural styles, it initially looks French in style, but there is a pagoda-style entrance gate and Chinese characters around the stained-glass windows and altar crucifix. Cha Tam is infamous as the place where the Catholic president of South Vietnam, Ngo Dinh Diem, and his brother took refuge on 1 November 1963 after fleeing Gia Long Palace during a coup sanctioned by the US government. Having surrendered, they were assassinated on their way to central Saigon. A small plaque on a rear pew indicates where Ngo awaited his fate before being escorted away.

The adjacent **Tran Hung Dao Street** is the main artery linking Cholon to the city centre. This street's western section is known as "garment district" due to its continuous succession of open-sided garment workshops and wholesale warehouses stacked with rolls of textiles.

## Quan Am Pagoda

Heading east along Tran Hung Dao Street and then north along Luong

*The Cha Tam Church was used as a hiding place by Ngo Dinh Diem, former president of South Vietnam.*

**BELOW:** spiral coils of incense at Quan Am Pagoda.

*A statue of a deity at Thien Hau Pagoda.*

**BELOW LEFT:** Thien Hau Pagoda.
**BELOW RIGHT:** dried herbs for sale at a Chinese medicine shop.

Nhu Hoc Street takes you to **Quan Am Pagoda** ㉑ (Chua On Lang or Chua Quan Am; daily 8am–5pm; free), located on Lao Tu Street. This is one of the city's most stunning pagodas. Built in 1740 by Chinese Fukien immigrants, it's also probably the oldest.

Dedicated to the Goddess of Mercy (Quan Am), not surprisingly, the two statues of Quan Am dominate. Many of the 16 deities that are worshipped here are festooned with flashing fairy lights in the large open courtyard area at the back. Constantly busy with worshippers, the burning votive paper offerings and hanging spiral incense coils result in a permanent smoky haze.

The pagoda is a heady riot of red and gold, with decorative details and striking relief wall murals. The showstopper is the entrance; its ridged roof and wall edged with exquisite ornamental glazed ceramic figurines and sculptures. Opposite the pagoda is a small pond with terrapins and fish.

## Thien Hau Pagoda

South along Nguyen Trai Street at No. 710 is **Thien Hau Pagoda** ㉒ (Hoi Quan Tue Thanh; daily 8am–5pm; free), one of Cholon's most important pagodas. Cantonese immigrants established this temple-pagoda in 1760, dedicating it to Thien Hau (Tin Hau), the Goddess Protector of Seafarers, and giving thanks for a safe passage across the perilous South China Sea. The entrance is dark and imposing but beyond this the second open-air courtyard has three statues of Thien Hau standing one behind the other. To the left is a bed with feather-like fans to keep her cool.

A festival in Thien Hau's honour is held here in March, on the 23rd day of the lunar calendar. Thien Hau is also known as the **Women's Pagoda** (Chua Ba) because local women make offerings and prayers to Me Sanh, the Goddess of Fertility, and Long Mau, the Goddess of Mothers and Babies, statues of whom are displayed on other altars.

## Tam Son Temple

Diagonally across from Thien Hau, at 118 Trieu Quang Phuc Street, is the **Tam Son Temple** ㉓ (Hoi Quan Tam Son; daily 8am–5pm; free). Built by Fukien migrants in the 19th century,

this temple is less elaborate in terms of architecture and sees fewer tourists. Instead, the temple is hectic with a constant flow of women in search of blessings to improve their chances of conceiving children. The deities worshipped here include Me Sanh, Quan Cong and Thien Hau.

### Ong Pagoda

Back on Nguyen Trai Street at No. 678 is Thien Hau Pagoda's counterpart, **Ong Pagoda** (Chua Ong Nghia An; daily 8am–5pm; free), also known as the Men's Pagoda. An intricate carved wooden boat stands over its entrance and a statue of Quan Cong (a famous Chinese military general) with a ruddy face, long black beard and ornate regalia presides over the main altar, flanking General Chau and the mandarin called Quan Binh.

### Cholon Jamial Mosque

The minimalist blue and white **Cholon Jamial Mosque** (Thanh Duong Hoi Giao Cholon; daily 8am–5pm; free), nearby at 641 Nguyen Trai Street, sits in sharp contrast with the area's highly decorative Chinese pagodas and temples. It was built by Tamil Muslims, most of whom fled the country around 1975.

### Hai Thuong Lan Ong Street

Head south down Trieu Quang Phuc Street to get to **Hai Thuong Lan Ong Street ㉔**, or "Medicine Street". This lengthy street is named in honour of Lan Ong, an 18th-century physician, mandarin and master of Vietnamese herbal medical practice. Shops specialising in traditional Chinese and Vietnamese medicine have long proliferated here; nowadays they are mostly located in a concentrated hub in the eastern section of the street, around the intersection with Trieu Quang Phuc Street. From here, the shops run along both sides of Hai Thuong Lan Ong Street, especially between Nos 43–61 and opposite, Nos 70–108 and 134–142.

These old, open-fronted shophouses, some which date back to French colonial times, are stocked full of weird concoctions purported to cure all sorts of ailments. Huge hessian sacks overflow with odorous fungi, strange dried plants and gnarled roots spill out onto the pavements, and dried sea horses are packed into plastic bags. Unfortunately, also for sale are preserved animal parts, like powdered rhino horn and ivory, flagons of coiled snakes and sharks' fins.

## NORTH OF CHOLON

### Giac Vien Pagoda

From Cholon head north to District 11, where a bright red-and-yellow entrance gate at 247 Lac Long Quan Street will lead you down a long alley to the **Giac Vien Pagoda ㉕** (Chua Giac Vien; daily 8am–5pm; free). Built in 1803, Giac Vien was previously known as Earth Pit Pagoda (Chua Ho Dat), due to the vast amounts of earth required to fill the site before the pagoda – said to be frequented by Emperor Gia Long of the Nguyen dynasty – could be constructed.

*Muslim devotees pray at the Cholon Jamial Mosque.*

**BELOW:** Buddhist and Taoist images at the Giac Vien Pagoda.

*A monk's humble abode at the Giac Vien Pagoda.*

Within its dimly lit and cluttered interiors enveloped in joss-stick haze are 153 beautifully carved wooden statues, with many Buddhist and Taoist deities located on the multi-tiered altar in the main sanctuary. The front hall has rows of old dark-wood tables, flanked by funerary tablets and time-worn photographs of the deceased. Monks here are not the only residents; bats have made the wooden rafters their home. As it is quite far removed from the city centre, about 6km (4 miles) away, the pagoda has a refreshingly tranquil feel and does not see many tourists.

## Dam Sen Park and Water Park

Bordering Giac Vien Pagoda with two entrances nearby (319 Lac Long Quan Street and 3 Hoa Binh Street) lies the enormous **Dam Sen Park** ㉖ (tel: 08-3963 4963; www.damsenpark. com.vn; daily 9am–9pm; charge). One of the largest and most modern theme parks in Vietnam, it covers 50 hectares (124 acres) of landscaped parkland and offers an array of attractions for families, including a haunted castle, 3-D and 4-D cinemas, roller-coaster,

**BELOW:** intricate carving at the Giac Lam Pagoda.

Ferris wheel and several other theme-park rides. There is also a boating lake, crocodile farm, bird and animal enclosure, plus an "explore the jungle" section. Visitors get around by mini-electric cars and monorail. It isn't quite Disneyland, but it is a good option if travelling with children. It has been a huge hit with the locals since its opening in 1999. For Vietnamese middle-class families, it represents the epitome of modern recreational activity.

Part of the sprawling grounds is given over to **Dam Sen Water Park** (tel: 08-3858 8418; www.damsenwaterpark. com.vn; Mon–Sat 8.30am–6pm, Sun 8am–7pm; charge; access at a separate main entrance next to Dam Sen Park). It offers a multitude of water-based fun rides and slides, including the Boomerang, Wild River, Kamikaze Ride, and Space Bowl Slide. Gentler options for younger children include the Wave Pool and Wandering River. Weekends at both parks are packed, and they offer a good chance to see Vietnamese families at play.

## Giac Lam Pagoda

Heading north into Tan Binh District, about 7km (4 miles) from the downtown area at 118 Lac Long Quan Street, is **Giac Lam Pagoda** ㉗ (Chua Giac Lam; daily 8am–6pm; free). It is recognised as the city's second-oldest pagoda and is an important historical site. Built in 1744 (and reconstructed in 1909), Giac Lam's design reflects the typical architectural style of pagodas in south Vietnam. The large complex incorporates several sections, including monks' living and study quarters. Although larger than Giac Vien (*see page 297*) and receiving more visitors, there are many similarities between the two mustard-hued pagodas.

Giac Lam is supported by 98 carved ironwood pillars, inscribed with gilded *Nom* characters, an ancient Vietnamese script based on Chinese ideograms. Amongst its dark, well-worn interiors are around more than 100 statues, some over 250 years old. The large front hall, or Altar of Patriarchs, is filled with ancestral

altars, portraits of monks from previous generations and rows of funerary tablets.

A small adjoining courtyard is edged by exquisite wall decorations and roof edges studded with blue-and-white porcelain saucers – these contrast with gruesome paintings of the 10 Buddhist images of hell. The main sanctuary at the opposite end houses beautifully carved, gilded wooden statues of the Buddha, reincarnations of the Buddha as well as judges and guardians of hell. The 49 oil lamps balanced on a tree-shaped wooden frame symbolise the 49 days the Sakyamuni Buddha meditated under the Bodhi tree to attain enlightenment.

The extensive grounds feature several tombs of monks and a seven-storey tower, Bao Thap Xa Loi, which can be climbed for excellent views of the city.

## Museum of Vietnamese Traditional Medicine

Heading east back towards the city centre, at 41 Hoang Du Khuong Street in District 10, is the **Museum of Vietnamese Traditional Medicine** ㉘ (Bao Tang; tel: 08-3864 2430; www.fitomuseum.com.vn;

Mon–Sat 8.30am–5.30pm; charge). The city's newest museum, it is a refreshing alternative to the war and Ho Chi Minh-themed offerings elsewhere. The privately owned enterprise was founded in 2007 by FITO, a Vietnamese manufacturer of traditional medicinal products. The building alone is worth seeing as it's a remarkable replica of a traditional northern house, complete with dark-wood interiors and authentic furnishings.

Ranged over six floors and 18 exhibition rooms, the origins and chronology of time-honoured traditional Vietnamese medicine are explained. Meticulously displayed and labelled in English, there are around 3,000 items sourced by the owner – many dating back centuries – including ancient Vietnamese *Nom* script books and encyclopaedias of traditional Vietnamese medicine, plus various implements used for the preparation and storage of medicines, such as stone pestle-and-mortars and foot-powered grinding machines. Life-size dioramas include a 19thcentury Chinese-style medicine shop. The free guided tour and short introductory film will take about 45 minutes to complete.

*Giac Lam Pagoda houses the seven-storey Xa Loi Tower.*

**BELOW:** a recreation of an apothecary's shop at the Museum of Vietnamese Traditional Medicine.

# RESTAURANTS AND CAFÉS

Prices for a three-course dinner per person:
**$** = under US$5
**$$** = US$5−10
**$$$** = US$10−20
**$$$$** = over US$20

Ho Chi Minh City is Vietnam's culinary capital, with a diverse range of both Vietnamese and international cuisines. The city's economic boom and expat population, coupled with rising affluence, has created a cosmopolitan range of culinary choices and chic eateries. With cheap and excellent street fare available, Western fast food has yet to make a major impact. Most restaurants are clustered in District 1, the main tourist hub.

## District 1

### Vietnamese
### 3A3 Bun Bo Hue
39A Ngo Duc Ke St. Open: daily L & D. **$**
Specialising in noodles from the central city of Hue, the broth served up here is rich and flavoursome. The eponymous bun bo hue dish comes packed with Vietnamese pork sausages and pork tenderloin, while the spring rolls are filled with pork, beansprouts and fresh herbs.
### Banh Xeo
46a Dinh Cong Trang St. Tel: 08-3824 1110. Open: daily L & D. **$**
Established since 1941, this is one of the city's most popular eateries. Frantic at night-time, the house speciality is banh xeo − crispy folded pancakes stuffed with pork, beansprouts and shrimp − cooked over open fires out front. Other Vietnamese dishes are served, too. Basic, open-air dining off the street.
### Ben Thanh Night Market
Junction of Tran Hung Dao, Le Loi and Ham Nghi streets. Open: daily D. **$**
Once Ben Thanh Market shuts around dusk, open-air makeshift eateries start firing up their woks on the surrounding streets, serving a huge selection of authentic regional Vietnamese fare, including fresh seafood, at very low prices. Lively and packed nightly with both locals and tourists.
### Lemongrass
4D Nguyen Thiep St. Tel: 08-822 0496. Open: daily L & D. **$$$$**
Lemongrass provides the ideal introduction to the very best of Vietnamese cuisine. This 80-seat restaurant has a welcoming, homely feel and offers a reasonable choice of classic dishes. Prices are on the high side, but then so is the quality.
### Minh Duc
100 Ton That Tung St. Tel: 08-3839 2240. Open: daily B, L & D. **$**
Fast, busy and noisy − this place is always packed thanks to fresh, tasty Vietnamese dishes. The English menu isn't very helpful ("tasteless simmered fish" anyone?) so just go to the front and point at what you want.
### Pho 24
5 Nguyen Thiep St. Tel: 08-3822 6278. Open: daily B,L & D. **$**
www.pho24.com.vn
A thriving domestic chain, taking national dish pho (rice noodle soup) off the street and into spotless and air-conditioned premises. Apart from its beef pho variations and standard chicken pho, other street foods are available, too. Especially popular with locals, this is Vietnam's answer to McDonald's, with numerous outlets across town (check website).
### Quan An Ngon
138 Nam Ky Khoi Nghia St. Tel: 08-3825 7179. Open: daily B,L & D. **$**
Occupying a low-rise colonial villa, the main dining section is a shaded courtyard framed by mock street stalls cooking up regional dishes like bun cha and banh cuon. Evenings and lunchtimes are a madhouse (part of its chaotic charm) as diners tuck into its incredibly good-value fare.
### Temple Club
29−31 Ton That Thiep St. Tel: 08-3829 9244. Open: daily L & D. **$$$**
The dining choice of celeb A-list couple Brad Pitt and Angelina Jolie, when in town. Set in a colonial villa and former Hindu pilgrim guesthouse, the refined ambience, objects d'art and cosy interiors are evocative of times past − almost overshadowing its traditional Vietnamese cuisine, like steamed clams in lemongrass. Have a pre-dinner aperitif on velvet couches in the plush lounge.

### Vietnamese & Western
### Bier Garden
125 Dong Khoi St. Tel: 08-3521 0691. Open: daily B,L & D. **$$$**
With Spanish guitars playing in the background, football on the televisions and German bottled beers aplenty, this is one of HCMC's busiest spots. The extensive menu includes pasta, ribs and Vietnamese standards. Portion sizes are more than generous.
### Barbecue Garden
135A Nam Ky Khoi Nghia St. Tel: 08-3823 3340. Open: daily B,L & D. **$$**
www.barbecuegarden.com
Large, alfresco garden setting. Cook your own skewered meats, fish and vegetables at your own table with a central grill. Both Vietnamese and international dishes served at this family-friendly place.

### Bonsai Cruise
Passenger Quay of HCMC (Ben Tau Khach Thanh Pho), junction Ham Nghi and Ton Duc Thang streets. Tel: 08-3910 5560. Open: daily B, L & D. **$$$$**
www.bonsaicruise.com.vn
The best of the Saigon River dinner cruises, with an extensive buffet dinner featuring a range of international, Vietnamese and Asian dishes. The two-hour river cruise also features live entertainment.
### Xu Restaurant-Lounge
71−75 Hai Ba Trung St. Tel: 08-3824 8468. Open: daily L & D. **$$$**
www.xusaigon.com
Ultra-sleek Xu serves contemporary Vietnamese cuisine, true to its roots yet with an international twist, like tuna spring rolls with mango salsa. The menu also includes traditional Vietnamese and Western dishes. The more casual ground-floor **Café-Bar** (daily 7am−midnight) serves breakfasts, tapas and cocktails.

### Chinese
### Crystal Jade Palace
Legend Hotel Saigon, 2A−4A Ton Duc Thang St. Tel: 08-3827 2387. Open: daily L & D. **$$$**
www.legendsaigon.com
The finest Cantonese cuisine and dim sum in town. Sunlit, understated contemporary interiors and impeccable service reflect its pedigree. Dim sum is served at lunchtime only; on Sunday the dim sum feast starts at 10am and is always packed.
### Kabin
Renaissance Riverside Hotel, 1st Fl, 8−15 Ton Duc Thang St. Tel: 08-3822 0033. Open: daily L & D. **$$$**
Authentic Chinese cuisine by Hong Kong master chef, with a contemporary twist. Dim sum for lunch and gourmet Cantonese and Sichuan menu for lunch and dinner.

The elegant dining space offers great riverside views.

## Indian

### Tandoor

74/6 Hai Ba Trung St. Tel: 08-3930 4839. Open: daily L & D. **$**
www.tandoorvietnam.com
Popular family-run Indian restaurant with contemporary decor. Authentic northern and southern dishes from four regional chefs include various curries, clay oven-broiled kebabs and vegetarian *dosa* pancakes. Good-value buffet lunches (Mon–Fri), plus excellent vegetarian selection.

## International

### Al Fresco's (two outlets)

27 Dong Du St. Tel: 08-3823 8424; 21 Mac Dinh Chi St. Tel: 08-3823 8427/9. Open: daily B, L & D. **$$**
www.alfrescosgroup.com
Family-style restaurant – perfect for those craving Western fare. Expect friendly staff and huge portions, including Aussie steaks and the house speciality, barbecued ribs. Also Tex-Mex dishes, pizza, pastas and salads. Child-friendly, with crayons and paper tablecloths.

### Amigo Grill Restaurant

55 Nguyen Hue St. Tel: 08-3824 1248. Open: daily L & D. **$$$**
Sublime steak is served up here in an open kitchen, which allows diners to watch the chefs work their magic. The restaurant is rather thin but well designed, with a well-stocked bar and stylish dark-wood decor.

### Hog's Breath

2 Hai Trieu St. Tel: 08-3915 6006. Open: daily L & D. **$$**
Sitting in the shadow of the 262-metre (859ft) -high Bitexo Financial Tower is Hog's Breath. Specialising in steaks of all kinds, from prime ribs to T-bone, and the atmosphere is usually lively.

### Reflections

Caravelle Hotel, 3rd Fl, 19 Lam Son Sq. Tel: 08-3823 4999. Open: daily D. **$$$$**
www.caravellehotel.com
Its intimate, old-world interior plays second fiddle to the innovative and sophisticated European cuisine – think red wine-braised veal cheeks with tomato onion jam – created by its European chefs. Be sure to leave room for the outrageously sinful ice creams.

### The Refinery

74 Hai Ba Trung St. Tel: 08-3823 0509. Open: daily L & D. **$$$**
French-style bistro housed in a restored colonial-period opium refinery. Contemporary European dishes given a light touch, like roast sea bass with garlic-olive mash, and also salads, sandwiches and home-made ice creams. Good-value weekend brunches are popular.

### Warda

71/7 Mac Thi Buoi St. Tel: 08-3823 3822. Open: Mon–Sat, L & D, Sun D only. **$$$**
www.wardavn.com
Hidden down a narrow alleyway, expect an authentic Middle Eastern experience – from its music and stunning Arabic interiors to its regional Gulf cuisine. The menu features tajines, barbecued meats and fish, kebabs and

mezes, plus sticky sweet desserts. Enjoy an infused Martini while dragging on a shisha pipe at the terrace under a Bedouin-style canopy.

## Spanish

### La Habana

6 Cao Ba Quat St. Tel: 08-3829 5180. Open: daily B, L & D. **$**
www.lahabana.com
This little corner of Cuba just oozes atmosphere. As if the 50-plus types of tapas and mojitos weren't enough, there is live music, perfect paella and the quintessential cigar to round the night off in style. For those who visit earlier, there is high-tea time when cakes and pastries are served. La Habana – Spanish for the Cuban capital Havana – is easy to find as it's close to the Opera House – just look for the Cuban-Spanish architecture and listen out for the sounds of salsa.

## Thai

### Golden Elephant

34 Hai Ba Trung St. Tel: 08-3822 8554. Open: daily L & D. **$**
Don't let the cramped interior deter; its authentic Thai cuisine is endorsed by all the Thais who dine here. Extensive photo-menu includes regional favourites of stir-fries, seafood, noodles, soups, piquant curries and salads, prepared by Thai chefs and well priced. Vegetarian dishes and traditional desserts also feature on the menu.

District 3

## Vietnamese

### Com Nieu

6C Tu Xuong St. Tel: 08-3932

6388. Open: daily L & D. **$**
Diners throng its famous bare-bones premises for its clay-pot fragrant rice (*com nieu*) and entertaining spectacle of waiters smashing pots and throwing the crispy rice across tables. Its flavoursome southern cooking is highly recommended, especially pork simmered in coconut flesh. Touristy, yet little English spoken.

### Tib

187 Hai Ba Trung St. Tel: 08-3829 7242. Open: daily L & D. **$$$**
www.tibrestaurant.com
Established by a celebrated music composer and named after his niece, this cavernous restaurant specialises in authentic imperial Hue cuisine, like tiny rice pancakes with shredded shrimp. Decorated in traditional imperial style and set in a colonial villa, Tib attracts an eclectic crowd; reservations essential.

## French

### La Camargue

191 Hai Ba Trung St. Tel: 08-3520 4888. Open: daily. D. **$$$**
Renowned French finedining venue with a romantic ambience. Option to sit either alfresco or in elegant, air-conditioned rooms. Expect classic French and Mediterranean cuisine with Asian accents – think duck confit samosas with balsamic and shallot dipping sauce. Extensive wine selection and immaculate service.

# CAFÉS

The café culture in Ho Chi Minh City is a throwback to French colonial times and is an integral part of life here. Caffeine connoisseurs don't need to look far to find a cup; there's a café on almost every corner.

### Ciao Café

74–76 Nguyen Hue St, District 1. Tel: 08 3823 1130. Open: daily B, L & D. **$$**

Looking as though a little part of Italy has been dropped into old Saigon, this charming café serves plenty of dishes, but it's the coffee and ice cream that impress the most.

### Gloria Jean's Coffee

106 Nguyen Thi Ninh Kha St. District 3. Tel: 08-3825 8239. Open: daily B, L & D. **$**
One of several branches, this

gets the nod as it's conveniently situated between the War Remnants Museum and Reunification Palace. Food is limited to muffins and pastries, but the choice of drinks is good and the quality excellent. The iced blueberry espresso takes some beating.

### Sozo

176 Bui Vien St. Tel: 08-6271

9176. Open: daily B, L & D. **$**
www.sozocentre.com
For some karma with your coffee, head to Sozo, which helps disadvantaged families. Its marzipan-coloured walls and wood furnishings lift it above the backpacker street it's set on, while its cakes and coffee are excellent.

# AROUND HO CHI MINH CITY

There are numerous interesting sights within striking distance of Ho Chi Minh City. Pick from the Cu Chi tunnels, the gaudy Cao Dai Church, a national park and the beaches at Vung Tau, Mui Ne and Con Son Island

The area surrounding **Ho Chi Minh City ❶** encompasses a diverse landscape. To the northwest are the flat plains that contain the tunnels of Cu Chi and the town of Tay Ninh, the birthplace of the Cao Dai cult. Northeast is the lush expanse of forest designated as Cat Tien National Park, while the coastline to the east is lined with sandy beaches extending from Vung Tau through Phan Thiet and on to the mountains that overlook Ca Na Beach. The Cham towers near Phan Thiet represent the southern reaches of the ancient Champa kingdom, with other areas east of Ho Chi Minh City once controlled by the Khmer and ancient Funan empire (in Vietnam referred to as "Oc Eo").

Religious diversity (Cao Dai, Muslim Cham and whale-worshipping fishermen), the military history of Cu Chi and the beach resorts of Mui Ne and Con Son Island (and, to a lesser extent, Vung Tau) are the main highlights of the area.

## CU CHI TUNNELS

Located 70km (44 miles) to the northwest of Ho Chi Minh City is **Cu Chi ❷** (daily 7am–5pm; charge), famous for its extensive network of underground tunnels. The tunnels were first used by the Viet Minh against the French in the 1940s, and later became

hideouts for the Viet Cong, who reportedly extended the labyrinthine network until it reached beneath the Mekong Delta headquarters of the US Army's 25th Division.

From these hiding places, the Viet Cong were able to spring devastating surprise attacks on their enemies. In fact, by the mid-1960s, it is believed that over 200km (124 miles) of tunnels laced the region around Cu Chi. Located at the end of the Ho Chi Minh Trail, and straddling both Highway 1 and the Saigon River (both

**Main attractions**
CU CHI TUNNELS
CAO DAI GREAT TEMPLE
VUNG TAU
CAT TIEN NATIONAL PARK
PHAN THIET
TA CU MOUNTAIN
MUI NE BEACH
WHITE SAND DUNES
CON DAO ARCHIPELAGO

**LEFT:** Cao Dai followers at the temple in Tay Ninh. **RIGHT:** military tank, Cu Chi tunnels.

## Phu Quoc

Rach Gia
Ha Tien

Bai Thom
Bai Bung
Bai Thom
Day Nui Ham Ninh
Ham Ninh
Bai Sao (Kream Beach)
Suoi Da Ban
Khai Hoan Fish Sauce Distillery
Phu Quoc Pearl Farm
Ap Thoi
Vuon Quoc Gia Phu Quoc (Phu Quoc National Park)
538
Chua
Khu Tuong
Ong Lang
Duong Dong
Ba Keo
Ham Ninh
Bai Truong (Long Beach)
Cua Can
Cua Can
Phu Quoc
Gulf of Thailand
Sor
Ganh Dau
Bai Dai
Duong To
Nha Lac Cay Dua (Coconut Prison)
An Thoi
Roi
Thom
Vong
Xuong
My Rut

0   10 km
0   10 miles

## Southern Vietnam

BIEN DONG

N

0   50 km
0   50 miles

Nha Trang
Phan Rang
Thap Cham
An Phuoc
Vinh Hao
Ca Na
Me Ly
152

Da Lat
Di Linh
1864
Lam Dong
Bao Loc
Gia Bac
Thon Lac Nghiep

Cho Lau
Phan Ri
Ap Long Hoa
Nha Trang (White Sand Dunes)
Ap Thien Ai
Mui Ne   10

Binh Thuan
Ham Thuan Bac
Thap
Muong Man
Ham Thuan Nam
Phan Thiet   7
Ta Cu Mountain Nature Reserve   9   Poshanu
Ham Tan   8
Khe Ga

Bao Tung
1648
Dinh Diep
Da Huoa
Tin
Xa Phuong
Dak Meroa
Binh Phuoc
20

Song Dinh
Pho Tri
Duc Linh
Vo Dat
Ap Rung La
Phuoc Tuy

Dong Nai
Vung Quoc Gia Nam Cat Tien (Cat Tien National Park)   6
Ho Tri An
Xa Gia Kiem
Dau Giay
Xuan Loc
Long Thanh
51
Cho Phuoc Hai   Long Dat
Phuoc Hai
Ba Ria-Vung Tau
Ba Ria
Vung Tau   5

Binh Phuoc
Chon Thanh
14
13
Bau Bang
Binh Duong
Thu Dau Mot
Bien Hoa
Thu Duc
Nha Be

Tay Ninh
986
22
Nui Ba Den   4
Chiphu
Trang Bang
Cu Chi (Tunnels)   2
Ho Chi Minh   1
Binh Chanh
Can Giuoc   Go Cong
Cua Tieu

CAMBODIA
Phnum Penh (Phnom Penh)
Long An
Ben Luc
Tan An
My Tho   12
Tan Thanh
Cho Gao
Cua Dai
Thoi Thuan
Ba Dong

Svay Rieng
Moc Hoa
Tien Giang
Cai Lay
Ben Tre   14
Ap An Thuan
Ba Dong

Tran Chim Tam Nong (Stork Sanctuary)
Trai Ran Dong Tam (Dong Tam Snake Farm)
Ben Tre   13
San Chim Vam Ho (Bird Sanctuary)
Tra Vinh   16
Tra Vinh
Ap Tram
Ba Cai

Dong Thap
Hong Ngu
Tien Giang
Cho Moi
Vinh Long   15
Vung Liem
Cang Long
Cau Ngang
Long Phu

Chau Doc
Sa Dec
Can Tho   17
Tra On
Ke Sach

An Giang
Long Xuyen   19
Thanh Hung
Nhon Ninh
Soc Trang   18
Vinh Chau

Rung Tram Tra Su (Bird Sanctuary)   22
Nui Sam   23
230
Oc Eo   21
Kien Thanh
Hau Giang
Ap Dau Giong
Xom Vam
Cai Cung

Chau Doc
Nha Bang
An Giang
Rach Gia   24
Vinh Rach Gia
Cai Rang
Vinh Thanh
Phung Hiep
Thanh Tri
Ap Vinh Phu
Bac Lieu
Vinh Loi

Hang Mo So   27
Kien Luong
Hon Chong
25   Chua Hang
Kien Giang
Hon Dat
Vinh Thuan
An Bien
Ong My
Ca Mau
Rung Duoc U Minh (Mangrove Forest)
1
Tan An

Ha Tien
Dao Phu Quoc
Hon Minh Hoa
Hon Tre
Hon Rai
Ca Mau
Vinh Thuan
Tho Binh
Ngoc Hien
Duong Keo

Gulf of Thailand

Hon Trung Lon
Hon Trung Nho

Vuon Quoc Gia Con Dao (Con Dao National Park)   11
Con Dao
Hon Bai Canh
Con Son

Mui Ca Mau
Song Bay Hap
Cai Nuoc
Cai Doi
Rach Tau

heading to Saigon), the tunnels were of vital strategic importance.

Individual tunnels ran up to 10 metres (33ft) deep, each with a breadth of between 0.5 to 1 metre (1.5–3ft), and stacked up to three levels. The top tier could support the weight of a 50-tonne tank, the middle layer could withstand moderate mortar attacks, while the lowest level was virtually impregnable.

The ground through which the tunnels burrowed is red clay, well suited to this kind of excavation. To avoid detection, the earth that had been removed was often dumped in bomb craters, rice fields or the Saigon River. The Americans often used trained dogs to sniff out the tunnels, but the Viet Cong would deflect them by scattering pepper at the tunnel entrances and vents. It is said that they would even use the same soap as Americans to confuse the dogs.

While the tunnel system included kitchens, meeting rooms, barracks, makeshift hospitals and storage for supplies, the tunnels were not intended for long-term accommodation (contrary to what is often written), as conditions inside them were quite deplorable. Likewise, a number of war anecdotes, including accounts of how doctors performed surgeries at the underground hospitals and administered blood transfusions via bicycle pumps, are highly implausible and probably concocted by overzealous government officials bent on glorifying the accomplishments of the Viet Cong.

Nevertheless, the tunnels are a vivid testament to the ingenuity and perseverance of the Vietnamese that eventually helped them win the war against the vast technical superiority of the Americans. Numerous tactics were used by the US troops to eliminate the tunnels' effectiveness, but with little long-term success until the B-52s began their relentless carpet-bombing. Although the Americans eventually destroyed much of the subterranean network, it was a temporary and Pyrrhic victory. The tunnels had already fulfilled their function by giving the Viet Cong not only the advantage of surprise but also the control of many surrounding villages.

Visitors often shudder when they crawl through a small section of tunnel, which has been enlarged and "improved" for the benefit of tourists. Reforested eucalyptus trees attest to the area's recovery from the ravages of chemical defoliants and carpet-bombing.

## TAY NINH

Further to the northwest, Highway 22 passes through Tay Ninh province before continuing on to Cambodia. From the 7th to the 14th centuries, this area belonged to the powerful Funan empire before being absorbed into the Chen La kingdom, the forerunner of the Khmer kingdom. In the early 18th century, the Nguyen Lords defeated the last of the Champa people here and assumed control.

During the war against the French, Tay Ninh was a hotbed of anti-colonial

**TIP**

Due to the sensitive political nature of Cu Chi, you will probably receive conflicting versions of the site's history from your tour guide and from the museum film and displays.

**BELOW:** the Cu Chi Tunnels offer a fascinating experience.

sentiment, and in the 1950s a hero of the armed resistance forces made Black Lady Mountain (Nui Ba Den) his hideout. The mountain went on to become an important strategic point of bloody confrontations in the war against America.

## Cao Dai Great Temple

Tay Ninh's greatest attraction is found approximately 100km (60 miles) northwest of Ho Chi Minh City, in the township of **Tay Ninh** ❸ itself. Here, in all its resplendent gaudiness, stands the **Cao Dai Great Temple** (Thanh That Cao Dai). Cao Dai was founded in 1926 by Ngo Minh Chieu, and its followers believe that all major world faiths offer pieces of the truth, but that Cao Dai arose in a third age to unite them all. While Cao Dai borrows saints and divinities from other religions and philosophies, it is principally a repackaging of Buddhism, Confucianism and Taoism with a new liturgy and leadership hierarchy. Adherents believe in one ultimate deity with many subordinate divinities, and also believe that the faithful

receive divine revelations from a variety of spiritual entities, including their principal saints: Sun Yat-sen, Victor Hugo and Nguyen Binh Khiem. Today, there are an estimated 2.5 million Cao Dai followers in Vietnam and 400 temples, all with a similar design.

Most tours arrive at the temple for the noon prayer ceremony, though there are also daily ceremonies at 6am, 6pm and midnight. Followers in their colourful ceremonial gowns of azure, red, yellow and white cut striking figures in their procession towards the altar, entering from opposite sides.

The temple blends Buddhist and Catholic architectural conventions. The Holy See is oriented with the entrance facing the west, so that the congregation faces the east. The general shape is longitudinal, as in a basilica. Unlike a cathedral, the temple is not built on an axis but it does have a central domed tower built where a cathedral transept would normally be. The temple also has striking twin towers at the front, and a smaller tower at the east end. On the outside a large eye symbolising the Cao Dai religion guards the entrance.

The interior has a blue, starstudded vaulted ceiling and an altar supporting a giant orb gilded with an all-seeing eye. The inner Church hall is divided into a nave with an aisle on either side, separated by columns encircled by Buddhist dragons. The ceremony is usually completed in less than 30 minutes, after which visitors are free to explore the temple.

### Nui Ba Den

The most outstanding natural feature around Tay Ninh is **Nui Ba Den** ❹ (Black Lady Mountain), at 986 metres (3,235ft) the loftiest mountain in southern Vietnam. It has been a strategic military stronghold through every major conflict. Its name centres around the story of a principled lady who chose death over dishonesty – a common theme in Vietnamese folklore. Although heavily scarred by war,

**BELOW:** the Cao Dai Great Temple is akin to a fantasy movie set.

over the past decades nature has made something of a comeback and the slopes are now protected as a nature reserve where many species of birds as well as primates thrive.

Visitors can hike from a temple at the base or take the cable car (daily 8am–5pm; charge) to a series of three cave temples halfway up the mountain, featuring numerous Buddhas in a variety of forms. However, while Nui Ba Den makes a pleasant outing, most will find Ta Cu Mountain (*see page 311*) near Phan Thiet a more convenient alternative, with similar features.

## VUNG TAU

The port city of **Vung Tau ❺** is situated 125km (80 miles) southeast of Ho Chi Minh City (HCMC). Located on a peninsula straddling two mountains, **Nui Nho** (Small Mountain) and **Nui Lon** (Big Mountain), Vung Tau offers some of the most stunning coastal scenery anywhere in Vietnam. The city has maintained its status as a popular weekend getaway for residents of HCMC, despite falling out of favour in the past decade with foreign

visitors, who prefer the charms of Phan Thiet further down the coast.

Vung Tau is a modern city, with all the conveniences of HCMC, including Western fast-food chains, high-rise shopping centres and other trappings of 21stcentury life. Despite its popularity as a domestic vacation spot, the offshore oil industry dominates the local economy and actually owns many of the hotels.

### The statue of Jesus

At the far end of the peninsula, perched on top of Nui Nho, is a 30-metre (100ft) **statue of Jesus**, arms outstretched to the sea and reminiscent of the famous *Christ the Redeemer* image of Rio de Janeiro in Brazil. The statue was erected by the Americans in 1971. Park your vehicle at the foot on Ha Long Street and hike up the path for about 30 minutes for incredible views of the coast.

Many locals enjoy their evening walks up the other side of Nui Nho via Hai Dang Street (across from the wharf) for unmatchable views of **Front Beach** (Bai Truoc), **Back Beach**

*Vung Tau Lighthouse sits atop Nui Nho (Small Mountain).*

**BELOW LEFT AND RIGHT:** views of Vung Tau.

**TIP**

If you wish to explore
Cat Tien National Park
bring plenty of mosquito
repellent, sunscreen, a
flashlight and batteries,
rain poncho, binoculars
and, last but not least,
leech-proof leggings.

(Bai Sau) and the cityscape between. Back Beach is the only sizeable sandy beach around the city. It is largely denuded of trees and has suffered from small oil spills in the past, but it's still a pleasant – albeit somewhat urban – place to swim and sunbathe.

Taking both left-hand forks on Hai Dang Street will lead about 1km (0.6 miles) to the very top of the mountain and the blinding-white **Vung Tau Lighthouse** (daily 7am–5pm; free), originally built by the French in 1910. Taking a left and then a right fork will lead you to an old **abandoned military bunker**, dating from the same period. You can freely explore the crumbling fort, whose walls are being torn apart by the roots of young Tung trees *(Tetrameles nudiflora)*. Already the bunker is starting to look like a mini version of the famous Ta Prohm Temple at Angkor Wat in Cambodia.

Alternatively, the other favourite evening hike leads you up Nui Lon peak via Vi Ba Street, past numerous Buddhist and Taoist temples, as well as one devoted to the Cao Dai faith. Big Mountain's premier landmark is

**Villa Blanche** (Bach Dinh; daily 7am–5pm; charge), built at the end of the 19th century for the French governor-general, Paul Doumer. Doumer was called back to France before the villa was completed, and never actually resided there. A new cable car (daily 8am–5pm; charge) runs from the base of the mountain, on the north side of the harbour, to the peak.

One of the Nguyen emperors, Thanh Thai, was held in Villa Blanche for some time before his exile to Reunion Island off Africa in 1909. Later, it became the residence of presidents Ngo Dinh Diem and Nguyen Van Thieu. Beautifully set above a forest of frangipani trees, the house contains ceramics and other items recovered from a Chinese junk shipwrecked off Cau Islet in the Con Dao Islands in 1690.

## Whale Temple

Like many coastal towns in southern Vietnam, Vung Tau has a fishermen's temple devoted to whale worship, **Lang Ca Ong** (also referred to as **Dinh Than Thang-Tam**, the Whale Temple; daily 8am–5pm; free). Dating from 1911, it is situated on the corner of Hoang Hoa Tham and Xo Viet Nghe streets, halfway between Front and Back beaches.

In this region, whales are highly revered by local fishermen, who see the mighty creatures as man's saviour from the perils of the high seas. Whales are depicted in beautiful murals with dragons and sea monsters, and skeletons of beached whales – some of them measuring 4 metres (13ft), and dating back to the 1860s – are displayed in glass cases. The Vietnamese adopted the whale cult from the people of Champa, who worshipped the whale deity. Cham people believed that a powerful god called Cha Aig Va assumed the form of a whale in order to rescue fishermen in peril. Every year, from the 16th to the 18th day of the eighth month of the lunar calendar,

**BELOW:** over 440 species of butterfly are found at Cat Tien National Park.

the Cau Ngu Festival is held at the temple.

## Other temples and pagodas

A large number of Buddhist temples are scattered around town and across both Nui Nho and Nui Lon mountains. **Hong Ba Pagoda** is located on an islet below the statue of Jesus and reachable only at low tide. **Quan Am Bo Tat Tu**, to the northwest on Tran Phu Street at Dau Beach, has a giant statue of the female Buddha (at odds with the statue of the taller Virgin Mary and Baby Jesus next door). About 3km (2 miles) away, **Thich ca Phat Dai** is notable for its beautiful pagoda, seen from Tran Phu Street on the north side of Big Mountain.

## CAT TIEN NATIONAL PARK

About halfway between Ho Chi Minh City and Dalat lies **Cat Tien National Park** ⑥ (tel: 061-379 1228; www.cattiennationalpark. vn and www.namcattien.org; daily daylight hours; charge), one of

Vietnam's best areas for wildlife. The large expanse of forest shelters some 105 species of mammals, 360 species of birds and 120 species of reptiles and amphibians. There are significant populations of yellow-cheeked gibbons, green peafowl, hornbills, civets, sambar deer and gaur, as well as a few tigers, elephants, Asian black bears and sun bears. Tragically, the last Javan rhinoceros in mainland Southeast Asia was killed by poachers in Cat Tien in 2010. The park has 14 excursions and hiking trails, with more under development. These include a variety of hikes through rainforest, grassland and wetland habitats as well as night-time safaris, and visits to S'Tieng minority tribes in Ta Lai village. The government no longer permits foreigners to visit the ancient temple ruins beside the park.

The crown jewel of the park is **Crocodile Lake** (Bai Sau). Getting here involves a drive and a long trek, but it's well worth it for the chance it gives to see some of the park's wildlife,

*Statues at Thich Ca Phat Dai Pagoda.*

**BELOW LEFT:** a mural of whales and dragons at Vung Tau's Whale Temple.

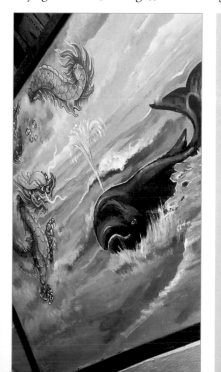

## The Whale Worshippers

In coastal communities of southern Vietnam there is a little-known festival called Cau Ngu, celebrated by local fisherman who follow an ancient whale-worshipping cult. In the Cau Ngu (Fish Prayer) Festival, fishermen pray to whales, dolphins and even sharks, asking their spirits to watch over them in the coming year. The festival usually includes the Nghinh Ong procession: when a whale or dolphin dies and is washed ashore, there is an elaborate funeral to welcome its spirit, with performers dressed in traditional costumes, stilt walkers, musicians and dragon dancers. After the funeral, the remains of the creatures are then buried at the local fishermen's temple near the beach. Three to five years later, the bones are exhumed and carried around the town in a similar procession until they are finally returned to the temple to be worshipped. In communities where there are several temples, the temples may share a single skeleton and take turns hosting Cau Ngu.

The practice also manifests itself in other ways. Fishing boats are adorned with eyes and fins, both to honour the whales and ward off sea monsters. There are also additional holidays and festivals tied to individual temples.

The most important whale temples are located in Phan Thiet *(see page 311)* and Vung Tau *(see page 308)*, but smaller versions are found in many fishing communities along the south-central coast.

*Phan Thiet Water Tower is a city landmark.*

including the Siamese crocodiles that were reintroduced in 2000.

It is possible to explore the park on your own, but trained English-speaking guides (who add to the experience) as well as cars and bicycles are available for hire. Air-conditioned bungalows can also be rented at the park headquarters, or you may opt to stay in a tent. Be sure to tell someone when and where you'll be hiking if you go it alone, as people have been known to get lost along the trails.

A **rescue centre** (open daylight hours; free) run by Wildlife at Risk or WAR (www.wildlifeatrisk.org) houses sun bears and wild cats, and is open to the public. Additionally, the Endangered Asian Species Trust (www.go-east.org) has built the new Dao Tien Endangered Primate Species Centre, which cares for rescued gibbons, langurs and slow loris. It too is open to the public.

Despite recent recognition for Cat Tien as a Unesco Biosphere Reserve, the Vietnam government has begun plans for several hydroelectric dams

**BELOW:** altar, Duc Thang Temple.

within the park which not only threaten many of the endangered species living there, but Cat Tien's future in general.

## PHAN THIET

**Phan Thiet ❼**, 200km (125 miles) from Ho Chi Minh City on the Ca Ty River, was once a sleepy little fishing port known only for its pungent *nuoc mam* (fish sauce) and dragon fruit. As tourism developed on the nearby beach of Mui Ne, however, the economy of Phan Thiet quickly grew. The riverfront is a lovely place to walk both day and night, offering the best views of colourful wooden fishing boats in the harbour and **Tran Hung Dao Bridge**, as well as **the mountains** to the north. The **Phan Thiet Water Tower** – at the eastern end of Le Hong Phong Bridge – designed by Prince Souphanouvong of Laos in the 1930s, is the symbol of both the city and the province. The tower, no longer in use as a receptacle to collect and store water, is lit up in the evenings until about 10pm.

Be sure to stop at **Nguyen Viet Vui's Butterfly Shop** (daily 8–11am and 5–8pm) on Trung Trac Street next to the Tran Hung Dao Bridge. Vui is one of Vietnam's leading naturalists, and an authority on native butterflies. He holds the national record for the largest collection of butterflies, and some of his specimens are more than a century old.

About 250 metres/yds further down Trung Trac Street, past the Le Hong Phong and Duc Thanh bridges, sits **Duc Thanh School**, where Ho Chi Minh himself taught in 1910 before "finding the road to national salvation". Across the street sits the **Ho Chi Minh Museum** (Tue–Sun 7.30–11.30am and 1.30–4.30pm; charge), at the site of his former home. The museum is of little interest other than to view some of Ho Chi Minh's personal effects, which

are of questionable authenticity (unless he really had a hat, cane and shirt for every museum in Vietnam).

On the other side of the town market is **Duc Thang Temple** (daily 8am–5pm; free), built in 1847. The jagged roof is decorated with numerous undulating dragons, and phoenixes and lions. Inside is a collection of ancient wooden scripture panels.

**Van Thuy Thu Temple** (daily 7.30–11.30am, 2–5pm; charge) at 20A Ngu Ong Street is the oldest temple (built in 1762) dedicated to whale worship in Vietnam (see page 309). The temple contains over 100 whale skeletons, but the main draw is a restored specimen more than 22 metres (72ft) long – the largest in the country. Like all such temples, Thuy Thu was originally built by the edge of the sea, but as water levels have changed over the centuries, this temple is now stranded in the middle of a busy neighbourhood. Fishermen can be seen mending nets and building boats in the temple, which is thought to bring them luck.

## Ta Cu Mountain

The **Ta Cu Mountain Nature Reserve** ❽ (Mon–Fri 6.30am–5pm, Sat–Sun 6.30am–6pm; charge) towers high above the town of Ham Tan, about 30km (19 miles) west from Phan Thiet, along Highway 1A. Take a ride on the **gondola** to the top, or hike the forest trail for a better glimpse of the local birdlife. The old pagoda that nestled on the other side of the peak for over 130 years was torn down in late 2007 and replaced with a more kitschy, theatrical version complete with dragon-head pillars and an ornate Chinesestyle curved roof. The temple is surrounded by a cluster of stupas (relic shrines), a trio of smaller Buddha statues and – the main attraction – Vietnam's largest reclining Buddha, some 49 metres (161ft) long. A small cave is hidden in the boulders far to the right of the statue. Legend says that a boy once followed the cave all the way to the sea, 20km (12 miles) away.

## Khe Ga Lighthouse

Heading southwest of Phan Thiet, the coastal road passes through the **Landing Zone Betty**, a former

*Chinese temples often commemorate New Year festivities with dragon dancing, which is thought to bring good luck and prosperity.*

**BELOW:** reclining Buddha at Ta Cu Mountain Nature Reserve.

# Dragon Fruit and Fish Sauce

Southern Vietnam is a land of plenty, typified by its luscious fruit and the national staple, *nuoc mam*

W hile tourism and its associated activities in Mui Ne are an important engine of growth in Phan Thiet's economy, the other two pillars of local commerce – dragon fruit and fish sauce – which existed long before the first pleasure-seeking tourists appeared, have an even greater significance to the country as a whole.

## Dragon fruit

Dragon fruit comes from an enormous creeping cactus *(Hylocereus undatus)*, native to Central and South America, where it is known as *pitaya*. With a preference for dry climates, it grows extraordinarily well in Binh Thuan and Ninh Thuan provinces, where it is known as *thanh long*, and produces some of the highest yields of the fruit in the world.

The bright-green cactus grows much like a vine. If left uncultivated it will climb trees and rock faces, anchoring itself with sturdy tendrils. Farmers keep

them manageable by fastening plants to rows of short posts, continuously re-grafting hundreds of arms back into the base. The result looks like a writhing Medusa's head.

The plant's enormous, white, trumpet-like flowers bloom only at night, and are easily stimulated by manipulating light levels. Thus farmers place lights at the base of the plant every evening to induce multiple harvests in a single year. The peel of the fruit is pink, with green scale-like protrusions. The fruit is white with thousands of tiny black seeds, which can be eaten. The taste and texture are often compared to a kiwi, although dragon fruits are much larger, often reaching the size of an ostrich egg.

## Fish sauce

Fish sauce, known in Vietnam as *nuoc mam*, is the foundation of Vietnamese cuisine. It's used as a seasoning, salt substitute, the base for broths and soups, and also a condiment. The best variety comes from Phan Thiet and Phu Quoc island. *Nuoc cham*, a mix of fish sauce, water, lime juice, sugar, chilli and garlic, is the most common dipping sauce in Vietnam.

Fish sauce is made from fresh anchovies and sea salt, which are allowed to ferment. The mixture of one part salt to two or three parts fish is placed in large vats. A bamboo mat is placed over the slurry and weighted down to keep the fish from floating to the top as the mixture liquefies. The jars are then covered and left in direct sunlight for nine months to a year. Periodically the lids are removed to ventilate the sauce and allow sunlight to stimulate further fermentation. Once the mixture is sufficiently reduced to an oily liquid, it is either siphoned or drained through a spigot in the bottom of the vat. The fluid is poured into clean jars and allowed to air for a few more weeks to reduce the fishy smell.

Top-grade fish sauce is always a clear amber colour, without any sediment, and has a fragrant and briny aroma (although it will always retain some of that inimitable fishy smell).

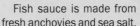

**LEFT:** Phan Thiet's famous fish sauce. **ABOVE:** dragon fruit thrives in the climate of southern Vietnam

American base, and straddles an enormous canyon along the beach.

Further down the coast is the **Khe Ga Lighthouse ❾**, located on a small island off Tien Thanh Beach, the longest continuous beach in the province. This is the tallest lighthouse in Vietnam, built by the French in 1897. It's still a beautiful spot, with large orange-and-red striated boulders jutting out of enormous windswept dunes. Just don't look to the west, where the beach is usually piled with rubbish, or at the resorts that are scheduled to be torn down to build a new port which will ship bauxite to China and deposit toxic red mud behind the beach.

## MUI NE BEACH

In 1995, when it was declared to be the best spot in Vietnam to view the solar eclipse, **Mui Ne Beach ❿** caught the attention of resort developers looking for fresh territory to stake out. Within a few years, this obscure little fishing community nestled in a coconut grove had morphed into the premier beach-resort capital of southern Vietnam, and it continues to be one of the country's fastest-growing tourist areas, with dozens of major new hotel properties under development.

In 2004, when the Boxing Day Tsunami struck Southeast Asia, it initiated another turning point for Vietnam: the Russian invasion. Scores of Russian tourists, who used to vacation in Thailand, suddenly came to Vietnam instead. Henceforth Mui Ne became a favourite spot of Russian tourists, many of them from Vladivostok.

Mui Ne is located 10km (6 miles) north of downtown Phan Thiet. The unique geography of Binh Thuan Province has endowed it with not only one of the driest climates in Southeast Asia, but also one of the windiest. With an average of 229 days per year with winds above 12 knots, it didn't take long for the world's kiteboarding and wind-surfing community to discover its attractions. One drawback to having dozens of kiteboarding centres along the beach-front is that swimming or sunbathing can be a bit hazardous in the afternoons when the bay is crowded with enthusiasts, along with newly introduced jet-skis and illegal fishing nets.

Not to be outdone, the golfers are the next group to have arrived in force, following the construction of the 18-hole **Sea Links Golf & Country Club** now rebranded "Sea Links City" to incorporate a private beach, high-rise condos, shopping centre, villas and upscale hotel-resort).

Mui Ne Beach, a name actually coined by the tourism industry, is made up of several wards within Phan Thiet City. Ham Tien Ward, and its Rang Beach, is the central tourism area where the bulk of resorts, restaurants and bars are located. This is the area most mean when they say Mui Ne Beach. The west end has the best beach and the most upscale venues, with the associated higher prices. The east end is prone to greater erosion and pollution. The cape on the east end is the "real" Mui Ne Village. The quaint hilltop community retains much of

*A wakeboarder in action off Mui Ne Beach.*

**BELOW:** fisherman at Mui Ne Beach.

*Southern Vietnam has notable Indian and Khmer influences, as seen in the Thap Poshanu towers.*

**BELOW:** White Sand Dunes.

the original fishing-village charm that has evaporated from Ham Tien with development. Further north, on the way to the dunes, are less-visited resort areas at Ganh and Suoi Hong Beaches, Hon Rom Village, and a newly invigorated resort area of Suoi Nuoc Beach.

## Thap Poshanu Cham Temple

While the beach itself is the main draw in Mui Ne, there are a few other sights worth visiting, too. The three Cham towers of **Thap Poshanu** (daily 8am–5pm; charge) at KM5 Nguyen Thong were built in the 8th century to honour Shiva and other deities. The primary tower (usually locked) contains a pair of phallic *linga-yoni*. The tower beside is devoted to Agni, the fire deity, and the smallest tower to Nandi, the buffalo deity. The site offers the best view of Phan Thiet City, the Phu Hai River and Song Len Mountain. A new pagoda, abandoned French military outpost and a shop selling Cham crafts and local gemstones are all located on site.

## White Sand Dunes

The **White Sand Dunes** (also known as Bau Trang or "White Lake") are an immense Saharan-like series of gold-and-snow-white dunes, located around 45 minutes' drive, 30km (19 miles) northwest of Mui Ne village. Nestled in the dunes are two large reservoirs and a series of smaller lakes, which offer excellent opportunities to observe local bird-life, including four species of heron, the red-wattled lapwing and several species of bee-eaters (contact Vietnam Birding, www.vietnambirding.com, in HCMC for guided, expert tours). There are always village kids standing by, waiting to rent sleds to visitors for a spot of "dune surfing". Be sure to bring plenty of water, sunscreen and a hat – the glare is intense. The best time to visit is early in the morning or late in the afternoon to avoid the intense heat and also to take advantage of the dramatic lighting for photos. At night when there is a full moon the dunes are particularly impressive, but watch for snakes, scorpions and bandits.

On the way to the dunes, it's hard to miss the **titanium mining** operations along the highway. Some of the world's richest deposits are located along the coast of Binh Thuan province. This is a frequent source of unhappiness for resort owners, who fear the noise and known radioactive pollution that the mining operations bring.

Other than fishing, goatherding has been the traditional vocation for many locals in the surrounding villages. They are raised for their meat rather than milk – goat hotpot and grilled goat meat are local specialities here. With the rising demand for lizard meat, however, many residents are switching to lizard-farming (lizards are said to be delicious stir-fried with lemongrass and chilli). Both goat and lizard pens can be seen amid the dunes.

Quad bikes (four-wheelers) have begun to dominate the once peaceful dunes. It can be a fun way to traverse them, but be mindful that neither the safety nor the wisdom of this activity is ensured.

## Red Sand Dunes

The **Red Sand Dunes** are another popular sight on the way, but are not as impressive as the white dunes. The **Fairy Stream** (Soui Tien), however, that flows through the dunes is a lovely walk (30 minutes each way) through layers of blood-red, gold and silver sand dunes undulating through the countryside. Leave your shoes at the shop near the last bridge before Mui Ne village, as you'll be wading in ankle-deep water all the way to the small waterfall at the other end. An ostrich farm (a local fad) has been set up along the way. A crocodile farm sits out of view, above the small waterfall at the end of the stream, and across the road.

## CON DAO ARCHIPELAGO

Once a feared prison known as "Devil's Island", **Con Son Island**, the largest of 14 islands that make up the **Con Dao Archipelago ⑪**, is now the heart of a national park famous for its hawksbill and green marine turtles as well as the dugong – a relative of the manatee. The World Wildlife Fund has been actively involved in programmes here to protect these amazing creatures. Since 1995,

more than 300,000 baby turtles have been released into the sea and around 1,000 mature turtles have been tagged.

Originally known as Poulo Condore, Con Son, which covers about 20 sq km (8 sq miles), was first settled by the British East India Company in 1703, but the Bugis mercenaries from Sulawesi, hired to build the garrison, murdered all their employers. Due to the remoteness of the island, the French used it later as a prison for Vietnamese anti-colonial protesters. The island became notorious for torture and death, but the full extent of the horrors – which continued under the South Vietnamese government – were not fully known until the end of the war in 1975. Prisoners were kept in 11 prisons on Con Son, and often held in tiny underground boxes with metal grille roofs, known as "tiger cages". Grisly dummies now shackled together in the prisons shed light on the horrors the inmates endured.

**Hang Duong Cemetery** holds the remains of the many prisoners who died here – most in unmarked graves. One of the best-known graves belongs to nationalist heroine **Vo Thi Sau**, in 1952

*Prisoners in Con Son Island were housed in "tiger cages" and often subjected to torture and abuse.*

**BELOW RIGHT:** Con Son's infamous "tiger cages" were used to hold prisoners.
**BELOW LEFT:** Con Son Island vista.

*Hang Duong Cemetery is dotted with the unmarked graves of prisoners.*

the first female to be executed here, at the age of 18. Her grave is decorated with offerings of mirrors and hairbrushes, a tribute to her gender and youthful age.

Occupying the former French governor's residence and overlooking the main bay is a small **Revolutionary Museum** (Mon–Sat 7.30–11am, 1.30–5pm; charge). The four rooms cover Con Dao's history, most of which revolves around the penal colony.

Con Son is mountainous and covered in rainforest, with great hiking trails for viewing endemic wildlife. The best information source is the **National Park Headquarters** (tel: 064-383 0150; www.condaopark.com.vn) at 29 Vo Thi Sau Street.

There are several good beaches on Con Son – like **Bai Dat Doc Beach** and **Bai Nhat Beach** – and also on some of the smaller islands, such as Bai Canh, which is also a major nesting area for turtles.

The waters around the Con Dao Archipelago encompass the country's most pristine and varied dive sites. Con Dao is also the only place in the country with an officially diveable wreck. That

**BELOW:** aquamarine waters of Bai Nhat Beach on Con Son Island.

being said, the waters here have not entirely escaped the destructive fishing practices that have obliterated reefs in other parts of Vietnam. Things are not quite as untouched as they were a few years ago, and many divers suggest that the last dugong was sold on the butcher block in the market, some years ago. Still, there are over 1,000 hectares (2,500 acres) of pristine coral reefs and over 1,300 marine species identified thus far. It is possible to see turtles, manta rays and reef sharks around Con Dao, and others such as devil scorpionfish, cowfish, giant moray eels, clownfish and many more are still very common.

The weather in this area is at its best from February to May, while the turtle-nesting season is May to September, overlapping with the prime diving between June and September. Rainbow Divers (see page 373) is the only dive shop operating on the island.

Traffic is mercifully light on Con Son's few roads, and the main resort hotels are found between the principal coastal road and Con Son Bay, including the luxury new **Six Senses** resort.

# RESTAURANTS

Prices for a three-course dinner per person:
**$** = under US$5
**$$** = US$5–10
**$$$** = US$10–20
**$$$$** = over US$20

Dining options in the areas outside Ho Chi Minh City range from sparse to plentiful. The most options are found in Mui Ne, with a few new restaurants added every month. Vung Tau has some good foreign food selections along the main road, and lots of seafood at the beaches. In Tay Ninh there's really nothing worth recommending, and in Cat Tien there's nothing but the park cantina.

## Vung Tau

### Vietnamese and Western
**Belly's Restaurant & Bar**
94 Ha Long St. Tel: 064-385 6305. Open: daily B, L & D. **$$**
Belly's is an old standard in Vung Tau, with an enormous menu (literally) of Vietnamese, Italian, French, Tex-Mex and American favourites, among other things. Service is friendly, the beer is cold, and the view across Front Beach is enticing.
**Tommy's Restaurant & Bar**
94 Ha Long St. Tel: 064-385 3554. Open: daily B, L & D. **$$**
Friendly Australian-Vietnamese sports bar with a big widescreen to watch international games. The menu serves a great mix of steaks, burgers and local fare. There is also a deli for takeaway meats.

### Italian
**Good Morning Vietnam**
6 Hoang Hoa Tham St. Tel: 064-385 6959. Open: daily B, L & D. **$$**
www.goodmorningvietnam.com

Expect consistent quality from the original outlet of a chain of authentic Italian restaurants. Pizzas are their claim to fame, but their breads (free with every meal), pastas and meat dishes are exceptional, too. Manager Franco Anastasi is a real gem, and will assist travellers with local info.

## Phan Thiet

### Vietnamese and Western
**Café Win**
Corner of Ton Duc Thang and Thu Khoa Huan St. Open: daily B, L & D. **$**
Win is the largest and most popular café in Phan Thiet, and despite otherwise being a fairly standard, though upscale, Vietnamese café, its burgers, pizza and fried noodles are at least as good (and certainly cheaper) than any of the restaurants in Mui Ne. Win has air conditioning, free Wi-fi and multiple widescreen TVs with cable.
**Ocean Dunes Golf Club**
1 Ton Duc Thang St. Tel: 08-3824 3640. Open: daily B, L & D. **$$$**
www.oceandunesgolf.vn
Overlooking the golf course and right next to old Novotel. American comfort food and Mexican dishes are the main draws. The spicy buffalo wings and giant chicken burritos are amazing. Portions are generous and flavours authentic.

## Mui Ne Beach

### Vietnamese
**Au Viet Restaurant**
81B Nguyen Dinh Chieu St. Tel: 062-3246 1881. Open: daily L & D. **$$**
A brand-new seafood restaurant serving both local Vietnamese cuisine and western favourites. The

decor is traditional bamboo and thatched roof, recalling the Mui Ne of a decade ago, before the tourists arrived in droves. The owner also runs a guesthouse, and a sister restaurant, Sunrise, a few doors down.
**Dragon Fly**
Nguyen Dinh Chieu St (across from Blue Ocean Resort). Tel: 062-384 7038. Open: daily L & D. **$$**
A roadside restaurant with fairly typical decor but surprisingly delicious Thai, Vietnamese and Western dishes. The speciality is fresh local seafood, grilled, steamed or stir-fried. Try the red snapper steamed with lemongrass and onions.
**Forest Restaurant (Rung)**
67 Nguyen Dinh Chieu St. Tel: 062-384 7589. Open: daily L & D. **$$$**
www.forestrestaurant.com
One of the most delightful Vietnamese restaurants in Mui Ne, it has a garden setting with fishponds and bamboo water music. The interior is immaculately decorated with rare hill-tribe minority crafts. Nightly demonstrations of weaving by Cham minorities, as well as performances by a live Cham band. The menu covers mainly seafood and local Vietnamese flavours.
**Vietnam Home**
125A, B Nguyen Dinh Chieu St. Tel: 062-384-7687. Open: daily B, L & D. **$$**
Set in an atmospheric bamboo tree house of sorts, Vietnam Home offers a varied menu of local favourites and regional specialities. The food is top-notch at reasonable prices. Occasionally there is a live band – either ethnic Cham or highlands music.

### French
**Champa Restaurant**
Coco Beach Resort, 58 Nguyen

Dinh Chieu St. Tel: 062-384 7111. Open: daily D only. **$$$$**
Offering French *cuisine bourgeoisie*, Champa offers some of the finest food in Mui Ne. The restaurant is decorated with Cham crafts and the large terrace overlooks the pool and gardens. The adjoining bar serves inventive cocktails to go with your Cuban cigar.

### Fusion
**Snow**
109 Nguyen Dinh Chieu St. Tel: 062-374 3123. Open: daily B, L & D. **$$$**
This Russian-owned restaurant (serving East-West fusion fare), club and sushi bar is set in the centre of the beach and is definitely the trendiest spot in town. The all-white decor with deep-blue ceiling is striking. More of an evening hangout for gourmet seafood and cocktails, but the breakfasts are great too. Free pick-up from your hotel.

### Indian
**Shree Ganesh**
57 Nguyen Dinh Chieu St. Tel: 062-374 1330. Open: daily B, L & D. **$$$**
This popular venue serves North Indian and tandoori dishes to the sounds of lively Indian music. Curry is king here, but you can't go wrong with anything on the menu.

### International
**Joe's Cafe**
139 Nguyen Dinh Chieu, Ham Tien (Mui Ne), Phan Thiet Tel: 062-374 3447. Open: daily B, L & D. **$**
The only local venue open 24 hours, offering Italian coffee, pizzas, burgers, pasta, a wide selection of sandwiches and breakfast. Live music is performed every night after 8pm.

# THE MEKONG DELTA

Known as Vietnam's rice bowl, the Mekong Delta is a region of lush green fields, traditional villages and floating markets, connected by countless canals that are fed by the mighty Mekong

Travelling through the serpentine, sleepy canals of the Mekong Delta is like taking a trip back in time. Its patchwork of fields and canals creates a scenic landscape, while its people are so relaxed and welcoming that the Delta often detains visitors for longer than they had expected.

The Vietnamese name for the Mekong is **Song Cuu Long**, meaning the River of Nine Dragons, in reference to the nine principal tributaries that empty into the South China Sea. The vast Mekong Delta is formed as the river fans out and deposits alluvium along its many smaller channels, creating a fertile landscape rich in agriculture.

The Mekong descends from its source high in the Tibetan Plateau and follows a 4,500km (2,800-mile) course through China, Myanmar (Burma), Laos, Thailand, Cambodia and southern Vietnam before emptying into the sea. For years it was nothing more than vast marshland, but by the end of the 18th century, two huge canals – the Thai Hoa, which linked Rach Gia and Long Xuyen, and the Vinh Te, linking Chau Doc and Ha Tien – were in use. Today, the region covers almost 40,000 sq km (15,400 sq miles) and its inhabitants include Khmer, Chinese and Cham.

## Travelling around

An adequate road network serves the delta's 13 provinces, and, until recently, more than 100 ferries also operated. Now only nine remain as the myriad of canals and bamboo bridges are slowly being upgraded into cable bridges and four-lane highways. In larger cities, the paved roads are in good condition, but in more rural spots, the "roads" are often little more than a series of loosely connected potholes. This can add hours onto journey times (particularly in the

**LEFT:** using water buffaloes to till the land in Ba Chuc. **BELOW:** Phu Quoc womenfolk.

*My Tho Market, a typical Mekong Delta produce market.*

wet season), but also allows travellers to fully appreciate the charming palm-thatched wooden huts and lush green landscape around them. The river and its network of tributaries carry a busy and varied flow of traffic, and jumping in a boat to explore the islands' narrow waterways is a key part of any trip to the delta.

## Agricultural heartland

During the Vietnam War the region was thick with Viet Cong, and so was heavily bombed with chemical defoliants. Today, you would never know this – the delta is the most densely populated area in Vietnam, and markets here overflow with fish and other produce yielded by the delta's rich alluvial soil: sesame, peanuts, cashews, pineapples, pumpkins, tangerines, melons, cabbages, coconuts, sugar cane, dragon fruit, durians and rice are just a few of the crops produced here. Most grow year-round, but the end of the rainy season in March is a good month to visit and sample the enormous variety of seasonal fruits. The flat, moist land is perfect for rice

**BELOW:** Dong Tam Snake Farm.

cultivation; in many places there are three full harvests during the year, and the delta produces enough rice to feed the whole nation, with a sizeable surplus exported to provide a substantial percentage of the country's earnings.

As well as fields, there are good beaches on the western coast, the most popular of which is Hon Chong. Sand-worshippers can fly direct from HCMC to Phu Quoc Island, with its beautiful beaches and lush forests, just off the Hon Chong coast.

Despite the march of development across the rest of Vietnam, life in the Mekong Delta remains virtually unchanged – agriculture is still the dominant industry and the landscape is a tapestry of green paddy fields, mirror-like pools and expansive fields of exotic fruits, all fed by the life-giving brown waters of the river that snakes between them.

## MY THO

**My Tho** ⑫, about 70km (43 miles) from HCMC through Long An province, is the gateway to the Mekong Delta. The sleepy capital of Tien Giang province, it was founded in 1680 by political refugees fleeing China at the end of the Ming dynasty, afraid that their affiliation to the Chinese would translate into a death sentence under their new masters. With a population of 300,000, this provincial town lies on the left bank of the My Tho River (Song My Tho), the northernmost branch of the Mekong. Along the waterfront are the main hotels and restaurants, along with a large tourist information centre that houses several companies. Thu Khoa Huan Park is a popular place to hang out in the evenings, as food traders set up stalls and children play on fairground rides. There are a couple of good cafés here too, making it an ideal place to people-watch. Café 30/4 is so retro it seems to be swathed in sepia, while Lac Hong plays blues and jazz tunes and has saxophones and vinyl records stuck to the walls.

The Catholic **My Tho Church**, on Ly Thuong Kiet Street, was built at the end of the 19th century, and there is still a Catholic congregation of more than 7,000 followers. At 60 Nguyen Trung Trac Street is the **Vinh Trang Pagoda** (Chua Vinh Trang; daily 8am– 5pm; free). Built in 1849 and the largest in the province, the temple is an eclectic mix of French, Chinese, Vietnamese and Khmer architectural styles.

My Tho's busy **Central Market** on Trung Trac and Nguyen Hue streets is a great place to flex your bartering skills and haggle over succulent fruits plucked fresh from the trees. Fishing is one of the mainstays of the local economy, and although fish are sorted for wholesale at night, during the day the market is a great source of dry fish products, including the pungent *kho muc*, or dried squid, often eaten with shrimp paste. Be sure to sample the town's famously tasty pork and vermicelli noodle soup, *hu tieu My Tho*, and beef meatballs, *bo vien*, from one of the busy stalls outside. A more sanitised, but not necessarily sanitary, undercover market is also here inside a

three-storey building, but most traders prefer to operate outside. Still, if you do go upstairs they sell fake perfume for US$2, which may just eradicate all those fishy smells.

From HCMC, My Tho is often the first stop for those embarking on a delta adventure. Scenic six-hour trips run by river ferry, chugging alongside boats carrying fresh produce to the city or manufactured goods from it. The province has a more than adequate road network, and a new cable bridge connects My Tho to nearby Ben Tre township.

## My Tho's islands

My Tho is the ideal spot from which to reach the natural canals and mangrove-covered inlets of the neighbouring islands. They are known locally as the "Coconut Islands" due to the huge concentration of the trees cultivated by locals. The fruit is sold for consumption, while its wood is used for handicrafts and the fibre for rope and mats. **Unicorn Island** (Con Lan) is the largest, with a population of 7,000, followed by **Phoenix Island**

**TIP**

A phenomenal number of fruits grow in the Mekong Delta. Look out for roadside stalls selling coconut, mangosteen, mango, pineapple, rambutan and durian – although the latter is so smelly most hotels won't let it through their doors.

**BELOW:** Ha Tien

## Doing the Delta

**G**etting to the heart of the Delta means taking to the water. Boat tours run all around the region, most following a similar trail. From My Tho, a four-hour trip will visit some of the four islands closest to the town. After stopping briefly at a fish farm and beehive, tourists are usually taken to listen to a performance of traditional music, before moving on to see women making candy coconut – something that Ben Tre is famous for. A horse and carriage await in Ben Tre along with a brief bicycle ride past rice fields, followed by the chance to feed crocodiles on Phoenix Island before catching the boat home. The cost is about US$15, but this can change depending on numbers. If this seems a bit touristy for your tastes, another option is to find local boat owners who can make a tailor-made itinerary that tends to be cheaper than the tour companies.

Other trips involve visiting the floating markets in Can Tho, and these tours can easily be booked in Can Tho itself. They start early to avoid the heat. To reach the picturesque town of Tra Vinh you can go by bus or hire a motorbike driver for VND500,000, stopping at villages and rice fields along the way. See Activities Travel Tips *(page 373)* for more information on Delta tours.

**TIP**

The best time to visit the Mekong Delta is between January and March, when temperatures are around 22°C to 34°C (72°F to 93°F). From May onwards, the rainfall and humidity increase. During the wettest months – July to October – some provinces are flooded and travel is restricted.

**BELOW LEFT:** Nguyen Dinh Chieu Temple in Ben Tre.
**BELOW RIGHT:** coconut candy factory in Ben Tre.

(Con Phung) and **Dragon Island** (Con Long), and then the tiny **Turtle Island** (Con Qui). Most of the boat tours from HCMC will include visits to small coconut candy factories and handicraft workshops, which have been set up solely for tourists. Note: Phoenix and Turtle islands are a part of Ben Tre province.

### Dong Tam Snake Farm

Some 12km (7 miles) to the west of My Tho is **Dong Tam Snake Farm** (Trai Ran Dong Tam; tel: 073-385 3204; daily 8am–5pm; charge). Converted from a former US army base, the pythons, cobras and king cobras reared here yield a variety of substances used in traditional medicines. Snake meat is believed to be an effective remedy against a number of ailments ranging from mental disorders to rheumatism and paralysis, and snake gall is combined with other drugs to treat coughs and migraine. Most Vietnamese men believe snake to be a virility enhancer, and an intriguing tonic is obtained by steeping three varieties of snake in alcohol

– if you need a boost it's sold at the gift shop.

### BEN TRE

The Rach Mieu cable bridge immediately put Ben Tre on the tourist radar when it opened in 2008. As well as providing easy access to Ben Tre from My Tho, crossing the bridge also shows visitors just how vast the waterways here are.

Crisscrossed by many small canals, **Ben Tre province** has perfect conditions for rice-growing, but is also prone to flooding during the rainy season. Competing with the area's extensive rice fields are coconut plantations: more coconut palms are grown in Ben Tre than in any other province in the country. Look out for *banh dua*, a sticky rice and banana combo that is beautifully wrapped in banana leaves and is unique to Ben Tre. The provincial capital, **Ben Tre** ⑬ ("Bamboo Boat Port"), is 10km (6 miles) from the My Tho ferry dock on the Ham Luong tributary, and is named after the little wooden vessels that used to dock there. A boat trip

along the Ba Lai–Ham Luong waterway is the ideal way to get a feel of everyday life on the river. Bee farms and fruit orchards are scattered all over the area, and can be reached by the network of small canals.

Ben Tre town has a modest museum (daily 7–11am and 1–5pm; free) that focuses on the conflict with America but does also house a giant crocodile skull, from the time when tigers and elephants also roamed these parts. The **Vien Minh Pagoda** (Chua Vien Minh; daily 8am–5pm; free) is the head office of the province's Buddhist association and the town's main centre of worship. Rebuilt in 1958, it is thought to be around 100 years old.

## Around Ben Tre

Located 70km (44 miles) from Ben Tre town is **Ba Tri ⓮**, where the **Nguyen Dinh Chieu Temple** (daily 7.30–11.30am, 1.30–7pm; free) is dedicated to a 19th-century poet born in the town. The bird sanctuary of **San Chim Vam Ho** (daily 7am–6pm; charge), 38km (24 miles) southeast of Ben Tre or 15km (9 miles) northwest of Ba Tri, has a good collection of storks. Many visit here hoping to get that classic photo of Vietnam: a stork on the back of a water buffalo. The best time to visit is at dusk, when the birds fill the skies as they return to roost.

## VINH LONG

The fruit-laden islands and floating market around Vinh Long make it a popular stopping-off point. West of Ben Tre province and 66km (41 miles) from My Tho, **Vinh Long ⓯** has several islands ripe for exploration. Boats leave regularly from in front of the **Cuu Long Hotel** for trips to nearby **An Binh Island** and **Binh Hoa Phuoc Island**; both are 5km (3 miles) from Vinh Long. The official booking office is at **Cuu Long Tourist** (tel: 070-382 3616) at 1 Thang 5 Street, but it is often cheaper to organise a trip privately with a local boatman. Mekong

Travel Company (tel: 070-383 6252) has great staff who can also arrange bicycling tours in nearby countryside, or you can rent a bike for US$3 a day.

The boat trip is a treat for fruit-lovers, as the excursion takes in villages with gardens and orchards heavy with juicy seasonal fruits. Visitors are also taken to see several cottage industries, such as potteries and rice-paper making, before strolling through well-tended bonsai gardens or staying overnight with one of a dozen local families on the islands. Many of the homes here are built on stilts, due to the constant threat of flooding. Boat trips can also include **Cai Be** floating market on the other side of An Binh. The market operates from 5am to 5pm daily, but the mornings are best, when the market is at its busiest. If time is short, private jeeps can be hired for a swifter journey to the market. For the truly frugal, a ferry crosses to An Binh for VND1,000.

The town itself has several Chinese pagodas but the main action is around the day market. Several cafés, notably Hoang An, have pleasant riverside views.

*An exhibit at Can Tho Museum depicting a Chinese herbalist selling traditional medicine.*

**BELOW:** fresh fish, My Tho Central Market.

*Clay figurine at Dat Set Pagoda.*

## TRA VINH

Leafy, sleepy **Tra Vinh** is a beautiful town filled with strong Khmer influences. Some 40km (25 miles) southwest of Ben Tre, Tra Vinh province is bordered by the Tien and Hau rivers and washed by over 65km (40 miles) of coastline. Well off the tourist path, **Tra Vinh** is known locally as Go Do ("City in the Forest") after its ancient trees. A third of Tra Vinh's 96,000-strong population are ethnic Khmer who make their living from farming. Around 140 Khmer pagodas are dotted throughout the province.

The town is easy to walk around and has a couple of attractions, including a day market that runs along the Long Bing River. Ong Pagoda, in the centre of town, is a wonderfully dramatic-looking Chinese pagoda, while 200 metres/yds north is Ong Met Pagoda, which has Khmer carvings on the main wall and a more Thai style main hall. About 5km (3 miles) out of town is Ho Chi Minh Temple (daily 7am–5pm; free), which was built in 1971 and features a simple memorial at its centre and a patriotic exhibition of

**BELOW:** floating market, Can Tho.

Ho Chi Minh's life all around it. Tree-fringed **Ao Ba Om** (Ba Om Lake) is a recreational area about 7km (4 miles) southwest of Tra Vinh town which also has a Khmer pagoda and museum nearby. Some 58km (36 miles) southwest of town is **Co Pagoda** (Chua Co) or Stork Pagoda, a Khmer pagoda that shelters hundreds of storks after sunset each day.

## CAN THO

**Can Tho** is the capital of Can Tho province and the largest and most modern city in the delta, with a population of 1.2 million. Situated 34km (21 miles) southwest of Vinh Long on the banks of the Hau River (Song Hau), it is an important commercial centre and river port, bustling with energy.

As the hub of the Mekong Delta, Can Tho is a prosperous and vibrant city, best for strolling around and soaking up the atmosphere. One of the few places to visit in town is the **Can Tho Museum** at 1 Hoa Binh Street (daily 8–11am and 2–5pm; free), with exhibits detailing local history.

The **Munirangsayaram Pagoda** at 36 Hoa Binh Street (daily 8am–5pm; free), built in 1946, is a centre of worship for the area's small Khmer community. This Hinayana Buddhist temple is similar to those found in Cambodia. Missing are the Taoist spirits and *bodhisattvas* found in Mahayana Buddhist temples that are more typical of Vietnam.

The city's **Central Market** is the largest fruit market in the Mekong Delta region, and although the main building is at the intersection of Hai Ba Trung and Nam Ky Khoi Nghia streets, the market hustle stretches along the length of Hai Ba Trung Street. Several restaurants on the waterfront serve regional specialities: frog, turtle, snake and many kinds of fish.

### Can Tho's floating markets

Boat trips on the Hau River are one of the highlights of Can Tho, and it is probably the best place in the

Mekong Delta from which to tour the floating markets. Trips can be booked with the local tourism office, but a better option is to explore the markets by small motorboat; enquire along the dock or in guesthouses about chartering a boat (around VND50,000–60,000 an hour). Rise early for the 10km (6-mile) ride southeast to lively **Cai Rang**, the largest floating market in the delta. Here, all manner of boats and sampans gather, their occupants busily engaged in buying or selling a wide variety of fruit, fish and vegetables. Photo opportunities at this wholesale market are endless.

For a different experience, head to **Phong Dien**, about 20km (12 miles) southwest of Can Tho. This is a much smaller, and some say more authentic, floating market, thanks to the fact that fewer tourists bother to travel this far. Here, ladies in conical *non la* hats are happy to select, peel and slice fresh *buoi* (pomelo) or *xoai* (mango) for tourists from the mountain of fruit stacked high on their boats.

## SOC TRANG

The Khmer-influenced province of Soc Trang is about 35km (22 miles) south of Can Tho. It is home to 300,000 Khmer people and its capital, **Soc Trang** ⑱, has a number of interesting Khmer temples and pagodas. The best of these is the luridly painted **Kh'leng Pagoda** (daily 8am–5pm; charge). Originally constructed more than 400 years ago, this pagoda was rebuilt in 1907 and is richly decorated on the outside with carved griffins, snakes and statues of dancing maidens. Inside, a gilded bronze statue of Sakyamuni Buddha presides over the main altar. About two dozen monks are in residence and 170 monks attend the Buddhist College on the premises. The ancient Dharma (Buddhist scripture), written on palm leaves, is one of the pagoda's most treasured relics.

### Dat Set Pagoda

Near the centre of town, along 68 Mau Than Street, is the fascinating **Dat Set Pagoda** (Chua Dat Set; daily 8am–5pm; free), or the Clay Pagoda. Made entirely of clay, this Chinese pagoda

*A villager of Cham origin, Dong Thap.*

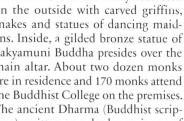

**BELOW RIGHT:**
Khmer-style
Kh'leng Pagoda.
**BELOW LEFT:**
reclining Buddha,
Doi Pagoda.

**TIP**

Homestays are a great way to experience what life is really like around this region. A growing number is now available, and they tend to offer basic accommodation but also the chance to cook, fish and live like locals for a few days.

houses statues and figurines sculpted from the same material by the monk Ngo Kim Tong. Look out for the intricately sculpted Bao Thap tower with its small Buddha figurines that rest on every lotus petal. There are also six giant paraffin candles, two of which have been burning in honour of the artist since 1970, when they were first made.

## Doi Pagoda (Bat Pagoda)

On the outskirts of town, just 4km (2 miles) away, is **Doi Pagoda** (Chua Doi; (daily 8am–5pm; charge), a popular stopping point for tourists. Less ornate than Kh'leng Pagoda, this Khmer temple is more famous for the thousands of screeching fruit bats residing in its gardens than for the colourful murals of the Buddha's life decorating the walls. It is said that while these bats may attack the fruit trees in other orchards, they know not to eat from the trees that shelter them. The best time to visit is around dawn and an hour before sunset, when the bats swoop out from the trees in a dense black cloud as they go hunting for food.

## DONG THAP

Bordering Cambodia in the north, Dong Thap province is one of the three provinces lying in the marshy area known as **Dong Thap Muoi** ("10 Tower Field"). The province takes its name from the 10-storey Thap Muoi tower that was built in ancient times in the commune of An Phong. The tower, which no longer stands, was used as a lookout by the resistance forces against the French during colonial times. The area is populated primarily by people of Chinese, Khmer, Cham and Tai origin. Agriculture has always been the dominant industry, but recently industrial parks at Sa Dec, Song Hau and Tran Quoc Toan have been attracting business from around the delta.

## Around Cao Lanh

The provincial capital of Dong Thap province, **Cao Lanh** ⑲, has little of interest for tourists. More interesting are the sights around it. About 1km (0.6 miles) south of Cao Lanh is the **grave of Nguyen Sinh Sac**, Ho Chi Minh's father, who lived from 1862 to 1929.

### The Oc Eo Civilisation

Some 40km (25 miles) southwest of Long Xuyen, in the hilly area of Ba The, are the ruins of Oc Eo, a major trading port during the first few centuries AD. Oc Eo lay submerged for many years until it was rediscovered in the 1940s after a French archaeologist took an aerial photograph of the area. Remnants of architectural structures and other finds made by researchers indicate that it was a city closely linked with the ancient pre-Angkor Indianised kingdom of Phu Nam (Funan), which dates back to the 1st century AD and was at the peak of prosperity during the 5th century.

It is possible to visit the ruins, but there's little to see, as the artefacts have been moved to museums throughout Vietnam. The museum in Long Xuyen has some exhibits from the site.

**BELOW:** Long Xuyen rural scene.

About 20km (12 miles) southeast of Cao Lanh and accessible only by boat is **Rung Tram**, a forested area that harboured an underground Viet Cong camp called **Xeo Quit Base** (daily 7am–5pm; charge) during the Vietnam War. For nearly 15 years, key Viet Cong personnel lived here in underground bunkers while planning strategic attacks against the American forces.

**Tran Chim Tam Nong is** a stork sanctuary located 45km (28 miles) north of Cao Lanh in the Tam Nong area. This wildlife reserve is home to rare red-headed cranes, lots of fish and innumerable water chestnut trees, all best seen by boat (VND100,000 per hour).

## AN GIANG

To the west, **An Giang province** ("Splitting River") borders the Cambodian province of Takeo. Here, the Mekong enters the province and divides into two branches, forming the Tien and Hau rivers, which every year deposit millions of cubic metres of alluvial soil in the adjacent areas.

This prosperous region, intersected by numerous natural canals and small rivers, is rich in natural resources and fertile land, and produces many varieties of fruit trees and crops of rice, soya bean, tobacco, groundnut and mulberry; it's also known for its silk industry.

An Giang is home to a sizeable number of Vietnam's ethnic minorities, of which Khmer Krom (southern Khmer) is the largest. It is believed that An Giang was once an important centre of the ancient Oc Eo culture (see panel).

## Long Xuyen

Ang Giang province's capital, **Long Xuyen** ❷, in the east of the province 190km (118 miles) from HCMC and 45km (28 miles) from the Cambodian border, is a thriving commercial town, the streets lined with cafés and motorbikes. The town's name refers to the shape of the river and literally means "dragon running through". Home to over 300,000 people, the predominant industries are rice production and the processing of fish (mainly catfish) for export, which have made the town the second-most prosperous town in the delta, after Can Tho.

Long Xuyen was home to the Hoa Hao sect, the region's major military force and army until 1956, and was the birthplace of Vietnam's second president, Ton Duc Thang.

Dominating the town with its tall bell tower at Hung Vuong Street is the grey-stone Catholic **Long Xuyen Cathedral**. Built between 1963 and 1973, the church can seat 1,000 worshippers and is the largest in the Mekong Delta. At 77 Thoai Ngoc Hau Street is the small **An Gian Museum** (Bao Tang An Giang; daily 7.30–10.30am and 2–4.30pm; charge). Displayed here are a few exhibits on the **Oc Eo** ❷ as well as personal effects of Ton Duc Thang and pictures of Long Xuyen in the 1930s.

## Chau Doc

A stone's throw from the Cambodian border, this town is situated on the

*The fishermen of Chau Doc live in houses that float on the Hau Giang River.*

**BELOW RIGHT:** Chau Phu Temple, Chau Doc.

*The Mekong Delta produces more rice for Vietnam than Japan and Korea combined. The entire delta is also home to a staggering amount of wildlife. The World Wildlife Fund reported in 2008 that a form of rat, thought to have been extinct for centuries, and a cyanide-producing millipede were among the most interesting finds.*

**BELOW:** view from Sam Mountain.

right bank of the **Hau Giang River** (Song Hau Giang) and is the usual entry or exit point for people on a boat tour between HCMC and the Cambodian capital Phnom Penh. With a population of 100,000, **Chau Doc ㉒** has a lively feel, and there is plenty to see and do on day trips from the town.

The **Chau Phu Temple** (Dinh Than Chau Phu; daily 8am–5pm; free) in the middle of Chau Doc town at the junction of Tran Hung Dao and Nguyen Van Thoai streets was built in 1926. Here, the locals worship Thai Ngoc Hau, the man responsible for building the nearby Chau Doc Canal, which opened the frontier between Cambodia and Vietnam. Thai was a high-ranking and important official during the time of the Nguyen dynasty.

Across the river in nearby Chau Giang is the **Chau Giang Mosque**, which serves the district's Muslim Cham community, as well as ethnic Vietnamese who have returned from Malaysia and Indonesia. The Cham number around 20,000 in the Chau Doc area, and typically live in stilt houses on the water, making their living from fishing and weaving.

Chau Doc is renowned for its quaint **floating villages**. Living in houses built over empty metal tanks to keep them afloat, many villagers make a living from fishing. Metal nets under the houses allow the families to farm and catch fish, which are then sold at local markets and transported all over the region. The houses stay stationary, anchored to poles sunk deep into the river bed by rope.

## Around Chau Doc

Some 4km (2 miles) away from Chau Doc is the 230-metre (755ft) -high **Sam Mountain ㉓** (Nui Sam), named after the sea cucumbers that once thrived nearby. Buddhist and Taoist shrines scatter the mountain slopes, visited by ethnic Chinese and pilgrims from Vietnam and abroad. You can climb up the south side of the mountain or get a motorbike to take you to the summit (the road is on the east side). Either way you will be greeted by spectacular views of the surrounding countryside at the summit. On a clear day even Cambodia is visible. A military outpost with a few soldiers is found at the top; the latter are more interested nowadays in their badminton games than the prospect of possible military incursions from Cambodia. The outpost is a legacy of the days when the Khmer Rouge would cross the border and slaughter Vietnamese civilians.

At the foot of the mountain is the tomb of Thai Ngoc Hau (the Nguyen-dynasty architect of the Chau Doc Canal), which also holds his two wives and some of the workers who died during the construction of the canal.

## Tay An Pagoda and Temple of Lady Xu

Sharing the base of the mountain are the Indian-style **Tay An Pagoda** (Chua Tay An) and **Temple of Lady Xu** (Mieu Ba Chua Xu). Famous for its numerous finely carved religious figures, Tay An Pagoda was established in

1847 by a Buddhist monk from Dong Thap province named Doan Minh Huyen, who wanted to help feed and heal the province's poor people.

Nearby, the Temple of Lady Xu reputedly marks the spot where looting Siamese troops left her granite statue after carrying it down from its original seat at the top of the mountain. According to folklore, Lady Xu came from the sky and helped the locals cultivate rice and develop their agriculture and fishing industries. Worshippers, including many Chinese from HCMC, Hong Kong and Taiwan, regularly visit bearing money, gifts and food, making it one of the richest temples in Vietnam. Every year on the 22nd day of the fourth lunar month, a large procession of followers begins a week-long series of festivities to celebrate their pilgrimage.

### Rung Tram Tra Su

The vast bird sanctuary of **Rung Tram Tra Su** (daily 7am–7pm; charge), covering 845 hectares (2,088 acres), is along the road to Sam Mountain, around 30km (19 miles) southwest of Chau Doc and 10km (6 miles) from the Cambodian border. This area around the Hau River became a protected forest reserve in 2005, and is home to many different animals and over 70 species of birds, notably the Indian crane, which is listed in the Vietnamese *Red Book* as a rare and endangered species.

Scientific research is a key component of the sanctuary, and of the 140 types of plants found in this reserve, 79 reportedly have medicinal properties. Rangers here offer hour-long motorised sampan rides along the waterways to visit hides elevated above the forest canopy.

### Ba Chuc

About 40km (25 miles) southwest of Chau Doc en route to Ha Tien are Vietnam's killing fields, **Ba Chuc**. For two weeks in April 1978, Khmer Rouge soldiers from Cambodia tore through this small border commune, mercilessly hacking adults to death with machetes and ripping young children limb from limb. In total, the raiding forces massacred 3,157 civilians,

*The remains of the Khmer Rouge genocide victims at Ba Chuc.*

**BELOW:** street scene, Chau Doc.

*Mac Cuu Family
Tombs.*

reducing the population of Ba Chuc to only two. A pagoda built in 1991 contains the skulls and bones of 1,159 victims. On display in the temple are some graphic photos depicting the aftermath of the slaughter.

## KIEN GIANG

**Kien Giang province**, in the southwest of the Mekong Delta, shares a common border in the northwest with Cambodia. In the west, it is washed by waters from the Gulf of Thailand. The border crossing from Ha Tien into Kampot in Cambodia is now open, but would-be travellers must hold a visa before entering Cambodia. Forests, plains, offshore islands and a 200km (124-mile) -long coastline make Kien Giang one of the delta's most geographically diverse and scenic provinces.

### Ha Tien

Nestling in a cove formed by the **Gian Thang River** (Song Gian Thang) is the town of **Ha Tien ㉔**, with a population of 120,000. Only 10km (6 miles) from the Cambodian border, Ha Tien's natural beauty, easy-going atmosphere and hospitality attract many visitors. To the east of Ha Tien, scenic **East Lake** (Ho Dong) – actually a sea inlet – is usually the first sight to greet visitors. The town is well known for its plentiful seafood and abundant black pepper plantations. It does a lively trade in items handcrafted from the shells of sea turtles, although it is best not to buy such goods as it only encourages this unfortunate trade.

### Mac Cuu Family Tombs

Ha Tien town has several temples dedicated to the legendary Mac family and an even greater number of tombs that rest on the eastern flank of **Binh San Mountain** (Nui Binh San). These 49 tombs are built of bricks and contain the remains of both Mac Cuu, a Chinese immigrant who founded the town, and his relatives. **Mac Cuu Family Tombs** (Lang Mac Chu), built in 1809 in a traditional Chinese architectural style, is the largest and is decorated with finely carved figures of the traditional Blue Dragon and White Tiger.

## Phu Dung Pagoda

If you only have time to visit one temple, head to 374 Phuong Thanh Street to see the **Phu Dung Pagoda** (Chua Phu Dung; daily 8am–5pm; free), founded by Mac Cuu's second wife, Nguyen Thi Xuan, in 1750. Her tomb is built on the hillside behind the pagoda's main hall, and the pagoda contains some interesting statues. In the centre of the main hall is one of the newborn Sakyamuni Buddha, in the embrace of nine dragons; on the main dais enclosed in a glass case is a bronze Chinese Buddha. Overcome by jealousy, Mac Cuu's first wife tried to kill her beautiful rival by placing her in an empty tank, intending her to drown as the rains slowly filled it up. Mac Cuu found and rescued her in time, and today visitors to Phu Dung Pagoda are predominantly women, intrigued by her story.

## Around Ha Tien

Some 8km (5 miles) northwest of Ha Tien are the twin beaches of **Mui Nai** and **Bai No**, which flank the sides of a small peninsula. The beaches are unremarkable, but they are popular with holidaying Vietnamese; expect lurid plastic picnic seats, kayaks, souvenir shops, and plenty of company at weekends.

## Thach Dong Cave Pagoda

About 4km (2.5 miles) away, past scenic paddy fields filled with water buffalo, is **Thach Dong Cave Pagoda** (Thach Dong Thon Van), the "Grotto that Swallows the Clouds". The cave shelters a Buddhist sanctuary and several funerary tablets, while altars to Quan Am and to Ngoc Hoang, the Jade Emperor of Heaven, can be found in several of its chambers. Lookout points at the cave reveal breathtaking views of the surrounding rice fields and smaller offshore islands. Near the grotto is a mass grave where 130 people massacred by Khmer Rouge troops in 1978 are buried; they are commemorated by a stela known as **Bia Cam Thu** – the Monument of Hatred – to the left of the sanctuary's entrance.

## Hon Chong and surroundings

The road from Ha Tien southeast to the provincial capital, Rach Gia, is generally good, and passes many small farms and picturesque villages. About 20km (12 miles) from Ha Tien, a detour off the main road in Ba Hon leads to the seaside town of **Hon Chong** ㉕. Unlike much of the pancake-flat Mekong Delta, this area is studded with impressive towering limestone formations. They are slowly becoming slightly less towering these days as these mountains are a prime source of quality limestone for the cement factories near Hon Chong, so are continually blasted with dynamite.

Once you pass the factories on the main road out to the beach, Hon Chong itself is relatively peaceful and beautiful. The best is **Duong Beach** (Bai Duong), which takes its name

*Fishermen at Mui Nai Beach.*

**BELOW:** Thach Dong Cave Pagoda.

**TIP**

With its reasonably flat terrain, the countryside around Ha Tien lends itself very well to bicycle touring. Several of the hotels in Ha Tien rent bikes by the day at modest rates.

from the *duong* (casuarina) trees growing beside it. Its clear waters and picturesque surroundings make it an ideal spot to break the journey with a swim.

At the tip of the beach, a toll gate leads to **Chua Grotto** (Chua Hang). The grotto is entered from behind the altar of the main pagoda, which is set back into the base of the hill. Small shrines line the cave, and a short walk through the rock leads you to the beach on the other side. For a small fee, tour boats here take you on a 20-minute cruise around the three islands, known locally as a mini Halong Bay.

Looking out to sea, you will see the famous **Father and Son Rocks** (Hon Phu Tu), the grottoes of which are a favourite haunt of sea swallows. A lightning strike in 2006 "killed" the father, knocking the stone column into the sea, so now only the son remains.

You can take a boat out to the islands, and then on to stalactite and stalagmite-riddled **Tien Grotto** (Hang Tien), or Coin Grotto. The cave is named after the zinc coins

**BELOW:** Khai Hoan Fish Sauce Distillery.

found buried within it by Nguyen Anh – the future Emperor Gia Long – and his troops, who camped here while battling the Tay Son rebels. A boat runs from a tiny dock on the beach from 7am to 4pm; the ticket costs VND9,000, but the boat only leaves once it has 25 passengers.

Leaving Hon Chung, around 3km (2 miles) before Ba Hon on the main road is **Mo So Grotto** (Hang Mo So). Open to the sky and encircled by sheer stone walls, a torch and a local guide will come in handy when exploring the labyrinth of tunnels beyond the three main caverns.

## Rach Gia

Ken Giang province's capital town is **Rach Gia** ㉖, located 100km (60 miles) southeast of Ha Tien. It is an active fishing port with a population of around 220,000, and is bordered by marshlands, many of which have been drained for rice cultivation. Well known for its seafood, Rach Gia has a good selection of restaurants serving both Chinese and Vietnamese food. The town also has a few interesting temples and pagodas, but does not offer as much as other delta towns; it's mainly used as a jumping-off point for travellers taking the ferry or plane to Phu Quoc Island.

## PHU QUOC ISLAND

Vietnam's largest island, **Phu Quoc** ㉗, is a mountainous retreat with 150km (94 miles) of sandy coastline. Situated 45km (28 miles) west of Ha Tien and part of Kien Giang province, the mountainous forest-island is 50km (30 miles) long and covers 1,300 sq km (500 sq miles). In the 18th century, Nguyen Anh (who later became Emperor Gia Long of the Nguyen dynasty) was sheltered here from the Tay Son rebels by French missionary Pigneau de Behaine, who himself used the island as a base between the 1760s and 1780s.

In 1869 the French occupied the island, establishing rubber and coconut plantations and also a notorious prison. During the Vietnam War, the South Vietnam government reopened the penal centre and incarcerated nearly 40,000 Viet Cong between 1969 and 1972.

In the past decade tourism has exploded here and things are about to get even bigger – there is a plan to build a US$4 billion casino and resort on 130 hectares (321 acres), while the government aims to attract up to 3 million visitors a year by 2020.

## Main sights

Today, the old prison near **An Thoi** port at the southern end of Phu Quoc Island has been turned into a museum. Called **Coconut Prison** (Nha Lao Cay Dua; Tue–Sun 7am–5pm; charge), it displays photographs of torture techniques and escape attempts, and lays bare the brutal conditions experienced by the inmates.

Phu Quoc has bountiful fishing grounds, black pepper trees and high-quality *nuoc mam* (fish sauce). Mats covered with fish drying in the sun can be seen (and smelt from afar) all over the island, and there are a number of local factories, including one of the island's best distilleries, **Khai Hoan Fish Sauce Distillery** (daily 8–11am and 2–5pm; free), where you can brave the stink to see how fish sauce is made. The factory is located at Hung Vuong Street, near the main port and town of **Duong Dong**, on the west coast of the island.

The island's pristine waters also provide perfect conditions for the cultivation of pearl-bearing oysters. The **Phu Quoc Pearl Farm** (tel: 077-398 0585; www.treasuresfromthedeep. com; daily 8am–5pm; free), just south of Duong Dong along Truong Beach (Bai Truong), provides an interesting insight into the world of pearl cultivation.

Half a kilometre from Duong Dong's main market, on a tiny spit of land at the mouth of Duong Dong River, is **Cau Castle** (Dinh Cau; on Truong Beach, daily 8am–6pm; free). This is not really a castle but a temple-cum-lighthouse that acts as a spiritual beacon for Phu Quoc's fishermen.

*Oysters are cultivated for pearls at Phu Quoc Island.*

**BELOW:** Long Beach is on the western side of Phu Quoc Island.

Built to honour the Goddess of the Sea, local fishermen and their families pray for her protection every time they put out to sea.

Phu Quoc can be accessed by a 2.5-hour boat ride from Rach Gia, Ha Tien or Hon Chung, or more easily via Vietnam Airlines flights from Ho Chi Minh City or Rach Gia. The best time to visit Phu Quoc is during the dry season from May to November.

## Phu Quoc's beaches

The real draw here is the coastline and its virtually uninterrupted fringe of spectacular white-sand beaches, washed by clear waters. **Dai Beach** (Bai Dai) in the northwest offers the perfect vantage point to enjoy the sunset, while remote **Thom Beach** (Bai Thom) in the northeast is usually deserted. **Truong Beach** (Bai Truong), better known as **Long Beach**, runs 20km (12 miles) along the western side of the island, stretching from Duong Dong almost to An Thoi Port in the south. This is where most of the

island's resorts are located, so finding a bite to eat or an ice-cool cocktail to sip under coconut palms is never a problem.

Locals will tell you that **Sao Beach** (Bai Sao), also known as Star Beach, and **Khem Beach** (Bai Khem), or Cream Beach, 25km (16 miles) from Duong Dong town on the far southeastern coast, are the island's most beautiful stretches. They are correct, and super-fine white sand and crystal waters await those who make the trek there, but these beaches are also the most undeveloped.

## Phu Quoc National Park

Established in 2001 in the hilly northeastern part of the island is **Phu Quoc National Park**. The highest of the 99 peaks in the island, **Chua Mountain** (Nui Chua) is found within the confines of the nature reserve. Little is known about the biodiversity of the park's 37,000 hectares (91,427 acres) of lowland evergreen forest, which covers two-thirds of the island. Check with your hotel about jungle-trekking tours of the reserve.

A few kilometres east of Duong Dong in the middle of the island is **Suoi Da Ban** (Stony Surface Spring), which flows through rocky pools pleasant enough for a swim. About 5km (3 miles) south, **Suoi Tranh** (Picturesque Stream) flows down from Ham Ninh Mountain (Nui Ham Ninh) to form an inviting waterfall called **Ben Tranh**.

## An Thoi Archipelago

To the south of the island is the **An Thoi Archipelago** ㉘, a group of 15 islands that has become enormously popular with divers and snorkellers. The surrounding waters are home to the endangered dugong as well as leatherback and hawksbill turtles, although underwater enthusiasts are more likely to see a huge variety of small, colourful reef and coral fish, many of which are endemic to Vietnamese waters.

**BELOW:** Mango Bay Resort, Phu Quoc.

# RESTAURANTS

Prices for a three-course dinner per person:

**$** = under US$5
**$$** = US$5 -10
**$$$** = US$10–20
**$$$$** = over US$20

Given that the Mekong Delta is largely water, it's no surprise that it serves up some of the best seafood in Vietnam. Certain towns have dishes with strong Khmer or Chinese influences, while much of the food takes advantage of the coconuts that grow so abundantly here.

My Tho

**Bach Tung Vien**
171B Anh Giac St. Tel: 073-388 8989. Open: daily B, L & D. **$**
Not far from Vinh Trang Pagoda, this open-sided, thatched-roof spot is popular with tour groups day-tripping from HCMC in the afternoon, before it morphs into a more local haunt at night. Delta specialities such as elephant ear fish and glutinous rice are menu staples, and the Hong Kong spring rolls are a speciality of the Chinese owners.

**Chuong Duong**
DC 10, 30/4 Duong. Tel: 073-870 875. Open: daily B, L & D. **$$$**
Set within the grounds of the Chuong Duong Hotel, the menu is largely seafood, with a few Japanese dishes also available. The decor may be dated, but the food quality is excellent.

**Vinh Long**

**Nem Nuong**
12 Duong 1/5. Tel: 070-3082 7127. Open: daily B, L & D. **$**
A fantastic little noodle shop near the market with detailed explanations, in English, of what's being served. *Xao nem*, a brilliant combination of barbecued meatballs, shredded pork

and vermicelli with roasted peanuts, is fantastic.

**Thien Tan**
56e Pham Thai Buong St. Tel: 070-382 4001. Open: daily L & D. **$$$**
One of the most popular, and biggest, places in town offers standard dishes and a few house specialities. Seating arrangements are unusual but pleasant: tables of eight have their own thatched pavilion. Portions are generous and the quality is excellent.

**Tra Vinh**

**La Trau Xanh**
Nguyen Thi Minh Khai. Open: daily B, L & D. **$$$**
The only large-scale restaurant in town, it offers dishes that range from the norm (beefsteak) to the more ambitious (braised tortoise and stewed snake). The menu offers English explanations; the staff do not.

**Can Tho**

**Nam Bo**
50 Hai Ba Trung St. Tel: 071-382 3908. Open: daily B, L & D. **$**
This crumbling colonial villa on the waterfront is one of the town's more Westernised restaurants, serving local Vietnamese specialities as well as some French-influenced dishes. Head to the breezy terrace for great views over the river as you tuck in.

**Spices Restaurant**
Victoria Can Tho Hotel, Cai Khe Ward. Tel: 071-381 0111. Open: B, L & D. **$$$**
www.victoriahotels-asia.com
Victoria's French chef, David Lacroix, rustles up the best fare that the Mekong Delta has to offer – try his speciality gazpacho of Vietnamese blue crab. The restaurant overlooks the Hau River, and offers casual all-day dining with both European and Vietnamese cuisine. Indoor

and outdoor seating is available.

**Long Xuyen**

**Long Xuyen Hotel**
19 Nguyen Van Cung. Tel: 076-384 1659. Open: daily B, L & D. **$**
On the ground floor of the hotel, with both indoor and streetside seating, this lively eatery is popular with local families keen to feast on fresh seafood in big portions.

**Chau Doc**

**Bassac Restaurant**
Victoria Chau Doc, 32 Le Loi St. Tel: 076-386 5010. Open: B, L & D. **$$$**
www.victoriahotels-asia.com
Looking out onto the Bassac River, this upscale restaurant has indoor and pleasant garden seating. Vietnamese chef Pham Van Quang has spent 20 years cooking in 5-star hotels, and a spot on the river-bank terrace is the best place to enjoy his Vietnamese specialities from all over the country.

**Thuan Loi**
18 Tran Hung Dao St. Tel: 076-386 5380. Open: daily B, L & D. **$**
Bring your mosquito repellent to this delightful, bamboo-screened floating restaurant on the river. Whether you choose Khmer and Vietnamese dishes à la carte or fresh from the tank, they will be served along with a smile and friendly conversation.

**Ha Tien**

**Hien**
07 Duong Dan Cau St. Tel: 077-385 1850. Open: daily B, L & D. **$**
Hien is a basic eatery that prides itself on dishing up the freshest seafood plucked straight from the sea. The menu stretches far beyond the printed card, and Hien can rustle up pretty much any Western or Vietnamese

speciality. Ordering is a lot easier if you have a Vietnamese-speaker with you.

**Huong Bien**
3–4 Tran Hau St, Lot Mac Thien Tic. Tel: 077-385 2072. Open: B, L & D. **$**
Another popular haunt for drinks and food, it has a reputation for being one of Ha Tien's "pricier" dining options (mains are actually a pinch at VND40,000) and dishes are tasty and fresh.

**Phu Quoc Island**

**Mai House**
Mai House, Duong Dong City. Tel: 077-384 7003/384 8924, mobile tel: 091-812 3796. Open: B, L & D. **$**
www.maihouseresort.com
Set on the "main strip" near the cluster of resorts and restaurants in Duong Dong town, this spot has a tempting array of local seafood specialities as well as a range of European favourites. More rustic than other options on the strip, but good value.

**Mango Bay**
Mango Bay Resort, Ong Lang Beach. Tel: 077-398 1693. Open: B, L & D. **$$$**
www.mangobayphuquoc.com
An open-air timber-frame restaurant where mouth-watering Asian and Western dishes and a superb range of cocktails are served right on the beach. Expect the freshest seafood and locally grown produce.

**Peppertree Restaurant**
La Veranda Duong Dong Beach. Tel: 077-398 2988. Open: D. **$$$$**
www.laverandaresort.com
Peppertree Restaurant is Phu Quoc's most upscale eatery and dishes up the best in Vietnamese, Asian fusion and international fine dining with an emphasis on fresh local produce. Perfect for a romantic sunset dinner.

# INSIGHT GUIDE   TRAVEL TIPS
# VIETNAM

# TRANSPORT

# GETTING THERE AND GETTING AROUND

## GETTING THERE

### By Air

#### Flying into Vietnam

Vietnam receives a small amount of air traffic compared with major Southeast Asian hubs such as Singapore and Bangkok. The main international airports are in Ho Chi Minh City (HCMC), Hanoi and Danang. HCMC is the prime gateway to the country, with fewer international flights going to Hanoi. Danang only receives international flights from Singapore, Bangkok and Hong Kong.

While Vietnam Airlines still has the largest number of international flights, as part of the country's WTO obligations (signed in 2006), the country has opened up the aviation industry to a number of international carriers. As a result, new carriers are flying in to HCMC and Hanoi all the time, including budget favourite Air Asia (from Bangkok) and JetStar Airlines (from Singapore).

From Europe, it is possible to fly to Vietnam direct from several countries, including France, Germany and the Netherlands, while many Asian countries now offer direct routes. Flight time from Europe is about 12 hours.

Other carriers from Europe and the USA have to fly through Bangkok, Hong Kong, Kuala Lumpur, Singapore, Seoul, Tokyo or Taipei to reach either HCMC or Hanoi.

Flight time from the USA (via Taipei or Tokyo) to Hanoi or HCMC is around 19 hours.

From Australia, there are nonstop flights from Sydney and Melbourne to either Hanoi or HCMC. Flight time from Sydney to HCMC is approximately 8 hours.

### Hanoi

**Noi Bai International Airport** is about 45km (28miles) north of downtown Hanoi. Apart from being a departure and arrival point for domestic flights, it is also served by flights from Europe, Australia and Asia. Aside from Vietnam Airlines (www.vietnamairlines.com), there are some 24 international airlines serving Noi Bai Airport. The main international destinations are Bangkok and Singapore.

Small and with few frills, the airport has only one terminal through which all travellers – both domestic and international – arrive and depart. There are plans for a Terminal 2 to serve international flights only. The airport carries close to its maximum capacity of 10 million passengers a year.

At present, both domestic and international departures check in on the second level, while arrivals are handled on the first level. On the first level are ATMs, foreign exchange counters, a restaurant and café, and a few duty-free shops.

For flight information, call the Operation Control Centre, tel: 04-3827 1513.

### Ho Chi Minh City

HCMC's **Tan Son Nhat International Airport** – just 7km (4 miles) from the city centre – is Vietnam's busiest airport hub, and accounts for nearly two-thirds of international arrivals and departures into Vietnam. At the time of press, 43 airlines operate out of Tan Son Nhat International Airport. Built in the 1930s and developed with US help in the 1950s, today it handles more than 15 million passengers a year.

Terminal 2, which services international flights, opened in September 2007, and is linked to the older Terminal 1 by a covered walkway. Terminal 2 has separate floors for Arrivals (first level) and Departures (second level).

Terminal 1 is used solely for domestic flights (namely Vietnam Airlines, Jetstar Pacific Airlines and VASCO). Both terminals have tourist information desks and food-and-drink outlets, but the larger, more upscale Terminal 2 has better facilities and swankier shops and restaurants. There are plans to open a new airport 50km (31 miles) away from HCMC by 2020.

For flight information, call the **Operation Control Centre**, tel: 08-3844 6662, 08-3848 5383.

### Danang

**Danang International Airport**, the main hub for central Vietnam, is just a few kilometres southwest of the city centre. Although designated as an international airport, Danang only receives direct flights from Singapore (Silk Air) and Bangkok (PB Air). Among the domestic airlines that serve the airport are Vietnam Airlines, Jetstar Pacific Airlines and VASCO. The airport is small and with few facilities, although a new terminal opened in 2011 to increase capacity. For flight information call 0511-382 3377. Airport taxis (tel: 0511 327-2727) and xe om are readily available.

From Danang, major places of interest like Hoi An and Hue are easily accessible by road.

### By Road

From **China**, it is possible to enter

Vietnam at the Lang Son and Lao Cai border crossings in the north and at Mong Cai near Halong Bay, where you can enter from Dongxing.

One can also enter Vietnam from several border points in **Laos**. Painfully slow buses bring passengers to the central towns of Lao Bao and Cau Treo.

Travellers can also enter Vietnam by crossing the border with **Cambodia** at Moc Bai, only a few hours by road from HCMC, or at Vinh Xuong, located about 30km (18 miles) north of Chau Doc in south Vietnam.

## GETTING AROUND

### From Major Airports

#### Hanoi

The best way to get to cover the 35km (21-mile) distance from **Noi Bai International Airport** to downtown Hanoi is by an **airport taxi** (tel: 04-3873 3333). The trip into town can take 40–60 minutes, depending on traffic and the actual destination. The taxi stand is directly outside the Arrivals area. Airport taxis charge a fixed rate of US$15, payable in US dollars or the dong equivalent, and are exempt from tolls. As the airport is located in Hanoi's northernmost Soc Son District, private vehicles heading to Hanoi from Noi Bai are subject to a road toll of US$2.60. Although taxis have meters it is often more economical to agree a price first.

Upmarket hotels tend to offer an airport pick-up service; ask in advance if this is available and the cost. Occasionally, some smaller guesthouses will say they do free airport pick-ups, but will then try to charge for the trip. Establish in advance if the service really is free. Airport minibuses cost US$2 but only leave once full. They drop passengers off in the heart of the Hoan Kiem District.

**Public buses** (daily 5am–10pm) are slow and crowded, so forget about this option unless you are travelling light. The yellow and red No. 07 or **No. 17** buses connect Noi Bai Airport with Hanoi's downtown. The bus stop is on the right side of the terminal exit. The fare is VND5,000 per person and the trip takes about an hour. Passengers are dropped off at Long Bien Bridge, on the eastern edge of the Old Quarter.

#### Ho Chi Minh City

**Tan Son Nhat International Airport** is only 7km (4 miles) northwest of the centre, but the ride into town can take 30 or 40 minutes. The airport offers few transport options: there are no airport shuttle buses, and it can be quite overwhelming for visitors, especially with unlicensed taxi "reps" hassling arrivals for business. Many hotels, especially 5-star establishments, offer pre-arranged transfer services, and, although sometimes costly, these are recommended.

Otherwise, your best option is an **airport taxi**, outside both Terminal 1 and Terminal 2. When leaving the international terminal, turn right and walk 200 metres/yds to the domestic terminal for more taxi options. There are no pre-arranged fixed rates, so be sure to establish the fare before departing (around US$10 for a ride to downtown HCMC is reasonable). Note: if you agree to go by meter, some taxi drivers may take long, circuitous routes into town; and if you're heading to the backpacker area (around Pham Ngo Lao and De Tham streets), a common scam is to try to convince you that your hotel closed down recently. The taxi driver will then offer to take you to an alternative hotel where he will get a commission from the owner. There are some reputable firms, such as Vinasun, but there are also copycat taxis with exactly the same name but displayed in a different font.

Alternatively, public bus **No. 152** travels into District 1, stopping at convenient places like Dong Khoi and Nguyen Hue streets, the backpacker area, and Ben Thanh Bus Station; it operates from outside Terminal 1 (6am–8.30pm); tickets, VND3,000.

### Domestic Travel

#### By Air

**Vietnam Airlines** (www. vietnamairlines.com) operates domestic flights to the following destinations: Buon Ma Thuot, Cam Ranh, Dalat, Danang, Dien Bien Phu, Haiphong, Hue, Nha Trang, Phu Quoc, Pleiku, Quy Nhon, Rach Gia, Tuy Hoa and Vinh – as well as Hanoi and HCMC.

**Jetstar Pacific Airlines** (www. jetstar.com) is a budget airline that flies to Buon Ma Thuot, Can Tho, Dalat, Danang, Hai Phong, Hanoi, HCMC, Nha Trang and Vinh.

**VASCO Airlines**, a former subsidiary of Vietnam Airlines, connects HCMC with Ca Mau in the

deep south and Con Son Island (Con Dao archipelago) as well as Da Nang.

Flying is by far the best way to travel if you intend to visit only a few cities in Vietnam. A Vietnam Airlines flight from Hanoi to HCMC costs under US$180 return (with taxes and fuel charges included). Vietnam Airlines also flies to out-of-the-way places like Phu Quoc Island.

You can use credit cards to buy airline tickets in Hanoi and HCMC, but in other cities you may be asked to pay cash. Tickets are sold by most travel agents in the big cities(see pages 360–3), or book directly with the airline office at HCMC and Hanoi.

### By Train

Train travel, operated by **Vietnam Railways** (www.vr.com.vn) in Vietnam, is very slow. Due to the existence of just a single track along the coast, train travel can often be hit by delays. The fastest express train from Hanoi to HCMC (called the *Reunification Express*), the SE4, covers 1,730km (1,073 miles) in 29 hours, with the slower ones (like the TBN) taking up to 41 hours because of the numerous stops they make. If you need to get somewhere fast, forget about the train. However, if you want to soak up the Vietnamese countryside the train has a lot to offer, including a chance to take in the beautiful scenery and – with long-distance trains being such a sociable means of travel – an opportunity to interact with Vietnamese people.

There are five classes of train travel in Vietnam: hard seat, soft seat, hard sleeper, soft sleeper and soft sleeper with air conditioning – this last option available only on certain trains. Expect to pay at least US$60 for a berth in a four-person compartment on the fastest express train from Hanoi to HCMC (or vice versa). There are five trains that make this run every day, and berths are reserved quickly, so try to make reservations early. There is a dining car on most trains, or you can buy snacks from the vendors that service the train at local stops.

There are also local train services on the Hanoi–HCMC line that branch out to various coastal cities. Lines also run from Hanoi northwest to Lao Cai, east to Hai Phong, and north to Lang Son. Overnight trains, with a sleeper ticket, can be a good way to travel as you save on a night's accommodation and wake up at your destination.

Note: hardly any English is spoken at local train stations, so do yourself a favour and get a travel agency to organise this for you for a small, but worthwhile, fee.

### Hanoi

Hanoi's Railway Station is at 120 Le Duan St, tel: 04-3942 3697 (located at the far western end of Tran Hung Dao St). The ticket office is open daily from 7.30am to 12.30am and 1.30pm to 7.30pm. Another ticket office to the right of the station entrance is for north-bound trains. Book a day ahead if you want to guarantee a sleeper carriage.

### Ho Chi Minh City

Trains leave HCMC for the northern coastal towns from the railway station, which is located at 1 Nguyen Thong St, District 3 (tel: 08-3843 6528). The ticket office is open daily from 7.15am to 11am and 1pm to 3pm.

At the railway station forecourt is the private joint-venture **Golden Trains** (tel: 08-3526 1683; daily 8am–8pm), which operates more upscale trains in the south with better services, security and facilities. These comprise daily overnight services between HCMC and **Nha Trang** (10 hours 20 minutes) and HCMC and **Quy Nhon** (11 hours 30 minutes), plus a daily daytime service (five hours) between HCMC and **Phan Thiet**. Features include LCD TVs, air conditioning, luxury cabin berths and recliner chairs with power points.

### Hanoi to Sa Pa

From Hanoi, the trip to Sa Pa requires an overnight train trip to Lao Cai, followed by a 45-minute bus ride from Lao Cai up to Sa Pa. Train tickets and transportation are best arranged through a travel agent in Hanoi as they get discounts on ticket purchases and will also arrange the final leg of the journey from Lao Cai to Sa Pa.

The Hanoi–Lao Cai train runs three times a night and once during the day. The daytime route doesn't have cabins with sleeping berths or air-conditioning, and so is best avoided. Evening trains have a selection of soft and hard sleepers, both with air-conditioning. A soft sleeper with air-conditioning costs about US$25 if you book tickets yourself at the station. More luxurious trains are on offer (www.sapatrain.com), which can be arranged via travel agents, and offer stylish carriages and superior service from US$50 return.

Transfers from Lao Cai are easy as numerous minibuses ply the road

up to Sa Pa for anywhere between US$1.50–3, depending on your bargaining skills. Drivers wait until the bus is full, which sometimes takes a while.

### By Bus

Bus travel in Vietnam can be gruelling, so it's best to opt for the more comfortable "Open Tour" air-conditioned express services. Departing every day, the bus allows you to get on or off anywhere along the route from either Hanoi or HCMC (for example, in Hue, Hoi An, Danang, Nha Trang, Dalat or Mui Ne) with few restrictions. The buses make stops every couple of hours for food and bathroom breaks. In contrast to standard local buses, you are guaranteed a seat to yourself and space to stretch your feet. The bus will pick you up from your hotel and drop you off at any hotel at your destination. The buses often work in partnership with sister travel agencies and hotels, but there is no undue pressure to stay at one of their recommended hotels. The ticket remains good for a month, but the clock starts ticking from the day you buy it, not when you first use it.

With a HCMC–Hanoi ticket costing about US$45 (including stops in between), this is certainly one of the cheaper ways of getting around, but one of the more time-consuming.

To book tickets, visit the offices of **Sinh Café** in Hanoi (66 Hang Than St; www.sinhcafe.com), or contact the call centre on tel: 04 3836 4212. Alternatively, your hotel can make all the arrangements for a fee.

If you're feeling adventurous and want a truly "local" experience, you could take local public buses. Expect to get overcharged (at three or four times the local rates) and be stuck in an overcrowded deathtrap with a suicidal driver. It might be "authentic", but the fun tends to wear off quickly so these rides are better for short-distances only.

### Mekong Delta

The best place to access the Mekong is from HCMC, and the easiest way to do it is to book yourself on an organised tour. Local travel agents will pick up from your hotel and a day trip typically costs from VND220,000 including lunch.

To blaze your own trail, head for the **Mai Linh** buses (64–68 Hai Ba Trung St; tel: 08-3929 2929) in HCMC, which offer express bus services to the Mekong Delta that

always depart on time and go straight through without stopping to pick up more passengers. Book in advance to guarantee a seat. Ticket prices vary from US$3–7, depending on distance travelled. The local bus station is based in Cholon.

### By Car and Minivan

In Hanoi, HCMC and the other major cities, you can hire cars and minivans to go on day trips or week-long excursions. Hiring a driver and vehicle in Vietnam is good value if your travelling party is large enough to share the cost. Ask to go for a test ride before making a commitment to a driver to see if the car is running properly. Expect to pay a minimum of US$60 a day (US$35 for half-day) for a good car (with driver). The best way to arrange this is to book through an established travel agency as it is required to take responsibility for your safety. If you need an English-speaking guide, the travel agency can also arrange this.

Sometimes, drivers from one part of the country are reluctant to drive to another. Drivers from HCMC, for example, are usually hesitant to drive to Hanoi. Licence plates on cars denote what province the car is from, and drivers often fear that the police will give cars from outside the region trouble. A driver in HCMC might agree to take you as far as Danang, for example, and then help you find another driver to take you further.

Think very carefully about whether you should drive yourself. With the crazy road conditions and the near absence of traffic rules, you are better off hiring a car with a driver. In any case you will be hard-pressed to find car rental companies that cater to tourists in Hanoi and HCMC. Car rentals start from around US$30 per day.

### Motorbike Rentals

Motorbike rental is available, especially from mini-hotels and in tourist hubs: prices range from around US$3–7 per day for a reliable 100–110cc bike, although weekly and monthly rentals are available. Driving in Hanoi and HCMC, however, is really only for the more experienced (or crazy) driver. Apart from the sheer volume, traffic in Vietnam has its own unique rhythms and "logic". Always wear a helmet and buy accident insurance.

For those who want to explore Vietnam by motorcycle, contact

Hanoi-based **Offroad Vietnam** (tel: 04-3926 3433; www.offroadvietnam. com), which has the best bikes and guides. Owner Anh Wu is a wealth of information on biking and trekking in the north. **Motortours Asia** (tel:04-3926 2373; www.voyagevietnam.net. com) can arrange for bikers to pick up their machines in Sa Pa, Hue, Danang or HCMC for an extra fee.

Dalat and the Central Highlands are a popular place for hiring motorbikes, given the beautiful scenery, pleasant roads, and little traffic. They can be rented from Phat Tire Ventures (109 Nguyen Van Troi St, mobile tel: 091-843 8781; www.phattireventures. com), Groovy Gecko Adventure Tours (65 Truong Cong Dinh St, mobile tel: 091-824 8976; www. groovygeckotours.net), and The Hangout, 71 Truong Cong Dinh St, tel: 063-351 0822; www.thehangoutcafe. com. *See page 372 for more information.*

## Cycling

Cycling around parts of Vietnam is possible thanks to tour companies who can provide good-quality bikes. Just as importantly, they can also provide guides who can suggest the best routes and attractions along the way. The most popular rides are near Halong Bay, through the Mekong Delta, or around Hoi An and Hue. Cycling can also be a good way of getting around the cities, particularly Dalat.

## Boats

### Mekong Delta

A high-speed hydrofoil operates twice daily to Can Tho from the pier at the end of Ham Nghi Street in HCMC for about US$12. Other boat services are available between other towns – enquire locally. The construction of several new bridges in the Delta has resulted in fewer boat services (the My Tho-Ben Tre service no longer exists, for instance). This means more previously remote towns, such as Tra Vinh, are now relatively simple to access.

Hydrofoils operating between HCMC and **Vung Tau** (around 80 minutes) terminate and depart from the **Passenger Quay of HCMC** (Ben Tau Khach Thanh Pho), 2 Ton Duc Thang St, District 1. **Vina Express** (tel: 08-3825 3333/3829 7892; www. vinaexpress.com.vn) and **Greenlines** (tel: 08-3821 5609; www.greenlines. com.vn) operate six departures daily

from both cities, from 6am to 5pm. **Viet Bamboo Travel** (tel: 08-3822 192; www.mekongriverboattrips.com) have boats that take guests from My Tho to Chau Doc, Long Xuyen and Can Tho over three days. Other trips start in HCMC and take in Vinh Long, Can Tho, Chau Doc and then finish back in HCMC. *See Activities page 373 for more details.*

### Cat Ba Island

The best way to get to Cat Ba Island is by booking a tour through an agency in Hanoi, as it will arrange the rather complicated transportation links.

For those doing it on their own, travel from Haiphong or Halong Bay (Bai Chay) to Cat Ba Island via hydrofoil or ferry; the hydrofoil will take an hour and the ferry at least twice as long. The ferry and hydrofoil schedules change according to the season, but at least one hydrofoil departs from both Haiphong and Halong Bay to Cat Ba daily, and there are at least two ferries. Confirm hydrofoil and ferry schedules at your hotel or the pier.

## City Transport

### Hanoi

**Taxis**

Taxis are omnipresent and are, on the whole, a cheap and quick way to get around. The majority are air-conditioned, and those operated by the more reputable companies are in fairly good condition. Taxis charge by the meter with a flagfall rate that ranges from VND8,000–15,000 for the first 2km (1.2 miles), followed by about VND2,000 for every kilometre travelled. Note: the taxis with the more expensive base rates often work out cheaper (and less stressful) overall, as they are highly regulated and the meters are likely not to have been tampered with.

There are dozens of different taxi firms that have cars out cruising the streets, but to guard against being ripped off, travellers should try to stick to the major recommended taxi companies: **Hanoi Taxi**, tel: 04-3853 5353; **CP Taxi**, tel: 04-3826 2626; **ABC Taxi**, tel: 04-3719 1919; and **Mai Linh Taxi**, tel: 04-3822 2555.

The operators at these major taxi companies speak English and will dispatch a cab to almost anywhere in less than 15 minutes. Few drivers speak English, but most will recognise the English names of the popular tourist sites. Be sure to take a card from your hotel to show your taxi

driver the hotel name and address (on your return trip), and the name of your destination in Vietnamese.

If you find yourself in a taxi that obviously has a rigged meter (the fare will rise very quickly), demand the driver stop, tell him the meter is broken and get out of the cab.

**Motorbike Taxis (xe om)**

*Xe om*, the Vietnamese phrase for motorbike taxis, are the most popular and prevalent form of public transport, but they do require nerves of steel and a slice of good fortune. *Xe om* can be found on almost every street corner and they generally charge US$1–2, depending on the destination. Settle the price beforehand and make sure the driver has an extra helmet for you – Vietnam's helmet laws have only been in place since December 2007 and many drivers still go without, especially in Hanoi.

For short distances, *xe om* can be the best way to get around, but there is some risk to life and limb, so be aware of this. Some *xe om* drivers drive very aggressively. Women should never take a *xe om* anywhere alone at night, especially if leaving a bar or club. Day or night, never accept a ride from an inebriated *xe om* driver.

**Cyclos**

Hanoi's front-seater cyclos *(xich lo)* are three-wheeled rickshaws pedalled by drivers. By far the most fun way to travel, Hanoi's cyclos are unique in that they can carry two passengers instead of one (unlike in HCMC). Cyclos are the perfect way to take in the city's wide, tree-lined streets, so take a ride on one at least once.

There is persistent talk from the government that cyclos will eventually be banned, so visitors to Vietnam should not miss an opportunity to experience this most enjoyable form of transportation. Hiring a cyclo is no problem in Hanoi's Old Quarter; the drivers will try to get the attention of passing tourists. Generally, an hour's tour around the Old Quarter or Truc Bach Lake will cost US$7, although cyclo drivers will press you to pay a higher price.

Cyclos can also be hired for short rides to specific destinations, though the price will have to be decided on first before you clamber onboard.

**Buses**

Hanoi's large Korean-made city buses ply most major streets. The network is quite extensive and fares are a flat VND3,000 per person, no matter where in the city you're heading. At 16 Cao Ba Quat St in Ba Dinh District, the **Hanoi Bus Company** office (tel: 04-3825 4250; www.hanoibus.com.vn) hands out a free map outlining the city's bus routes.

Despite the efficient network, few foreign travellers use the public buses as the routes are not clearly indicated on the outside and taxis are so affordable. Buses can also be very crowded and slow during rush hour, and most stop running by 9pm. Avoid buses if you are carrying a lot of luggage.

### Ho Chi Minh City

### Taxis

Taxis are the safest and most comfortable way of getting around. Most are air-conditioned, and fares are relatively cheap. The usual flagfall rate is VND10,000 for the first 1.5km (1 mile), followed by VND9,000 for each additional kilometre travelled. Stay clear of unlicensed taxis (especially around the airport and backpacker area); these either have rigged meters, or tend to quote over-inflated prices. Although taxis can be easily flagged down anywhere, especially downtown, stick to taxis operating outside upscale hotels or use the companies listed here: **ML (Mai Linh Taxis/M taxis)**, tel: 08-3822 2666; **Saigon Tourist**, tel: 08-3845 8888; **Vina Taxi**, tel: 08-3811 1111; **Vinasun**, tel: 08-3827 2727; and **SASCO Airport Taxis**, tel: 1800 1565/08-3844 6448).

Carry small notes, as drivers always claim they don't have enough change. As English is not commonly spoken, have your destination down in Vietnamese to show to the driver.

### Motorbike Taxis

The more adventurous may opt for motorbike taxis, known locally as *xe om* (literally translating as "to embrace"). Drivers invariably hang round at most street corners and call out "Motorbike?". Most are friendly and speak basic English, although increasingly many are from the countryside and do not. *Xe om* are a cheap, quick and adrenaline-packed means to beat the traffic jams, but they are more susceptible to accidents. Since 2007 all riders in Vietnam have been required to wear helmets; this is strongly enforced in HCMC with fines for offenders. The driver should supply you with a helmet; if he doesn't, find another driver. Always agree a price, preferably in writing, beforehand: short hops around town should cost

around US$1–2. Motorbike taxis are not advisable after dark, especially for women.

### Cyclos

Cyclos have traditionally been a novelty transport option for tourists, a uniquely Vietnamese, unhurried (and cheap) way to see the sights. Unfortunately, with increasing noise, pollution and traffic, cyclos are not such an attractive option any more. In HCMC, cyclos were officially banned by the city authorities in 2008. Some cyclos still ply the streets, but you have to search hard. They can be found in the backpacker area, Cholon and Ben Thanh Market, or book through your hotel.

Many tour companies invariably use cyclos as part of city tours, so this is another option. Never take a cyclo after dark (for security and safety reasons) and always agree on the price (about US$2 per hour) beforehand in writing so there are no misunderstandings.

### Buses

HCMC's fleet of buses are modern and offer an extensive city network with well-marked bus stops and a flat-rate ticket of VND3,000 that takes you anywhere in the city. The most you will pay for a ticket is around VND10,000. This is also one of the speediest forms of city transport – buses plough through traffic like Grand Prix drivers with little regard for anything in their path. Unfortunately, signs or instructions are only in Vietnamese and drivers can't speak English. As the city's main public transport mode, buses are often jam-packed during peak hours.

The main bus station for local routes is **Ben Thanh Bus Station** (Ben Xe Ben Thanh; tel: 08-3821 4444), located opposite Ben Thanh Market, junction of Tran Hung Dao, Le Loi and Ham Nghi streets, District 1; bus maps are available here. Another city bus hub is **Cholon Bus Station**, on Le Quang Sung St, District 6, near Binh Tay Market.

Useful bus routes include No. 1 (Binh Tay Market and Cholon Bus Station, Cholon); No. 13 (Cu Chi); No. 45, No. 49 and No. 96 (Cholon); No. 44 (Binh Quoi tourist area); No. 11 (Dam Sen Park); and No. 152 or No.147 (airport).

### Local Transport elsewhere in Vietnam

### Sa Pa

Sa Pa is a small town best explored

on foot. To get from one end of town to the other takes a maximum of 10 minutes, and there are a number of ethnic minority villages within walking distance.

Many visitors to Sa Pa choose to rent motorbikes to explore the surrounding mountains. Most guesthouses and hotels rent motorbikes for about US$6 a day.

Cars, vans and 4WDs are also available for hire through hotels, guesthouses and travel agents. Rates will vary depending on the destination, distance and time of year. Most Sa Pa hotels can easily recommend reliable vehicles with a driver and guide.

### Haiphong

Haiphong has a number of taxi companies that use reliable, metered, air-conditioned vehicles. The best are **Haiphong Taxi**, tel: 031-383 8383; **Mai Linh Taxi**, tel: 031-383 3660; and **Hoa Phuong Taxi**, tel: 031-364 1641. Rides within the city shouldn't cost more than US$2. There are plenty of motorbike taxis – don't pay more than US$1 for short hops, and always wear a helmet. Cyclos often cruise around town looking for customers. Short trips around town cost under US$1; an hour's tour of the city should cost about US$6.

### Halong City

When travelling in Bai Chay, metered taxis are a good option. **Mai Linh Taxi**, tel: 033-362 8628, and **Halong Taxi**, tel: 033-362 6262, are reliable companies. Rates begin at VND6,000 for the first kilometre and go up by VND1,200 for each additional 100 metres travelled.

Motorbike taxis are probably the best way to get around in Bai Chay and Hon Gai. The drivers are also an excellent source of information on where to find good restaurants and hotels. Expect to pay about US$1–2 for rides around the city, depending on your bargaining skills.

### Cat Ba Island

Cat Ba Town is tiny and can easily be covered on foot. For local transportation, *xe om* is the best bet are the best.

Many visitors to the island rent motorbikes (large smoky Russian Minsks) for about US$6 a day and tour the island independently. Motorbikes can be rented from any number of shops and guesthouses along the main street.

## Hue

Taxis, *xe om* and cyclos are found throughout the city and around all the major tombs. **Mai Linh** (tel: 054-389 8989) is one of the best companies, with new, comfortable cars, but even their drivers have been known to cheat their customers as much as any other company by rigging the meters and driving around in circles. Always be wary, and if you think the fee is climbing too steeply, simply stop and find another ride.

Hue is a fairly safe city to ride a bicycle. It's also an ideal mode of transportation to explore the royal tombs. Most hotels rent bicycles for US$1–2 per day. Motorbikes cost US$5–7 per day, while a car with driver runs to about US$40 per day.

Tourists who go alone by bicycle and motorbike tend to be targeted by local scam artists. Strangers will approach offering to show travellers the way to tombs and villages that are off the beaten path. All are ultimately looking to make money from you; some may actually rob victims once they are lured to a remote location. If you need a guide, ask your hotel to arrange one for you.

## Danang

Motorbike taxis wait on every street corner. **Mai Linh Taxis** (tel: 0511-356

### Street Mayhem

The streets of Vietnam's two largest cities, Hanoi and HCMC, are a crowded maze of bicycles, motorbikes, taxis, SUVs and trucks, all competing with thousands of pedestrians. Crossing the street can be a daunting prospect. To add to the chaos, the drivers of cars and motorbikes (there are thousands of the latter on the roads) use their horns incessantly – beeping to indicate a turn or to let you know they're overtaking. Driving the wrong way up one-way streets and on the pavements, plus ignoring red lights, are all par for the course. Traffic in Hanoi's Old Quarter area and HCMC's Dong Khoi Street is simply overwhelming.

As a pedestrian, remember that the Vietnamese are adept at manoeuvring around obstacles. As long as you don't make any sudden or abrupt movements when crossing busy roads, the traffic will flow around you like water. Be mindful but bold when crossing streets and never dash across the street.

5656) are recommended. Motorbikes can be rented from most hotels for around US$5 per day.

## Hoi An

Everything within the Old Town is reachable by foot. In fact, a motorbike or bicycle would be more of a hindrance than a help, and they are banned during the Full Moon festivals. Cars are banned from the Old Town at all times. For trips to My Son, Cau Dai Beach or the Marble Mountains, rent a motorbike from any hotel for US$5–10 per day. Longboats for up to 8 people can be hired along the riverfront for US$5 per hour.

## Quy Nhon

**Mai Linh** (tel: 056-354 6666) is the best choice for taxis in Quy Nhon. Local transport costs here are a bit out of touch with the rest of the country. Expats here have traditionally been big spenders and have driven up the costs. Expect to pay as much as US$10 per day to rent a motorbike, and double the normal rates you'll find elsewhere for other forms of transport and tours.

## Quang Ngai

Rent a motorbike from almost any hotel for US$6 per day. **Mai Linh Taxis** (tel: 055-383 8383) are also available.

## Dalat

Motorbikes can be rented for about US$5 per day. A *xe om* for short distances around the city will cost about US$2. A taxi ride for quick trips around town will cost under US$5. **Mai Linh Taxis** (tel: 063-351 1511) is one of the more reputable taxi companies, but always double check the rate on the meter.

Dalat can be a fun place to ride a bicycle, but casual riders may find it challenging due to the many hills.

## Nha Trang

Bicycles can be rented from most hotels for around US$2. All the major sights are within riding distance. Taxis, cyclos and *xe om* are found everywhere; drivers of the last two will pester you as you walk down the streets. Motorbikes can be rented from most hotels for around US$5. **Mai Linh Taxis** (tel: 058-381 1811) offer the best taxi service, but keep your eye on the meter to make sure the numbers all add up correctly.

## Phan Thiet

Motorbike rentals and **Mai Linh** taxis (tel: 062-389 8989) can

be arranged through your hotel. Cyclos are not common in Phan Thiet, and it's not advisable to ride bicycles here because of the chaotic traffic.

## Mui Ne

*Xe om* and **Mai Linh Taxis** (tel: 062-389 8989) are very common in Mui Ne. Motorbikes can be rented from most hotels for US$5–8 per day and bicycles for US$2–3 per day. Cyclos are not available. Most tour companies can arrange jeep tours to the Sand Dunes (US$25–30), Ta Cu Mountain (US$50) and other local sights. Great care should be taken when exiting the beach and heading west to Phan Thiet. Locals as well as tourists are killed in traffic accidents on an almost weekly basis, so go carefully..

## Mekong Delta

To sightsee locally in the Mekong Delta area, sign up for a bus tour at a local agent, or hire a car or *xe om*, making sure your itinerary is clear and the price has been fixed before you set off. For a *xe om*, a good guide is US$2.50 per hour, or US$12 per day.

*Xe dap loi*, a bicycle hitched to a carriage and the Mekong's version of the cyclo, should cost around US$6 an hour. A *xe loi* (carriage with motor bike instead of a bicycle) should be the same price as a *xe om*, but expect to pay more for two or more people.

The Mekong's diverse tracks are made for touring by motorbike. Enquire at your hotel. Rates are usually US$7–10 a day. Riding a bicycle is another possibility – self-pedalling will cost US$2 a day.

As much exploration is best done by boat, particularly the floating markets and tiny Mekong River islands, ask a local to ferry you around. Small motorboats can be hired from US$3 an hour.

## Vung Tau

Most hotels can rent motorbikes for US$6–9 per day and bicycles for US$2–3 per day. Stand on any street corner, and a taxi, *xe om* or cyclo will stop right under your nose.

## Con Dao Islands

There are no taxis or *xe om* on the island, although it's possible to rent a motorbike (less than US$10 per day) or bicycle (US$2–3 per day) from one of the hotels. Boats may be rented from the park service for about US$75 per day.

# ACCOMMODATION

# HOTELS IN VIETNAM

### Choosing a Hotel

Until the mid-1990s, Vietnam's hotel infrastructure, particularly in the north and centre of the country, was far below international standards. Rooms were often under-equipped or kitted out with fixtures and appliances that did not work, and there were frequent power cuts. Room rates were also relatively high.

Demand for accommodation often outstripped supply, but following a hotel boom in the mid-1990s onwards in Ho Chi Minh City and Hanoi, today's rooms offer far better value. Hotel development in the country is flourishing and visitors are spoilt for choice. International chains, with service standards and prices to match, can be found in all the major cities. Luxury hotels and resorts with business centres, high-speed internet access and/or Wi-fi, and spas and fitness centres, are the norm these days, but there is also plenty of choice in the budget lodgings category, where a room can go for US$10 a night.

The easing of restrictions on foreign investment has resulted in a boom in upmarket accommodation. The Hyatt, Sheraton, Hilton and Sofitel chains are well represented in Ho Chi Minh City and Hanoi, and along the coast the Six Senses and GHM (which is linked to the high-end Aman chain) hotel groups have opened luxury properties in Vietnam.

Hotel staff are generally friendly and helpful, and adequate English is spoken in the major tourism and business centres. In more remote areas, communication in English can be a real problem. State-run hotels tend to have indifferent staff and low standards of service, which is a pity because some of Hanoi and HCMC's most atmospheric historic hotels are state-run enterprises.

### Mini Hotels and Homestays

If you're on a tight budget, try the so-called "mini hotels", small, often family-run hotels with fairly modern (but modest) facilities. These abound in Hanoi and HCMC, but are also increasingly common in popular resort towns.

There are smaller family-run guesthouses that offer homestay accommodation. These are mainly found in the Mekong Delta area and offer a more personal touch (you will probably have dinner, go fishing or end up singing karaoke with the family). In the northern highlands, it's possible to arrange a stay with hill-tribe minority communities, particularly in and around Sa Pa. These would have to be booked with a travel agency that specialises in trekking tours.

### Rates and Bookings

When booking your accommodation, always check the hotel website first to see what the best rates are. If it's a smaller outfit without a website, call directly to ask. Hotel-booking websites should be your next port of call; these companies can often get you better rates because of the volume of business they bring in.

The published rates listed here should only be taken as a guide, as actual prices can be quite elastic – depending on seasonal discounts. Note: higher-end hotels usually charge a tax of about 10 percent and a service charge of about 5 percent.

As disposable income increases, more and more Vietnamese are travelling. During the school holidays (June–August) the beaches get very crowded, and during the annual Tet festival (in late January or early February) buses and trains are packed to the rafters with domestic travellers. On those days that the lunar calendar indicates as auspicious for weddings, you'll also find many honeymooners flocking to Dalat. Hotel rates also spike during the Christmas and New Year periods. If you are making a trip during any of these times, it would be a good idea to book ahead.

Note: archaic communist-era Vietnamese laws insist that all hotel guests be registered with the local police. This could mean leaving your passport with the reception for the entire duration of the stay or just overnight. In Hanoi and HCMC, the practice is either to make a photocopy or to record details from your passport and landing card.

**BELOW:** Sheraton Saigon Hotel & Towers.

# HANOI

Hanoi has a wide variety of hotels to satisfy all budgets. The central Hoan Kiem District (which includes the Old Quarter) has the largest choice of luxury and expensive hotels. Most budget hotels and guesthouses are concentrated in the side streets of the Old Quarter. The West Lake area (Tay Ho) has two excellent 5-star hotels, though little else in terms of moderate or budget lodgings. In Hai Ba Trung District, south of downtown Hanoi, mid-range hotels catering to businesspeople do a booming trade, although they are quite a trek from the city centre and you will need a taxi.

## Hoan Kiem District

**Hilton Hanoi Opera**
1 Le Thanh Tong St. Tel: 04-3933 0500.
www.hanoi.hilton.com
An architecturally impressive hotel – on the outside at least – built to complement the neighbouring Opera House. Rooms are large, airy and modern, and the Vietnamese-style pads are a particular treat. The wide, spacious lobby features live music and free WWi-fi. There is also a great pool, gym facilities and beauty salon/spa. **$$$$$**

**Melia Hanoi**
44B Ly Thuong Kiet St. Tel: 04-3934 3343.
www.meliahanoi.com
Located in Hanoi's business and diplomatic district, the elegant Melia features large rooms with modern amenities. On site are five excellent restaurants, bars, a deli and a pool. The icing on the cake is a helipad on its rooftop and the largest pillarless ballroom in Vietnam. **$$$$$**

**Sofitel Metropole Hanoi**
15 Ngo Quyen St. Tel: 04-3826 6919.
www.accorhotels-asia.com
Built in 1901 and renovated by the French Sofitel company in 2005, this grande dame has maintained its colonial-era atmosphere while improving on comfort

levels. Former guests include kings, princes, presidents and an assortment of celebrities. Rooms in both the original Metropole Wing and newer Opera Wing are beautifully appointed, but the latter has larger and more contemporary-style rooms. It features two excellent restaurants, three bars and a swimming pool. **$$$$$**

**De Syloia Hotel**
17A Tran Hung Dao St. Tel: 04-3824 5346.
www.desyloia.com
A small but pleasant boutique hotel just south of the Old Quarter, with an excellent restaurant and small but good gym facilities. Rooms are clean, well appointed and spacious, and the windows are soundproofed so they remain blissfully quiet. Staff are helpful, if a little curt. **$$$$**

**Army Hotel**
33C Pham Ngu Lao St. Tel: 04-3825 2896
Owned and operated by the army, this eclectic hotel features a large saltwater pool and well-appointed if kitschy rooms. The grounds are spacious and quiet, and the hotel is just a few steps from two museums. **$$$**

**Church Hotel**
9 Nha Tho St. Tel: 04-3928 8118.
www.churchhotel.com.vn
This gem of a boutique hotel, just steps away from St Joseph's Cathedral was built in 2004 and features stylishly appointed (though not huge) rooms overlooking trendy Nha Tho Street and the Ba Da Pagoda. Try to get a room facing the back, where it's quieter. Features free Wi-fi and made-to-order breakfast. **$$$**

**Hanoi Paradise Hotel**
53 Hang Chieu St. Tel: 04-3929 0026.
www.hanoiparadisehotel.com
One of few Old Quarter hotels to boast a pool, this spotlessly clean hotel features large, well-kept rooms and very helpful staff. Opened in 2006, all rooms have an internet-connected

computer. Free bottle of red wine, fruit and flowers on arrival. **$$$**

**Hoa Binh Hotel**
27 Ly Thuong Kiet St. Tel: 04-3825 3315.
www.hoabinhhotel.com
A small and elegant hotel with a sweeping wooden staircase and lovely French colonial touches. The staff are friendly and helpful, but rooms facing the street can be noisy in the morning. French and Vietnamese restaurant on site. **$$$**

**Blue Sky**
2 Hang Ga St. Tel: 04-3923 0514
A clean mini hotel offering well-appointed single, double and triple rooms. Free breakfast and wWi-fiWi-fi, as well as free airport pick-up if you stay two nights. Extremely helpful and friendly staff can help with tour bookings or visa renewals. **$$**

**Espacen Hotel**
28 The Xuong St. Tel: 04-3824 4401
This simple but well-maintained hotel was remodelled in 2006 and features large en-suite single and double rooms. Spotlessly cleaned each day, the hotel also provides free internet. Basic accommodation but great value. **$$**

**Hanoi Elegance Hotel II**
85 Ma May St. Tel: 04-3926 3451.
www.hanoieligancehotel.com
A stylish, modern hotel built in 2006 right in the heart of the Old Quarter. Large, airy, well-furnished rooms and helpful English-speaking staff. **$$**

**Phoenix Hotel**
43 Bat Su St. Tel: 04-3923 2683
Formerly known as the Ocean Stars Hotel, the Phoenix Hotel changed hands and was renovated in 2008. It features beautiful wooden floors, comfy rooms and exceptionally helpful staff. Some of the rooms on the lower floors do not have windows. Includes breakfast and wWi-fiWi-fi. **$$**

**The Ritz Hotel**
32 Le Thai To St. Tel: 04-3928 9897.
www.theritzhotelhanoi.com
This mini hotel built in 2007 is just a minute's walk from Hoan Kiem Lake and features clean, well-appointed rooms and probably the most helpful staff in Hanoi. The bathrooms are huge and spotless, and the owners provide a free room for a few hours if you need to freshen up after checking out. **$$**

## Hai Ba Trung District

**Hotel Nikko Hanoi**
84 Tran Nhat Tong St. Tel: 04-3822 3535.
www.hotelnikkohanoi.com.vn
The Nikko is a high-rise, Japanese-owned hotel with airy, modern rooms and excellent, attentive service. Geared towards Japanese

## PRICE CATEGORIES

Price categories are for a standard double room in peak season.

**$** = under US$20
**$$** = $20–50
**$$$** = $50–100
**$$$$** = $100–150
**$$$$$** = over $150

**ABOVE:** bathroom at the colonial-style Sofitel Metropole.

businesspeople and over-looking Thong Nhat Park, the hotel has a good-sized pool and fitness centre. It also has three restaurants (Chinese, Japanese and French), bar and bakery. Disabled-friendly. $$$$$

**Sunway Hotel**
19 Pham Dinh Ho St. Tel: 04-3971 3888.
www.sunway-hotel.com
This pleasant but slightly dated boutique hotel out-side of the city centre has good facilities and a busi-ness centre. Rooms are spacious and quiet, though most could use some refur-bishing. $$$$

**Zenith Hotel Hanoi**
96–98 Bui Thi Xuan St.
Tel: 04-3822 9797
A distinguished hotel with all the expected amenities. The lobby is a bit shabby, but the rooms are quiet, comfortable and well main-tained. Also has a good res-taurant, bar and a fitness centre. $$$$

**Fortuna Hotel Hanoi**
6B Lang Ha St. Tel: 04-3831 3333
www.fortunahotels.com
A large business hotel with spacious rooms and all the usual mod cons, including large LCD flat-screen TVs.

Rooms on the lower floors can be a bit noisy. The lobby staff are very helpful. It includes three restaurants, outdoor pool, a large gym and spa, as well as a casino. $$$$

**Hanoi Daewoo Hotel**
360 Kim Ma St. Tel: 04-3831 5000
www.hanoi-daewoohotel.com
This immense complex in western Hanoi has every con-ceivable facility. Rooms are large, quiet, comfy and equipped with all the expected amenities. Rooms on the uppermost floors have amazing views over Hanoi. Has one of the city's best Chinese restaurants. $$$$

**Hanoi Horison Hotel**
40 Cat Linh St. Tel: 04-3733 0808
Located adjacent to the British Council, this tower-ing hotel has tastefully designed and well-appointed rooms with all the expected amenities for busi-ness and leisure travellers. Particularly popular among Asian businesspeople, the hotel staff are multilingual and helpful. The hotel was undergoing major renova-tions at time of going to press. $$$$

**Sofitel Plaza Hanoi**
1 Thanh Nien St. Tel: 04-3823 8888

www.accorhotels-asia.com
The 20-storey Sofitel Plaza dominates the skyline at the edge of West Lake and is home to the best indoor/outdoor swimming pool in the city. The hotel has quiet, stylish rooms, two restau-rants, three bars and a spa. Views over Truc Bach Lake are a bonus. $$$$

**Anise Hotel Hanoi**
22 Quan Thanh St. Tel: 04-3927 4670
Located on the border of the Old Quarter, this small bou-tique hotel features clean, quiet and comfortable accommodation (cheaper standard rooms do not have windows, while more expen-sive rooms on the higher floors have excellent views). The staff are helpful and polite. All rooms outfitted with wWi-fiWi-fi and LCD flat-screen TVs. $$$

**Bro and Sis Hotel**
65 Cua Bac St. Mobile tel: 090-438 7467
This 12-storey hotel, for-merly known as the Hang Nga, is popular with busi-ness travellers. Rooms are spacious and well main-tained. Features a café and rooftop restaurant. $$$

**Intercontinental Westlake Hanoi**

1 Nghi Tam St. Tel: 04-6270 8888.
www.intercontinental.com
The Intercontinental is a luxurious new hotel, built over a picturesque part of West Lake and overlooking an 800-year-old pagoda. It features gorgeous rooms and top-notch facilities geared toward business travellers. The rooms are large, comfortable and ele-gantly outfitted, and the hotel pool and gym are unmatched in Hanoi. Staff are helpful, though restrained. Features three restaurants and two bars. Watching the sunset at the Sunset Bar is a must. $$$$$

**Sheraton Hanoi Hotel**
11 Xuan Dieu St. Tel: 04-3719 9000
www.sheraton.com/Hanoi
This high-rise hotel boasts all the modern amenities of a Sheraton. The lobby decor is looking a bit faded, but the lakeside swimming pool, floodlit tennis courts, con-ference facilities and staff are all excellent. All rooms are tastefully appointed and have spacious bathrooms. The more expensive rooms have lake views. Features three restaurants and a rather raucous late-night bar. $$$$$

# NORTHWEST VIETNAM

If not staying at the **Mai Chau Lodge**, there are only a handful of other options. In the villages of **Lac** and **Pom Coong**, visitors can stay in a traditional Thai stilt house that has been converted into a guest-house. Pom Coong is slightly more rural and less developed than Lac, mak-ing it the better choice. Accommodations are basic: a mat on the stilt house floor, thick blankets and a mosquito net. Both villages offer a rustic experience at a mere US$5 per person, which includes dinner and, at weekends, traditional dance performances in the

evenings. Both villages have plenty of stilt guest-houses, so advance book-ings are not necessary.
A fourth option, requiring a couple days' stay in the area, is to trek to a village and do a homestay with a local family. This is best arranged through a tour operator in Hanoi. **Buffalo Tours** (tel: 04-3828 0702; www.buffalotours.com) is a pioneer in the area and can organise such trips .

**Mai Chau Lodge**
Mai Chai Town. Tel: 0218-386 8959.
www.maichaulodge.com
This gorgeous resort/lodge has large, comfortable rooms decorated in natural

woods and local minority handicrafts. A full-service resort with English-speaking staff, guests are treated to a free bottle of rice wine on arrival. The outdoor swim-ming pool is impressive and there's a good spa on site; ideal after a day of trekking. $$$$ .

**People's Committee (Uy Ban Nhan Dan) Guesthouse**
Off Highway 6. Tel: 022-385 2080
An interesting government-run guesthouse which has been expanded and reno-vated and offers clean, com-fortable rooms with all the

standard amenities. Has great views over the nearby hills. $

**Phong Lan 1 Hotel**
Chu Van Thinh St. Tel: 022-385 3515
Just opposite the Central Market, this hotel features clean and comfortable but basic rooms with A/C and breakfast included. Can get rather noisy in the evenings. $

**Thanh Binh Guesthouse**
7 Chu Van Thinh St. Tel: 022-385 2969
This warm and homey little guesthouse is tucked away down an alley in a pleas-ant courtyard. Rooms are spotlessly clean with com-fortable beds, and the staff

are helpful (but not very proficient in English). **$**

## Dien Bien Phu

Most hotels in Dien Bien Phu are government-run, which generally means poor service, low standards and a less than enthusiastic staff. While a handful of hotels have begun renovating and improving on the back of increased tourism, visitors shouldn't expect too much.

**Brewery Guesthouse (Khach San Cong Ty Bia)**
Tran Can St. Tel: 023-382 4635
This brewery-operated guesthouse has clean and comfy rooms, with the best ones featuring hot water and TV. For the full experience, spend the night drinking at one of the countless *bia hoi* (local bars) lining the nearby streets. **$**

**Dien Bien Party Hotel**
Thanh Binh St. Tel: 023-383 0337
Small hotel located down by the river near the bridge. The rooms are simple but well kept, and the beds are quite comfortable. The family who run the hotel – some members of whom speak basic English – are helpful. **$**

**Dien Bien Phu Hotel**
279A Duong 7/5. Tel: 023-382 5103
This large hotel is right on the main strip, and offers clean and well-maintained rooms with TVs, desks and bathtubs. Staff are friendly, though only one or two speak any English. Attached is a massage parlour and 200-seat restaurant. **$**

**Dien Bien Phu-Hanoi Hotel**
849 Duong 7/5. Tel: 023-382 5103
This renovated government-run hotel has simple but large and clean rooms, though the decor is a bit tacky. Some rooms have balconies, and the larger ones have desks. Seedy massage parlour comes as standard. Very little English spoken, but the staff get by. **$**

**Muong Thanh Hotel**
25 Him Lam St. Tel: 023-381 0038
Quirky old hotel featuring large, bizarre concrete statues, a great restaurant and many simple yet acceptable rooms, plus karaoke and massage facilities. Avoid the murky swimming pool at all costs, however. Book ahead, as it's popular with tour groups. English-speaking staff. **$**

## Lai Chau

**Huyen Tran Guesthouse**
Tel: 023-387 5829
This quaint and comfy little guesthouse along the main road is popular with Vietnamese businessmen, and offers nice rooms (pay the extra US$1 for the larger room) with A/C, TV and a balcony that looks out over the rice paddies. More expensive than Tay Bac but still good value. **$**

**Tay Bac Hotel**
3 Phong Chau St. Tel: 023-387 5879
Easily the best hotel in Lai Chau, the Tay Bac has a number of different types of rooms available, though the best are undoubtedly the quaint stilt houses. Other options include small but clean rooms with fans, or larger units with A/C. Staff speak passable English. **$**

## Sa Pa

From December to February, Sa Pa can be cold, windy and wet. Few hotels have heating; instead, most prefer to offer fireplaces, though these rarely warm the rooms.

Many visitors to Sa Pa opt to do a homestay in an ethnic minority village in the valley. The treks range from two days to a week and can be booked at any travel agency in Hanoi or in Sa Pa at any guesthouse or hotel.

**Victoria Sa Pa Resort**
Sa Pa Town. Tel: 020-387 1522.
www.victoriahotels-asia.com
This charming chalet-style resort is located just above the town, and offers stunning views of the valley and Mount Fansipan. Rooms are warm and luxurious with unique Vietnamese accents. Features a beautiful pool, garden and spa. Prices in the restaurant are through

**ABOVE:** Intercontinental Westlake Hanoi.

the roof, so you may wish to eat elsewhere in town. The resort can arrange its own train transfers on board the exclusive Victoria Express from Hanoi. This is Sa PaPa's best hotel if you're looking for a bit of luxury. **$$$$$**

**Topas Eco Lodge**
24 Muong Hoa St. Tel: 020-387 2404.
www.topas-eco-lodge.com
Located south of Sa PaPa, this environmentally friendly lodge generally has warmer weather and clearer views because of its location. The 25 rooms are contained within bungalows, each powered by solar panels. Rooms are sparse but comfortable and clean, and the staff mostly comprise local ethnic minorities. This is a great place to stay and has amazing views, although it isn't suitable for families with young children or guests with mobility issues. **$$$$**

**Cha Pa Garden Boutique Hotel and Spa**
23B Cau May St. Tel: 020-387 2907.
www.chapagarden.com
Once Sa PaPa's best-kept secret, this gorgeous little boutique hotel features clean, comfortable and well-appointed rooms in a renovated French villa. The friendly owners, Tommy and Chai, go out of their way to make their guests happy. In mid-2009, 10 additional rooms and the Zen Spa were added. The owners are helpful with arranging treks, homestays and local transport. **$$$**

**Chau Long Sapa Hotel**
24 Dong Loi St. Tel: 020-387 1245.
www.chaulonghotel.com
This renovated hotel has large, elegantly designed rooms with stunning views over the valley. If possible, ask to be roomed in the new wing. The friendly and knowledgeable staff are a great source of information. Also features a spa, but give the pool a miss. **$$**

**Bamboo Sapa Hotel**
18 Muong Hoa. Tel: 020-387 1076.
www.bamboosapahotel.com
A great location and with friendly staff. Try to secure one of the rooms with a balcony and views of Mt Fansipan. Facilities include a spa and massage centre, free Wi-fi in rooms and a well-kept garden area. **$$**

**Cat View Hotel**
Cat Cat St. Tel: 020-387 1946.
www.catcathotel.com
Don't confuse this long-established favourite with the numerous copycats; this is the authentic Cat Cat Hotel. Located on the Cat Cat village side of town, its comfortable rooms are located up a hillside, making for breathtaking views at the top. A newly installed lift makes the trek up even easier. Ask for a room with a

### PRICE CATEGORIES

Price categories are for a standard double room in peak season.

**$** = under US$20
**$$** = $20–50
**$$$** = $50–100
**$$$$** = $100–150
**$$$$$** = over $150

TRANSPORT

ACCOMMODATION

ACTIVITIES

A – Z

LANGUAGE

fireplace. The reception can arrange treks and homestays at local minority villages. **$$**

**Lotus Hotel**
5 Muong Hoa St. Tel: 020-387 1308
The Lotus is a pleasant little guesthouse right on the main drag, next door to the Auberge. It offers huge, well-appointed rooms

(fireplaces, TV, balcony, bathtub) for low rates. Staff are friendly and can arrange treks and homestays at local minority villages. **$$**

**Sapa Rooms Boutique Hotel**
81 Phan Xi Pang St. Tel: 020-387 2131.
www.saparooms.com
A gem of a boutique hotel featuring clean, comfortable

rooms with amazing views and interesting tribal decor. With good service and friendly staff, this is an all-round great deal. Has a fantastic gourmet restaurant on site. **$$**

**Thai Binh Hotel**
Ham Rong St. Tel: 020-387 1212.
www.thaibinhhotel.com
This cosy and beautifully

maintained hotel features clean, quiet rooms (with fireplaces) and a warm, family atmosphere. Located at the foot of the Ham Rong Botanical Gardens, it's blissfully removed from the vendors and touts on the main strip. Owner Nam Hong can help arrange guides and suggest interesting treks. **$$**

# NORTHEAST VIETNAM

## Cao Bang City

**Bang Giang Hotel**
1 Kim Dong St. Tel: 026-385 3431
A government-run hotel located beside the bridge with large and clean but characterless rooms. Excellent views from the top floors. **$**

**Huong Thom Hotel**
45 Kim Dong St. Tel: 026-385 5888
This well-maintained mini hotel has bright, clean rooms, some with A/C and TV. Located near the market, the top floor has a great panorama of the Bang Giang River. **$**

## Lang Son City

**A1 Guesthouse**
32 Dinh Tien Hoang St. Tel: 025-381 2221
Basic but decent government-run guesthouse located in the city's Old Quarter, and featuring clean(ish) rooms with attached bathrooms. **$**

**Dong Kinh Hotel**
25 Nguyen Du St. Tel: 025-387 0166
Simple but comfortable hotel located near the market. It offers both shared and private rooms, with the latter featuring TV, A/C and mini bar. **$**

**Kim Son Hotel**
3 Minh Khai St. Tel: 025-387 0378
The Kim Son is a clean and comfortable Chinese joint-venture hotel with well-appointed rooms with A/C and private bathrooms, as well as a pretty good Chinese restaurant on site.
**$**

## Haiphong

**Harbour View Hotel**
4 Tran Phu St. Tel: 031-382 7827.
www.harbourviewvietnam.com
This lovely old colonial hotel has huge, well-appointed rooms with views over the bay and friendly staff. Located on the edge of downtown Haiphong, it has a nice pool, the Mandara Spa and an excellent fitness centre. Easily the best hotel in Haiphong. **$$$$**

**Huu Nghi Hotel Haiphong**
60 Dien Bien Phu St. Tel: 031-382 3244
Centrally located, with large, nicely furnished rooms and all the amenities required for its primarily business-oriented clientele. Has a good pool and tennis court, as well as massage facilities. **$$$**

**Hôtel du Commerce**
62 Dien Bien Phu St. Tel: 031-384 2706
This attractive and renovated colonial-style hotel offers large, well-appointed rooms. Rates at the more expensive rooms include breakfast. **$$**

**Quang Minh Hotel**
20B Minh Khai. St. Tel: 031-382 3404
A great little budget hotel with huge, spotlessly cleaned rooms and an extremely friendly staff. Free breakfast included in the room rate. **$$**

**Thang Nam Hotel**
55 Dien Bien Phu St. Tel: 031-384 2818
Clean, comfortable and affordable. Decor is nothing to write home about, but it's centrally located and all

rooms have A/C and satellite TV. **$$**

## Halong City

Most visitors to Halong Bay book their tours in Hanoi, and many opt to stay overnight on board one of the bay's many cruise boats or on Cat Ba Island. Any of the Hanoi-based travel agents *(see page 370)* can book you on a boat trip to Halong Bay. For those who prefer to base themselves in Halong City, there is a huge variety of hotels and guesthouses to choose from, so feel free to bargain hard for the best rates.
In touristy **Bai Chay**, there are two areas teeming with hotels: on Halong Street, set back from the beach, and on Vuon Dao Street.
In **Hon Gai**, the majority of guesthouses and hotels are clustered around Le Thanh Tong Street.

## Bai Chay

**Saigon Halong**
168 Halong St. Tel: 033-384 5845.
www.saigonhalonghotel.com
This large, imposing hotel has seen better days, but still offers spotlessly clean rooms with amazing views of the bay. Offers heavily discounted room rates during the low season. Very popular with tour groups. **$$$$**

**Halong 1**
Halong St. Tel: 033-384 6320
Catherine Deneuve stayed in this beautiful French colonial villa during the filming

of *Indochine* (room 208, to be exact). Features charming rooms with huge bathrooms and amazing views. This small hotel fills up early, so be sure to book in advance. **$$$**

**Halong Plaza**
8 Halong St. Tel: 033-384 5810.
www.halongplaza.com
This boxy but elegant Thai joint venture has tastefully furnished rooms with excellent views over the bay. Also has a large swimming pool to laze by.

**Novotel Halong**
Halong St. Tel: 033-3848 108.
www.novotelhalong.com.vn
Fantastic views of the bay are perhaps the biggest selling point here, closely followed by the slick service and spacious rooms. **$$$**

**Thanh Nien Hotel**
Halong St. Tel: 033-384 6715
A small hotel located on a narrow neck of land right on Bai Chay Beach. Cute little bungalows, all with A/C, TV and hot water. Can be a bit noisy due to nearby cafés and karaoke parlours, but good value nonetheless. **$**

**Vuon Dao Hotel**
Halong St. Tel: 033-384 6427
This large, concrete behemoth set at the top of a hill is popular with tour groups and has spacious, airy rooms at bargain rates. **$**

## Hon Gai

**Halong Hotel/Guesthouse**
80 Le Thanh Tong St. Tel: 033-382 6509
A small but spotlessly clean guesthouse with private bathrooms, A/C and hot

water. Great value for money. **$**

**Hien Cat**
252 Ben Tau St. Tel: 033-382 7417
Just next door to the ferry wharf, this homey little hotel offers clean, bright rooms with fans, hot water and shared bathrooms. The staff are extremely friendly and helpful. **$**

### Cat Ba Island

Yet another boom town, there are dozens of mini hotels and guesthouses on Cat Ba Island, and many more still being built. The majority are found along the main seafront stretch, Nui Ngoc Street. To complicate matters, there are no street numbers, and many of the hotels have the same or similar names. The ones listed below are some of the better hotels and guesthouses.

Note: it's possible either to rent a bamboo beach hut or pitch tents and camp out on Cat Co 2 Beach for about US$6 per night. Just make your way down there and enquire.

**Catba Island Resort and Spa**
Cat Co 1 Beach. Tel: 031-368 8686.

www.catbaislandresort-spa.com
Set on a hill and surrounded by forest, this plush resort features tastefully outfitted rooms with gorgeous views of the bay and Cat Co Beach. Great free-form pool with water slides and private beach to laze by. Restaurant on site serves Asian, Western and seafood dishes. **$$$$**

**Sunrise Resort**
Cat Co 3 Beach. Tel: 031-388 7360.
www.catbasunriseresort.com
This beautiful and well-regarded resort is a bit off the beaten track, but the landscaping, design, rooms and view make it well worth the trek. Gorgeous private beach and pool; many rooms have jacuzzis. Two restaurants and a tour desk on site. **$$$$**

**Holiday View Hotel**
Nui Ngoc St. Tel: 031-388 7200.
www.holidayviewhotel-catba.com
On the edge of Cat Ba Town, this towering hotel features large, immaculate rooms with sea views. Popular with tour groups and often offers great room deals. **$$$**

**My Ngoc Hotel Restaurant**
Nui Ngoc St. Tel: 031-388 8199
This basic but quiet and comfortable hotel has a

**ABOVE:** poolside at Sunrise Resort, Cat Ba Island.

streetside restaurant and offers tour information and kayak rentals. Ask for a room with a balcony, and get all your questions answered by the helpful staff. **$**

**Noble House**
Nui Ngoc St. Tel: 031-388 8363
Funky little Australian-run guesthouse directly across from the pier and offering clean, comfortable accommodation with an English-pub vibe. Has a good bar and restaurant. **$**

**Princes Hotel**
Nui Ngoc St. Tel: 031-388 8899.
www.princeshotel-catba.com
The Princes is a comfortable, well-appointed hotel with lots of character and

large, airy rooms. Also features an inner courtyard with a garden. The staff are friendly, and they accept credit cards. Great rooftop bar. **$**

**Quang Duc Family Hotel**
Nui Ngoc St. Tel: 031-388 8231
Charming little hotel where the owner and staff do indeed treat guests like family. Offers a range of tour and activity options. **$**

**Sunflower 1 Hotel (Huong Duong 1)**
Nui Ngoc St. Tel: 031-388 8429
Nice, clean hotel with large, well-appointed rooms. Not all have views of the bay, but there are large family rooms available upon request. Rooftop billiards bar. **$**

# THE TONKIN COAST

### Nam Dinh City

**Vi Hoang Hotel**
153 Nguyen Du St. Tel: 0350-384 9290
Located in the centre of Nam Dinh City, this hotel faces the large Vi Xuyen Park and is right next door to the city's cultural house. Features large rooms, a swimming pool, massage facilities and a restaurant. Staff are all business here, so don't expect small talk. **$**

### Ninh Binh City

**Ngoc Anh Hotel**
30 Luong Van Tuy St. Tel: 030-388 3768
Built in 2005, this baby-blue mini hotel has large, spotlessly clean rooms and a fairly good restaurant.

Owners are extremely friendly and helpful. Rents motorbikes and arranges tours. **$**

**Thuy Anh Hotel**
55A Truong Han Sieu St. Tel: 030-387 1602
This clean and comfortable family-run hotel is located right in the centre of town. Popular with tour groups, the nicer, quieter rooms are found in the new wing, though the old wing rooms are decent too. Great restaurant and rooftop bar, and excellent tour desk. **$**

**Xuan Hoa Hotel**
31 Minh Khai St. Tel: 030-388 0970. www.xuanhoahotel.com
A great little hotel which recently added a whole new building (Xuan Hoa 2) and

has clean, comfortable and well-appointed rooms for low rates. Nice family atmosphere, and the café is a great place to chat with the owner and other travellers about the area's sights. Arranges tours and transportation. **$**

### Hoa Lu

**Van Xuan Hotel**
National Road 12, Hoa Lu (just off Highway 1). Tel: 030-362 2615
Managed by the Communist Youth League of Ninh Binh province and surprisingly well run, this hotel is located in a lush garden at the bottom of Thien Ton Mountain – just a few kilometres from Hoa Lu and Tam Coc. Empty

most of the time, the rooms are large and bright. Larger villas are also available. **$**

### Cuc Phuong N.P.

Nho Quan District, Ninh Binh Province. Tel: 030-384 8006
For visitors wishing to stay a night or two in Cuc Phuong National Park, there are three types of lodgings in three different areas of the park. At the headquarters

#### PRICE CATEGORIES

Price categories are for a standard double room in peak season.

**$** = under US$20
**$$** = $20–50
**$$$** = $50–100
**$$$$** = $100–150
**$$$$$** = over $150

TRANSPORT

ACCOMMODATION

ACTIVITIES

A – Z

LANGUAGE

(park entrance) visitors can choose a hotel room (basic with A/C, hot water and TV), a stilt house (hot water, fan) or a detached bungalow (en-suite bathroom, hot water, TV, A/C). At Mac Lake, there are detached bungalows; large groups can rent a stilthouse dormitory (no hot water, separate bathroom). Furthest into the park, the Bong substation offers detached bungalows and stilt houses, though the electricity is only turned on during the day.

**Thanh Hoa City**
**Ben Ngu Guesthouse**
5 Ben Ngu St. Tel: 037-385 4704
This motel-style guesthouse features clean, comfortable rooms overlooking a leafy courtyard. The friendly staff can arrange tours, though their English skills aren't the best. **$**
**Kim Ngan Hotel**
92 Nguyen Truong To St. Tel: 037-371 4223
A pleasant little hotel overlooking the dried-up Nha Tho Lake, it's situated just down

the street from the Cathedral. The staff only speak a little English but are friendly and accommodating. **$**
**Sao Mai Hotel**
20 Phan Chu Trinh. Tel: 037-371 2888
Opened in 2005, this supposedly four-star hotel has large, well-appointed rooms and a swimming pool, though the service leaves a little to be desired. Good value for what you get. **$**

**Vinh**
**Huu Nghi Hotel**

74 Le Loi St. Tel: 038-384 2520
Rooms and service much like the Saigon Kim Lien(see below), with prices a little cheaper. Rooms on the uppermost floors are quiet and have great views. **$**
**Saigon Kim Lien Hotel**
25 Quang Trung St. Tel: 038-383 8899
This quality business hotel features all the expected amenities (TV, A/C, mini bar and safe) at reasonable prices. Often offers room discounts. **$**

# HUE, DANANG AND HOI AN

**Hue**
**Ana Mandara Hue**
Thuan An Town, Phu Vang District. Tel: 054-398 3333
www.epikurean.ws/ana-mandara-hue
Exclusive resort located about 15km (9 miles) east of Hue at Thuan An beach. All the five-star facilities you'd expect in this price range, with special mention for the spa and the quality of the cuisine. **$$$$$**
**Celadon Palace Hotel**
105A Hung Vuong St. Tel: 054-393 6666.
www.celadonpalacehue.com
Billing itself as "Hue's only world-class hotel", the new Celadon Palace is also the largest hotel in town and by far the most visually impressive. There are enormous suites with opulent decor inspired by the Nguyen dynasty. **$$$$$**
**La Residence Hotel & Spa**
5 Le Loi St. Tel: 054-383 7475.
www.la-residence-hue.com
This boutique hotel occupies the former home of the French governor. The lovely rooms have three themes: *Monuments d'Egypte*, *Voyage en Chine* and *Suite d'Ornithologue*. Each has Art Deco furnishings, four-poster beds and terraces overlooking the Perfume River and the flagstaff of the Royal Citadel. A spa and fine-dining options are on site. **$$$$$**
**Century Riverside Hotel**
49 Le Loi St. Tel: 054-382

3391.
www.centuryriversidehue.com
Once past the rather unappealing reception area, guests will enjoy the lovely, spacious rooms with balconies overlooking the Perfume River. Facilities include a riverside swimming pool, on-site restaurant and bar, and conference room. **$$$$**
**Hoa Hong Hotel**
1 Pham Ngu Lao St. Tel: 054-382 4377
An oldie but goodie. Rooms are decked out with all the expected comforts for the price, including A/C and satellite TV. The spacious bathrooms have spa bathtubs and shower curtains. Located in the heart of the busy tourist district. **$$$**
**Hue Heritage Hotel**
9 Ly Thuong Kiet St. Tel: 054-383 8111
A fine faux colonial-style hotel with wooden floors, a rooftop swimming pool, bar and restaurant. The elegant rooms have A/C, satellite TV and private balconies. The spacious bathrooms have invigorating massage shower-heads. **$$$**
**Huong Giang**
51 Le Loi St. Tel: 054-382 2122.
www.huonggianghotel.com
This riverfront hotel is walking distance from the railway station. Facilities include a tennis court, spa and swimming pool. Large rooms with private

balconies overlook the Perfume River. Rooms are equipped with A/C, internet and satellite TV. **$$$**
**Duy Tan Hotel**
12 Hung Vung St. Tel: 054-382 5001. Email: nkduytan@dng.vnn.vn
Located in the city centre, this government-run hotel is good value, with all the basic amenities like A/C and satellite TV. The pricier rooms are located on the upper floors and have balconies. **$$**
**Ngoc Huong Hotel**
8–10 Chu Van An St. Tel: 054-383 0111.
www.ngochuonghotel.com
Friendly service and a convenient location on the edge of the tourist district. The comfortable and clean rooms have A/C, hot water and satellite TV. Walking distance from all the best restaurants, bars and shopping. **$$**
**Ngoc Binh Hotel**
6/34 Nguyen Tri Phuong St. Tel: 054-381 9860.
www.ngocbinhhotel.com
Conveniently located in the centre of town, with pleasant staff and disabled-friendly facilities. There is free pick-up from the train and bus stations. **$**
**Thanh Noi Hotel**
57 Dang Dung St. Tel: 054-352 2478. Email: thanhnoi@dng.vnn.vn.
www.thanhnoihotel.com
One of the few hotels north of the Perfume River, the

Thanh Noi is located in the heart of the Royal Citadel. The hotel is surrounded by quiet streets shaded by trees and bridges that cross over the citadel's many lakes and canals. Well-kept gardens and a swimming pool. **$$**

**Lang Co Beach**
**Lang Co Beach Resort**
Lang Co Beach. Tel: 054-387 3555.
www.langcobeachresort.com.vn
This most luxurious resort in Lang Co is surrounded by lush tropical gardens and built in the style of traditional Hue wooden houses. The grounds include two large restaurants serving European and Asian dishes, bars, a swimming pool, spa and gym. Rooms are spacious and all have balconies with ocean or garden views. Free Wi-fiWi-fi on site. **$$**

**Danang**
**Green Plaza Hotel**
238 Bach Dang St. Tel: 0511-322 3399.
www.greenplazahotel.vn
Green Plaza is conveniently located in a high-rise building overlooking the Han River and right in the centre of town. Facilities include a rooftop swimming pool, spa, jacuzzi, gym, and some of the best views of the city and coastline. **$$$**
**Bamboo Green Harbourside Hotel**
177 Tran Phu St. Tel: 0511-382 2722.

www.bamboogreenhotel.com
Not to be confused with Bamboo Green Riverside or Bamboo Green Central; this one is conveniently located across from the Catholic church in the middle of town. The comfortable rooms include A/C, hot water and satellite TV. The in-house restaurant serves Vietnamese, Chinese and European food. Breakfast included in the price. **$$**

**Bamboo Green Riverside Hotel**
68 Bach Dang St. Tel: 0511-383 2591.
www.bamboogreenhotel.com
Located next to the Song Han Bridge, rooms in this new addition to the Bamboo Green chain have great views, bathtubs, A/C, hot water and satellite TV. Facilities include internet access, restaurant and bar. The cheapest of the three hotels bearing the name. **$$**

**Dai A Hotel**
51 Yen Bai St. Tel: 0511-382 7532
Located southwest of the cathedral and about a block away from the Han Market, this small, friendly hotel has great views of the cityscape and free internet access. Rooms have A/C, fridge, phone, satellite TV and hot water. A popular venue for long-term guests and businessmen. **$$**

### China Beach

**Furama Resort Danang**
68 Ho Xuan Huong St. My An Beach. Tel: 0511-384 7333
www.furamavietnam.com
One of Vietnam's premier luxury resorts is located right on My An Beach, which is one of several white-sand beaches on the stretch collectively known as China Beach (where American GIs hung out while on R&R from the Vietnam War). The spacious rooms are surrounded by landscaped gardens, and there are two swimming pools (one with waterfalls), a private beach, and a golf driving range. Rooms have all the amenities you would expect in a 5-star hotel. Also has a fully equipped fitness

centre and several excellent, albeit expensive, restaurants. **$$$$$**

**Fusion Maia Resort**
Son Tra - Dien Ngoc Coastal St. My Khe Ward. Tel: 0511 396-7999.
www.fusion-resorts.com
The Fusion resorts are a one-of-a-kind luxury experience with unlimited spa treatments included in the price. Each room comes with its own private pool, sunken black granite bathtub, fully loaded iPod and free Wi-fi. **$$$$$**

### Hoi An

**Life Heritage Resort Hoi An**
1 Pham Hong Thai St. Tel: 0510-391 4555.
www.life-resorts.com
Located on the banks of the Thu Bon River just next to Hoi Ang town, this is one of Hoi An's top resorts, with all the amenities one would expect from a hotel in this price bracket. The Senses Restaurant and Vienna Café serve Asian-European fusion cuisine, as well as "wellness" dishes designed to complement the resort's spa treatments. Expect the full range of facilities. **$$$$**

**Ha An Hotel**
6–8 Phan Boi Chau St. Tel: 0510-386 3126.
www.haanhotel.com
Ha An is a friendly, family-run hotel set in a quiet alley close to town. The two houses that make up the hotel are built and decorated in traditional Chinese and French colonial styles, and enclose a small garden courtyard. Rooms have A/C, hot water, TV and telephones. Located on the far eastern end of the Old Town. **$$$**

**Vinh Hung Resort**
An Hoi Peninsula. Tel: 0510-391 0577.
www.vinhhungresort.com
This high-end resort is just south of the Old Town on the Thu Bon River. Rooms have either river or garden views. Services include a free shuttle boat to the Old Town, complimentary English magazines and newspapers, and a nightly

"Countryside Market" where you can sample local specialities. **$$$**

**Vinh Hung I Hotel**
143 Tran Phu St. Tel: 0510-386 1621.
www.vinhhungresort.com
This Chinese trading house exudes the atmosphere of old Hoi An on the outside. Only the more expensive rooms carry that theme on the inside, however. Two rooms were used by Michael Caine while filming *The Quiet American* – a stay in either costs a premium, but the other rooms are nice too. **$$$**

**Nhat Huy Hoang Hotel**
58 Ba Trieu St. Tel: 0510-386 1665.
Email: nhathuyhoang.coltd@vnn.vn
Overall the best value in a city where accommodation is generally overpriced. This small, quiet hotel has friendly, English-speaking staff, and amenities that cost double the price at other hotels in town. The rooms have A/C, satellite TV, hot water, phone and fridge. Located just a few minutes' walk north of the Old Town. **$**

**Vinh Hung II Hotel**
Corner of Hai Ba Trung & 96 Ba Trieu St. Tel: 0510-386 3717.
www.vinhhungresort.com
This Chinese-themed hotel is larger than its older sister hotel and has a swimming pool in the courtyard. Located on the edge of the Old Town, which means you don't quite wake up in the heart of things, but it is a comfortable place. **$$**

### Cua Dai Beach

Many people combine the charms of Hoi An town with a relaxing beach holiday. Lovely Cua Dai Beach is only about 5km (3 miles) east of Hoi An and lined with several nice beach resorts; most provide free shuttle services for their guests to Hoi An town and back.

**The Nam Hai**
Thon 1, Dien Duong Village, Cua Dai Beach. Tel: 0510-394 0000.
www.ghmhotels.com
Its pedigree alone – chairman Adrian Zecha of the GHM hotel group also owns

the legendary Aman resorts – assures this resort of both style and substance. Stratospheric prices aside, this is easily Vietnam's most exclusive beach resort (and probably one of its most expensive). The smallest room is an oversized 80 sq metres (860 sq ft) villa while the one-bedroom villas with their own private pools are a mere 250 sq metres (2,690 sq ft). Occupying prime beachfront land about 10km (6 miles) from Hoi An town, this designer's dream resort has all the expected facilities one would expect of a resort of this calibre, including three stunning infinity-edged swimming pools and an exquisite spa. **$$$$$**

**Palm Garden Resort**
Cua Dai Beach. Tel: 0510-392 7927.
www.palmgardenresort.com.vn
A secluded resort on a private stretch of beach, just 5 minutes' drive from Hoi An. Facilities include a fitness centre and four eateries. The resort has a full suite of services, including free internet and free shuttle to Hoi An. There are plenty of water-sports activities available at the beach, including windsurfing, sea kayaking, sailing, jet-skiing and parasailing. **$$$$$**

**Swiss-Belhotel Golden Sand Resort & Spa**
Cua Dai Beach. Tel: 0510-392 7555.
www.swiss-belhotel.com
This beachfront resort comprises eight chalet-style buildings, housing rooms with their own private balconies and surrounded by landscaped gardens of frangipani, hibiscus and palm trees. The resort features one of the largest outdoor swimming pools in Vietnam, five restaurants, bars, spa,

### PRICE CATEGORIES

Price categories are for a standard double room in peak season.

**$** = under US$20
**$$** = $20–50
**$$$** = $50–100
**$$$$** = $100–150
**$$$$$** = over $150

and Wi-fi throughout. **$$$$$**
**Victoria Hoi An Resort**
Cua Dai Beach. Tel: 0510-392
7040.
www.victoriahotels-asia.com
This is a charming hotel
located right on a white,
sandy beach and only 5km
(3 miles) away from Hoi An.
There are several room
options, with either French,
Vietnamese or Japanese-
inspired decor. Also features

a large swimming pool and
several restaurants. The
hotel operates a free shuttle
bus to and from Hoi An.
**$$$$$**
**Hoi An Beach Resort**
Cua Dai Beach. Tel: 0510-392
7011.
www.hoianbeachresort.com.vn
Flanked by the beach
(across the road) on one
side and the river on the
other, this resort is popular

with well-to-do Vietnamese
tourists. Facilities
include two swimming
pools, spa and fitness
centre, free shuttle to
and from Hoi An town,
internet access and water-
sports facilities. Delicious
seafood is served in the
evenings at its restaurant.
**$$$$**
**Hai Yen Hotel**
Cua Dai Beach. Tel: 0510-386

2445.
www.khachsanhaiyen.com
Hai Yen is a quiet refuge
located on the beach
road just outside the
centre of town. This
old favourite has comfo
rtable rooms with all the
typical amenities plus internet access, a pool and a
restaurant. The friendly staff
speak English reasonably
well. **$$**

# SOUTH TO QUY NHON

## Quang Ngai
**Central Hotel**
784 Quang Trung St. Tel: 055-
282 9999.
www.centralhotel.com.vn
The Central Hotel is not
exactly centrally located, but
it's not too far out. The hotel
is clean and has friendly,
English-speaking staff,
although it's beginning to
show signs of its 10-year
age. There is a rooftop
swimming pool and tennis
court. ADSL internet is avail-
able in all but the standard
rooms. **$$**
**Dong Khanh Hotel**
16–17 Be Trieu St. Tel: 055-382
4481
Dong Khanh is good value
with friendly staff and conveniently located near
plenty of eateries, internet
cafés and the local post
office. Rooms are nicely furnished and include A/C,
cable TV and a bathtub with
hot water. **$**
**Kim Thanh Hotel**
19 Hung Vuong St. Tel: 055-382
3471

This small, family-run hotel
is right across from the town
square. Although the building is a little old, the large
rooms here are the best
value in town, with hot
water, A/C, fridge and satellite TV. The service is both
helpful and friendly, and
English is spoken. **$**

## Sa Huynh
**The Vinh Hotel**
Highway 1A. Tel: 055-386 0385
A simple, quiet hotel
located on the south end of
town on a pristine strip of
golden-sand beach. The tidy
rooms have A/C or fan, hot
water and TV. You probably
won't find English spoken
here, or anywhere else in
Sa Huynh for that matter,
but the staff are friendly
and will do their best to
meet your needs. **$**

## Quy Nhon
**Life Wellness Resort Quy
Nhon**
Ghenh Rang, Bai Dai Beach. Tel:
056-384 0132.

www.life-resorts.com
The beautifully designed
resort with Cham-influenced
architecture is set on a
secluded section of beach.
All the rooms overlook the
sea. There are two bars and
a large cliff-side seafood
restaurant. The hotel can
also arrange boat trips to
nearby craft villages and
sights, including the hotel-
owned Hon Dat Island. Its
award-winning spa is out-
standing and offers a variety
of massages, treatments
and wellness programmes.
**$$$$**
**HAGL (Hoang An) Resort –
Quy Nhon**
1 Han Mac Tu St. Tel: 056-374
7100.
www.hotels84.com
This nice resort is set on the
southernmost stretch of
sandy beach close to the
city. Rooms have private
balconies, and many face
the ocean. Facilities include
a health club, two swimming
pools and tennis courts.
Queen's Beach is just next

door, and Banh It Cham
Towers are just a little to the
west. **$$$**
**Seagull Hotel**
489 An Duong St. Tel: 056-384
6377.
www.seagullhotel.com.vn
Seagull is a well-estab-
lished hotel with a recent
high-rise addition and over-
all renovation. Located on
the south end of town, it
has its own stretch of white
sandy beach. The restau-
rant is decent but only
serves Vietnamese cuisine.
The facilities are conveni-
ent with free Wi-fiWi-fi and
cable TV in all the rooms.
**$$**
**Lan Anh**
102 Xuan Dieu St. Tel: 056-389
3109
Lan Anh offers spacious, private rooms – some with
balconies overlooking the
beach. Rooms include A/C,
bathtub, satellite TV, work-
desk, fridge and Wi-fi. The
staff are helpful and friendly,
and the housekeeping is
impeccable. **$**

# NHA TRANG

## Nha Trang
**Evason Ana Mandara**
Tran Phu St. Tel: 058-352 2811.
www.sixsenses.com
Part of the luxury Six Senses
resort chain, the Ana
Mandara occupies a slice of
urban beach, albeit a nice
one. This elegant property –
undoubtedly Nha Trang's
best, despite the presence
of newer kids on the block –
has two swimming pools,

two restaurants and two
bars, a water-sports centre
and a PADI scuba-diving
facility. The villas (either garden view, sea view, de luxe
sea view or suite) are not
overly huge, but each is
beautifully furnished and
well appointed, with everything you'd expect from a
hotel of this standard. **$$$$$**
**Novotel Nha Trang**
50 Tran Phu St. Tel: 058-625

6900.
www.accorhotels.com
The new Novotel resort is a
modern facility with many
basic safety features that
are rare elsewhere in
Vietnam – like smoke
alarms, sprinkler
systems and a security
peephole. Most rooms are
non-smoking. Facilities
include a rooftop swimming
pool, sauna, fitness centre

and Wi-fi access. The
Novotel is also family-
friendly, with an indoor playground and a babysitting
service. **$$$$**
**Vinpearl Resort**
Hon Tre Island. Tel: 058-395
8188.
www.vinpearlresort.com
Located on Bamboo Island
(Hon Tre), this resort is managed by the Sofitel group
and had the distinction of

hosting the Miss Universe swimsuit competition in 2008. The island can be accessed from Nha Trang by either cable car or speedboat. Rooms are spacious and elegantly furnished in dark wood and rattan. The sprawling resort grounds include two swimming pools, four restaurants, a truly private beach (something most resorts claim falsely) and an adjoining theme park. **$$$$**

### Mia Resort Nha Trang

Bai Dong, Cam Hai Dong, Cam Lam, Khanh Hoa Province. Tel: 058-3989 666.

www.mianhatrang.com

Mia is the newest edition to the Nha Trang Sailing Club resort-bar-restaurant-spa group. This luxurious eco-resort is located just south of the city on the way to Cam Ranh Bay, so it's best to arrange transport (most likely from the airport in Cam Ranh) before you arrive. The signature Sandals Restaurant serves seafood, Asian fusion and imaginative pizzas (try the bacon and banana). Be sure to book a massage at their Xanh Spa. **$$$$**

### Nha Trang Lodge

42 Tran Phu St. Tel: 058-352 1500.

www.nhatranglodge.com

The lodge bills itself as a business hotel, but performs admirably for most travellers. Spacious rooms on the 12 floors face the beach and have spectacular views of the coast. Facilities include a rooftop swimming pool, and internet access throughout. **$$$**

### Sunrise Nha Trang Beach Hotel and Spa

12–14 Tran Phu St. Tel: 058-382 0999.

www.sunrisenhatrang.com.vn

Architecturally this is one of the most striking – some say ostentatious – hotels in Nha Trang. You'll be met by a cool, jasmine-scented breeze when you walk into its vast, white-granite reception, reinforced by tall columns and accented by striking black-iron sculptures. Three excellent

in-house restaurants. Live classical music is performed nightly in the lounge. Facilities also include a spa, gym and swimming pool. It's all a bit over the top, but the resort has its fans. **$$$**

### Asia Paradise Hotel

6 Biet Thu St. Tel: 058-352 4686.

www.asiaparadisehotel.com

One of Nha Trang's few upscale hotels that does not face the beach. Targeted at business travellers, its facilities include a spa, gym, rooftop pool and Wi-fi access throughout. This is a good option if you want some of the luxury you'll find at the Melia Sunrise, at a much lower price. **$$**

### Phu Quy 2 Hotel

1 Tue Tinh St. Tel: 058-352 5050.

www.phuquyhotel.vn

This new high-rise hotel is centrally located and offers beautiful views of the beach and cityscape. Also features a rooftop swimming pool and elegant restaurant. The de luxe rooms have natural wood floors and are smartly decorated. Rooms include Wi-fi, A/C and cable TV. **$$**

### Nha Trang Beach Hotel

4 Tran Quang Khai St. Tel: 058-352 4468.

www.nhatrangbeachhotel.com.vn

This hotel is conveniently located just 2 minutes from the Sailing Club and the beach. There is a large reception area, and rooms are spacious and have beach views, but no balconies. The rooftop restaurant is a great place to meet other travellers and watch the sun set. Spa with massage services on site. **$**

### Perfume Grass Inn

4A Biet Thu St. Tel: 058-352 6433.

www.perfume-grass.com

Stylishly decorated, each room in the hotel has its own character. Rooms have cable TV, A/C, a bathtub, and mini bar. Facilities include a family-run restaurant and bar, as well as a rooftop terrace and complimentary internet access. **$**

### Sao Mai Hotel

99 Nguyen Thien Thuat St. Tel: 058-352 6412.

Email: Saomai2ht@yahoo.com

This friendly, family-run hotel is one of the best-value digs in town. The large, tidy rooms have fan or A/C, hot water, fridge and TV. The place is owned by the family of photographer Mai Loc, who leads popular guided tours of central Vietnam. **$**

## Hon Heo Peninsula and Doc Let

### Six Senses Ninh Van Bay

Ninh Van Bay, Ninh Hoa. Tel: 058-372 8222.

www.sixsenses.com

A favourite getaway of the rich and famous, this is perhaps Vietnam's most expensive resort, and certainly one of the most exclusive (white-sand Ninh Vanh Bay is only reachable by boat). There are 5 villa types to chose from, each with its own butler. The focus here is luxury and relaxation. Each private villa, with its own pool, feels like a haven of tranquillity; some villas even have their own private mini spas. Dine in one of several restaurants, or have your meals delivered and prepared right on your private deck. Many celebs have been guests, including the British royals. **$$$$$**

### Doc Let Beach Resort

Doc Let Beach. Tel: 058-384 9152.

www.docletresort.com

A lovely little resort right on the beach. The staff are friendly but very little English is spoken. The grounds include two restaurants, a swimming pool and tennis courts. Rooms have A/C or fan, and satellite TV. Most customers here are Vietnamese, which means the hotel has the obligatory karaoke and massage facilities. **$**

### Jungle Beach

Ninh Phuoc Village. Tel: 058-362 2384.

www.junglebeachvietnam.com

This resort is set on one of

the most pristine beaches in the country. The water is calm, shallow and clear year-round. The staff are exceptionally friendly and hospitable – they won't let you sit or stand without a glass of free lemonade in your hand. Rates include three meals a day. **$$**

### Paradise Beach Resort

Doc Let Beach. Tel: 058-367 0480.

Email: Paradise_doclech@hotmail.com

Rooms and meals here are similar to Jungle Beach, with rustic huts and three meals per day included in the price, as well as drinking water. The setting is different, however: a bustling little fishing village with an abandoned American guard tower nearby. Internet access is available. Run by a lovely French-Vietnamese family. **$$**

## Phan Rang

### Ho Phong Hotel

363 Ngo Gia Tu St. Tel: 068-392 0333.

www.hophong.vn

Just off the main drag on the south side of town, Ho Phong is a lovely hotel, with clean and spacious rooms. Rooms have A/C or fans and satellite TV. Complimentary internet access. Minimal English is spoken, but the staff are friendly and do their best to meet your needs. **$**

### Huu Nghi Hotel

300 Thong Nhat St. Tel: 068-392 0434.

www.ninhthuantourist.com.vn

This relatively new hotel has spacious, clean rooms with A/C, fridge and satellite TV. The more expensive "High-Class" suites have an additional office space and guest room. In-house restaurant, massage services and ADSL internet access. **$**

### PRICE CATEGORIES

Price categories are for a standard double room in peak season.

**$** = under US$20
**$$** = $20–50
**$$$** = $50–100
**$$$$** = $100–150
**$$$$$** = over $150

TRANSPORT

ACCOMMODATION

ACTIVITIES

A – Z

LANGUAGE

# DALAT

**Ana Mandara Villas Dalat**
Le Loi St. Tel: 063-355 5888.
www.anamandara-resort.com
This is the most luxurious resort in Dalat, and is set in an unlikely, secluded neighbourhood on the southwest side of town. The resort's take on rustic elegance is not lost on the 17 beautifully restored French colonial villas dating from the 1920s and 30s. Service and pampering are the focal points, with private butlers assigned to every room. Facilities include a heated swimming pool, fitness centre, DVD library and Wi-fi throughout. The only drawbacks are the long uphill walks between buildings. **$$$$$**

**Dalat Palace**
12 Tran Phu St. Tel: 063-382 5444.
www.dalatpalace.vn
Dalat's original luxury hotel is the best choice if you want to be transported back into the time of the French colonials. The hotel originally opened in 1922, and although it was completely renovated in 1995, it still drips with old-world charm and elegance. Rooms are furnished in period French style and have fireplaces, but also mod cons like satellite TV, Wi-fi and ADSL internet access, 24-hour

room service and in-room safes. The Le Rabelais French Restaurant, Larry's Bar and the L'Apothiquaire Spa complete the scene. Expect nothing but impeccable service from the staff. **$$$$$**

**Best Western Dalat Plaza Hotel**
09 Le Dai Hanh St. Tel: 063-625 0999.
www.bestwestern.com
The new Best Western is a surprising option for Vietnam, and even more unexpected is the price (all in a good way). The hotel is located in the centre of town with views of the lake. The onsite restaurant provides room service, which is not common in Vietnam at this price level. Facilities include spa, fitness centre and free Wi-fi. **$$**

**Golf 3 Hotel**
4 Nguyen Thi Minh Khai St. Tel: 063-382 6042.
www.vilagolf.vn
Part of the Golf hotel chain in Dalat, this one sits on the southern edge of Central Market and offers package deals with the Dalat Palace Golf Club. The spacious rooms have sunken bathtubs, wood or tiled floors, satellite TV with DVD players, and Wi-fi. The top-floor Sky View Café offers beautiful vistas of the

lake and market area while you dine. **$$**

**Hôtel du Parc**
7 Tran Phu St. Tel: 063-382 5777.
www.hotelduparc.vn
Dalat's second hotel was built in 1932 and renovated in 1997. It is located across the street from Café de la Poste, offers package deals with the Dalat Palace Golf Club, and shares a number of amenities with its partner, the Dalat Palace. This is a good, moderately priced option for those seeking some of the history and atmosphere of the Sofitel, without paying hefty room rates. Wi-fi internet access available throughout. **$$$**

**Dreams Hotel**
151 & 164B Phan Dinh Phung St. Tel: 063-383 3748 & 063-382 2981
Unmatched comfort on the cheap. The natural wood floors and double-panelled windows (to block off street noise), along with a rooftop jacuzzi, sauna and steam room, make this hotel an incredible bargain. The hotel is immaculately clean and looks brand new, despite its 8-year age. **$**

**Hotel Long Binh**
4K1 Bui Thi Xuan St. Tel: 063-382 0526
Long Binh is a Vietnamese tavern, which isn't as

romantic as it may sound. The customers on the ground floor can be rather noisy in the early morning and the late evening, but fortunately they cannot easily be heard in the upper-floor rooms. The spacious rooms are tidy with satellite TV, large bathrooms and balconies. **$**

**Phuong Thanh**
65 Truong Cong Dinh St. Tel: 063-382 5097
This cosy, family-run hotel is located right in the centre of Dalat's backpacker area. The tidy rooms are mostly downstairs, and have satellite TV and hot water. The Central Market is just a few minutes' walk up the hill. The steep, one-way lane winding down the hill here ensures limited noise and traffic and, therefore, a much quieter night's sleep. **$**

**Thien An Hotel**
272A Phan Dinh Phung St
Email: thienanhotel@vnn.vn
This relatively new hotel was built by the family of the woman who owns the Dreams hotel chain, and follows the same successful philosophy. The rooms are spacious, and the service is friendly. Rates include a great buffet breakfast, internet access as well as complimentary bicycles. **$**

# HO CHI MINH CITY

Ho Chi Minh City has a staggering number of hotels, and a remarkable number of these are international 5-star stunners – a reflection of the city's escalating number of business travellers. These luxury digs are mostly located in the downtown area in District 1, the epicentre being Dong Khoi Street. At the other end of the spectrum is budget-priced accommodation, which is mostly concentrated in the backpacker zone of De Tham, Pham Ngo Lao and Bui Vien streets (western

District 1) – with dozens more crammed cheek-by-jowl down narrow alleyways.
Inexplicably, mid-range hotels are less well represented in HCMC, although more are starting to emerge as developers see a potential market to be tapped.
There are very few hotels in District 3 and the Chinatown/Cholon area as they are too far removed from the heart of the action.

**District 1**

**Caravelle**

19 Lam Son Sq. Tel: 08-3823 4999.
www.caravellehotel.com
Opened in 1959, the 5-star Caravelle is one of the city's most celebrated international hotels, yet it is not part of a generic chain. A glitzy 24-floor edifice, the original low-rise wing was famously home to foreign press corps during the Vietnam War. Expect luxuriously appointed rooms and suites, including the old-wing Executive Suites with prime views over the Municipal Theatre.

Award-winning yet personable, the Caravelle offers excellent wining and dining choices. **$$$$$**

**Hotel Continental Saigon**
132–134 Dong Khoi St.
Tel: 08-3829 9201.
www.continentalvietnam.com
The antithesis of HCMC's slick and modern downtown hotels, the charming, historic Continental has a to-die-for location. Today state-run, this 1880s-built colonial-era hotel seems hardly to have changed since the time Graham Greene was holed up in

Room 214. The rooms and suites are spacious, simple and endearingly old-fashioned, some with balconies looking across the Municipal Theatre or the inner courtyard. Limited facilities and no pool. $$$$$

**Duxton Hotel Saigon**
63 Nguyen Hue Blvd. Tel: 08-3822 2999. www.duxton.com

The city's first 4-star, this Singapore-owned hotel is one of the city's boutique favourites among leisure and corporate travellers. Key factors are good downtown location and impeccable level of service. The guest rooms and suites – some with river views – are slightly dated but still comfortable. Facilities include the largest gaming centre in town, meeting rooms, fitness centre and swimming pool. $$$$$

**Legend Hotel Saigon**
2A–4A Ton Duc Thang St. Tel: 08-3823 3333. www.legendsaigon.com

If you seek great service and high standards, this Japanese-owned 5-star easily fits the bill. Located alongside the Saigon River, the elegant rooms and suites offer immaculate bathrooms (with Japanese-style toilets) and wonderful river views, although many face a noisy thoroughfare. First-class facilities include the city's premier Cantonese and Japanese restaurants (the former serving excellent dim sum lunches) and large landscaped outdoor pool. $$$$$

**Hotel Majestic**
1 Dong Khoi St. Tel: 08-3829 5517.
www.majesticsaigon.com.vn

This historic five-star landmark is one of Southeast Asia's classic colonial hotels. State-run, it radiates old-world charm, with dapper bell-boys, violin players serenading at afternoon tea and a grand marbled lobby with chandeliers and stained-glass skylights. Built in 1925, all rooms and suites have elegant colonial designs and features – including black-and-gold

marble bathrooms and high ceilings – but vary in size and views. The fifth-floor Breeze Sky Bar gives stunning panoramic views of the Saigon River. $$$$$

**Nguyen Du Park Villas**
111 Nguyen Du St. Tel: 08-3822 0788.
www.ndparkvillas.com.vn

Surrounded by lush greenery, this boutique residence comprises luxury apartments, pool, spa and gym. The generously sized one-bedroom apartments to four-bedroom duplex units come fully serviced and are equipped with every conceivable comfort. A remarkably good-value change from HCMC's usual hotel-style accommodation. $$$$$

**Norfolk Hotel**
117 Le Thanh Ton St. Tel: 08-3829 5368.
www.norfolkhotel.com

This personable boutique hotel, located on a pleasant leafy street, is popular with business and independent travellers. Most of the well-appointed guest rooms have balconies. There is no swimming pool, but guests can use the sister apartment complex. $$$$$

**Park Hyatt Saigon**
2 Lam Son Sq. Tel: 08-3824 1234.
www.saigon.park.hyatt.com

Relatively new, the elegant Hyatt evokes a nostalgic feel from the city's French Indochina era, while offering all manner of modern facilities. With a vantage point overlooking the Municipal Theatre, this 5-star hotel oozes class and luxury. The rooms feature colonial touches like four-poster beds and modern amenities like rain showers and huge flat-screen TVs. The hotel's exquisite Xuan Spa, Park Lounge and two restaurants are all highly recommended. Its room rates are probably the highest in the city, but justifiably so. $$$$$

**Renaissance Riverside Hotel Saigon**
8-15 Ton Duc Thang St. Tel: 08-3822 0033.
www.renaissancehotels.com/sgnbr

Located downtown along

the river, this Marriott-managed 5-star offers high standards with a boutique-style vibe and exceptionally friendly service. Most of the rooms and suites are on the small side, but designed with both business and leisure travellers in mind and offer superb (albeit noisy) river views and luxurious bedding. Highlights include the 22nd-floor rooftop terrace pool, elegant 5th-floor Atrium Lounge and Chinese restaurant. $$$$$ .

**Sheraton Saigon Hotel and Towers**
88 Dong Khoi St. Tel: 08-3827 2828.
www.sheraton.com/saigon

Luxurious and opulent in the heart of downtown, the city's largest 5-star hotel offers two choices. The original 23-floor hotel with 371 rooms and suites has consistently been an award-winning favourite. Just adjoining it, the cutting-edge, 25-floor Grand Tower takes Vietnam's accommodation to new world-class levels, with 112 sophisticated studios and suites serviced by your own personal butler. Chic wining and dining, shopping and spa options are all on site. $$$$$

**Sofitel Plaza Saigon**
17 Le Duan St. Tel: 08-3824 1555.
www.accorhotels.com/asia

Opened in 1998, this was one of the city's pioneering new crop of 5-star digs. Located off downtown in the diplomatic enclave, the high-rise hotel is a favourite with European and corporate guests. Stylish, contemporary flair extends from the atrium-style lobby to the sleek rooms and suites. Facilities include rooftop pool, plus fitness centre and ground-floor Martini bar. $$$$$

**Somerset Chancellor Court**
21–23 Nguyen Thi Minh Khai St. Tel: 08-3822 9197.
www.somerset.com

Part of the Singaporean Ascott group, this luxury serviced apartment complex near the downtown area

offers great value – ideal as a hotel alternative or for longer stays. The contemporary yet comfortable apartments – ranging from studios to three-bedroom units – are spacious, fully furnished and feature well-equipped kitchens. Most have balconies. Facilities include outdoor pool, supermarket and gym. $$$$$

**Somerset Ho Chi Minh City**
8A Nguyen Binh Khiem St. Tel: 08-3822 8899.
www.somerset.com

The same set-up as sister Chancellor Court, this de luxe apartment complex near the city zoo is more family-orientated and with a resort feel. The two- to four-bedroom spacious apartments are fully furnished, serviced and equipped, plus offer homely touches and en-suite bathrooms for each bedroom. Indoor and outdoor children's playrooms, landscaped pool with alfresco dining area, plus regular children's events, makes this a premier family-friendly accommodation option.

**Lavender Hotel**
208–210 Le Thanh Ton St. Tel: 08-2222 8888.
www.lavenderhotel.com.vn

A much-needed new boutique hotel in this price category, the Lavender Hotel is already a firm favourite for its stylish, intimate ambience and great pricing. Located behind Ben Thanh Market, all rooms are nicely appointed and feature rain showers in the bathrooms and flat-screen TVs (note some rooms don't have windows). The owners' obsession with lavender extends to omnipresent flower arrangements and decor. $$$$

**Hotel Metropole**
148 Tran Hung Dao St. Tel:
08-6295 8944.
www.metropolesaigon.com
Located on Cholon's main
artery and near the back-
packer area, the govern-
ment Saigontourist-run
Metropole offers one of the
most reliable and popular
3-star options in HCMC,
plus friendly service. There
are standard, superior and
de luxe room options plus
suites; the latter offers spacious living room areas.
Other features include gym,
conference centre, small
rooftop pool and snooker
room. **$$$$**
**Grand Hotel Saigon**
8 Dong Khoi St. Tel: 08-3823
0163.
  www.grandhotel.vn
With an impressive all-white
lobby and friendly service,
this 4-star hotel has been in
business since 1930, mak-
ing it one of the oldest
establishments in town. The
hotel was completely renovated in 1997 but the
1930s feel remains, with
rooms that are both elegant

and spotless. The Belle Vue
rooftop restaurant comes
with riverside views and
cracking cocktails.
**Elios**
233 Pham Ngu Lao St. Tel:
08-3838 5585.
www.elioshotel.vn
Located in the heart of
backpackerville and opened
in 2007, this is already a
favourite – and justifiably
so, as it's a new 3-star with
slightly higher standards
than others in this price
category. The rooms are
bright, comfortable and
modestly sized; superior
rooms are a bit larger. The
rooftop restaurant-bar
offers good views and is a
great place to unwind. Also
has a gym, meeting rooms
and lift. Staff are super-
friendly and always happy to
answer your questions.
**$$$$**
**May Hotel**
28–30 Thi Sach St. Tel:
08-3823 4501.
www.mayhotel.com.vn
Another new mid-range
hotel, conveniently located
on a quiet leafy side street,

yet within the city's nightlife
zone. A sweeping staircase
leads up to a grandiose
lobby area, complete with
chandeliers and wall-to-ceil-
ing glass frontage. The
rooms and suites are bright
and clean, with faux marble
floors, bathtubs and strong
showers. De luxe rooms
have balconies and higher
rooms have river views.
**$$$$**
**iPeace**
175/8 Pham Ngu Lao St. Tel:
08-3838 0207.
www.ipeacehotel.com
Among the backpacker bus-
tle of Pham Ngu Lao Street
is this excellent-value hotel.
Although it appears tiny
from the outside it manages
to fit 20 rooms between its
narrow walls, each with
cream and brown rooms,
and free Wi-fi. Breakfast is
included. **$$$$**
**Hai Long 5 Hotel**
Hai Long 559 Hai Ba Trung St.
Tel: 08-3823 4455.
www.hailonghotel.com.vn
Right in the heart of District
1, this simple but stylish
boutique hotel has

compact, neat rooms with
soft yellow tones. Little
extras include a buffet
breakfast, free Wi-fi and a
reasonable spa on site. It's
especially good for those
who come to shop as it's
within walking distance of
Dong Khoi St. **$$$$**

**District 5**
**Windsor Plaza Hotel**
18 An Duong Vuong St. Tel:
08-3833 6688.
http://hotel-windsorplaza.com/
Marking Cholon's bounda-
ries, the 25-floor Hong-
Kong-owned 4-star offers
an astounding array of in-
house facilities and ser-
vices, including casino,
Vietnam's largest nightclub,
three-floor shopping plaza
and several food and bever-
age outlets, including a
rooftop restaurant-cocktail
lounge with spectacular
views. From the 9th floor
upwards, the well-
appointed rooms also offer
great views of Cholon. A
bustling, family-friendly
hotel with a distinctly Asian
feel. **$$$$**

# AROUND HO CHI MINH CITY

**Tay Ninh**
**Hoa Binh Hotel**
210D 30/4 St. Tel: 066-382
7306
This Soviet-era, govern-
ment-run concrete box is
about the only tolerable
hotel in town. It has simple
but clean rooms with A/C,
hot water and TV. No English
is spoken, but the staff are
friendly and manage to
communicate the essentials
to English-speaking guests.
Walking distance to the Cao
Dai Temple. **$$$**

**Vung Tau**
**Imperial Hotel**
159 Thuy Van St. Tel: 064-362
8888.
www.imperialhotel.vn
Ostentatious design fea-
tures hardwood floors and
furnishings together with
marble counters and foun-
tains offset by plentiful art-
work and lush drapes. There
is a large swimming pool

and private beach club
across the street. **$$$$$**
**Ky Hoa – Vung Tau Hotel**
30–32 Tran Phu St. Tel: 064-
385 2579.
www.kyhoahotel.com.vn
This new French Vietnamese
castle-like hotel takes the
prize for the most stunning
architecture in the city.
Nestled at the foot of Big
Mountain near Villa
Blanche, pagodas rise from
its garden of bougainvillea,
frangipani and palm trees.
Rooms have A/C and large,
flat-screen satellite TVs. A
restaurant, swimming pool
and sports club are located
on site. **$$$$**
**Grand Hotel**
2 Nguyen Du St. Tel: 064-385
6888.
www.grand.oscvn.com
This government-owned
hotel shares some facilities,
including the pool and gym,
with nearby sister property
the Palace Hotel, but offers

a much better view of Front
Beach. A bar, restaurant,
café and nightclub are all on
site, and a buffet breakfast
is included in the rate. The
apartments are perfect for
small families. **$$$**
**Rex Hotel**
01 Le Quy Don St. Tel: 064-385
2135.
www.rexhotelvungtau.com.vn
Don't let the grumpy reception area put you off. The
Rex (government-run but no
relation to the Rex in hcmc)
offers immaculate rooms
with beautiful wooden furniture and some of the best
views of Front Beach.
Rooms include whirlpool
bathtub, A/C and satellite
TV. A swimming pool, tennis
court and internet access
are offered on site. **$$$**
**Hotel Lam Phuc**
19 Phan Van Tri St – P. Hang
Tam. Tel: 064-352 1666.
This high-rise hotel is set in
an alley behind Back Beach,

and offers great views of the
beach and the surrounding
cityscape. Clean, sunny
rooms include A/C, flat-
screen satellite TV and an
elevator (which is unusual in
small hotels and guest-
houses). **$**

**Con Dao Islands**
**Six Senses Con Dao**
Dat Doc Beach. Tel: 064-383
1222.
www.sixsenses.com
The most remote and exclu-
sive resort in all of Vietnam.
The Con Dao property is
similar to the Six Senses
Ninh Van Bay (outside Nha
Trang) in overall feel and
range of facilities. Villas
each have their own private
pools and butler service.
Their renowned fine dining
and spa services are entirely
customised to the desires of
each guest. Jolie, Pitt and
family stayed here in 2011.
**$$$$$**

### Con Dao Resort
8 Nguyen Duc Thuan St, An Hai Beach. Tel: 064-383 0939.
www.condaoresort.com.vn
Located right on An Hai Beach, this modern hotel with a swimming pool is less than a kilometre south of town. Next to the Six Senses resort being built, this is the next best option on the island – with rates that are at the opposite end of the spectrum. Rooms have mountain or ocean views, and a buffet breakfast is included. **$$$$**

### ATC Hotel
8 Ton Duc Thang St, Loi Voi Beach. Tel: 064-383 0345.
Email: atc@fmail.vnn.vn
A friendly, family-run resort separated from Loi Voi Beach by a road. The somewhat cluttered rooms have A/C, hot water and private terraces. Both brick bungalows and thatched-roof stilt houses are available. An excellent restaurant is on site. **$$**

## Mui Ne Beach

### Anantara Mui Ne Resort & Spa
KM10, Nguyen Dinh Chieu St. Tel: 062-374 1888.
www.anantara.com
Formerly known as the L'Anmien and now under new international management, Anantara is the first 5-star resort on the strip. Accommodations include basic rooms, suites and villas, all with separate rain showers and tubs. Other facilities include a spa, wine cellar and the best fitness centre in Mui Ne. **$$$$$**

### Seahorse Resort & Spa
Km 11, Ham Thien St. Tel: 062-384 7507.

www.seahorseresortvn.com
This beautifully landscaped property is one of the largest hotels in Mui Ne but it is still able to maintain an intimate feel. Offers windsurfing, kiteboarding, tennis, resort-wide Wi-fi, a large pool and beachside restaurant. Childcare and cribs are also available. All rooms have open-air bathrooms, A/C and satellite TV. **$$$$$**

### Coco Beach Resort
58 Nguyen Dinh Chieu St. Tel: 062-384 7111.
www.cocobeach.net
Mui Ne's original pioneer resort, Coco Beach offers a tropical escape like no other. TVs are absent from all rooms, except Danny's Pub, to help you focus more on the surroundings. The property is cleverly hidden from the main road by a private enclosure. Coco Beach is one of the few spots in Mui Ne where one can play in the sea and sunbathe without the threat of stray surf kites. **$$$$**

### Mia Resort
24 Nguyen Dinh Chieu St. Tel: 062-384 7440.
www.miamuine.com
A favourite of expats and water-sports enthusiasts, Mia (previously known as the Sailing Club) offers private bungalows hidden among tropical gardens. The beachside pool and bar is a favourite hangout of both guests and expats. A spa is located on site, as is an excellent kiteboarding centre. **$$$$**

### Victoria Phan Thiet Beach Resort & Spa
Km 9, Phu Hai St. Tel: 062-381 3000.
www.victoriahotels-asia.com

A landmark in Mui Ne, the French-managed Victoria Phan Thiet has a long-standing reputation for quality and service. The resort is set on its own private stretch of beach just outside the main drag of resorts and restaurants, which means it's always peaceful. Facilities include horse riding, fitness centre, spa, two swimming pools, Wi-fi access and childcare services. **$$$$**

### Joe's Garden Resort
86 Nguyen Dinh Chieu St. Tel: 062-384-7177.
www.Joescafegardenresort.com
Formerly known by many names simultaneously, including Mai Khanh Resort, Paradise Huts and Chez Nina Resort, the property is now under new management, renovated, and the new home of the famous Joe's Café as well. The seaside bungalows are equipped with minibars, free Wi-fi, porches with hammocks, and include free breakfast. **$$**

### Mai Am Guesthouse
148 Nguyen Dinh Chieu St. Tel: 062-384 7062.
www.guesthousemaiam.com
This Swiss-run mini beach resort is tidy and well kept. Each room has two beds, a safe, A/C and cable TV. Unique to Mai Am, nursing care for the elderly is available (the owners run a certified care facility in Switzerland). **$$**

### Ocean Valley Hotel
187 Nguyen Dinh Chieu St. Tel: 062-377 7777.
email: hoteloceanvalleymuine@gmail.com
A small hotel overlooking the beach from across the street. Rooms are basic but clean and offer all the essentials like A/C, hot water and cable TV. Most rooms have balconies, half of which face the sea. **$$$**

### Little Way (Loi Nho) Guesthouse
93/1 Nguyen Dinh Chieu St. Tel: 062 374-1171
A quiet little guesthouse set off behind the road and nestled in an aquatic garden. The newly built rooms are clean and cosy, with cable TV, A/C and hot water. Sunrise restaurant, known for great coffee and seafood, is just outside. **$**

### Mui Ne Backpackers Resort
88 Nguyen Dinh Chieu St. Tel: 062-384 7047.
www.muinebackpackers.com
This guesthouse is one of the nicest in the budget price range. There is a small swimming pool, and there is a wide variety of room types to choose from, including dorms. **$**

## Phan Thiet

### Novotel Ocean Dunes & Golf Resort
1 Ton Duc Thang. Tel: 062-382 2393.
www.novotel.com
A destination in itself, the Novotel is one of the few reasons to stay in Phan Thiet rather than Mui Ne. Whether your room faces the private beach or overlooks the Ocean Dunes Golf Course and the rugged mountains beyond, your private balcony will have great views. Facilities include several restaurants and bars, a café, spa, fitness centre, swimming pool and water-sports centre. **$$$$$**

# MEKONG DELTA

## My Tho

### Hotel Chuong Duong
10 Duong 30/4. Tel: 073-387 0875.
www.chuongduonghotel.com
Opened in 1999, this is still My Tho's best option, with tastefully decorated rooms and all the mod cons. A popular spot for local weddings,

the open-air Vietnamese restaurant offers great views across the river. **$$**

### Song Tien Hotel
So 101 Trung Trac. Tel: 073-387 2009.
www.tiengtourist.com
One of the brightest hotels in town, rooms are great value and service is good.

The hotel includes a massage service, karaoke rooms and free Wi-fi. **$**

## Ben Tre

### Thai Homestay
Ap 2, Xa Quo Son, Huyen Chau, Thanh Tinh. Tel: 09-1455 7386
The eponymous Mr Thai, and several neighbouring

### PRICE CATEGORIES
Price categories are for a standard double room in peak season.
**$** = under US$20
**$$** = $20–50
**$$$** = $50–100
**$$$$** = $100–150
**$$$$$** = over $150

**ABOVE:** Mui Ne Beach is a windsurfing and kiteboarding hotspot.

families, offer basic facilities and the chance to fish, eat, cook, sing and generally embrace the rural way of life. Thai is a former soldier-turned-guide who speaks English and has a story for every occasion. **$**

**Ham Luong Hotel**
200 Nguyen Van Tu St. Tel: 075-356 0560.
www.hamluongtourist.com.vn
Easily Ben Tre's best hotel is a government-run affair with a swimming pool, sauna and karaoke rooms. Rooms have neutral cream tones with crisp linen. **$$**

## Vinh Long

**Cuu Long Hotel**
02 Phan Boi Chau, Ward 1. Tel: 070-382 3656.
www.cuulongtourist.com
Set right by the river, rooms here are modern, clean and spacious. The old block has now closed, so only this new wing remains. **$**

## Tra Vinh

**Hoan My**
105a Nguyen Thi Minh Khai Road. Tel: 074-862 211.
A beautifully kept hotel with great service and rooms with character makes this amazingly good value. Free Wi-fi is available in every room. **$**

## Can Tho

**Victoria Can Tho**
Cai Khe Ward. Tel: 071-381 0111.
www.victoriahotels-asia.com

This elegant colonial-style resort lies on the banks of the Hau River. Close to town, but tucked away from the action, all its well-appointed rooms feature furnishings that blend traditional handicrafts with colonial-style design. Balconies overlook either the river, pool or gardens. **$$$$**

**Golf Can Tho**
2 Hai Ba Trung St. Tel: 071-381 2210.
www.golfhotel.vnn.vn
One of Can Tho's better options; ask for a room on one of the upper floors to get a balcony facing the river. A buffet breakfast is served at the rooftop café. **$$$**

## Soc Trang

**Ngoc Suong Hotel**
Km 2127, 1A Road, An Hiep, My Tu, Soc Trang. Tel: 079-361 3106
This 3-star hotel is Soc Trang's most upscale option, with well-appointed rooms, an inviting restaurant and a large, clean swimming pool. **$$**

## Long Xuyen

**Dong Xuyen**
9A Luong Van Cu St. Tel: 076-394 2260.
www.angiangtourimex.com.vn
Slap-bang in the middle of town, this is Long Xuyen's most upscale lodgings, and a favourite of travelling businesspeople. Bright and modern, all the rooms have

en-suite bathrooms, A/C and satellite TV. **$**

## Chau Doc

**Victoria Chau Doc**
32 Le Loi St. Tel: 076-386 5010.
www.victoriahotels-asia.com
Built in the traditional French, low-rise architectural style, with tastefully decorated wooden-floor rooms. The swimming pool, restaurant and spa are excellent, and most rooms have river views. **$$$$**

## Ha Tien

**Ha Tien Hotel**
36 Tran Hau St. Tel: 077-385 1563
Centrally located, near the market and waterfront, this is the town's most modern and upscale hotel. Rooms have carpeted floors, tasteful wooden furnishings and soft lighting. Vietnamese and Western cuisine is served in the elegant restaurant. **$**

**Hai Van Hotel**
55 Lam Son St. Tel: 076-385 2872
This is a bright, cheerful and large six-storey hotel. It's worth paying extra for a de luxe room; the comfy bed, windows with views over the town, A/C and cable TV, plus a modern bathroom, make for a pleasant stay. **$**

## Phu Quoc Island

**La Veranda**
Duong Dong Beach, Tran Hung

Dao St. Tel: 077-398 2988.
www.laverandaresort.com
Aiming to re-create a colonial seaside mansion ambience, this luxury boutique resort and spa is the ultimate in romantic indulgence. Centrally located on Duong Dong Beach, its rooms and villas are scattered throughout well-tended tropical gardens. Swimming pool and restaurant. **$$$$$**

**Long Beach Ancient Village Resort and Spa**
Duong To Village. Tel: 077-398 1818
A sanctuary of Vietnamese atmosphere and tradition, this luxury resort blends ancient architectural style with modern touches to create the ultimate island hideaway. Well-appointed guest rooms (basic rooms, duplex and beach-front suites) overlook the blue waters of a natural lagoon. Also features a spa with an amazing variety of indulgent massages and treatments. **$$$$$**

**Mango Bay**
Ong Lang Beach. Tel: 077-398 1693, 0916-488 044.
www.mangobayphuquoc.com
Driven by a passion for the environment, Mango Bay is a truly back-to-nature experience. There is no A/C, TV or telephone in its bungalows made of packed earth. The resort – around 15 to 30 minutes' drive from Duong Dong town – occupies a sprawling site with two splendid beaches and protected forest at its doorstep. Restaurant and bar on site. **$$$**

**Maï House Resort**
Duong Dong City. Tel: 077-384 7003/384 8924, 0918-123 796.
www.maihouseresort.com
Set on a private beach, this resort offers simple yet tastefully decorated rustic bungalows nestled in 2 hectares (5 acres) of well-manicured tropical gardens. Choose from sea-view bungalows, garden-view bungalows or the large hexagonal bungalows on a gentle grassy incline that slopes down to pristine soft sands and shady palm trees. **$$$**

# ACTIVITIES

# FESTIVALS, THE ARTS, NIGHTLIFE, SHOPPING AND SPECTATOR SPORTS

## THE ARTS

The main centres for the arts are Hanoi and, to a lesser degree, Ho Chi Minh City. Outside of these two cites, the pickings are generally slim. Hanoians have an abiding love for the arts, and that love is reflected in the city's numerous venues for traditional art forms. Apart from the enduringly popular water puppet performances, visitors will have difficulty appreciating some of its more esoteric art forms as most are targeted at local audiences. HCMC is less exciting as a centre for the arts. Traditional music, dance and theatre are in decline, and the city's youth is more besotted with Western art forms and culture, although the Opera House does offer quality performances.

## Hanoi

### Performing Arts Venues

**Opera House**, 1 Trang Tien St, Hoan Kiem District, tel: 04-3993 0113; www.ticketvn.com (for ticket booking and reservations). Built in the early 1900s by the French, Hanoi's Opera House holds regular performances of classical and traditional music, as well as dance, by local and foreign artists of note. The performance space is quite small, making for an intimate evening. Call the office or check the booking website for details of performances.
**Youth Theatre**, 11 Ngo Thi Nham St, Hai Ba Trung District, tel: 04-3943 0820; www.ticketvn.com. Home to a performance troupe established in 1978, the stable of

actors who perform at the Youth Theatre (Nha Hat Tuoi Tre) focuses on three art forms: drama, music and dance. The 150-member company regularly performs both Vietnamese and Western classics, and its mime and dance troupes are among the best in the country. Particularly worthwhile are its staging of contemporary Vietnamese dramas, though few have English translations.

### Traditional Vietnamese Theatre

**Cheo Hanoi Theatre**, 15 Nguyen Dinh Chieu St, Hai Ba Trung District, tel: 04-3943 7361. *Cheo* theatre is a uniquely northern Vietnamese folk art that originated in the Red River Delta. The shows – which incorporate dance, music and drama – depict the ordinary struggles and successes of rural Vietnamese, and often without English translation.
**Vietnam National Tuong Theatre**, 51 Duong Thanh St, Hoan Kiem District, tel: 04-3828 7268; www.vietnamtuongtheatre.com. This beautifully restored national theatre has regular performances of excerpts from traditional *tuong* (Vietnamese classical opera). Shows on Wed and Thur at 5pm. Brochures available at the ticket counter provide an English translation of the action on stage.

### Water Puppetry

**Thang Long Water Puppet Theatre**, 57B Dinh Tien Hoang St, Hoan Kiem District, tel: 04-3824 9494; www.thanglongwaterpuppet.org. Skilled puppeteers standing waist-high in an indoor pond bring traditional legends and historic tales to life. An explanation of the plot in English begins the show, but there is no English narration

throughout. Mon–Sat 5.15pm, 6.30pm and 8pm, Sun 9.30am.

### Art Galleries/Shops

Vietnam's art galleries are not formal venues where art is displayed strictly for viewing. They are commercial operations for the most part, aimed at promoting and selling the works of established and up-and-coming artists. Both Hanoi and Ho Chi Minh City have dozens of art galleries and shops, some of which specialise solely in creating reproductions of classic and contemporary pieces. Usually there is no pressure to buy, so feel free to visit to get a better understanding of Vietnamese art.
**Aroma DD**, 2A Ngo Trang Tien St, Hoan Kiem District, tel: 04-3936 1914. Operates as an art dealer as well as an artist-management agent. Specialises in engaging works by established Vietnamese artists as well as newcomers.
**Art Vietnam Gallery**, 7 Nguyen Khac Nhu St, Hoan Kiem District, tel: 04-3927 2349; www.artvietnamgallery.com. One of the city's best, Art Vietnam features compelling and challenging works by a number of talented new and established artists, including Kristine McCarroll and Pham Quang Vinh. Also has an amazing photography section.
**Dogma**, 13 Hang Bac St, Hoan Kiem District, tel: 04-3926 3419; www.dogmavietnam.com. This funky store specialises in reproductions of the country's most famous propaganda art posters. The prints also appear on its range of sweatshirts, T-shirts and mugs.
**Green Palm Gallery**, 15 Trang Tien St, Hoan Kiem District, mobile tel: 091-321 8496; www.greenpalmgallery.com.

This large gallery specialises in typical works featuring scenes from traditional Vietnamese life, as well as some abstract pieces.

**Hanoi Studio**, 13 Trang Tien St, Hoan Kiem District, tel: 04-3934 4433; www.arthanoistudio.com. Founded in 1997, this place exhibits a mixed bag of works by new and established artists. Don't miss the works of Co Chu Pin and Nguyen Lieu.

**L'Espace – Centre Culturel Français de Hanoi**, 24 Trang Tien St, Hoan Kiem District, tel: 04-3936 2164; www.ambafrance-vn.org. Though not exactly an art gallery, L'Espace – the French Cultural Centre – often features works of talented young artists that can't be shown elsewhere. While the government still decides whose works can be publicly shown, it has little say about what goes on display here. Check their website for event details.

**Mai Gallery**, 113 Hang Bong St, Hoan Kiem District, tel: 04-3828 5854; and 3B Phan Huy Chu St, Hoan Kiem District, tel: 04-3825 1225; www.maigallery-vietnam.com. A giant of the Hanoi art scene, the acclaimed Mai Gallery (in both locations) features the works of the country's most renowned contemporary artists, including Nguyen Bao Ha and Nguyen Cong Cu.

**Salon Natasha**, 30 Hang Bong St, Hoan Kiem District, tel: 04-3826 1378. Natasha Kraevskaia and her partner artist Vu Dan Tan established this funky, bohemian art space in 1990. Used as a meeting and work space by a number of renowned and emerging contemporary artists, it features offbeat, eclectic works that never fail to cause a stir.

## Hue

### Performing Arts Venues

**Nha Hac Mua Roi Co Do Hue**, Century Hotel, 49 Le Loi St, tel: 054-383 4779. A small outdoor theatre specialising in water puppetry. The theatre looks more impressive from the outside, but it puts on a decent show, and has a small gift shop selling some of the simpler puppets. Shows are held daily at 3pm, 4.30pm and 8.30pm.

**Royal Theatre**, tel: 054-351 4989, www.nhanhac.com.vn. Located in the heart of the Forbidden City, the Royal Theatre has 30-minute shows

daily at 9.30am and 10.30am, and 2.30pm and 3.30pm. Performances include five or six traditional songs and dances (including lion dancers) in elaborate costumes backed by an orchestra.

## Hoi An

### Performing Arts Venues

**Hoi An Artcraft Manufacturing Workshop**, 9 Nguyen Thai Hoc St. Traditional costumed music and dance shows Mon–Sat at 10.15am and 3.15pm. Admission is part of the Old Town Ticket system.

**Traditional Arts Theatre**, 75 Nguyen Thai Hoc St. Traditional music and dance shows Mon–Sat 9–10pm.

## Ho Chi Minh City

### Performing Arts Venues

**Ho Chi Minh City Conservatory of Music**, 112 Nguyen Du St, District 1, tel: 08-3824 3774; www.hbso.org.vn. Founded in 1956, the conservatory is southern Vietnam's centre for classical (Western) music training, closely affiliated with the Ho Chi Minh City Ballet, Symphony Orchestra and Opera (HBSO). Occasional classical music performances are hosted here.

**IDECAF**, 31 Thai Van Lung St, District 1, tel: 08-3829 5451; www.idecaf.gov.vn. HCMC's French Cultural Centre (L'Institut d'Echanges Culturels avec La France) hosts a variety of performing arts, aimed at promoting French-Vietnamese artistic cooperation. This includes theatre productions, including comedy, drama and a Festival of Music every year on 21 June.

**Municipal Theatre (Opera House)**, 7 Lam Son Square, District 1, tel: 08-3829 9976; www.hbso.org.vn; box office, 8am–8pm performance day; otherwise Mon–Sat 8am–5.30pm; tickets, tel: 08-3925 2265. The grand Municipal Theatre (Opera House), opened in 1899 and renovated a century later, is mainly used by the Ho Chi Minh City Ballet, Symphony Orchestra and Opera (HBSO) and visiting artistes. Classical dance and music performances, including concerts, are held every month on the 9th and 19th. Programmes available at the box office; banners outside advertise forthcoming events.

### Traditional Vietnamese Theatre

Unique, traditional Vietnamese theatre integrates music, singing, dance, recitation and mime with plots, songs and characters familiar to audiences. The three main forms are **Cheo**, **Hat Tuong** and **Cai Luong** (see page 75). Several dedicated Cai Luong theatres still operate, including: Tran Huu Trang, 136 Tran Hung Dao St, District 1, tel: 08-3836 9718. Saigon No. 3 Cai Luong Troupe, 961 Tran Hung Dao St, District 5, tel: 08-3923 5423.

### Water Puppetry

Although a northern tradition, HCMC has its own dedicated water puppet theatre with daily performances. Part of Vietnam's cultural heritage, this is a delightful must-see, especially for children.

**Golden Dragon Water Puppet Theatre**, 55B Nguyen Thi Minh Khai St, District 1, tel: 08-3827 2653; www.goldendragonwaterpuppet.com; daily performances (50 minutes) 6.30pm and 8pm.

### Cultural Dinner Shows

Binh Quoi Tourist Village, 1147 Binh Quoi St, Binh Thanh District, tel: 08-3556 6020; www.binhquoiresort.com.vn. Amid riverside gardens, a cultural show of songs and dances from a traditional southern wedding ceremony are performed while an elaborate Vietnamese dinner is served indoors. Contact travel agent **Saigontourist** (tel: 08-3824 4554), which operates a sunset cruise (Tue, Thur, Sat, 5.30–9.30pm; tour boats depart Bach Dang Pier) along Saigon River to Binh Quoi Tourist Village.

**Cuong Dinh Restaurant**, Rex Hotel, 146–148 Pasteur St, District 1, tel: 08-3829 2185; www.rexhotelvietnam.com. Re-creating the ambience of the Nguyen-dynasty royal court within the Rex Hotel, this elaborate restaurant features traditional folk music and dance performances during lunch and dinner. Popular with tour groups; reservations are advised.

### Art Galleries

Art galleries in HCMC, like those in Hanoi, are generally private art shops with works for sale. The only exception is the **Ho Chi Minh City Fine Arts Museum** (see page 289) and the Duc Minh Art Gallery (31C Le Quy Don St, District 3, tel: 08-3933 0498; daily 9am–noon and 2–6pm; free). Housed in a colonial mansion, this private gallery-museum displays some of the finest pieces of modern-era Vietnamese art (1920s–1980s). The private collection covers more than 1,000 valuable artworks by Vietnamese masters. The basement section displays a rotating collection of these revered paintings, featuring celebrated artists like Bui Xuan Phai. Two upper floors sell more recent contemporary paintings.

### Art Galleries/Art Shops

The influx of wealthy foreign visitors to HCMC has led to a corresponding surge in the city's contemporary art scene. HCMC now has a huge number of art galleries with varying reliability – some sell openly mass-produced art reproductions, while others carry more exciting cutting-edge pieces. The better ones are listed here.

**Apricot Gallery**, 50–52 Mac Thi Buoi St, District 1, tel: 08-3822 7962; www.apricotgallery.com.vn. One of the finest galleries in town, renowned for its savvy art knowledge and collection of paintings by both Vietnam's leading "old masters" and contemporary artists. A sister branch is in Hanoi, and it also owns Thanh Mai Gallery (see below).

**Dogma**, 1/F, 43 Ton That Thiep St, District 1, tel: 08-3821 8272; www.dogmavietnam.com. Displays original propaganda art paintings – Vietnam's historic, unique art form (1945–85); these are not for sale, but the excellent poster reproductions are, along with kitsch propaganda art-adorned gifts, clothing and souvenirs.

**Galerie Quynh**, 65 De Tham St, District 1, tel: 08-3836 8019; www.galeriequynh.com. Deals in contemporary art with an edgy, intellectual slant, by both established and promising young artists. One of the most progressive avant-garde galleries in Vietnam, acknowledged as a main contributor to HCMC's cutting-edge art scene.

**Thanh Mai Art Gallery**, 52 Dong Khoi St, District 1, tel: 08-3824 6076; www.apricot-artvietnam.com. Long-established and reputable, Thanh Mai is an elegant multi-level gallery – one of the largest in town – which mainly focuses on emerging young Vietnamese artists.

**Tu Do Gallery**
53 Ho Tung Mau St, District 1, tel: 08-3821 0966; www.tudogallery.com. One of the city's first privately run art galleries (and owned by a female artist), this family-run gallery focuses

on an eclectic array of artworks by established and emerging artists from south Vietnam.

## FESTIVALS

### Jan–Mar

#### Tet Nguyen Dan

The biggest festival in Vietnam by far, this event marks the Vietnamese lunar new year. Held on the same day as Chinese New Year, it lasts for three days. Rituals include paying respects to their ancestors, visiting friends on New Year's Day and handing "lucky" money placed in red envelopes to children.

#### Ba Den Mountain Festival

Held at Nui Ba mountain, near Tay Ninh, in January or February, this festival honours the daughter of a guard who was forced into an unhappy marriage. She left home to become a nun and eventually died at Nui Ba. Southerners embark on a pilgrimage up the mountain, stopping en route at Ling Son Temple, where vegetarian meals are offered by very hospitable monks.

#### Cau Ngu

Held to honour fishing guru Truong Thieu, this event takes place in mid-January on the coast around Hue. Truong Thieu was a northerner but moved to Thai Duong and taught villagers how to fish and do business. The festival involves a ceremony, where everyone prays for abundant supplies of fish, and is followed by sea-based activities.

#### Quan The Am (Cultural Festival)

Taking place every February, the games and dances that occur here make it a great event for those wanting to better understand local life. Based on Ngu Hanh mountain in Danang, it is part-religious festival and part-excuse for a party. Folk songs, lion dances, floating lamps on the river, chess and handicrafts are just some of the events. First held in 1962, the event honours an Avalokiesvara Bodhisattva statue within a cave in the Marble Mountains.

#### Huong Perfume Pagoda Festival

Held in Ha Tay, around 70km (44 miles) from Hanoi, from January until mid-March, the festival is a chance to visit various pagodas and caves

and mingle with nature-loving locals. Festivals are held in most pagodas as locals pray to the Buddha for good fortune.

### Apr–June

#### Thanh Minh (Holiday of the dead)

During the third lunar month Vietnamese make a point of visiting their ancestors' graves and offering flowers and incense sticks as a way of remembering the dead. This ancient festival was once presided over by royalty.

#### Truong Yen

The former capital of Hoa Lu comes alive every April to remember King Dinh Tien Hoang, who united the country, and King Le Dai Hanh, who saw off foreign invaders. A mock battle, lighting of incense sticks and exhibition of Chinese characters are the highlights.

#### Hung Temple Festival

Sword-fighting, wrestling and rope-climbing are some of the activities held at Nghia Linh Mountain in Phu Tho province each April. The event remembers King Hung I, the nation's founder.

#### Tet Doan Ngo (Summer Solstice)

This mid-year festival aims to help prevent disease and deter pesky evil spirits. Locals believe that everyone has an inner spirit "bug" that needs exterminating, and the best way to do this is by eating sticky rice and downing ruou nep, a type of stodgy rice wine. The wine, as well as killing off any sobriety, is also thought to rid the body of any nasty parasites.

### July–Sept

#### Trung Nguyen (Wandering Souls Day)

This festival takes place all around the country every July. Buddhist in origin, the idea is that worshippers pray that unfounded allegations and gossip about their ancestors be forgotten. It is also a time when souls are said to be set free until sunset, and so food is offered to these wandering souls to keep them placated. If for some reason the spirits don't take up the offerings, the food is given to the poor in the community.

#### Trung Thu (Autumn Festival)

One of the most pleasant of Vietnam's festivals, Trung Thu is held so parents who have been busy harvesting rice can make up for lost time with their children. Youngsters take to the streets clutching brightly decorated lanterns. Moon cakes are one of the traditional offerings. The festival is usually held on 15 August.

### Do Sun (Buffalo Fighting Festival)

One of the more extreme events on the calendar is the buffalo fighting that takes place in Hai Phong each August. The diet, preparation and training that goes on before this event is meticulous, with qualifying matches being held in May ahead of the main festival. The buffaloes go head-to-head (sometimes literally) until one gives up and the other progresses to the next round, until a champion is declared.

### National Day

On 2 September, the whole country remembers Ho Chi Minh's declaration of independence in 1945. Official ceremonies are held, along with less formal events and performances.

## Oct–Dec

### Oc Om Bok Festival

Every mid-November in Soc Trang province, Khmer residents pray to the moon goddess for bumper crops and good fortune. The main spectacle is a wooden boat race.

## Year-round

### Full-Moon Festival

On the 14th of every month, the central town of Hoi An is decorated with silk lanterns to mark the full moon. Men don traditional costumes and play board games, people sing folk songs, and local food, such as *cau lau*, a noodle soup, is eaten. To cater for tourism, similar events now take place every Saturday, full moon or not.

## NIGHTLIFE

In a country where people habitually rise by 5am, it is little surprise that a drink at 9.30pm is considered a wild night out. In the big cities, where incomes are rising and foreign influences felt, this attitude has all but disappeared as a rash of bars and clubs is making its presence felt.

Note: legal drinks licensing in Vietnam is only valid until midnight. Therefore any place of entertainment that stays open later is at the mercy of the enforcement authorities, making Vietnam's nightlife scene a constantly shifting one.

## Hanoi

There are few glitzy clubs or bars as Hanoi's "morality police" are notorious for shutting down any venue that becomes too popular or stays open too late. However, there are a few tried-and-tested venues that do their best to serve the city's late-night crowd.

Depending on the mood of the police and the scheduling of official Party gatherings, even these places can occasionally find themselves forced to shut their doors at midnight or refrain from opening at all.

### Dance Clubs

**Diamond D**, 319 Duong Tay Son St, Thanh Xuan District. A mix of house and electro music attracts a young local crowd. The place can get busy at weekends but service remains friendly and slick.

**Dragonfly**, 15 Hang Buom St, Hoan Kiem District, tel: 04-3926 2177. A newly relocated Hanoi favourite, Dragonfly features good drinks, a dance floor and an upstairs shisha lounge. Welcomes a wide mix of patrons, with nightly drinks specials.

**Funky Buddha**, 2A Ta Hien St, Hoan Kiem District, mobile tel: 091-488 6689. A slick and shiny dance club/lounge on the bar street of Ta Hien. Cool decor, competent staff and a varied clientele of expats, locals and tourists make this a fun spot.

**Ho Guom Xanh Club**, 32 Le Thai To St, Hoan Kiem District, tel: 04-3828 8806. This loud, garish club boasts costumed pole dancers, live singing, gregarious DJs and drinks for triple the going rate. For those wanting to see how Hanoi's young and wealthy live it up, this is the place to go.

**Nutz Bar**, 11 Xuan Dieu St, Tay Ho District, tel: 04-3719 9000. This bar, located in the basement of the Sheraton Hotel, can be relied upon to stay open late (until at least 2am) after all other venues have closed their doors. Drinks are expensive, and the clientele includes a mix of tourists, businessmen and "working girls". Dress code is smart casual.

### Bars and Pubs

**Daluva**, 33 To Ngoc Van, Tay Ho District, tel: 04-3243 4009; www. daluva.com. This wine bar/restaurant serves great tapas and excellent wine and cocktails. The restaurant has a children's room with a nanny available during the daytime, and the bar stays open late.

**G/C Bar**, 5A Bao Khanh St, Hoan Kiem District, tel: 04-3825 0499. Though not explicitly a gay bar, this is known to be LGBT-friendly, and it attracts quite a crowd on weekend nights. Not much to look at in terms of decor, but drinks are cheap and it boasts an excellent pool table.

**Half Man, Half Noodle**, 68 Dao Duy Tu Street, tel: 04-3926 1934. Almost worth visiting for the name alone, this downmarket bar has cheap drinks, good Western music and reasonable food. The second floor has a popular games room.

**Le Pub**, 25 Hang Be St, Hoan Kiem District, tel: 04-3926 2104; www. lepub.org. This is one of those places where travellers, expats and locals mix easily. The location in the Old Quarter is excellent, the music is up to date, there are nightly drinks specials, the food is diverse and good, and the staff are very friendly.

**Mao's Red Room**, 7 Ta Hien St, Hoan Kiem District, tel: 04-3926 3104. This rustic, homely bar offers cheap drinks and cheerful company, and has a devoted clientele of mainly expats.

**Noc Bar – La Scala**, 671 Hoang Hoa Tham St, Ba Dinh District, tel: 04-3761 6812. A chilled rooftop bar and restaurant outside of the city centre overlooking West Lake, and some of the best views over the city.

**R&R Tavern**, 47 Lo Su St, Hoan Kiem District, tel: 04-3934 4109; www.rockandrolltavern-hanoi.com. Probably the first American-run joint in Hanoi, R&R Tavern opened in 1995 and has established itself as the classic American bar in the capital. Spacious and airy, the downstairs bar area features live bands while upstairs has more of a lounge feel. Serves some of the city's best Mexican food.

## Hue

There aren't a lot of options for nightlife in Hue, but the few bars in town are well patronised and lively.

### Bars and Pubs

**B4 Bar**, 75 Ben Nghe St. A Belgian-run bar with imported Belgian beer. Happy hours are from 4–7pm. The atmosphere is relaxed and friendly.

**DMZ Bar & Café**, 60 Le Loi St, tel: 054-382 3414; www.dmz-bar.com. The liveliest backpacker bar in town,

with very loud music. The top floor is an outlet of **Little Italy Restaurant** (tel: 054-382 6928). There is a pool table and free internet with computer terminals upstairs. Open until late.
**Why Not? Bar**, 21 Vo Thi Sau St, tel: 054-382 4793. A small but popular corner bar owned by a couple of foreigners. It has a pleasant atmosphere with eclectic decor and serves typical backpacker food. Pool table downstairs.

## Danang

Danang is relatively quiet in the evenings. Other than two cinemas on Tran Phu Street or walking along the riverfront, most locals spend their evenings at one of the city's many cafés that serve both booze and food.

### Bars, Pubs and Cafés

**Bao Nam Tran**, 27 Nguyen Chi Thanh St, tel: 0511-388 9889. An excellent café with a long list of cheap drinks and snacks. The atmosphere is enchanting (housed in traditional, 200-year-old wooden houses lit by Hue lanterns) and the service is excellent.
**Camel Club**, 16 Ly Thuong Kiet St, tel: 0511-388 7462. This is the only truly lively nightspot in town. The music is loud and the drinks pricey.
**Paloma Café**, Lot 1, Nguyen Chi Thanh St, tel: 0511-388 9833. This lively corner café has two floors and several flat-screen satellite TVs. The dance tunes shake up the room. Open from 8pm nightly.

## Hoi An

Quiet, quaint Hoi An has surprisingly lively nightlife. All the best bars are within walking distance of most hotels, and open until late.

### Bars

**Before & Now**, 51 Le Loi St. Tel: 0510-910 599. A popular spot with funky, modern decor and a broad menu of Vietnamese, Italian and fusion cuisine.
**Green Chili**, 122 Nguyen Thai Hoc St, tel: 0510-392 8199; www. greenchilihoian.com. As much a great restaurant as a bar, Green Chili serves great Vietnamese, Mediterranean and Tex-Mex dishes.
**Lounge Bar**, 102 Nguyen Thai Hoc St, tel: 0510-391 0480. Set in an old merchant house, this watering hole has a long list of drinks, tasty snacks and nice local atmosphere.
**Tam Tam Café**, 110 Nguyen Thai

Hoc St, tel: 0510-386 2212. The downstairs is a clone of the Cargo Club across the street, but upstairs has numerous private sitting areas and large open spaces, as well as a pool table.
**Treat's Café**, 158 Tran Phu St, tel: 0510-386 1125. This backpacker favourite is always full, especially during happy hours from 4–9pm. There are several other places around town by the same (or similar) name, but this original is the most popular.
**White Marble Restaurant & Wine Bar**, 98 Le Loi St, tel: 0510-391 1862. A foody favourite with lots of vegetarian options; be sure to try the "Hoi An Money Bags". As expected, there is an extensive wine list that won't disappoint.

## Nha Trang

After HCMC and Hanoi, Nha Trang has the most active nightlife in the country. There are numerous bars and pubs and, unlike other centres of tourism, the night-time venues here stay open until after midnight. Unfortunately, the presence of tourists and large amounts of alcohol also attract the underbelly of society; men should guard their wallets when approached by prostitutes. Nha Trang's working girls have a habit of walking up to strangers and putting one hand around their shoulders while rifling through their pockets with the other.

### Bars, Pubs and Clubs

**007**, 3 Hung Vuong St. Located along a strip of cafés and billiards halls at the north end of the backpacker district. This dance club with loud music is open until late and attracts a trendy crowd.
**Guava**, 17 Biet Thu St, tel: 058-352 4140. A very social hangout – the cushioned sofas are arranged so that no matter where you sit you'll be in the thick of things and quickly making new friends. Some evenings feature live music.
**Krazy Kim's**, 19 Biet Thu St, tel: 058-352 3072. Krazy Kim's is a very popular backpacker bar with varied music, great pizzas and bar food, themed party nights and a wide selection of drinks. Happy hours 10am–10pm.
**Louisiane Brewhouse**, Lot 29, Tran Phu St, tel: 058-352 1948. This popular beachside bar with swimming pool offers a great selection of drinks (including a selection of in-house brews) and international food. Expat bands play three times weekly (Wed, Fri and Sat). This is one of the few

places that are just as happening any time of the day. Open until very late.
**The Sailing Club**, 72–74 Tran Phu St, tel: 058-352 4628; www. sailingclubvietnam.com. This Australian-owned hangout is one of the best-known nightspots in Vietnam. The orange stucco walls, thatched roofs with dark-wood pillars, and spacious sitting areas make it feel more like a resort than a bar or restaurant. Famous for its wild, party atmosphere (in high season) on the beach-front terraces. Open until late.

## Dalat

Dalat has a very subdued nightlife. The market – particularly the stairs and ramps leading to it – is full of vendors in the evenings selling local snacks and souvenirs. The strip of cafés above the market is a popular hangout in the evenings for Vietnamese and tourists alike.

### Bars and Cafés

**Larry's Bar**, Dalat Palace, 12 Tran Phu St, tel: 063-382 5444. Charming place with old stone walls and hidden in the former wine cellar of the hotel. This is one of the few relaxed bars in Vietnam where backpackers, English-language teachers, golf pros and Dalat's expat crowd mingle freely after hours.
**My Town**, 98 Truong Cong Dinh St, tel: 063-352 2099. This eclectic bar, art gallery and vegetarian restaurant is a popular hangout for backpackers and career-aged travellers, with funky bamboo decor and furniture. Pool table upstairs.
**The Hangout**, 71 Truong Cong Dinh St, tel: 063-351 0822; www. thehangoutcafe.com. The friendly owners have created a perfect place for backpackers and other travellers to chill, with pool tables, TV and beer.
**U & Me**, 14 Nguyen Chi Thanh St, tel: 063-383 1876. The front porch is a popular hangout after dark, facing the central market. The food and drinks are good, and occasionally you can pick up Wi-fi signals from the surrounding cafés.
**Whynot Café**, 24 Nguyen Chi Thanh St, tel: 063-383 2540. The classiest café in town. This café has a large flat-screen TV on each floor, showing American films. After 7pm the dance music upstairs cranks up to mind-numbing volumes. Free Wi-fi.

## Ho Chi Minh City

During the Vietnam War, Saigon was legendary for its notorious bars and

**ABOVE:** Sax n' Art in HCMC

clubs catering to American GIs. HCMC has never quite recaptured that heady wartime spirit – a long-running, police-enforced midnight curfew for bars and some clubs helps ensure that such a scene is unlikely to return soon.

As the main commercial hub of Vietnam, HCMC has many hip, cosmopolitan bars that keep the burgeoning ranks of expats, business travellers, tourists and moneyed locals happy. Although HCMC's clubbing scene lags behind other major Asian cities, its club and bar scene is getting better. The scene is extremely fickle, however, with clubs opening, closing and losing favour on a regular basis.

The official midnight curfew has exceptions, and closing times fluctuate; those in the backpacker area (around Pham Ngo Lao and De Tham streets) seem to stay open until much later. Practically all bars and clubs are located in District 1.

### Dance Clubs

**Apocalypse Now**, 2B Thi Sach St, District 1, tel: 08-3825 6124. This legendary club has been going more than 20 years and is now something of an institution. Named after the iconic movie that was based on the war in Vietnam, the club has contemporary dance music, pool, occasional live bands and is gay-friendly. The 150,000VND cover charge includes a drink.
**Bounce**, 4/F, Parkson Saigontourist Plaza, 35–45 Le Thanh Ton St, District 1, tel: 08-3824 8555. Intimate club on the fourth floor of

a glitzy department store – popular with the local business crowd and trendy people. Resident DJs play the latest sounds, including hip hop, to keep dancers happy on the compact dance floor.
**Gossip**, 79 Tran Hung Dao St, District 1, tel: 08-3824 2602. This long-time nightspot is popular with young Saigonese (and some foreigners) into serious clubbing. A cavernous two-floor establishment with one of the few proper dance floors in town. Creative lighting, and groovy sounds and DJs keep the atmosphere electric.
**Lush**, 2 Ly Tu Trong St, District 1. Established by a San Francisco native, this is one of HCMC's hippest, hottest clubs, jam-packed most nights with an eclectic crowd. Lush offers an infectious party atmosphere with cool sounds and trendy DJs. Gay-friendly.
**Nightspot Level 23**, 23/F, Sheraton Saigon Hotel, 88 Dong Du St, District 1, tel: 08-3827 2828; www.sheraton. com/saigon. Smart nightclub in the Sheraton, with nightly live performances by international bands and large dance floor. Service and drinks prices reflect the 5-star surroundings. If you don't like the music, the fabulous 23rd-floor views should compensate.
**Sax n' art**, 28 Le Loi St, District 1, tel: 08-3822 8472; www.saxnart. com. HCMC's premier jazz and blues club is a suave, intimate venue, with black-and-white photos and vintage saxophones displayed on the walls. Live performances nightly (after 9pm), featuring well-known saxophonist-owner Tran Manh Tuan with his house band,

plus occasional international guest musicians.

### Bars

**GO2 Bar**, 187 De Tham St, District 1, tel: 08-3836 9575. One of the most popular haunts in the heart of the backpacker area, this airy, neon-lit spot has a busy bar spilling out on the street. Packed most nights with a wildly diverse crowd – all attracted by the late opening hours and informal, buzzing atmosphere.
**La Habana**, 6 Cao Ba Quat St, District 1, tel: 08-3829 5180; www.lahabana-saigon.com. Delightful piece of Cuba in downtown HCMC. Intimate Cuban-Spanish bar with Cuban-inspired interiors and drinks, including carajillos, sangria and mojitos. Also hand-rolled cigars, traditional Spanish tapas and seafood paella. Live guitar performances plus salsa classes.
**Park Lounge**, Park Hyatt Saigon, 2 Lam Son Square, District 1, tel: 08-3520 2359; www.saigon.park.hyatt.com. Expect old-world elegance, with floor-to-ceiling louvred windows, teak floors and chaises longues. Classical resident pianist and a jazz/blues singer add to its refinement.
**Q BAR**, 7 Lam Son Square, District 1, tel: 08-3823 3479; www.qbarsaigon.com. Ensconced in the Opera House, the long-established, cavernous Q Bar features Renaissance-inspired wall murals that contrast with leopard-print couches and ultraviolet-lit bars. With its guest European DJs, themed party nights and sophisticated cocktails, glamorous Q attracts a cosmopolitan ensemble of locals, expats and celebrities.

**Rex Rooftop Garden Bar**, Rex Hotel, 141 Nguyen Hue St, District 1, tel: 08-3829 2185; www.rexhotelvietnam. com. The service may leave a lot to be desired, but this fifth-floor, rooftop terrace bar is a HCMC institution and tourist "must-do". Expect great views over central downtown, live nightly music, old-fashioned charm and the rare attraction of all-night drinking.

**Saigon Saigon Bar**, 10/F, Caravelle Hotel, 19 Lam Son Square, District 1, tel: 08-3823 4999; www. caravellehotel.com. During the Vietnam War, this was an infamous watering hole for war correspondents. Today, the 10th floor rooftop bar is still popular for its superb skyline views from the outdoor terrace, excellent drinks list and upbeat, nightly live entertainment.

**Sheridan's Irish House**, 17/13–17/14 Le Thanh Ton St, District 1, tel: 08-3823 0793; www. sheridansvietnam.com. Traditional Irish pub interior and a welcoming, family-orientated ambience. Live bands perform nightly. The extensive menu offers hearty Irish and British dishes, including Sunday roasts.

**Velvet Bar**, 26 Ho Huan Nghiep, District 1, tel: 08-222 262. A stylish lounge bar with a mix of trendy locals and foreigners, Velvet Bar has its own DJ playing contemporary tracks.

**Xu Restaurant-Lounge and Café-Bar**, 71–75 Hai Ba Trung St, District 1, tel: 08-3824 8468; www.xusaigon. com. Upstairs is an über-hip lounge-restaurant with contemporary decor, while downstairs is the informal café-bar with minimalist blonde-wood furnishings and chandeliers. Expect snappy service, gourmet all-day cuisine, mellow sounds, fine wines and innovative cocktails (like coconut Martinis and lemongrass sake-tinis).

## Vung Tau

Vung Tau is a very quiet place in the evenings, unless you care to join the crowds from HCMC at its karaoke bars, or expats at one of the town's dingy hole-in-the-wall bars. The nicest evening spots are the local cafés, with cheap drinks and lively atmospheres.

### Cafés

**Bluenote Café**, 6 Tran Hung Dao St, tel: 064-353 2246. This inexpensive but nice Vietnamese café, set on the corner of Tran Hung Dao Square, is a great place to watch the evening buzz from the terrace. Inside has air conditioning and satellite TV.

**Café Hoa Su**, 6 Tran Phu St (below Villa Blanche), tel: 064-385 5963. Ocean-side views under a canopy of frangipani blooms. There is no English menu, but with all drinks under a dollar, you can afford to experiment.

## Mui Ne Beach

Until a few years ago, Mui Ne was dead by 9pm. New bars and pubs are springing up quickly today, offering something for every taste. Most of the large resorts have bars with mediocre live music; more appealing are the independent spots that are open late.

### Bars and Pubs

**Dany's Pub**, 58 Nguyen Dinh Chieu St, tel: 062-384 7111; www. cocobeach.net. A small and simple Irish pub inside the resort, Dany's is the best place to catch sports games on their widescreen.

**Déjà Vu Restaurant**, Bar & Garden, 21 Nguyen Dinh Chieu St, tel: 062-374 1276. Popular with Russian tourists, Déjà Vu is a good family option with billiards, projection TVs and plenty of games.

**Hoa Vien Brauhaus**, 2A Nguyen Dinh Chieu St, tel: 062-374 1383; www.hoavien.vn. The newest outlet of the well-known HCMC and Hanoi microbrewery chain has great beer – both dark and light – and one of the loveliest locations on the beach.

**Hot Rock**, tel: 062-374 3086. Decent food, loud music, a pool table and a central location have made this old haunt a popular spot.

**Jibes**, 90 Nguyen Dinh Chieu St, tel: 062-384 7405; www.windsurf-vietnam.com. Jibes is a haven for kiteboarders and backpackers. One of the only two beachside bars in town, this is also the oldest bar in town. Plays the latest tunes at head-pounding decibels.

**Joe's Café**, 155 Nguyen Dinh Chieu St, tel: 062-374 3447. Joe's is one of the only 24-hr venues in Mui Ne, with live music in the evenings and great sandwiches, pasta and pizza. Owned by an American-Vietnamese husband and wife team; the food, entertainment and service is of an international standard..

**Snow**, 109 Nguyen Dinh Chieu St, tel: 062-374 3123. Another popular spot for Russian families, Snow is the only bar with A/C and live piano music.

## SHOPPING

## Hanoi

For those with money to burn and space in their suitcase, Hanoi is a shopper's paradise. Exquisite silks, colourful lacquerware, gems, silver and hand-tailored clothing can all be found at reasonable prices within the city centre.

In the Old Quarter, Hang Gai (Silk Street) has a clutch of top-notch silk shops, while south on trendy Nha Tho Street, clothing, handbags and home-decor items abound.

Throughout the Old Quarter, shops flog all manner of water puppets, scarves, fake war mementoes and old-fashioned Tin Tin posters.

The general rule when shopping is that if there's no price tag, the price can be negotiated. In higher-end shops, items will have fixed prices.

In the city's bright, air-conditioned malls, shops selling brand-name electronics, clothing and cosmetics do a booming business thanks to a new generation of affluent Vietnamese consumers. But for tourists, aside from revelling in the cool air or escaping a sudden downpour, there's little reason to linger in these places.

### Antiques

Vietnam has very strict regulations on the sale and export of genuine antiques, and as such, most "antique" art pieces sold to tourists are fakes or copies. If someone claims they are selling an original piece, ask to see a certificate of authenticity and ownership.

For the best "antique" repros, the small shops along Hang Gai and Hang Bong in the Old Quarter are a good source, as is Nghi Tam Street in Tay Ho District. Whereas Hang Gai and Hang Bong shops deal in tourist items, the ones along Nghi Tam specialise in pricier high-quality cast-iron statues, stone Buddhas and other fascinating bric-a-brac.

### Silk

No trip to Hanoi – or Vietnam – would be complete without purchasing some ridiculously cheap but exquisite silk. Compared with Thailand, Vietnamese silk is of slightly inferior quality, but the prices are lower and tailoring services are top-notch. In the many silk shops along Hang Gai Street, customers can choose from rolls of taffeta, Vietnamese silk and organza, and have gorgeous suits, dresses and gowns made to fit in record time. Many visitors opt to have a tailor-made ao dai, Vietnam's national dress, which comprises silk trousers under a fitted, elegant tunic-style dress.

**F Silk**, 82 Hang Gai St, Hoan Kiem

District, tel: 04-3928 6786. This long-established silk shop has an endless selection of beautiful silks and well-designed garments at prices slightly lower than the upscale Khai Silk.

**Kenly Silk**, 108 Hang Gai St, Hoan Kiem District, tel: 04-3826 7236; www.kenlysilk.com. This silk and clothing shop can count the USA's Clintons and a few Southeast Asian royals among its clientele.

**Khai Silk**, 96 Hang Gai St, Hoan Kiem District, tel: 04-3825 4237; 121 Nguyen Thai Hoc St, Ba Dinh District, tel: 04-3823 3508; and 56 Ly Thai To St, Hoan Kiem District, tel: 04-3934 8968 (inside Metropole Hotel); www.khaisilkcorp.com. The Khai Silk empire – which includes numerous restaurants, a resort, and shops all over the country – is the brainchild of Hoang Khai, whose skill with silk and tailoring is unmatched. Today the biggest name in the country, Khai Silk offers an expensive range of stunning silks, fabrics and gorgeous clothing.

## Fashion

Not exactly renowned as a fashion capital, Hanoi does have a number of exciting new designers working hard to establish their labels and opening shops throughout the country. Some of the best include:

**Ipa-Nima**, 34 Han Thuyen St, Hai Ba Trung District, tel: 04-3933 4000; www.ipanima.com. Christina Yu from Hong Kong started this often imitated handbag and accessory company in 1997. Features high-quality handbags and purses along with funky jewellery. Has a sister shop named **Tina Sparkle** (17 Nha Tho St, Hoan Kiem District, tel: 04-3928 7616) in the Old Quarter.

**Le Vent**, 7B and 31C Ly Quoc Su St, Hoan Kiem District, tel: 04-3628 6774. Run by a young Vietnamese designer, traditional designs are given a modern slant. The items are simple, of high quality and all handmade.

**Marie-Linh**, 11 Nha Tho St, Hoan Kiem District, tel: 04-3928 6304; www.marie-linh.com. This Vietnamese-run clothing and accessory store does beautiful pants, shirts and dresses in linen, and also features a slew of home-decor items.

**Song**, 27 Nha Tho St, Hoan Kiem District, tel: 04-3928 8733; www.valeriegregorimckenzie.com. The French designer who creates the elegant clothing at Song named her boutique after the Vietnamese word for "life". The flagship store on Nha Tho features simple but beautiful clothing in international sizes, as well as quilts, blankets and home-decor items.

## Gems and Jewellery

Hang Bac (Gold Street) is home to many of Hanoi's gold and gold jewellery dealers. These small street-side shops generally have their wares displayed in glass cabinets, mainly thick gold chains, jade and Buddha pendants, and some silver. Few shop owners speak English as they serve a primarily Vietnamese clientele. The shop listed below deals mainly in original jewellery designs.

**Huong's Jewellery Shop**, 62 Hang Ngang St, Hoan Kiem District, tel: 04-3828 1046. This small jewellery shop may not look like much from the outside, but inside it has the best Vietnam has to offer in terms of silver jewellery, pearls and jade. Mrs Huong, the owner, is also proficient at copying and reproducing treasured pieces of jewellery.

## Handicrafts and Home Decor

**Chi Vang**, 17 Trang Tien St, Hoan Kiem District, tel: 04-3936 0027. This little boutique is famous for its hand-embroidered bed linens, tablecloths, curtains, pillowcases and cushions.

**Craftlink**, 43 Van Mieu St, Ba Dinh District, tel: 04-3843 7710; www.craftlink.com.vn. This not-for-profit organisation/shop provides a place where ethnic minority people can sell their crafts and clothing at fair rates. Pick up some beautiful jewellery, embroidery and small souvenirs with the knowledge that your money is going back into the community.

**Dome**, 71-B6 Hang Trong St, Hoan Kiem District, tel: 04-3928 7677; www.dome.com.vn. This high-end furniture and home-accessory shop is a favourite among Hanoi's expats. For those not in the market for lusciously thick pillows and sofas, the home-wares section has some beautiful lacquer boxes, bags, shoes and picture frames.

**Lacquers Shop**, 10A Dinh Liet St, Hoan Kiem District, tel: 04 3934 1165. The English-speaking owner in this shop is knowledgeable and offers quality handicrafts.

**La Boutique**, 9 Xuan Dieu St, Tay Ho District, tel: 04-3716 0400. Features gorgeous blankets, pillows, throws and other home-decor pieces by **Velvet Underground**, one of the country's best home accessory brands.

**Mosaique**, 22 Nha Tho St, Hoan Kiem District, tel: 04-3928 6181; 6 Ly Quoc Su, Hoan Kiem District, tel: 04-6270 0430; www.mosaiquedecoration.com. Long-established boutique known for its high-quality furnishings and house wares that blend traditional

Vietnamese motifs with modern styles. Also features jewellery and clothing by local designers.

**Nagu**, 20 Nha Tho St, Hoan Kiem District, tel: 04-3928 8020; www.zantoc.com. This Japanese-run shop sells a funky mix of decorative knick-knacks – candle holders, laundry baskets, picture frames – along with some stylish clothing.

**Tes Décor**, 9 Lot 14B Trung Yen St, Trung Hoa, Cau Giay District, tel: 04-3784 8802. For the serious shopper, this excellent home-decor and lighting shop features handmade Vietnamese furniture and exotic and unique imported crafts from abroad.

**Vietnam Quilts**, 16 Hang Tre St, Hoan Kiem District, tel: 04-3926 3682; www.vietnam-quilts.org. This not-for-profit quilt shop provides employment for rural women so that they can remain in their communities and care for their children. The beautiful handmade quilts can be made to order in any design.

## Shopping Centres

**Hanoi Towers**, 49 Hai Ba Trung Street, Hoan Kiem District. Nothing flash. Only one floor of shopping, which includes a grocery store, a clothing store and some home-decor shops.

**Vincom City Towers**, 191 Ba Trieu Street, Hai Ba Trung District. This large shopping mall has multiple floors of shopping (Western clothing, electrical appliances, cosmetics), as well as Hanoi's first and only multiplex cinema on the sixth floor. Popular with Hanoi's upper classes.

## Hue

Hue has some great shopping, but most of it is spread out in the main tourist districts. A number of artists have opened galleries around the hotels and restaurants where tourists congregate, selling fine art rather than the cheap reproductions found in most backpacker areas.

The larger of the two tourist districts, on the lanes between Le Loi and Tran Cao Van streets – where the Perfume and Nhung rivers meet – is one of the best shopping areas in the city. Here you'll find a number of art galleries and shops selling lanterns, lacquerware, woodcarvings and antiques. Beware of the perfume jars and other items made of ivory. While most are probably fakes, the few that aren't are illegal.

## Markets

**Dong Ba Market**. Hue's Central Market sits to the right of Trang Tien

Bridge on the Citadel side of the Perfume River. It's more for locals than tourists, but some souvenirs can be found, including conical hats. It's also a great place to sample local food and sweets.

### Shopping Centre

**Coop Mart**. At the time of press, this new shopping centre was being built at the southwest corner of Don Ba Market. Coop Mart typically have a Western-style grocery store, department store, a bookstore, food court and souvenir shops.

### Lacquer Work and Painting

**Newspace Art Gallery**, 28 Pham Ngu Lao St, tel: 054-384 9353; www.newspacearts.com. Modern lacquerworks by twin brothers Le Duc Hai and Le Ngoc Thanh. Motifs include human faces, fish, birds and other animals.

**Paintings by Pham Trinh**, 24 Pham Ngu Lao St, tel: 054-382 5287; www.phamtrinhart.com. Award-winning artist Pham Quang Trinh's gallery features modern lacquer and oil on canvas pieces. Themes include daily village life, agriculture and fishing. Fish and water buffalo are prominent motifs.

### Silk Embroidery

**Thien Nam**, 7 Vo Thi Sau St, tel: 054-222 9036. High-quality embroidery with beautiful compositions and tight stitch-work. Excellent value.

**XQ**, 49 Le Loi St, tel: 054-382 5026; www.xqhandembroidery.com. This outlet of Vietnam's top producer of silk embroidery is a smaller version of the XQ Historical Village in Dalat. Besides having a large selection of fine artwork for sale, there are also nightly live music performances and a small snack bar.

### Clothing

**Bambou**, 21 Pham Ngu Lao St, tel: 054-383 0482; www.bamboucompany.com. This is an outlet of the popular T-shirt company and one of the few local brand-name clothing vendors that produces quality stuff.

## Danang

Danang has many excellent shopping venues, although they are spread out around town. Expect cheaper prices than you'll find in Hue or Hoi An, since there are fewer foreign tourists in the city.

### Markets

**Con Market** (Cho Con), on the corner of Ong Ich Khiem and Hung Vuong streets. A daily-needs sort of market, this is the largest in Danang, although it's recently been somewhat displaced by the new Big C shopping centre.

**Han Market** (Cho Han), on the corner of Hung Vuong and Tran Phu streets. A great place to find candied fruits, dried seafood snacks and souvenirs. This market is popular with both foreign and Vietnamese tourists.

### Shopping Centre

**Big C**, opposite corner from Con Market. This is a Saigon-style shopping centre with a modern grocery store, department store, jewellery and handbag shops, a Highlands Café, Lotteria fast-food restaurant and a cinema.

### Crafts

**Thanh Tam School Gift Shop**, 47 Yen Bay St, tel: 0511-382 4735; http://homepage.internet.lu/spcdanang. Sells a variety of local crafts including minority-doll bookmarks and embroidery, made by disabled children under the care of the Catholic nuns at Danang Cathedral.

### Silk Fabrics and Tailors

**Lan Huong Silk Shop**, 65 Phan Chu Trinh St, tel: 090-645 0031; www.danangsilk.com. Besides custom-tailored clothing, this shop also sells retail and wholesale fabrics as well as embroidery.

**Ngoc Diep**, 114 Hoang Dieu St, tel: 0511-382 8949. Another silk and tailor shop recommended by local expats. Fast turnaround. An alternative to Hoi An's touristy shops.

### Traditional Crafts

**Gom Viet**, 176 Tran Phu St, tel: 0511-382 6714. This is an outlet of the popular national chain, offering modern ceramics and pottery based on ethnic designs.

**Khanh Ha**, 77 Tran Quoc Toan St, tel: 0511-322 6359. Specialising in pictures made of embroidered silk and exotic materials like stone, sand, butterfly wings, bamboo, feathers and other natural materials.

**XQ Danang**, 39–41 Nguyen Thai Hoc St, tel: 0511-381 6847. A small outlet store of Vietnam's top silk embroiderer. Also sells its trademark silk paintings.

## Hoi An

Hoi An's Old Town has some of the best shopping in Vietnam. For many years, Hoi An has been known as the centre of silk fabric and tailor shops, many of which are housed in the old Chinese merchant shophouses. While tailoring is key to Hoi An's economy, in recent years an increasing number of souvenir shops have joined the commercial fray.

### Markets

**Hoi An Central Market**. Located across from Quang Cong Temple at the end of Nguyen Hue Street. You will find better bargains on souvenirs here than at any of the shops in town.

### Jewellery

**Memory Jewellery Design**, 04 Hoang Van Thu St, tel: 04-3910 1314. Beautiful, decorative jewellery made with semi-precious stones and natural materials.

**Ngoc Duc**, 147 Tran Phu St, tel: 0510-386 2390. Handmade gold and silver jewellery with pearls and semi-precious stones.

### Souvenirs and Crafts

**Art Handicraft Workshop**, 09 Nguyen Thai Hoc St, tel: 0510-391 0216; www.hoianhandicraft.com. An extensive collection of traditional crafts, woodcarvings, silver jewellery and stonework. The highlight is the large display of traditional lanterns.

**Hung Phat**, 10 Nguyen Thai Hoc St, mobile tel: 090-631 5896. Hand-carved wooden frames and pictures made from coloured wood and bamboo. The shop occupies a traditional merchant shop.

**Reaching Out**, 103 Nguyen Thai Hoc St, tel: 0510-386 2460; www.reachingoutvietnam.com. Next to the Tam Ky House. This is one of the nicest shops in town; its high-quality crafts are made on the premises by disabled youth. The large selection includes brass work, jewellery, ceramics, dolls and puppets made with ethnic fabrics.

### Tailors

If you're planning to have clothing tailored in Hoi An, try to do it as soon as you arrive in town. This is to allow time for fittings and alterations in case the finished product is not up to standard. Tailors have a tendency to rush their work, knowing full well that their customers are only here for a few days and that most won't bother coming back to complain if they're not satisfied with their outfits. Below are two of the more reputable tailors in town.

**BiBi Silk**, 13 Phan Chu Trinh St. Fine garments tailored from silk, wool and linen. The service is fast, friendly and the staff are knowledgeable.

**Yaly Fashion Town**, 358 Nguyen Duy Hieu St, tel: 0510-391 4995; www. yalycouture.com. Hoi An's top tailor has an extensive showroom and open factory. No deposits are required – pay only when you are satisfied. Other products include hand embroidery, hand-woven silk rugs, shoes and jewellery.

## Nha Trang

Nha Trang has decent souvenir shopping around the tourist district. You'll mostly find the sort of speciality stores seen in other big cities. There aren't a lot of products made locally, apart from the Cham crafts at nearby Po Nagar.

### Market

**Dam Market**. Set in the old Chinese Quarter, this atmospheric market spills onto the streets and occupies several old Chinese merchant shops. Here you'll find everything from dried seafood to inexpensive clothing, snacks and a plethora of souvenirs. This is one of the least touristy points of interest in the city.

### Cham Crafts

**Hue-Duong**, Po Nagar Cham Towers, 2/4 St, Vinh Hai Ward, mobile tel: 091-882 4235. This shop sells hand-woven blankets, bags and crafts that incorporate traditional Cham designs and fabrics. Many are created on site using wooden looms.

### Silk Embroidery

**XQ Nha Trang**, 64 Tran Phu St, tel: 058-352 6579; www. xqhandembroidery.com. This outlet of the country's leading silk embroidery company sells both embroidered paintings and traditional ao dai outfits. Visitors can watch the women create the artwork here in the craft village. The prices are high, but so is the quality.

## Dalat

Most of the shopping in Dalat revolves around edible treats, but good buys in exquisite silk embroidery and minority fabrics also abound.

### Markets

**Dalat Central Market** is a haven for treats like candied fruit, deer jerky, artichoke tea and strawberry wine. Cheap clothing can be found on the upper floors, interspersed with souvenirs here and there. You'll find fresh produce on the lowest level,

while the second floor of the middle building has numerous food stalls.

### Miscellaneous

**Domain du Marie Convent**, 6 Ngo Quyen St. This French convent has a wonderful gift shop with an extensive selection of home made fruit candies and wines. There is also a small section of unique, silk-embroidered pictures with designs that you won't find anywhere else and a large selection of knitted sweaters and other clothing. Proceeds benefit local orphans, the homeless and the disabled.

### Silk Embroidery

**XQ Historical Village**, 258 Mai Anh Dao St, tel: 063-383 1343; www.xqhandembroidery.com. This is the home office of the country's top silk embroidery company. This location is a theme park for the art, with embroidered paintings, ao dai (Vietnamese traditional dress), jewellery, handbags and silk crafts for sale.

## Ho Chi Minh City

Shopping in HCMC has dramatically improved in recent years, and it is fast emerging as a key Asian shopping and design hub. Although still a source of mass-produced cheap goods, Vietnam's undisputed shopping capital now offers stylish, home-grown stores selling contemporary stuff at down-to-earth prices. Local talent and HCMC-based international designers create exceptional home accessories, furniture, lighting, modern art and clothing. The shopping scene is still dominated by Vietnam's centuries-old traditional crafts, like silk, lacquer, ceramics and embroidery, which are all enjoying a remarkable renaissance. Many innovative designers combine ancient artisanal techniques with contemporary designs to create both decorative and practical goods.

### Ceramics

**Authentique**, 6 Dong Khoi St, tel: 08-3823 8811. Piles of delicate ceramics in many styles, colours and sizes, some displayed warehouse-style in baskets. Everything from sake pots and espresso cups to large vases.
**Gom Viet Fine Arts**, 91A Pasteur St, tel: 08-3823 1636; www.gomviet.net. Rich brown earthenware created with traditional techniques, but moulded into modern home accessories, ornaments and art pieces.

### Home Decor, Furniture and Gifts

**Dong Duong**, 45 Dong Khoi St, tel: 08-3827 3748. Fantastic little pieces are on sale here, from Chinese board games to all manner of smoking paraphernalia.
**Gaya**, 1 Nguyen Van Trang St, tel: 08-3914 3769; www.gayavietnam. com. Vietnam's first international designer showroom, showcasing stylish, quality home decor, furniture, lighting, accessories and gifts, all hand-crafted in Vietnam but designed by locally based international designers.
**Saigon Kitsch**, G/F, 43 Ton That Thiep St, tel: 08-3821 8019. This kooky, brightly coloured store has an equally kitsch collection of home wares, accessories and gifts – many with Vietnamese propaganda-art themes.

### Embroidery and Needlework

**Catherine Denoual Maison**, 15C Thi Sach St, tel: 08-3823 9394; www. catherinedenoual.com. Resident French designer's exclusive store showcases bedding and table linens made from top-notch imported fabrics with hand-embroidered patterns inspired by nature.
**Kim Phuong**, 110A Nguyen Hue St, tel: 08-3823 2094; www.kimphuong. net. Operating since 1989, Kim Phuong and sister branch **Bao Nghi** (4–6 Le Loi St) specialise in traditional hand-embroidered bedding and table linens on fine white cottons and crisp linens.
**Vietnam Quilts**, 26/1 Le Thanh Ton St, tel: 08-3825 1441; www.vietnam-quilts.org. This non-profit community development organisation offers ongoing employment for women in impoverished southern areas through the sales of lovely handmade cotton bed quilts. Can also custom-make.

### Fashion

**Ipa-Nima**, 85 Pasteur St, tel: 08-3824 2701; www.ipa-nima.com. Flamboyant, coquettish and vintage high-end handbags (all locally made) created by a Vietnam-based Hong Konger designer-founder.
**Mai's**, G/F, Hotel Continental, 132–134 Dong Khoi St, tel: 08-3827 2733; www.mailam.vn. Mai's hand-made classic, yet funky, urban fashions and accessories for men and women feature embroidery on distressed, natural fabrics.
**Minh Hanh**, Rex Hotel Arcade, 77 Le Thanh Ton St; 155 Nguyen Hue St (two entrances); tel: 08-3291 3611. Haute couture boutique owned by a leading Vietnamese designer,

showcasing unorthodox, theatrical-style ao dai that blends traditional and modern designs.

**SONG**, 76D Le Thanh Ton St, tel: 08-3824 6986; www.SONG-life.com. SONG retails high-end men's and women's resort-orientated clothing and accessories (like bags and scarves) blending embroidery with eco-friendly, natural fabrics.

**Zen Plaza**, 54–56 Nguyen Trai St, tel: 08-3925 0339. A compact, multi-level shopping plaza aimed at locals. The lower floors specialise in home-grown designer fashions. Fresh, original and affordable Vietnamese fashions – albeit mainly in small sizes.

## Lacquer

**Appeal**, 41 Ton That Thiep St, tel: 08-3821 3614; www.christianduc. fr. Minuscule upscale store retailing high-quality crushed-eggshell lacquer pieces – furniture, lighting and home decor – in striking designs by Vietnamese French designers.

**Nga Art and Craft**, 49–57 Dong Du St, tel: 08-3823 8356; www.vietnam-art-craft.com. Renowned and long-established local company producing quality lacquer gifts, home decor and furniture that combine traditional craftsmanship with contemporary art. A second branch (103 Le Thanh Ton St) retails lacquer lighting, mainly in Art Deco style.

**SaiGon Craft**, 74 Dong Khoi St, tel: 08-3829 5758; www.saigoncrafts. com. Specialises in quality lacquer home decor, souvenirs and gifts. Both traditional and contemporary styles feature in multi-sized bowls, trays, photo frames and more.

## Silk

**Khai Silk**, 107 Dong Khoi St, tel: 08-3829 1146; www.khaisilkcorp. com. Besides top-notch silk clothing (both ready-to-wear and custom-made) for men and women in a wide range of styles, Vietnam's most exclusive silk boutique chain retails luxurious silk accessories, including ties, kimonos, embroidered scarves, lingerie, brocade shawls and bed quilts.

**XQ Saigon Silk Hand Embroidery**, 106 Le Loi Street, tel: 08-3829 8693; www.xqhandembroidery.com. Intricately made silk wall hangings of all sizes, with some incredibly beautiful pieces.

**Mosaique Decoration**, 98 Mac Thi Buoi St, tel: 08-3823 4634; www. mosaiquedecoration.com. Gorgeous handmade gifts, lighting and home decor made of silk – like embroidered

cushion covers and wall hangings, bed quilts and multi-sized lanterns.

## Souvenirs

Souvenirs like buffalo-horn servers, marble stone boxes, ceramic tea sets, silk lanterns and more are sold at the countless souvenir stores located along Dong Khoi and Le Loi streets, plus around the backpacker area of De Tham and Pham Ngo Lao streets. For one-stop souvenir blitzes, try the following two outlets:

**Ben Thanh Market**, Intersection of Ham Nghi, Le Loi and Tran Hung Dao streets. The city's best-known covered market sells plenty of cheap and cheerful souvenirs and handicrafts (like lacquerware, ceramics, coffee beans, T-shirts, conical hats and more) in a relatively compact ground-floor area. Bargaining is optional.

**Saigon Tax Trade Centre**, 135 Nguyen Hue St, tel: 08-3821 3849; www.thuongxatax.com.vn. The two upper floors of this open-plan, hybrid market-mall sell a huge selection of slightly better-quality souvenirs and handicrafts than Ben Thanh at slightly higher prices, but with less hassle and in A/C comfort.

## Vintage Goods and Bric-a-Brac

There are scant genuine antiques in HCMC, plus it's illegal to export antiques out of Vietnam. However, amongst the fake copies, some reputable dealers sell decent authentic reproductions, vintage goods, plus also bric-a-brac.

**Le Cong Kieu Street**. Shophouses along this charming narrow stretch, previously known as "Antique Street", sell mainly mass-produced repros. Vintage oriental and Indochina bric-a-brac, objets d'art and furniture can also be found here.

**Nguyen Frères**, 2 Dong Khoi St, tel: 08-3823 9459. Atmospheric store resembling a traditional-style northern Vietnamese house. Inside is a veritable Pandora's Box of bric-a-brac and vintage items like restored French Indochina-era furniture.

**Red Door Deco**, 20A Thi Sach St, tel: 08-3825 8672; www.reddoordeco. com. Has an eclectic stock of original vintage and reproduction items, including furniture, statues and objets d'art, including old black and white photos, glass-beaded chandeliers and carved wood Buddhas.

## Shopping Malls

Compared to the rest of Vietnam, HCMC has some of the glitziest shopping malls and plazas – but

compared to the rest of Asia, these are pale comparisons. Still, for air-conditioned bliss and the finest international goods the city can offer, the following are recommended.

**Diamond Department Store**, 34 Le Duan St, tel: 08-3822 5500; www. diamondplaza.com.vn. Upscale department store with sophisticated, open-plan interiors, retailing mainly high-end international brands including jewellery, watches and cosmetics. Men's and women's fashions, home ware, electronics and sports goods also feature in addition to a café, food court and supermarket.

**Parkson Hung Vuong**, 126 Hung Vuong St, District 5, tel: 08-2222 0383. Large department store in Cholon occupying the first four floors of Hung Vuong Plaza (featuring offices, apartments, bowling alley and cineplex).

**Parkson Saigontourist Plaza**, 35–45 Le Thanh Ton St, tel: 08-3827 7636. This glamorous, upscale department store was one of Vietnam's first outlets to retail luxury international brands – like Dolce & Gabbana – as well as introduce retail concepts like customer-service desks, loyalty cards and valet parking. Luxury international brands dominate, but well-known local brands also feature, from fashion and footwear to stationery, plus a food court, supermarket and amusement arcade.

**Rex Hotel Arcade**, 155 Nguyen Hue St. The swish ground-floor arcade, attached to the Rex Hotel, houses individual boutiques from top luxury international designers like Chloe, Balenciaga, Tara Jamon, Sergio Rossi and Marc Jacobs.

## Vung Tau

Vung Tau's only notable shopping is at its modern shopping centres. The souvenir shops out on the street specialise in products pillaged from the local reefs – like lacquered sea turtles and painted coral – and are probably best avoided.

## Shopping Centres

**Hodeco Plaza**, 36 Nguyen Thai Hoc St. This all-purpose shopping centre includes a grocery store, bookshop, small department store, and KFC and Lotteria (fast food).

**Imperial Shopping Centre**, 163 Thuy Van St (Back Beach). This small upscale shopping mall has jewellery, cosmetics, designer clothes and handbags, plus a fine restaurant and café.

## Mui Ne

In the last few years Mui Ne's shopping selection has expanded greatly to include sports equipment, jewellery, handbags, fashion, art and a wide variety of souvenirs. There are a few items that are unique to Mui Ne, like local Cham textiles and pottery, Phan Thiet fish sauce, and sand paintings made from the coloured sands of Binh Thuan province.

### Markets

**Rang Market**. This little market at the centre of the beach is open from sunrise to 10.30pm. It's a great place to eat breakfast and buy fresh fruit and banana-sesame candies, coconut cakes and peanut brittle. There are also fruit vendors in the evening.

### Leather Goods

**Minh Nhung Crocodile Shop**, 34 Nguyen Dinh Chieu St, tel: 062-374 1428. Crocodile and snake bags, wallets, belts and other items are popular in Mui Ne now. The fixed prices are a little high, but the merchandise is high-quality.

### Water-sports Gear/Beachwear

**Mellow**, 117C Nguyen Dinh Chieu St, tel: 062-374 3086. Sells Ozone kiteboarding equipment and clothing.

### Jewellery

**Thinh & Sabine**, 79A Nguyen Dinh Chieu St, mobile tel: 090-993 1192. This German-Vietnamese couple produce exquisite handmade jewellery.

### Souvenirs

**Shop Thai**, 29 Nguyen Dinh Chieu St, tel: 062-374 1267. This is one of the largest of many large souvenir shops in Mui Ne, selling virtually every popular trinket and craft item from all over the country. Rigorous haggling is necessary. The marked prices are overly optimistic.
Vietnam Home, 125A, B Nguyen Dinh Chieu St, tel: 062-384 7687; www.vietnamhomerestaurant. com. An excellent restaurant as well as a great shop with an extensive selection of leather goods, handbags, clothing, jewellery and local souvenirs.

## Mekong Delta

Save it for Saigon – coconut shell and shell-inlaid wooden trinkets can be found along the Mekong Delta tourist trail, but most items are invariably cheaper in HCMC.

## TOURS AND ACTIVITIES

### Hanoi

### Travel Agents

In the Old Quarter, just about every second shopfront seems to be a small travel agent or guesthouse, and all seem to offer the same tour excursions at relatively similar prices. Booking a tour with one of these small agencies isn't a bad idea, as long as customers ask the right questions. When booking a trip to a destination outside of Hanoi (like Pefume Pagoda, Mai Chau, Halong Bay, Sa Pa, etc), be sure to ask how many people will be in the group, what kind of transportation will be arranged, and whether the cost includes meals, entrance fees and other incidentals. The main advantage of booking through an established, well-known travel agent is that it is more likely to be concerned about its reputation, and will ensure that tour groups are small and all costs are clearly spelt out.

**ET-Pumpkin Adventure Travel**, 89 Ma May St, Hoan Kiem District, tel: 04-3926 0739; www.et-pumpkin. com. Best used for booking cheap and reliable train, plane and bus tickets. Also rents vehicles and drivers at reasonable rates. Its tour packages are quite ordinary.

**Exotissimo Travel**, 26 Tran Nhat Duat St, Hoan Kiem District, tel: 04-3828 2150; www.exotissimo.com. This travel agent specialises in tailor-made vacations for those with bigger budgets to blow. Also offers high-end tour packages, including a 14-day cross-country excursion.

**Handspan Tours**, 78 Ma May St, Hoan Kiem District, tel: 04-3926 2828; www.handspan.com. This long-established travel agent offers reliable and reasonably priced tours of Vietnam's major destinations. Small groups and private tours available. Also offers sea-kayaking, mountain biking and 4WD adventures.

**Kangaroo Café Tours**, 18 Bao Khanh St, Hoan Kiem District, tel: 04-3828 9931; www.kangaroocafe.com. This Australian-run travel agent and café organises cheap but reliable (and fun) tours of Sa Pa and Halong Bay, as well as shorter day trips. Offers excellent travel advice.

**Offroad Vietnam**, 36 Nguyen Huu Huan St, Hoan Kiem District, tel: 04-3926 3433; www.offroadvietnam. com. The best option for those

wanting to explore northern Vietnam on motorbike. Uses 4-stroke Honda 160cc motorcycles tried and tested in the field. Owner Anh Wu is one of the friendliest and most knowledgeable travel agents in town.

**Sinh Café Travel**, 14 Cua Bac St, Ba Dinh District, tel: 04-3836 4212; www.sinhcafe.com. This long-established travel agent is the backpacker's ally when it comes to cheap tours. Most famous for its long-distance "Open Tour" bus transport services.

**Topas Adventure Travel**, 52 To Ngoc Van St, Tay Ho District, tel: 04-3715 1005; www.topasvietnam.com. A high-end tour and travel company that specialises in package trips to Sa Pa, as well as tours of Vietnam, Laos and Cambodia. Excellent guides. Manages a great eco-lodge in Sa Pa.

**Vietnam Sunshine Travel**, 49 Luong Ngoc Quyen St, Hoan Kiem District, tel: 04-9262 2239; www. vietnamsunshinetravel.com. Particularly good for trips to Halong Bay.

### Walking Tour

**Hidden Hanoi**, 137 Nghi Tam St, Tay Ho District, mobile tel: 091-225 4045; www.hiddenhanoi. vn. This small, locally run company offers some of the best walking tours of Hanoi. Choose from tours of the Old Quarter, the French Quarter, street food and temples. The guides are young, energetic and excellent English-speakers, and the company also offers cooking and language classes.

### Golf

**Hanoi Club Driving Range**, 76 Yen Phu St, Tay Ho District, tel: 04-3823 8115; www.hanoi-club.com. Part of the Hanoi Club, golfers at this driving range smack golf balls into West Lake. Call for bookings.

**King's Island Golf Course**, Dong Mo, Son Tay Town, Ha Tay province, tel: 34-368 6555; www.kingsislandgolf. com. With two 18-hole courses, King's Island is the first 36-hole facility in northern Vietnam, and it makes excellent use of the region's dramatic natural environment. Located about 45km (28 miles) from Hanoi; advance bookings required.

**Tam Dao Golf & Resort**, Hop Chau Commune, Tam Dao District, Vinh Phuc province, tel: 21-189 6554; www.tamdaogolf.com. This golf club is about two hours outside of Hanoi, nestled at the foot of the mountains near Tam Dao. Offers a free shuttle-bus service from Hanoi.

## Dien Bien Phu

The Dien Bien Phu battleground sites are toured independently, but for those unfamiliar with the battle it would be a good idea to hire a guide who can explain the history behind the most important sites. Guides are best booked at the **Muong Thanh Hotel** (25 Him Lam, tel: 023-381 0038), where staff can also arrange transportation, or by asking around on the street. Many of the city's xe om drivers double as guides, though finding one who speaks good English is a challenge.

## Sa Pa

### Travel Agents

Tours of Sa Pa, including train tickets, are usually organised by Hanoi-based tour operators.

### Mountain Climbing

For hardy travellers hoping to scale Vietnam's highest peak, Mount Fansipan, the three-day trip (including guides) can be organised by any of the hotels listed under Sa Pa in Accommodation (see page 347). The climb can also be booked in Hanoi with travel agents like **Buffalo Tours** and **Sinh Café Travel**. Also try the well-regarded **Active Travel Vietnam** (3/F, 303 Nguyen Du St, Hoan Kiem District, tel: 04-3944 6230; www. activetravelvietnam.com).

### Biking

A great way to see the countryside outside of Hanoi is on two wheels. Several companies organise trips that run from one-day trips to epic two-week slogs. Several routes are available around Sa Pa, where the scenery is great and the cooler weather much more geared towards pedal power.

### Trekking

To book treks to Sa Pa's surrounding villages, hire a guide from a local hotel. All of the hotels listed under Accommodation (see page 347) have a stable of energetic English-speaking guides, usually young Hmong women, who are well experienced in leading groups of foreigners through the picturesque valleys. Non-English-speakers can request French-, German- or Chinese-speaking guides.

## Halong Bay/Cat Ba Island

### Travel Agents

Tours of Halong Bay and Cat Ba Island, including kayaking trips, are usually organised by Hanoi-based tour operators.

### Trekking

Trekking in **Cat Ba National Park** (tel: 031-368 8686; daily 7–11.30am and 12–5.30pm) is one of the main draws of Cat Ba Island, and offers numerous excellent hiking trails for the intrepid traveller. Bring sturdy shoes, breathable clothing and lots of water – it can get extremely hot and humid in the summertime.

### Kayaking

Kayaking is also very popular in Cat Ba, and a number of hotels and guesthouses along Nui Ngoc Street rent kayaks for visitors wanting to tour the calm waters of the bay. Expect to pay about VND40,000 an hour.

### Biking

Biking is a great way to see Cat Ba Island. The majority of hotels and guesthouses rent out cheap Chinese-made bicycles. For those hoping to do more serious trips, good-quality mountain bikes can be rented at the **Flightless Bird Café** (tel: 031-388 8517; south end of Nui Ngoc St).

## Hue

### Travel Agents

Other than the Royal Citadel, most sights in this area are rather spread out. Therefore, using the services of a tour operator is a good way to visit all of the sights. All of the local companies tend to offer the same cookie-cutter tours.
**Café on Thu Wheels**, 3/34 Nguyen Tri Phuong St, tel: 054-383 2241; email: minhthu1970@hotmail.com. A very popular company that leads tours by motorbike and bicycle.
**Camel Travel**, 5 Nguyen Thai Hoc St, tel: 054-384 9643; email: phigreentravel@yahoo.com. Offers group tours of the city, the royal tombs, Perfume River boat trips, Bach Ma National Park and the DMZ.
**Sinh Café**, 12 Hung Vuong St, tel: 054-384 5022; email: mandarin@dng.vnn.vn. Offers a similar range of tours as Camel Travel.

## Danang

The Danang area has incredible opportunities for outdoor sports, but so far only a few companies have moved in to capitalise on the opportunity. China Beach has the best surfing in Vietnam, and the mountains around Ba Na, Bach Ma and Monkey Mountain offer superb spots for rock climbing – but you'll have to bring all your own gear to enjoy these activities.

## Hoi An

### Travel Agents

Hoi An is an excellent hub for sightseeing tours of Hue, My Son and nearby islands in the Cu Lao Cham Marine Park. The following travel agents are recommended:
**Hoian Ecotours**, Phuoc Hai Village, Cua Dai District, tel: 0510-392 7808; www.hoianecotour.com.vn. River tours, fishing trips and tours of the Hoi An Delta focusing on local culture, history and agriculture.
**Nga**, 22 Phan Boi Chau St, tel: 0510-386 3485; email: lenga22us@yahoo.com. Offers tours to Hue and My Son; also books boat trips and sells bus, plane and train tickets.
**Sinh Café Travel**, 587 Hai Ba Trung St, tel: 0510-386 3948; www.sinhcafevn.com. Offers tours of Hue, My Son and boat tours of Cu Lao Cham Marine Park to visit the traditional Thanh Ha ceramics village and Kim Bong carpentry village.

### Diving

Situated on a delta with numerous rivers, tributaries and islands encircled by fertile reefs, it's no wonder that Hoi An's outdoor activities all revolve around the water.
**Cham Island Diving Centre**, 88 Nguyen Thai Hoc St, tel: 0510-391 0782; www.chamislanddiving.com. Offers day trips for beginners (diving or snorkelling) and certified divers. PADI training courses available.
**Hoian Jet Ski Adventure Tours**, Karma Waters, 63 Cau Dai Beach, tel: 0510-392 7632; www.jetskivietnam.com. Exciting jet-ski tours from the Hoi An Delta all the way to the Laos border.
**Rainbow Divers**, 39B Tran Hung Dao St, tel: 0510-391 1914; www.divevietnam.com. Vietnam's top dive centre offers dives around the Cu Lao Cham Marine Park, and training for a variety of professional dive certifications.

## Quy Nhon

### Travel Agent

**Barbara's Kiwi Connection**, 102 Xuan Dieu St, tel: 056-389 2921; email: nzbarb@yahoo.com. Barbara is a backpacker's best friend. She provides free information on how to do self-guided tours and can also arrange tours by taxi to nearby Cham temples, ancient pagodas, Quang Trung Museum and Ham Ho. The itineraries are perfectly spaced and make for a very relaxing day.

## Nha Trang

### Travel Agents
Most of Nha Trang's sightseeing tours revolve around the islands and coral reefs out in the bay. Unfortunately, local tour operators focus more on providing transport than actually explaining to their customers about what they are seeing. Mai Loc, listed below, is one of the few exceptions.

**Long Phu Tourist**, 84 Hung Vuong St, tel: 058-352 7022; www. longphutourist.com. Provides package boat tours of all the surrounding islands. Note: Long Phu is contracted by many tour companies.

**Mama Linh's Boat Tours**, 140 Hung Vuong St, tel: 058-352 2844. Boat trips to the islands as well as snorkelling. This is essentially a party boat – there's loud music and plenty of alcohol. It's not the safest combination, and, not surprisingly, is very popular with backpackers.

**Mai Loc**, Sao Mai Hotel, 99 Nguyen Thien Thuat St, tel: 058-352 6412; email: mailoc98@hotmail. com. Mr Loc, an award-winning photographer who has received international recognition, leads motorbike tours around Nha Trang, the central coast, and up into the central highlands. This knowledgeable guide, with exceptional English skills, comes highly recommended.

**Sinh Café Travel**, 2 Biet Thu St, tel: 058-352 2982; www.sinhcafevn. com. Leads city tours and books boat tours of the bay (sometimes through Long Phu), with visits to surrounding islands, and snorkelling on the reefs.

### Amusement Parks
**Phu Dong Water Park**, Tran Phu St (south of Louisiane). This water park is right on the beach and has shallow pools, water slides and fountains.

**Vinpearl Land Amusement Park**, Hon Tre, tel: 058-395 8188; www. vinpearlland.com. Central Vietnam's largest amusement park, with carnival rides, upscale shopping, a water park, aquarium, several restaurants, and a large performance centre. The US$20 ticket includes the gondola ride, park and aquarium access.

**ABOVE:** Diving with Rainbow Divers in Nha Trang

### Diving
**Rainbow Divers**, 90A Hung Vuong St, tel: 058-352 4351; www.divevietnam. com. Vietnam's top dive centre, and the only National Geographic centre in the country, has its head office here in Nha Trang. PADI certification from basic to advanced available, or take an introductory Discovery Dive. Branches all over Vietnam.

**Sailing Club Diving**, 72–74 Tran Phu St, tel: 058-352 2788, www. sailingclubdiving.com; and Octopus Diving, 24 Biet Thu St, tel: 058-352 1629. These two outlets are run by the same reputable dive centre, offering PADI certification and dive trips.

### Water sports
**Mana Mana Water Sports**, Louisiane Brewhouse, Lot 29, Tran Phu St. Offers a full range of water sports and equipment rental right on the beach, including kayaking, windsurfing, kite-boarding, wake-boarding, water-skiing and more.

## Dalat

Dalat has some of the best opportunities for adventure activities in the country, including trekking, mountain biking, rock climbing, abseiling and paragliding. Always ask questions before you engage in any risky activity. Make sure you have insurance; often Vietnamese companies do not, and expect their customers to assume all risk and liability.

**Groovy Gecko Adventure Tours**, 65 Truong Cong Dinh St, mobile tel: 091-824 8976; www.groovygeckotours. net. Tin and his eight experienced, English- and French-speaking guides

lead popular trekking adventures on Langbiang Mountain; mountain biking to Mui Ne; and canyoning, abseiling and rock climbing at Datanla Waterfall. In addition they also do trekking tours to hill-tribe minority villages around Dalat and the central highlands (including Buon Me Thuot, Kontum and Pleiku).

**Phat Tire Ventures**, 109 Nguyen Van Troi St, mobile tel: 091-843 8781; www.phattireventures. com. The original Dalat adventure guides, offering many of the same activities as Gecko, with a little more experience, and higher prices. Kayaking and local biking treks are also on the menu.

**Sinh Café Travel**, 4A Bui Thi Xuan, tel: 063-382 2663; www.sinhcafevn. com. Provides tours of local sights around Dalat, as well as 2–4-day trips through the central highlands, with stops in Buon Me Thuot and Kontum.

**Vietwings**, mobile tel: 090-382 5607; www.vietwings-hpg.com. Offers rock climbing, camping and paragliding on Langbiang Mountain.

### Golf
**Dalat Palace Golf Club**, Phu Dong Thiet Vuong St, tel: 063-382 1201; www.dalatpalacegolf.com. This 18-hole, par-72 championship golf course features bent-grass greens, fairways and tees. The renovated clubhouse (which has an excellent restaurant) was built in 1956.

## Ho Chi Minh City

City-based tour operators (and some hotels) in HCMC all offer standard half-day city tours that take in the key sites, plus day tours that cover the historic Cu Chi Tunnels and Cao Dai Temple. In addition, HCMC is the perfect base for tours of the Mekong Delta, ranging from multi-day bus/ boat tours and de luxe cruises to budget boat tours. Another option is Cat Tien National Park, one of the best places in Vietnam to spot wildlife.

### Travel Agents

**Buffalo Tours**, Suite 601, Satra House, 58 Dong Khoi St, District 1, tel: 08-3827 9169; www. buffalotours.com. This privately owned Vietnamese company offers quality scheduled and customised tours for adventure or luxury travel. Known for its well-informed guides and low-impact responsible tourism.

**Exotissimo Travel Vietnam**, 20 Hai Ba Trung St, District 1, tel: 08-3827 2911; www.exotissimo.com. One of the longest-established tour operators in Indochina, Myanmar and Thailand, offering upmarket, tailor-made and scheduled tours and adventure trips.

**Handspan**, F7, Titan Building, 18A Nam Quoc Cang St, District 1, tel: 08-3925 7605; www.handspan. com. Established 1997, this young adventure travel company offers a range of good-value tours – anything from kayaking and mountain biking to luxury boat cruises in the Mekong Delta – with experienced guides and environmentally sensitive operations.

**Saigontourist Travel Service**, 49 Le Thanh Ton St, District 1, tel: 08-3829 8914; www.saigontourist. com. State-run tour company that offers standard travel services and tours, including regional and city day tours and Mekong Delta cruises.

**Sinh Café Travel**, 246 De Tham St, District 1, tel: 08-3836 7338; www. sinhcafevn.com. The granddaddy of budget tour operators: long-established outfit with headquarters in the backpacker area, specialising in no-frills multi-day budget trips as well as long-distance bus trips.

**STA Travel**, 70 Bui Vien St, District 1, tel: 08-3920 9479; www. statravelvietnam.com.vn. The super-friendly staff here is well informed and can arrange a good variety of tours in HCMC and beyond. Hotel and travel bookings are also possible.

### Speciality Tours

**Vespa Tours**; http:// vietnamvespaadventures.com/.

Why tour southern Vietnam on a bus, when you can do it on a Vespa? This American-owned, HCMC-based outfit runs personalised, small group five-day tours on classic Vespas through Vung Tau, Mui Ne, Dalat and Nha Trang, past magnificent scenery and with the wind in your hair.

**Mekong Delta Cruises**, Bassac Boat (TransMekong), tel: 071-382 9540; www.transmekong.com. French company operates two large, luxury wooden boats designed like rice barges, with en-suite cabins and all mod cons. Overnight and multi-day cruises into the heart of the Mekong Delta can be customised.

**Mekong Eyes Cruise**, tel: 071-546 0786; www.mekongeyes.com. Can Tho-based, local company operating two-day boat cruises on a traditional rice barge, with en- suite cabins. Side-trips by small sampans offer an up-close experience of the delta.

### Golf

**Vietnam Golf and Country Club**, Long Thanh My Ward, District 9, tel: 08-6280 0103; www.vietnamgolfcc. com. Vietnam's first 36-hole golf club features two challenging, championship 18-hole courses – one designed by golfer Lee Trevino – plus driving range and recreational area.

### Water Park

**Dam Sen Water Park**, 3 Hoa Binh St, District 11, tel: 08-3858 8418; www. damsenwaterpark.com.vn; Mon–Sat 8.30am–6pm, Sun 8am–7pm. HCMC's premier water park, with numerous exhilarating water slides like Kamikaze Ride and Twister Space Bowl; attractions are regularly updated. Gentler options feature wave pool and wandering river. Very crowded at weekends.

### Vung Tau

### Travel Agent

**OSC Vietnam Travel**, 09 Le Loi St, tel: 064-625 4007; www. oscvietnamtravel.com.vn. Offers a variety of package tours, as well as visa extensions and transport bookings.

### Con Dao Islands

### Diving

**Rainbow Divers**, mobile tel: 090-516 2833; www.divevietnam.com. A reputable outfit that runs a range of dive courses with certification.

### Phan Thiet

### Golf

**Ocean Dunes Golf Club**, 1 Ton Duc Thang St, tel: 062-382 3366; www. oceandunesgolf.vn. Designed by Nick Faldo, this par-72 links course offers 18 holes of challenging golf beside the Novotel Hotel and Doi Duong Beach. Currently the most popular course within driving distance of HCMC.

### Mui Ne Beach

### Travel Agents

**Mr Binh Sahara Tour**, 81 Huynh Thuc Khang St, mobile tel: 098-929 7648; email: mrbinhmuine@hotmail. com. Visitors to Mui Ne rave about Mr Binh, a highly knowledgeable Vietnamese who speaks fluent English and specialises in off-the-beaten-path tours of the Mui Ne area as well as southern and central Vietnam.

**Fish Egg Tree Tours**, mobile tel: 090-443 4895; email: muinehung@gmail. com. Mr Hung is a knowledgeable, English-speaking tour guide who provides more than a transport service, unlike most local travel agents.

### Golf

**Sea Links Golf and Country Club**, tel: 062-374 1741; www.sealinkscity. com. Complete with resort, villas, restaurant and 18 holes of golf. The panoramic views of the coast from the dunes above Mui Ne are spectacular.

### Kiteboarding and Windsurfing

**Storm Kiteboarding Center**, Mia Resort (Sailing Club), 24 Nguyen Dinh Chieu, St; www.stormkiteboarding. com. Experienced one-on-one instruction in a relaxed atmosphere, where safety comes first.

**C2Sky Kite Center**, Sunshine Beach Resort, 82 Nguyen Dinh Chieu St, mobile tel: 091-665 5241; www. c2skykitecenter.com. C2Sky's instructors are all IKO certified and together speak as many as 8 languages. The owners also run a popular local cooking school.

**Windchimes Kite – Surf – Windsurf School**, 56 Nguyen Dinh Chieu St, mobile tel: 090-972 0017; www. kiteboarding-vietnam.com. One of the largest kiteboarding centres, with IKO instructors who speak several languages. Cabrinha, Naish and North kites for rent, as well as up to 40 boards to choose from.

## SPAS

### Hanoi

Massage parlours, spas and beauty salons abound in Hanoi, ranging from dingy, hole-in-the-wall venues to high-end, luxurious health centres. Whatever you do, avoid the grungy neon-lit businesses – they are often simply covers for brothels.

Most high-end hotels will offer spa services; these are usually good but can cost a pretty penny. Only independent spas are listed here.

**Anam QT Spa**, 28 Le Thai To St, Hoan Kiem District, tel: 04-3928 6116; www.qtanamspa.com. This comfortable and clean downtown spa features excellent massage services, as well as relaxing facials.

**Exotical Spa**, 57 Nguyen Khac Hieu St, Ba Dinh District, tel: 04-3715 0316. Popular with tour groups, this all-purpose spa offers top-notch massage services. The foot reflexology massages are among the best in the city.

**Qi Spa**, 27 Ly Thuong Kiet St, Hoan Kiem District, tel: 04-3824 4703; www.qispa.com.vn. With several locations throughout Vietnam, the elegant Qi Spa has built a name for itself with its spa and massage packages. Also sells its own line of body lotions and fragrances.

**Siam Spa**, 341 Kim Ma St, Ba Dinh District, tel: 04-3846 3120; www. spasiam.com.vn. This Thai-inspired spa and salon offers a wide range of massage and spa treatments, including a package geared towards stressed-out office workers.

**Spa La Madera**, 18 Tong Duy Tan St, Hoan Kiem District, tel: 04-3938 0549. A self-styled well-being centre that uses natural, local products in foot reflexology and traditional Vietnamese body massages.

**Zen Spa Red River**, Lane 310, Nghi Tam St, Tay Ho District, tel: 04-3719 9889; www.zenspa.vn. This tranquil spa is tucked away down a lane near the banks of the Red River. The massages and spa treatments take place inside traditional wooden houses over a sprawling area. Though pricey, the spa treatments are out of this world.

### Ho Chi Minh City

Although lagging behind its experienced Asian neighbours like Bali and Thailand, HCMC's spas and salons are the most sophisticated in Vietnam. Most luxury hotels like the Sheraton and Hyatt have expensive, albeit exquisitem, spas. Like the Hanoi listings, only spas outside of hotels are listed here.

**Glow Spa**, Mezzanine, Eden Mall, 106 Nguyen Hue St, District 1, tel: 08-3823 8368; www.glowsaigon. com. With its hip, retro-contemporary decor, Glow has treatments and massage therapies selected to meet specific skin and body types.

**Jasmine**, 45 Ton That Thiep St, District 1, tel: 08-3827 2737. Long-established salon-spa popular with expats. Jasmine is noted for its aromatherapy body massages, as well as invigorating scrubs and rejuvenating facials.

**Just Men**, 40 Ton That Thiep St, District 1, tel: 08-3914 1407. A sister outet of Jasmine, this slick salon is HCMC's first quality establishment dedicated to male body maintenance and grooming.

**La Maison de L'Apothiquaire**, 64A Truong Dinh St, District 3, tel: 08-3932 5181; www.lapothiquaire. com. Set within a 1950s Art Deco villa with tranquil gardens and pool, HCMC's only full-scale wellness centre takes inspiration from the traditions of French herbalist-healers. A smaller downtown spa is located at 61–63 Le Thanh Ton St, District 1 (tel: 08-3822 1218).

## COOKERY CLASSES

### Hanoi

**Hidden Hanoi**, 137 Nghi Tam St, Tay Ho District, mobile tel: 091-225 4045; www.hiddenhanoi.com.vn. This local tour company that organises walking tours of Hanoi also runs hands-on cookery classes. There are five different menus (including a vegetarian one) to choose from and each has four courses.

**Highway 4 Restaurant**, 575 Kim Ma St, Ba Dinh District, tel: 04-3771 6372; www.highway4.com. A popular chain of restaurants that also runs cookery classes at its Kim Ma branch (meeting point at Hang Tre branch). The class starts with a market visit to the Old Quarter followed by a hands-on cooking class during which students whip up three dishes.

**Metropole Cookery School**, Sofitel Metropole Hotel, 15 Ngo Quyen St, Hoan Kiem District, tel: 04-3826 6919, www.accorhotels-asia.com. Started in 1999, this popular cookery school is well regarded but pricey. The four-hour classes start with a visit to the market followed by a cooking demo by the instructor. Perfect for those who don't want to get their hands messy.

### Hoi An

**Morning Glory Cooking School**, 106 Nguyen Thai Hoc St, tel: 0510-391 1431; www.hoianhospitality.com. Classes are taught by either Ms Vy, the owner of four superb restaurants in Hoi An – Cargo Club, Mermaid, Morning Glory and White Lantern – or her assistant, Ms Lu. A wide range of classes in Vietnamese cuisine is offered, from an hour to a full day. Highly recommended, especially the longer classes for the serious cook.

**Red Bridge Cooking School**, Thon 4, Cam Thanh, tel: 090-545 2092; www.visithoian.com. One of the most popular local cookery schools, it begins with a trip to the local market, a lesson in the herb garden, and then a very informative class teaching several Hoi An specialities, including creative garnishes.

### Ho Chi Minh City

**Bonsai Floating Cookery Classes**, departs Passenger Quay of HCMC (Ben Tau Khach Thanh Pho), junction Ham Nghi and Ton Duc Thang streets, District 1, tel: 08-3910 5560; www. bonsaicruise.com.vn. Learn to cook traditional Vietnamese cuisine while cruising along the Saigon River on a traditional royal dragon boat. Morning, afternoon or evening cookery classes (three-course set menu) are held on the deck on request.

**Saigon Culinary Art Centre (Mai Home)**, 36/13–14 Lam Son St, Phu Nhuan District, tel: 08-3551 2400; email: sgncookeryart@vnn. vn. Small, dedicated cookery centre set in a traditional-style southern home. Hosts on-request morning or afternoon cookery classes. Standard class involves hands-on preparation of three dishes, but also ask about its more intensive or specialist classes.

**Vietnam Cookery Centre**, M1 Cu Xa Tan Cang St, 362/8 Ung Van Khiem St, Binh Thanh District, tel: 08-3512 1491; www.vietnamcookery. com. Professional and privately run dedicated cookery centre in a charming colonial villa. Daily classes include a standard class with hands-on preparation of four Vietnamese dishes, enjoyed afterwards for lunch or dinner.

# A – Z

## A HANDY SUMMARY OF PRACTICAL INFORMATION, ARRANGED ALPHABETICALLY

**A**

### Addresses

Finding a residential or business address can be surprisingly tricky in Vietnam. Streets often change names when they run through different neighbourhoods, and in rural areas come won't have names at all. Street prefixes include "D" for Duong, "P" for Pho, and "DL" for Dai Lo. For the sake of clarity, we have added the suffix St to all street names; therefore Duong Tran Hung Dao is referred to as Tran Hung Dao St.

When a street number includes a slash, such as 98/6, your first task is to find number 98, go down the alley, and then hunt for building number 6. When a number is followed by a letter, such as 48C, it means a whole block of buildings is numbered 48, and you must find the third office in the block. Odd and even numbers are typically on opposite sides of the street and do not necessarily correlate with each other, so don't expect 31 to always be close to 32. To make matters worse, sometimes houses have no numbers at all. Be thankful you're not a postman in Vietnam.

### Budgeting for Your Trip

While still inexpensive for most Western travellers, Vietnam is not as cheap as it was a few years ago. In 2008, inflation sky-rocketed to an all-time high, thanks to the rising price of oil, grains and other commodities around the world.

Accommodation in Vietnam can be cheap, but is generally more expensive than many other Southeast Asian countries. The US$5 rooms of old, with a bed, fan and little else, are now rare. Hostels with dorms only began to appear recently, and are still uncommon. Most guesthouses in the cities will cost around US$15–20 per night, which will get you air conditioning, a TV, fridge, hot water, up to two beds, and Wi-fi. Mid-range beach hotels cost between US$20 and US$50. Service improves considerably as the price rises to US$100. Above that, you are in five-star territory.

Street food is cheap and convenient, with meals costing between US$0.50 and US$1.50. Mid-range Vietnamese and backpacker restaurants will charge US$2–3 per dish. A typical restaurant catering to tourists will cost US$5–8 for three courses and drinks. There are few truly high-end restaurants outside of Ho Chi Minh City and Hanoi, where the top tables can easily top US$25 per person.

Budget travellers can realistically get by with as little as US$20 per day for food, drinks, room, transport and sightseeing. A mid-range budget is about US$40–50 per day. Beyond that the sky is the limit if you have cash to burn.

It is common practice for Vietnamese to charge different rates for foreigners and locals. This was once mandated in government-run establishments, but has largely been abolished. Despite this, most Vietnamese see foreigners as an opportunity to make extra profit and so continue to charge above the norm. One should generally assume that a quoted price, especially when shopping, is at least double the normal rate (although more than four times is not uncommon), and bargain the price down. Knowing the street price can help, but it doesn't mean the seller will be willing to agree to it.

Note: it's not uncommon for restaurants to have an expensive English menu and a cheaper Vietnamese one. If you're watching your dong, ask to see the Vietnamese version too to compare prices.

### Business Hours

Most banks, public services and state-run offices work from Monday to Friday between 7.30 and 8.30am, and 4 and 5pm, with a lunch break between 11.30am and 1.30pm. Museums roughly follow the same hours, but many close on Mondays (sometimes Fridays). Tourist-orientated shops open daily from 9am to 7–9pm, and may close for lunch. Markets open au daily as 5.30 to 6.30am, and are finishing up come lunch time. Markets in tourist areas (or during festivals) may open again in the evening. Only very large markets in city centres stay active all day. Pagodas and temples are open daily from early morning until the evening. There are no fixed hours, however, and sometimes the door may be shut because there is a special event going on inside – or the caretaker is away.

**C**

### Children

Bringing children to Vietnam is not a major issue, as they will be welcome everywhere and there is plenty for them to enjoy. Most big cities have a water park and/or a zoo of some description. There are also good beaches along the entire coast and excellent national parks to explore. Be sure to leave the buggy at home as footpaths in most Vietnamese cities and towns are not pedestrian-friendly; a chest-mounted baby carrier is far more practical. Children should be warned never to approach dogs, monkeys and other small animals; those wandering the streets tend to be feral, and rabies is a risk.

The tropical sun is intense, so high-factor sunblock and hats are essential. Make sure children keep their hands clean; those who frequently suck their thumbs can easily pick up stomach bugs.

## Climate

Given Vietnam's length – it stretches 1,650km (1,000 miles) from north to south – its topography and the effect of the monsoon tropical climate, temperatures and rainfall patterns can vary widely from one region to another. In the north, temperatures can dip to as low as 10°C (50°F) and be accompanied by a biting winter wind. In the south, however, it is hot all year round.

The south has two seasons, wet and dry. During the rainy months between May and November, it rains fiercely for about 30 minutes a day (but some days not at all), normally in the afternoon or early evening. The dry season runs from December to April, with the hottest months stretching from March to late April, with temperatures well over 30°C (86°F) and with high humidity levels. Seasons are extreme along the coast between Vung Tau and Phan Rang – one of the driest spots in Southeast Asia, where it almost never rains during the dry season.

The north experiences four seasons. The summer months from May to September are almost always hot and humid, with the most rainfall occurring during this period. Winter, from late December to early March, is often grey, drizzly and cool.

Central Vietnam from Danang to Nha Trang has its own weather patterns due to the monsoons: the dry season is from February to September, with the most rainfall from October to December. The seasons are not as pronounced here, however, and it can rain at any time of the year, but the hottest months are June/ July while the coolest months are December/January.

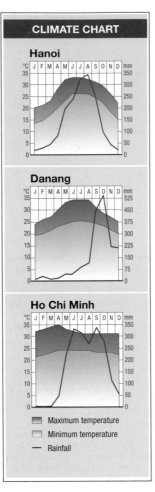

**CLIMATE CHART**

**Hanoi**

**Danang**

**Ho Chi Minh**

■ Maximum temperature
□ Minimum temperature
— Rainfall

It's near-impossible to find a time of the year when the north, centre and south have equally good weather, but the safest bet – if you're travelling the length of Vietnam – is between March and April. The rains will have abated, humidity levels are still bearable, and it will be relatively warm and dry throughout Vietnam. However, if you are just visiting north and south Vietnam and skipping the centre, November and December are good months too.

## Clothing

Bring casual, lightweight clothing of natural fabrics, which offer the most comfort in the humidity and heat. If you plan to spend time in the highlands, then a light jacket or fleece and long trousers – especially in winter – are advisable. Rain gear, including a small foldable umbrella,

is a good idea, as it's always raining somewhere in Vietnam.

Sandals or footwear that can be easily slipped off are best. Shoes should be removed before entering homes, and even some shops.

## Crime and Security

In general, Vietnam is a safe country to travel in and violent crimes against foreigners are rare, though they do happen. Petty theft and robbery, on the other hand, are very common. In big cities, especially Ho Chi Minh City, tourists are often the victims of pickpockets and snatch-and-grab thieves. Always leave valuables in a hotel safe, and when you must carry cash, put it in a money belt worn inside your clothes. When walking, or travelling in a cyclo, keep one hand firmly on handbags and cameras. When travelling on buses or trains, always stay with your bag. If you travel by train, bring a cable lock to secure your bags to your bed frame when you are sleeping.

Be careful of pavement vendors selling maps, books and souvenirs or people begging for money, especially in Hanoi and HCMC. They can easily distract you while a friend slips a hand into your pocket, grabs your wallet and vanishes. Mobile phones are easy prey, and it's not uncommon to have MP3 players, laptops and even sunglasses snatched by passing motorcyclists. Pickpockets could be children and women with babies as well.

The Vietnamese are extremely friendly and generous, but caution must be taken when making casual acquaintances. Vietnam has its fair share of con artists who hustle everything from Cambodian gems to "genuine" bones of missing American servicemen. Beware of people who suddenly approach you in tourist areas (especially in HCMC) and engage you in conversation, or try to persuade you to go somewhere with them. This is almost always a scam.

### Women Travellers

Women should take extra precautions when travelling alone, as some Vietnamese men can be very aggressive. Their behaviour may range from following you to your hotel room to physically touching you (usually after being egged on by their male friends).

Also, Vietnam can be a very difficult country for an Asian woman, or a woman of Asian descent, travelling with a white male companion. Some Vietnamese men mistakenly assume such women to be Vietnamese and prostitutes (the same is true for a younger Asian man travelling with an older Western man), and can often be verbally abusive.

Women staying alone in budget hotels may want to consider using an extra lock on the door at night. Quiet streets and isolated beaches should also be avoided late at night. It's a good idea to travel in groups or to arrange transportation ahead of time. Paying a little extra to have a driver wait for you after a late night out is better than having to find a way of getting home late at night.

### Police Registration

By law, all tourists are required to be registered with the local police station. When checking in at hotels and guesthouses in the smaller and more remote towns, the staff will take your passport to the police for registration. They will normally return it to you the next morning, although sometimes the staff may insist on holding your passport for the entire duration of your stay. In Hanoi, HCMC and the bigger cities, the staff generally only ask to see your passport and landing card, from which they will fill in details in a book and then return it. If you must turn over your passport, make sure that the correct one – and the landing card – are returned to you. Hotel staff are prone to misplacing passports; don't wait until you are at the airport before you check.

If you plan on staying with family or friends then you should visit the local police station to avoid any late-night visits by the police, as nosy neighbours often report suspicious foreigners. Although you may consider this a nuisance, you will be saving your hosts quite a bit of trouble from authorities.

Be aware that in some remote areas in the central highlands, internal travel permits are required for travel. Tourists have reported being arrested by provincial police in the central highlands and Mekong Delta for travelling in restricted areas. Occasionally, innocent tourists walk unknowingly into sensitive border areas and military installations unaware that they are breaking the law. The best advice is to play it safe in very remote areas and always contact the police. Spending your holiday under house arrest is not much fun.

### Customs Regulations

#### Entry Formalities

Visitors to Vietnam are required to fill

## Big Brother

In an archaic throwback to old-style communism, movements of "suspicious" foreigners may be monitored by the local police. Tour guides have been known to be instructed to report the activities of their clients, while some private tour companies, and certainly state-owned ones, are said to employ members of the country's internal security apparatus.

In reality, most tourists will never come in direct contact with police. However, visitors who spend more than a few days off the beaten path may receive visits from inquisitive policemen and even be followed. Persons suspected of engaging

in a detailed customs declaration in duplicate upon arrival. Customs may inspect your luggage to verify that you have made a correct declaration. Currency in excess of US$7,000, as well as most electronic items – cameras, computers, video cameras – should be declared. Books, reading material and videos are supposed to be declared, but it doesn't seem to be expected. Your items may be inspected to check for anything considered culturally or politically sensitive (including religious items), but this is usually only a concern for mailed parcels.

You must keep a copy of the customs declaration form to show customs officials upon leaving Vietnam. They may check to see if you are leaving with the items declared, such as computers and cameras.

#### Exit Formalities

Official authorisation from the Ministry of Culture is required to take antiquities out of the country. Visitors are not allowed to take ancient artefacts, Buddha images, antiques or "items of value to Vietnamese culture". An antique is defined as anything more than 30 years old. Travellers have reported problems in trying to leave with items that appear to be antiques, even if they are reproductions. It is a good idea to take a detailed receipt from the shop with a description of the item.

When leaving Vietnam, you may be stopped to have film, video and reading materials inspected. Usually this is just an annoyance, but if you are a journalist, your equipment may be seized unless you have express permission to take them out from the government's Foreign Affairs Press Department.

in criminal or politically sensitive activities will also be closely watched. Likewise, any mail or parcels sent or received in Vietnam may be searched for political or religious materials. Don't put your new Vietnamese friends in jeopardy – leave your political views at home.

Censorship is a way of life in Vietnam. Every form of media – including pop songs, newspapers, TV shows and children's books – must be submitted for prior approval before being printed, broadcast or performed. Even churches must submit their sermons and song lists for prior approval.

## D

### Disabled Travellers

With all the traffic, the scarcity of lifts, clogged pavements, squat-type toilets and the sheer amount of people out and about on the streets, Vietnam is not designed for disabled travellers. The roads are extremely treacherous and traffic doesn't tend to stop, even for disabled travellers, especially in the major cities. It's a contentious issue that a country with so many disabled citizens hasn't done more to accommodate them. Thankfully, it's not impossible for adventurous disabled people with an easy-going attitude to get by. Make sure you plan well ahead and find out about hotel access. Generally the bigger hotels have wheelchair access, toilets and lifts for the disabled.

## E

### Electricity

The voltage in the cities and towns is generally 220V, 50 cycles, but sometimes 110V in the rural areas. Electric sockets are standard European and/or American, but bring an adaptor just in case. If you bring a computer to Vietnam, you should consider using a surge suppressor to protect its circuit.

### Embassies and Consulates

#### Embassies in Hanoi

**Australia**, 8 Dao Tan St, Ba Dinh

District, tel: 04-3831 7755, fax: 04-3831 7711; www.vietnam. embassy.gov.au.
**Canada**, 31 Hung Vuong St, tel: 04-3734 5000, fax: 04-3734 5049; www.dfait-maeci.gc.ca/vietnam.
**New Zealand**, 63 Ly Thai To St, tel: 04-3824 1481, fax: 04-3824 1480; www.nzembassy.com.
**Singapore**, 83B Ly Thuong Kiet St, tel: 04-3823 3966, fax: 04-3825 1600; www.mfa.gov.sg/hanoi.
**United Kingdom**, 31 Hai Ba Trung St, tel: 04-3936 0500, fax: 04-3936 0562; www.uk-vietnam.org.
**United States**, 7 Lang Ha St, tel: 04-3831 4590, fax: 04-850 35010; http://vietnam.usembassy.gov.

### Consulates in Ho Chi Minh City

**Australia**, 5B Ton Duc Thang St, District 1, tel: 08-3829 6035, fax: 08-3829 6031; www.hcmc.vietnam. embassy.gov.au.
**Canada**, 235 Dong Khoi St, District 1, tel: 08-3827 9899, fax: 08-3827 9935.
**New Zealand**, 235 Dong Khoi St, District 1, tel: 08-3822 6907, fax: 08-3822 6905.
**Singapore**, Saigon Centre, 8th Floor, 65 Le Loi St, District 1, tel: 08-3822 5174, fax: 08-3914 2938; www.mfa. gov.sg/hochiminhcity.
**United Kingdom**, 25 Le Duan St, District 1, tel: 08-3829 8433, fax: 08-3829 5257; email: bcghcmc@ hcm.vnn.vn.
**United States**, 4 Le Duan St, District 1, tel: 08-3822 9433, fax: 08-3822 9434; http://hochiminh.usconsulate. gov.

## Entry Requirements

### Tourist and Business Visas

Nationals from most Southeast Asian countries do not need a visa for stays of less than 30 days, while citizens from Korea, Japan, Russia and Scandinavian countries can go visa-free for 15 days.

For all other nationals, getting a visa is fairly straightforward, but one important change is that unless you are from the countries mentioned above, you cannot just turn up in Vietnam and get a visa on arrival. Most travellers apply for a one-month, single-entry tourist visa beforehand that costs a minimum US$25 (depending upon where you arrange it). Multiple-entry tourist visas up to six months in duration start at around US$70.

The easy way of getting a visa is to use the travel agent from whom you buy your air ticket. There will be

a commission charge on top of the usual visa processing fee paid to the Vietnamese embassy or consulate. In addition to the application form, you must submit a valid passport and two passport-size photos. Allow two working days for approval. A letter will be issued and visitors then need to present this when they arrive at any Vietnamese airport.

Individual travellers may also apply directly for a visa with the Vietnamese embassy or consulate in their home country, but this might prove tedious. For a list of Vietnamese foreign missions overseas, check the Ministry of Foreign Affairs website (www.mofa. gov.vn).

Many travellers who stop over in Bangkok apply for visas there. Travel agents in Bangkok offer attractive round-trip flight and visa packages. The best place to acquire visas however, is Phnom Penh, where travel agencies can arrange to have both multiple-entry business and normal tourist visas issued in as little as 24 hours – depending upon how much you are willing to pay.

Other types of visa available include press, family visit and official visit. To enter Vietnam on business, technically you should contact your Vietnamese sponsor, who will then submit an application form and letter to the embassy. Such visas allow for multiple-entry and are valid for up to six months. In practice, however, business visas can be arranged easily, just like tourist visas, from most travel agencies in Phnom Penh or in Bangkok. Processing business visas costs more, with prices starting at around US$120.

Most major tour agents are now able to offer pre-arranged visas when you arrive in Hanoi, Danang and HCMC airports, for US$50 or more. The agent will fax you an "invitation letter" which you will need to present to immigration on arrival.

Note: visas must be used within one month of their issue. The period of your visa begins on the date you specify on the application form – not on the date you actually enter the country. Postponing your visit by two weeks means that your month-long visa will only be valid for two weeks.

### Extension and Renewal of Visas

Most travel agencies in Vietnam can arrange 30-day extensions of tourist visas for US$22–30. Often this can only be done once, without having to leave the country to apply for a new visa altogether. However, these rules change frequently, and it also

depends on how well connected your agent is. Six-month multiple-entry business visas can be renewed in Vietnam for around the same price as the original visa.

## Etiquette

Arguing in a loud and aggressive manner will get you nowhere very fast in Vietnam. Complaining about bad service in an international-standard hotel is one thing, but such actions will fall on deaf ears at a humble guesthouse. The very notion of service is alien to the majority of the Vietnamese, and vociferous complaining won't persuade them otherwise. On the other hand, a smile can go a long way, open doors and win favours. The Vietnamese prefer a cooperative rather than confrontational approach.

As with many other parts of Asia, Confucian attitudes remain strong, and seniority demands respect whatever the circumstances. The eldest male member of any group is invariably "in charge". At any party it is the eldest who is served first, gets to eat first and generally dictates the course of events.

### During Meals

Most meals are eaten "family style" with shared courses. It is considered polite for hosts occasionally to dish out the best morsels, using their chopsticks, into the guests' bowl throughout the meal. In many dining establishments it is common to discard table scraps on the floor or even on the table itself. Observe what others do, and do likewise. You do not have to accept every food item or drink (especially alcohol) that you are offered, but you should empty your rice bowl. Do not leave chopsticks sticking upright in your bowl as it symbolises an offering to the dead.

### At Temples

Anyone visiting the inner sanctum of a Buddhist temple will be required to remove their shoes and hat. Temples administered by the government as "cultural relics" (tourist attractions) generally require men to wear shirt and trousers, and women to wear a modest top with skirt or trousers. Contrary to what is often written, however, such dress is not required to visit most pagodas, and Vietnamese men and women will often show up in shorts and T-shirts. Be respectful when inside and always point your feet away from any Buddha image.

## Festivals

Nearly all of Vietnam's festivals coincide with the lunar calendar. For an extensive list of festivals with detailed information and precise dates, check www.vietnamtourism. com. *See also page 258.*

## Gay and Lesbian Travellers

Travel in Vietnam is a relative breeze for gay people. Legally there is no law against homosexuality, but police are known to harass Vietnamese homosexuals observed loitering. Same-sex couples will not be questioned about sharing the same hotel room at first, but if guests stay for an extended period, there will be presumptions made.

It is quite common to see open affection between the same sexes in cafés or on the street among the Vietnamese. Men can often be seen holding hands, and women too, even though they are not homosexuals; it's just a sign of deep friendship. On the other hand, it is quite rare to see open affection between men and women.

In 2002, Vietnamese writer Bui Anh Tan won a literary prize for his novel *A World without Women*, which tackles the issue of homosexuality in Vietnam. However, the fact that one of the novel's main characters is suddenly "cured" of homosexuality and becomes attracted to women makes the whole premise of the novel somewhat laughable. Still, the very fact that a novel like this was published (and made into a television series in 2007) in Vietnam shows a measure of progress in attitudes.

For more information on Vietnam's gay scene, check the Asian-wide gay portal **Utopia** at www.utopia-asia. com/tipsviet.htm.

## Health and Medical Care

### Vaccines

The only vaccination required is for yellow fever, a prerequisite for travellers coming from Africa. Immunisation against hepatitis (A and B), Japanese encephalitis and tetanus is strongly encouraged.

It is a good idea to consult a physician a month to six weeks before departing to leave enough time to obtain the immunisations.

Malaria and dengue fever are prevalent throughout Vietnam, but are rarely seen outside the central highlands and the Mekong Delta. The best protection is prevention. Sleep under a mosquito net at night when visiting rural areas, use potent DEET repellent on exposed skin at all times, and where possible try to wear long-sleeved tops and trousers. Malaria-carrying mosquitoes are most active during the night, but the mosquitoes that spread dengue are most active during the day.

If you are travelling in remote areas, consult with a knowledgeable doctor to determine what anti-malarial drugs are best suited for your travels. For more information check the website of the Centre for Disease Control (CDC) in Atlanta, United States: www.cdc.gov.

### Food and Water

Food is often prepared in insanitary conditions. Ice is delivered to rest-aurants and hotels each day by motorbike and laid bare on the doorsteps. Market produce is doused with canal and river water to keep it looking fresh. Butcher shops hang meat along dusty streets for hours in the hot sun.

Fruit and vegetables should be peeled before eating. Cooking them is a better idea. Savvy travellers advise against eating the raw herbs and lettuce served with Vietnamese noodle soup *(pho)* and spring rolls. However, most tourists ignore these recommendations with out consequences. Because most places do not have refrigeration, food is thrown away at the end of the day. If a place is crowded, it is a good sign that it serves freshly cooked food.

Do not drink tap water unless it has been boiled properly. It is safest to avoid ice in drinks as well. Imported bottled water is available in most cities, but beware of bottles that are refilled with tap water. Check to make sure the bottle has a seal. And don't forget to drink plenty of liquids to guard against dehydration.

### Emergencies

Should you have an accident or an emergency health problem in Vietnam, you may want to consider evacuation to Singapore or Bangkok for treatment. Visitors to Vietnam should therefore have health insurance that includes repatriation (or at least travel to Bangkok or Singapore for emergency treatment).

### Medication

Imported pharmaceutical drugs are available throughout the country, but it is best to bring a small supply of medicine to cope with diarrhoea, dysentery, eye infections, insect bites, fungal infections and the common cold.

## Hospitals and Clinics

### Hanoi

**Hanoi French Hospital**, 1 Phuong Mai St, Dong Da District, tel: 04-3577 1100. A full-service hospital that caters to French nationals and wealthy Vietnamese. The health-care services are expensive and of acceptable standards.
**International SOS Clinic**, 31 Hai Ba Trung St, Hoan Kiem District, tel: 04-3934 0666. The most expensive clinic in Hanoi. Staffed with international doctors and nurses. Refers patients abroad to Bangkok or Singapore for hospital treatments.
**Vietnam-Korea Friendship Clinic**, 12 Chu Van An St, Ba Dinh District, tel: 04-3843 7231. Excellent Korean-run clinic that is both affordable and clean. Has new facilities, and patients can choose either a Korean or Vietnamese doctor.

### Ho Chi Minh City

**Columbia Saigon**, 8 Alexandre de Rhodes St, tel: 08-3829 8520. Good reputation with international doctors and emergency evacuation.
**HCMC Family Medical Practice**, Diamond Plaza, 34 Le Duan St, tel: 08-3822 7848. International doctors offering vaccinations, dental services and emergency evacuation.
**International SOS Clinic**, 65 Nguyen Du St, tel: 08-3829 8424. The top choice in the city has international doctors and 24-hour emergency services. Refers patients abroad to Bangkok or Singapore for hospital treatments.

## Internet

Internet cafés with computer terminals are quickly losing popularity with the rapid proliferation of free Wi-fi, and the fact that most hotels have one or two computers with free

**TRANSPORT** · **ACCOMMODATION** · **ACTIVITIES** · **A – Z** · **LANGUAGE**

access to the internet for their guests. Still, you are likely to find at least one or two venues with computer terminals in most tourist areas and large towns. Most Vietnamese cafés with indoor seating have free Wi-fi, as do many bars, restaurants and hotels that serve foreigners.

## Left Luggage

Tan Son Nhat Airport (tel: 08-3844 6665), which services Ho Chi Minh City, has left-luggage facilities (daily 7.30am–11pm) at both terminals.

All hotels and guesthouses offer a left-luggage service; usually it is free, but some may levy a small daily fee for extended periods.

## Lost Property

If you lose or have any valuable property stolen, report it as soon as possible to the local police to receive an insurance statement. Travellers who are very vocal about lost or stolen wallets have reported that their wallets were returned, including passports and credit cards (but minus any cash). Similarly, some thieves and opportunists who find lost items may return them – in exchange for a small ransom.

## M

## Maps

Most travel agencies offer free maps of the city in which they are located. Sinh Café Travel (see *Tours and Activities section in Activities Travel Tips*) has a handy free booklet that includes maps for all the cities they service. Popular bookstores like Fahasa and Phuong Nam sell maps for the cities and provinces in which they are located. Large bookstores in HCMC and Hanoi sell maps and detailed atlases for most parts of the country. There is usually a free local map (with advertisements) available at popular hotels and restaurants in each city as well. Most cities and provinces also have their own guidebooks (printed in English) which are sold at local bookstores.

## Media

All Vietnamese media, whether print, broadcast, recordings or performances, must undergo a lengthy government censorship and approval process before they go public. In recent years, however, government-run newspapers have begun criticising corruption and some government policies, albeit in a somewhat timid manner.

Foreign newspapers and magazines can be purchased in larger bookstores in downtown HCMC and Hanoi, as well as some upscale hotels (although they aren't always current). Street vendors in tourist areas often sell second-hand copies too.

### Newspapers

Vietnam has several English-language government-run newspapers, including *Viet Nam News* (http://vietnamnews.vnagency.com.vn), *Vietnam Investment Review* (www.vir.com.vn) with its helpful weekly supplement called *Timeout* (www.vir.com.vn/client/timeout), and *Vietnam Economic Times* (www.vneconomy.vn), with its weekly supplement The Guide.

### Magazines

*Vietnam Pathfinder* (www.pathfinder.com.vn) and *Vietnam Discovery* are free government publications developed for tourists. Both have decent listings and reviews.

### Radio

Voice of Vietnam (www.vov.org.vn), the official government radio station, began as a propaganda tool during the wars. Two stations transmit English-language programmes on a variety of subjects several times a day on FM radio.

### Television

Most hotels, restaurants, bars and cafés now have cable or satellite television with access to CNN, BBC, Australia Network, Star TV, Discovery: Travel & Living, HBO, Cartoon Network, MTV Asia and more. The quality of transmission is generally poor in rural areas; it's not uncommon to be interrupted in the middle of a programme with a sudden switch to another channel.

## Money Matters

Vietnam's unit of currency, the dong (pronounced *dome*, and abbreviated as VND), currently circulates in bank-notes of 500,000, 100,000, 50,000, 20,000, 10,000, 5,000, 2,000, 1,000, and now infrequently, 500, 200 and 100. Coins of 5,000, 2,000, 1,000, 500 and 200 denominations are common in cities but not small towns. Notes from 10,000 to 500,000 are now made of polymer plastic, which ensures a longer life span and and is difficult to counterfeit. The dong's value against the dollar has begun to slide in the past few years: at the time of writing it was about VND1,700 to US$1. Care should be taken when exchanging money or receiving change. The old 20,000 notes and the 5,000 are the same size and colour (blue) and easily confused. The 100,000 and new 10,000 (both green) as well as the 500,000 and new 20,000 (both blue) are also easily confused, though of different sizes.

All transactions are supposed to be conducted in Vietnamese dong; in practice, a dual-currency system exists. That is, most purchases can be made with US dollars as well as Vietnamese dong.

Vietnamese have an obsession with unblemished US dollars and larger dong notes. They will often refuse notes with tears or handwriting on them, although they can usually be turned in at banks. Counterfeiting of US notes $5 and higher, as well as VND100,000 and higher, is very common. Most of it actually comes through the government banks.

At the time of writing US$1 = 20,800VND.

### Exchanging Money

Changing money on the street is never a good idea. Most money-changers on the street are scam artists who will try to cheat you by offering ridiculously poor exchange rates or attempt to slip counterfeit notes into wads of the genuine stuff. It's best to stick to a bank.

Apart from banks, establishments that cater to foreigners, like hotels, travel agencies, restaurants and cafés, will also exchange dollars at bank rates. It is also possible to change dollars at almost any jewellery or gold shop; sometimes the rate is slightly higher than the bank rate. Look for a shop with the sign *Vang* (gold). They are easily identifiable because the signs usually have bright, gold-coloured letters. Be prepared to be offered two exchange rates: one for denominations of 50 and 100 US dollars, and a lower rate for smaller denominations.

### Traveller's Cheques and Credit Cards

Traveller's cheques in US dollars are accepted in most banks and in major hotels, but not in shops and not in smaller hotels or any restaurants.

Major credit cards are accepted at upscale hotels, restaurants, shops and many tour offices.

Note: fairly high commission rates – usually 3 percent – are tacked onto your bill when using credit cards.

Cash advances can be withdrawn using major credit cards (again with the 3 percent commission) from a few banks, including branches of Vietcombank and Sacombank. Vietcombank will also provide cash dollars for US dollar traveller's cheques – for a 2 percent surcharge.

## Photography

Everything the photographer may need is readily available in most cities. Camera shops and photo-development outlets are commonly found in the tourist areas, and all now offer digital transfers onto CD and hard-copy photos from digital memory cards. Traditional and digital equipment of all kinds are available. Cameras are often more expensive than in Western countries but accessories are usually cheaper.

Photographing government buildings, policemen and military installations is prohibited. Virtually any other subject matter is fine.

## Postal Services

Post offices are generally open every day from 7am to 8pm, and are the telecommunications hub of Vietnam. In the smaller towns, they often don't even identify themselves as post offices (buu dien) at all, but rather by the name of the cell-phone plans (Vinaphone or Mobiphone) they sell.

Post offices usually offer computers with internet access (although very slow), fax services, and courier services like FedEx, UPS, DHL and EMS. However, these services are not as reliable in Vietnam as they might be in other countries. It is common for foreigners to be charged extra for postal and courier services, although there is usually no official reason given for this.

### Central Post Offices

**Dalat**, 2 Le Dai Hanh St, tel: 063-382 2586.
**Danang**, Bach Dang St, near Song Han Bridge, tel: 0511-382 1327.
**Hanoi**, 75 Pho Dinh Tien Hoang St, tel: 04-3825 7036 (domestic), 04-3825 2030 (international).
**Ho Chi Minh City**, 2 Cong Xa Paris St,

tel: 08-3829 6555.
**Hoi An**, 6 Tran Hung Dao St, tel: 0510-386 1480.
**Hue**, 8 Hoang Hoa Tham St, tel: 054-382 3468.
**Nha Trang**, 2 Tran Phu St, tel: 058-382 1002.
**Phan Thiet**, corner of Nguyen Tat Thanh St, tel: 062-382 7892.

## Public Holidays

The most important celebration of the year in Vietnam is Tet, or Lunar New Year, which falls either in late January or early February each year (see also page 69), on the day of the full moon between the winter solstice and the spring equinox. Officially, there are three public holidays, but in reality almost all of Vietnam shuts down for an entire week.

It is best to avoid being on the road during this period (relaxing at a beach hotel is fine). As the celebrations begin the week before the actual festivities, roads, trains and planes become clogged with local and overseas Vietnamese rushing home for their family reunions. It may be difficult to arrange transportation and book hotels during this period.

The dates of nearly all festivals vary from year to year because they follow the lunar calendar. By counting the days from a new moon, it's fairly easy to determine when, say, "the third day of the second lunar month" falls on the familiar Gregorian calendar. But it's easier to consult a Vietnamese calendar, which always comes with both systems.
**1 Jan**: New Year's Day
**Jan/Feb**: Tet
**3 Feb**: Founding of Vietnamese Communist Party
**30 Apr**: Liberation Day
**1 May**: International Labour Day
**19 May**: Ho Chi Minh's Birthday
**June**: Buddha's Birthday (8th day of the fourth lunar month)
**2 Sep**: National Day/Independence Day

## Public Toilets

Most bus trips that cater to foreign tourists include scheduled stops at places that have Western-style toilets. Shopping centres, most hotels and the better restaurants and cafés also normally have Western-style toilet facilities. However, go off the beaten tourist track and you will come face to face with squat toilets that you may not be used to. Be sure to carry a pack of tissue paper as toilet paper is unlikely to be available.

## Religious Services

Foreigners are free in most cities to attend registered, government-authorised temples and churches, but their attendance may be noted by authorities, especially at churches. Foreigners who visit unregistered places of worship, or churches in remote areas, may be detained and questioned at length by the local police.

Buddhists and Catholics will have no difficulty finding convenient places of worship. Most large towns have at least one Protestant and one Catholic church each. Cities with large Catholic and Protestant populations, such as HCMC and Danang, have a dozen or more authorised churches. HCMC also has several mosques, Hindu temples, and at least one Chabad Lubavitch (Jewish centre). Outside of Hanoi and HCMC, it's best to ask your hotel receptionist for the address of the local place of worship, and then go there directly to enquire about times for services.

## Taxes

Vietnam has a standard 10 percent Value Added Tax. Usually this is already included in quoted prices for goods and services. However, upscale hotels and restaurants serving mostly foreign tourists may add it as a separate fee to the final bill.

## Telephones

Calling home from abroad is a lot cheaper than it used to be. The exception to this is at 5-star hotels, where IDD calls are still prohibitively expensive.

When calling a city in Vietnam from overseas, dial the country code **84**, followed by the area code, but drop the prefix zero. When making a domestic call from one province or city to another in Vietnam, dial the area code first (including the prefix zero). Note: local calls within the same province/city do not require the area code. See list of area codes below.

Vietnam upgraded its phone systems in October 2008 by adding an additional digit (which can be any number between 2 and 6) after the area code to all land-line phone numbers. The specific number addition is dependent upon

TRANSPORT

ACCOMMODATION

ACTIVITIES

A – Z

LANGUAGE

the service provider and not the region. Most land lines are serviced by VNPT and so have a "3" inserted before the existing phone number. The exceptions are newly issued phone numbers and land lines in rural areas.

Land lines in HCMC and Hanoi now have 8 digits plus a 2-digit area code (08 for HCMC and 04 for Hanoi). Danang and Quang Nam province (including Hoi An) land lines now have 7 digits plus a 4-digit area code (0511 and 0510, respectively). All other locations now have 7 digits with a 3-digit area code.

Voice Over Internet Protocol is the standard method of placing overseas calls from Vietnam. Calls can be made in any internet café, or via any telephone by first dialling 17100, followed by the country code and number. Rates average US$0.50 a minute. Or you can just Skype.

### Mobile Phones

Local mobile phone numbers are 10 digits, starting with the prefix 09 (the most common being 090, 091, 095 and 098, with more added from time to time).

Most mobile phone users from overseas who have signed up for roaming facility with their service providers back home will be able to hook up with the GSM 900 or 1800 network that Vietnam uses. The exceptions are users from Japan and North America (unless they have a tri-band phone). It's best to check with your service provider. Alternatively, cheap phones using prepaid cards can be purchased in Vietnam for a few hundred thousand dong, along with a local number for an additional VND75,000. These prepaid cards are available at Vina-phone and Mobiphone shops, post offices, or any shop that sells mobile phones. Sim cards can be bought for about $7.

### Time Zones

Vietnam is seven hours ahead of GMT. Since it gets dark between 6pm and

7pm uniformly throughout the year, Vietnam does not observe daylight-saving time.

### Tipping

Tipping is not part of the traditional Vietnamese culture, although it is becoming more common in areas that are frequented by foreign tourists. If you've received particularly good service, a tip of VND5,000 to 20,000 is reasonable; avoid giving excessive amounts. Upscale hotels and restaurants usually add on a 5 to 10 percent service charge to their bills.

### Tourist Offices

Vietnam's tourism industry lags behind other Asian countries (and for some travellers this may be a good thing). The official representative for Vietnam's tourism – domestically as well as overseas – comes under the purview of the government-operated **Vietnam National Administration of Tourism** (VNAT; www.vietnamtourism.com). However, it is more involved in the construction of new hotels and infrastructure development than in providing tourist services. State-run "tourist offices" under the VNAT are merely tour agents out to make money and are not geared towards meeting the requirements of most travellers. For tours, car hire and travel-related information, you are better off with privately run travel and transport agencies (see Tours and Activities page 370).

### W

### Websites

### General

**www.vietnamtourism.com**
Vietnam National Administration of Tourism.

### Area Codes: Provinces

| | |
|---|---|
| Ben Tre | 075 |
| Binh Dinh | 056 |
| Can Tho | 071 |
| Chau Doc | 076 |
| Ha Tien | 077 |
| Ha Tinh | 039 |
| Hoa Binh | 018 |
| Khanh Hoa | 058 |
| Lai Chau | 023 |
| Lao Cai | 020 |
| Quang Nam-Danang | 0511 |
| Quang Tri | 053 |
| Rach Gia | 077 |
| Soc Trang | 079 |
| Son La | 022 |
| Tay Ninh | 066 |
| Thai Binh | 036 |
| Thanh Hoa | 037 |
| Thua Thien-Hue | 054 |
| Tien Giang | 073 |

**www.mofa.gov.vn/en**
Ministry of Foreign Affairs.

### Regional Sites

**www.dalattourist.com.vn**
Government tourism office for Dalat.
**www.haiphong.gov.vn**
Government and tourism site for Haiphong.
**www.halong.org.vn**
Tourism site of Halong Bay.
**www.hanoi.gov.vn**
Government and tourism site for Hanoi.
www.longwallofquangngai.com
Tourism site on the Long Wall of Quang Ngai and surroundings.
**www.newhanoian.com**
Reviews of Hanoi's shops, restaurants and hotels along with classifieds.
http://hochiminhcity.gov.vn/default.htm
Ho Chi Minh City's Department of Tourism.
**www.muinebeach.net**
Tourism information and local news in Mui Ne Beach and surroundings.

### Special Interest

**www.thingsasian.com**
Travelogues, stories and recommendations for much of Asia, with a special focus on Vietnam.
**www.panda.org**
WWF Indochina's Greater Mekong Programme.

### Weights and Measures

Vietnam uses the metric system. Temperatures are measured in degrees Celsius. Measurements in this book are given in metric with the imperial equivalents in brackets.

### Area Codes: Cities

| | | | | |
|---|---|---|---|---|
| Buon Ma Thuot | 050 | Hue | 054 |
| Can Tho | 071 | Long Hai | 064 |
| Chau Doc | 076 | My Tho | 073 |
| Danang | 0511 | Nha Trang | 058 |
| Dalat | 063 | Phan Thiet | 062 |
| Haiphong | 031 | Quy Nhon | 056 |
| Hanoi | 04 | Rach Gia | 077 |
| Ho Chi Minh City | 08 | Vinh | 038 |
| Hoi An | 0510 | Vung Tau | 064 |

# LANGUAGE

# UNDERSTANDING THE LANGUAGE

## Origins and Intonation

Vietnamese, the national language, is spoken by nearly the entire population. Significant variations in pronunciation, some vocabulary, and even the tones themselves exist between northern, central and southern dialect. However, small differences can even be found between cities and surrounding villages. Through the centuries of Chinese occupation the Vietnamese adopted the Han characters. In the 13th century they developed their own written variation – Nom. In the 17th century, on the initiative of a French Jesuit priest, Alexandre de Rhodes, missionaries translated the language into its Romanised form, Quoc Ngu, which was first used by the Catholic Church and the colonial regime's administration. Gradually its use spread, replacing the old written form in the 20th century.

Although Vietnamese uses compound words frequently, individual word fragments are always monosyllabic (unless borrowed from another language). Each syllable (word) can be spoken with one of six different tones (central and southern dialects only have five tones), which could convey six unrelated meanings. These tones are expressed by five diacritical accents and one atonic, where the word has no accent. For example, the word bo can mean "a toilet for children", "father", "lover", "to chop", "impolite", or "a government ministry". While these tones are clearly important, their significance can be overstated. Context is equally important. If the person on the receiving end is patient, most meanings can be conveyed eventually, even if the tones are not entirely correct. After all, tones disappear entirely when Vietnamese

is set to music, yet the meaning is still clear, due to context.

Thankfully, Vietnamese has no verb conjugations or tenses (instead, five modifier words are used to convey tense), no masculine or feminine, and no plural noun forms (a universal modifier word is used – cac). To compensate for such simplicity, Vietnamese employs numerous confusing pronouns and titles, mimicking family relationships (for instance, you might address a man as young, middle or older "uncle", younger or older "brother", "friend", or even "grandfather", depending upon his age and the formality of the situation).

Learners often fret over which dialect they should learn. Ultimately, you should learn the dialect of the area where you plan to spend most of your time. Beginners are often told they should learn the Hanoi accent of the northern dialect, because it is the linguistic standard. Indeed, most language courses teach this dialect. Reasons given include the idea that the Vietnamese culture (and thus the language) began in the north and moved southward (thus the northern dialect is the most original), or that Hanoians pronounce the language exactly as it is written. However, it has been argued that these justifications tend to be based more on politics and elitism than logic and pragmatism.

## Phonology

The Vietnamese alphabet has 29 letters, although it lacks the English letters **f**, **j**, **w** and **z**. Most consonants are pronounced as they are in English, with a few exceptions: **c** takes on the sound of g or k. A **ch** sound at the end of a word sounds like k. The letter **d** with a crossbar sounds like a d in English,

but a **d** without a crossbar sounds like z in the north and a y in the south. A **g** normally has the same hard sound as in English, but when followed by an i, it sounds like a z in the north and a y in the south. When a word begins with **ng** or **ngh**, the letters sound like the ng in the English word long. However, when a word ends in **ng**, the letters sound like m. The letter combination **nh** sounds like ny as in canyon. As in English, **ph** sounds like f. In the south, an **r** sounds as it does in English, but in the north, it sounds like a z. A **th** at the beginning of a word sounds like a strongly aspirated t. A **tr** at the beginning of a word usually sounds like ch, but can also sound like a very hard tr. Finally, an **x** always sounds like the letter s.

Vowels are a much more complicated affair. There are 12 vowels in the alphabet, and each can be altered by the addition of five different diacritic marks to change the tone of the word. Furthermore, vowels routinely appear in series of up to three letters per word, creating new sound combinations. With such extensive variability, it takes a lot of practice to learn all the possibilities. Beginners should not be deterred, however. Vietnamese pronunciation is very consistent (within each of the regional dialects), so once a pattern is learnt, it can generally be applied to every reoccurrence of that pattern.

Five of the six tones correspond to individual diacritic marks above and below the key vowel in each word. The mid tone does not have an associated diacritic mark.
**Mid Tone**: Voiced at the speaker's normal, even pitch.
**Low Falling Tone**: Pitched slightly lower than the mid tone and falls lower.
**High Rising Tone**: Pitched slightly higher than the mid tone and rises sharply.

**Low Dipping-Rising Tone**: Pitched lower than the mid tone, dips and then rises.
**High Breaking-Rising Tone**: Pitched slightly higher than the mid tone, dips and then rises sharply.
**Low Falling Constricted Tone**: Pitched lower than the mid tone, drops lower, and then stops abruptly.

## Numbers

**0** *khong*
**1** *mot*
**2** *hai*
**3** *ba*
**4** *bon*
**5** *nam*
**6** *sau*
**7** *bay*
**8** *tam*
**9** *chin*
**10** *muoi*
**11** *muoi mot*
**15** *muoi nam*
**20** *hai muoi* (north), *hai chuc* (south)
**50** *nam muoi* (north), *nam chuc* (south)
**100** *mot tram*
**1000** *mot nghin* (north), *mot ngan* (south)
**1,000,000** *mot trieu*

## Days of the Week

**Monday** *thu hai*
**Tuesday** *thu ba*
**Wednesday** *thu tu*
**Thursday** *thu nam*
**Friday** *thu sau*
**Saturday** *thu bay*
**Sunday** *chu nhat*

## Basics

**Yesterday** *hom qua*
**Today** *hom nay*
**Tomorrow** *ngay mai*
**Yes** *vang* (north), *da* (south)
**No** *khong*
**Hello** *xin chao*
**Goodbye** *tam biet*
**My name is…** *ten toi la…*
**How are you?** *ban co khoe khong?*
**Thank you** *cam on*
**Thank you very much** *cam on rat nhieu*
**Sorry/Excuse me** *xin loi*
**Can you help me?** *Ban co the giup toi duoc khong?*
**No problem/you're welcome** *khong co gi*
**Do you speak English?** *Ban co noi duoc tieng Anh khong?*
**I don't understand** *Toi khong hieu*

## Directions and Travel

**Go** *di*
**Come** *den*

**Where** *o dau*
**Right** *ben phai*
**Left** *ben trai*
**Turn** *re* (north), *queo* (south)
**Straight ahead** *phia truoc*
**Stop here** *ngung o day* (north), *dung tai day* (south)
**Fast** *nhanh*
**Slow** *cham*
**Hotel** *khach san*
**Street** *duong*
**Lane** *duong nho, con hem*
**Bridge** *cai cau*
**Police station** *don canh sat*
**Ferry** *pha*
**Aeroplane** *may bay*
**Taxi** *tac xi*
**Train** *tau lua* (north), *xe lua* (south)
**Bus** *xe buyt*
**Cable car** *cap treo*
**Rickshaw** *xich lo*
**Pier** *ben tau*
**Bus stop** *tram xe buyt*
**Bus station** *noi do xe*
**Train station** *nha ga*
**How do I get to… the bus stop?** *Toi di den… tram xe buyt… nhu the nao?*
**Can you show me on the map where I am?** *Ban co the chi cho toi biet toi dang o dau tren ban do?*
**Where's the… tour office?** *Van phong du lich… o dau?*

## Accommodation

**The air conditioning doesn't work** *May dieu hoa khong hoat dong.*
**The light doesn't work** *Den khong sang.*
**There's no hot water** *O day khong co nuoc nong.*
**Do you have… toilet paper?** *Ban co… giay ve sinh… khong?*

## Shopping

**How much?** *Bao nhieu?*
**Expensive** *rat dat*
**Do you have a cheaper price?** *Ban co gia nao re hon khong?*
**Can I try it on?** *Toi co the thu no khong?*
**Too big** *rat rong*
**Too small** *rat chat*
**I'll take it** *Toi se mua no.*
**I don't like it** *Toi khong thich no.*
**Do you have another colour?** *Ban co mau nao khac khong?*

## Colour

**White** *mau trang*
**Black** *mau den*
**Red** *mau do*
**Yellow** *mau vang*
**Blue** *mau xanh nuoc bien*
**Green** *mau xanh la cay*
**Orange** *mau cam*

## Eating Out

**May I have the menu, please?** *Lam on cho toi cai thuc don?*
**Nothing too spicy, please** *Lam on moi thu khong qua cay*
**I'm vegetarian** *toi an chay*
**Hot (heat hot)** *nong*
**Hot (spicy)** *cay*
**Cold** *lanh*
**Sweet** *ngot*
**Sour** *chua*
**Delicious** *ngon*
**Water** *nuoc*
**Coffee** *ca phe*

## Other Handy Phrases

**Can I hire a… bicycle?** *Toi co the thue… xe dap… khong?*
**Do you accept credit cards?** *Ban thanh toan bang the tin dung?*
**I'd like a cash advance** *Toi lay tien mat.*
**Where's the… toilet?** *Nha ve sinh… o dau?*
**I do not feel well** *Toi cam thay khong khoe lam.*
**Can you get me a doctor?** *Ban co the goi bac si cho toi khong?*
**Is it safe to swim here?** *Noi day boi co an toan khong?*
**Is it all right to take pictures?** *Toi co the chup hinh khong?*

## Glossary of Terms

**Vietnam unit of currency** *dong*
**foreigner** *nguoi nuoc ngoai*
**map** *ban do*
**ticket** *ve*
**museum** *tang*
**market** *cho*
**go out for fun** *di choi*
**holiday** *ky nghi* (vacation), *ngay le* (festival)
**pagoda** *chua temple*
**tomb** *lang mo*
**church** *nha tho*
**Buddhist** *Nguoi theo dao Phat*
**Catholic** *Nguoi theo dao Thien Chua*
**Protestant** *Nguoi theo dao Tin Lanh*
**restaurant** *nha hang*
**toilet** *nha ve sinh*
**ship/boat** *tau/thuyen*
**motorbike** *taxi xe om*
**beach** *bai bien*
**island** *dao*
**gulf/bay** *vinh*
**city** *thanh pho*
**village** *lang/xa*
**cave** *thung lung*
**mountain** *nui*
**river** *song*
**waterfall** *thac nuoc*
**clinic** *tram xa*
**pharmacy** *nha thuoc*

# FURTHER READING

## Colonial History

**A Dragon Apparent** by Norman Lewis. Eland, 2003. Travels through Indochina in the waning days of the French empire.
**The Smaller Dragon: A Political History of Vietnam** by Joseph Buttinger. Praeger, 1958. Prehistory to the French conquest.

## War with America

**Born on the Fourth of July** by Ron Kovic. Akashic, 2005. Memoirs of a Vietnam veteran paralysed by a bullet.
**A Bright Shining Lie** by Neil Sheehan. Pimlico, 1998. A compelling account of the war from a journalist's perspective.
**Dispatches** by Michael Herr. Picador, 1991. Perhaps the most compelling account of the war in all its gruesome and, at times, surreal detail.
**Fire in the Lake** by Frances Fitzgerald. Vintage Books, 1972. A classic on the Vietnam War.
**The Nightingale's Song** by Robert Timburg. Simon & Schuster, 1995. Explores the war experiences of several noteworthy veterans.
**The Sorrow of War** by Bao Ninh. Pantheon, 1995. A North Vietnam war veteran who writes one of the first realistic novels from a northern soldier's perspective.
**A Vietcong Memoir** by Truong Nhu Tang. Vintage, 1986. The voyage of a scion of the Saigon bourgeoisie to the jungle, to the National Liberation Front, to victory and finally to escape as a boat person.

## Politics and Post-War

**Behind the Red Mist** by Ho Anh Thai. Curbstone Press, 1998. Contemporary short stories about post-war life in Vietnam.
**Catfish and Mandala** by Andrew X. Pham. Picador, 2000. Illuminates the Vietnamese-American experience by describing a family's struggle to reach America.
**Paradise of the Blind** by Duong Thu Huong. Harper Perennial, 2002. The writer has been imprisoned for her

writings that included veiled criticisms of the government.
**Vietnam Notebook** by Murray Hiebert. Review Books, 1996. An insightful collection by one of the first Westerners in Hanoi after the onset of *doi moi*.
**Vietnam, Now: A Reporter Returns** by David Lamb. Public Affairs, 2003. A journalist in the south from 1969 to 1975, Lamb returned to Vietnam in 1999 to open the peacetime office for the LA Times. His experiences with the two Vietnams – the embattled and the post-war – are recounted in depth and with great sensitivity.
**Vietnam: Rising Dragon** by Bill Hayton. Yale University Press, 2010. A comprehensive overview of contemporary Vietnamese history.
**The Will of Heaven** by Nguyen Ngoc Ngan. Dutton, 1981. A collection of memoirs by survivors of communist re-education camps.

## Culture and General History

**Champa and the Archaeology of My Son**, Andrew Hardy, Mauro Cucarzi & Patrizia Zolese (eds). Singapore: NUS Press, 2009. A detailed history of the Cham civilisation.
**Dumb Luck: A Novel** by Vu Trong Phung. University of Michigan Press, 2002. A hilarious tongue-in-cheek satire of hip Hanoians in the 1930s who want to be "modern".
**The Eaves of Heaven: A Life in Three Wars** by Andrew X. Pham. Harmony, 2008. The author tells his father's story as it unfolds through the French occupation, the Japanese invasion and the war with America.
**Ho Chi Minh: A Life** by William J. Duiker. Hyperion, 2001. An exhaustive biography of the man who fought for Vietnam's independence.
**The Tale of Kieu** by Nguyen Du. Yale University Press, 1987. The classic epic poem is a foundation of Vietnamese literature. Chronicles the struggle of the main character to maintain grace and dignity in spite of her life of suffering.

## Stories and Travel in Modern Vietnam

**Hanoi Stories** by Pamela Scott. New Holland Publishers, 2004. Tales of people and everyday life in Hanoi.
**To Vietnam with Love: A Travel Guide for the Connoisseur** by Kim Fay. Things Asian Press, 2008. A collection of recommendations with anecdotal stories from expats, seasoned travellers and locals.
**Phaic Tan: Sunstroke on a Shoestring** by Tom Gleisner and Rob Sitch. Quadrille, 2004. A witty spoof guide to Vietnam that tells you everything the tourist authority won't.

## Cookery

**Communion: A Culinary Journey Through Vietnam** by Kim Fay. Things Asian Press/Global Directions, 2010. A beautifully photographed journey through Vietnam and Vietnamese cuisine.

# ART AND PHOTO CREDITS

# INDEX

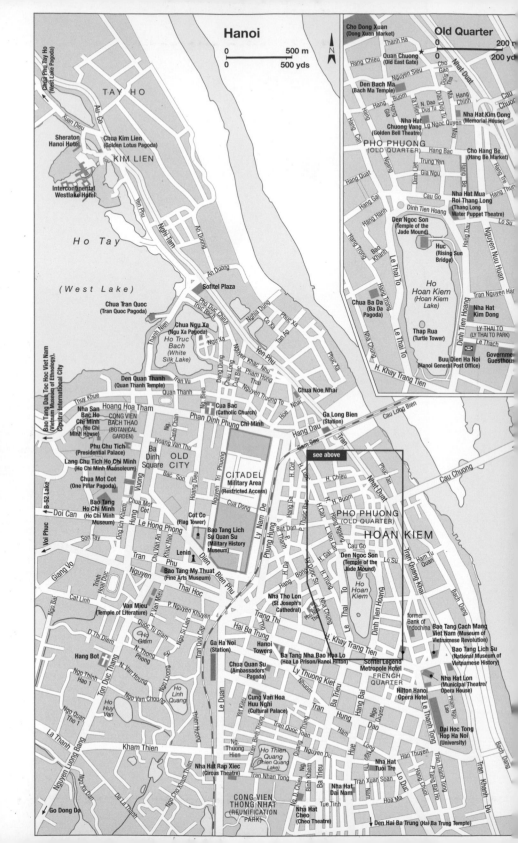

**Hanoi**

0        500 m
0        500 yds

N

**Old Quarter**

0     200 m
0     200 yds

Chua Phu Tay Ho
(West Lake Pagoda)

TAY HO

Sheraton
Hanoi Hotel

Chua Kim Lien
(Golden Lotus Pagoda)

KIM LIEN

Intercontinental
Westlake Hotel

*Ho Tay*

*(West Lake)*

Chua Tran Quoc
(Tran Quoc Pagoda)

Sofitel Plaza

Chua Ngu Xa
(Ngu Xa Pagoda)

*Ho Truc
Bach
(White
Silk Lake)*

Den Quan Thanh
(Quan Thanh Temple)

Cua Bac
(Catholic Church)

Chua Noe Nhai

Bao Tang Dan Toc Hoc Viet Nam
(Vietnam Museum of Ethnology),
Cputra International City

Nha San
Bac Ho
Chi Minh
(Ho Chi
Minh House)

CONG VIEN
BACH THAO
(BOTANICAL
GARDEN)

Phan Dinh Phung Chi Minh

Ga Long Bien
(Station)

Cau Long Bien

Phu Chu Tich
(Presidential Palace)

Lang Chu Tich Ho Chi Minh
(Ho Chi Minh Mausoleum)

Ba
Dinh
Square

OLD
CITY

CITADEL
Military Area
(Restricted Access)

see above

Chua Mot Cot
(One Pillar Pagoda)

Bao Tang
Ho Chi Minh
(Ho Chi Minh
Museum)

Chua Mot
Cot

Cot Co
(Flag Tower)

Bao Tang Lich
Su Quan Su
(Military History
Museum)

PHO PHUONG
(OLD QUARTER)

HOAN KIEM

B-52 Lake

Doi Can

Lenin

Den Ngoc Son
(Temple of the
Jade Mound)

*Ho
Hoan
Kiem*

Voi Phuc

Bao Tang My Thuat
(Fine Arts Museum)

Van Mieu
(Temple of Literature)

Nha Tho Lon
(St Joseph's
Cathedral)

former
Bank of
Indochina

Bao Tang Cach Mang
Viet Nam (Museum of
Vietnamese Revolution)

Hang Bot

Ga Ha Noi
(Station)

Hanoi
Towers

Ba Tang Nha Bao Hoa Lo
(Hoa Lo Prison/Hanoi Hilton)

Sofitel Legend
Metropole Hotel

Bao Tang Lich Su
(National Museum of
Vietnamese History)

Chua Quan Su
(Ambassadors'
Pagoda)

Hilton Hanoi
Opera Hotel

FRENCH
QUARTER

Nha Hat Lon
(Municipal Theatre/
Opera House)

Cung Van Hoa
Huu Nghi
(Cultural Palace)

*Ho Linh
Quang*

Dai Hoc Tong
Hop Ha Noi
(University)

Kham Thien

*Ho Thien
Quang
(Thien Quang
Lake)*

Nha Hat Rap Xiec
(Circus Theatre)

Nha Hat
Tuoi Tre

Go Dong Da

CONG VIEN
THONG NHAT
(REUNIFICATION
PARK)

Nha Hat
Dai Nam

Nha Hat
Cheo
(Cheo Theatre)

Den Hai Ba Trung (Hai Ba Trung Temple)

**Old Quarter detail:**

Cho Dong Xuan
(Dong Xuan Market)

Quan Chuong
(Old East Gate)

Den Bach Ma
(Bach Ma Temple)

Nha Hat Kim Dong
(Memorial House)

Nha Hat
Chuong Vang
(Golden Bell Theatre)

PHO PHUONG
(OLD QUARTER)

Cho Hang Be
(Hang Be Market)

Dinh Tien Hoang

Nha Hat Mua
Roi Thang Long
(Thang Long
Water Puppet Theatre)

Den Ngoc Son
(Temple of the
Jade Mound)

Huc
(Rising Sun
Bridge)

Chua Ba Da
(Ba Da
Pagoda)

*Ho
Hoan Kiem
(Hoan Kiem
Lake)*

Nha Hat
Kim Dong

Thap Rua
(Turtle Tower)

LY THAI TO
(LY THAI TO PARK)

Buu Dien Ha Noi
(Hanoi General Post Office)

Governme
Guesthous